Dimensions of Political Analysis

Dimensions of Political Analysis

An Introduction to the Contemporary Study of Politics

Cyril Roseman

Charles G. Mayo

F. B. Collinge

School of Behavioral and Social Sciences
San Francisco State College

Prentice-Hall, Inc.
Englewood Cliffs, New Jersey

© 1966 by
PRENTICE-HALL, INC.,
Englewood Cliffs, New Jersey
All rights reserved. No part of this book may be reprinted
in any form, by mimeograph or any other means, without permission
in writing from the publisher.
Library of Congress Catalog Card No.: 66–13643
Printed in the United States of America C–21438

Current Printing (Last Digit):
10 9 8 7 6 5 4 3 2 1

c

231151

Politics

PRENTICE-HALL INTERNATIONAL, INC., *London*
PRENTICE-HALL OF AUSTRALIA, PTY. LTD., *Sydney*
PRENTICE-HALL OF CANADA, LTD., *Toronto*
PRENTICE-HALL OF INDIA (PRIVATE) LTD., *New Delhi*
PRENTICE-HALL OF JAPAN, INC., *Tokyo*

Preface

Beginning students of political science rarely, if ever, have been given the opportunity to acquire first-hand familiarity with the orientation and methods of prominent twentieth-century studies in political science. This book of readings is designed to reflect, as accurately as possible in one introductory volume, the diversity and vitality of modern political science by delineating the major concerns of political science, the methods by which political phenomena are studied, the central concepts of the discipline, and some of the major questions which confront professional students of government and politics. Naturally such an enterprise has demanded reappraisal and successive modification of the organizational structure of the volume. The framework ultimately employed has provided the editors with a useful device for presenting introductory students with a coherent overview of the discipline without preconceived, doctrinaire conceptions of what political science ought to be.

In selecting the readings the editors tried, wherever possible, to meet each of the following criteria: that the selections be written in language that the beginning student can understand; that the selections be drawn from a variety of subfields of political science; that the selections illustrate the concepts operationally employed (where conceptualization is not self-conscious they should illustrate the ideas implicitly at work); and that the selections provide a tenable combination of commonly accepted perspectives, widely acclaimed selections, less orthodox foci, and imaginative, lesser-known materials. The selections have been ordered in part by the complexity of excerpted materials, in part by the relationship of the concepts illustrated, and in part in terms of the gradual development of the volume from simple ideas at the outset to more sophisticated, challenging notions toward the conclusion. Finally, it has been our intention to use as large a number of selections illustrating the American scene as possible, because we have felt that the students could gain the most from this familiar terrain.

We wish to acknowledge our gratitude to the following persons whose advice was invaluable: James M. Burns, Fred I. Greenstein, Herbert Kaufman, Donald R. Matthews, Jack W. Peltason, J. Roland Pennock, and David G. Smith; our colleagues and students at San Francisco State College; James J. Murray, III, social science editor for Prentice-Hall; and Patricia Collinge and Karen Whissen, who typed and assisted in editing the manuscript. In the last analysis, of course, we must assume responsibility for any failings of this book.

San Francisco, California

C. R.
C. G. M.
F. B. C.

Contents

Contributors   xi

1. The Study of Politics   1

The Work of Political Scientists, 1

The Ingredients of a Discipline, 3

Reconstruction in Political Science, 7

>   The Traditional Study of Political Science, 8
>   The Behavioral Innovation, 12

Political Science as a Discipline, 16

Diversity and Vitality in Contemporary Political Science, 20

2. Elements of Analysis   22

Introduction, 22

A. Governmental Institutions—The Constitutional Framework, 28
>   Clinton Rossiter
>   *President and Congress in the 1960's*

B. Public Law and Judicial Philosophy, 43
>   C. Herman Pritchett
>   *Equal Protection and the Urban Majority*

C. Ideals, 52
>   Alexis de Tocqueville
>   *Liberty, Equality, and Individualism in Democratic Nations*

D. Political Parties, 58

V. O. Key, Jr.
Democratic Party Organizations in the South

E. Interest Groups, 67

David B. Truman
The Dynamics of Access in the Legislative Process

F. Public Policy Issues, 83

Hans Morgenthau
A Political Theory of Foreign Aid

3. Perspectives on Political Behavior   95

Introduction, 95

A. Decision Making, 102

Theodore C. Sorensen
Presidential Advisers

B. Psychological Determinants, 108

Richard E. Renneker
Some Psychodynamic Aspects of Voting Behavior

C. Social and Economic Factors, 117

Arthur J. Vidich and Joseph Bensman
The Prosperous Farmers in Town Government

D. The Small Group, 125

Eloise C. Snyder
The Supreme Court as a Small Group

E. Language, Culture, and Politics, 133

Paul Friedrich
Language and Politics in India

4. Competition, Conflict, and Control   144

Introduction, 144

A. Campaigning for Office, 151

Theodore H. White
Kennedy vs. *Nixon: The T.V. Debates of 1960*

B. Interparty Competition, 157

William Nisbet Chambers
The Choice of 1800

C. The Struggle for Organizational Control, 166

James Q. Wilson
New York: The Struggle for Power

D. The Dynamics of Controversy, 176

James S. Coleman
The Escalation of Community Conflict

E. The Politics of Totalitarian Control, 186

Raymond A. Bauer
The Soviet Party Secretary: A Vignette

5. Power   196

Introduction, 196

A. Leadership, 204

James C. Davies
Political Leaders and Followers

B. Authority, 217

Richard E. Neustadt
The President's Power to Persuade

C. Influence, 223

Harold L. Wilensky
The Influence of the Staff Expert

D. Elites, 232

Edward C. Banfield
The Mythology of Elite Influence

E. The Study of Cliques—Some Methodological Considerations, 242

John C. Wahlke *et al.*
The Bonds of Legislative Friendship

6. Communications   253

Introduction, 253

A. Language and Action, 260

Eric Hoffer
Men of Words

B. Socialization and Opinion Formation, 267

William C. Mitchell
The Socialization of American Citizens

C. Mass Media, 276

Bernard C. Cohen
The Use of News in Foreign Policy Making

D. Bureaucratic Politics and Organizational Behavior, 285

Norton E. Long
Administrative Communication

7.   Approaches to the Science of Politics   **294**

Introduction, 294

    A.   Comparative Analysis, 302

        Seymour Martin Lipset
        Economic Development and Democracy

    B.   Quantification and Statistical Analysis, 309

        Donald R. Matthews and James W. Prothro
        Social and Economic Factors in Negro Voter
        Registration in the South

    C.   Functional Analysis, 331

        Robert K. Merton
        The Latent Functions of the Political Machine

    D.   Conceptualization and Research Design, 339

        Lewis J. Edinger
        Military Leaders and Foreign Policy Making

    E.   Experimentation, 353

        Richard C. Snyder
        Some Reflections on Experimental Techniques
        in Political Analysis

Index   **361**

Contributors

Edward C. Banfield

Raymond A. Bauer

Joseph Bensman

William Buchanan

William Nisbet Chambers

Bernard C. Cohen

James S. Coleman

F. B. Collinge

James C. Davies

Lewis J. Edinger

Heinz Eulau

Leroy C. Ferguson

Paul Friedrich

Eric Hoffer

V. O. Key, Jr.

Seymour Martin Lipset

Norton E. Long

Donald R. Matthews

Charles G. Mayo

Robert K. Merton

William C. Mitchell

Hans Morgenthau

Richard E. Neustadt

C. Herman Pritchett

James W. Prothro

Richard E. Renneker

Cyril Roseman

Clinton Rossiter

Eloise C. Snyder

Richard C. Snyder

Theodore C. Sorensen

Alexis de Tocqueville

David B. Truman

Arthur J. Vidich

John C. Wahlke

Theodore H. White

Harold L. Wilensky

James Q. Wilson

Dimensions of Political Analysis

1

The Study of Politics

The thoughtways of political science are too often taken for granted by the professional student of politics and, partially as a result, are too often misunderstood, overlooked, ignored, or avoided by the passing undergraduate. Those being formally introduced to political science are usually not treated to any survey of the purposes and processes of political analysis, largely, it would appear, because political science has only recently become self-conscious about its scope and methods, and such concerns are thus reserved for the advanced student. But before one can appreciate the significance of specific work, he must have some understanding of the general field within which this work has been undertaken.

It is our purpose in this book, and particularly in this chapter, to discuss the most common characteristics of contemporary political science as a field of study. This work has been designed primarily to aid the undergraduate student, and one of our primary intentions has been to clarify certain subjects that are widely acknowledged to be unclear. This, we feel, has been accomplished without oversimplification and should render the book useful not only to the beginning student, but to the more advanced student of politics as well.

Since we shall have to enter into some rather tangled issues before too long, it makes sense to begin the analysis and commentary at a fairly concrete level —with a discussion of the work normally performed by political scientists. The remainder of this chapter is devoted to more abstract considerations on the nature of political science as a discipline. The student should consider this discussion of political science on two levels: the study of politics as *actually debated* by political scientists, and the field of political science, *as the authors observe this debate.*

The Work of Political Scientists

There is more to political science than academic study. That is, professors of political science use their professional training in a variety of ways, some of which take them outside the classroom.[1] They may work as consultants

1 *Political scientists can be found in nonacademic professions, such as journalism. But for our purposes we have found it useful to consider political scientists as professors. We might note in passing that it is the range of ways in which political science can be appropriately used*

or professional staff members with domestic and/or international public agencies, with political parties, or with nonpublic bodies, such as interest groups, associations, and civic organizations. A good bit of their classroom attention is devoted to the training of future professionals, such as lawyers, public administrators, public officeholders, politicians, foreign affairs specialists, political news commentators and reporters, diplomats, and governmental research analysts—to say nothing of future professors of political science. There is, in addition, another kind of student training, for education in political science is in part designed to broaden the base of intelligent participation by providing training in citizenship. Other types of students in political science classes, such as social science majors, are interested in government as it affects their own fields of interest. And there are those who are learning about politics simply because it interests them. These latter types demand education more than training. They highlight the need for political scientists to function as educators in the liberal arts tradition and not just as professional experts.

The professor of political science also has an important responsibility in the area of political and governmental research. He must keep abreast of the burgeoning literature of the field as well as the avalanche of governmental publications and news reports, a time-consuming activity. In addition, many political scientists are continually engaged in the conduct and preparation of original research. Some of these projects are smaller experiments or investigations reported in professional journal articles, while others are larger in scope, resulting in full-length books or monographs. And, of course, secondary research is of great importance in the preparation of textbooks, another type of enterprise resulting in publication.

This does not imply that teaching and research in political science are ideally separated. They are actually closely related, for both depend on a thorough awareness of the field under study—an awareness that should be based on a continuous survey of the purpose, methods, scope, and findings of the works in the field. In research such a survey is essential, for it provides the researcher with the ideas, guidelines, and criticisms of others for the conduct of his own work. In teaching it is equally essential, for it is in terms of the approaches and findings of a large community of scholars that the scope and content of the field is defined. When research and teaching are based on such surveys there ensues a professional dialogue among political scientists—a dialogue whose object is to define the nature of political science itself.

Of course political science, like any field of study of similar scope, cannot be surveyed in its entirety by any one individual. Consequently there exist

---

that makes it difficult to state its professional responsibilities. Moreover, the basis of professional status is not clearly established, although membership in a political science association is commonly considered evidence of a professional commitment to political science.

a number of subfields within political science that form the context within which individual scholars work. Political scientists are likely to specialize in the conduct of research, while at the same time teaching courses spread more broadly in the discipline at large. Thus at the core of any discussion of the profession there must be an analysis of the framework of the field as an area of study.[2]

But there are several problems confronting one involved in such an analysis. First of all, there is little possibility of clearly and simply identifying the full scope and dimensions of political science. The work undertaken by political scientists has covered a wide variety of subjects and has employed many different techniques and methods of inquiry. It is not clear, moreover, where political science leaves off and sociology, economics, or geography begins. Second, no introductory review of the organization of the field would provide an understanding of the difficulties normally faced by political scientists in the conduct of their work, and a simple outline might well mislead the student about the critical issues confronting the profession. Finally, it seems appropriate to review the field of political science from the vantage point of the structure of inquiry and learning in general. Only in this way can one develop an understanding of the special characteristics of political science as a field of study. Indeed, preliminary analysis reveals that a most important facet of the field is its claim to be a discipline—a distinctive kind of academic specialty. The claim to disciplinary status is significant, for reasons above and beyond prestige and the self-satisfaction of a field's students. The distinctiveness of a discipline rests in its ability to lay down guidelines for rigorous work in that field. It can and does offer its students criteria by which to evaluate their own and other's work. It provides the analytic tools by which the state of knowledge or understanding in the field can be advanced. Political science's claim to be a discipline rests in part on its desire to be something more than a haphazard study of politics. It has traditionally stressed carefully focused analysis. Before we evaluate this claim in greater detail, however, we must examine the ideal characteristics of a discipline, especially those characteristics that might be related to political science.

The Ingredients of a Discipline

In one sense political science surely is a discipline: it has come to be recognized, along with anthropology, economics, geography, history, psychology, and sociology, as one of the established social science disciplines. But there are no judgmental standards evident in such recognition. We believe that there are in fact criteria by which fields of study can be evaluated in terms of their disciplinary status. Does political science meet these standards? Our answer is a qualified "yes." After we review the standards we will discuss how political science measures up to them and will explain the reasons for our

2 *See footnote 15 of this chapter for a listing of the subfields of political science.*

qualifications. We do not expect full agreement with our judgment in this analysis, but we feel that the basic ideas we offer are in line with those articulated by other students of social and political science.

A review of generally recognized academic disciplines, such as anthropology, biology, history, linguistics, mathematics, physics, and sociology, suggest that eight ideal ingredients can be delineated:

1. Disciplinary self-consciousness, reflected in the emphasis placed on critical analysis of the growth and development of the field of study.

2. A body of classic works that often stand as milestones in the evolution of the discipline—works such as Newton's *Principia Mathematica* and Einstein's *Relativity: The General and Special Theory.*

3. Specialization of personnel within the field in terms of commonly agreed-upon subfields. These specialists and their subfields may, in some cases, focus on multidisciplinary concerns, as in the case of biophysics, political sociology, and economic history.

4. An easily differentiated subject matter. That is, a subject matter which can be clearly distinguished from that of other allied or related disciplines.

5. A body of generalizations or abstractions, part of which are added, deleted, or modified over time as deemed necessary and appropriate. Such generalizations include the several different types of abstractions appropriate for the development of sound, supportable ideas in the discipline. These types include the following:

Laws—statements of uniformities used as explanations of specific phenomena, which, because of their explanatory character can be viewed as predictive statements. Newton's Law of Gravity is such a law. It is frequently asserted that the vagaries of human behavior make it difficult and perhaps impossible to develop laws in the social sciences similar to those in the physical sciences.

Theories—those explanations of uniformities that, although widely held, nevertheless require empirical validation for confirmation. A theory is distinguishable from a law in that a theory offers at one and the same time less certainty and greater explanatory power: it explains in effect why laws work, but it is not as useful as a law in predicting particular events.

Theory in political science has also been used to refer to high-order abstractions regarding normative aspects of politics (prescriptive or recommendatory aspects; what *ought to be* rather than what *is*), based primarily on conjecture and much a priori analysis, and designed to link normative considerations of politics to some world-view or other larger philosophical conception. Such normative theory may be vigorously systematic or focused on a specific but omnipresent and eternal issue of politics. Plato's *Republic* offers a systematic normative theory of the State; John Stuart Mill's *On Liberty* offers a specific normative theory of politics.

Of course there have been efforts to develop predictive theories of politics, but the very tradition of normative theory in political analysis has created special problems in the use of the idea "theory" in political science in anything other than a normative way. The distinction between explanatory-predictive theory and normative theory is an important one and has contributed to much controversy in political science, as noted below, pp. 295–96.

Principles—basic laws or theories used as major premises in the deduction of other general ideas or propositions useful in explaining, predicting, or recommending action. The classic example of a principle in political science is Jeremy Bentham's principle of utility, or "the greatest happiness for the greatest number," upon which Bentham based his system of hedonistic calculus, or the measurement and calculation of pleasure resulting from different rules of conduct or public policies.

The word "principles" has been used very loosely to cover a wide variety of propositions, thus making it difficult to specify one generally applicable definition. Moreover, it is frequently asserted that the term has been misapplied to certain normative statements in the social sciences, creating a false sense of certainty and authority in the statements so labeled. Such "principles" are often nothing more than their author's preferences or biased perceptions passed off as logically and empirically assailable Truth. The statement of principles, in short, sounds more scientifically impressive than it might were the term "principles" not applied to it.

Hypotheses—tentative explanations, assertions, or suppositions that are created to be tested and, when extensively tested and confirmed, either themselves take on the character of laws or theories or else modify existing laws. Hypotheses are what normally are tested in scientific inquiry.

Facts—those phenomena observable by normal human beings through sensory perception and whose existence is generally assumed to be noncontroversial because they are empirically verifiable. Of course there are individual differences or distortions in human perception, and as a result the facts are actually very much in dispute in many disciplines. Political facts are particularly prone to such controversiality. In every field of study, save perhaps mathematics, facts are considered necessary ingredients in the development of sound and supportable ideas.

Values—the importance individuals or groups attach to phenomena and ideas in terms of their views of the world. One of the major controversies in the development of a discipline is the appropriate emphasis to be placed on values in the establishment of the discipline's body of abstractions—a controversy ranging from the issue of value-distortion of fact to the question of the possibility or desirability of either value-laden or value-neutral theory. Many scholars tend to take polar positions on this matter: either that values ought to be central to the discipline or that they ought to be absolutely eliminated as subjective and unscientific. The nature of any given discipline is perhaps best approached at first through the question of values—how the discipline understands and uses them.

Concepts—the terms of analysis by which the major ideas of a discipline are expressed and by which the data is organized, explained, and studied. Conceptual framework is the ordering of all the terms of any particular analysis. There are invariably assumptions underlying the construction of a conceptual framework, and these assumptions cannot be empirically validated but must be accepted as more or less useful to the study underway. Conceptualization is the building of such frameworks or the definitions that are an endemic part of them—not to be confused with theorizing, which, as noted above, demands prediction, explanation, or prescription.

Taxonomy—one form of the conceptual ordering of data, primarily in terms of classification of phenomena into mutually exclusive categories in such a way that the interests of the investigation are best served thereby. Examples of taxonomy are the use of species and genus in biology, or types of political parties in political science.

6. Concepts *peculiar to the field of study*. Though some concepts may be borrowed from other fields of study, without a specialized vocabulary and abstract ideas designed especially for analysis of the field in question, a discipline cannot exist.

7. Generally accepted and relatively standardized methods of analysis by means of which to confirm or invalidate theories. The standardization of methods permits all students of the discipline to retest, or replicate, the original analysis by retracing the steps taken.

8. A body of data and accessible, possibly indexed, reports of data or factual summaries useful in empirical analysis. Mathematics is nonempirical in character and thus, as the rare exception, does not and cannot meet this criterion.

These eight points do not easily distinguish disciplines from ordinary fields of academic specialization. This checklist merely provides a catalogue of desirable or ideal characteristics, not a statement of minimum qualifications. It is unlikely that any real discipline will match it perfectly, though each one should come close. But coming close can conceal many important problems. There can, for instance, be a lack of agreement among scholars in a discipline as to the emphasis to be given to one or another of its features. There may be disagreements as to the definitions of such terms as "theory" or "principle" or "law." There may be a number of radically different conceptual systems within the discipline. In short, there can be considerable disagreement over characteristics and objectives, resulting in deep-seated conflict over the question of professional outlook, and thereby creating difficulty in maintaining the necessary communication among scholars in that discipline. Such considerations affect the use of our list or of any set of abstract standards.

Moreover, no discipline can prosper if controversy over such matters inhibits the exchange of ideas among its specialists. In the last twenty years political science has sustained a challenge to what had been its established intellectual order. A communications failure has developed between defenders and challengers of the old order; some students have considered it so serious that the pedigree of political science as a discipline has been called into question. Our first task, then, must be to analyze this dispute. Only after we review the basic developments of recent decades, in particular that of a radically new approach to political science, can we return to the question of its position as a discipline.

Reconstruction in Political Science

This new approach to political science is called *behavioralism*, a term drawn from the field of psychology, in which John B. Watson (*Behaviorism*, 1925) introduced the idea of focusing on empirically observable psychological data, rather than on Freudian abstractions, such as psyche, id, ego, and so on. Watson stressed experimentalism and therefore turned his attention away from clinical problems of psychopathology. Political scientists who consider themselves behavioralists[3] do not subscribe to Watson's conception that science should deal only in "hard" data, such as stimuli and responses, and should therefore disregard preferences and values; rather, they are committed to the inclusion of ideas and values as part of the relevant political phenomena to be considered in shaping their research plans. Behavioralism in political science does not offer ready answers to all questions of how to build an empirical political science, but it does have this general concern at its core. Moreover, the behavioralists have sought to introduce greater precision into the study of political phenomena by applying some of the methodology of the natural and physical sciences and by adapting some of the concepts developed in sister social science disciplines, such as psychology and sociology.

The behavioral reconstruction, like any fundamental change in academic outlook, did not occur overnight. Since World War II the "new look" in political science has been especially apparent, but almost all behaviorally inclined students of politics acknowledge their debt to the early works of Arthur F. Bentley (*The Process of Government*, 1908), Graham Wallas (*Human Nature in Politics*, 1908), Charles E. Merriam (*New Aspects of Politics*, 1927), Stuart A. Rice (*Quantitative Methods in Politics*, 1928), Harold D. Lasswell (*Psychopathology and Politics*, 1930; *Politics: Who Gets What, When and How*, 1935), Herman C. Beyle (*Identification and Analysis of Attribute-Cluster-Blocs*, 1931).

It is not the historical specifics that concern us here, however, but rather the nature of the transformation that behavioralists recommend. To appreciate better the behavioral persuasion, it is necessary first to set out the traditional or orthodox mode of political analysis prior to the postwar debate, and second, to explain the reasons for the emergence of the new wave in terms of changes in thought in the larger academic community. After reviewing these matters we can return to the central characteristics of the behavioral approach.

---

3 *Note the terminological distinction. While generally applauding the motives behind Watson's behaviorism, a good many social scientists wished clearly to distinguish their efforts from Watson's psychology—hence behavioralism. On this and related issues see David Easton, "The Current Meaning of 'Behavioralism' in Political Science," in James C. Charlesworth, ed.,* The Limits of Behavioralism in Political Science *(Philadelphia: American Academy of Political and Social Science, 1962), pp. 1–25.*

The Traditional Study of Political Science

For at least the last twenty-three hundred years, since the time of Plato, politics has been a subject of great interest to philosophers and social commentators of the Western world. It is not surprising, therefore, that continuities in the traditional study of politics are difficult to state in short, simple form. There have been gaps in the flow of ideas over the centuries, and occasionally new directions in thought have been opened up that cannot be squared with prior developments. Our task is to cite those traditions that have in fact influenced twentieth-century political science, for prior to the twentieth century there was almost no recognition of political science as a distinguishable field of study, let alone a discipline.[4]

The most apparent aspect of traditional political science stems from the fact that political science was assumed to be part of moral philosophy or social ethics. Political theory was, and continues to be in many colleges, the study of the political aspects of the thought of great philosophers—Immanuel Kant, John Locke, St. Augustine, Thomas Aquinas, Karl Marx—together with other thinkers who devoted their major attention to politics *per se:* Niccolò Machiavelli, Jean Bodin, Thomas Hobbes, Jean-Jacques Rousseau. Distinguished social critics have also focused their attention on political affairs. Such critics have included, among others, Thomas Jefferson, Alexis de Tocqueville, and James Bryce. Thus the "predisciplinary" stress on moral philosophy and social criticism provided a rationale for the later, twentieth-century attachment to normative, or evaluational and prescriptive, modes of theorizing in political science.

In particular, traditional political science has concentrated on the formulation of utopian systems, i.e., ideal states or societies that have never existed and are unlikely to exist, but whose hypothetical workings represent the philosopher's logically organized recommendations about how the world *ought* to be constituted. They are thus both a goal toward which to strive and a set of marks by which to judge the politics of the real world. At least those are the presumptions underlying utopian analysis. The concern with ideals, at both the societal and the individual citizen levels, is naturally part of the normative commitment: the ultimate objective of traditional political science is to offer judgments, and to help its students make judgments, about the good society and the good life (at least about the political aspects thereof).

Concern with ideals also encourages the analysis of ideologies—bodies of doctrinal statements woven together by their adherents to form a system of beliefs or myths that are accepted with little or no questioning by their supporters. Some ideologies, such as fascism, communism, socialism, and capital-

4 *Note that the* American Political Science Review, *acknowledged as the leading United States professional journal in the field, was not established until 1906. Few colleges or universities in the nineteenth century recognized political science as a curricular specialty.*

ism, are readily recognized as such in the modern world. But many other social movements also have ideological underpinnings—a fact studied by traditional political scientists, and this permits the assertion of the existence of ideologies not commonly recognized even by adherents of the supposed ideology. It is because ideologies are aggregations of normative or value-laden descriptive statements, unchallenged by adherents, that traditional theorists have maintained an interest in them, even sometimes in economic or social, as distinct from political, ideologies.

Ideologies and mass movements are two sides of the same coin; traditional political scientists have long been interested in those movements that espouse or spawn ideological expression of belief. They have wanted to understand the roots of political belief and commitment, and so they have examined these obvious sources of political emotion and faith. Only in recent years has attention been devoted to the intrinsic importance of such movements to the world of political behavior.

Traditionalists have been unable and reluctant to restrict their involvement with ideas to the ideals of others. They themselves are ideologically involved with the politics of their times.[5] Most apparent in this regard is their commitment to reform. Not all traditionalists have been so inclined, but those that have involved themselves with contemporary politics have leaned in this direction—reform, or nonviolent transformation of the *status quo* in order to improve the political system in terms of its conformity to the established ideals that are part and parcel of the reformer's accepted ideology. The reform outlook among political scientists has been of three kinds: structural reform (the transformation of organizational or institutional arrangements), procedural reform (modification in manner or mode of political or governmental action), and redistribution of rewards in society (modification of public policy or law to provide for greater equality among the populace). Reformers have had different objectives during the past century, from the early interest in paper money, curbs on monopoly power, destruction of the political machine, and the introduction of the civil service system, through the turn-of-the-century municipal efficiency-and-economy reorganization movement, to the postwar civil rights movement. Political scientists have played leading roles in some of these reform movements, and rarely have they stood foursquare against the proposed changes in the *status quo.*

It is particularly interesting to note the traditionalists' concern with public policy. Much traditional political science was written about policy questions being publicly discussed immediately prior to or during the writing

---

[5] *Behavioral political scientists are perhaps no less ideologically oriented toward their own individual political worlds. What is being argued here, however, is that the traditional emphasis on ideals encourages ideological commitment among political scientists, while the behavioral emphasis either fails to stimulate or actually discourages such involvement on the part of political scientists as political scientists.*

of the work, and in most monographs written during the last forty years there can be found a concluding chapter that draws attention to the implications of the study for public policy. The focus of such work has been recommendatory rather than simply analytical or predictive. One might say that the *sine qua non* of traditional political science was that the investigation would produce findings which would highlight deficiencies and suggest correctives—correctives that were packageable in public policy, preferably statutory law.

Of course this evaluative or value-laden approach to the study of politics presented a major difficulty, of which traditionalists themselves have been aware. It is *necessarily* subjective and thus raises questions about the standardization of methods of analysis and even the validity of the substantive generalizations developed in this unstandardized way. Although there have been recognized limits to the subjectivity of judgment permitted within the traditional approach (at a minimum, Aristotelian logic must be employed in deducing conclusions from premises), nevertheless it has been felt necessary by the most orthodox traditionalists themselves to impose deliberate limitations on the freedom of the scholar in marshaling facts in support of his arguments. To prevent the use of subjectively derived or interpreted data, and simultaneously to preclude the use of imprecise and ambiguous "evidence," traditionalists have focused their empirical investigations on the formal, legal, institutional aspects of governmental systems.[6] By so restricting their field of vision they have been able to use easily observable and recordable phenomena. They have tended to disavow any interest in the dynamic side of governmental affairs—the personalities, the informal groups, those elements of politics that when stated as fact are open to challenge. Thus the noncontroversiality of admissible evidence, as in a court of law, has become the hallmark of sound traditional political science. This can be called the institutional mode of traditional analysis.

Coupled with this has been a concentration on what can be called the juridical focus, or a focus on the legal bases of politics. Often this involves viewing *all* politics as *necessarily* related in some way to government and its several agencies; it involves the use of the *state* (the national body politic, incorporating territoriality, resident populace, authoritative government, and national independence) as the central, unifying concept of the discipline. This juridical focus also nicely accommodates the long-standing interest of students of politics in *jurisprudence* (the study of legal philosophy and the

---

6 *It is not intended to convey here the impression that the traditionalists in any self-conscious way adopted the institutional mode as a means of limiting subjectivity in analysis. However, it seems apparent that the original emergence of political science at the turn of the century was clearly related to the establishment of certain standardized analytic procedures, which at that time included primarily the institutional mode referred to above. Thus there seems to have been at least a subconscious desire to set up an "empirical" science of politics—one not so obviously based on subjective evaluation.*

meaning and nature of law) and *sovereignty* (the independent and autonomous character of modern nation-states).[7]

To complement the institutional mode and the juridical focus, the traditionalists have stressed historical-descriptive methods of investigation and
analysis. It has generally been felt that the burden of careful scholarship lay
in detailed review of the specific conditions and changes introduced in institutions at each point in time.

Finally, it should be noted that there came to be a conflict between the
two underlying approaches: the idealistic approach, which attempts to explain the perfect, the ideal order inherent in nature so that men might strive
to approximate it; and the empirical approach, which tries to evade the subjectivity of the pure ideal approach by elaborating upon the formal, legal,
and institutional aspects of politics. These two approaches *can* be combined;
and, as we have indicated, most traditionalists have in fact done so—typically
by investigating political institutions empirically while assuming that the
long life and evolutionary development of such institutions were some sort
of testimony to their connection with the order of nature. But this connection is an unstable one that can be and has been attacked from solid logical
grounds—and initially by the traditionalists themselves. The outcome of this
attack is the origin of behavioralism.

The idealists—or, to use the more descriptive term coined by one political
scientist, the transempiricists[8]—were prone to attack the empiricist approach.
They did so because empiricism was at best merely useful to the task of
political analysis and at worst involved the denial of it. This was so because,
while reality as depicted by empirical evidence is somehow connected with
the ideal, no simple counting of evidence or generalizing about it can ever
reveal the ideal. For this a wholly different approach is required: logical
definition of basic concepts, deduction, and consequent metaphysical speculation in order to construct hypotheses that then, and only then, might possibly be "tested" empirically—although such a test is by no means considered
conclusive since, as Plato tried to demonstrate, reality might only be a degenerate copy of the ideal. Clearly, if political science were to concentrate on
empirical counting, it would be denying the essence of political theory: speculation about nature's ideal order for man.

But there were those among the traditionalists who clearly distrusted such
an approach. They knew full well that, to paraphrase a common complaint,
"the idealists agree about the sublime perfection of their deductive method.

---

[7] *The juridical focus and the concepts of state and sovereignty have been criticized from a
number of viewpoints, but perhaps most successfully from the vantage point of their ineffectiveness in explaining contemporary world politics, where state and sovereignty are not clearly
evident in the case of many nations.*
[8] *See Robert A. Dahl,* Modern Political Analysis (*Englewood Cliffs, N.J.: Prentice-Hall, Inc.,
1963*), pp. 101ff.

Only they agree on nothing else."[9] Subjectivity was the curse of transempiricist method for a very simple reason: its results depended entirely on the assumptions—the definitions put into it—from which all conclusions were deduced. There was no agreement on these assumptions among the transempiricists and no possible formal way of reaching agreement; their method of reasoning began only *after* the assumptions were stated. This, to canny empiricists, indicated that there was something drastically wrong with the urge toward the ideal on which, intellectually and historically, traditionalism was based. If political inquiry were to explain politics, perhaps it would have to do so empirically, and not transempirically.

Clearly, the traditional approach was caught in a bind, partly of its own making; but as we shall now see, only partly, for this idealist-empiricist friction was symptomatic not only of trouble in political science, but also of trouble throughout virtually all of Western thought. It represented, in short, a crisis in that basic philosophy on which all inquiry rests: shall inquiry be based on ideal speculation or empirical verification? It was those who pursued the thrust of empiricism, exploring its logic and implications, who were to carry the battle (though not yet the war) and were to remake the character of Western inquiry, and with it political science.

The Behavioral Innovation

Thus the proximate impetus for behavioralism was the empirical deficiency of traditional analysis. Any and all efforts to elevate the study of politics in terms of methodological rigor and solution of the empirical dilemma can be considered part of the behavioral innovation. But the new wave involves more than just this general objective. Before presenting the several dimensions of behavioralism we must note the deeper sources of reconstructionism.

Just as philosophy accounted for the traditional emphasis on normative theory, so the extreme contemporary emphasis in philosophy on *non*normative matters—philosophy of science, theory of knowledge, studies of language, symbolism, and meaning—in what might generally be called the "age of scientific inquiry," has encouraged a shift in political science to what Robert Dahl has called "empirical theory."[10]

Contemporary philosophy, particularly that most influential school called "logical positivism," has deveoped an idea of central significance to the evolution of the behavioral approach—in fact, to all of modern thought. It is commonly referred to as the "fact-value dichotomy." According to this position, it is logically necessary to separate statements about facts (which may be empirically verified) from statements about values and from the subjective

9 *Charles Sanders Peirce, "Some Consequences of Four Incapacities,"* Journal of Speculative Philosophy, *Vol. II (1868), 140–157, reprinted in Philip Wiener, ed.,* Values in a Universe of Chance *(New York: Doubleday & Co., Inc., 1958), pp. 39–72, reference at p. 40.*
10 *Dahl, op. cit. See especially Chap. 8, "Political Evaluation," pp. 93–110.*

preferences of the observer (which cannot be empirically verified). Not only must facts be separated from values, but this fact-value position tends to relegate normative concerns to at best a poor-relation status in thought. It does so because, as contemporary philosophy and science insist, claims to knowledge must be objectively (empirically) verified—a process in which subjective values can have no part. Normative inquiry has come to be regarded as a suspicious, unsatisfactory, and perhaps illogical form of thought. Furthermore, associated with such notions is the idea of value-relativism— that there is no universal scale by which man's values can be weighed objectively and that there is no eternal order from which absolute values can be derived.

Thus it has been the general position of contemporary philosophy that no good purpose is served by searching for the ideal world, the world of so-called "essence," since by its very nature such a world would have to be outside the realm of any possible experience and empirical evidence. Only the subjective dreams of a philosopher could attest to such a world, and science does not deal in dreams. It should be perfectly clear that such a powerful school of thought would have to have profound effects on the traditional school of political inquiry. Not only did it undermine the use of such absolute ideals as "justice" and "the good state" in meaningful discourse about politics, but it also attacked the very normative core of traditionalism itself.

In part the behavioral innovation can be traced to the changes that have occurred in the other social sciences in the last few years. Sociology, economics, psychology, and even history and geography have to some extent been critically examined by their own students in the light of the scientific revolution that has swept through all phases of contemporary life since the turn of the century. The concern in each case has been with more than just the introduction of the methods and trappings of the physical sciences, though this aspect should not be overlooked. But in almost every field of study criticized the central concern has been a re-evaluation of the purposes of the discipline. Gradually, in every social science there has been emerging a general commitment to the development of *explanatory and predictive ideas that are empirically tested*. Often coupled with this has been a devotion to the task of ordering such ideas into systems of thought that can serve as the theoretical framework of a field, or subfield, of study. A minor, but connected theme in the development of the contemporary social sciences has been the emergence of an interdisciplinary outlook as an accepted and necessary element in the effective investigation of any question regarding human behavior—which, after all, is not political or economic or cultural, but all of these at once.

Scientific methods, predictive-explanatory theory, empirical testing, and systematic theory construction are earmarks of the new thinking in the social sciences in the last half century. All of these developments have naturally generated interest among political scientists in how such changes might or should affect the study of politics. In short, behavioralism in political science is only part of a larger scientific movement that has occurred within virtually all social sciences over a longer period of time.

Technological innovation in research is another development in the academic community that has provided an impetus for the behavioral innovation. The creation of a variety of applied mathematical techniques, the steady improvement in data-processing equipment, and the use of computers in complex problem solving have made it difficult for political scientists to remain convincing professionals without utilizing these devices for their research activities.

These three factors—changes in philosophy, changes in the social sciences, and technological innovation in research—do not completely account for the behavioral innovation in political science. But for our purposes they provide an adequate explanation for the growth and prosperity of that movement. Let us move then to a refinement of the characteristics of the reconstruction in political science.

One central aspect of the reconstruction is a shift away from the state as the central organizing concept of the discipline. As noted above, the juridical focus fails to account for much of what happens in international relations. Within the domestic realm it likewise removes from view many politically significant phenomena that occur only on the outer fringes of a political system having government at its core—such phenomena as the activities of pressure groups or the voting behavior of citizens. Behavioralists have become conscious of the value of having a smaller, more manageable unit than the state as the central unifying concept of the field. In the early days of behavioralism this new unit was taken to be *power,* the ability of an individual or group to affect the behavior of others in conformance to his or its wishes. More recently the unit taken has been the *decision* (the choice among alternative lines of action), and individual and group decision making has been of great interest as the subject of political inquiry.

There have been other units of analysis that have been employed in different works by different men, and we need not review them here. What is important about these efforts is that all can be characterized as concentrating on *politics,* as distinguished from the state, as the central idea of the discipline. Of course politics is not a new ingredient in political science; but what *is* new is that politics *not necessarily directly related to government* is of central importance to political science.

Politics traditionally has been viewed in terms of a polity, or political system—as activity carried out in support of, or in response to, or in provocation of government and its leaders. According to the behavioral view of politics as ubiquitous phenomena, we offer the definition: "the way satisfactions, or opportunities for achieving satisfaction, are distributed among people." According to this definition, and it is not too different from others offered recently in political science literature,[11] it is now possible for political scientists to examine any aspect of social life, however nonpolitical in the traditional sense, to learn more about politics. Political science has claimed its place as a modern social science by turning its attention to empirical investigation of relationships among people.

The institutional mode of analysis has in turn been replaced by the process mode of analysis in the behavioral reconstruction. Behavioralists study the behavior of persons or groups rather than structures, institutions, ideologies, or events. The reason for the shift in emphasis (and note that here, as elsewhere in the discussion of the behavioral reconstruction, we are examining changes still underway and not at all uniformly adopted or necessarily to be so adopted) is in large part a reflection of the interest in change, adaptation, or innovation in politics. The process mode avoids the static quality of structural analysis; it has a dynamic dimension that is extremely valuable in accurately capturing the mercurial quality of political life.

Just as the more fundamental behavioral perspectives—like the interdisciplinary focus, the concern with conceptual clarity, the emphasis on empirical hypothesis testing—are distinct by-products of the changes in philosophy and social science in general, so too are certain specific innovations of behavioralism. One is the development of the systems analysis approach. Atomic theory stands as "grand" or comprehensive theory in the physical sciences, and systems analysis is considered by some to be its analogue in social and political science. It tries to depict social and political life as a system in which all parts are regularly and functionally related, a kind of regular and self-consistent universe. Systems analysis sometimes tends to reflect the presumed scientific rigor of social scientists who believe that the first order of business of science is the creation of precise conceptual frameworks by which the variety of existence can be explained. This approach presently involves a good deal more speculation and a priori judgment than empirical evidence, and its adherents have often been charged with the same sort of subjectivity that is associated with traditional transempiricism: they "enact" their preferences and idiosyncratic viewpoints into "law."

Such criticism suggests another innovation: the stress placed by other behavioralists on the interdependence of theory and empirical research. This development is in part a reaction to the deficiencies of grand theory, but it is also a result of the great interest found in philosophy regarding the procedural rules for gathering evidence and is manifested in a concern with methodology in behavioral social science.[12] Directly related to this concern is a third innovation: the emphasis placed upon quantification and statistics

---

11 *Cf. the definition offered by Lewis A. Froman, Jr.,* People and Politics: An Analysis of the American Political System *(Englewood Cliffs, N.J.: Prentice-Hall, Inc., 1962), p. 3. "Politics, in its broadest sense, is concerned with the distribution of advantages and disadvantages among people."*
12 *For an elaboration and illustration of this and other innovations noted, see Chap. VII.*

in empirical research. This emphasis on quantifiable data is in part a response to the computerization of research noted above, but even more is it a response to the need felt to step away from subjectively interpreted data.

These innovations have, of course, generated much loud criticism among the traditionalists, who have not sat idly by and watched their discipline change before their very eyes. They have, quite appropriately we think, publicly opposed and criticized some or all of the innovations introduced, depending on the degree of their orthodoxy and their devotion to the tradition. There has in fact been a period of internecine warfare, sometimes quite acrimonious, within the ranks of political science. But there was much to criticize in traditionalism, and most traditionalists knew it; likewise there was much to criticize in early behavioralism, and the behavioralists have largely admitted it. It appears now that the battle, while by no means resolved, has been narrowed to more negotiable issues. The extremes in each camp have moved from the center of the stage, and the moderates have begun to carry on the debate. Indeed, one scholar has recently noted:

> Where will the behavioral mood, considered as a movement of protest, go from here? I think it will gradually disappear. By this I mean only that it will slowly decay as a distinctive mood and outlook. For it will become, and in fact already is becoming, incorporated into the main body of the discipline. The behavioral mood will not disappear, then, because it has failed. It will disappear rather because it has succeeded. As a separate, somewhat sectarian, slightly factional outlook it will be the first victim of its own triumph.[13]

Political Science as a Discipline

Now that the behavioral reconstruction of political science has been reviewed, it is possible to return to the question originally posed: how does political science measure up to the criteria of a discipline?

Political science does meet most of the criteria. It has a body of abstractions that has gradually evolved into its present form, including theories, hypotheses, facts, values, conceptual frameworks, and classificatory schemes; it has developed a variety of analytic methods, special concepts, and data banks; its internal division of labor, disciplinary self-consciousness, and classic works all mark it as an established discipline. Yet, for all this, there are still important qualifications on its disciplinary status. Its subject matter is not clearly differentiated from that of sister social studies. And perhaps more importantly, it lacks internal consensus regarding its basic objectives and *modus operandi*. Evaluation of political science as a discipline requires a careful examination of these deficiencies and characteristics.

The lack of differentiation of subject matter is only partially explained by the interdisciplinary outlook of the behavioralists. The subject matter itself —politics—can be found in social and economic, as well as in governmental

13 *Robert A. Dahl, "The Behavioral Approach in Political Science: Epitaph for a Monument to a Successful Protest,"* American Political Science Review, *Vol. LV (December, 1961), 770.*

and political institutions. In part it rests in a state of mind, a cultural environment, a set of economic and diplomatic conditions or public policy needs. It is a reflection of historical evolution; it is generated in crowds, families, and friendship groups. Even the focus on government or the state takes the student of political science into legal studies, examination of societal causes or stimulants of governmental action, and exploration of philosophical implications of authority, freedom, and responsibility. Moreover, political science is no different from any other social science in maintaining subject-matter boundary lines that run through the terrain claimed by another social science. Sociology, history, and political science have at times each laid claim to being *the* overarching study of man within which all other social sciences could be organized. Thus political science cannot be denied disciplinary status on this ground alone.

But the internal cohesiveness of political science is a more important consideration. The behavioral innovation in political science has enlarged the range of disciplinary concerns and commitments; debates have grown up on several issues of disciplinary objectives, foci, and methods. In this sense, political science has become something less than a cohesive discipline.

The arguments between traditional and behavioral political scientists have been centered on the issues surrounding most of the characteristics of a discipline. Traditionalists and behavioralists disagree about what constitutes the field's body of generalizations; in general they argue about whether to *in*clude (à la traditionalism) or *ex*clude (à la behavioralism) prescriptive theories. Though neither has claimed to have formulated *laws,* there has been argument over whether behavioralists have been attempting to model political science after the physical sciences, particularly in focusing on the "uniformities" of human behavior in their attempt to develop more universally valid and "unchallengeable" explanations. On the other hand, behavioralists have criticized traditionalists for their tendency in certain cases —such as in the subfield of public administration—to focus their professional attention on the development of prescriptive "principles." Traditionalists have scant use for hypotheses, because much of their work does not permit any kind of scientific experimentation or testing. They tend to look askance at what they feel is the "scientistic"[14] tendency to state ordinary problems in the language of experimentation, especially where this beclouds the subjective character of the testing of hypotheses so stated. Behavioralists have argued that traditionalists have too often shown a disregard for facts, either by oversight or by deliberate disengagement from any empirical investigation.

In one sense the debate is centered on the role of values in political inquiry. Each side debates before its own supporters, however, in that they are unable to agree on any basic premises concerning the role of values. The

---

[14] *A pejorative reference to the imitation of the method of the natural sciences by the social sciences.*

debate becomes particularly bitter when traditionalists accuse behavioralists of considering their conceptual frameworks as the only "grand theory." Behavioralists respond with the charge that lack of conceptual rigor and clarity has destroyed whatever insight might otherwise have been of theoretical value in traditional analysis. The traditionalists have warned behavioralists about the confusion of overrefinement of taxonomies; behavioralists have questioned the value of what appear to them to be oversimplified classifications of political phenomena.

The debate has focused on methodology as well. In general, traditionalists are indifferent to this aspect of their work; they often fail to explain how they arrived at their conclusions. This is a point of much concern to behavioralists, who feel that methods affect findings and that different methods might produce different findings. However, behavioralists often fall to quarreling among themselves about the correctness of certain methods in a particular case and, even more important, about different methodological approaches in general. Traditionalists have been quick to point out that the absence of generally accepted principles of scientific method in behavioral analysis calls the scientific basis of behavioralism into serious question—indeed, it dashes the hopes for any immediate breakthrough in the development of a *science of politics,* the objective frequently stated by behavioralists.

Traditionalists have resisted the development of specialized terminology in political analysis, largely because their humanistic origins provide little support for such specialization. Many traditionalists see themselves as men of letters, able to communicate freely with men in all walks of life and all fields of study. Moreover, it is too often true that the terminological innovation of some behavioral analysis contributes little in the way of new findings. It serves simply to permit the rephrasing (in clumsy and incoherent form) of old matters without any apparent gain in new ideas. Yet with nothing but the terms of traditional political analysis, it appears that political scientists would be unable to communicate about many phenomena and would frequently run the risk of confusion through imprecise expression and its resultant ambiguity.

On the remaining four ingredients of a discipline—subfield specialization, disciplinary self-consciousness, classic works, and reported data—there is much less significance to whatever disagreements exist. Traditionalists, of course, favor the retention of the established subfields of public administration, international relations, comparative government, political theory, and American government and politics.[15] Behavioralists opt for less attention to

---

15 *It should be understood that different colleges and universities recognize slightly different subfields, combining the areas of study in the subfields in different ways. Also, the areas themselves are given separate recognition as professional fields of specialization. A typical breakdown of fields of specialization would be the following:*

Public Administration
  administrative theory and philosophy
  administrative behavior
  fiscal and budgetary administration

jurisdictional divisions and institutional distinctions and more emphasis on the processes of politics. They argue in some cases for the establishment of a separate subfield dealing with political behavior. But this dispute can usually be settled by compromise. Both traditionalists and behavioralists have been pleased with the continued awareness of the emergence of the discipline in the last fifty years, but of course their descriptions of this development might be drastically different. They see different classic works as having different worth to students of politics, but behavioralists, no less than traditionalists, subscribe to the idea that political science has had its share of seminal thinkers. Finally, only a few traditionalists oppose the call for data and repositories of data, though again the kind of data desired is markedly different between the two camps. Traditionalists want data about constitutional or legal matters, governmental structure and procedures, political rules and regulations, and any other clearly observable and formally acknowledged "facts." Behavioralists' interest in data runs toward the quantifiable, because such data are amenable to statistical testing of hypotheses. But this issue, like the others noted in this paragraph, is not fundamentally disruptive of disciplinary communications. The important question is: "to what extent do issues regarding the other four ingredients adversely affect the status of political science as a discipline?"

---

   public personnel administration
   administrative law
International Relations
   international law
   international organization
   international politics
   American foreign policy
   diplomatic history
   theory of international relations
Comparative Government
   theory of comparative government
   Western Europe
   Asia
   Soviet and Eastern Europe
   Commonwealth
   geographic specialties in developing areas, e.g., Africa, Latin America, or Southeast Asia
American Government and Politics
   political parties and interest groups
   public opinion
   Constitutional law
   legislative behavior
   public policy formation
   state and local politics
   theory of American government
Political Theory
   history of political ideas, subdivided as follows:
      ancient (Plato to Machiavelli)
      modern (Machiavelli to the present)
   contemporary ideologies
   Marxism
   American political thought
   jurisprudence
   analytic or systematic theory

The answer depends on the intensity of the dispute both on each separate issue and in general. So long as behavioralists and traditionalists square off against each other it will be difficult to preserve the discipline's integral unity. But as each camp grows less hostile toward the other, as has become the case in the last decade, then the chances for preserving—and, indeed, improving—the discipline are greatly increased. For a discipline depends upon much more than unanimous acceptance of a type of Hippocratic oath. The very essence of disciplinary vigor can be measured by the interchange of opinion among the field's specialists on basic questions regarding the ingredients of the discipline. But the differences of opinion among field specialists work to the discipline's advantage only when there is an exchange of ideas. It is of utmost importance to political science that the dialogue between traditionalists and behavioralists be preserved, for there *are* issues, particularly the role of values in analysis, that represent problems for which there are no apparent solutions.

The Diversity and Vitality of Political Science

It might appear from the foregoing comments that the field of political science includes just two armed camps, facing each other in solid phalanxes with little or no internal disagreement within each camp. Actually, however, the traditional and the behavioral approaches are not monolithic schools of thought within political science. Indeed, it is sometimes difficult to determine whether a particular scholar or a particular work is behavioral or traditional when no explicit identification or label is used. Moreover, there are, if anything, so many different perspectives among political scientists that students, and sometimes teachers, are confused about where to draw the line between groupings of scholars. It is this diversity of political science, rather than any simple traditional-behavioral split, that should be explored in depth in an introduction to contemporary political analysis. The remainder of this volume is devoted to an examination and illustration of this diversity and vitality of political inquiry.

It should be understood, however, that the terms of our presentation do not represent schools of thought or distinct doctrinal commitments. Any effort to set forth the dimensions of political analysis in such a fashion would be doomed from the start. The discipline today is too much in flux, too responsive to the changing world around it, to become committed to fixed conceptions of what ought to be studied. The difficulty that one must face in constructing a lasting conceptual overview of political science is found in this very diversity and vitality. We hope that our effort at constructing such an overview will not be taken for more than it is—an introductory, heuristically useful ordering of what appear to us to be the central concerns of the contemporary study of politics.

Suggestions for Additional Reading

Charlesworth, James C., ed., *The Limits of Behavioralism in Political Science.* Philadelphia: American Academy of Political and Socal Science, 1962.

Crick, Bernard, *The American Science of Politics.* Berkeley: University of California Press, 1959.

Dahl, Robert A., "The Behavioral Approach in Political Science: Epitaph for a Monument to a Successful Protest," *American Political Science Review,* Vol. LV (December, 1961), 763–772.

————, *Modern Political Analysis.* Englewood Cliffs, N.J.: Prentice-Hall, Inc., 1963.

Easton, David, *The Political System.* New York: Alfred A. Knopf, Inc., 1953.

Eulau, Heinz, *The Behavioral Persuasion in Politics.* New York: Random House, Inc., 1963.

Hacker, Andrew, *The Study of Politics: The Western Tradition and American Origins.* New York: McGraw-Hill Book Company, 1963.

Hyneman, Charles S., *The Study of Politics.* Urbana: University of Illinois Press, 1959.

Lasswell, Harold D., *The Future of Political Science.* New York: Atherton Press, 1963.

Redford, Emmette S., "Reflections on a Discipline," *American Political Science Review,* Vol. LV (December, 1961), 755–762.

Somit, Albert, and Joseph Tanenhaus, *American Political Science: A Profile of a Discipline.* New York: Atherton Press, 1964.

Storing, Herbert, ed., *Essays on the Scientific Study of Politics.* New York: Holt, Rinehart & Winston, Inc., 1962.

Van Dyke, Vernon, *Political Science: A Philosophical Analysis.* Stanford, Calif.: Stanford University Press, 1960.

Young, Roland, ed., *Approaches to the Study of Politics.* Evanston, Ill.: Northwestern University Press, 1958.

2
Elements of Analysis

The American political system,[1] in spite of its complexity, offers the student of politics readily accessible case materials for political analysis. This section thus provides illustrations of orthodox political analysis as reflected in studies of American politics.

The starting point for political analysis traditionally has been the constitutional framework, particularly as it delineates the major governmental institutions of a state and their interrelations. Clinton Rossiter has drawn up such a basic statement of the leading American governmental institutions—the Presidency and the Congress. In his view there is a mystery in American government that lies at the very core of the constitutional system—the doctrine of separation of powers. How is it, he asks, that twentieth-century America can be governed by an eighteenth-century doctrine based on the notion that governmental power is inherently dangerous and that its concentration should be resisted and prevented by constitutional fragmentation of authority? How, under the separation of powers doctrine, can responsive and responsible government be achieved in contemporary America, with its need for executive-legislative cooperation in meeting the crises that have regularly confronted the nation in the last fifty years?

The key to the success of the separation of powers doctrine lies in the flexibility of the Presidency and the Congress in their mutual dealings. In Rossiter's terms, the two branches have learned mutual respect rather than mutual distrust. A working partnership has been devised that permits dispute within consensus, that encourages cooperation within a context of independent rivalry and contention. Rossiter claims that members of both branches agree on fundamental objectives: the structure of government, the nature of the economy, and the identity and threat of the external enemy. Other factors accounting for this cooperation are party ties (Democratic Presidents in the past thirty-five years have usually been blessed with Demo-

---

[1] *That is, the government (all of its separate branches, levels, and agencies), political parties, interest groups, citizenry, laws and public policies, ideological tendencies and "political culture" within which political expression is generated, expressed, and interpreted. Thus the concept of a political system involves the interrelatedness of the institutions, processes, and beliefs affecting the way satisfactions (or opportunities for achieving satisfactions) are distributed among people.*

cratic Congresses), the traditions of political barter, and the morality of compromise in democratic politics.

Within the context of "cooperative independence," the President stands out as the key factor in the governmental formula—the first among equals. The President leads, and Congress is either to tag along or be left in the dust.

Modern Presidents have tended to be liberals on national unity over sectional diversity, on racial equality, on public regulation and welfare in the economic realm, and on internationalism in foreign policy. Congress tends to be more conservative on these matters. As a result, the cooperative tendency and its corollary of Presidential ascendancy have tended to favor the liberal viewpoint. Many feel that the twentieth century has demanded liberal imagination in the Presidency for coping with the crises of the times. Moreover, it has been argued that Presidential activism plants the nation firmly in the footsteps of its greatest forefathers—Jefferson, Jackson, Lincoln, and Theodore Roosevelt. The American heritage is rooted in liberal idealism.

The American liberal heritage places particular emphasis on the Bill of Rights, and in postwar years the Supreme Court has become perhaps the stanchest institutional defender of this heritage. As Professor C. Herman Pritchett notes, the Court was not always so ready to defend the constitutional rights of minorities. But its 1954 *Brown v. Board of Education* decision, by overturning the "separate but equal" doctrine in public education, placed the Court in the center of perhaps the major domestic political issue confronting contemporary America—the problem of racial relations—and squarely on the side of "equal protection of the laws" under the Fourteenth Amendment. The reasons for the Court's new-found defense of liberal doctrine can perhaps be traced to complex legal issues, but it is more likely that Professor Pritchett is right in stressing the Court's awareness of the need to respond to the "urban majority," particularly the disadvantaged racial, religious, and ethnic groups of the cities. The Court has followed the philosophy of judicial activism in the recent legislative apportionment cases reviewed by Pritchett as well as in the defense of Negro rights to equal and unsegregated education. Pritchett defends the Supreme Court's broad interpretation of the Constitution in the handling of questions of such political magnitude. Thus his analysis of contemporary public law dramatizes the age-old issue of the role of the Court in a representative democracy: how far shall it go in making public law? Pritchett takes an unequivocal stand in defense of a vigorous Court. He argues that "judges who endeavor to speak for the constituency of reason and justice may truly represent the enduring principles of a democratic society."

Alexis de Tocqueville was concerned about another problem regarding the enduring principles of a democratic society: how the ideals of freedom, equality, and individuality would be promoted in the American democracy. When he came to the United States early in the nineteenth century to do research for a study of the young republic, certain questions were obvious. Since the American Revolution had provided a model and impetus for the French Revolution, had it, nevertheless, been able to avoid those excesses of democratic politics that had deformed democracy in France? Could American democracy stand for liberalism (nineteenth-century variety)[2] support the conservative ideal of respect for law, and resist tyranny of the masses, while maintaining its democratic devotion to equality?

Early America, it must be remembered, was an *experiment* in democracy, founded on a revolution against a mother country and bolstered by a new constitutional order. The state was republican in form, but in spirit there was a natural devotion to democracy not unlike that which became prevalent in France in the early nineteenth century. What were the ingredients of the American spirit of democracy that distinguished it from the less successful ones, such as the French?

Tocqueville found the important ingredients to be a devotion to free institutions and an understanding of the need to rely upon more than simple representation of majority views and for locally based representation to guard against the dangers of despotism born of overemphasis on equality. He also noted that rich and poor were on speaking terms in America, unlike on the continent. He found an American commitment to the idea of every man's responsibility to his fellow men, a commitment reinforced by the reminder that free institutions and political rights are shared by all in society.

Tocqueville, no defender of democracy in France, acknowledged that in America political freedom protects society against one danger of equality: unbridled individualism. The electoral process, more than anything else, accounts for the success that Tocqueville found in American democracy. It is elections, he argued, that turn individual selfishness and social irresponsibility, so common to democratic countries and democratic revolutions, away from majoritarian tyranny and despotism toward the achievement of individual freedom.

Elections are meaningful only where there are contending forces, programs, or personalities vying for voter support. In America it is the competition between Democrats and Republicans in Presidential and many Congressional and state elections that is the focus of electoral attention. Yet competitive, two-party politics is still only an ideal in many districts and states, especially in the South, where the Democrats generally held undisputed control at the state, county, and local levels from the 1800's until 1964, when votes for Barry Goldwater accelerated the trend toward conserva-

2 *Nineteenth-century liberalism stresses the* freedom *of the individual and the protection of his liberty against governmental encroachment. Twentieth-century liberalism stresses the* welfare *of the individual in an urban, industrialized society. The older ideals of liberalism, with the exception of defense of the civil rights and civil liberties of minorities, have in the twentieth century become the sacred principles of conservatives.* [See Louis Hartz, The Liberal Tradition in America *(New York: Harcourt, Brace & World, Inc., 1955).*]

tive Republicanism in the Deep South. In the late 1940's V. O. Key, Jr., published a definitive study of politics in the Southern states, with particular emphasis on party politics, and this work still stands as a valuable analysis of the dynamics of Southern politics, even though the trend toward competition in that section has clearly begun. Selections from his chapter on party organization are included below. In this chapter he compares the Southern Democratic party organization with its Northern cousin.

In the noncompetitive Southern situation Key found the party rather impotent, restricted largely to the performance of routine jobs. The more entrenched the Democratic party, the more likely it was to act as a framework for the settlement of intraparty factional disputes and electoral contests in the important primary—the winner of which was in most cases (until the post-World War II years) unchallenged in the general election. "Usually," Key writes, "the party machinery is impartial toward personalities and factions competing in the primaries." Yet in certain states where one faction has been particularly strong—such as the Crump machine in Tennessee, the Byrd machine in Virginia, and the Long machine in Louisiana—the party leadership has been drawn from the dominant faction, and this leadership then supports its faction in the performance of official duties, wherever it is possible and advantageous to do so.

Overall, Key found Southern politics to be atomistic, lacking continuity, responsiveness, or accountability. It is interesting to note that these are the same criticisms that have been levied against the nonpartisan system of local elections. Perhaps competitiveness between parties, rather than organizational structure or legal restrictions on the party electoral role, is the critical element in maximizing the benefits and minimizing the dangers of powerful but responsive political parties in a democracy. We will analyze interparty competition in greater detail in Chapter 3.

Another important question of democratic politics is how much response to interest group demands ought to be embedded in public law. Too much pressure, of course, like too little recognition of affected groups by the lawmakers, has a deleterious effect on the representative process. But the groups themselves cannot be expected to restrain themselves in the interests of society at large. Instead, they act, as David Truman has revealed in his classic work, *The Governmental Process,* in terms of the costs and benefits to the group itself. To paraphrase George Washington Plunkitt, a Tammany Hall politician during the 1870's, the interest group "sees its opportunities and it takes them."[3] In Truman's terminology and more scholarly perspective, it is the structure of government and the differential access thereby provided to interest groups that accounts for variations in lobbying—the exertion of group pressure on governmental officials.

[3] *See William L. Riordan,* Plunkitt of Tammany Hall *(New York: Alfred A. Knopf, Inc., 1948), p. 4. In this statement Plunkitt sums up his concept of "honest graft."*

Truman analyzes the differential influence of groups, whose action is channeled by the constitutional framework, the structure of the political parties, and legislative organization in America. In particular, he singles out federalism, the separation of powers and checks-and-balances system, bicameralism, decentralization of party power, the seniority rule in Congressional committee assignments and leadership, the power of the House Rules Committee, and the loosely integrated legislative party organization in Congress and most state legislatures[4] as factors permitting certain groups—especially those whose grass-roots support is strong—to exercise greater influence than those who lack the support of voters in certain "safe" constituencies. For safe districts frequently re-elect incumbents, thus gaining representatives who profit by the seniority rule; in safe districts (rural Southern districts, for example) interest groups that are strong, such as conservative farm organizations, thereby gain in overall legislative access. This "localistic" bias of American legislative politics has affected the substance of American public policy—foreign as well as domestic—which is evidence of the importance of differential access in the legislative process.

Truman's analysis highlights the fact that a group may be influential without deliberately exerting more pressure than others against which it is struggling. There are systematic biases in the legislative systems of the country (state and municipal legislative systems as well as the Congressional system) on behalf of certain groups and to the detriment of others. Influence, in short, may exist without any overt evidence of group pressure.

There are important implications of Truman's conception. For example, the influence relationship between interest group official (or legislative advocate, as lobbyists are politely termed) and legislator is two-way: because of their mutual interdependence they can, within limits, extract promises of support from each other. It is often difficult to tell who is influencing whom. Chapter 4 illustrates this ambiguity regarding power and influence in the larger context of political systems in general. For the moment it is enough to note the mutuality of power in all symbiotic political contexts, such as the legislative arena in a democracy.

Of course pressure groups are not the only forces operating on legislators in the shaping of public policy. Hans Morgenthau, in the article reprinted below, analyzes the foreign aid debate in Congress in terms of the arguments offered on behalf of, and in opposition to, different types of foreign aid. It is arguments over policy matters and internalized ideals and ideology that in some cases are more important in conditioning legislative decisions than influence wielded, threats of reprisal, or those biases generated by the formal or informal characteristics of legislative politics.

Yet for all the force of argument and the presuasiveness of a legislator in dealing with his colleagues, it often happens that at the core of the legislative

---

4 *Truman mentions Maryland and Pennsylvania as exceptions to this Congressional pattern.*

debate there is a vacuum in theory. Morgenthau argues that the annual debate over the level of foreign aid expenditure reflects basic disagreements over the *kind* of foreign aid, rather than the amount of money to be spent. But these disagreements about basic policy and programs are rarely recognized by the legislative disputants and even less frequently brought into open debate.

In delineating six different types of foreign aid, Morgenthau highlights the unfortunate consequences of ideological commitment in dealing with a complex policy problem. The myth of economic development as the basic purpose of foreign aid, for example, can create misunderstandings and resentment on the part of both the benefactor and the recipient when it finally becomes evident that economic development is not a possible product of the transaction. Morgenthau argues that it is advantageous for the giver of foreign aid to distinguish the kind of aid the receiver most needs and wants; it may be cheaper and less upsetting than dealing in myths and misconceptions.

Once major innovation in the economic system is introduced, there is no telling where it will lead in terms of social and political upheaval. Can the United States risk such upheaval? Clearly not to the same degree that the Soviet Union can, argues Morgenthau. Economic development is not even likely to produce an absence of belligerency in the foreign policy of the receiving nation. In short, foreign aid for the economic development of Asia, Latin America, and Africa may have serious unintended consequences for the United States.

While we may disagree with this view that foreign aid policies are simply "weapons in the political armory of the nation," we must agree that the analysis of this field of public policy, like others that may readily come to mind, requires the inclusion of judgments about the political consequences and efficacy of alternative actions. Analysis of public policy should include the *art* of political analysis, i.e., judgment regarding probabilities and possibilities. An awareness of the need for such judgment on the part of the public policy maker is what political scientists have long been pleading for.

Suggestions for Additional Reading

Bickel, Alexander M., *The Least Dangerous Branch*. Indianapolis: Bobbs-Merrill Company, Inc., 1962.

Boorstin, Daniel, *The Genius of American Politics*. Chicago: University of Chicago Press, 1953.

Brogan, Denis W., *Politics in America*. New York: Harper & Row, Publishers, 1954.

Bryce, James, *The American Commonwealth*, edited, abridged, and introduced by Louis M. Hacker. New York: G. P. Putnam's Sons, 1959.

Burns, James McGregor, *The Deadlock of Democracy*. Englewood Cliffs, N.J.: Prentice-Hall, Inc., 1963.

Goldwin, Robert A., ed., *A Nation of States: Essays on the American Federal System*. Chicago: Rand McNally & Co., 1961.

———, *Political Parties, U.S.A.* Chicago: Rand McNally & Co., 1961.

Keefe, William J., and Morris S. Ogul, *The American Legislative Process: Congress and the States*. Englewood Cliffs, N.J.: Prentice-Hall, Inc., 1964.

Key, V. O., Jr., *Politics, Parties and Pressure Groups*, 5th ed. New York: Thomas Y. Crowell Company, 1964.

Koenig, Louis W., *The Chief Executive*. New York: Harcourt, Brace & World, Inc., 1964.

Lowi, Theodore J., ed., *Legislative Politics, U.S.A.*, 2nd ed. Boston: Little, Brown & Co., 1965.

McCloskey, Robert G., *The American Supreme Court*. Chicago: University of Chicago Press, 1960.

Milbrath, Lester W., *The Washington Lobbyists*. Chicago: Rand McNally & Co., 1963.

Minar, David W., *Ideas and Politics: The American Experience*. Homewood, Ill.: The Dorsey Press, Inc., 1964.

Monsen, R. Joseph, Jr., and Mark W. Cannon, *The Makers of Public Policy: American Power Groups and Their Ideologies*. New York: McGraw-Hill Book Company, 1965.

Riker, William H., *Federalism: Origin, Operation, Significance*. Boston: Little, Brown & Co., 1964.

Sorauf, Frank J., *Political Parties in the American System*. Boston: Little, Brown & Co., 1964.

Woll, Peter, *American Bureaucracy*. New York: W. W. Norton & Company, Inc., 1963.

Zeigler, Harmon, *Interest Groups in American Society*. Englewood Cliffs, N.J.: Prentice-Hall, Inc., 1964.

A. Governmental Institutions— The Constitutional Framework

President and Congress in the 1960's

Clinton Rossiter

Constitutional Separation of Powers: The Mystery of American Government

The study of government is always and everywhere the study of the dimensions, powers, procedures, and limitations of the instrumentalities that make and administer public policy. In the United States it is most certainly the study of all these things, but it is also—perhaps more certainly than it is in any other country in the world—the study of the relationships among these instrumentalities. No one can begin to understand the operations of our extraordinary system of government until he has looked long and hard at the points of contact, both formal and informal, among the four great organs established in the Constitution: President, House of Representatives, Senate, and Supreme

Clinton Rossiter, "President and Congress in the 1960's," in Marian D. Irish, ed., *Continuing Crisis in American Politics*, pp. 86–106. © 1963 by Prentice-Hall, Inc., Englewood Cliffs, N.J. Reprinted by permission. Originally offered in the Government Lecture Series at Florida State University, 1961–1962.

Court. This is, perhaps, the most instructive aspect of the government of the United States, and also the most fascinating.

One element in the fascination that envelops the relationships between the President and Supreme Court, or House and Senate, or Senate and the President is a quality that is always present where men are fascinated—whether by women on earth or by stars in the heavens—and that quality is mystery. If the texts and commentaries on comparative government may be believed, the largest single unsolved mystery in the whole realm of political science is the success we have had in governing ourselves according to the frugal, subtle, and exasperating directions of the Constitution of 1787. Although it may not appear a mystery to all of us who dwell in the midst of it, it most assuredly does to most of those who observe us from afar, and especially to those who can congratulate themselves (and they do, almost daily) on living under what they like to call *"responsible* government." They cannot understand, not when they are being entirely frank, first, why we should want to govern ourselves on the basis of the separation of powers and, second, how we are able to do it without making a total mess out of the complicated process of transmuting popular wish into public policy. It is, indeed, a source of never-ending surprise to even our best friends in Canada and England and India that the nation which prides itself on having the most advanced and flexible of economic systems should be governed under the most retarded and rigid of political systems. The sight of an eighteenth-century constitution existing in a twentieth-century world is enough to amuse them; the recognition that the constitution appears to work with tolerable efficiency leaves them shaking their heads in disbelief.

The purpose of this essay is to probe this mystery, and to probe it at that point of contact—the varied and delicate relations of the President and Congress— where it seems most significant, instructive, and fascinating. To any American

who doubts that this relationship is all these things one can only ask, Where were you during the second session of the Eighty-Seventh Congress? The hard campaign waged by John F. Kennedy and every last one of his battalions in behalf of tariff reduction, the appeal to executive privilege in the "splendid little war" between Strom Thurmond [R., S.C.] and Robert J. McNamara (over the censorship of speeches to be given by military men), the collision of personalities and constitutional principles in that other splendid little war between Carl Vinson [D., Ga.] and the President (over the future of the RS-70, if not of the Constitution)—these were several of the best acts ever staged in a play that has been running for 170 years and will run, let us hope, for at least as many more.

I do not propose to solve the mystery of *why* we govern ourselves as we do, because as a citizen of the United States I deny that this is a mystery at all. I do propose to explore (if not to solve) the mystery of *how* we do it, although this exploration may not take us very far toward the heart of the mystery. As a general rule I agree with Sir Winston Churchill that a little mystery in the prosaic business of government is a Very Good Thing. Always a first-rate political scientist, he was never more insightful than when he acknowledged, some thirty years ago, the "enormous and unquestionably helpful part that humbug plays in the social life of great peoples dwelling in a state of democratic freedom."[1] A constitution without any humbug would be a constitution for either angels or drones, and ours, if nothing else, is a constitution of, by, and for imperfect human beings.

The Powers and Functions of Our "Irresponsible" Executive

As a first and essential step toward a sharper understanding of the relationship between the President and Congress, let

1 *Winston Churchill,* My Early Life *(London: Odhams Press, Ltd., 1958), p. 64.*

us take a quick reading of the current dimensions of these great organs of government. In particular, I would call attention to the condition of the Presidency and Congress in terms of five basic qualities of any instrument of constitutional government: power, prestige, independence, responsibility, and support.

The *powers* of the modern Presidency (or would it be more exact to say *functions?*) are so numerous, far-ranging, and consequential that it is becoming increasingly difficult for the man who holds this office to bear his burden with anything like the efficiency we have been taught to expect from twentieth-century administrators. He is nominated by the Constitution to fill four fairly distinct roles, and no one who watches him go through his daily paces can doubt that each brings a vast accretion of personal and constitutional authority.

He is, first of all, Chief Executive, and as such is held primarily and often exclusively accountable for the efficiency, frugality, loyalty, and ethics of the 2.3 million Americans in the national administration. From the Constitution he draws, explicitly or implicitly, the twin powers of appointment and removal, as well as the primordial duty, which no law or plan or change in social circumstance can ever tear from his grasp, to "take care that the laws be faithfully executed." From Congress he has received such remarkable confirmations of his position as the Budget and Accounting Act of 1921, the succession of Reorganization Acts, and Section 631 of Title 5 of the United States Code.[2]

The Constitution designates the Presi-

dent specifically as "Commander-in-Chief of the Army and Navy of the United States." In peace and war he serves as the unchallenged, indeed unchallengeable director of the armed might of the nation. In time of peace he raises, trains, supervises, and deploys the forces that Congress is willing to maintain, and he has a great deal to say about the size and makeup of these forces. In time of war he makes all major decisions of strategy (and many of tactics as well), mobilizes the economy for maximum production of the weapons of victory, and draws on the example of Lincoln to institute measures that cut deeply into the liberties of the people.[3] And thanks principally to the nature of war, he has a good deal more to say than does Congress about the manner and timing of the transition from peace to hostility.

He is also, by common consent of Constitution, Congress, custom, and history, our Chief Diplomat; in the still fresh words of John Marshall he is "the sole organ of the nation in its external relations, and its sole representative with foreign nations."[4] He dominates the making of foreign policy; he monopolizes the direction of foreign affairs. If ever there was any question about his primacy in this area, there is no longer; for he is, as we have just noted, Commander-in-Chief, the man who controls and directs the armed might of the United States in a world in which might, real or threatened, is the essence of diplomacy.

The last of the President's constitutional roles finds him serving as a "third house of Congress." Not even the most hard-bitten Republican Congressmen can deny that he is a kind of Chief Legislator, a man possessed of a large arsenal of weapons—the veto, the special message, the White House conference, the fireside chat,

[2] *A deceptively simple grant of authority that reads:* "The President is authorized to prescribe such regulations for the admission of persons into the civil service of the United States as may best promote the efficiency thereof, and ascertain the fitness of each candidate in respect to age, health, character, knowledge, and ability for the branch of service into which he seeks to enter; and for this purpose he may employ suitable persons to conduct such inquiries, and may prescribe their duties, and establish regulations for the conduct of persons who may receive appointment in the civil service."

[3] *Ernest R. May, ed.,* The Ultimate Decision (*New York: George Braziller, Inc., 1960*); *Clinton Rossiter,* Constitutional Dictatorship (*Princeton, N.J.: Princeton University Press, 1948*), *Chaps. 15–16, 18.*

[4] *March 7, 1800,* Annals of Congress, *6th Congr., 1st Sess., p. 613.*

the bagful of appointments and defense contracts and favors—with which to influence, if never to dominate, the legislative process. While Congress has a wealth of strong and talented men, the complexity of the problems they are asked to solve by a people who assume that all problems are solvable has made external guidance a requisite of effective operation, and the President alone is in a constitutional, political, and practical position to provide such guidance.

The pressures of history have added at least four subsidiary and yet highly influential tasks—and therefore powers of command and persuasion—to the strictly constitutional burden of the President: first, the leadership of his party, which makes it possible for him to achieve a reasonably cohesive administration and also to make the appeal of fraternal loyalty to roughly half the members of Congress; second, the shaping and expression of what Woodrow Wilson called "the real sentiment and purpose of the country,"[5] that is to say, the service Theodore Roosevelt performed when he used the White House as a "bully pulpit"; third, the many-sided function of acting as the grand protector of "the peace of the United States," under which he can muster troops, experts, food, money, loans, equipment, medical supplies, and moral support to rescue Americans stricken by natural or social disaster; and fourth, the management (within the limits imposed by the facts and ideology of American capitalism) of the national economy, which calls upon him to take the lead in wielding what President Eisenhower described as the "formidable arsenal of weapons" now at "the disposal" of the national government for "maintaining economic stability."[6]

When one puts all these roles together, then particularizes this total responsibility in terms of the constitutional authority to command, negotiate, veto, appoint, remove, pardon, and supervise and also in terms of the statutory authority to make budgets, reduce tariffs, close banks, and cool off strikes, one is bound to conclude that never in history have free men put so much power in a single office. This is a remarkable display of confidence in the good intentions of one man, a display rendered all the more remarkable by the fact that the man enjoys a kind of *prestige* that is unique among elected heads of government. For he is, by implicit direction of the Constitution and common consent of the people (thanks to the memory of George Washington), the Chief of State in the American system. He is, as it were, a republican king, the figurehead as well as the working head of the government of the United States, "the personal embodiment" (in the words of President Taft) of the "dignity and majesty" of a mighty nation.[7]

If there is much that is trivial about many of the President's activities as Chief of State, there is nothing at all trivial about the role itself. Indeed, no modern President can fail to realize that all his powers are invigorated, even given a new dimension of authority, by the aura of legitimacy and mystery—Sir Winston would be the first to call it "humbug," and do so approvingly—that envelops this office. No one who deals with the President of the United States . . . can ever forget that he deals with no ordinary head of government. The framers of the Constitution, who may not have been quite sure what they were doing,[8] took a momentous step when they fused the dignity of a king and the authority of a prime minister in one elective office.

Remarkable in the way it mingles power and prestige, the Presidency is ren-

[5] *Woodrow Wilson,* Constitutional Government in the United States *(New York: Columbia University Press, 1908), p. 68.*
[6] *In his message to Congress accompanying the Economic Report, January 28, 1954, Congressional Record, 83rd Congr., 2nd Sess., Vol. 100, p. 965.*

[7] *William Howard Taft,* The Presidency *(New York: Columbia University Press, 1916), p. 51.*
[8] *On this interesting point, see John P. Roche, "The Founding Fathers: A Reform Caucus in Action," American Political Science Review, Vol. LV (1961), 799.*

dered even more remarkable as an instrument of democratic government by its *independence* of most of the day-to-day, week-to-week checks and pressures to which even the most exalted of prime ministers in parliamentary systems of government must be alert. If we may use the word in a technical sense, the President of the United States is virtually *irresponsible:* he is entirely exempt from votes, even motions of no confidence; he is asked no questions that he is bound to answer; he can look forward confidently, as no prime minister can, to a full term in office. Rarely does the Supreme Court find itself in a mood as well as a position to check or deflect a Presidential action;[9] the process of impeachment is now, for all practical and political purposes, a "rusted blunderbuss, that will probably never be taken in the hand again."[10] Even the process of election holds few fears for the resolute and knowing President—the one thing he ought to know about that process is that in an electorate as large as the one he faces (and in which there is only one real alternative to voting for him) the desires of various groups to punish him for wrong behavior have a way of cancelling each other out. In any case he faces this electorate, as President, only once.

The President's unique freedom of action must be exercised, of course, within the institutional and moral boundaries of a democratic government and plural society. Although he may be technically irresponsible, he bears a large burden of responsibility for his actions. His actions have consequences which can be disastrous for his influence and reputation. While his powers are huge, they are of no real effect unless exercised through proper forms and within both constitutional and customary limits. The Presidency is nothing if not a constitutional office.

This fact finds overwhelming confirmation in the history of the United States: 170-odd years, thirty-four Presidents—and still no gross abuse, and no likelihood of a gross abuse, of the confidence of the American people or of the terms of their Constitution. The reasons for the success of the Presidency as a constitutional office —and the magnitude of this success can be judged by contrasting it with the failure of almost every constitution ever modeled on our own—are essentially three: first, the screening process of nomination and election that keeps men such as Thaddeus Stevens, Huey Long, and Joseph McCarthy far from the White House, and opens the way only to what Hamilton described as "characters pre-eminent for ability and virtue";[11] second, the dictates of both public and private morality, which, for a variety of sociological and historical reasons, operate more powerfully on the President than they do upon almost any other person of authority in the United States; third, the vast network of likewise independent centers of power—House, Senate, Supreme Court, parties, regulatory commissions, state governments, corporations, labor unions, foundations, mass media—that sets limits to his striving and keeps him almost always within what Harold Laski called "the range of common expectation."[12] The President, indeed, is a "lion on a reservation," a man who can "roam widely and do great deeds" as long as he does not try to break out of the pluralistic system of restraints that is the mark of our open society.[13] The system is designed to keep him from going out of bounds, not to paralyze him in the splendid fields that have been set aside for his use. This, not quite incidentally, is why I made a distinction at the outset of

[9] *Glendon Schubert,* The Presidency in the Courts *(Minneapolis: University of Minnesota Press, 1957), pp. 3–4; Clinton Rossiter,* The Supreme Court and the Commander in Chief *(Ithaca, N.Y.: Cornell University Press, 1951), pp. 2–10, 126–131.*
[10] *Henry Jones Ford,* The Rise and Growth of American Politics *(New York: The Macmillan Company, 1898), p. 288.*

[11] *In No. 68 of* The Federalist *(New York: New American Library, Inc., 1961), p. 414.*
[12] *Harold Laski,* The American Presidency *(New York: Harper & Row, Publishers, 1940), p. 37.*
[13] *Clinton Rossiter,* The American Presidency, *2nd ed. (New York: Harcourt, Brace & World, Inc., 1960), pp. 72–73.*

these remarks between *function* and *power*. Function can take the form of power only when the President has the acquiescence of most of the other centers of power in our society, particularly of Congress—and the more acquiescent they are, the more genuinely powerful he is.

Finally, a word about what I have labeled *support:* by this, I mean simply the character of the constituency that has elected him and can be prevailed upon to back him in the pursuit of his aspirations. In one sense, of course, his constituency is the whole nation, and he is, as Andrew Jackson long ago insisted, peculiarly entitled to think of himself as the one "direct representative of the American people."[14] In another sense, however, his support is that part of the nation which elected him, and it has become increasingly plain in recent years that, thanks to the imperatives of the electoral system (in particular, the special importance of the large states), his constituency is one in which cities, minority groups, and consumers are given extra weight—whether in the calculations of delegates in the nominating conventions or the calculations of aides in the White House. It is, if we may put it this way, the more restless, problem-plagued, reform-minded classes and groups in his party—and therefore in America—from which the President draws his principal support.

The Functions and Powers of Our "Responsible" Legislature

When we scrutinize the Congress of the United States in these same terms, we find first of all that it, too, is an instrument of immense *power* for good or ill. During Franklin D. Roosevelt's first term we heard a great deal about the notion of delegated powers. Indeed, it was more than a notion; it was a fact, as the Supreme Court was able to prove in *Schechter Bros. v. U.S.* and *U.S. v. Butler.*[15]

Today, for better or worse, we talk rather differently about Article I, Section 8 of the Constitution, because the new and apparently established fact is that the sweep of vast events abroad and the pressures of an industrial civilization at home have blown the restrictive concept of delegated powers into a balloon of immense proportions. Congress, it would seem, now has the constitutional authority (and the implicit blessing of the Supreme Court)[16] to pass laws dealing with just about any problem that appears to be "national" in scope—including problems of agriculture, health, education, morals, civil rights, and urban renewal—without much concern about the admonishing words of Amendment X. The opening words of Article I, Section 8 + the war powers + the commerce clause $\times$ "necessary and proper" = the full sovereignty of a modern legislature—that, I think, is the equation of Congressional authority, real or potential, in modern America.

The powers that Congress brings to the struggle with the President for its fair share of their joint responsibility for shaping the American future are the particular concern of this scrutiny, and one should certainly call attention in passing to the whole range of formal and informal techniques through which it acts today as a kind of Grand Inquest of the Nation.[17] If the members of Congress, whether gathered together in committees or operating as lone gladiators, can never quite get at the President himself to demand a public explanation of this policy or to force a reconsideration of that decision, they can exercise a considerable amount of supervision and control of even his most powerful lieutenants. If the President does not feel the hot breath of Congressional

14 *J. D. Richardson,* Messages and Papers of the Presidents *(New York: Bureau of National Literature, Inc., 1896), Vol. III, p. 90.*
15 *295 U.S. 495 (1935); 297 U.S. 1 (1936).*

16 *See the cases reviewed in* The Constitution of The United States of America: Analysis and Interpretation, *Sen. Doc. 170, 82nd Cong., 2nd sess. (1953), pp. 71–82.*
17 *Ernest S. Griffith,* Congress: Its Contemporary Role, *3rd ed. (New York: New York University Press, 1961), Chap. 5; Charles S. Hyneman,* Bureaucracy in a Democracy *(New York: Harper & Row, Publishers, 1950), Chap. 9.*

leaders, then his department heads certainly do.

The cutting edge of the power of Congress, whether the power to hand the President fifty billion dollars or to make it hard for him to spend it flexibly, is the pride with which almost all its members contemplate the past, present, and future of the institution. The Congress of the United States yields not one inch to the President in point of *prestige*. Although he may be the Chief of State, the tribune of the people, and the high priest of national ritual, Congress is the mirror of the nation; and in its own opinion it presents a more accurate image of the hopes and fears and needs of the American people than does even the most alert and dedicated of Presidents.

Almost all Presidents, be it noted, have tended to agree at least halfway with Congress, and not just because they have had favors to ask. It would be impossible for any President to deal open-mindedly with Congress without coming to realize, perhaps more sharply than the rest of us, how much depends upon the skill, courage, and good will of this now quite venerable body. We may shake our heads over the lapses from dignity that have marked every session of Congress from the first to the latest, or chuckle over the slightly ridiculous figures that Herblock or Mauldin uses to represent the House or Senate, yet one is bound to ask the question, and to ask it altogether rhetorically (except, perhaps, for the House of Commons—I am not sure that even this exception should be made): what legislature in the world is a match for Congress in its claims upon the respect of the nation it serves? Surely there is no upper house that is remotely comparable to the Senate, and even the recollection of some few demagogues and mavericks cannot spoil the sense of awe one must feel in the presence of the history, authority, and dignity of this body.

Much of the authority and dignity of Congress derives, of course, from its *independence*, which is every bit as unique and fateful as the independence of the President. Let us refix attention on the power of Congress to check or persuade him, and in doing so let us take particular note that the essence of this power is quite simply the untrammeled right to say "no" to his requests for legislation, which includes the untrammeled right of the Senate to say "no" to his requests for confirmation of nominations and treaties. Two points are worth recalling in this connection. First, no important policy, domestic or foreign, can be pursued for long by even the most forceful President unless Congress comes to his support with laws and money. Second, the Constitution makes it impossible for him to force Congress to pass a law or spend money against its will. Ours is almost the only legislature in the world over whose decisions the executive has no final power of persuasion. The President has influence over the legislative process, and the influence can be great, but he has no power—not until Congress presents him, gladly or grudgingly, once in a while maliciously, with a bill for approval or disapproval. If the members of Congress cannot force him to resign by a vote of no confidence, neither can he send them packing with a proclamation of dissolution. If his term is rigidly fixed, so, too, is theirs. Congress, indeed, is a uniquely independent legislature.

This is not to say that it is free of restraints. To the contrary, Congress is a legislature that bears large responsibility for its decisions and behavior. Apprehension of the next election presses hard upon the political consciousness of most members of Congress; the President's power of veto remains a weapon of immense efficiency; even the Supreme Court's power of judicial review is not quite so rusty from disuse as some observers would have us think. As to the restraints of what we like to call "public opinion," these operate far more immediately upon the minds of all but the most imperious members of Congress than they do upon the most timid of Presidents.

The most consequential restraint of all upon the will of Congress, however, operates internally rather than externally, although little attention is paid to it by those who fuss a good deal about the checks and balances in our system of government. This restraint is quite simply the existence of two equal chambers of the legislature, each of which maintains a committee to range at will through every large area of political concern, each of which has strong men who strike bargains with bureaucrats, each of which must give its assent to a bill before it can be presented to the President for his consideration. If there is no way for the President to force his will upon Congress, there is also no way for one house to force its will upon the other. The sovereign independence that marks the relationship of President and Congress is matched by the sovereign independence that marks the relationship of House and Senate. This is one country in which bicameralism, real as well as nominal, continues to flourish grandly.[18] Not only are the House and Senate very nearly equals in power and prestige; there is no machinery, constitutional or customary, for resolving deadlocks or animosities against the will of either.

Congress draws no less support from the American people than does the President. The important point to remember is that "the people" that elects, sustains, and restrains Congress is not exactly the same "people" with which the President is concerned. For one thing, his constituency is far more of a piece than is the constituency of the House or Senate, which is, after all, a collection of constituencies. For him the American people is more often than not just that: the American people, a society of individuals who share a common interest in the freedom and prosperity of the United States. For Congress, however, it is more often than not a swarm of groups that divide with one another over the spoils of freedom and prosperity. His constituency is, in effect, a nation of citizens, that of Congress a nation of interests.

The natural distinction between the sources of support for President and Congress has been sharpened in recent years by the way in which his constituency seems to be gerrymandered in behalf of the cities and their more restless groups, the constituency of Congress in behalf of the rural areas and their more conservative interests. Whether one good gerrymander deserves another is a question about which we can all dispute with a will, but there can be no disputing that the President is tugged by the imperatives of his nationwide electorate toward the left, the House of Representatives is tugged by the imperatives of its diverse constituencies toward the right, and the Senate, for reasons too numerous and tangled to unravel here, sits just about on dead center of the American political spectrum.[19] Presidential proposals for legislation in such areas as health, education, and economic growth encounter a good deal less opposition in the Senate than they do in the House—and a good deal more opposition in both than the Administration can cope with comfortably.

Executive-Legislative Relations: Cooperation in Contention

This has been a perhaps familiar recital of details about President and Congress, yet it has also been a necessary one. Only those who are thoroughly familiar with these details can recognize that it is in fact something of a mystery with which we are dealing. Only those who understand the way in which power is set against power, prestige rubs against prestige, independence evokes independence, responsibility overlaps responsibility, and support fails to match support can savor the fascination of the central question: how can such a system work? How can two (three, really) equally proud, unmanageable, often intractable instruments of the

---

18 George B. Galloway, The Legislative Process in Congress (*New York: The Thomas Y. Crowell Co., 1953*), *pp. 249–254.*

19 Andrew Hacker, "Voice of Ninety Million Americans," The New York Times Magazine (*March 4, 1962*).

popular will ever get together and stay together long enough to bring a major policy to life and move it forcefully on its way to fruition? How, in short, can cooperation ever emerge from this pattern of contention?

Two facts about executive-legislative relations in twentieth-century America are worth noting at this juncture. The first is that, although cooperation in pursuit of national purposes is not guaranteed in the Constitution (indeed, is made difficult to achieve), cooperation on a broad and continuing basis is now essential to effective operation of the system. There have been famous periods (and at least one that was infamous) when the conduct of public affairs in the United States was marked by a condition of patent noncooperation—in which the President and Congress spent most of their energies attacking one another instead of the problems of the nation or went their respective ways pretending that the other branch hardly existed. The bitter, protracted, demoralizing struggle between Andrew Johnson and the Fortieth Congress is the most familiar instance of the first kind of noncooperation, the cool and distant relationship between Lincoln and the Thirty-Seventh Congress the most inexplicable example of the second—inexplicable, that is, to modern minds.

Neither savage conflict nor splendid isolation is now a tolerable pattern of executive-legislative relations. The problems of a convulsive world and a runaway technology fall much too thickly upon us. They demand solution, or at least confrontation, and the President who refuses to give a tactful lead to Congress, like the Congress that lets its investigators run riot in the gardens of State, Defense, and Treasury, is a luxury we can no longer afford. . . . We have now become a positive state—a state with 2.3 million civil servants and a ninety billion dollar budget. And this positive state demands an annual outpouring of legislation and a day-to-day practice of efficient administration that can be achieved only if its

great political organs work closely and continuously with one another. If the President and Congress were ever again to war openly and massively, or simply to operate in a state of mutual indifference, the American system of divided government would come crashing to the ground.

The second fact is that, a spate of superficial evidence to the contrary, cooperation on this broad and continuing basis is now the normal pattern of operation in most areas of national concern. By and large the President and his lieutenants provide Congress with detailed and tactful guidance, Congress churns out the laws and pours out the dollars that keep the positive state from foundering, and the laws are executed and money spent by men who feel the touch of Congress but are not thrown off stride by it.

It is true, of course, that Congress, especially the House, has been more than usually recalcitrant in the last few years in responding to the pleas and pressures of the President in such areas of national concern as education, health, civil rights, and urban dislocation, but the refusal of Congress to act more decisively in these areas strikes me as a failure of national will rather than a stoppage in our political machinery. The imperatives of American pluralism, indeed the very dictates of our time-tested Constitution, require us to muster a "persistent and undoubted majority" before taking the sort of decisive steps that President Kennedy advocate[d] in beckoning us toward the New Frontier. That kind of majority . . . simply [did] not yet exist in most of those areas in which the ultraconservatives in Congress . . . seem[ed] to be calling the tune. When it [did] finally emerge, . . . it [began to] get its way—and [got] it largely through processes of cooperation.

This is one of those instances in which our view of reality is distorted by the way in which we gather our information. A fight between President and Congress is news; we read about it avidly. Cooperation between President and Congress is not news; most of the time we do not get to read about it at all. I do not mean to criticize the political scientists of the United States too harshly—not least because I would have to include myself in the criticism—but I do think that the eyes of teachers and scholars, like the eyes of readers of the daily press, are fixed much too rigidly on the occasional spats between the President and the gentlemen of Congress and much too casually, if at all, on the usual pattern of cooperation.

All things considered, the essence of Presidential-Congressional relations in the past few years has been harmony rather than dissonance, cooperation rather than dissension, mutual respect rather than mutual mistrust. The American system may not work as smoothly as the British to produce a joint attack of executive and legislature on national problems, but if one probes beneath the surface, one discovers just about as much cooperation as can be expected in a constitutional system designed to prevent action not willed and supported by a thoughtful majority. Once we accept, as accept we must, the notions that this is still an open, plural society, that Congress should not be denied the right to be a genuine legislature, and that the President ought not to be given all the laws and dollars he asks for from Congress (and would not know what to do with if he got them), then we will be in a position to recognize the remarkable extent to which this working partnership of equal and independent organs has been carried in recent years.

New Factors in the Equation of Cooperation

How, then, does this system work, in particular to generate cooperation and to dampen antagonism? To answer this question fully and convincingly is quite impossible. Here is one of those problems in understanding that defies the "science" of political science, that mocks the pretensions of those who claim to know the unknowable and want to measure the immeasurable. One cannot say exactly *how* the American system manages to beget the

degree of cooperation it does and must: one can say only that it *does*, and then call attention to several forces and tendencies of vague and variable dimension that have helped to beget it.

The first is the consensus in principle and policy that is the distinguishing mark of American politics. We have had our political differences in America, and there have been times in the past seventy-five years—1896 and 1936 are probably the best remembered—when it seemed to many sober observers that the class struggle had come at last to these shores. For the most part, however, we have been uniquely exempt from the tensions, hatreds, and unresolved feuds that have made it almost impossible for so civilized a people as the French to govern themselves constitutionally; and despite the accusation of "the radical Right" that at least half of us are traitors, we remain a remarkably united nation in a world full of disunited ones.

The result of all this is that the President and Congress, the political instruments of the nation, are in fundamental, largely unforced agreement on issues that in other countries, and at other times in this country, have divided men hopelessly. To put the matter concretely, not more than two or three eccentric Congressmen now look upon the President as a violent political enemy, as a man who might be found sometime on the other side of the barricade in a war of classes or ideologies. It takes a united country to run a divided government, and much of the cooperation that keeps ours running today arises out of the American consensus in such matters as the dictates of ideology, the structure of government, the ownership and control of the economy, and the identity of the enemy. A consensus is by no means an unmixed blessing, for it tends to discourage fresh views and thus to stifle debate on important issues, yet no one can doubt the overall benevolence of its influence upon the course of executive-legislative relations in our constitutional system.

A second factor in the equation of co-

operation is the political ties that bind
the President to roughly half the members of Congress, and that bind all but
the most secure and factious of them to
him. Party government in the United
States, as we have been taught by Professor
Schattschneider and others,[20] is a pallid
phenomenon compared with party government in Britain, Canada, Belgium, and
Germany. It nevertheless exists, and there
can be no doubt that it could be a major
influence in creating an air of good will
and mutual trust between President and
Congress. At the same time, the fuzzy nature of party divisions and the tolerant
sway of party loyalties make it possible for
both the leaders and followers of the opposition in Congress to cooperate with
the President on many kinds of issues
without surrendering their claims to respectability. When all the pluses and
minuses are cancelled out, the influence
of our unique pattern of party politics
comes down rather visibly on the side of
cooperation as opposed to dissension.

Another factor is the simple truth that
the key element in a good horse-trade is
always present in our system of divided
power and shared responsibility: Congress
has things the President wants; he has
things they want; each of the principals
has goods to buy and sell. If he wants
laws, dollars, confirmations, and expressions of good will (and committees that
leave his chief lieutenants alone), they
want loaves, fishes, and acts of friendship
(and lieutenants who acknowledge the
right of committees to be informed and to
offer guidance). There is nothing, surely,
more conducive to cooperation than anticipation of the fruits of friendly compromise, and this sense of anticipation, in the
White House as well as on Capitol Hill,
has much to do with the mysterious process of creating harmony out of dissonance.

The rules of the game, especially as it is
played by the members of Congress, are

[20] *See* Toward a More Responsible Two-Party System (*New York, 1950*), *a document produced by
the Committee on Political Parties of the American Political Science Association.*

certainly more favorable to cooperation
than they were, say, fifty years ago. Most
of these rules are the product of custom,
and custom now decrees that the President
need not confine himself to the points of
input and output on the legislative transmission belt. Rather, he is now expected
by most Congressmen, at least, to make detailed recommendations to Congress, to
watch their progress closely on the floor
and in committee, and to use every honorable means within his power to bring
about their enactment. The rules that govern his dealings with the leaders of both
parties in both houses are especially conducive to cooperation. The relations of a
Truman with a Rayburn would have surprised our grandfathers, the relations of
an Eisenhower with a Johnson would
amaze them, the relations of a Kennedy
with a Dirksen would stun them into disbelief. Yet the polite and even chummy
give-and-take of intensely Democratic President Kennedy and professionally Republican Minority Leader Dirksen seems quite
natural to us. Times have changed—and
with them, the rules of the game.

Finally, one would want to point, and
point with some pride, to the morality
that appears to govern the strivings of
even the most deeply committed men in
American politics. There exists today both
in the White House and in Congress a
clear recognition that the struggle does
have limits, that the game does have rules,
and that the first rule reads: "Play to win
but not to disgrace or demoralize or destroy." It would be hard to imagine a President who would take delight in a really
compliant Congress, hard to imagine a
majority of Congressmen behaving like
the Radical Republicans of 1867–1868.
What we are seeing at work today is a general disposition to stay within the bounds
of common sense and fair dealing, a disposition sharpened by a rather false but
useful memory of the imperious quality of
Franklin D. Roosevelt's leadership of Congress during the Hundred Days in 1933
and the first elating months of 1942, and
by a rather more true and altogether use-

ful memory of the extent of Senator McCarthy's challenge not merely to the decencies of the Constitution but to the responsibility of the President for the good order of his Administration. While the bounds are, like all bounds, by no means unbreachable, they are clearly more visible today than they have been at any time in the past fifty years.

Presidential Ascendancy

Consensus, politics, horse-trading, rules, customs, morality—each of these is an important element in the modern pattern of executive-legislative cooperation, yet all of them together are no guarantee that the cooperation will be of the kind that impels men to grapple with problems rather than of the kind that encourages them to stand pat or perhaps to run and hide. Cooperation pure and simple is not enough; cooperation that moves and shakes, that faces life and takes chances, is the kind we must have in the 1960's.

Such cooperation, I am convinced, is far more of a reality in the American system today than it was only a generation ago, largely because an element has now been added permanently to the pattern we have just been examining: the element of Presidential ascendancy. The essence of the situation, the basic reason why the President and Congress work together far more often and readily than they fall out —and work together to get things done —is that he now has a visible edge over Congress in most of their dealings. In the Soviet Union, we have been told, all men are equal, except that some are "more equal" than others. In the American system of government, it can be argued, all branches are equal, except that one is "more equal" than the others. The President of the United States—any President, no matter how modest and moderate a man he may be—is in a position of clear and almost effortless superiority over Congress in the contest for the right to direct the course of the American future. If I may borrow the language and ideas of Stephen Potter[21] (a great student, not only of politics and social behavior, but of life itself), the President is now "one-up" on Congress at all times, and "two-up" if he is disposed to exploit the advantages of his position with tact and vigor.

He is one-up because, if we may think of the governing process in America as a great game, he as executive is usually on the offensive, and Congress as legislature usually on the defensive. His natural posture is that of the active leader, the posture of Congress that of the grudging follower. His great power is essentially positive, the great power of Congress essentially negative. He is a hammer, and hammers are made for striking; Congress is an anvil, and anvils must bear. This has always been true in our constitutional system, and it is doubly true today because of the internal and external pressures under which the system now operates. Action, which is his forte, is at a premium; delay, which is the style of Congress, is at a discount. All over the world, even in the home of parliamentary government, it is a good season for executives and a poor one for legislatures.

The tactical one-upness of the President is most readily apparent in the broad field of "national security," in which he plays the twin roles of Chief Diplomat and Commander-in-Chief. The ingredients of successful diplomacy in time of peace—unity, continuity, dispatch, secrecy, and access to information—have always been properties of his office; none of them has ever been a property of Congress. The ingredient that must be added to the formula in time of cold war—the capacity to threaten or actually use military force —is one that not even the most Coolidge-minded of Republicans would deny the President. And not even the most Stevens-minded Republicans (if there are any still alive) would today presume to give orders

21 *Stephen Potter,* Gamesmanship *(New York: Holt, Rinehart & Winston, Inc., 1948),* Lifemanship *(New York: Holt, Rinehart & Winston, Inc., 1951), and* One-Upmanship *(New York: Holt, Rinehart & Winston, Inc., 1952).*

to fighting generals. The pace of military technology has laid to eternal rest the pretensions of the famous Joint Committee on the Conduct of the Civil War,[22] just as the pace of events in Asia and Africa has destroyed any lingering hopes of the supporters of the Bricker Amendment.

So long as America plies a diplomacy of involvement, as it must into the indefinite future, Congress can hope to play no more than a delaying, harassing, critical role in this vast area of national security: while it will be, as always, a powerful role, it will also be an essentially negative one. For example, it can make life miserable for a President who even thinks about recognizing Red China, and could make it unendurable for one who decided to go ahead in spite of everything and extend recognition, but it cannot recognize Red China itself, nor could it undo the consequences of a Presidential act of recognition. For another example, it can authorize the President to enlarge the Air Force (as it authorized Mr. Truman) or add to the strength of the Marine Corps (as it authorized General Eisenhower) or get on with the development of a supersonic bomber (as it authorized Mr. Kennedy), but it cannot force him (and is reluctant even to "direct" him) to spend the money appropriated for such a purpose.[23] Whatever else we learned in March, 1962, we cannot doubt that, while the President must be excessively polite to Congressional leaders, he takes no orders from them in the performance of his duties as Commander-in-Chief.[24] The President, it may be added, could have drawn on the authority of Congress itself in a real showdown, for Sections 665 (c-2) and 665 (g) of

Title 31 of the United States Code authorize him, in effect, to "establish reserves in any appropriation"—an astounding yet altogether logical recognition of his permanent one-upness.

Presidential "Liberalism" and Congressional "Conservatism"

One-up on the level of tactics, the President goes two-up on the level of strategy if he is in fact a *modern* President. He is now more likely than Congress to be in touch with what seem to be the great trends of American history, and thus more likely to deal from a position of moral strength.

The United States of America is launched, for better or worse, on four massive courses that have already run an astounding distance in the past thirty years and bid well to run even farther in the next thirty: from diversity toward unity in our national habits and sentiments, from easy acceptance of discrimination toward at least a rough equality of opportunity for men of all races in our social structure, from a free-swinging capitalism toward a pattern of regulation and welfare in the economy, and from disdainful isolation toward almost frenetic involvement in diplomacy. I do not mean to exaggerate the impact of these four closely related developments upon the American way of life as it was willed to us by Calvin Coolidge and Warren G. Harding, yet the changes of the recent past have been, for a nation as fundamentally conservative as the United States, something almost deserving of the label of "revolution."

The significance of these changes for the American system of government centers upon the indisputable fact that our last [five] Presidents have been, with no exceptions, purposeful leaders or at least permissive patrons of this long revolution, our last fifteen Congresses, with few exceptions, recalcitrant roadblocks, or at best grudging followers. It is our Presidents, by and large, who have emphasized the

22 *W. W. Pierson, "The Committee on the Conduct of the Civil War,"* American Historical Review; *Vol. XXIII (1918), 550; T. H. Williams, "The Committee on the Conduct of the War,"* Journal of the American Military Institute, *Vol. III (1939), 139.*

23 *See the excerpts from the report of the House Armed Services Committee printed in* The New York Times *(March 9, 1962), 14.*

24 *See the dispatches signalling the termination of "The Battle of the RS-70" in* The New York Times *(March 22, 23, 1962).*

power and glory of the nation at the expense of the states, who have hacked away as best they could at the roots of racial and religious discrimination, who have called for new weapons to deal with the problems of an advanced industrial society, and who have taken us adventuring beyond our shores. Even the most conservative of the last [five] Presidents (and, not at all incidentally, the only one who was a Republican) proved himself more national-minded, more impatient with prejudice, more conscious of the problem of economic growth, and more dedicated to the United Nations and NATO than were the Congresses with which he dealt —certainly more so than the members of his own party in these Congresses.

The causes of this interesting and not yet fully understood situation of what we should not be afraid to call *Presidential "liberalism"* and *Congressional "conservatism"* are too numerous and complicated for me to probe here, yet I must at least mention certain arrangements, attitudes, or developments in the American system which invite the attention of researchers in political science.[25]

1. The whole complicated process of election, which far too often places men with narrow views and special interests in the seats of power in Congress, yet acts remorselessly to reserve the Presidency for men with broad views and general interests, and thus with a deeper insight into the needs of the national community.

2. The relative immunity of the President from the self-interested pressures—most of which are, in the nature of our system, "conservative" in character—that beat daily upon all but the most secure members of Congress.

3. The double gerrymander in our electoral system, which asks the President to serve a constituency in which the residents of great cities have the highest visibility, and Congress (especially the House of Representatives) to serve a constituency in

which the residents of small towns and rural areas are distinctly overrepresented.

4. The sharp contrast between the traditions of the Presidency, which call for strength and action, and the rules and customs of Congress, which place a high premium on caution and compromise.

5. The relative weakness of party government in Congress, which forces the President willy-nilly to assume the responsibility for hard problems that ought in the first instance to be solved by imaginative legislation.

6. The development of a political instinct in the American people, many of whom now seem to expect the President to look out for one set of their interests (the big ones) and their Congressman to look out for the other set (the small ones)—and at least some of whom split their tickets accordingly.

7. Finally, the distinction that Andrew Jackson injected forcefully into the American pattern of politics: between the President as the representative of the people-as-community and Congress as the representative of the people-as-interests.

Only a foolhardy political scientist would try to give each of these factors its exact value in this double equation of Presidential liberalism and Congressional conservatism, yet they all add up to a fact of huge consequence for the historical relationship between the President and the men of Congress, indeed for the course of events: that *he* is clearly more likely than *they* to be ready and willing to take the next and, as it often seems, inevitable steps along the American road. To put the matter as simply and yet dramatically as possible, he is in closer touch with history than they, and that is the one compelling reason for the strategical one-upness that he now enjoys in the American constitutional system. In domestic affairs, he tends to take the broad and progressive point of view; in world affairs, the adventurous and cooperative. In the former, Congress tends to be more parochial and desultory; in the latter, more cautious and nationalistic.

In closer touch with history—that is to

25 *For a pioneering attempt to lay out the dimensions of this cleavage, see Willmoore Kendall, "The Two Majorities,"* Midwest Journal of Political Science, *Vol. IV (1960), 317.*

say, with the realities of the American future—he seems also to be in closer touch with the objective "right"—that is to say, with the ideals of the American tradition. The truth of this generalization is perhaps most clearly demonstrated in the field of civil liberties, in which each of the last [five] Presidents has behaved with considerable restraint and has taken at least a few stands in defense of unpopular persons and ideas. By contrast some Congressmen have been spoilers of democracy and many more have sat by and, faithful to the rules of the club, have let them get away with it. I do not mean to say that the President's personal virtues are generally superior to the collective virtues of Congress, but I do say that the President of the United States can be counted on to behave tactfully and tolerantly most of the time. On the other hand, the rules and customs of Congress sometimes permit unpleasant and unbridled characters to take undue advantage of their privileged position in legislative debates; and the highly developed pluralism of the committee system sometimes allows a chairman or even a single member to assume unwarranted authority in Congressional hearings or investigations. These remarks quite plainly have the character of a value judgment, yet it is the kind of judgment that one can make with the feeling that he is standing squarely on the best American traditions of tolerance and fair play.

The Road Ahead

These, then, are the outlines of the modern pattern of executive-legislative relationships in the United States; to be more precise, this is the context of law, custom, and historical imperative within which the executive branch works with the legislative to make policies that meet the needs of a high and powerful civilization. If we put the roughly harmonizing forces of consensus, politics, horse-trading, rules, customs, and morality together with the tactical and strategical ascendancy of the President, then thrust this whole complicated pattern of decision making into the crucible of a world full of tensions and a nation full of rather healthy self-doubts, we may begin to understand why we are getting just about as much harmony between the two great and independent political organs of our federal government as we could expect or perhaps even want in the 1960's. We are getting it because the President's power is now perceptibly greater than the power of Congress, because his prestige is now more solidly based, because his independence is now more real, because his responsibility is now less pressing, and because his support is now of a character to propel him forcefully down the road to the future. Whether the road leads to freedom or serfdom is well worth arguing, but that the President is some years ahead of Congress on the journey along this road can no longer be doubted. . . .

No one can look for long at the antics of this Congress and grimaces of this President without recognizing the persistence of areas of genuine disagreement between them about the policies to be pursued (if not the fundamentals to be honored) in the next decade. Yet a certain amount of dissension, obstinacy, and just plain angry disagreement is, after all, both a sign and a condition of the operations of constitutional democracy. It is a rare political scientist who interprets the dissensions in the British Parliament today—and indeed in the ranks of each of the major parties active in it—over such fateful issues as the pattern of defense or membership in the Common Market as evidence if a bad or badly performing system of government, and perhaps something of the same kind of tolerance should be shown in interpreting the dissensions in our system. We, too, are arguing about some fateful steps, and to ask our system of government to take them smoothly and agreeably would be to ask something of it that no system, certainly no free system, can produce. What one can ask is that, as our disagreements should not be smothered, so they should not be needlessly exacerbated by the cranky operations of an eighteenth-century constitution. As a matter of fact, they are not needlessly exacerbated; ours is more of a twentieth-century constitution than some people seem to realize; and the ongoing dissensions of President and Congress are products of political nature rather than of constitutional art.

All in all, there is a remarkable degree of purposeful cooperation now built into the American system of government. It would surprise the framers and yet also, upon reflection, make sense to them; and they, wiser men than we, would see that it was perhaps not so much of a mystery after all. They would tell us, I am sure, what the logic of our politics has already told us: that if America fails to do what it has to do at home and abroad in the next generation, it will not be a failure of the American Constitution but of the American character. That Constitution will prove itself equal to any reasonable demand we decide to put upon it.

B. Public Law and Judicial Philosophy

Equal Protection and the Urban Majority

C. Herman Pritchett

. . . On May 17, 1954, nine judges, sworn to defend a Constitution which guarantees equal protection of the laws, speaking for a country which declared its independence on the proposition that all men are created equal and which is fighting for moral leadership in a world predominantly populated by people whose skin color is other than white—these nine men unanimously concluded that segregated educational facilities are "inherently unequal."*

Even those who were in full sympathy with the holding must nevertheless have been awed by the responsibility the Supreme Court had undertaken and shaken by some doubts whether the judicial institution could engage in a controversy so charged with emotion and bitterness without running the risk of political defeat and possible permanent impairment of judicial power.

. . . [Today] we know that they made the right decision. The decision was right

* Brown v. Board of Education, *347 U.S. 483 (1954)*—ED. NOTE.

because it got the United States on the right side of history at a crucial time in world affairs. By its action the Court raised a standard around which men of good will might rally. Under the Court's leadership the issue of racial segregation was forced on the American conscience. Segregation could persist only if it could be ignored; once the case for segregation had to be examined, it was lost. Without either the purse or the sword, the weakest of the three branches of government proved to be the only one with the conscience, the capacity, and the will to challenge the scandal, the immorality, the social and economic waste, and the positive international dangers of racial discrimination. Eventually the executive, through Presidents Kennedy and Johnson, and the Congress began to assume their responsibilities for achieving the broad purposes of racial equality. But if the Court had not taken that first giant step in 1954, does anyone think there would now be a Civil Rights Act of 1964?

Today, the Supreme Court stands with

C. Herman Pritchett, "Equal Protection and the Urban Majority," *American Political Science Review*, Vol. LVIII, No. 4 (December, 1964), 869–875. Reprinted by permission.

respect to the issue of legislative districting and apportionment where it stood in
1954 on the issue of racial segregation.
Though the differences are substantial, I
suggest that the similarities are even
greater. Now, as then, the Court has
taken sides in the crisis of our times.
Where the Court in 1954 was demanding
a social revolution, today it is presiding
over a political revolution. Once again
the Court has unlocked the explosive potentialities of the equal protection clause,
staking its prestige and its reputation on
its ability to remake the nation in the image of its constitutional concepts.

I

The Supreme Court has never been
detached from the major political issues of
the times. As Edward S. Corwin once said:
"Constitutional law has always a central
interest to guard."[1] Under John Marshall
the central interest was in the heroic task
of legitimizing a strong national government. Under Roger Taney the Court's
attachment was to narrower, more frag-
mented goals, principally the economic
interests of the South and West. In the
latter part of the nineteenth century the
Court's role was to encourage the economic freedom which a rapidly expanding
economy demanded. In the New Deal
period the Court was striving toward a
balance of governmental power, strong
enough to prevent depressions yet restrained enough not to threaten individual freedom.

When we come to the recent past, we
stand in our own light and may not see
what will be obvious from a longer perspective. But certainly a central focus of
constitutional law since World War II has
been on problems of what may be called
"the urban majority." The census of 1920
revealed that rural America, which from
the beginning of the nation had dominated American politics and social values,

had become a minority. Since that time
white, Protestant, rural America has been
on the defensive, seeking to maintain in
race, religion, and politics its former
superiority. Urban America, the new majority, has offered to the Negro the opportunity to escape from the bondage of
rural peonage, as it had earlier permitted
European immigrants to rise in economic
and social status. Urban America has had
to develop a tolerance which did not exist
in rural America, so that various races and
religions could live together in peace. Urban America has needed the political
power which would make possible governmental recognition of its staggering problems of housing, transportation, recreation, juvenile delinquency, disease, and
social disintegration.

Faced with this challenge, the rural
minority could preserve its political power
and its social system only by a denial of
that equality which had been a major
tenet of the American credo, though often
"honored in the breach" rather than the
observance. Conversely, the drive of the
urban majority required the assertion and
the practice of equality in race, equality
in religion, equality in political power.
As Alan Grimes says in his thoughtful
book on *Equality in America,* the urban
majority has proved to be "a liberating
force in American politics, redistributing
freedom by equalizing the claims of the
contestants." He continues:

> American politics has always made a prag-
> matic adjustment to its immediate needs,
> tempering its idealism with expediency. To-
> day, ironically, the imperatives of urban
> life are making expedient the fulfillment
> of the historic ideal of equality.[2]

II

The idea of equality indeed has roots
deep in Western political thought. It
reaches back to the Greek and Roman
Stoics and the Christian fathers, and was

---

[1] The Constitution and What It Means Today
(*Princeton: Princeton University Press, 1946*), *p.
viii.*

[2] Equality in America: Religion, Race and the
Urban Majority (*New York: Oxford University
Press, 1964*), *p. x.*

carried forward by seventeenth- and eighteenth-century political philosophers such as Hobbes and Locke. The Declaration of Independence announced the "self-evident" truth that "all men are created equal," but no language specifically reflecting egalitarian concern found a place in the Constitution. In fact, that document in several provisions accepted and guaranteed the institution of human slavery.

The idea of equality finally appeared in the Constitution when the Fourteenth Amendment was adopted in 1868, forbidding the states to deny to any person within their jurisdiction "the equal protection of the laws." This formulation was conceived primarily as a protection for the newly freed slaves. Justice Miller in *The Slaughter-House Cases*[3] said that this was "the one pervading purpose" of the Civil War amendments. Speaking specifically of the equal protection clause, he doubted very much "whether any action of a State not directed by way of discrimination against the negroes as a class, or on account of their race, will ever be held to come within the purview" of the clause.

This expectation was doubly confounded. The Court proved very reluctant to use the equal protection clause as an instrument for the protection of the civil rights of the "newly made freemen," and at the same time eager to invent uses for it as a bar to business regulation. Robert J. Harris, in his fine study of the equal protection clause,[4] located some 554 decisions of the Supreme Court up to 1960 in which this provision was invoked and passed upon by the Court. Of these, 426 (77 per cent) dealt with legislation affecting economic interests, while only 78 (14 per cent) concerned state laws allegedly imposing racial discrimination or acts of Congress designed to eliminate it.

The generally low regard in which the equal protection clause was held as late as

1927 is indicated by Justice Holmes's deprecatory characterization of equal protection in *Buck v. Bell* as "the usual last resort of constitutional arguments."[5] It was not until the early 1930's that the Supreme Court "returned to the Constitution," as Harris puts it, and began the rehabilitation of the equal protection clause in a series of cases dealing with racial discrimination which finally led in 1954 to the epoch-making decision in *Brown v. Board of Education.*[6]

In the meantime there had been a tentative exploration on the Court of the possible application of the equal protection clause to legislative districting and apportionment. Serious complaints had accumulated in most of the states as to inequality of population in Congressional and state legislative districts. Inequality resulted both from failure to redraw district lines as population changes occurred, and from provisions in many states basing legislative districts on factors other than population. The problem of unequal Congressional districts was raised in the 1946 case of *Colegrove v. Green,*[7] and three members of the Court asserted there for the first time that equal protection required the election of Congressmen from districts generally equal in population. But there was no follow-up on this suggestion. Over the next fifteen years efforts to get the Court to intervene in other kinds of legislative election problems were met, in Harris's words, with "bland unconcern for equitable representation." Consequently it came as a considerable surprise in 1962 when the Court in *Baker v. Carr*[8] by a six to two vote reversed the result of the *Colegrove* case and directed a federal court to hear a challenge to the constitutionality of Tennessee's legislative arrangements, where no reapportionment of seats in the state legislature had taken place since 1901.

While this decision did not indicate

---

[3] *16 Wall. 36 (1873).*
[4] The Quest for Equality (*Baton Rouge: Louisiana State University Press, 1960*), *p. 59.*

[5] *274 U.S. 200 (1927).*
[6] *347 U.S. 483 (1954).*
[7] *328 U.S. 549 (1946).*
[8] *369 U.S. 186 (1962).*

what standards the judiciary should apply in passing on complaints about legislative apportionment, that was soon to come. In 1963 the Court in *Gray v. Sanders*[9] by a vote of eight to one invalidated the Georgia county unit system of primary elections for statewide offices, a system deliberately designed to give control of the electoral process to rural minorities. The Court held:

> Once the geographical unit for which a representative is to be chosen is designated, all who participate in the election are to have an equal vote—whatever their race, whatever their sex, whatever their occupation, whatever their income, and wherever their home may be in that geographical unit. This is required by the Equal Protection Clause of the Fourteenth Amendment.

This was the Court's first approach to the rule of one-man-one-vote. *Gray v. Sanders* was not, of course, a legislative apportionment case. But in 1964 the Court held that the same principle covered election of representatives in Congress and the apportionment of seats in the state legislatures. In *Wesberry v. Sanders*[10] the Court by a vote of six to three applied the one-man-one-vote principle to the Congressional districts of Georgia, holding that the Constitution had the "plain objective of making equal representation for equal numbers of people the fundamental goal for the House of Representatives." Four months later the rule of one-man-one-vote was responsible for holding unconstitutional the legislatures in no less than fifteen states, as the Court decided *Reynolds v. Sims*[11] and fourteen other cases by varying majorities of from six to eight justices. Probably more than forty state legislatures in all are vulnerable to challenge under the principle of *Reynolds v. Sims*.

III

The apportionment decisions have been bitterly criticized on many grounds,

but there are two basic objections to the constitutional position asserted by the Court. First, it is argued that the equal protection clause has no relevance to and does not control matters of political representation, and consequently that there are no constitutional limits on legislative arrangements. Second, even if there are some limits, it is alleged that they are not judicially enforceable. So this is partly an argument about constitutional standards for apportionment systems, and partly an argument about the proper role of the courts.

Let us examine first the question of constitutional standards. Only Justices Frankfurter and Harlan on the recent Court contend that there are no constitutional limitations on legislative discretion in setting up apportionment arrangements. With Frankfurter's retirement, the Court's position is eight to one against Harlan on this score.

Six members of the Court majority say that the proper standard is one-man-one-vote. In *Wesberry v. Sanders* Justice Black derived the principle of equal Congressional districts from certain of Madison's statements at the Constitutional Convention and in *The Federalist,* and from the provisions in Article I for the choosing of representatives "by the people of the several States." In *Reynolds v. Sims* Chief Justice Warren replied on general principles of representative government and majority rule to support the Court's conclusion that "the Equal Protection Clause guarantees the opportunity for equal participation by all voters in the election of state legislators." "Legislators represent people, not trees or acres," he said, adding: "To the extent that a citizen's right to vote is debased, he is that much less a citizen."

Obviously the Court is here creating new law, just as it did in the *Brown* decision. The Court never likes to admit that it is creating new law. In *Brown* the Court had hoped that it could find some support for overruling its precedents in the "intention of the framers," some definite indica-

[9] *372 U.S. 368 (1963).*
[10] *376 U.S. 1 (1964).*
[11] *377 U.S. 533 (1964).*

tion of concern with segregated education when the Fourteenth Amendment was adopted, and so it had asked counsel to undertake research on the historical background of the amendment. But no clear voice spoke from the past, and consequently the Court had to ground its interpretation of equal protection on the "present place" of public education in American life and present psychological knowledge and present standards of morality. In the same way the Court in *Reynolds v. Sims* relates equal protection to present concepts of representative government.

It is charged, however, that these are simply the concepts of a "particular political philosophy" which seems wise to the present majority of the Supreme Court, and without constitutional standing. Justices Stewart and Clark deny that the rule of one-man-one-vote can be logically or historically drawn out of the equal protection clause, and they contend that the rule is much too rigid in its effect on systems of representation. Holding every state to the one-man-one-vote rule, they say, would deny "any opportunity for enlightened and progressive innovation in the design of its democratic institutions." The goal of equal protection as they see it is a broader one, "to accommodate within a system of representative government the interests and aspirations of diverse groups of people, without subjecting any group or class to absolute domination by a geographically concentrated or highly organized majority."

This is a rather vague standard. How is one to judge whether it has been achieved? There are two tests, according to Stewart. First, the plan of representation must be "rational," in the light of the state's own characteristics and needs. Second, "the plan must be such as not to permit the systematic frustration of the will of a majority of the electorate of the State." Determining whether a state is meeting this test might seem to require the employment of whole cadres of political scientists, but Stewart suggests that a liberal arrangement for use of the initiative and referendum in approving or reviewing apportionment plans should be regarded as an acceptable guarantee against frustration of the basic principle of majority rule.

Application of this twofold test led Stewart and Clark to uphold the legislative apportionments of New York, Colorado, Illinois, and Michigan, all of which were condemned by the six-judge majority as violative of one-man-one-vote. In addition, Stewart, but not Clark, would have approved the Ohio apportionment. The Stewart-Clark standard gave the same result as one-man-one-vote in the ten other states which the Court considered in the spring of 1964.[12]

Which of these standards has the better claim to validity? The Stewart-Clark rule of rationality has the pragmatic merit of flexibility. It does not clamp down so strictly on the discretion the states have traditionally exercised in making representation decisions, and consequently it may be more politically acceptable.

By contrast, one-man-one-vote is a rigorous rule. But I believe that it comes closer to summarizing current notions of democracy in representation than any other. For example, the Twentieth Century Fund in 1962 assembled a conference of sixteen distinguished research scholars and political scientists to discuss the problems of legislative apportionment. With only one dissent, they concluded that "the history of democratic institutions points compellingly in the direction of population as the only legitimate basis of representation today."[13]

Moreover, the Court's one-man-one-vote rule may not be as rigorous as it sounds. Chief Justice Warren's opinion in *Reynolds v. Sims* specifically disclaimed the intention "to spell out any precise constitutional tests." All that the Court asked was that apportionments be "based substantially on population and the equal-

12 *In four of these cases, however, Stewart voted to remand for further proceedings.*
13 One Man-One Vote (*New York: The Twentieth Century Fund, 1962*), *p. 4.*

population principle   . not [be] diluted in any significant way." He also granted that "a State can rationally consider according political subdivisions some independent representation in at least one body of the state legislature, as long as the basic standard of equality of population among districts is maintained." It therefore appears possible that one-man-one-vote may in practice be tempered by some of the same rationality which is the foundation of the Stewart and Clark approach.

IV

Fortunately for us, however, this comparison of the Court's two standards can be left to another occasion. For present purposes their similarity is more important than their differences. The significant fact is that eight members of the Court, though disagreeing as to the standard, have agreed that the Court must assume responsibility for bringing legislative apportionments under the coverage of the equal protection clause. And the more lenient of the two standards is still strict enough to invalidate ten of the first fifteen state legislatures to which it has been applied.

The basic division on the Court, then, is not over standards but over the proper role of the Court in handling political questions. In *Colegrove v. Green,* Justice Frankfurter first made the argument that legislative districting and apportionment was a "political thicket" which courts must shun. When he lost this argument in *Baker v. Carr,* he had to develop a positive justification for inequality of voting and representation arrangements in order to continue his posture of judicial nonintervention. His argument was that population had never been the sole basis for representation systems, either in the past or the present, and so it could not be part of the concept of equal protection. He presented a long historical review of the various systems of representation, and wound up with the conclusion that there

had been "a decided twentieth-century trend away from population as the exclusive base of representation." Only twelve state constitutions, he reported, provided for a substantially unqualified application of the population standard for even a single chamber. This appeared to Frankfurter to constitute a conclusive case against one-man-one-vote.

Frankfurter is, of course, correct on the mathematics. There *has* been a trend away from population as the exclusive base of representation in state legislatures. Such a trend has manifested itself, for example, in the state of Illinois, which affords an interesting commentary on Frankfurter's statistics. The Northwest Ordinance of 1787, the Illinois Enabling Act of 1818, the Illinois Constitution of 1848, and the present Constitution of 1870 all provided for two houses based on population. From 1818 to 1901 both houses were redistricted fourteen times in conformity with population changes. In 1870 Cook County contained only 14 per cent of the state's population. But by 1900 it had grown to 38 per cent, and 1901 was the last reapportionment that could be put through the legislature, because the population growth of Cook County would have had to be recognized. Efforts to force remapping in the courts failed. Finally, in 1954 a compromise constitutional amendment was presented to the voters—the lower house to be redistricted every ten years on a population basis, the senate to be drawn permanently with area the prime consideration to guarantee downstate control. The amendment was ratified by 87 per cent of Illinois voters.

This is a sample of how Frankfurter's trend was established. It is a trend resulting from rural legislators' persistent refusal to recognize state constitutional requirements and metropolitan expansion, and final acquiescence by city dwellers in permanent underrepresentation as the price of getting any reapportionment at all. Somehow Frankfurter's trend seems less impressive when put in this light. The principle of representation which his research has discovered is simply the principle that power holders do not willingly give up power.

Since Frankfurter did not recognize this as the operative principle of representation in the twentieth century, he did not have to defend it. But his colleague Justice Harlan did in fact do so in his several opinions. In *Baker v. Carr,* supplementing Frankfurter's dissent, he announced that he would not regard it as unconstitutional for a state legislature to conclude (a) "that an existing allocation of senators and representatives constitutes a desirable balance of geographical and demographical representation," or (b) "that in the interest of stability of government it would be best to defer for some future time the redistribution of seats in the state legislature," or (c) that "an electoral imbalance between its rural and urban population" would be desirable "to protect the State's agricultural interests from the sheer weight of numbers of those residing in the cities."

Bear in mind that in *Baker v. Carr* the legislature which was making these decisions was a legislature elected from districts drawn in 1901 and not subsequently revised, in defiance of the state constitution. So what Harlan was saying was that legislators representing the state as it was in 1901 could legitimately decide in 1962 that the 1901 balance of geography and demography had been preferable, that the political situation in the state would be more stable if the clock had been stopped in 1901, and that the rural interests as of 1901 could themselves decide, contrary to the state constitution, that they deserved protection against the cities and that it should take the form of keeping city representation in a minority.

Justice Harlan did not even stop with this. In the 1963 case of *Gray v. Sanders,* he was, alone on the Court, rash enough to argue that Georgia's county unit caricature of a representation system was not irrational. He said in its defense:

Given the undeniably powerful influence of a state governor on law and policy mak-

ing, I do not see how it can be deemed irrational for a State to conclude that a candidate for such office should not be one whose choice lies with the numerically superior electoral strength of urban voters. By like token, I cannot consider it irrational for Georgia to apply its County Unit System to the selection of candidates for other statewide offices in order to assure against a predominantly "city point of view" in the administration of the State's affairs.

The amazing doctrine here announced is that a state can rationally, and therefore lawfully, set up an electoral system under which the governor and other statewide officers must be chosen by the minority because if they represented the majority they might abuse the "legitimate interests" of the minority. By the same logic it could be argued that Negroes, who are in every state a minority more abused than rural interests ever were, could rationally be given the right to control the naming of public officials. Actually, Harlan suggests in his *Baker* dissent that he would accept as rational *any* legislative plan of allotting representatives short of throwing dice.

V

Justice Harlan would have been better advised not to try to find rational excuses for misrepresentation, and simply to confine himself to stating the case against judicial involvement in political questions. He does elaborate on Frankfurter's *Colegrove* reasoning, as in the following statement from the *Wesberry* case:

What is done today saps the political process. The promise of judicial intervention in matters of this sort cannot but encourage popular inertia in efforts for political reform through the political process, with the inevitable result that the process is itself weakened.

My response is that it is a naïve, static view of politics which holds that if the courts do more, the legislature and executive will do less. If the courts act, it is quite possible that they will stimulate

others to act. In fact, within four days
after the *Wesberry* decision was handed
down, the Georgia legislature, its political
process not sapped but invigorated, passed
a bill redistricting the state's Congressional seats for the first time since 1931
and giving Atlanta the representation in
Congress to which it was entitled by population.

The *Wesberry* decision also motivated
the House Judiciary Committee to take
up a long-pending measure drafted by
Representative [Emanuel] Celler (D., N.Y.)
providing that Congressional districts must
be composed of compact and contiguous
territory, varying not more than 15 per
cent from the average population of the
state's Congressional districts.[14] Prospects
for eventual passage of the bill are regarded as favorable. Representative William McCulloch (R., Ohio) was quoted as
saying, when the bill was being considered
in committee: "With hindsight, we probably would have been well-advised to have
taken some action heretofore."[15] Now that
the Supreme Court has said that there is
no defense for unequal Congressional districting, everyone agrees and the districts
are being made equal. But until the Supreme Court acted, there was no legislative action and no prospect of legislative
action.

Justice Harlan puts his objection to judicial activism in a somewhat different way
when he castigates the "current mistaken
view . . . that this Court should 'take
the lead' in promoting reform when other
branches of government fail to act." Stated
this broadly, Harlan's criticism must include the Court's historic accomplishment
achieved by "taking the lead" in *Brown v.
Board of Education*. The Court in 1954
could have decided that ending racial segregation was not a task for them—indeed,
not a task for a court at all. The justices
could have said, this is a job for Congress,
which is specifically authorized by Section
5 of the Fourteenth Amendment to en-

force the equal protection clause by "appropriate legislation." They could have
said, this is a job for the President, who
has resources for marshalling opinion and
providing the leadership and quite possibly the coercion that will be required to
make equal protection a reality in many
parts of the nation. The *Brown* Court
could have said these things—but it did
not. It took the lead.

Now, in 1964 the Court has taken the
lead to achieve equality in the representative process at the state level. It has taken
the lead in demanding that the naked
power struggle, which up to the present
has determined how state legislatures are
composed, be subjected to the rule of law
—specifically, equal protection of the laws.
The Court has stirred the stagnant waters
in the rotten boroughs. It has challenged
the beneficiaries of the various systems of
malapportionment and underrepresentation to justify if they can their privileged
status. The Court has cut through the
sophistry that to prevent the problems of
rural minorities from being ignored, it is
necessary to ignore the problems of urban
majorities.

But stirring the waters is not enough,
of course, and here is where Justice Harlan's reservations about judicial leadership
have some relevance. Courts cannot lead
unless someone will follow. The burden of
achieving racial integration was too heavy
for the courts to bear alone; they needed
the executive and legislative assistance
they have recently received. Just so the
Supreme Court cannot expect to carry
through a massive reform of American
state legislatures unless there is substantial
legislative support for the goals it has announced. It is true that some courts, when
reapportionment deadlines imposed on
state legislatures have not been met, have
themselves carved up a state into legislative districts. But few can be happy to see
courts assume such functions, for which
they have so little qualification.

The Supreme Court, needing legislative
support, must anticipate the possibility
that this support may be less than com-

14 *H. R. 2836 88th Congr.*
15 The New York Times (*March 19, 1964*).

plete. Many proposals for constitutional amendments have been put forward to modify in one respect or another the impact of the Supreme Court decisions on state legislatures. The principal proposal, backed by the Republican party platform in 1964 and the Republican leadership in Congress, would accept the position that one house must be based on population, but would allow representation in the second house to take into account factors other than population if the people of the state approved in a referendum vote.[16]

If such an amendment were to be adopted, it would be regarded as a rebuff to the Supreme Court. But its adoption would actually require most of the states to revise their legislative apportionments in the direction of greater equality of representation than now exists, and the Court, even with its mandate thus limited, would have been responsible for stimulating the political process to accomplish the

most sweeping reform of state legislative composition in American history.

In a very real sense, then, the Court's decision in *Reynolds v. Sims* is not an order. It is an opinion offering itself for belief; it is a recommendation proposing action. The Court proposes, but politics disposes.

The Court was justified in taking the lead on reapportionment in state legislatures because no other channels of protest were open to an aggrieved citizenry. The Court was justified in concluding that the stalemate of legislative representation could be broken only by holding one-man-one-vote to be a constitutional mandate. In a nation which is 70 per cent urban, the Court is saying to rurally dominated legislatures that the way to regain the position and prestige the states once had is to establish contact with the real world of the second half of the twentieth century. The Court is opening the way for state legislatures, which all too often have seemed engaged in an organized conspiracy against the future, to play a positive role in dealing with the staggering problems of metropolitan America.

"Courts are not representative bodies," said Justice Frankfurter in his concurring opinion in *Dennis v. United States*.[17] "They are not designed to be a good reflex of a democratic society." It is one of the strengths of the American system that this is not necessarily true. Not all elective institutions are representative, and not all representative institutions are elective. Students of public administration have demonstrated how much we rely on the representative character of the American civil service. Now *Brown* and *Baker* have again reminded us that judges who endeavor to speak for the constituency of reason and justice may truly represent the enduring principles of a democratic society.

16 *In an effort to delay judicial enforcement of the Supreme Court reapportionment decisions until a constitutional amendment could be considered by Congress, several legislative measures were considered in the closing days of the Eighty-Eighth Congress. Senator Everett Dirksen sponsored H.R. 11380 as a rider to the foreign aid bill, providing that federal courts may not interfere with the election of state legislatures before January 1, 1966, and that they must allow states "a reasonable opportunity" to reapportion their legislative seats in regular legislative sessions, except in "highly unusual circumstances." Adoption of the rider was prevented by a filibuster, and eventually a compromise was approved in the Senate. It declared the "sense of Congress" that any order of a federal district court concerning apportionment of a state legislature could properly allow the legislature the length of time of its regular session plus thirty days, but no longer than six months, to apportion itself in accordance with the Constitution. House conservatives, angered at the mildness of H.R. 11380 as amended, forced its elimination from the foreign aid bill in conference, so the Eighty-Eighth Congress adjourned without taking any action relating to the Court's apportionment decisions.*

17 *341 U.S. 494 (1951).*

C. Ideals

Liberty, Equality, and Individualism in Democratic Nations

Alexis de Tocqueville

Why Democratic Nations Show a More Ardent and Enduring Love of Equality than of Liberty

The first and most intense passion that is produced by equality of condition is, I need hardly say, the love of that equality. My readers will therefore not be surprised that I speak of this feeling before all others.

Everybody has remarked that in our time, and especially in France, this passion for equality is every day gaining ground in the human heart. It has been said a hundred times that our contemporaries are far more ardently and tenaciously attached to equality than to freedom; but as I do not find that the causes of the fact have been sufficiently analyzed, I shall endeavor to point them out.

It is possible to imagine an extreme point at which freedom and equality would meet and blend. Let us suppose that all the people take a part in the government, and that each one of them has an equal right to take a part in it. As no one is different from his fellows, none can exercise a tyrannical power; men will be perfectly free because they are all entirely equal; and they will all be perfectly equal because they are entirely free. To this ideal state democratic nations tend. This is the only complete form that equality can assume upon earth; but there are a thousand others which, without being equally perfect, are not less cherished by those nations.

The principle of equality may be estab- lished in civil society without prevailing in the political world. There may be equal rights of indulging in the same pleasures, of entering the same professions, of frequenting the same places; in a word, of living in the same manner and seeking wealth by the same means, although all men do not take an equal share in the government. A kind of equality may even be established in the political world though there should be no political freedom there. A man may be the equal of all his countrymen save one, who is the master of all without distinction and who selects equally from among them all the agents of his power. Several other combinations might be easily imagined by which very great equality would be united to institutions more or less free or even to institutions wholly without freedom.

Although men cannot become absolutely equal unless they are entirely free, and consequently equality, pushed to its furthest extent, may be confounded with freedom, yet there is good reason for distinguishing the one from the other. The taste which men have for liberty and that which they feel for equality are, in fact, two different things; and I am not afraid to add that among democratic nations they are two unequal things.

Upon close inspection it will be seen that there is in every age some peculiar and preponderant fact with which all others are connected; this fact almost always gives birth to some pregnant idea or some ruling passion, which attracts to it-

Alexis de Tocqueville, *Democracy in America* (New York: Alfred A. Knopf, Inc., 1945), Vol. II, Second Book, Chaps. 1–4, pp. 94–105. Henry Reeve text, revised by Francis Bowen; Phillips Bradley edition. Reprinted by permission.

self and bears away in its course all the feelings and opinions of the time; it is like a great stream toward which each of the neighboring rivulets seems to flow.

Freedom has appeared in the world at different times and under various forms; it has not been exclusively bound to any social condition, and it is not confined to democracies. Freedom cannot, therefore, form the distinguishing characteristic of democratic ages. The peculiar and preponderant fact that marks those ages as its own is the equality of condition; the ruling passion of men in those periods is the love of this equality. Do not ask what singular charm the men of democratic ages find in being equal, or what special reasons they may have for clinging so tenaciously to equality rather than to the other advantages that society holds out to them: equality is the distinguishing characteristic of the age they live in; that of itself is enough to explain that they prefer it to all the rest.

But independently of this reason there are several others which will at all times habitually lead men to prefer equality to freedom.

If a people could ever succeed in destroying, or even in diminishing, the equality that prevails in its own body, they could do so only by long and laborious efforts. Their social condition must be modified, their laws abolished, their opinions superseded, their habits changed, their manners corrupted. But political liberty is more easily lost; to neglect to hold it fast is to allow it to escape. Therefore not only do men cling to equality because it is dear to them; they also adhere to it because they think it will last forever.

That political freedom in its excesses may compromise the tranquillity, the property, the lives of individuals is obvious even to narrow and unthinking minds. On the contrary, none but attentive and clear-sighted men perceive the perils with which equality threatens us, and they commonly avoid pointing them out. They know that the calamities they apprehend are remote and flatter themselves that they will only

fall upon future generations, for which the present generation takes but little thought. The evils that freedom sometimes brings with it are immediate; they are apparent to all, and all are more or less affected by them. The evils that extreme equality may produce are slowly disclosed; they creep gradually into the social frame; they are seen only at intervals; and at the moment at which they become most violent, habit already causes them to be no longer felt.

The advantages that freedom brings are shown only by the lapse of time, and it is always easy to mistake the cause in which they originate. The advantages of equality are immediate, and they may always be traced from their source.

Political liberty bestows exalted pleasures from time to time upon a certain number of citizens. Equality every day confers a number of small enjoyments on every man. The charms of equality are every instant felt and are within the reach of all; the noblest hearts are not insensible to them, and the most vulgar souls exult in them. The passion that equality creates must therefore be at once strong and general. Men cannot enjoy political liberty unpurchased by some sacrifices, and they never obtain it without great exertions. But the pleasures of equality are self-proffered; each of the petty incidents of life seems to occasion them, and in order to taste them, nothing is required but to live.

Democratic nations are at all times fond of equality, but there are certain epochs at which the passion they entertain for it swells to the height of fury. This occurs at the moment when the old social system, long menaced, is overthrown after a severe internal struggle, and the barriers of rank are at length thrown down. At such times men pounce upon equality as their booty, and they cling to it as to some precious treasure which they fear to lose. The passion for equality penetrates on every side into men's hearts, expands there, and fills them entirely. Tell them not that by this blind surrender of themselves to an exclusive passion they risk their dearest interests; they are deaf. Show them not freedom escaping from their grasp while they are looking another way; they are blind, or rather they can discern but one object to be desired in the universe.

What I have said is applicable to all democratic nations; what I am about to say concerns the French alone. Among most modern nations, and especially among all those of the continent of Europe, the taste and the idea of freedom began to exist and to be developed only at the time when social conditions were tending to equality and as a consequence of that very equality. Absolute kings were the most efficient levelers of ranks among their subjects. Among these nations equality preceded freedom; equality was therefore a fact of some standing when freedom was still a novelty; the one had already created customs, opinions, and laws belonging to it when the other, alone and for the first time, came into actual existence. Thus the latter was still only an affair of opinion and of taste while the former had already crept into the habits of the people, possessed itself of their manners, and given a particular turn to the smallest actions in their lives. Can it be wondered at that the men of our own time prefer the one to the other?

I think that democratic communities have a natural taste for freedom; left to themselves, they will seek it, cherish it, and view any privation of it with regret. But for equality their passion is ardent, insatiable, incessant, invincible; they call for equality in freedom; and if they cannot obtain that, they still call for equality in slavery. They will endure poverty, servitude, barbarism, but they will not endure aristocracy.

This is true at all times, and especially in our own day. All men and all powers seeking to cope with this irresistible passion will be overthrown and destroyed by it. In our age freedom cannot be established without it, and despotism itself cannot reign without its support.

Of Individualism in Democratic Countries

I have shown how it is that in ages of equality every man seeks for his opinions within himself; I am now to show how it is that in the same ages all his feelings are turned toward himself alone. *Individualism* is a novel expression, to which a novel idea has given birth. Our fathers were only acquainted with *égoïsme* (selfishness). Selfishness is a passionate and exaggerated love of self, which leads a man to connect everything with himself and to prefer himself to everything in the world. Individualism is a mature and calm feeling, which disposes each member of the community to sever himself from the mass of his fellows and to draw apart with his family and his friends, so that after he has thus formed a little circle of his own, he willingly leaves society at large to itself. Selfishness originates in blind instinct; individualism proceeds from erroneous judgment more than from depraved feelings; it originates as much in deficiencies of mind as in perversity of heart.

Selfishness blights the germ of all virtue; individualism, at first, only saps the virtues of public life; but in the long run it attacks and destroys all others and is at length absorbed in downright selfishness. Selfishness is a vice as old as the world, which does not belong to one form of society more than to another; individualism is of democratic origin, and it threatens to spread in the same ratio as the equality of condition.

Among aristocratic nations, as families remain for centuries in the same condition, often on the same spot, all generations become, as it were, contemporaneous. A man almost always knows his forefathers and respects them; he thinks he already sees his remote descendants and he loves them. He willingly imposes duties on himself toward the former and the latter, and he will frequently sacrifice his personal gratifications to those who went before and to those who will come after him. Aristocratic institutions, moreover, have the effect of closely binding every man to several of his fellow citizens. As the classes of an aristocratic people are strongly marked and permanent, each of them is regarded by its own members as a sort of lesser country, more tangible and more cherished than the country at large. As in aristocratic communities all the citizens occupy fixed positions, one above another, the result is that each of them always sees a man above himself whose patronage is necessary to him, and below himself another man whose cooperation he may claim. Men living in aristocratic ages are therefore almost always closely attached to something placed out of their own sphere, and they are often disposed to forget themselves. It is true that in these ages the notion of human fellowship is faint and that men seldom think of sacrificing themselves for mankind; but they often sacrifice themselves for other men. In democratic times, on the contrary, when the duties of each individual to the race are much more clear, devoted service to any one man becomes more rare; the bond of human affection is extended, but it is relaxed.

Among democratic nations new families are constantly springing up, others are constantly falling away, and all that remain change their condition; the woof of time is every instant broken and the track of generations effaced. Those who went before are soon forgotten; of those who will come after, no one has any idea: the interest of man is confined to those in close propinquity to himself. As each class gradually approaches others and mingles with them, its members become undifferentiated and lose their class identity for each other. Aristocracy had made a chain of all the members of the community, from the peasant to the king; democracy breaks that chain and severs every link of it.

As social conditions become more equal, the number of persons increases who, although they are neither rich nor powerful enough to exercise any great influence over their fellows, have nevertheless acquired or retained sufficient education and

fortune to satisfy their own wants. They owe nothing to any man, they expect nothing from any man; they acquire the habit of always considering themselves as standing alone, and they are apt to imagine that their whole destiny is in their own hands.

Thus not only does democracy make every man forget his ancestors, but it hides his descendants and separates his contemporaries from him; it throws him back forever upon himself alone and threatens in the end to confine him entirely within the solitude of his own heart.

Individualism Stronger at the Close of a Democratic Revolution than at Other Periods

The period when the construction of democratic society upon the ruins of an aristocracy has just been completed is especially that at which this isolation of men from one another and the selfishness resulting from it most forcibly strike the observer. Democratic communities not only contain a large number of independent citizens, but are constantly filled with men who, having entered but yesterday upon their independent condition, are intoxicated with their new power. They entertain a presumptuous confidence in their own strength, and as they do not suppose that they can henceforward ever have occasion to claim the assistance of their fellow creatures, they do not scruple to show that they care for nobody but themselves.

An aristocracy seldom yields without a protracted struggle, in the course of which implacable animosities are kindled between the different classes of society. These passions survive the victory, and traces of them may be observed in the midst of the democratic confusion that ensues. Those members of the community who were at the top of the late gradations of rank cannot immediately forget their former greatness; they will long regard themselves as aliens in the midst of the newly composed society. They look upon all those whom this state of society has made their equals as oppressors, whose destiny can excite no sympathy; they have lost sight of their former equals and feel no longer bound to their fate by a common interest; each of them, standing aloof, thinks that he is reduced to care for himself alone. Those, on the contrary, who were formerly at the foot of the social scale and who have been brought up to the common level by a sudden revolution cannot enjoy their newly acquired independence without secret uneasiness; and if they meet with some of their former superiors on the same footing as themselves, they stand aloof from them with an expression of triumph and fear.

It is, then, commonly at the outset of democratic society that citizens are most disposed to live apart. Democracy leads men not to draw near to their fellow creatures; but democratic revolutions lead them to shun each other and perpetuate in a state of equality the animosities that the state of inequality created.

The great advantage of the Americans is that they have arrived at a state of democracy without having to endure a democratic revolution, and that they are born equal instead of becoming so.

That the Americans Combat the Effects of Individualism by Free Institutions

Despotism, which by its nature is suspicious, sees in the separation among men the surest guarantee of its continuance, and it usually makes every effort to keep them separate. No vice of the human heart is so acceptable to it as selfishness: a despot easily forgives his subjects for not loving him, provided they do not love one another. He does not ask them to assist him in governing the state; it is enough that they do not aspire to govern it themselves. He stigmatizes as turbulent and unruly spirits those who would combine their exertions to promote the prosperity of the community; and, perverting the natural meaning of words, he applauds as good citizens those who have no sympathy for any but themselves.

Thus the vices which despotism produces are precisely those which equality fosters. These two things perniciously complete and assist each other. Equality places men side by side, unconnected by any common tie; despotism raises barriers to keep them asunder; the former predisposes them not to consider their fellow creatures, the latter makes general indifference a sort of public virtue.

Despotism, then, which is at all times dangerous, is more particularly to be feared in democratic ages. It is easy to see that in those same ages men stand most in need of freedom. When the members of a community are forced to attend to public affairs, they are necessarily drawn from the circle of their own interests and snatched at times from self-observation. As soon as a man begins to treat of public affairs in public, he begins to perceive that he is not so independent of his fellow men as he had at first imagined, and that in order to obtain their support he must often lend them his cooperation.

When the public govern, there is no man who does not feel the value of public good will or who does not endeavor to court it by drawing to himself the esteem and affection of those among whom he is to live. Many of the passions which congeal and keep asunder human hearts are then obliged to retire and hide below the surface. Pride must be dissembled; disdain dares not break out; selfishness fears its own self. Under a free government, as most public offices are elective, the men whose elevated minds or aspiring hopes are too closely circumscribed in private life constantly feel that they cannot do without the people who surround them. Men learn at such times to think of their fellow men from ambitious motives; and they frequently find it, in a manner, their interest to forget themselves.

I may here be met by an objection derived from electioneering, intrigues, the meanness of candidates, and the calumnies of their opponents. These are occasions of enmity which occur the oftener the more frequent elections become. Such evils are doubtless great, but they are transient; whereas the benefits that attend them remain. The desire of being elected may lead some men for a time to violent hostility; but this same desire leads all men in the long run to support each other; and if it happens that an election accidentally severs two friends, the electoral system brings a multitude of citizens permanently together who would otherwise always have remained unknown to one another. Freedom produces private animosities, but despotism gives birth to general indifference.

The Americans have combated by free institutions the tendency of equality to keep men asunder, and they have subdued it. The legislators of America did not suppose that a general representation of the whole nation would suffice to ward off a disorder at once so natural to the frame of democratic society and so fatal; they also thought that it would be well to infuse political life into each portion of the territory in order to multiply to an infinite extent opportunities of acting in concert for all the members of the community and to make them constantly feel their mutual dependence. The plan was a wise one. The general affairs of a country engage the attention only of leading politicians, who assemble from time to time in the same places; and as they often lose sight of each other afterward, no lasting ties are established between them. But if the object be to have the local affairs of a district conducted by the men who reside there, the same persons are always in contact, and they are, in a manner, forced to be acquainted and to adapt themselves to one another.

It is difficult to draw a man out of his own circle to interest him in the destiny of the state, because he does not clearly understand what influence the destiny of the state can have upon his own lot. But if it is proposed to make a road cross the end of his estate, he will see at a glance that there is a connection between this small public affair and his greatest private affairs; and he will discover, without its being shown to him, the close tie that unites private to general interest. Thus far more may be done by entrusting to the citizens the administration of minor affairs than by surrendering to them in the control of important ones, toward interesting them in the public welfare and convincing them that they constantly stand in need of one another in order to provide for it. A brilliant achievement may win for you the favor of a people at one stroke; but to earn the love and respect of the population that surrounds you, a long succession of little services rendered and of obscure good deeds, a constant habit of kindness, and an established reputation for disinterestedness will be required. Local freedom, then, which leads a great number of citizens to value the affection of their neighbors and of their kindred, perpetually brings men together and forces them to help one another in spite of the propensities that sever them.

In the United States the more opulent citizens take great care not to stand aloof from the people; on the contrary, they constantly keep on easy terms with the lower classes: they listen to them, they speak to them every day. They know that the rich in democracies always stand in need of the poor, and that in democratic times you attach a poor man to you more by your manner than by benefits conferred. The magnitude of such benefits, which sets off the difference of condition, causes a secret irritation to those who reap advantage from them, but the charm of simplicity of manners is almost irresistible; affability carries men away, and even want of polish is not always displeasing. This truth does not take root at once in the minds of the rich. They generally resist it as long as the democratic revolution lasts, and they do not acknowledge it immediately after that revolution is accomplished. They are very ready to do good to the people, but they still choose to keep them at arm's length; they think that is sufficient, but they are mistaken. They might spend fortunes thus without warming the hearts of the population around them; that population does not ask them for the sacrifice of their money, but of their pride.

It would seem as if every imagination in the United States were upon the stretch to invent means of increasing the wealth and satisfying the wants of the public. The best-informed inhabitants of each district constantly use their information to discover new truths that may augment the general prosperity; and if they have made any such discoveries, they eagerly surrender them to the mass of the people.

When the vices and weaknesses frequently exhibited by those who govern in America are closely examined, the prosperity of the people occasions, but improperly occasions, surprise. Elected magistrates do not make the American democracy flourish; it flourishes because the magistrates are elective.

It would be unjust to suppose that the patriotism and the zeal that every American displays for the welfare of his fellow citizens are wholly insincere. Although private interest directs the greater part of human actions in the United States as well as elsewhere, it does not regulate them all. I must say that I have often seen Americans make great and real sacrifices to the public welfare; and I have noticed a hundred instances in which they hardly ever failed to lend faithful support to one another. The free institutions which the inhabitants of the United States possess, and the political rights of which they make so much use, remind every citizen, and in a thousand ways, that he lives in society. They every instant impress upon his mind the notion that it is the duty as well as the interest of men to make themselves useful to their fellow creatures; and as he sees no particular ground of animosity to them, since he is never either their master or their slave, his heart readily leans to the side of kindness. Men attend to the interests of the public, first by necessity, afterward by choice; what was intentional becomes an instinct, and by dint of working for the good of one's fellow citizen, the habit and the taste for serving them are at length acquired.

Many people in France consider equality of condition as one evil and political freedom as a second. When they are obliged to yield to the former, they strive at least to escape from the latter. But I contend that in order to combat the evils which equality may produce, there is only one effectual remedy: namely, political freedom.

D. Political Parties

Democratic Party Organization in the South

V. O. Key, Jr.

Chairmanship of Democrats Goes Begging"[1]

"County Democratic Jobs A-Begging in 59 Areas"[2]

"Thirty Qualify for 40 Posts on Committee—Election Assured to Democratic Body"[3]

"Lone Contest for Post in Party Slated —Democratic Committeemen Unopposed Except in Precinct 16-B"[4]

[1] Richmond Times-Dispatch (*June 19, 1948*).
[2] Dallas Morning News (*June 16, 1948*).
[3] Richmond Times-Dispatch (*June 12, 1947*).
[4] (*Jacksonville*) Florida Times-Union (*March 18, 1947*).

V. O. Key, Jr., *Southern Politics in State and Nation* (New York: Alfred A. Knopf, Inc., 1949), Chap. 18, "Party Organization," pp. 386–405. Reprinted by permission.

These headlines spell the spirit of Democratic party organization from Virginia to Texas. Few southerners really care much about "the party." In North Carolina the governor expressed confidence that some "patriot" could be found to take the vacant Democratic state chairmanship. A Texas county chairman, over 40 per cent of whose precinct posts were unfilled, implored good citizens to file as candidates for precinct committeemen. The dollar an hour they could earn as election judges would, he said, offset the dollar filing fee. He appealed also to higher motives: "Our precinct committeemen are the very grass roots of our system of government and the party machinery. Unless our citizens offer themselves for these positions, neither our government nor party can operate very well."[5]

The bald fact is that in most of the South most of the time party machinery is an impotent mechanism dedicated largely to the performance of routine duties. It has few functions that lend it prestige or power. Its officers in many states exert little influence in politics. They are often, as one Democratic county chairman put it, "a bunch of do-nothings." It is not literally true that southern party officials do nothing at all. Nor are their duties always limited to administrative routine. And it is manifestly untrue that the governing bodies of the parties—conventions and committees—have no significance whatever. They appear devoid of significance only in contrast to party organizations of states with dual party competition.

In two-party states party machinery is often moribund, but at times it takes on vitality. Party organizations may be ladders to political power, channels for the distribution of patronage, agencies of partisan discipline, campaign mechanisms. Each "organization"—those who control the party posts—may occupy an important position in the operation of its own party. It frequently sponsors a slate of candidates for party offices and for party nominations.

5 Dallas Morning News (*June 16, 1948*).

Those who control the party organization often control access to the general election ballot and hence the access to public office.

None of these characteristics can be ascribed to party organizations where parties have nothing to do with the election of public officials. Within the South the Democratic party becomes a framework, presumably and usually nonpartisan, for the settlement of factional contests. Its organization can scarcely be considered partisan machinery. The more secure the Democratic party is in its dominance, the more applicable is this observation. Prestige and influence rest with personal and factional leaders rather than party functionaries. Party jobs are routine and frequently obscure. No wonder many of them go begging.

Party Machinery: Neutral, Not Partisan

Conventional ideas about party organization have little relevance in one-party states. Our common notions about it spring from the workings of party functionaries in two-party states. Supposedly in such states disciplined armies of party workers, ranging from precinct captains through ward committeemen, district leaders, county chairmen, to the state chairman spring to life during campaigns to fight the party's battles and to elect its candidates. Once the election is won, a common cause—the desire for future re-election—holds together its elected officials in all branches of the government. Furthermore, patronage and perquisites contribute to party unity.

When the party does not have to fight campaigns—i.e., when it is not a vote-getting institution—party organization departs radically from the usual conception of it. Democratic nominees in the South win with only the most feeble electioneering in the general elections. Lacking opposition, no external pressure drives the party toward internal unity and discipline. Patronage does not function as a cohesive force; it remains beyond the reach of party functionaries as such: the party has little to do with putting into office those who control patronage. The party organization, therefore, becomes merely a framework for intraparty factional and personal competition. It has the usual complement of conventions, committees, and officials, but the resemblance to genuine party organization is purely formal.

Although the absence of the necessity for intensive general election campaigning influences the character of southern party machinery, in some states some of the time some campaign effort precedes the general election. It is in those states that party organization most closely approximates the usual concept of a party. The Democratic party conducts the most elaborate campaigns in North Carolina, Virginia, and Tennessee; the biggest show is usually put on in Presidential years and in counties of sharpest local competition. State headquarters are opened, speakers sent on circuit, and campaign funds raised. Radio broadcasts, newspaper advertising, and even some transportation of voters to the polls reflect a concern over the outcome uncommon in other southern states. Usually the regular party machinery handles general election campaigns. The more active the local Republicans are, the more alert the local Democratic organization is likely to be. When party officials fail, other Democrats may fill the breach.[6]

In the more predominantly Democratic states the party sometimes goes through the motions of a general election campaign, especially in Presidential years in such states as Texas and Florida where

6 *Thus, in 1946 in a North Carolina county with few Republicans the Democratic county chairman showed no signs of activity before the general election. A local supporter of the Democratic Congressional nominee hustled around a few days before the election, rounded up funds from loyal Democratic officeholders, had some radio announcements made urging a large vote, and hired a few cars to carry voters to the polls. Supporters of the Congressional candidate were interested in the race because other counties in the district had Republican majorities and it was important to get out a large vote in the Democratic counties.*

the margin of Democratic supremacy is not so wide. In Deep South states such as South Carolina, Georgia, and Mississippi there is hardly any campaign. When a show of activity is needed, the regular organization is sometimes so untrained in the campaign arts that it is incapable of performing the chore. Mr. Wilkie in 1940 aroused some fears among Florida Democrats. The state committee tried to run a campaign through the county committees. "They got into the damndest mess yet," one politician recalls, and it was necessary to call in an old campaigner of broad experience in the primaries to run the show.

Aside from its responsibility for campaigns, such as it is, the party's duties vary from state to state. The most onerous task, assigned to the party in several states, is the conduct of the primaries. The party sometimes makes and enforces party loyalty standards which have a peculiar significance in the southern milieu. Earlier the party had an important role in the fixing of suffrage requirements. Occasionally party committees or conventions make an unaccustomed splash when it falls their lot to make nominations for special elections or to replace nominees removed from the ballot between the primary and the general election. In most states the selection of national convention delegates and Presidential electors falls to party organs, and . . . the party organization assumes its greatest significance in its relation to national affairs.

The role of party organization in the South can best be understood by contrast with party hierarchies elsewhere. When parties are parties, the inner core of workers and officials who make up the "organization" exert considerable influence in party nominations. As a disciplined minority they often can put over, in convention or primary, their favored candidates. Often contests for nominations are between the regular or organization slate and others who aspire to control of the party. Battles are waged for control of the party machinery also because of its power in intraparty affairs, such as the channeling of patronage. The southern contrast is marked. Usually the party machinery is impartial toward personalities and factions competing in the primaries. There is considerable variety, however, in the types of individuals who hold party posts and in the nature of their political interests. As individuals, they often have preferences among contests for nominations, but they usually do not employ the party organization as weapons of favoritism—and often they could not, if they wished. Sometimes patriarchs with no real power serve the party dutifully and take little personal interest in primary squabbles.

In states with powerful factional machines the line between party organization and faction is sometimes thin, but in reality, the faction has independent foundations and takes over party posts as an incident to its general dominance. In Virginia, for instance, where the local units of the Byrd organization are usually the most active political forces in their communities, Byrd supporters control most conventions and party posts. Similarly, in Tennessee the Crump faction has in past years dominated much of the party machinery, especially the state committee. As the most cohesive political force in the state, its local candidates for state committee places were often unopposed in the primaries. When opponents offered, they seldom could overcome the organization bloc of votes. Yet Crump's use of the state committee was not, even in Tennessee, in accord with the locally orthodox doctrine of the party's role. That doctrine was expounded in editorial discussion in 1948 of the naming of a successor to J. Frank Hobbs, Crump state chairman:

> . . . The chairman is a very important man in Democratic primary elections. The committee, among other things, sits as judge over primary election contests.
>
> The chairman, because of his position, should remain impartial in primary elections. He should represent both sides. Mr. Hobbs never did. Altho technically not McCord's manager while chairman of the committee, Hobbs always acted more or less

—more rather than less—as director of the McCord campaigns.

> This certainly did not make for impartiality in any matters which came before him. It was bad for the Democratic party—and it was bad for Tennessee.

In Louisiana Huey Long lost little time in taking over control of the Democratic party. In later years slates of candidates identified with the important contenders for the governorship have sometimes included candidates for state or parish Democratic committees.

* * *

At lower party levels Democratic committees display the widest variance in favoritism toward candidates. From one end of the South to the other, however, one is told that county committees, with rare exceptions, remain aloof from factional and personal primary fights. Individual committee members and party officers have their preferences among contestants, but there is seldom unanimity of viewpoint or concerted partisan action. In states such as Florida the paucity of duties entrusted to the party makes it immaterial who controls the county committee. One veteran politician remarked that when he was county chairman the competition for county committee posts was so slight that he had to name 90 per cent of the candidates, who ran, unopposed, in the primary.

* * *

In some instances party organs that are neutral on candidates use their position to advocate a policy about which there may be the deepest controversy among party members. Alabama's state Democratic chairman has been particularly energetic in this wise. In 1946, for example, the state committee, under his leadership, went on record in favor of the Boswell amendment—a scheme to limit voting by Negroes and perhaps others—and spent party funds in support of the proposition, which won the approval of only 53.7 per cent of the voters. The state committee sought to rally county Democratic committees to its line; some followed and others did not. In 1948 an extraordinary use of committee prestige for factional advantage occurred. The state committee spent party funds, collected as fees from all primary candidates, to advocate the election of anti-Truman candidates, including its chairman, as delegates to the Democratic national convention and as Presidential electors.

Party authorities sometimes express themselves officially on issues about which there appears to be general agreement among members. In 1948, for instance, the Texas Democratic state committee (and the Republican state committee) went on record in support of federal legislation to grant the states title to tidelands oil. By and large, however, party officials are confined to an impartial administration of their offices free from political controversy, at least in intrastate politics.

* * *

Government of the Party

The party machinery, which sometimes conducts primaries, chooses national convention delegates, and performs other duties, differs little in form from party organization in two-party states. The supreme governing authority in each state is either a state convention or a state committee, which is chosen by election in the primary. . . .

As the supreme governing authority of the party, the convention . . . has little power to determine the party's mode of operation. . . . Party activity is closely regulated by statute. So detailed is this regulation that no party rules have been adopted in Florida, Alabama, Mississippi, Tennessee, Texas, and Louisiana.

* * *

The state convention, as the governing body of the party, assumes significance only when an issue arises that divides the party sharply and is within the purview of the convention. Its routine duties, such as the declaration of the party nominees selected in the primary and the adoption of a party platform, customarily receive only pro forma attention. In all the convention states in 1948 convention action was highly important in the decision whether to instruct Presidential electors for the states' rights candidates, although only two convention states refused to go along with the national nominees, Mississippi and South Carolina. In 1944 the same sort of question arose in the Texas and Mississippi conventions. Forces opposed to the renomination of President Roosevelt captured the 1944 Mississippi convention by careful maneuvering in the precinct mass meetings and county conventions. The ease of their success, according to one of the leaders, demonstrated the facility with which a little concerted action can overcome the will of the people untranslated into organized effort.

Generally, however, party conventions do not settle major controversies. They are more often sounding boards for a few of the state's politicos, a time for formal organizing of the party, a day of whoop and holler. In some states any qualified voters willing to pay their own transportation are permitted to go as delegates from their county. From the precinct up, the process is largely in the hands of the professionals—so much so that there is cynical reference to the "office mass meetings" which some political leaders have been known to call in their places of business when a few cronies drop around. By design or by default, in most southern states the general electorate plays small part in the convention.

* * *

Between conventions, and in states that do not have conventions, party affairs are conducted by a hierarchy of committees similar in general contour to party structures outside the South. In all states of the South there are at least two levels, a committee for each county and a committee for the state as a whole. [Most Southern] states . . . have an intermediate layer of district committees. Where the latter exist a separate committee is usually set up for each district office: a Congressional district committee, a state senatorial district committee, a state representative district committee, and so on. Where they do not exist, the state committee exercises jurisdiction over offices for which nominations are made by the electorate of more than one county. County committees, in most of the states, follow the usual pattern in that their members are chosen from precincts or whatever the local title of subcounty electoral units is.

The thorough ward and precinct organization usually associated with urban machines in the North and East appears only rarely in the South. The famed Choctaw Club of New Orleans, a factional organization like Tammany Hall, has off and on for a great many years been indistinguishable from the Democratic organization of Orleans parish. The Old Regulars, as its members are called, have secured their votes and offices by the time-honored techniques of machine politics. In recent years the rival Crescent City Democratic Association has contested with it for control of the parish and the city of New Orleans. Outside New Orleans the nearest approach to the traditional urban party structure is found in the few southern cities with well-organized machines. Crump's in Memphis is most famous and most thorough. Charleston has sported one of the most effective machines for one of the longest periods of time. Other cities have had them, including Savannah, Augusta, Jacksonville, Chattanooga, Montgomery, and San Antonio. In all these instances the organizations have been private affairs designed to maintain the power of a boss or series of bosses and have not been extensions of the organization of the Democratic party. They have operated within the party, not as the party.

* * *

The chairmen and secretaries of county and state committees constitute the continuing party machinery between primaries and conventions. Since there is little concern among serious politicians with party machinery, especially outside the conventions, the county or state party office becomes a one-man show. The office of chairman or secretary can be to a large extent what the individual wishes to make it. The chairman of the Democratic state executive committee in Alabama, for instance, has exerted marked personal leadership of his committee. On the contrary in Arkansas, where the successful gubernatorial candidate customarily names his campaign manager as the state chairman, the office when occupied by one recent chairman was hardly more than titular. In South Carolina the state chairman is vested with great responsibilities because of the party's discretion in the conduct of its affairs, including the primaries. A recent chairman, however, was generally regarded as an errand boy for a more potent state leader who was credited with his selection. In one state the secretary of the state committee was a veteran home from the wars put in office by his seniors as window dressing. He had only the faintest notion of party affairs and referred inquiries about the party to the secretary of state. . . .

Indicative of the low regard for party organization is the haphazard way in which most party records are kept. Fortunately many party officials turn over their tabulations of primary results to some public office, such as the secretary of state or department of archives and history, but in some instances even this precaution is not observed. Otherwise, party records—minutes of meetings, copies of resolutions and regulations, certifications of returns—usually lie in disorder until the office of secretary changes hands and then are destroyed or stored in some inaccessible attic. The general attitude is that the conduct of the party's business, like the secretaryship of a dancing club, is a chore to be performed with as little effort as possible. Hence, persons drafted to fill the office are sometimes of lesser caliber who can be counted upon to do faithfully but incompetently an onerous job.

County chairmen frequently go unnoticed. Occasionally a local patriarch will be repeatedly selected for the post because of the confidence in which he is held by his compatriots. Thus in one Mississippi delta county "a paragon of southern virtue" has been county chairman for more than two decades. He is known for his unequivocal views, but his integrity and determination to administer the party's affairs impartially are respected.

The plight of party dignitaries in one-party states has been most heart-rendingly dramatized in Texas. In that state the chairmen of the county committees have formed the Texas Association of Democratic Chairmen. They sounded the lament: "they are tired of being the forgotten men of party politics."[7] In 1947 the secretary-treasurer, apparently with a completely straight face, solemnly announced the three purposes of the organization:

> That each county chairman head the delegation from his county to the state convention to exercise his prerogative as titular leader in his county.
>
> That the county chairman of the county executive committee be the presiding officer and permanent chairman of all county conventions.
>
> That all county chairmen, regardless of the size of the county, be recognized as the key man in the party in the county and that credit be given where credit is due.[8]

Campaign Organization

When the formal party organization fights no general campaigns and is virtually precluded by its position from taking a hand in primary campaigns, other organizational mechanisms must be created to perform the electioneering function usually assigned to the party machine. In a sense campaign organization in the South is the counterpart of party organization outside the South, though campaign organization is unlike the usual party machinery in many respects.

Party machinery has continuity. It survives campaign after campaign no matter how overwhelming the victory or how crushing the defeat. It functions—with varying degrees of enthusiasm—for whatever candidates the party puts up. It can campaign for a relative newcomer or for an old warhorse. Its institutional nature provides established channels of communication, a ready reserve of personnel, and a body of "technical knowhow" which can be marshalled with a minimum of lost motion. The call to arms is dependent mainly on party patriotism, nourished partly by an orderly allocation of favors in which party officialdom often plays a commanding part.

A candidate's problems of organization in a primary campaign depend largely on his experience in state politics, the character of his opposition, and the nature of his appeal to the voters. One type of southern politician is singularly independent of normal campaign machinery. Notable men of this sort have been the brothers Blease of South Carolina: Cole, who served as governor and United States Senator, and Eugene, a former chief justice of South Carolina, who ran for the Senate in 1942. Even their enemies admitted that they did astonishingly well without the normal campaign funds and mechanics. They relied on stump appeal and on the host of followers built up over Cole's long career, persons who spontaneously volunteered their electioneering efforts and who did not require the prodding or incentives offered by an alert and energetic hierarchy beginning with a state headquarters and extending down to county and precinct chairmen.

Most candidates, however, face at the outset of each race the necessity of creating an entire campaign engine *de novo*. The machinery employed and the manner of recruitment of personnel to man it vary from race to race and from state to state. Conversations with experienced managers of state, district, and county primary campaigns reveal numerous individualities. They indicate, too, certain practices and necessities that recur.

[7] Dallas Morning News (*November 15, 1947*).
[8] Ibid. (*September 19, 1947*).

Managers generally point to four important phases of a full-scale, adequately financed, statewide campaign for governor or United States Senator: central direction, provided by a strategy committee composed of three or four of the candidate's highest counselors; the raising of funds, assigned to a single individual, usually not prominently identified with the campaign although he may be a prominent citizen, who may have a small committee working with him; the conduct of the open campaign, involving publicity in its many forms and the work of the state headquarters, all of which is often directed by a small committee; and the organization of support in the counties, the most delicate and most critical phase of campaigning.

State headquarters performs the publicity routine—preparation and distribution of literature, posters, press releases, radio addresses—in a manner much like that of a party-conducted campaign. Key technical personnel in the process are frequently on salary but most workers volunteer. Occasionally an advertising firm handles publicity for a fee.[9] More frequently newspapermen sympathetic to the campaign direct publicity work, sometimes at a salary when on leave rather than loan from their employers. Decisions on major policy matters, such as the line the candidate is to take on a hot campaign issue, are sometimes made by the publicity committee if there is one, or more often by the strategy committee. The publicity staff is usually confined to the technical implementation of such decisions through their professional skills.

The finance director of the campaign is ordinarily a man of standing in the community whose knowledge of the responsive sources of funds has been acquired from long observation or experience. It is usually part of his job to keep the candidate and the campaign manager (and most other people) in ignorance of the exact channels through which the sums flow, how much is given by "X" and how much is given to "Y."

A factional or personal candidate has no established party hierarchy—state chairman, county chairmen, precinct committeemen—to carry the message to the voters. Substitute mechanisms have to be constructed. Factions with continuity, such as the Byrd machine, or leaders long on the scene, such as Gene Talmadge [D., Ga.] or Olin Johnston [D., S.C.], develop a set of followers on whom the candidate depends in campaign after campaign. When their usefulness and devotion have been tested they come to occupy positions in the grand scheme of factional affection and loyalty, a hierarchy that resembles vaguely a formal party organization.

The need for experienced counsel and skillful aid in the conduct of a statewide campaign is met by individuals whose services are frequently for sale to the highest bidder, or to the most persuasive talker, or to the most likely winner. Often campaign managers are purely decorative. In 1946 many veterans were put in front positions for the sake of appearances. The real management, however, remained in the hands of experienced practitioners, some of whom are irrevocably wed to one candidate—as A. B. Friend was to Senator Bilbo in Mississippi—and may, at the behest of their principal, put in a helping hand in other campaigns. Some managers acquire independent stature of their own, such as Homer Adkins of Arkansas, who made himself governor after establishing a reputation as the state's best organizer by managing several successful campaigns for others. Some are frankly technicians, as Boyce Williams in Florida or Ed Reid in Alabama, who may be in one camp one year and another the next. Occasionally one of these persons develops so much influence of his own that he tends to dominate the candidate for whom he works, as many have thought to be the relationship

9 *In Texas public relations firms play a more significant role in campaign management than in other southern states. The huge population and area of the state accentuate the importance of publicity as a campaign technique.*

between Roy Harris and Herman Talmadge of Georgia.

The special asset of these men is not
their organizing ability or their political
acumen alone; it is their intimate acquaintance with county politics and politicians. The entire machinery for distrib-
uting publicity, arranging rallies, beating the partisan drums, advising on local
issues and local reactions to campaign efforts, punching doorbells or contacting
farmers, the whole business of preparing
for election day, arranging for transportation, designating watchers or officials, the
complete procedure for appealing to
voters where the voters are, in the countries and in the precincts, must be set up
anew for each primary. To launch a successful operation in a county requires
knowledge of local points of sensitivity
and familiarity with politicos of potency,
those to be solicited and those to be
avoided, those who are buddies and those
who are mutually incompatible.

. . . In setting up county machinery
the candidate who is an old campaigner
has [the] advantage, for over the years he
has won followers in almost every county
who will handle his affairs. The problem
of central headquarters under those circumstances is to activate the local leaders
and to keep tab on their efforts. The new
candidate may have personal friends of
varying political usefulness around the
state, but his major task is to get competent county managers and allied helpers.
Failing to get satisfactory volunteers, he
may have to hire local managers.

When a county or portion thereof is
"deliverable," negotiations with county,
or more often subcounty, bosses can be
conducted in an atmosphere of reality
only by a politician of sufficient experience to treat with them as equals. He must
not be duped by a pretender to influence
over votes. He must not accept support
that will alienate more important influences. He must know the vital interests at
stake in intracounty politics—from family
feuds to the location of the needed highway. The experienced campaigner will

know, too, how the greatest support can
be extracted from groups like labor unions, business associations, and Negro
clubs.

A candidate in his first statewide race
particularly needs the aid of professionals
who can recruit county leaders. The candidate himself can impress some local bigwigs into his service. A veteran organizer,
however, can by his personal influence
gather to the fold political cronies that he
has used and who have used him in previous years.

The relationship between the state
command and county managers must be
direct if the local boys are to feel that they
are really part of the show. Some campaigns . . . have used district managers,
an intermediate layer of administrators
between the top and the counties and
precincts. They are most useful, however,
in informal roles as traveling emissaries
who keep an ear to the ground and are
enough at home in their section not to
arouse antagonism or suspicion. Seldom
will a county's "patriotism" permit a
neighbor to come in and "tell it what to
do." State headquarters always has an important set of employees rarely in the
public eye: a corps of troubleshooters who
spend most of the campaign going from
one hot spot to another, sometimes on
the call of local managers, coordinating
campaign efforts, negotiating about money
needed from above, advising on strategy.

A significant adjunct to many campaigns is an instrument for checking campaign progress in local areas. State managers must determine the effectiveness and
faithfulness of local adherents. One leader
sends out periodically during the campaign a questionnaire tailored specifically
for each stage of the contest. The persons
reporting do so in strictest confidence and
are not known to be informants by the
political workers in their counties. Another manager has used the facilities of a
retail credit firm to get confidential reports. In one state an old hack, whose political influence is so meager "he couldn't
carry his wife," has an unerring instinct

for political evaluation. He is for hire in any campaign, and when he hits the road everyone knows what he is up to, yet the valuable reports he brings in after nosing around the precincts assure him ready employment in every race. Other managers use anonymous individuals who have a similar intuitive judgment, who can spend half a day in a county and come out with a fair appraisal of what the score is, what will improve it, and who has been falling down on the job.

Only rarely are primary campaigns in the South . . . jointly conducted for more than one office. Joint campaigns are not feasible in an atomistic, individual politics. Campaigns for governor steer scrupulously clear of formal connections with other state races and races for federal and local offices. Campaign organizations for each office are entirely separate, in sharp contrast with party campaigning in a general election in a two-party state. But the subrosa operations of professional politicos, especially in the counties and precincts, breed crisscrossing of lines and complexities of alliances which the politicians themselves seldom can identify and which may often be contradictory.

Although the organization set up for the primary campaign in a one-party state serves the same purpose as party organization in two-party states, it is almost invariably less tenacious, less cohesive, less continuous. Hence, as an instrument of popular leadership, it is less responsible or accountable. Primary campaign organizations, even when successful, hold together only loosely after the campaign. Local leaders closely identified with a particular candidate are called upon by their fellow citizens when communication must be had with the throne on matters of grievance or patronage. Similarly, the officeholder calls for counsel from his trusted local lieutenants. In some cases, therefore, a person gets to be known as "a big Folsom man" or "the Laney leader" in the county. A network of such persons over the state might be called a factional machine. It can be kept together to some extent by the judicious distribution of benefits. Such a development is infrequent, however, except in the states with formal factional organizations. . . . A candidate's ultimate ascent to power (or its retention) is less certain than a party's, and there is little adhesive influence within the factional organization other than personal loyalty to the candidate.

E. Interest Groups

The Dynamics of Access in the Legislative Process

David B. Truman

. . . The legislature traditionally has been the major focus of attention for political interest groups. Though this interest in legislation has not been an exclusive preoccupation, the established importance of group activities in legislatures is reflected in a popular synonym for the political interest group, the word *lobby*.

Though for tactical reasons many groups profess slight or no concern with lobbying, legislative activity has been for the layman the distinguishing feature of the political interest group.

It follows that access to the legislature is of crucial importance at one time or another to virtually all such groups. Some

David B. Truman, *The Governmental Process: Political Interests and Public Opinion* (New York: Alfred A. Knopf, Inc., 1951), Chap. 11, "The Dynamics of Access in the Legislative Process," pp. 321–343. Reprinted by permission.

groups are far more successful in this pursuit than others. Moreover, access is not a homogeneous commodity. In some forms it provides little more than a chance to be heard; in others it practically assures favorable action. Some groups achieve highly effective access almost automatically, whereas it is denied to others in spite of their most vigorous efforts.

It will be appropriate, therefore, to begin an exploration of the role of groups in the legislative process by examining some of the factors that affect the kind of access that various groups are able to achieve. For the sake of convenience these may be divided into two types: first, a set of formal, structural factors whose importance will be readily apparent; second, a set of informal determinants whose effect is somewhat more subtle but of at least equal significance.

Governmental Structure and Differential Access

The formal institutions of government in the United States do not prescribe all the meanderings of the stream of politics. They do mark some of its limits, however, and designate certain points through which it must flow, whatever uncharted courses it may follow between these limits. Such is the character of formal organization in any setting. . . . Although the effect of formal structural arrangements is not always what its designers intended, these formalities are rarely neutral. They handicap some efforts and favor others. Debate over proposals to eliminate such a ritualistic bit of procedure as the electoral college, for example, reveals the fact that, although no one knows the exact consequences that would follow if it were to be abandoned or modified, a change would affect various segments of the community unequally. Such, inevitably, is the influence of formal structure.[1]

Access is one of the advantages unequally distributed by such arrangements; that is, in consequence of the structural

peculiarities of our government some groups have better and more varied opportunities to influence key points of decision than do others. Take as an example the provision for equal representation of states in the Senate of the United States. This has allowed agricultural interest groups that are predominant in many thinly populated states more points of access in the Senate than urban groups whose members are concentrated in a few populous states. Thus, were it not for this structural provision, the United States would not have been so solicitous for the sugar beet or silver-mining interests as it has been over the years. It is obvious, moreover, that a group such as the American Farm Bureau Federation, which can cover a great many rural states, can gain readier access than urban groups concerning any matter on which it can achieve a satisfactory measure of cohesion. It is less obvious, but equally important, that an urban group whose interests are such that it can ally with the Farm Bureau derives an advantage in access over another urban group whose claims are such that it cannot effect an alliance of this sort. The National Association of Manufacturers and various trade associations, among others, have been the beneficiaries of such combinations.

Similar advantages, gained from the way in which the boundaries of legislative districts are drawn whether by legislatures or by constitutions, can be observed throughout the governmental system. They are clearly observable in the House of Representatives, many of whose districts, even in relatively urban states like Illinois, are defined by state legislatures in which rural groups predominate. The state legislatures, of course, show similar patterns.[2]

The existence of the federal system itself is a source of unequal advantage in ac-

[1] *Cf. E. Pendleton Herring, "The Politics of Fiscal Policy,"* Yale Law Journal, *Vol. XLVII, No. 5 (March, 1938),* 724–745.

[2] *Cf. Dayton D. McKean,* Pressures on the Legislature of New Jersey *(New York: Columbia University Press, 1938), p. 112; C. E. Merriam, S. D. Paratt, and A. Lepawsky,* The Government of the Metropolitan Region of Chicago *(Chicago: University of Chicago Press, 1933), Chap. 28.*

cess. Groups that would be rather obscure or weak under a unitary arrangement may hold advantageous positions in the state governments and will be vigorous in their insistence upon the existing distribution of powers between states and nation. As the advantage of access shifts through time, moreover, groups shift from defenders to critics of the existing balance. At the turn of the century, for example, the insurance companies were active in Washington to get the federal government to take over the regulation of insurance, despite the obstacle of an adverse Supreme Court decision handed down shortly after the Civil War. Since the Court in 1944 altered the prevailing doctrine, the insurance companies have been equally vigorous in the opposite direction, at least insofar as they have tried to gain exemption from the Sherman Antitrust Act.[3] A somewhat complicated symptom of a similar state of affairs is suggested by the contrast between argument and behavior in connection with the Tydings-Miller Act of 1937. This legislation, sponsored principally by the National Association of Retail Druggists, exempted from the provisions of the Sherman Act contracts fixing resale prices on goods sold in interstate commerce, provided that they were resold in a state which permitted such contracts. Proponents of the measure argued that it was simply a means of permitting the individual states to regulate their own affairs. When the law was passed, however, the N.A.R.D. set up an unofficial *national* board through which uniform contracts between manufacturers and retailers could be approved and administered. The policy was a national one, but the druggists' access to the states was more effective once the federal antitrust hurdle was eliminated.[4]

The separation of powers, especially between the legislature and the executive, and the accompanying system of checks and balances mean that effective access to one part of the government, such as the Congress, does not assure access to another, such as the Presidency. For the effective constituencies of the executive and the members of the legislature are not necessarily the same, even when both are represented by men nominally of the same party. These constituencies are different, not simply because the President is elected from the whole country rather than from a particular state or Congressional district, although this fact has significance under a system characterized by loose party discipline, but rather because within any state or district, for various reasons, the organized, active elements responsible for the election of a Senator or Representative are not necessarily the same as those which give the state's or district's support to a candidate for President. This situation is accentuated at the national level by the staggered terms of Senators, Representatives, and President. A Senator elected at the same time as a President must face re-election in an "off" year, and vice versa; a Representative must "go it alone" at least every four years. In consequence, as Herring has put it, "most Congressmen are still independent political entrepreneurs."[5] The Representative, the Senator, and the President each must give ear to groups that one or both of the others frequently can ignore.

An admirable illustration of this situation is the fact that four successive presidents—Harding, Coolidge, Hoover, and Franklin Roosevelt—found it possible to veto veterans' bonus legislation passed by the Congress, although on each occasion approximately four-fifths of the House of Representatives chose to override the veto. Somewhat the same circumstance is indicated by the periodic group demands that reciprocal trade agreements should be submitted to the Senate for ratification as

[3] *Paul v. Virginia, 8 Wallace 168 (1869). See Edward B. Logan, "Lobbying," supplement to the Annals, Vol. CXLIV (July, 1929), p. 6.* U.S. v. South-Eastern Underwriters Association, *322 U.S. 533 (1944).*
[4] *See* U.S. Federal Trade Commission, Report on Resale Price Maintenance (*Washington, D.C.: United States Government Printing Office, 1945*), *pp. 62, 145–146, 149.*

[5] *E. Pendleton Herring,* Presidential Leadership (*New York: Holt, Rinehart & Winston, Inc., 1940*), p. 27. . . .

treaties. Such requests imply less effective access to the executive than to the maximum of thirty-three senators sufficient to reject a treaty.

As the preceding paragraphs suggest, access to points of decision in the government is significantly affected by the structure and cohesion of the political parties considered not just as electioneering devices, but as instruments of governing within the legislature. A single party organization that regularly succeeds in electing an executive and a majority in the legislature will produce one pattern of access to the government. The channels will be predominantly those within the party leadership, and the pattern will be relatively stable and orderly. A quite different pattern will be produced if the party is merely an abstract term referring to an aggregation of relatively independent factions. Then the channels of access will be numerous, and the patterns of influence within the legislature will be diverse, constantly shifting, and more openly in conflict. Party discipline provides the power to govern because it permits stable control of access to the points of policy determination.

It is no novelty to observe that in the United States political parties, particularly on the national scene, correspond more closely to the diffused than to the disciplined type of structure. Because the legislator's tenure in office depends on no overarching party organization, he is accessible to whatever influences are outstanding in his local constituency almost regardless of more inclusive claims. Whether he carries the label of the majority or the minority party, he finds himself now in the majority and now in the minority on legislative votes. Majorities rarely are composed of the same persons in votes on successive measures. They are likely to be bipartisan or, more accurately, nonpartisan.

The dominant character of access and of influence under the American system is well stated in the remark of a Texas Representative in response to a query concerning his motives in advocating the repeal of federal taxes on oleomargarine: "If I were from the South and were not interested in a market for my people, I would indeed be unworthy to represent my people. Of course I am interested in the right of the cotton farmer to sell his seed. . . ."[6] Diffusion of access has its ramifications as well. During the struggle over the McNary-Haugen farm "relief" bill from 1924 through 1928 President Coolidge was hostile both to the measure and to its principal group sponsor, the American Farm Bureau Federation. Vice-President Dawes, however, gave "support and assistance," to quote the words of the group's president, that were "of the utmost importance."[7]

Advantages of access are likely to go to the group than can accentuate and exploit the local preoccupations of the legislator. Many corporations and trade associations have long made use of this tactic although the exact forms have been various. Railroad companies have worked through lawyers and doctors retained in the states and counties in which they practice to reach influential supporters of state and national legislators, as have other corporate enterprises. The Association of Railway Executives, predecessor of the Association of American Railroads, organized such a device in a rather complete form. As outlined by one of its officials:

> I had it in mind putting into effect a plan whereby we would be advised as to who are the influential men behind the several Congressmen, and the further thought that we might be able through personal contact or by the careful distribution of literature to influence in a perfectly proper way the judgment of the men upon whom the several Congressmen rely for support and advice.[8]

6 *U.S. House of Representatives, Committee on Agriculture,* Hearings on Repeal of the Oleomargarine Tax, *80th Congr., 2nd Sess. (1948), p. 36.*
7 *Orville M. Kile,* The Farm Bureau Through Three Decades *(Baltimore: The Waverly Press, 1948), p. 146.*
8 *U.S. Senate, Committee on Interstate Commerce,* Senate Report No. 26, *77th Congr., 1st Sess.*

Such a system has never been more completely organized than it has been by the Iowa Farm Bureau Federation. Although the group does not openly endorse candidates for election, after the election it sets up committees of five members in each legislative district, whose function it is to capitalize upon local support. The qualifications of the members of these committees, according to Kile, are four in number: (1) they must be "willing to put Farm Bureau policies ahead of any personal interest;" (2) they must be from the same party as the successful candidate; (3) they must be men who "individually helped get the candidate elected;" and (4) they must be "politically potent in the district."[9] A very similar plan of organization to exert local influence has been employed by, among others, the National Association of Retail Druggists. The Federal Trade Commission has described it as "the most important device" used by the association in its efforts to secure passage of desired legislation.[10]

Such is the effect of our disintegrated national party structure upon access. Although this structure may be in process of gradual change in the direction of greater integration and central control, as some competent observers believe,[11] conclusive evidence of this shift is not at hand. We can be sure, however, that an altered party structure will be reflected in an altered pattern of group access to the Congress.

The effects of party structure upon group access to many of the state legislatures are similar to its effects upon access to Congress. The channels of approach for various groups are numerous and varied, as in Congress, except in those cases where an individual party leader or

faction has been able to impose a high degree of discipline upon the rank and file. In the heyday of Boss Platt, access to the legislature of New York was available primarily through him, usually at a price.[12] When in 1935 the governor of Florida established temporary dominance over the state legislature, the Association of Life Insurance Presidents found that it could not even gain admission to legislative committee hearings until it had persuaded the governor of its point of view.[13] Other states, such as New York and New Jersey, have quite consistently shown a pattern of party government quite different from that at the national level.[14] Where the party structure is integrated and the legislators are under discipline, access is channeled and is more available to those groups upon which the party as a whole, rather than the individual legislator, is dependent.

Once it has established access, by whatever means, a group will exert tremendous efforts to retain the structural arrangements that have given it advantage. An illustration is afforded by the struggle over the adoption of the Twenty-First Amendment repealing the Eighteenth. When the prohibition amendment was submitted, the Anti-Saloon League favored the method of ratification by the state legislatures, since it had built up its access to most of those bodies and could be sure that the weapons at its disposal would assure favorable action by the required number of states. When the repeal proposal was passed by the Congress in 1933, however, the method of ratification by conventions called especially for the purpose was specified for the first time in the history of amendments to the federal Constitution. This means was employed in order to get around the established access of the league.

(1941), Part 2, pp. 51–53. Cf. N. R. Danielian, A. T. & T.: The Story of Industrial Conquest (New York: The Vanguard Press, 1939), pp. 321–325.

9 Kile, op. cit., pp. 381–382. . . .

10 U.S. Federal Trade Commission, op. cit., pp. 64–66.

11 Cf. E. E. Schattschneider, The Struggle for Party Government (College Park: University of Maryland Press, 1948), pp. 28–29.

12 Cf. Logan, op. cit., p. 5.

13 U.S. Temporary National Economic Committee, Hearings, Part 10, pp. 4380, 4758.

14 Cf. McKean, op. cit., Chap. 2; Warren Moscow, Politics in the Empire State (New York: Alfred A. Knopf, Inc., 1948), passim.

All the factors of a structural character that result in the unequal distribution of access among interest groups operating upon a legislature need not be discussed in detail. We must, however, even in this rough sketch, discuss one additional type, closely related to the structure of the party system—the structure of the legislature itself, including legislative procedure and the committee system. Legislative structure and rules of procedure are by no means neutral factors in respect to access. As Schattschneider observed with reference to the Smoot-Hawley Tariff Act of 1930: "Legislation cannot be understood apart from the manner in which it is made."[15]

No legislative assembly of whatever size can, of course, carry on its activities without some internal division of labor, without methods of setting the order of business, or without means of regulating the process of deliberation. The procedures for selecting those to whom the leadership of an assembly is entrusted, for example, have a direct bearing upon the kind of access to the legislature that various groups may be able to achieve. Thus the practice in Congress and most of the states of assigning committee memberships and designating their chairmen on the basis of seniority gives a special advantage to groups having access to members from "safe" constituencies who are likely to look with hostility on the demands of the less established groups. Organizations whose membership is concentrated in "close" districts, where the incidence of change and the consequent demands for adjustment are high, are less easily able to establish access to committee chairmen.

Whoever sets the timetable of a legislature and determines how long debate on a measure shall continue has a significant control upon access. This power, of course, is one of the principal means by which the British Cabinet leads the House of Commons. In American state legislatures a unified party leadership, both legislative and executive, may enjoy similar dominance, and in that case effective access will be through such leadership. In the Congress, and at times in all of the state legislatures, control of the timetable lies with a loosely integrated collection of men belonging to the majority party, sometimes acting in consultation with the minority leader. In the Senate this scheduling function is performed by the floor leader, his aides, and the chairmen of the standing committees. The party Steering Committee and its Policy Committee are nominally a part of this machinery, but their importance is slight. In the House the timetable is set by the Rules Committee, the floor leader, the Speaker, and the chairmen of standing committees. The Steering Committee is of as little functional significance as in the Senate. Depending on the nature of the legislation to be considered and on the skill of the leadership, the legislators who determine the schedule may work in concert, or they may operate at cross purposes. In the latter case the legislative timetable is a compromise or emerges from a test of strength among these various points of power, a process in which the President, if he is of the same party, may play a significant role.[16] Groups with access to parts of this machinery have a privileged influence upon the legislative program, especially if their objective is to obstruct rather than to promote a particular bill.

Both the power to limit debate and the practice of permitting unlimited debate on a measure have significance for the degree of access that various groups achieve. In the House of Representatives, where limitation on debate is customary, it usually takes the form of adopting a special rule reported by the Rules Committee. Practically all major legislation in the House is handled under this sort of procedure, which sets both the terms and the duration of debate. The committee is

---

[15] *E. E. Schattschneider*, Politics, Pressures and the Tariff (*Englewood Cliffs, N.J.: Prentice-Hall, Inc., 1935*), *p. 13.*

[16] *Cf. Floyd M. Riddick*, The United States Congress: Organization and Procedure (*Manassas, Va.: National Capitol Publishers, Inc., 1949*), *Chap. 6.*

thus in a position either to block or to expedite action on a bill, and access to its membership is a crucial advantage. Such access is likely to go disproportionately to established groups dominant in "safe" constituencies, since the seniority of all members of this committee is high. For example, in the Seventy-Seventh Congress, elected in 1940, no member of the Rules Committee had had less than four consecutive terms of service, and the average number of such terms represented on the committee was just under seven. Thus most of the members came from districts that had made no change in their representation since before the onset of the New Deal. A similar advantage accrues in the Senate to any defensive group that has access to even a small bloc of members. Under that body's practice of unlimited debate, such a minority can "talk a bill to death" through the filibuster, effectively preventing action by the Senate as a whole. In some cases this result has been achieved by one member alone. Although the Senate has had since 1917 a rule permitting closure of debate, it is rarely applied, and the effective veto power of a Senate minority remains virtually unchallenged.

Finally, the enormously complicated and technical rules under which debate is carried on in legislative chambers have an important influence upon relative access. In the first place, the rules themselves are not neutral; witness the heat frequently generated by an attempt to change them. At the beginning of the Eighty-First Congress in January, 1949, a successful effort was made to modify the House rules so that committee chairmen could call up bills that the Rules Committee failed to report out. The significance of such a modification was indicated both by the activity in the House and by the attention given the amendment in the press.[17] But groups gain advantages in access not just from the substance of such procedural regulations. They may derive tremendous

advantage if their representatives, whether in or out of the legislative halls, have a mastery of the ins and outs of parliamentary procedure. Like the technicalities of legal procedure in courts of law, procedural arrangements may be used as often to delay and obstruct action as to facilitate it. Thus the ability to command the services of a skillful parliamentary tactician may be the key to effective access to a legislature.

. . . [T]he place of committees in a legislative body has important effects upon the degree of access that various groups can achieve. It is as accurate today as it was nearly three-quarters of a century ago when Woodrow Wilson published his little classic, *Congressional Government*, to say that, although the Congress as a whole formally legislates, the real policy determination takes place in the standing committees.[18] Both because of the volume and the complexity of the problems coming before a modern legislature and because of the size of such bodies, they have had to leave the most important part of the examination, if not the preparation, of legislation to smaller units. Under the British system this function is performed primarily by the Cabinet, which is strictly speaking a committee of the legislature. Relatively minor use is made of other standing committees. In the Congress of the United States the sifting of legislative projects is pre-eminently the function of the committees, primarily the standing committees. Neither house, with rare exceptions, considers any measure that has not first been acted upon by one of these nominally subordinate bodies. Refusal to report a bill from a committee usually dooms the proposal. But perhaps the most significant feature of the system is that, although many major measures are altered by the Senate or the House after a committee has reported, both houses usually follow closely the recommendations of their committees. Few bills are passed in

17 Congressional Record, *81st Congr., 1st Sess. (January 3, 1949), pp. 10–11, A. 3–4, A. 6, A. 7 (daily edition).*

18 *Woodrow Wilson,* Congressional Government *(Boston: Houghton Mifflin Company, 1885), p. 56 et passim.*

a form substantially different from that given them at the committee stage.[19]

The effect that this system of committees has upon access stems not only from the relative finality of their actions but also from the comparative independence that they enjoy. These bodies are subject to little or no coordinating influence from any source. A committee majority, or even its chairman alone, effectively constitutes a little legislature, especially insofar as it blocks action on a proposal. Therefore access to a committee majority or even to a chairman may give a group effective advantage in the legislature itself, to the virtual exclusion of its competitors.

The role of committees in the state legislatures varies widely. In some their place is roughly similar to that of the Congressional committee, whereas in others it is sharply different. One general difference is that, since state legislative sessions are shorter and less frequent and since many state legislators perform their duties on a part-time basis, there is usually less opportunity for prolonged committee consideration in the states. In some states, New Jersey, for instance, the committees are of no significance, except as graveyards for bills, since control by the party leaders is pervasive. Access to the committee under such circumstances is almost meaningless.[20] In other states the committee function appears to be quite similar to that in Congress. Thus a study of several legislative sessions in Maryland and Pennsylvania shows that well over 80 per cent of the committee reports were accepted outright by these legislatures.[21]

This evidence would suggest that committees in Maryland and Pennsylvania

were indeed "little legislatures" and that access to them was crucial. Although such undoubtedly was the case in some instances, in these same two states there were other regularities that lay behind the acceptance of committee reports. The legislators followed the committees, to be sure, but the latter were dominated by chairmen who in turn cooperated closely with the governors and other legislative leaders.[22] Similar evidence on the New York legislature indicates that state legislative committees and their chairmen enjoy much less freedom of action than their Congressional counterparts. Political management by an informal conference of legislative leaders determines the content of major bills, not the individual committees operating independently.[23] Under such circumstances access to the legislature is not assured merely by establishing relationships with individual committeemen or chairmen. Lines of access tend to be integrated rather than diffused; consequently, the tactics of groups and relative advantage among them can be expected to show a pattern quite different from that characteristic of the Congress.

Aspects of formal structure, therefore, are significant determinants of the channels of access to legislatures, national and state. They afford advantages to some groups and impose handicaps upon the efforts of others to achieve influence in the legislature. Formal structure both reflects and sustains differences in power. It is never neutral.

The Role of Knowledge and the Effects of Overlapping Membership

Governmental structure is not the only factor creating advantages in access to the key points of decision in the legislature. It is the most obvious, but perhaps not the most important. The politician-legislator is not equivalent to the steel ball in a pin-

19 Cf. Riddick, op. cit., pp. 3, 153; E. Pendleton Herring, Group Representation Before Congress: Public Administration and the Public Interest (New York: McGraw-Hill Book Company, 1936), pp. 250–251; Paul D. Hasbrouck, Party Government in the House of Representatives (New York: The Macmillan Company, 1927), pp. 74–75.

20 Cf. McKean, op. cit., pp. 47–49.

21 C. I. Winslow, State Legislative Committees: A Study in Procedure (Baltimore: The Johns Hopkins University Press, 1931), pp. 7, 112ff., 139.

22 Ibid., pp. 118–121, 137. Cf. Robert Luce, Legislative Procedure (Boston: Houghton Mifflin Company, 1922), pp. 493–494.

23 Joseph P. Chamberlain, Legislative Processes, National and State (New York: Appleton-Century-Crofts, 1936), p. 90.

ball game, bumping passively from post to post down an inclined plane. He is a human being involved in a variety of relationships with other human beings. In his role as legislator his accessibility to various groups is affected by the whole series of relationships that define him as a person.[24] Most of these relationships, however, cannot be identified by viewing the legislator as a creature of the statute book. We need not go into the complicated area of motives to account more fully for differences in accessibility by observing such continuing relationships, remembering that their stability is as important an element in the equilibrium of the individual legislator as are predictable relationships in the well-being of any other human.

One important factor among the informal determinants of access is created by the legislator-politician's need of information and the ability of a group to supply it. Any politician, whether legislator, administrator, or judge, whether elected or appointed, is obliged to make decisions that are guided in part by the relevant knowledge that is available to him. In this deciding, however, the politician is in a position analogous to the late Lord Keynes's stock exchange investor, whose knowledge of the factors that will govern the future yield of an investment is necessarily partial or even negligible.[25] The politician also must rely on somewhat conventionalized assessments of trends, corrected by new information about the relevant facts.

The politician is in continuous need of current information because he is at the mercy of the changes as they occur. Like a college president, a politician, especially an elected politician, is expected to have a judgment on all matters ranging from the causes of an outbreak of Bang's disease among the local livestock to the latest strategy of the Kremlin. He must make decisions on many of these questions, decisions on the content of his public statements, on the causes and persons he will champion, on how he will vote on a roll call.

The penalty for numerous or conspicuous decisions made in ignorance or in neglect of relevant available knowledge is disturbance in the politician's established relationships. The disturbance may be minor and temporary or serious and lasting. It may be reflected in a diminution of "reputation" or in a threat to his leadership position in party, faction, or other group. Finally, it may lead to defeat at the polls, a penalty that no elected official can be expected to welcome. Forced to make choices of consequence and to minimize serious disturbances in his established relationships, the legislator is constantly in need of relevant information. Access is likely to be available to groups somewhat in proportion to their ability to meet this need.

For purposes of discussion the knowledge required by the politician may be divided into two types: technical knowledge that defines the content of a policy issue, and political knowledge of the relative strength of competing claims and of the consequences of alternative decisions on a policy issue. Any group may be in a position directly or indirectly to supply information of either type.

Representative of the first sort of knowledge is the specialized information about industry conditions that a trade association can provide for the politician, whether legislator or administrator. Almost any group is likely to regard knowledge of this sort as a major part of its stock-in-trade. Those who are preoccupied with moral judgments of group politics, in fact, normally treat the supplying of such information as a "legitimate" group activity. A measure of access almost inevitably accompanies the ability to provide this type of information. Where competing claims are not present, and where available knowledge of the likely political consequences suggests that the legislator

---

24 *See Theodore M. Newcomb*, Social Psychology *(New York: The Dryden Press, 1950), Chap. 10 et passim.*
25 *John Maynard Keynes*, The General Theory of Employment, Interest, and Money *(London: Macmillan & Co., Ltd., 1936), pp. 149ff.*

will be little affected whatever decision he makes, technical information may control his decision. The politician who comes from a "safe" district, confronted with an issue of no moment in his constituency, is in a position to act upon what he regards as the "merits" of an issue, to act like what the ward heeler calls a "statesman." Especially where official sources of information are deficient, command of technical knowledge may provide access for groups that can supply the deficiency, especially if other influences are operating in their favor.[26] Thus McKean noted that the absence of a legislative reference library, the impossibility of retaining technical staff on a legislator's salary, and the failure of the state government to provide such services as information on the progress of pending bills, gave privileged access to groups in New Jersey prepared to perform such functions.[27]

The second type, political information, is of at least equal importance. Many familiar expressions, such as "keeping one's ear to the ground" and "mending fences," testify to this fact. The legislator, as anyone knows who has had even an amateur's brush with politics, can never know enough in this sphere. Who are behind this measure? How well unified are they? What dormant elements in the constituency will be stirred up if the proponents' claims are acceded to? Will there be a later opportunity to pacify them? For questions such as these there is rarely a final answer, but the legislator often must act as if there were. Where the situation remains obscure, his behavior may be ambiguous. Thus he may vote to kill a bill by sending it back to committee, but when that motion is lost, he may change his position and vote for the measure's passage. It may be easier to defend such apparent vacillation than to face the consequences of an unequivocal stand.

In politically ambiguous circumstances,

and they are common, a group that can give the legislator an indication of the consequences of supporting or opposing a measure is likely to win his ear at least in some degree. Such "information," of course, is rarely taken at face value, since most groups find it expedient to exaggerate their influence and the cohesion of the rank and file. It is up to the legislator to apply a discount rate that seems appropriate. In some instances his knowledge of his constituency is such that he knows immediately how to evaluate such claims. In others he must be aided by trusted advisors, who may themselves, in consequence, become the objects of petitions from various interest groups. The evaluation of group claims may itself be a puzzling task, although a politician of any skill can often see through assertions that are largely pretense. Yet because pretense and exaggeration are common, a group may gain advantage in access if it is presented by agents who have a reputation for candor and realism. Few elected politicians are in a position requiring no reliable political knowledge.

The desire for information may not be the only informal factor leading the legislator to make himself accessible to particular interest groups. He is not simply a machine for calculating odds and acting on the most favorable ones. When he assumes office he does not cut himself off from all previous connections and divest himself of the attitudes he has acquired up to that time. The prevailing myths may hold that he does so or should do so, but to accept such folklore literally is to fall victim to the institutional fallacy, to look at formalities and to ignore relationships. As John Dewey has put it: "Those concerned in government are still human beings. They retain their share of the ordinary traits of human nature. They still have private interests to serve and interests of special groups, those of the family, clique or class to which they belong."[28]

---

[26] Cf. V. O. Key, Jr., "The Veterans and the House of Representatives," Journal of Politics, *Vol. V*, *No. 1 (February, 1943)*, 39–40.
[27] McKean, op. cit., pp. 203–205.

[28] John Dewey, The Public and Its Problems (New York: Holt, Rinehart & Winston, Inc., 1927), p. 76. . . .

Such was essentially the point argued by Madison in the following passage from *The Federalist,* No. 10:

> No man is allowed to be a judge in his own cause, because his interest would certainly bias his judgment, and, not improbably, corrupt his integrity. With equal, nay with greater reason, a body of men are unfit to be both judges and parties at the same time; yet what are many of the most important acts of legislation, but so many judicial determinations, not indeed concerning the rights of single persons, but concerning the rights of large bodies of citizens? And *what are the different classes of legislators but advocates and parties to the causes which they determine?* (Italics added.)

Madison concluded that legislators must inevitably have interest affiliations, and not infrequently we find evidence that members of Congress also assume so. Thus in 1929 the Senate committee investigating tariff lobbying criticized the head of a series of "paper" associations for pretending to an influence that he did not have. After commenting on his lack of technical qualifications, the committee added as further evidence of his fraudulent position: "He is on terms of intimacy with no Member of Congress so far as your committee has been able to learn."[29]

Since an elected representative cannot give up his already existing attitudes and relationships, the legislature and various political interest groups inevitably overlap in membership. Any of the latter that can claim members in the legislature will thus enjoy a measure of privileged access. Other influences aside, the value of this means of access will vary with the number of such members and with the importance that they attach to such affiliation. It is well known, for instance, that the organized bar has had advantages in access to state and national legislatures in consequence of the number of lawyers elected to those bodies. The American Legion usually can list among its membership one-third to one-half the members of Con-

gress, in addition to Cabinet members and even the President. Not all of these are equally accessible to the Legion, but at least a portion of them are likely to be readily so. Similarly the Chamber of Commerce of the United States constitutes, as one author has put it, "an unofficial functional constituency of the federal legislature" in consequence of having several of its members in the Congress.[30]

Where the claims of a group are or can be made sufficiently central for its members in the legislature, the latter can be formed into a "bloc" that is expected to act as a unit on as many as possible of the issues of concern to the group. At its height such was the "farm bloc" of 1921–1922, which included a quarter of the Senators (fourteen Republicans and ten Democrats) and a similar but less well defined segment of the House. Though a minority of both houses, it held a balance of power for the better part of four years.[31]

The National Rivers and Harbors Congress, whose membership overlaps with that of a variety of other groups, including Congress, has acquired almost as much influence in the area of its claims. It is made up of contractors and state and local officials, members of Congress, and ex-officio officers of the Army Corps of Engineers. The loyalties uniting this group have demonstrated their strength on many occasions. When the Rivers and Harbors Congress announces its opposition to the recommendation of the Hoover Commission that the flood control and rivers and harbors activities of the Corps of Engineers be transferred to the Department of

---

[29] Senate Report No. 43, 72nd Congr., 1st Sess., Congressional Record (*December 20, 1929*), *p. 994.*

[30] Cf. *Justin Gray,* The Inside Story of the Legion (*New York: Boni & Gaer, 1948*), *p. 99. Paul Studenski, "Chambers of Commerce,"* Encyclopaedia of the Social Sciences (*New York: The Macmillan Company, 1948*).

[31] E. *Pendleton Herring, "Farm Bloc,"* Encyclopaedia of the Social Sciences, op. cit., *and* Group Representation Before Congress, op. cit., *pp. 122–124; Kile,* op. cit., *pp. 188ff. Not infrequently men have entered the legislature after serving as officials of interest groups. Before he was governor and Senator, Styles Bridges was the paid secretary of the New Hampshire Farm Bureau Federation (Kile,* op. cit., *p. 386).*

the Interior, it is in effect announcing the opposition of a "bloc" to any effort to implement the suggestion. When Representative William M. Whittington of Mississippi testified in 1945 before a Senate committee in opposition to a proposal to establish a Missouri Valley Authority, he spoke not only as a member of Congress and as chairman of the Flood Control Committee of the House, but as vice president of the National Rivers and Harbors Congress and vice president of the related Mississippi Valley Flood Control Association.[32]

The variety of uses to which such multiple memberships can be put is almost infinite. The legislator who is a "member" of an active political interest group may, better than anyone outside the legislature, observe and report on developments within the legislative body and its committees; he may act as the group's spokesman on the floor; he may attempt to persuade key committee members; he may save the group postage by allowing it the use of his franking privilege; and so on. A few examples will suggest the range of relationships. When the retail druggists and their allies were attempting in the 1930's to secure passage of price-maintenance laws, full use was made of retailer-legislators, according to the manual on the subject issued by the National Association of Retail Druggists. In Iowa the druggists who were members of the legislature met as a group and selected the persons who were to sponsor the measure. In the State of Washington the bill was introduced by a collection of legislators, "several of whom were or had been in the retail business and knew the meaning of predatory price

cutting. Such men needed no prodding when it came to arguing the bill on its own merits."[33] Much the same procedures are followed by the veterans' organizations. The Legion distributes among its members in the Congress the responsibility for sponsoring its measures, and it supervises the tactics they employ. During the bonus drive of the 1930's the key member of the Veterans of Foreign Wars in Congress was Representative Wright Patman of Texas. He spearheaded the V.F.W.'s effort to secure immediate cash payment of the bonus.[34] When the tariff revision of 1929–1930 was in process, Senator Bingham of Connecticut placed on the payroll of the Senate the assistant to the president of the Connecticut Manufacturers Association. The latter not only advised Senator Bingham, but accompanied him to the meetings of the Senate Finance Committee, which prepared the measure, as an "expert" on tariff matters.[35]

An important possibility to bear in mind in connection with the effect of a legislator's group memberships upon his accessibility is that the willingness to aid a group's claims need not involve any overt act on the part of the group, any "pressure" on the legislator, and it need not involve formal membership in the group. A legislator-politician no less than any other man has . . . lived his life in a series of environments, largely group-defined. These have given him attitudes, frames of reference, points of view, which make him more receptive to some proposals than to others. As a specialist in politics he may be in possession of information that obliges him to choose between his preferences as a successful upper-middle-

32 The New York Times (*April 10, 1949*). See *U.S. Commission on Organization of the Executive Branch of the Government*, Task Force Report on Natural Resources (*Washington, D.C.: U.S. Government Printing Office, 1949*), esp. *pp. 79–88, 98–99, 149–182*; Robert de Roos and Arthur Maass, *"The Lobby that Can't Be Licked,"* Harper's Magazine (*August, 1949*), *21–30. The hearings on the M. V. A. are effectively discussed in James M. Burns,* Congress on Trial (*New York: Harper & Row, Publishers, 1949*), *pp. 94–97.*

33 U.S. Federal Trade Commission, op. cit., pp. 52ff.
34 Cf. Herring, Group Representation Before Congress, p. 222. Veterans of Foreign Wars, 35th National Encampment, Proceedings, House Document No. 45, 74th Congr., 1st Sess. (1935); U.S. Senate, Finance Committee, Hearings on Payment of Adjusted Compensation Certificates, 74th Congr., 1st Sess. (1935).
35 Senate Report No. 43, Part 1, 71st Congr., 1st Sess., Congressional Record (October 26, 1929), p. 4922.

class lawyer and the demands of a group of militant workers in his constituency. But in the absence of such conflicts, and even in the face of them, he is likely to be most accessible to groups or proposals that stem from sources comparable to those from which his own attitudes have been derived. Many, if not all, such legislators will insist in all sincerity that they vote as their own consciences dictate. They may even resent any effort from an otherwise acceptable group to force a particular decision from them. This is true; however, whether they are "liberals" or "conservatives," urbanites or country boys, their "consciences" are creatures of the particular environments in which they have lived and of the group affiliations they have formed.

Under such circumstances the notion of group "pressure" has limited value. Bailey makes this point extremely well in his discussion of the attitudes of those members of Congress who were on the joint conference committee that produced the Employment Act of 1946 in its final form. In accounting for the strongly hostile position of Senator Buck of Delaware, Bailey refers to Buck's close connections with the Du Pont family, including his marriage to the daughter of T. Coleman du Pont. No overt group act was necessary to secure Buck's vote against the measure, for, as Bailey observes, "it was not the pressure of Du Pont *on* Buck but the pressure of Du Pont *in* Buck which was at work."[36] Similarly it is scarcely necessary for an organized interest group to take overt action among members of Congress from the South in order to secure their votes against F.E.P.C. legislation and the like. Access for this point of view is assured in most cases by the attitudes which Southern legislators hold without promoting.

We encounter here again the fact that interest groups operate in a hierarchy of prestige. Some groups, as we have seen

previously, enjoy a prestige which makes it unnecessary for them to participate actively in elections. Such high status groups are likely to acquire favorable access to the legislature for the same reasons. A politician need not himself be a member of the Chamber of Commerce of the United States to listen with respect to the testimony of a business leader who is pleading its case. Among the attitudes he is likely to have acquired in the average constituency are ones involving deference toward those groups that enjoy high prestige in the country as a whole. In the legislative process, as in other aspects of politics, groups are affected by their position or status in the society.

In this connection some reference should be made to what is widely referred to as the "social lobby." An informal influence upon access, it provides material for the more lurid exposés of legislative life and lends itself to treatment in eye-catching headlines. Popular impressions to the contrary, there is no reason to revise Herring's judgment that the influence of this device is "decidedly secondary."[37] If the minor importance of the "social lobby" is not forgotten, however, examination of the phenomenon will provide instructive illustrations of the informal determinants of relative access.

The "social lobby," a technique rather than a type of group, is a device to create a feeling of obligation on the part of the legislator toward individuals who have established sociable relations with him through entertaining him and his family. It uses social intercourse to develop multiple memberships, on the not unwarranted assumption that in a conflict situation the face-to-face relations of the "social lobby" will be dominant.[38] It is harder to refuse someone who has been kind to you than to turn away a more or less complete stranger.

---

[36] *Stephen K. Bailey,* Congress Makes a Law *(New York: Columbia University Press, 1950), p. 192. . . . See also pp. 148–149, 182.*

[37] *Herring,* Group Representation Before Congress, *p. 40.*

[38] *Cf. Paul Lazarsfeld, et al., The People's Choice (New York: Columbia University Press, 1944), Chap. 16, esp. pp. 153–155.*

If the attempted seduction is successful, it probably works best with the new legislator who is just taking up residence in a strange community.[39] Having been a fairly large frog in a comparatively small pond, he suddenly finds the situation reversed. He may be disturbed by the abrupt interruption of his accustomed social relationships and feel the need for adequate substitutes. These may be supplied by the dinner and golf games of a "social set" or by the poker games and other diversions offered by an interest group representative. The implied penalty for sharp political disagreement is ostracism from the friendly group, and the legislator may quite unconsciously find himself avoiding this penalty by conforming. Reinforcement in this direction may come from the legislator's wife and daughters. They too need satisfactory personal relationships in the new community; once established these may involve none of the conflicts which the legislator himself feels, and the sanction then becomes the more unpleasant. Especially if the ladies are "socially ambitious," exclusion from "important" social functions may be acutely painful. The rationale of the device is suggested by the Georgia representative of the Association of Life Insurance Presidents in a report on the 1933 session of the state legislature. Accounting for their expenditures, they say in part: "This money has been spent in invitations to those of whom we wished to make friends, and seeing that their wives and daughters were looked after properly and courteously. . . ."[40] At its crudest the "social lobby" amounts to simple bribery, as the following case suggests. A new member of the House of Representatives, assigned to a committee considering a power bill, struck up a friendship with a "newspaper correspondent" to whom he had been introduced at a small luncheon. He did not know that the introduction was by prearrangement, nor did he develop suspicions as the men and their wives became quite intimate, the two couples enjoying dinners and weekend excursions together, and the genial "journalist" drawing the Congressman and his wife into a new set of friendships. The "reporter" and wife even aided in redecorating the legislator's apartment. After this kind of thing had gone on for some time, the "journalist" one day dropped in at the Congressman's office, stated his attitude toward the power bill and his assumption that the legislator also opposed the measure. When the Congressman announced that he favored the bill and would not be dissuaded, the pleasant social relations between the two couples ceased completely.[41]

Normally the technique is more subtle, along the lines of the following statement by a former state legislator:

> The legislator who remains aloof will find himself, if not quite ostracized, at least not "one of the gang," and will constantly be surprised at an unexpected solidarity on the part of a majority of his colleagues for or against a pending measure. His surprise will be dissipated when he learns that the night before the "gang" were at an entertainment at a downtown hotel, where probably the subject of legislation was not even mentioned, but in some subtle way an understanding was reached as to what was expected of those present as all around "good fellows."[42]

Part of the subtlety in this case, of course, depended upon the clique structure within the legislature itself. . . .

Although the "social lobby" illustrates a type of informal overlapping membership, the reasons for its comparative unimportance are fairly obvious. In the first place, the successful politician, like other leaders, is likely to be a person whose pattern of interpersonal relations is fairly

---

[39] *McKean found that the "social lobby" was almost nonexistent in New Jersey because most legislators commute to the capital from their homes (op. cit., p. 192).*
[40] *U.S. Temporary National Economic Committee, Hearings (1933), Part 10, p. 4770.*

[41] *Reported in Logan, op. cit., p. 53.*
[42] *Henry Parkman, Jr. "Lobbies and Pressure Groups: A Legislator's Point of View," The Annals, Vol. CVC (January, 1938), 97. . . .*

flexible and thus not readily subject to the sanction of ostracism. Secondly, since positions of power within the legislature customarily are occupied by experienced legislators rather than by newcomers, the seductive technique must operate in a limited field. The old hand does not need the flattery of the "social lobby" for his personal happiness; he may, in fact, favor a gathering by his presence rather than be favored by an invitation to it. Excepting, therefore, the occasional newcomer and the rare legislator who is undisturbed by bribery, the "social lobby" is at most a means of reinforcing the preferences already held by various members of the legislative body. Even among these it may not prevail over other devices in a legislative situation where opposing influences are present.

An important implication of the various multiple memberships of legislators is that their interactions with interest groups are not just one-way relationships. The popular view is that the political interest group uses the legislator to its ends, induces him to function as its spokesman and to vote as it wishes. As we have already seen, this is not an inaccurate view. But it is incomplete. In most of the examples discussed above the legislators were not subject to overt "pressure." They did not necessarily act in anticipation of group demands but rather behaved as persons in official position whose views of the pending legislation for various reasons approximated those of organized and potential interest groups. When a legislator arouses organized groups in connection with a proposal that he knows will involve them or when he solicits their support for a measure which he is promoting, the relationship becomes reciprocal. Even in connection with the development of a single bill from conception to enactment, the initiative may lie alternately with legislator and with group, including other outside influences.

The Employment Act of 1946 furnishes a good example of such reciprocal rela-

tionships, as Bailey's study indicates.[43] Perhaps because this legislation involved few concrete deprivations or indulgences and is, therefore, not entirely typical of many controversial measures, it highlights the use that members of Congress may make of a variety of interest groups. The impetus for the bill came in part, to be sure, from the National Farmers Union. Much of the drive behind the measure, however, was supplied by the most important of the Senate and House sponsors and their aides. These solicited the support of a diversity of groups and welded them into what Bailey dubs the "Lib-Lab Lobby." Some of these interest groups in turn attempted to win over other members of Congress and officials of the executive branch, so that it became difficult to determine who was influencing whom. Certainly, however, it was no simple, one-way pattern of group demands upon legislators. On the opposition side as well, moreover, testimony against the measure was solicited by members of Congress. In particular, Representative Carter Manasco of Alabama, Chairman of the House Committee on Expenditures in the Executive Departments, to which the bill was referred, took the initiative in mobilizing opposition witnesses.

Overlapping memberships of legislators, therefore, give privileged access to the interest groups involved, whether the membership is formal or of the "fellow-traveler" variety. Such membership does not mean simply that the legislator is "used" by the groups in a one-way, conditioned-response relationship. As "parties to the causes which they determine," legislators may equally function as leaders of the interest groups with which they identify.

* * *

Conclusions

The degree of access to the legislature that a particular group enjoys at a given

43 *Bailey, op. cit., Chaps. 3, 5, 7, et passim. For some good examples of this see James MacGregor Burns, Congress on Trial (New York: Harper & Row, Publishers, 1949), pp. 19–23.*

moment is the result of a composite of influences. These determining factors will include the peculiarities of formal governmental structure and of the political party as a legislative instrument, such informal influences as the knowledge-supplying functions of the group and the character of the legislator's group affiliations, the formal and informal structure of the legislative body, and the influence of the standardized expectations in the community concerning the behavior of a legislator. Depending on the circumstances and the relative importance of these factors in a given situation, some groups will enjoy comparatively effective access, and others will find difficulty in securing even perfunctory treatment. As conditions change, as some of these influences become more and others less potent, the fortunes of group claims upon the legislature will rise or decline.

The most important implication of this multiple-factor conception of the dynamics of access is that the legislature is not just a sounding board or passive registering device for the demands of organized political interest groups. The legislature as a part of the institution of government embodies, albeit incompletely, the expectations, understandings, and values prevailing in the society concerning how the government should operate. These expectations may cover now a wide and now a relatively narrow range of behavior; they may be fairly explicit or highly ambiguous. Although the legislator's role is in part defined by limited expectations and norms prevailing in his constituency and in the interest groups with which he identifies himself, it is also the creation of the norms more widely recognized in the society. Partly because his role as a legislator inevitably gives him a specialized kind of experience from which he learns the limits of his behavior, partly because he has learned some of these norms as a member of the society, he cannot behave simply and completely as a vehicle for organized group demands.

It does not follow from the [above] argument . . . that the widespread expectations about the legislature alone account for differences in ease of access or for all features of the legislative product. It is easy enough to identify cases in which the standardized expectations are ignored. The norms of official behavior inevitably partake of the quality of myth, of professed values. On the other hand, they are also operating values that affect all legislative behavior in some measure and that place limits upon both the methods and the content of group demands upon the legislature. In a stable political system the competing demands of organized interest groups are meaningless unless they are viewed in the context of these limiting and defining norms.

A second implication of this conception of the dynamics of access is that "pressure," conceived as bribery or coercion in various forms, is scarcely the distinguishing feature of interest groups in the legislative process. Such coercion is frequently attempted, of course, and it often has an observable effect. "Pressure" of group upon legislator, however, is at most one aspect of technique, one among many different kinds of relationships that exist within the lawmaking body. As indicated by the evidence we have examined, the belief that the relationship between groups and legislators is a one-way, coercive relationship simply does not explain the observed behaviors. The institution of government . . . is not so passive and cannot be understood in such oversimplified terms.

F. Public Policy Issues

A Political Theory of Foreign Aid

Hans Morgenthau

Of the seeming and real innovations which the modern age has introduced into the practice of foreign policy, none has proven more baffling to both understanding and action than foreign aid. The very assumption that foreign aid is an instrument of foreign policy is a subject of controversy. For, on the one hand, the opinion is widely held that foreign aid is an end in itself, carrying its own justification, both transcending, and independent of, foreign policy. In this view, foreign aid is the fulfillment of an obligation of the few rich nations toward the many poor ones. On the other hand, many see no justification for a policy of foreign aid at all. They look at it as a gigantic boondoggle, a wasteful and indefensible operation which serves neither the interests of the United States nor those of the recipient nations.

The public debate on foreign aid has contributed little to understanding. In the spring of every year the nation engages in such a debate, carried on almost exclusively in terms of the amount of money to be spent for purposes of foreign aid rather than of the substantive purposes which a policy of foreign aid is supposed to serve. The Administration tries, as it were, to sell a certain amount of foreign aid to Congress, and Congress refuses to buy that amount. Congress generally appropriates about 10 per cent less than what the Administration has requested, and the Administration spends what is appropriated as it sees fit within the general categories authorized. Only when glaring abuses and inefficiencies are uncovered . . . is the question of the substance of our foreign aid policy raised in public, and even then it is put in the negative terms of remedying the abuses and inefficiencies rather than in the positive terms of the purposes our foreign aid policy may be supposed to advance and the kinds of measures best calculated to serve these aims.

It is in fact pointless even to raise the question whether the United States ought to have a policy of foreign aid—as much so as to ask whether the United States ought to have a foreign political or military policy. For the United States has interests abroad which cannot be secured by military means and for the support of which the traditional methods of diplomacy are only in part appropriate. If foreign aid is not available, they will not be supported at all.

The question what kind of policy of foreign aid we ought to have can then not be evaded. As it has developed in recent years, the kind we have is fundamentally weak. It has been conceived as a self-sufficient technical enterprise, covering a multitude of disparate objectives and activities, responding haphazardly to all sorts of demands, sound and unsound, unrelated or only by accident related to the political purposes of our foreign policy. The United States, in short, has been in the business of foreign aid for more than two decades, but it has yet to develop an intelligible theory of foreign aid that could provide standards of judgment for both the supporters and opponents of a particular measure.

Hans Morgenthau, "A Political Theory of Foreign Aid," *American Political Science Review*, Vol. LVI (June, 1962), 301–309. Reprinted by permission.

I. Six Types of Foreign Aid

The first prerequisite for the development of a viable foreign aid policy is the recognition of the diversity of policies that go by that name. Six such can be distinguished which have only one thing in common: the transfer of money, goods, and services from one nation to another. They are humanitarian foreign aid, subsistence foreign aid, military foreign aid, bribery, prestige foreign aid, and foreign aid for economic development.

Of these distinct types, only humanitarian foreign aid is *per se* nonpolitical. The aid which governments have traditionally extended to nations which are victims of natural disasters, such as floods, famines, and epidemics, falls in that category. So do the services, especially in the fields of medicine and agriculture, which private organizations, such as churches and foundations, have traditionally provided in Asia, Africa, and Latin America.

While humanitarian aid is *per se* nonpolitical, it can indeed perform a political function when it operates within a political context. The foreign aid that private organizations provide will be attributed for better or worse to their respective governments insofar as humanitarian aid emanating from a foreign country is recognized by the recipient country or its inhabitants to perform a political function. Thus the agricultural aid which the Rockefeller Foundation has provided for many years to certain Latin American countries is likely to take on under contemporary conditions a political function which it did not perform previously. The same has from the beginning been true of the work the Ford Foundation has been doing in India. By the same token, humanitarian aid extended by a government may have political effects.

Subsistence foreign aid is extended to governments, such as those of Jordan and Niger, which do not command the resources to maintain minimal public services. The giving nation makes up the deficit in the budget of the recipient nation.

Subsistence foreign aid is akin to the humanitarian type in that it seeks to prevent the breakdown of order and the disintegration of organized society. But it also performs the political function of maintaining the *status quo,* without, however, as a rule, increasing its viability. Where a political alternative to a nonviable regime may exist, subsistence foreign aid diminishes the chances of its materializing.

Bribes proffered by one government to another for political advantage were until the beginning of the nineteenth century an integral part of the armory of diplomacy. No statesman hesitated to acknowledge the general practice of giving and accepting bribes, however anxious he might be to hide a particular transaction. Thus it was proper and common for a government to pay the foreign minister or ambassador of another country a pension, that is, a bribe. Lord Robert Cecil, the Minister of Elizabeth, received one from Spain. Sir Henry Wotton, British Ambassador to Venice in the seventeenth century, accepted one from Savoy while applying for one from Spain. The documents which the French revolutionary government published in 1793 show that France subsidized Austrian statesmen between 1757 and 1769 to the tune of 82,-652,479 livres, the Austrian Chancellor Kaunitz receiving 100,000.

The Prussian Ambassador in Paris summed up well the main rule of this game when he reported to his government in 1802: "Experience has taught everybody who is here on diplomatic business that one ought never to give anything before the deal is definitely closed, but it has only proved that the allurement of gain will often work wonders." It is worthy of note that the first appropriation act adopted by the first Congress of the United States in 1789 included a modest contingent fund for such purposes.

Much of what goes by the name of foreign aid today is in the nature of bribes. The transfer of money and services from one government to another performs here the function of a price paid for political services rendered or to be rendered. These bribes differ from the traditional ones exemplified above in two respects: they are justified primarily in terms of foreign aid for economic development, and money and services are transferred through elaborate machinery fashioned for genuine economic aid. In consequence, these bribes are a less effective means for the purpose of purchasing political favors than were the traditional ones.

The compulsion of substituting for the traditional businesslike transmission of bribes the pretense and elaborate machinery of foreign aid for economic development results from a climate of opinion which accepts as universally valid the proposition that the highly developed industrial nations have an obligation to transfer money and services to underdeveloped nations for the purpose of economic development. Thus, aside from humanitarian and military foreign aid, the only kind of transfer of money and services which seems to be legitimate is one ostensibly made for the purpose of economic development. Economic development has become an ideology by which the transfer of money and services from one government to another in peacetime is rationalized and justified.

The present climate of opinion embraces another assumption as universally valid: that economic development can actually be promoted through such transfers of money and services. Thus economic development as an ideology requires machinery that makes plausible the postulated efficacy of the transfer for the stated purpose of economic development. In contrast to most political ideologies, which operate only on the verbal level and whose effects remain within the realm of ideas, this political ideology, in order to be plausible, requires an elaborate administrative apparatus serving as an instrument for a policy of make-believe. The government of nation *A*, trying to buy political advantage from the government of nation *B* for, say, the price of twenty million dollars, must not only pretend, but also act out in elaborate fashion the pretense, that what it is actually doing is giving aid for economic development to the government of nation *B*.

This practice of giving bribes as though they were contributions to economic development inevitably creates, in the giver and the recipient, expectations which are bound to be disappointed. Old-fashioned bribery was a relatively straightforward transaction; services were to be rendered at a price, and both sides knew what to expect. Bribery disguised as foreign aid for economic development makes of giver and recipient actors in a play which in the end they may no longer be able to distinguish from reality. In consequence, both may come to expect results in terms of economic development which in the nature of things may not be forthcoming. Thus both are likely to be disappointed, the giver blaming the recipient for his inefficiency and the recipient accusing the giver of stinginess and asking for more. The ideology, if taken for reality, gets in the way of the original purpose of the transaction, and neither side believes that it has received what it is entitled to.

For the past decade, military aid took the lion's share of the foreign aid programs of the United States. A shift in favor of nonmilitary aid occurred during the 1961 session, when Congress appropriated somewhat over two billion dollars for military aid, while the total voted for all the other foreign aid programs ran in excess of three billion dollars. To the latter amount must be added the equivalent of approximately one billion dollars in foreign currencies, the proceeds of the sale of agricultural commodities abroad, to be used for economic grants and loans to purchasing governments.

Foreign aid for military purposes is a traditional way by which nations buttress their alliances. Rome used to receive tribute from its allies for the military protections it provided. The seventeenth and eighteenth centuries are the classic period of military subsidies, by which nations, and especially Great Britain, endeavored to increase the military strength of their allies. Glancing through the treaties of alliance of that period, one is struck by the meticulous precision with which obligations to furnish troops, equipment, logistic support, food, money, and the like were defined. The loans which France extended to Russia after the conclusion of the alliance between the two nations in 1894 fall in the same category. This traditional military aid can be understood as a division of labor between two allies who pool their resources, one supplying money, matériel, and training, the other providing primarily manpower.

In contrast to traditional practice, military aid today is extended not only to allies, but also to certain uncommitted nations. The military aid the United States has been giving to Yugoslavia is a case in point. The purpose is here not so much military as political. It seeks political advantage in exchange for military aid. It obligates, by implication, the recipient toward the giver. The latter expects the former to abstain from a political course which might put in jeopardy the continuation of military aid. Military aid is here really in the nature of a bribe.

What appears as military aid may also be actually in the nature of prestige aid, to be discussed below. The provision of jet fighters and other modern weapons for certain underdeveloped nations can obviously perform no genuine military function. It increases the prestige of the recipient nation both at home and abroad. Being in the possession of some of the more spectacular instruments of modern warfare, a nation can at least enjoy the illusion of having become a modern military power.

As bribery appears today in the guise of aid for economic development, so does aid for economic development appear in the guise of military assistance. In the session of 1961, for instance, Congress appropriated 425 million dollars for economic aid to strategic areas, and it is likely that in the total appropriations of over two billion dollars for military aid other items of economic aid are hidden. This mode of operation results from the reluctance of Congress to vote large amounts for economic aid in contrast to its readiness to vote virtually any amount requested for military purposes. Yet the purposes of aid for economic development are likely to suffer when they are disguised as military assistance, as we saw the purposes of bribery suffer when disguised as aid for economic development. The military context within which such aid is bound to operate, even though its direct administration be in the hands of the civilian authorities, is likely to deflect such aid from its genuine purposes. More particularly, it strengthens the ever-present tendency to subordinate the requirements of aid for economic development to military considerations.

Prestige aid has in common with modern bribes the fact that its true purpose, too, is concealed by the ostensible purpose of economic development or military aid. The unprofitable or idle steel mill, the highway without traffic and leading nowhere, the airline operating with foreign personnel and at a loss but under the flag of the recipient country—all ostensibly serve the purposes of economic development and under different circumstances might do so. Actually, however, they perform no positive economic function. They owe their existence to the penchant, prevalent in many underdeveloped nations, for what might be called "conspicuous industrialization," spectacular symbols of, and monuments to, industrial advancement rather than investments satisfying any objective economic needs of the country.

This tendency sheds an illuminating light upon the nature of what is generally referred to as the "revolution of rising expectations." We are inclined to assume that the urgent desire to improve one's lot by means of modern technology and industry is a well-nigh universal trend in Asia, Africa, and Latin America. Actually, however, this trend is universal only in the sense that virtually all underdeveloped nations want to appear as having achieved industrialization, while only a fraction of the population, and frequently only small, élite groups within it, seek the social and economic benefits of industrialization and are willing to take the measures necessary to achieve them. For many of the underdeveloped nations the steel mill, the highway, the airline, the modern weapons, perform a function that is not primarily economic or military, but psychological and political. They are sought as the outward show of modernity and power. They perform a function similar to that which the cathedral performed for the medieval city and the feudal castle or the monarch's palace for the absolute state. Nehru is reported to have said, when he showed Chou-En-Lai a new dam: "It is in these temples that I worship." And the more underdeveloped and less viable a nation is, the greater is likely to be its urge to prove to itself and to the world through the results of prestige aid that it, too, has arrived in the mid-twentieth century.

The advantage for the giver of prestige aid is threefold. He may receive a specific political advantage in return for the aid, very much like the advantage received for a bribe. Also, the spectacular character of prestige aid establishes a patent relationship between the generosity of the giver and the increased prestige of the recipient. The giver's prestige is enhanced, as it were, by the increase of the recipient's prestige. Finally, prestige aid comes relatively cheap. A limited commitment of resources in the form of a spectacular but economically useless symbol of modernity may bring disproportionate political dividends.

The giver of foreign aid is therefore well advised to distinguish between prestige aid and aid for economic development, though both are justified by the prospective recipient in terms of genuine economic development. The prospective giver, if unaware of the distinction, is likely to fall into one of two errors. By mistaking prestige aid for aid for economic development, he may waste human and material resources in support of the latter when the purpose of prestige aid could have been achieved much more simply and cheaply. Or else he may reject out of hand a request for prestige aid because he cannot justify it in terms of economic development, and may thereby forgo available political advantages. The classic example of this error is the American rejection of the Afghan request for the paving of the streets of Kabul as economically unsound. The Soviet Union, pursuing a politically oriented policy of foreign aid, did pave the streets of Kabul.

II. Foreign Aid for Economic Development in Particular

None of the types of foreign aid discussed thus far poses theoretical questions of great magnitude; rather they raise issues for practical manipulation which can be successfully met by common sense tested by experience. Foreign aid for economic development has been the primary area for theoretical analysis and speculation, and these have been primarily of an economic nature. Economic thought, true to its prevailing academic tradition, tends to look at foreign aid as though it were a self-sufficient technical enterprise to be achieved with the instruments, and judged by the standards, of pure economics. And since Western economic development, from the first industrial revolution onward, has been due to the formation of capital and the accumulation of technical knowledge, we have tended to assume that these two factors would by themselves provide the impetus for the economic development of the underdeveloped nations of Asia, Africa, and Latin America. This tendency has been powerfully supported by the spectacular success of the Marshall Plan, the political origins and motivations of which were easily forgotten in its justification as a strictly economic measure for the provision of capital and technological know-how. Yet it is not always recognized that this success was made possible only by the fact that, in contrast to the underdeveloped nations of Asia, Africa, and Latin America, the recipients of Marshall aid were among the leading industrial nations of the world, whose economic systems were but temporarily in disarray.

The popular mind, on the other hand, and, through it, much of the practice of foreign aid have proceeded from certain unexamined assumptions, no less doubtful for being deeply embedded in the American folklore of politics. Thus the popular mind has established correlations between the infusion of capital and technology into a primitive society and its economic development, between economic development and social stability, between social stability and democratic institutions, between democratic institutions and a peaceful foreign policy. However attractive and reasuring these correlations may sound to American ears, they are borne out neither by the experiences we have had with our policies of foreign aid nor by general historic experience.

The first of these assumptions implies that underdevelopment is at least primarily the result of lack of capital and technological know-how. Underdevelopment is regarded as a kind of accident or at worst as a kind of deficiency disease, which can be taken care of through subcutaneous injections of the missing ingredients. Yet a nation may suffer from deficiencies, some natural and insuperable, others social and remediable, which no amount of capital and technological know-how supplied from the outside can cure. The poverty of natural resources may be such as to make economic development impossible. Nations such as Jordan and Somalia are in all likelihood permanently incapable of economic development for that reason. Many of the nations which are the perennial recipients of subsistence aid are likely to fall in the same category.

A nation may also suffer from human deficiencies which preclude economic development. As there are individuals whose qualities of character and level of intelligence make it impossible for them to take advantage of economic opportunities, so are there nations similarly handicapped. To put it bluntly: as there are bums and beggars, so are there bum and beggar na-

tions. They may be the recipients of charity, but short of a miraculous transformation of their collective intelligence and character, what they receive from the outside is not likely to be used for economic development.

Other nations are presently deficient in the specific qualities of character and intelligence that go into the making of a modern economic system, even though their general or inherent capabilities qualify them potentially for the necessary transformation sometime in the future. They are, to use a rough analogy, in a medieval stage of cultural development, still awaiting the equivalent of the moral and intellectual revolutions which in the sixteenth and seventeenth centuries created the cultural preconditions for the economic development of the West. Yet we tend to take the existence of these preconditions for granted, forgetting that without the secularization and rationalization of Western thought and society the industrialization of the West would not have been possible.

A civilization, such as the Burmese, which deprecates success in this world because it stands in the way of success in the other world, puts a cultural obstacle in the path of industrial development, which foreign aid by itself cannot overcome. Saving, that is, the preservation of capital or goods for investment or future use, has become so integral a part of our economic thought and action that it is hard for us to realize that there are hundreds of millions of people in the underdeveloped areas of the world who are oblivious of this mode of operation, indispensable to economic development. We have come to consider the productive enterprise as a continuum in the betterment of which the individual owner or manager has a personal stake. Yet in many underdeveloped areas the productive enterprise is regarded primarily as an object for financial exploitation, to be discarded when it has performed its function of bringing the temporary owner the largest financial return in the shortest possible time. Foreign aid poured into such a precapitalistic and even prerational mold is less likely to transform the mold than to be forced by it, in ways hardly predictable in advance, into channels serving the interests of a precapitalistic or prerational society.

The economic interests which tend to prevent foreign aid from being used for economic development are typically identified with the ruling groups in underdeveloped societies, which derive their political power in good measure from the economic *status quo*. The ownership and control of arable land, in particular, is in many of the underdeveloped societies the foundation of political power. Land reform and industrialization are in consequence an attack upon the political *status quo*. In the measure that they succeed, they are bound to affect drastically the distribution of economic and political power alike. Yet the beneficiaries of both the economic and political *status quo* are the typical recipients of foreign aid given for the purpose of changing the *status quo*. To ask them to use foreign aid for this purpose is to require a readiness for self-sacrifice and a sense of social responsibility which few ruling groups have shown throughout history. Foreign aid proffered under such circumstances is likely to fail in its ostensible purpose and, performing the function of a bribe to the ruling group, to strengthen the economic and political *status quo*. It is more likely to accentuate unsolved social and political problems than to bring them closer to solution. A team of efficiency experts and public accountants might well have improved the operations of the Al Capone gang; yet by doing so, it would have aggravated the social and political evils which the operations of that gang brought forth.

Given this likely resistance of the ruling group to economic development, foreign aid requires drastic political change as a necessary condition for its success. Foreign aid must go hand in hand with political change, either voluntarily induced from within or brought about through pressure from without. The latter alternative faces the giving nation with a dilemma. On the one hand, to give foreign aid for economic development without stipulating conditions that maximize the chances for success will surely maximize the chances for failure. On the other hand, to give aid "with strings" arouses xenophobic suspicions and nationalistic resentments, to be exploited both by the defenders of the *status quo* and the promoters of Communist revolution.

Furthermore, once one has decided to bring about political change in opposition to the ruling group, one must identify some alternative group as the instrument of political change. Sometimes, the only choice is among alternative groups which are equally unattractive. Sometimes, and not infrequently, the absence of any available alternative group leaves only the choice between creating one or doing nothing.

Finally, the promotion of drastic social change on the part of the giving nation may create the indispensable condition for economic development, but it also conjures up the spectre of uncontrollable revolution. In many of the underdeveloped nations peace and order are maintained only through the ruthless use of the monopoly of force by the ruling group. Determined and skillful foreign intervention may find little difficulty in weakening or even removing altogether the power of the ruling group. It is not so easy to finish what has thereby been started. While the interventionist nation may be able to control events up to the point of instigating drastic reform and revolution, it may well prove unable to control the course of the revolution itself. More particularly, a democratic nation, such as the United States, is greatly handicapped in competing with Communists in the control of a revolution. The revolution may start, as it did in Cuba, under the democratic auspices of unorganized masses dedicated to social reform and supported by the United States, and may in the course of its development be taken over by the highly organized and disciplined Communist minority, the only organized and disciplined revolutionary group on the scene.

Successful foreign aid for economic development may have similarly unsettling political results. Economic development, especially by way of industrialization, is bound to disrupt the social fabric of the underdeveloped nation. By creating an urban industrial proletariat, it loosens and destroys the social nexus of family, village and tribe, in which the individual had found himself secure. And it will not be able, at least not soon, to provide a substitute for this lost social world. The vacuum so created will be filled by social unrest and political agitation. Furthermore, it is not the downtrodden peoples living in a static world of unrelieved misery who are the likely protagonists of revolution, but rather those groups that have begun to rise in the social and economic scale have not enough to satisfy their aroused expectations. Thus, economic development is bound to disturb not only the economic *status quo* but, through it, the political *status quo* as well. If the change is drastic enough, the social and political effects of economic development may well bring about a prerevolutionary or revolutionary situation. And while the United States may have started the revolutionary process, it will again be uncertain under whose auspices it will be ended.

The United States faces a number of formidable handicaps in trying to control social and political change in the underdeveloped nations either as a prerequisite for, or a result of, foreign aid for economic development. First of all, as a Western capitalistic nation, the United States is a conservative power both domestically and internationally, and must appear particularly so to the underdeveloped nations. Both in its civilization and its social and economic structure, it belongs to that complex of nations which until recently were able to hold Africa, Latin America, and the outlying areas of Asia in a condi-

tion of colonial or semicolonial dependency. It has military alliances with these nations, and while it has generally shunned and even opposed outright colonial policies, it has actively and successfully participated in the semicolonial exploitation of backward nations. Thus the resentment against the former colonial powers attaches also to it, and its policies of foreign aid are frequently suspect, as serving in disguise the traditional ends of colonialism.

Furthermore, the United States, by dint of its pluralistic political philosophy and social system, cannot bring to the backward nations of the world a simple message of salvation, supported first by dedicated and disciplined revolutionary minorities and then by totalitarian control. In the nature of things, the advantage lies here with the Communist powers. They are, as it were, specialists in exploiting a revolutionary situation, which is bound to cause us embarrassment. For while the Communists are able to direct a revolution into the desired channels through their use of a disciplined minority, we, even if we are convinced that revolution is inevitable and therefore do not oppose it, tend to look on it with misgivings since we cannot control the direction it will take.

The Communist powers have still another advantage over the United States in that, at least on the surface, their problems and achievements are more meaningful to the underdeveloped nations than ours. The Soviet Union has achieved, and Communist China attempts to achieve, what the more enlightened underdeveloped nations seek: a drastic increase in national output through rapid industrialization. The Communist powers use totalitarian control as their instrument and Communist doctrine as rationalization. Seeking the same results, the underdeveloped nations cannot help being attracted by the methods which brought about these results elsewhere. In contrast, the slow process, stretching over centuries, through which the nations of the West achieved a high standard of living through industrialization must appeal much less to them. That appeal is further lessened by the economic processes of the free market and the political processes of liberal democracy through which in large measure Western industrialization was achieved. For these processes require a degree of moral restraint and economic and political sophistication which are largely absent in the underdeveloped nations. The simple and crude methods of totalitarianism must appear to them much more congenial.

Thus we arrive at the disconcerting conclusion that successful foreign aid for economic development can be counterproductive if the social and political goal of the giving nation is the recipient's social and political stability. In some cases at least, the failure of American aid for economic development may have been a blessing in disguise in that it did not disturb a stable *status quo* whose continuance was in our interest. Such aid, intended for economic development, actually performs the function either of a bribe or of prestige aid. Here again, however, these functions are likely to be impaired by disappointed expectations of economic development on the part of the giving and the recipient nation.

It is equally a moot question whether successful foreign aid for economic development is conducive to the development of democratic institutions and practices. Without stopping here to examine the complexities of the relationship between democracy and economic development, it is enough to observe, as recent history has made clear, that no necessary causal relationship exists between the two. The most impressive example is the Soviet Union. Its rapid economic development has gone hand in hand with totalitarian government, and a case could well be made for the proposition that the former would have been impossible without the latter. It is more likely than not that where the intellectual and moral preconditions for economic development are lacking in the

population at large and are present only in a small élite, as is true in many of the underdeveloped nations, the imposition of the will of that small minority upon the majority of the population is a prerequisite not only for the start of economic development but also for sustained economic growth.

As concerns the promotion of a peaceful foreign policy, economic development is likely to be counterproductive if a political incentive for a belligerent foreign policy is present. The contrary conclusion derives from the popular, yet totally unfounded assumption that "poor" nations make war on "rich" nations for economic advantage and that "rich" nations are by definition peaceful because they have what they want. In truth, of course, most wars have been fought not for economic but political advantage, and, particularly under modern technological conditions, only economically advanced nations are capable of waging modern war. We did not consider the Soviet Union a military threat as long as it was economically underdeveloped; it became one when its economic development had transformed it into a modern industrial power. Similarly, Communist China today, except to its immediate neighbors, is only a potential military threat by virtue of its economic potential, both likely to be activated by economic development.

Foreign aid for economic development, then, has a very much smaller range of potentially successful operation than is generally believed. Its success depends in good measure not so much upon its soundness in strictly economic terms as upon intellectual, moral, and political preconditions, which are not susceptible to economic manipulation, if they are susceptible to manipulation from the outside at all. Furthermore, the political results of successful foreign aid for economic development may be either unpredictable or counterproductive in terms of the political goals of the giving nation. In any event, they are in large measure uncontrollable. Foreign aid proffered and ac-

cepted for purposes of economic development may turn out to be something
different from what it was intended to be,
unless it is oriented toward the political
conditions within which it must operate.
Most likely, it will turn out to be a bribe
or prestige aid, or else a total waste. To do
too much may here be as great a risk as to
do too little, and "masterly inactivity"
may sometimes be the better part of wisdom.

III. Conclusions for Policy

The major conclusions for policy to be
drawn from this analysis are three: the
requirement of identifying each concrete
situation in the light of the six different
types of foreign aid and of choosing the
quantity and quality of foreign aid appropriate to the situation; the requirement
of attuning, within the same concrete situation, different types of foreign aid to each
other in view of the overall goals of foreign policy; and the requirement of dealing with foreign aid as an integral part of
political policy.

The task of identifying concrete situations with the type of foreign aid appropriate to them is a task for country and
area experts to perform. Can country *A*
not survive without foreign aid? Is its
government likely to exchange political
advantages for economic favors? Would
our military interests be served by the
strengthening of this nation's military
forces? Does this country provide the non-
economic preconditions for economic development to be supported by foreign aid?
Are our political interests likely to be
served by giving this nation foreign aid
for purposes of prestige? Can a case be
made for foreign aid in order to alleviate
human suffering? What kind and quantity
of foreign aid is necessary and sufficient to
achieve the desired result?

To answer these questions correctly demands first of all a thorough and intimate
knowledge and understanding of the total
situation in a particular country. But it
also requires political and economic judg-

ment of a very high order, applied to two
distinct issues. It is necessary to anticipate
the receptivity of the country to different
kinds of foreign aid and their effects upon
it. When this analysis has been made, it is
then necessary to select from a great number of possible measures of foreign aid
those which are most appropriate to the
situation and hence most likely to succeed.

In most cases, however, the task is not
that simple. Typically, an underdeveloped country will present a number of
situations indicating the need for different
types of foreign aid simultaneously. One
type given without regard for its potential
effects upon another type risks getting in
the way of the latter. One of the most
conspicuous weaknesses of our past foreign aid policies has been the disregard of
the effect different types of foreign aid
have upon each other. Bribes given to the
ruling group, for instance, are bound to
strengthen the political and economic
status quo. Military aid is bound to have
an impact upon the distribution of political power within the receiving country;
it can also have a deleterious effect upon
the economic system, for instance, by increasing inflationary pressures. Similarly,
the effect of subsistence foreign aid is
bound to be the support of the *status quo*
in all its aspects. Insofar as the giving nation desires these effects or can afford to
be indifferent to them, they obviously do
not matter in terms of its overall objectives. But insofar as the giving nation has
embarked upon a policy of foreign aid
for economic development which requires
changes in the political and economic
status quo, the other types of foreign aid
policies are counterproductive in terms of
economic development; for they strengthen
the very factors which stand in its way.

This problem is particularly acute in
the relations between prestige aid and aid
for economic development. The giving nation may seek quick political results and
use prestige aid for that purpose; yet it
may also have an interest in the economic
development of the recipient country, the
benefits of which are likely to appear only

in the more distant future. Prestige aid is at best only by accident favorable to economic development; it may be irrelevant to it, or it may actually impede it. What kind of foreign aid is the giving country to choose? If it chooses a combination of both, it should take care to choose an innocuous kind of prestige aid and to promote economic development the benefits of which are not too long in coming. Afghanistan is the classic example of this dilemma. The Soviet Union, by paving the streets of Kabul, chose a kind of prestige aid that is irrelevant to economic development. The United States, by building a hydroelectric dam in a remote part of the country, chose economic development, the very existence of which is unknown to most Afghans and the benefits of which will not appear for years to come.

It follows, then, from the very political orientation of foreign aid that its effect upon the prestige of the giving nation must always be in the minds of the formulators and executors of foreign aid policies. Foreign aid for economic development, in particular, which benefits the recipient country immediately and patently is a more potent political weapon than aid promising benefits that are obscure and lie far in the future. Furthermore, the political effects of foreign aid are lost if its foreign source is not obvious to the recipients. For it is not aid as such or its beneficial results that creates political loyalties on the part of the recipient, but the positive relationship that the mind of the recipient establishes between the aid and its beneficial results, on the one hand, and the political philosophy, the political system, and the political objectives of the giver, on the other. That is to say, if the recipient continues to disapprove of the political philosophy, system, and objectives of the giver, despite the aid he has received, the political effects of the aid are lost. The same is true if he remains unconvinced that the aid received is but a natural, if not inevitable, manifestation of the political philosophy, system, and objectives of the giver. Foreign aid remains politically ineffectual—at least for the short term—as long as the recipient says either: "Aid is good, but the politics of the giver are bad"; or "Aid is good, but the politics of the giver—good, bad, or indifferent—have nothing to do with it." In order to be able to establish psychological relationship between giver and recipient, the procedures through which aid is given, and the subject matter to which it is applied, must lend themselves to the creation of a connection between the aid and the politics of the giver which reflects credit upon the latter.

The problem of foreign aid is insoluble if it is considered as a self-sufficient technical enterprise of a primarily economic nature. It is soluble only if it is considered an integral part of the political policies of the giving country—which must be devised in view of the political conditions, and for its effects upon the political situation, in the receiving country. In this respect, a policy of foreign aid is no different from diplomatic or military policy or propaganda. They are all weapons in the political armory of the nation.

As military policy is too important a matter to be left ultimately to the generals, so is foreign aid too important a matter to be left in the end to the economists. The expertise of the economist must analyze certain facts, devise certain means, and perform certain functions of manipulation for foreign aid. Yet the formulation and overall execution of foreign aid policy is a political function. It is the province of the political expert.

It follows from the political nature of foreign aid that it is not a science but an art. That art requires by way of mental predisposition a political sensitivity to the interrelationship among the facts, present and future, and ends and means. The requirements by way of mental activity are twofold. The first is a discriminating judgment of facts, ends, and means and their effects upon each other. However, an analysis of the situation in the recipient country and, more particularly, its projection into the future and the conclusions from the analysis in terms of policy can only in part be arrived at through rational deduction from ascertainable facts. When all the available facts have been ascertained, duly analyzed, and conclusions drawn from them, the final judgments and decisions can be derived only from subtle and sophisticated hunches.

The best the formulator and executor of a policy of foreign aid can do is to maximize the chances that his hunches turn out to be right. Here as elsewhere in the formulation and conduct of foreign policy, the intuition of the statesman, more than the knowledge of the expert, will carry the day.

3
Perspectives on Political Behavior

The complexity of the contemporary world of politics is reflected in its study. From an earlier focus on the state and government, contemporary political science has increasingly turned its attention to political *behavior,* to the study of individual action and political attitudes, to social interaction and socioeconomic characteristics, to national belief-systems and their relationship to the values and psychological characteristics of national leaders. Not only has the focus shifted, but the field of vision has been expanded greatly. The discipline of political science, which once was composed of several distinguishable elements of analysis, in the post-World War II years has become a welter of overlapping and not readily differentiated perspectives regarding the study of political phenomena. This chapter highlights the breadth of contemporary perspectives in political science, stressing in particular the interdisciplinary character of these broadened perspectives. The selections also illustrate the central components of a behavioral conception of politics as a field of study.

One component of a behavioral conception of politics is the stress placed on individual and group decision making as the context within which political action is usually observed. Important governmental decisions, such as those that the President often must make, are products of both his own mental problem-solving and reasoning processes and the advice and ideas offered him by his advisers. Theodore C. Sorensen, Special Counsel to the late President Kennedy, in the selection below from his book *Decision-Making in the White House,* discusses this latter aspect of the process as he observed it firsthand in the shaping of Presidential action during the Kennedy years.

Sorensen argues that meetings, as settings within which the consultative function is normally performed, are themselves a prime conditioner of the decision-making process and its results. The exchange of ideas and the usefulness of the ideas developed are affected by the way in which the chief and his advisers behave in their meetings, the freedom felt by advisers to present controversial ideas, or the size of the group. The presence of a crisis, often the reason for the meeting, can temporarily dissolve differences in rank and permit freer criticism of the ideas of recognized authorities. Likewise, the position of those in attendance at the meeting, particularly the President's, can fundamentally alter the character of the deliberations. Different advisers assume different roles in the meeting; men with different outlooks behave in different ways, and such differences can and do affect the ideas expressed.

The variety found among advisers is perhaps the critical factor affecting group decision making in the White House. Experts tend to take the narrow view of the problem at hand. A Cabinet member tends to reflect the thinking of his department and its special clientele, often a limited segment of the affected public. The White House advisers, largely as a result of their isolation from Congressional affairs or governmental operations, lack contact with the day-to-day problems of politics and administration. And outside advisers, because of their irregular participation in governmental affairs, have no continuing appreciation of the complexities of public business. Sorensen reveals the dangers and opportunities confronting the President as he picks and chooses from among the bits and snatches of advice offered by these different types of advisers for his consideration in making decisions.

The individual's deliberations in political decision making have been studied more frequently in the context of voting decisions than in the making of executive decisions. Many factors affecting a man's choice in a voting booth have been cited—income, occupation, religion, and ethnic and racial identity among others. Dr. Richard E. Renneker reports on only one factor in voting behavior—the psychodynamic makeup of the voter. There is a difference of opinion among experts regarding the emphasis to be placed on psychological determinants of voting in the case of the majority of citizens. But when it comes to those voters who are known to be psychologically disturbed in the realm of their daily activities and responsibilities, many experts would probably agree that psychological factors play a large role in explaining their voting behavior. Dr. Renneker's findings are based on a review of the clinical records of forty-two patients undergoing psychotherapy or psychoanalysis during the election campaigns of 1948, 1952, and 1956. These findings cannot, of course, be taken as representative of the public at large; nevertheless, they may be valid representations of a larger universe of psychotic or neurotic individuals, even those who are not undergoing treatment for their problems.

Renneker finds that the party choice of the patients was affected by the dominant parent, usually the father. Where the father positively identifies with one party, the sons, after a period of rebellion and rejection, tend to reflect the political values of their fathers. Father-dominance in politics is also reflected in Presidential imagery and voter response, as several writers have noted particularly with regard to the Eisenhower years.

Where fathers provide no political direction, or where they provide only negative direction regarding politics and other forms of expression, the political attitudes of the patient-sons vary considerably, in some cases reflecting and in others counteracting the parental pattern of influence. Most often that influence is rejected and a negative concept of voting is adopted—voting *against* parties or candidates rather than *for* anyone or anything or any party in particular. Given the seeming frequency of negative voting in America (as noted in the press during elections), this finding is rather striking; it may help to explain patterns of voting among the populace at large.

No explanation or prediction of political behavior could be complete without heavy reliance on social and economic factors, and those most frequently cited are perhaps the social status and economic activities of the individual himself. Such matters affect not only political attitudes of voters, but also the conduct in office of public officials. The selection reprinted below from *Small Town in Mass Society* illustrates the impact of social rank and occupational differences on community politics.

The authors of that study, Arthur J. Vidich and Joseph Bensman, spent three years participating in the daily affairs of Springdale, a pseudonymous rural township of three thousand in upstate New York, gathering data for a systematic anthropological case study of community life. While the main focus of their volume is the community social system and its relation to the larger urban society beyond its boundaries—in particular, Springdale's growing dependence on this external urban world—the institutional forces of religion, government, local business, education, and their interrelationships within the community are highlighted. The authors are also quite conscious of the interplay of social and psychological pressures, and they do not hesitate to draw attention to the impact of community dependency on individual patterns of adjustment and self-delusion regarding the realities of contemporary community life. In the selection below the authors examine the subtle relations between different segments of the community in the control of local affairs, particularly the muted struggle between the businessmen of the village and the prosperous farmers of the township in seeking control of the township board.

Differences in class and occupational composition within each jurisdiction (village, town, and school district) account for the complex array of political ties and cleavages. The following class structure of Springdale is presented by the authors, the percentages referring to approximate percentages of the 750 households in the community:

I. The Middle Class 47%
    A. Independent Entrepreneurs 13
    B. Prosperous Farmers 25
    C. Professionals and Skilled
       Industrial Workers 9

II. The Marginal Middle Class 32
    A. Aspiring Investors 10

          B. Hardworking Consumers 10
       C. Economically and Socially
          Immobile Ritualists 10
          D. Psychological Idiosyncratics 2

   III. Traditional Farmers 10

   IV. Old Aristocrats 1

   V. Shack People   10
                                              ―――――
                                              100%

In the struggle for control over the town board, the various classes and occupations are concerned about public policy, particularly the tax burden of policies on them individually and on the several personalities competing for control. Three men—Lee, Jones, and Flint—each representing different economic and social forces, each relying on different political organizations and economic resources, try to shape local policy and tax rates to favor the interests they represent. Yet the very complexity of the political and socio-economic systems in the community make it necessary for the leaders to work together to keep the struggle from reaching a showdown. When a particularly important issue arises, such as road construction, it is these three men, and primarily Jones, who act as "an invisible government" in working out compromises so that action can be taken in spite of the "low tax ideology" that prevails among the members of the board. Nevertheless, certain groups, such as the prosperous farmers, are usually rewarded, while the less prosperous are provided with few benefits from public action.

The focus on social groups in politics has in recent years taken on another dimension. It has become apparent that the small, face-to-face group—a central object of study in social psychology for at least twenty years—may be of significance in analyzing and predicting political behavior. Studies of small-group leadership and intragroup dynamics could be used in the study of legislative or judicial voting and personal relationships in clique formation in legislatures[1] or courts. Eloise C. Snyder in her article on the Supreme Court examines the evidence bearing on clique formation in that body—how changes in alignments occur, how new members are assimilated, and how individual justices gradually adjust to the Court as a small group of which they are individual members.

Although the Court, because its members are loathe to discuss its inner workings with social scientists, does not permit investigation of actual social interaction among the justices, it is nevertheless possible to infer social interaction from the opinions of the individual justices in the cases reviewed.

---

[1] *See the selection below, pp. 242–52, from John C. Wahlke*, et al., The Legislative System: Explorations in Legislative Behavior (*New York: John Wiley & Sons, Inc., 1962*).

According to Professor Snyder's research design, whenever "two or more justices consistently tended to respond together in opposition to other members of the Court,"[2] a clique was considered to exist. On this basis she finds that over a thiry-year period the Supreme Court has had three basic cliques —a liberal, a conservative, and a pivotal clique. Most justices are consistently members of one, but when they change they tend not to switch radically from liberal to conservative or vice versa, but rather more moderately, by way of the pivotal clique. Moreover, the shifts that do occur are from liberal to conservative, never the other way. New justices tend to be moderates; as the years go by they tend to become more conservative (or else far more liberal, as in the case of certain individuals, such as Justices Black and Douglas). From this evidence it can be inferred that new members gradually gain the assurance to become more outspoken and committed to a more clearly articulated philosophy of constitutional interpretation. This pattern of individual adjustment is quite similar to the pattern of individual small-group relations evident in other, nonpolitical groups studied by social psychologists in recent years.

The environment to which individuals react, especially in the realm of political behavior, includes a much broader slice of society than the small groups to which they belong. In the postwar years social scientists have become interested in the interplay of politics and culture—that set of interrelated social ideas, folk beliefs, and group values that gives any people its character and differentiates it from others. Of the principal vehicles of culture, one stands out as primary: language, for it is through language that the terms of cultural expression are carried. It is language that permits, indeed facilitates, cultural insularity and that handicaps political integration or communication among peoples expressing themselves in different tongues. The problems and prospects of nationalism and internationalism are rooted in the cultural and linguistic diversity of man, and individual political behavior can profitably be understood in terms of its cultural and linguistic context.

Paul Friedrich's analysis of contemporary India dramatizes the political difficulties that a multilingual country faces. As he notes, India's problems as a modernizing nation are directly tied to the communications barriers that exist among the fourteen official languages, twenty-four tribal languages, and 720 minor languages and dialects native to India. Linguistic diversity has proved difficult to correct: efforts to establish Hindi as the one official

2 *The measure of consistency in agreement is not discussed by Professor Snyder in her article. Through the use of advanced statistical techniques, however, such a measure can be devised. Therefore at this point the student should not be concerned about this gap in the Snyder research design, but should instead focus his attention on the conceptual framework employed. For extended discussion of the methodological issues of the analysis of judicial behavior, see Glendon A. Shubert,* Quantitative Analysis of Judicial Behavior *(New York: The Free Press of Glencoe, Inc., and East Lansing: Michigan State University, Bureau of Social and Political Research, 1959).*

language, naturally of potentially great importance in economic development and national political identification, have faced a variety of social, religious, and educational obstacles, themselves at least partially generated by linguistic diversity. The very effort to unify the nation linguistically creates separatist resistance on the part of minor-language communities. This resistance has arisen in large part because of the religious-ideological overtones of the campaign for linguistic unification, a campaign originally waged by Mohandas K. Gandhi and his Congress Party when India gained independence at the end of World War II. Hindi has few literary masterpieces, many regional dialects, and almost no support from the intellectuals, who prefer to use other, more prestigious languages, such as Sanscrit, Tamil, or Bengali. It can boast of scant upper-class usage, an important factor in the resistance to its adoption. Moreover, the language issue has become highly controversial and politically dangerous as the political leaders of the nation have wrestled with it, and with each other, in efforts to establish one official medium of communication. As Friedrich notes, it will probably take dictatorial power to solve the language question, "but such power and the strategic vision to go with it are as yet absent."

This political dimension of linguistic diversity is manifested clearly at the state, as well as the federal level. Regional language usage does not fully coincide with state boundaries, and thus the sense of community or cultural individuality tends to cut across the major political subdivisions of the nation, at times seriously handicapping governmental effectiveness at the provincial level. At the same time, language differences and similarities are politically exploited by regional and local leaders in their efforts to gain a toehold in the state governmental machinery. As such leadership has arisen in the states, the chances for linguistic unification have diminished; *regional* language unification has been proposed by regional politicians as a viable alternative to total Hindization of the nation. Provincialism in language is thus tied directly to provincialism in politics.

The political and linguistic balkanization of India, particularly southern India, where these tendencies are most apparent, is to a large degree reflective of the cultural mélange of Indian society. National unification, whether political or linguistic in character, carries obvious implications of cultural homogenization and assimilation. Where assimilation is likely to take root, so might unification, but in India the long history and tradition of caste distinction and ethnic identification do not die easily. Cultural fragmentation in India stands as the chief barrier to linguistic reform, modernization programs, and the development of a sense of national identity.

Thus cultural and linguistic patterns, as they bear upon or are affected by political forces for and against integration, can form the basis of a nation's politics. The problems highlighted in Friedrich's discussion of Indian politics and language, moreover, are illustrative of the world at large, in which cultural and linguistic diversity combine with political forces to make the notion of "one world" (or even simply a powerful United Nations) an ideal not readily achieved. Clearly, the study of political behavior would not be complete without an analysis of language and culture as politically relevant phenomena.

Suggestions for Additional Reading

Alford, Robert R., *Party and Society*. Chicago: Rand McNally & Co., 1963.

Almond, Gabriel A., and Sidney Verba, *The Civic Culture: Political Attitudes and Democracy in Five Nations*. Princeton: Princeton University Press, 1963.

Berelson, Bernard, ed., *The Behavioral Sciences Today*. New York: Basic Books, Inc., 1963.

———— and Gary A. Steiner, *Human Behavior: An Inventory of Scientific Findings*. New York: Harcourt, Brace & World, Inc., 1964.

Campbell, Angus, *et al.*, *The American Voter*. New York: John Wiley & Sons, Inc., 1960.

Davies, James C., *Human Nature in Politics: The Dynamics of Political Behavior*. New York: John Wiley & Sons, Inc., 1963.

Erikson, Erik H., *Young Man Luther*. New York: W. W. Norton & Company, Inc., 1958.

Eulau, Heinz, Samuel J. Eldersveld, and Morris Janowitz, eds., *Political Behavior: A Reader in Theory and Research*. New York: The Free Press of Glencoe, Inc., 1956.

Eysenck, Hans J., *The Psychology of Politics*. New York: Frederick A. Praeger, Inc., 1955.

Froman, Lewis A., *People and Politics: An Analysis of the American Political System*. Englewood Cliffs, N.J.: Prentice-Hall, Inc., 1962.

Golembiewski, Robert, *Behavior and Organization: O & M and the Small Group*. Chicago: Rand McNally & Co., 1962.

Gore, William J., *Administrative Decision-Making*. New York: John Wiley & Sons, Inc., 1964.

Lane, Robert E., *Political Life: Why People Get Involved in Politics*. New York: The Free Press of Glencoe, Inc., 1959.

Lasswell, Harold D., *Power and Personality*. New York: W. W. Norton & Company, Inc., 1948.

Lipset, Seymour M., *Political Man: The Social Basis of Politics*. New York: Doubleday & Company, Inc., 1959.

MacIver, Robert M., *The Web of Government*. New York: The Macmillan Company, 1947.

Matthews, Donald R., *The Social Background of Political Decision-Makers*. New York: Doubleday & Company, Inc., 1954.

Milbrath, Lester W., *Political Participation: How and Why People Get Involved in Politics*. Chicago: Rand McNally & Co., 1965.

Polsby, Nelson W., Robert A. Dentler, and Paul A. Smith, eds., *Politics and Social Life*. Boston: Houghton Mifflin Company, 1963.

Snyder, Richard C., H. W. Bruck, and Burton M. Sapin, *Decision-Making as an Approach to the Study of International Politics*, rev. ed. New York: The Free Press of Glencoe, Inc., 1962.

Verba, Sidney, *Small Groups and Political Behavior*. Princeton, N.J.: Princeton University Press, 1961.

Wallas, Graham, *Human Nature in Politics*, 3rd ed. New York: Alfred A. Knopf, Inc., 1921.

Weldon, Thomas D., *The Vocabulary of Politics*. Mitcham, Australia: Penguin Books, Pty. Ltd., 1953.

A. Decision Making

Presidential Advisers

Theodore C. Sorensen

. . . Article II, Section 2 [of the constitution] provides that the President "may require the Opinion in writing of the principal Officer in each of the Executive Departments upon any subject relating to the Duties of their respective offices." But it does not prevent him from requiring their opinion *orally*, as [President Kennedy] frequently prefer[red] in the early stages of decision. It does not prevent him from obtaining a Cabinet member's opinion on subjects *not* relating to his respective office—if a Secretary of Defense has a business background, for example, that would be helpful in a dispute with the steel industry—or if a Secretary of the Treasury has experience in foreign affairs. Nor is the President prevented from seeking the opinions of those who are *not* principal officers of the Executive departments.

Meeting with Advisers

In short, each President must determine for himself how best to elicit and assess the advice of his advisers. Organized meetings, of the Cabinet and National Security Council, for example, have certain indispensable advantages, not the least of which are the increased public confidence inspired by order and regularity and the increased esprit de corps of the participants.

President Kennedy, whose nature and schedule would otherwise turn him away from meetings for the sake of meeting, . . . sometimes presided over sessions of the full Cabinet and National Security Council held primarily for these two reasons. Regularly scheduled meetings can also serve to keep open the channels of communication. This is the primary purpose, for example, of the President's weekly breakfast with his party's legislative leaders.

But there are other important advantages to meetings. The interaction of many minds is usually more illuminating than the intuition of one. In a meeting representing different departments and diverse points of view, there is a greater likelihood of hearing alternatives, of exposing errors, and of challenging assumptions. It is true in the White House, as in the Congress, that fewer votes are changed by open debate than by quiet negotiation among the debaters. But in the White House, unlike the Congress, only one man's vote is decisive, and thorough and thoughtful debate *before* he has made up his mind can assist him in that task.

That meetings can sometimes be useful was proven by the deliberations of the NSC executive committee after the discovery of offensive weapons in Cuba. The unprecedented nature of the Soviet move,

Theodore C. Sorensen, *Decision-Making in the White House* (New York: Columbia University Press, 1963), Chap. 5, "Presidential Advisers," pp. 57–77. Reprinted by permission.

the manner in which it cut across so many departmental jurisdictions, the limited amount of information available, and the security restrictions which inhibited staff work, all tended to have a leveling effect on the principals taking part in these discussions, so that each felt free to challenge the assumptions and assertions of all others.

Everyone in that group altered his views as the give-and-take talk continued. Every solution or combination of solutions was coldly examined, and its disadvantages weighed. The fact that we started out with a sharp divergence of views, the President . . . said, was "very valuable" in hammering out a policy.

In such meetings, a President must carefully weigh his own words. Should he hint too early in the proceedings at the direction of his own thought, the weight of his authority, the loyalty of his advisers, and their desire to be on the "winning side" may shut off productive debate. Indeed, his very presence may inhibit candid discussion. President Truman, I am told, absented himself for this reason from some of the National Security Council discussions on the Berlin blockade; and President Kennedy, learning on his return from a midweek trip in October, 1962, that the deliberations of the NSC executive committee over Cuba had been more spirited and frank in his absence, asked the committee to hold other preliminary sessions without him.

But no President—at least none with his firm cast of mind and concept of office —could stay out of the fray completely until all conflicts were resolved and a collective decision reached. For group recommendations too often put a premium on consensus in place of content, on unanimity in place of precision, on compromise in place of creativity.

Some advisers may genuinely mistake agreement for validity and coordination for policy—looking upon their own role as that of mediator, convinced that any conclusion shared by so many able minds must be right, and pleased that they could

in this way ease their President's problems. They may in fact have increased them.

Even more severe limitations arise when a decision must be communicated, in a document or speech or diplomatic note. For group authorship is rarely, if ever, successful. A certain continuity and precision of style, and unity of argument, must be carefully drafted, particularly in a public communication that will be read or heard by many diverse audiences. Its key principles and phrases can be debated, outlined, and later reviewed by a committee, but basically authorship depends on one man alone with his typewriter or pen. (Had the Gettysburg Address been written by a committee, its ten sentences would surely have grown to a hundred, its simple pledges would surely have been hedged, and the world would indeed have little noted or long remembered what was said there.)

Moreover, even spirited debates can be stifling as well as stimulating. The homely, the simple, or the safe may sound far more plausible to the weary ear in the Cabinet room than it would look to the careful eye in the office. The most formidable debater is not necessarily the most informed, and the most reticent may sometimes be the wisest.

Even the most distinguished and forthright adviser is usually reluctant to stand alone. If he fears his persistence in a meeting will earn him the disapprobation of his colleagues, a rebuff by the President, or (in case of a "leak") the outrage of the Congress, press, or public, he may quickly seek the safety of greater numbers. At the other extreme are those who seek refuge in the role of chronic dissenter, confining their analytical power to a restatement of dangers and objections.

Still others may address themselves more to their image than to the issues. The liberal may seek to impress his colleagues with his caution; idealists may try to sound tough-minded. I have attended more than one meeting where a military solution was opposed by military minds and supported by those generally known as peace-lovers.

The quality of White House meetings also varies with the number and identity of those attending. Large meetings are less likely to keep secrets—too many Washington officials enjoy talking knowingly at social events or to the press or to their friends. Large meetings are also a less flexible instrument for action, less likely to produce a meaningful consensus or a frank, hard-hitting debate. President Kennedy prefer[red] to invite only those whose official views he require[d] or whose unofficial judgment he value[d], and to reserve crucial decisions for a still smaller session or for solitary contemplation in his own office.

The difficulty with small meetings, however, is that, in Washington, nearly everyone likes to feel that he, too, conferred and concurred. For years agencies and individuals all over town have felt affronted if not invited to a National Security Council session. The press leaps to conclusions as to who is in favor and who is not by scanning the attendance lists of meetings, speculating in much the same fashion (and with even less success) as the Kremlinologists who study the reviewing stand at the Russian May Day Parade or analyze which Soviet officials sat where at the opening of the Moscow ballet.

Yet in truth attendance at a White House meeting is not necessarily a matter of logic. Protocol, personal relations, and the nature of the forum may all affect the list. Some basic foreign policy issue, for example, may be largely decided before it comes to the National Security Council —by the appointment of a key official, or by the President's response at a press conference, or by the funds allocated in the budget. Yet personnel, press conference, and budget advice is generally given in meetings outside the National Security Council.

Expert Advisers

Many different types of advisers, with differing roles and contributions, attend these meetings. President Kennedy met on his tax policy in the summer of 1962, for example, with professional economists from both inside and outside the government, as well as with department heads and White House aides. To the key meetings on Cuba were invited highly respected Foreign Service officers as well as policy appointees, retired statesmen as well as personal Presidential assistants.

There is no predictable weight which a President can give to the conclusions of each type. The technical expert or career specialist, operating below the policy-making level, may have concentrated knowledge on the issue under study which no other adviser can match. Yet Presidents are frequently criticized for ignoring the advice of their own experts.

The reason is that the very intensity of that expert's study may prevent him from seeing the broader, more practical perspective which must govern public policy. As Laski's notable essay pointed out, too many experts lack a sense of proportion, an ability to adapt, and a willingness to accept evidence inconsistent with their own. The specialist, Laski wrote, too often lacks "insight into the movement and temper of the public mind. . . . He is an invaluable servant and an impossible master."[1]

Thus the atomic scientist, discussing new tests, may think largely in terms of his own laboratory. The career diplomat, discussing an Asian revolt, may think largely in terms of his own post. The professional economist, in urging lower farm price supports, may think more in terms of his academic colleagues than of the next Presidential election.

But not all experts recognize the limits of their political sagacity, and they do not hesitate to pronounce with a great air of authority broad policy recommendations in their own field (and sometimes all fields). Any President would be properly

[1] *Harold J. Laski, "The Limitations of the Expert,"* Harper's Magazine, *CLXII (December, 1930), p. 106.*

impressed by their seeming command of the complex; but the President's own common sense, his own understanding of the Congress and the country, his own balancing of priorities, his own ability to analyze and generalize and simplify, are more essential in reaching the right decision than all the specialized jargon and institutionalized traditions of the professional elite.

The trained navigator, it has been rightly said, is essential to the conduct of a voyage, but his judgment is not superior on such matters as where it should go or whether it should be taken at all. Essential to the relationship between expert and politician, therefore, is the recognition by each of the other's role, and the refusal of each to assume the other's role. The expert should neither substitute his political judgment for the policy maker's nor resent the latter's exercising of his own; and the policy maker should not forget which one is the expert.

Expert predictions are likely to be even more tenuous than expert policy judgments, particularly in an age when only the unpredictable seems to happen. In the summer of 1962, most of the top economists in government, business, and academic life thought it likely that a recession would follow the stock market slide —at least "before the snows melted" was the cautious forecast by one economist from a cold northern state. But, instead, this year's thaw brought with it new levels of production—and, naturally, a new set of predictions.

In the fall of 1962, most specialists in Soviet affairs believed that long-range Soviet missiles, with their closely guarded electronic systems, would never be stationed on the uncertain island of Cuba, nearly six thousand miles away from Soviet soil and supplies. Nevertheless, each rumor to this effect was checked out; increasing rumors brought increased surveillance; and when, finally, the unexpected did happen, this did not diminish the President's respect for these career servants. It merely demonstrated once again that the only infallible experts are those whose forecasts have never been tested.

Cabinet Advisers

In short, a Cabinet of politicians and policy makers is better than a Cabinet of experts. But a President will also weigh with care the advice of each Cabinet official. For the latter is also bound by inherent limitations. He was not necessarily selected for the President's confidence in his judgment alone—considerations politics, geography, public esteem, and interest-group pressures may also have played a part, as well as his skill in administration.

Moreover, each department has its own clientele and point of view, its own experts and bureaucratic interests, its own relations with the Congress and certain subcommittees, its own statutory authority, objectives, and standards of success. No Cabinet member is free to ignore all this without impairing the morale and efficiency of his department, his standing therein, and his relations with the powerful interest groups and Congressmen who consider it partly their own.

The President may ask for a Secretary's best judgment apart from the department's views, but in the mind of the average Secretary (and there have been many notable exceptions) the two may be hardly distinguishable. Whether he is the captive or the champion of those interests makes no practical difference. By reflecting in his advice to the President his agency's component bureaus, some of which he may not even control, he increases both his prestige within the department and his parochialism without.

Bureaucratic parochialism and rivalry are usually associated in Washington with the armed services, but they in fact affect the outlook of nearly every agency. They can be observed, to cite only a few examples, in the jurisdictional maneuvering between the Park Service and the Forest Service, between the Bureau of Reclamation and the Army Engineers, between

State and Treasury on world finance, or State and Commerce on world trade, or State and Defense on world disarmament.

They can also be observed in Cabinet autobiographies complaining that the President—any President—rarely saw things their way. And they can be observed, finally, in case studies of an agency head paying more heed to the Congress than to the President who named him. But it is the Congress, after all, that must pass on his requests for money, men, and authority. It is the Congress with which much of his time will be spent, which has the power to investigate his acts or alter his duties. And it is the Congress which vested many of his responsibilities directly in him, not in the President or the executive branch.

White House Staff Advisers

The parochialism of experts and department heads is offset in part by a President's White House and executive staff. These few assistants are the only other men in Washington whose responsibilities both enable and require them to look, as he does, at the government as a whole. Even the White House specialists—the President's economic advisers or science adviser, for example—are likely to see problems in a broader perspective, within the framework of the President's objectives and without the constraints of bureaucratic tradition.

White House staff members are chosen, not according to any geographical, political, or other pattern, but for their ability to serve the President's needs and to talk the President's language. They must not . . . replace the role of a Cabinet official or block his access to the President. Instead, by working closely with departmental personnel, by spotting, refining, and defining issues for the President, they can increase governmental unity rather than splinter responsibility. A good White House staff can give a President that crucial margin of time, analysis, and judgment that makes an unmanageable problem more manageable.

But there are limiting factors as well. A White House adviser may see a departmental problem in a wider context than the Secretary, but he also has less contact with actual operations and pressures, with the Congress and interested groups. If his own staff grows too large, his office may become only another department, another level of clearances and concurrences instead of a personal instrument of the President. If his confidential relationship with the President causes either one to be too uncritical of the other's judgment, errors may go uncorrected. If he develops (as Mr. Acheson has suggested so many do) a confidence in his own competence which outruns the fact, his contribution may be more mischievous than useful. If, on the other hand, he defers too readily to the authority of renowned experts and Cabinet powers, then the President is denied the skeptical, critical service his staff should be providing.

Outside Advisers

Finally, a President may seek or receive advice from outside the executive branch: from members of the Congress; from independent wise men, elder statesmen, academic lights; from Presidentially named high-level commissions or special agents; or merely from conversations with friends, visitors, private-interest leaders, and others. Inevitably, unsolicited advice will pour in from the mass media.

This is good. Every President needs independent, unofficial sources of advice for the same reasons he needs independent, unofficial sources of information. Outside advisers may be more objective. Their contact with affected groups may be closer. They may be men whose counsel the President trusts, but who are unable to accept government service for financial or personal reasons. They may be men who are frank with the President because, to use Corwin's phrase, their "daily political salt did not come from the President's table."[2]

2 *Edward S. Corwin,* The President, Office and Powers 1787–1957. *New York: New York University Press, 1957, p. 298.*

Whatever the justification, outside advice has its own limitations. As national problems become more complex and interrelated, requiring continuous, firsthand knowledge of confidential data and expert analysis, very few outsiders are sufficiently well informed. The fact that some simple recommendation, contained in an editorial or political oration or informal conversation, seems more striking or appealing or attention-getting than the intricate product of bureaucracy does not make it any more valid.

Moreover, once the advice of a distinguished private citizen or committee is sought and made public, rejection of that advice may add to the President's difficulties. The appointment by the last [four] Presidents of special advisory committees on civil rights, world trade, and foreign aid was, in that sense, a gamble—a gamble that the final views of these committees would strengthen, not weaken, the President's purpose. Should the outside report not be made public, the Gaither Report being a well-known example, a President who rejects its advice may still have to face the consequences of its authors' displeasure.

Qualifications of Advisers

Finally, a President's evaluation of any individual's advice is dependent in part on the human characteristics of both men. Personalities play an intangible but surprisingly important role. Particular traits, social ties, recreational interests, or occupational backgrounds may strengthen or weaken the bonds between them. Some Presidents pay more attention to generals, some to businessmen, some to politicians, some even to intellectuals who have "never met a payroll and never carried a precinct."

In truth, a political background, not necessarily at the precinct level, is helpful. It gives the adviser a more realistic understanding of the President's needs. Those without such experience will tend to assume that the few Congressmen in touch with their agency speak for all the Congress, that one or two contacts at a Washington cocktail party are an index of public opinion, and that what looms large in the newspaper headlines necessarily looms large in the public mind.

Those with a political base of their own are also more secure in case of attack; but those with political ambitions of their own—as previous Presidents discovered—may place their own reputation and record ahead of their President's. (Such a man is not necessarily suppressing his conscience and forgetting the national interest. He may sincerely believe whatever it is most to his advantage to believe, much like the idealistic but hungry lawyer who will never defend a guilty man but persuades himself that all rich clients are innocent.)

Other advisers may also be making a record, not for some future campaign, but for some future publication. "History will record that I am right," he mutters to himself, if not to his colleagues, because he intends to write that history in his memoirs. The inaccuracy of most Washington diaries and autobiographies is surpassed only by the immodesty of their authors.

The opposite extreme is the adviser who tells his President only what he thinks the President wants to hear—a bearer of consistently good tidings but frequently bad advice.

Yet there is no sure test of a good adviser. The most rational, pragmatic-appearing man may turn out to be the slave of his own private myths, habits, and emotional beliefs. The hardest-working man may be too busy and out of touch with the issue at hand, or too weary to focus firmly on it. (I saw firsthand, during the long days and nights of the Cuban crisis, how brutally physical and mental fatigue can numb the good sense as well as the senses of normally articulate men.)

The most experienced man may be experienced only in failure, or his experience, in Coleridge's words, may be "like the stern lights of a ship which illumine

only the track it has passed." The most
articulate, authoritative man may only be
making bad advice sound good, while
driving into silence less aggressive or more
cautious advisers.

All this a President must weigh in hearing his advisers. He need not weigh them
equally. For toward some, he will have
more respect. With some, he will communicate easier. For some, he will have more
affection.

President Kennedy's confidence in the
Attorney General, for example, on a wide
variety of issues, [was] based not on fraternal ties alone but on long years of
observing and testing his brother's judgment and dependability. The more active

role taken by Secretary of Labor Gold-
berg, also assumed by his successor but in
contrast with that of his predecessors,
resulted not from an upgrading of that
post but from a closer relationship with
the President.

There are countless other examples. My
emphasis on the role of the President has
not made me a turncoat to the distinguished class of Presidential advisers. On
the contrary, while his perspective may be
more limited, the career specialist, the
Cabinet Secretary, the White House aide,
or any other adviser still has a valuable
contribution to make; and his limited perspective is a danger only if both he and
the President are blind to that limitation.

B. Psychological Determinants

Some Psychodynamic Aspects of Voting Behavior

Richard E. Renneker

This [study] is based on a review of the
clinical records of forty-two patients in
psychoanalytic psychotherapy or psychoanalysis during the elections of 1948, 1952,
and 1956. The review covered the two-
month periods preceding and following
the election dates. Clinical histories frequently included a lifelong Presidential
voting record. No attempt will be made
to present these data statistically since the
major emphasis will be devoted to the
multidetermined nature of psychological
influences upon political choice, candidate
preference, and voting behavior. Focus is
fixed upon the importance of understanding the individual conscious and unconscious emotional motivations for political
behavior and the different combinations
of intensities of the basic psychological
factors involved.

I make practically no attempt to deal

with the voting realities of geographical
distribution, socioeconomic factors, basic
election issues, and the like. . . . This is
a presentation of the psychodynamics of
voting behavior as seen by a psychoanalyst
from his privileged seat at the edge of the
patient's unconscious.

There was *always* some sort of meaningful relationship between the voting
history of the patient and of the *dominant*
parent. The most expected finding was
that party-fixated parents generally tended
to influence their offspring toward the
same party orientation. The effect of religion did not appear to be nearly as important a factor in these patients' material
as the governing emotional influence of
the significant parent. It has been commonly noted in voting studies that socioeconomic status, religious affiliation,
urban *vs.* rural residence all allow for fairly

Richard E. Renneker, "Some Psychodynamic Aspects of Voting Behavior," in E. Burdick and
A. Brodbeck, eds., *American Voting Behavior*, pp. 399–413. Copyright © 1959 by The Free
Press, a corporation. Reprinted by permission.

reliable predictions regarding the percentage of Democrats *vs.* Republicans in each group. The clinical data indicated that the various external pressures associated with each of these variables were important in molding the cultural values of the individuals, but that party choice seemed transmitted more by *identification* with the parents. This was more true for sons than daughters, since the primary political figure from childhood seemed almost without exception to be the father.

The Positive Father and the Son as Voter

Father's party preference and pet political opinions were found to be part of the pattern of *primary identification . . .* within the core of the male patient. This political frame of reference became something which the patient subsequently treated in one or all of the following ways:

1. Blind perpetuation as a symptomatic manifestation of failure of maturation.
2. Total rejection as a symptomatic manifestation of neurotic rebellion against father with acceptance of a completely different set of beliefs.
3. Confrontation and testing of various portions with the facts of changing reality of the self and the external world. This was part of the natural process of differentiation of the self and usually resulted in an *individualistic* set of political ideas which were different [from] father's but still in the same philosophical or party direction.

The latter could be disrupted and either one of the previous two instituted or vice versa.

Example 1: A thirty-three-year-old Protestant lawyer with a long history of sexual impotency, work inhibitions, and feelings of inadequacy faithfully followed and echoed his strong father's unswerving political convictions. The working through of the unresolved paternal conflicts was accompanied by a continued challenging of the old political concepts during the pre-election months. It progressed to a temporary decision to vote for the opposite party. This was given up in favor of return to the primary party which best reflected the actual values of his current life. He was, however, no longer a "follower" but assumed a postelection course of activity aimed at helping to institute some "progressive changes" within the local party. His political activities were for the first time experienced with enthusiasm. Passive, noncritical voting compliance was thus a symptomatic manifestation of his inability to compete with and to complete separation of himself from the powerful father.

Example 2: A twenty-two-year-old medical student with disturbing periods of depression, sporadic anxiety, and hypochondriasis had gotten himself deeply involved in Communist causes and party-line activities. This was quite disturbing to his stanchly Republican physician father who worried greatly about the possible negative social and professional consequences of such behavior. The symptoms were most centrally related to guilt over conflictful hostile destructive impulses directed toward father. His communistic activities not only provided other targets as substitutes for father, but also managed to "hurt" him through worry. Guilt was neutralized by the pain of social ostracism which came to him because of a need to talk about his activities.

Diminution of rage against father within therapy was followed by a de-emphasis of his "radical" orientations. The fortunate establishment of a really functioning relationship with the male parent was accompanied by a comfortable acceptance of certain of father's candidate preferences and a shift into the company of "independent" voters.

Example 3: A forty-three-year-old chemical engineer came for therapy because of a chronic depressive reaction of five years' duration. His wife complained of a gradual personality change in him from a lighthearted, easygoing, understanding fellow into a serious, worrisome, and authoritative man. He had been relatively inactive politically with no definite party affiliation, but with the change came much self-recrimination about his past "shirking of social responsibilities." He became deeply committed to one party, and in the election months spent more time in political work than with his family. Analysis revealed that the chain of events was precipitated by the man's unresolved guilt over the sudden death of father, whose character traits were unconsciously assumed by the patient as a means of magically attempting to neutralize guilt by undoing father's death. Father was still living in a sense—through the son.

There were a small number of instances in which death of the father *freed* the son to express or to develop his own political beliefs.

Example 4: A forty-seven-year-old university instructor had never completed his partially carried through individualization from the primary father identification. He lived in a stage of arrested, halfhearted revolution against the parental figure. This was beautifully expressed through his voting record. He prided himself upon his thorough knowledge regarding party stands on basic issues, records of the candidates, and so on. He had always functioned as an independent voter. We discussed his voting performance in six previous national elections. On three occasions his carefully thought out Presidential choice was at variance with his father's, so he voted without mishap. The other three times his candidate turned out also to be father's pick. He failed to vote each time because of varying, unconsciously supplied interferences on election day. His intellectual integrity demanded that he vote for the father-shared candidate, but his semiactive, unconsciously perpetuated adolescent defiance of father was so strong that solution to the conflict each time was an "unfortunate" or "accidental" occurrence which prevented voting. We had opportunity to see this pattern because of a "strange" association which flitted across his mind during father's funeral. He felt a sense of sad relief and was suddenly conscious of the thought that now he could vote for any candidate. This remained puzzling until it was recalled in therapy because it had never occurred to him that he wasn't free to vote for whomever he selected.

There seemed to be a tendency for first voting young men to deviate from father's established political preferences. The passively compliant, deeply identified, party-line son was the chief exception, otherwise the male first voter at least seriously considered divergent voting. Our culture has set twenty-one as the age when "now you are a man." This seems more linked to assumption of the right to vote than to anything else. The initial vote is therefore an initiation rite which formally recognizes the former youth as a man. It is something to be approached with great seriousness since voting choice is expected by the young man to be evaluated by his elders and peers for evidence of wisdom and independent thinking. He has been in the shadow of a parent for many years and a vote *with* father has to be instinctively explained and defended to others. A vote different from father's is like a declaration of manhood and stands distinct and separate from this parent.

The first vote did not seem to provide any consistent basis for predicting subsequent voting behavior. This appeared to be more dependent on the eventual degree of resolution achieved in the working through of the father-connected conflicts.

I had the impression that return to the general direction of father's party or political philosophy was determined by whether the basic father-son relationship had been positive or negative. History of positive relationship in the formative childhood years was correlated with change or shift toward father, whereas negative relationship always seemed to produce political divergence.

A pattern for those with positive father associations was the following:

1. Primary identification with father's masculine frame of reference, including

political attitudes if these were strongly felt and verbalized.

2. An early manhood phase of rejection of father's political convictions as part of the process of prematurely declaring total independence and separation from the male parent before it actually existed. This phase was bypassed by some in the political area because it was enacted in another part of his life (i.e., choice of profession, girl, etc.). It usually involves a selected area of rejection of father's values as a sort of battlefield upon which the battle for independence takes place. The political area can easily be selected if time for self-differentiation coincides with an election year and the "first vote."

3. Resolution of the unconscious conflicts impinging upon father, accompanied by development of the self into functioning manhood, allows a swing backward in which many of the values previously unconsciously rejected because of their father contamination are now reintegrated within consciousness. This is right because the nucleus of the developed man always remains his identification with the positive, strong portion of the loving father. Father's political ideas are logical extensions of his value systems, thus it would follow that some of them would make sense within the son's personality, which is founded upon the father's. These political values have been exposed to a shakedown cruise within himself and have been joined by new shipmates. They have been accepted as belonging to the crew, although originally held suspect because of the feeling that they represented another ship. Father's values of all kinds have been critically examined, subjected to various tests, and some have been discarded as nonfunctional within the son's world. The rest finally secure the son's seal of approval and thus become indefinably merged with the self. They are no longer "father's values" but are now the son's values. The final product is a combination of some new, acquired values of the son plus some old ones learned from the father. "Sowing one's wild oats" is the shakedown cruise

in which he reacts away from learned parental frames of reference in a too sudden and too far search for identity apart from father. The "wild oats" can be expressed in sexual, behavioral, and political areas.

There is another way in which the positive father identification reasserts itself in later life. We know that human beings when placed in difficult conflict situations which they seem unable to solve tend to react with regressive manifestations. Regression as a reaction to such a situation is movement backward in time to some past relationship or to some method of past adaptation, associated with feelings of security. The strong, dominant, loving father was obviously often the source of such security orientations, therefore such troubled times often result in regressive activation of unconscious need for reestablishment of the old parent-son relationship in which father could seemingly solve any problem or ward off any threat. These are the moments in a man's life when he deeply appreciates help from his boss, a friend, etc. It has political significance because *the Presidential candidate is commonly regarded by the unconscious as a father substitute* (e.g., Washington as the "father" of his country). This means that people displace onto him needs and hopes which were originally connected with the positive father or the quest for an ideal parent.

It is easy to see that there will always be a varied number of individually and temporarily dislocated people who will make a Presidential candidate the focus of their regressive needs for protection and help. They can be drawn outside of party lines by the particular personality characteristics, physical appearance, and behavior of one candidate. He might remind the person unconsciously of his longed-for dead father—no longer there to help him in his hour of need. The resemblance might be confined to a single physical feature. The candidate, consciously or unconsciously, endeavors *to act the part* of a strong, gentle, loving, interested, understanding, friendly, helpful father. After all, he kisses babies, puts in appearances at athletic contests, stumbles over rocky river beds to the accompaniment of clicking shutters. He smiles on all voters and looks properly strong and serious when discussing the acute problems of his times. He makes a point of understanding all groups, professions, and the like. His family clusters around him admiringly or else smiles reassuringly into the camera of the people. We must get the message of "this is a contented family." The children should appear properly clean-cut and secure. The wife has to be lost in love, deep admiration, and obvious compliance to her master. Her faith must be unswerving, so that she and the family become living proof of his infallible ability to meet and banish all obstacles. The deprecating, hostile behavior of Stevenson's wife during his two campaigns was the decisive factor in several patients' decisions not to vote for him although they otherwise felt that he perfectly represented their opinions. In each instance they were products of a matriarchally dominated family in which father was a mere figurehead for the proclamation of mother's policies. These men could not buy Adlai because he did not represent to them the sort of a man who could give security to their regressive needs.

The sights and sounds of the strong father have become essential equipment for Presidential candidates since the crash of 1929. Roosevelt's voice, electrifying mannerisms, and decisive actions generated such belief in his basic strength as to make most forget his physical incapacity. He was thus a fine figure for preserving hope in millions throughout the depression years. They were able to postpone hopelessness through regressive retreat to a feeling of almost total reliance upon the confident, strong voice which came into their homes with the story of what he was doing for them and what they must do to help. The concept of fireside talks was psychologically brilliant since it conveyed the essence of a calm, wise father speaking to his family. The only Republican candidate who was a worthy opponent on the level of father representation was Willkie. The war revitalized Roosevelt's political career since it seemed impossible to take a chance on someone else who couldn't conceivably be as strong "father-wise." His gradual physical deterioration was massively denied by millions because its recognition was the signal for collective irrational anxiety such as the child feels when he thinks about the possible death of the key parent. He was mourned as a father, and his passing reactivated unresolved oedipals all over the country. After Roosevelt, Truman was like a man seen through the wrong end of a telescope. He was said to look like the average man on the street because people, for a long time, couldn't really see him as a distinct person. They kept looking at him through the afterimage of Roosevelt. The feeling was like that of a family which loses the respected, loved father—no one can take his place. A new man starts coming around regularly but no one takes him seriously for awhile because "he isn't daddy." New events may gradually bring him into positive focus and so blur the memory of father. Truman imperceptibly emerged as the cocky, confident fighter who wouldn't back down for anyone. There was much critical press comment over his violent attacks upon the critics of his daughter, but more people felt vaguely reassured and pleased by them than otherwise. He was like a living demonstration of the Americanism: "My father can lick any father on the block." His courageous, jut-jawed campaign against the personally unconvincing Dewey pulled in the legions of those who would rather have a strong father figure in their corner just in case. Eisenhower by the same token never really had any competition from Stevenson. Potentially explosive and dangerous times seem to call for an unequivocally strong Presidential personality. For some reason the opposite seems to hold (e.g., Coolidge and Hoover) in times of unthreatened peace.

Nonpolitical Parents and Voting Behavior of the Sons

Those patients who came from families in which there was practically no political emphasis or interest during their childhood years tended to develop strong convictions about politics. They seemed to act out fantasies of what their parents should have been like in order to be saved the repeated social embarrassments suffered through mother and father's inert social behavior. It was also part of their defense against the partially nonfunctioning primary identification with these same parents.

There were other patients who represented the modern counterpart of such socially disinterested parents. They were the uninvolved, with long histories of disinterest and avoidance of what was outside of themselves. They were often nonvoters and generally unreachable with information about pertinent issues since they simply didn't try to understand. Some were the hugely narcissistic characters who frequently manage to go through life without sensing or meeting the needs of anyone other than themselves. For such a man life was with himself. He voted only because there seemed to be some immediate personal gain involved in the act.

Example 5: A middle-aged businessman temporarily trapped in therapy by his internist's frightening predictions about the outcome of a malignant essential hypertension admitted he had never voted. He didn't have the time. There was never time for anything but the pursuit of his own goals. People came into focus only as obstacles standing between himself and what he wanted. His wife and children were perpetually involved in the service of *his* needs. He thus taught them selfishness, interpersonal blindness, and one-way communication. Politics simply never entered the home because nothing was allowed to exist there except what was in

his head at the moment. He was the mirror image of a father who had lived an identical life. His philosophy was anchored in the idea that childhood had been governed by the needs of his father, thus he was entitled to get his as an adult.

A few nonvoters were deeply disturbed people whose life was spent on the brink of a psychotic break. They were the lonely ones who had pulled in their senses so that only the most literal aspects of the reality of their immediate environment filtered through to perception. Psychic energy was spent either in intrapsychic ruminations or in constant defensive attempts aimed at deceiving others and at times themselves.

Example 6: One man had cast his ballot in five elections without being able to remember for whom he had voted. It didn't matter really. The important fact was that he *had* gone into the voting booth; what happened then was not important because he either carelessly checked a few boxes or gravely handed in an unmarked ballot. He let everyone in his world in on his "social act" but sagely refrained from identifying his choice. He waited until the results were obvious and simply took credit for picking winners. His reputation was that of never having voted for a losing candidate. This pseudo personality expended all of his energies in an effort to prevent others from recognizing the vacuum within.

The Negative Father and the Son as Voter

Negative fathers with identifiable political views seemed to produce a variety of disturbed voting behavior in their sons. The term negative father is used here to denote a parent who contributed little to his son other than the repeated frustrations of his needs for love, dependency, and a masculine frame of reference. He usually used the boy for his own needs or ignored him. He often was crushing in his competitiveness or else totally discouraged it. He engendered pain, fear, hostility, and destructive impulses in his son. These were defended against in the offspring by various defensive intrapsychic maneuvers. The common denominator in the sons of these fathers was a peculiar sort of ambivalence. Ambivalence is ordinarily thought of as a mixture of opposing feelings struggling for dominance, but here the feeling was almost pure hatred camouflaged, with varying degrees of success, from the self and others. These patients were sometimes the superidealists whose hostility had been converted into a reaction formation of emotionless, pure theorizing. They all seemed possessed of the perpetual dream of finding a good, loving father. Their relationships with men, however, were disruptive ones since the unconscious hostility constantly interfered. They leaned occasionally toward paranoid defenses.

Father's political preferences were, of course, rejected, as was the image of father. Islands of father identification were disturbing parts of the personality since they inevitably represented nonfunctioning elements. Political campaigns, during late adolescence, usually represented a perfect opportunity for verbalizing in one more area their disagreement with everything that father stood for. The basic principle was to be sure what this *was,* and then to take the opposite viewpoint. Father was a Democrat, then be a Republican. Father was against an issue, then be for it. Many had histories of dipping into Communism because it represented the antithesis of the parents' conservatism. The only factor which silenced the loud sounds of their constant identification of areas of disagreement was continuing fear of the father. This diverted the process into nonverbal channels within the home (i.e., passive resistance) or into external channels of rebellion (i.e., antisocial acting out, or involvement in the youth Communist movements).

There was a startling repetition in the case notes of these men. They did not really speak *for* a candidate but always *against* one. Consciously this was not so to them, since in their minds they were vigorous forces working toward the election of a carefully chosen candidate. Records of their comments about candidates disclosed that they spent much more time and energy in attacking the other candidate than in extolling the virtues of their own. They seemed to specialize in first identifying the black characteristics of one party or candidate which had to be avoided or defeated at all costs. These were overdrawn and overemotionalized. There were dire predictions of national disaster if so and so [were] elected. The issues had to be clear-cut and opposing. They doctored them to become so in their minds. It was a dedicated struggle to defeat an evil force which was threatening the nation with a period of being used. The men pictured as behind the candidate were political prototypes of the hated father. The candidate was sometimes also so depicted, particularly if there was some real theory to distort into evidence—otherwise he was thought of as a well-meaning, but hopelessly impotent front man for the evil power behind the throne. I noticed that this latter version seemed to be found in men whose fathers were impotent, passive characters dominated by strong, masculine, protest women. It is easy to see the reduplication of this real-life family situation in their fantasied version of an evil force behind the hapless candidate.

This is a description of an extreme reaction, but it of course existed also in benign forms wherein emphasis was still on *defeating* a candidate rather than on *electing* one. Enthusiastic sounds *for* a candidate seemed to be rationalizing activity to cover up the real source of their efforts—to work *against* and defeat a despised and hated parental surrogate. It boiled down to a choice of evils, because when pushed several revealed that they wouldn't be a bit surprised to see their man turn out badly. This is understandable since their experiences with father figures had generally been repeated episodes of unrealistic hope of finding the ideal parent substitute, which inevitably had culminated in feelings of bitterness and frustration.

They were susceptible to good father

propaganda, but were especially sensitive to bad father information or rumors. The first step for such a one was to construct a case *against a candidate* or a party, then to construct a case *for the remaining side*. Both steps could be riddled with irrational distortions of the facts essential to the building of "airtight" cases *for* and *against*.

Example 7: A political scientist, who was a superpurist, reached the ultimate in this type of voting behavior. He set himself the professional task of identifying the negative qualities of *both* candidates. In order to do this he had decided not to vote and thus to avoid emotional blindness in the service of defending his choice against himself. This was a neat maneuver which freed him from the necessity of going through the motions of being *for* something. It also allowed free rein to his critical, hostile feelings unconsciously directed toward father figures. He was ostensibly operating in the interests of science, in fact, people admired him for greater purity of investigative method, therefore people—including himself—didn't dream that his real satisfaction came from the exercise of his hostility.

Women Voters

There isn't too much to be said here, since the female patients shared the political views of their husbands or, if unmarried, their fathers. They displayed a ready capacity for giving up father's views in favor of the husband's. Although, as patients, they were inevitably part of a disturbed, conflictful marriage, political disagreement somehow did not occur in *these* marital relationships. A few of them passively belonged to the League of Women Voters only because a friend, husband, or neighbor had talked them into it.

The women with strong political convictions and activities were the following:

1. *Masculine protest women.* These were like the sons of negative fathers since they specialized in the *against* technique. Unconscious gratification was derived through deprecation of the rival candidate. Father was either a defeated shell of a man, or a rigid, narcissistic character who encouraged daughter to seek security through masculine identification. One woman persisted in the fantasy that Roosevelt's really important decisions had actually been made by his wife. Mother tended to be the prototype of daughter or else a masochistic woman whose fate the patient was attempting to avoid through identification with the aggressor (father). Hostility toward father was a common factor. These women were, of course, competitive with their husbands and dominated the relationship. They said that there was no marital disagreement about choice of candidate, but one did worry that her husband had secretly changed his vote without her knowledge.

2. *Father seekers.* These were the ones, for the most part single, who were bound to spinsterhood, or to frigid, masochistic marriages by unresolved incestuous conflicts. They reacted strongly to the candidates in terms of the positive father image. The candidate of choice (selected by the husband) was aggrandized by them into somebody with a heart as big as a barrel, wisdom greater than that possessed by the high lama of Shangri-la, and so on ad infinitum. They wished to help him in the same fashion that they had worked to please father. Some of them were the best doorbell pushers in their precinct. They operated strictly in terms of *for* their candidate and *not against* the other one. I can easily imagine that they effectively convinced other women by the sheer purity and intensity of their love for the candidate (father). They must have rekindled hope in the breasts of women who had almost given up finding a good father. Their sincerity was possible because they identified the candidate with the overidealized father memories.

3. *Identity seekers.* These were the pseudopolitical interest women whose seemingly intense dedication covered up feelings of worthlessness, of nothingness, or the like. Such a woman's activity might be an imita-

tion of her husband's, necessary because she came to life only through imitating his enthusiasm. She could very well have had no political interests or voting record prior to marriage. She might have been single and deeply involved in the middle of party headquarters, but she was really there to suck in the excitement and dedication of others. Her work was an ego transfusion which brought her to life— temporarily. One such woman worked endlessly throughout a campaign and then didn't bother to vote since outcome of the election was not the point of her endeavors. She simply told her fellow workers that a vote had been cast.

Depth Interviews

Voting surveys have been aimed at securing information as to *how* a sample population is going to vote. This can be further broken down into statistical descriptions of the *how* of various cultural groups and subgroups. Predictions based on such *hows* have a fairly high degree of constancy but are static and completely miss the decisive fluctuations which determine the outcome of an election. . . . [Most] voting studies [try] to get at the *why* of voting choice primarily through tackling it on the level of the voter's *conscious explanation*. This [study] has presented many examples of the irrational unconscious element in voting behavior. It is therefore immediately obvious that unless one knows the deeper dynamics of the voting act in terms of its function and meaning within the total personality the conscious explanation can never be separated from the rationalization. The *why* was also sometimes confused with *what* happened, for example, the tendency of sons of Republican fathers to vote Republican.

I do not believe that we are yet at a place in the development of depth psychology where it will be easy to set up predictive studies of behavior. We have spent most of our energies explaining why something occurred in the past or present.

Prediction of the future has had to take a back seat because we haven't been ready. It is time to begin.

Voting behavior would be a fine place to start since it culminates in a single act executed at a time agreed upon in advance. The act, though based upon complex factors, narrows itself down to the selection of one element from each of a few units of two possible choices (i.e., Democrat *vs.* Republican; candidate *vs.* candidate). One difficulty is our inability to observe the act itself, thus we are left with no means of controlling for voter falsification in the reporting of voting choices.

The predictive study should be small and thorough, being based in depth interviewing aimed at eliciting adequate personal information for the understanding of the personality development, the neurosis, and the current dynamics. Special effort can be made to get more details in the areas critical to an understanding of the emotional background of voting behavior. These would stress the points touched upon in this paper: personality characteristics of each parent, nature of voter relationship with parents (past and present), with spouse, longitudinal voting histories on all, their pet political convictions, and the voter's description of the personality of each candidate.

The sample for interviewing could be selected from those who indicate indecision regarding their future voting act. Psychoanalytic evaluation of the depth interview data would allow for understanding of the individual's psychodynamics of voting. The data can be used in several different ways. The unconscious meaning of the act in his life at that time can be grasped by the voter. Predictions can be made regarding party and candidate. The psychoanalytic bases for the predictions must, however, be made explicit.

Summary

The following points were extracted from a review of the psychotherapeutic notes of forty-two patients in psychoanalytic psychotherapy or psychoanalysis.

1. The positive father with political convictions has decided influence upon his son's subsequent voting behavior. This tends eventually to resemble a contemporary, individualized version of father's.

2. The negative father with political convictions can produce strongly divergent political views in his son, who seems to work more *against* a candidate than *for* one.

3. Nonpolitical parents seemed to produce politically conscious sons.

4. Nonvoters were deeply narcissistic characters or semiwithdrawn, precariously balanced patients.

5. Women were in political agreement with their husbands.

6. These neurotic patients in psychiatric treatment seemed for the largest part to have intense feelings about voting behavior. They also tended to make up their minds early and to carry their decision into the final vote.

C. Social and Economic Factors

The Prosperous Farmers in Town Government

Arthur J. Vidich and Joseph Bensman

There are three major areas of politics in Springdale: village government, town government, and school government. However they do not involve the same constituencies or the same political interests. The village government is excluded from jurisdiction over those who live in the country, so that farmers do not participate in its affairs. The town government and the school district potentially include all residents of the township, but because each encompasses different interests and purposes—road issues in the one and school issues in the other—quite different groups, especially leadership groups, are involved in the political processes of each.

Because of the differences in the class composition of the groups interested in politics in each of the major jurisdictions, each jurisdiction exhibits a social and psychological climate different from the others. Each exhibits different political processes, different issues, and different connections to the mass society.

In addition to the local jurisdictional

levels, the township is, of course, connected to county, state, and national political jurisdictions. In this case, too, different combinations of groups and leaders are involved in the attempt which Springdale makes to come to formal and informal terms with the society of which it is a part.

* * *

The town board is made up of a supervisor (the chairman of the board), two board members, two police justices, a clerk, and a road supervisor. All these officials are elected and, with the exception of the clerk and the road supervisor, all are voting members of the board. The town supervisor is a member of the county board of supervisors and represents the township in an organization which deals with county problems.

* * *

. . . Although its actual functions pertain exclusively to activities outside the village, the entire township, including voters in the village, votes for the election of its officers. The village voting privilege arises from the fact that the general town tax applies to village property as well as to country property. In consequence, town government is partially supported by village taxpayers who derive no benefit from the activities of town government.

The Social Composition and Psychology of Board Members

. . . The clerk of the [town] board is Sam Lee, who has held this position for the past twenty years and whose father held the same position for thirty years before him. The two police justices tend to be older men, retired farmers or lifelong residents of the township who live either in the village or in the country. The board members are practicing farmers, one of whom is characteristically a traditional farmer[1] and the other in more recent years has been a prosperous Polish farmer. The road supervisor lives outside the village, usually has some knowledge of road construction, has lived there for a long time, and does not have a permanent or full-time job (small chicken farmer, manager of a rural postal station, etc.). . . .

Traditionally the town supervisor has been a farmer and a Republican who is active in village affairs. For fifteen years prior to 1949 he was a prosperous farmer, Melbin, who had become prosperous during the decade of the forties. Due to differences over party policies on the county board of supervisors, Melbin was not nominated by the local party to succeed himself in 1949. Instead, a popular local entrepreneur was nominated and defeated by a Democratic candidate, Richard Calvin, who has remained in office to the present time. Calvin is a part-time appliance dealer who lives just outside the incorporated limits of the village.

[1] *That is, one who views farming as "a way of life to be practiced in all its ceremonial and ritual complexity" unlike the "rational" farmer, who "conceive[s] of and work[s] at farming as a business." Almost all of the Polish farmers in Springdale are rational farmers.*—ED. NOTE.

The composition of the board at any time represents an ostensible balance between village and country members, the country members being drawn from different sections of the township. However, Lee, Calvin, and one police justice, while considered "village representatives," have strong connections with farm people and must profess or have some basis for implying a psychological identification with township affairs and farmers—i.e., having grown up on a farm, having many farm friends, being a retired farmer. A candidate for supervisor must ordinarily have extensions into both the village and the country. If he is a farmer, he is usually active in many village affairs, which also means that he lives relatively close to the village. If he is a businessman, he usually has a farm clientele and belongs to such farm organizations as the Grange. Psychologically the town supervisor must bridge, at least symbolically, the village-country difference.

The town board, like the village board, is oriented to keeping taxes down. The records show that at one time or another every member of the board has subscribed to the "keep taxes down" rhetoric. The candidate for town supervisor, whether Democrat or Republican, cannot be elected unless he is known as a "low tax man." However, the psychological atmosphere in which this rhetoric is voiced differs from that of the village board.

Combined town tax rates in relation to the village rate run in the ratio of ten to one. The town budget, including state road subsidies, comes close to one hundred thousand dollars and, even though a large percentage of this is allocated to fixed costs (automatically turned over to the county and the fire district according to fixed formulas), the board members must nevertheless approve what is regarded as a high tax rate and must approve a budget which runs into "six figures." More specifically, in terms of "free decisions," the board must annually approve expenditures of close to twenty-five thousand dollars for roads. Although the low tax ideology is central to the board, it must face up to its fixed commitments and to the necessity of roads.

Roads are, of course, highly visible to those who use them. If their condition is poor, if they have not been graded or graveled for a long time, or if the maintenance crew has not been seen working on them "since the spring thaw," the road supervisor and the board are held directly responsible. It is this fact more than any other which determines the psychological atmosphere of the town board. The immediate and visible consequences of poor road conditions make the board capable of approving what are regarded as a high tax rate and expenditures of large sums of money.

In addition, however, this circumstance in combination with the abdication of other functions and the low tax attitude leads to a psychological acceptance of *roads as the only jurisdiction* of town government. The acceptance of this limitation of jurisdiction is a primary qualification for membership on the board. Within this psychological atmosphere, however, the board must take due account of the existence of a village constituency which derives no benefits from the board's actions. Village property owners pay the town general tax and constitute an important and easily mobilized electorate in township elections. It is at this point that the low-expenditure ideology becomes partly understandable and that the connecting link between village and town government is provided by the invisible government of the community.

Personalities Embodying Farmer-Business Conflicts: The Invisible Government

. . . The major figures in the Republican party, that is, the effective Republican committee, are John Flint, Sam Lee, and Howard Jones. Flint is the legal counsel to the *village* board and, in his capacity as a member of the party, this board is his jurisdiction. He initiates the nomination proceedings for village elec-

tions and intimately guides the proceedings of the board itself. Flint, however, is not important in township politics. He does not attend town board meetings in either an official or unofficial capacity. He is not known to be intimate with any members of the town board and in township elections his activities are limited to getting out the village vote. Although he may privately voice dissatisfaction with the state of town government, his effective political reference group is the village, and his participation in town politics would be a direct challenge to Sam Lee.

Sam Lee is the link between the town board and the effective Republican committee. As clerk of the board since the death of his father twenty years ago, Lee has an intimate knowledge of the affairs of the town, and is the only man in town who knows the fiscal setup of town government. The public records of town government have been in the Lee family for fifty years and in many cases the system of record keeping and the whereabouts of the records themselves are known only to Lee.

Lee is also the owner and editor of the local weekly newspaper, the *Springdale Press,* which he inherited from his father along with the clerkship of the board. Until recently, when, for reasons of health, he sold out his interests in the newspaper, the office and meeting place of the town board and the repository of its records have been the front office and editorial room of the print shop. The daily business of the board as conducted by its clerk was transacted across the business counter of the newspaper, and board meetings took place in an atmosphere of printer's ink. The minutes which Lee kept as clerk of the board became the basis of a news item in the next issue of the newspaper. The town board office is now located in the abandoned railroad station and Lee continues with a more tangential interest in the newspaper; he holds the mortgage on the establishment and works "by the hour" for the new editor.

On several occasions in the past, Flint

as a member of the Republican committee has sought to nominate an alternative candidate for the position of town clerk. In each case Lee has successfully foiled the attempt by threatening to run for town supervisor if he should not be nominated for the clerkship. Except for one or two occasions, the Democrats do not back a candidate for the clerkship. Lee has been able to maintain his position as town clerk by his personal friendliness, by being critical of Flint, by being the champion of underdog causes (particularly in the village), and by his outspoken editorial views in the *Springdale Press*. Traditionally, Lee has assumed the position of attacker of the village board—editorials on village board members as money grabbers when they raised their own pay, agitation for board action on snow removal—while simultaneously he has carried out some of the major functions of the village board as president of the Community Club and chairman of the committee on the dam. In his capacity as chairman of the committee on the dam, he was largely responsible for raising the three thousand dollars necessary to preserving the dam. In the village he is known as a critic of a village government which does nothing, and as a man who accomplishes desirable social projects.

As editor and town clerk he has "social contacts" with a wide range of rural residents. The newspaper carries a social column for each of the rural areas ("Mrs. Smith and her daughter, Velma, went to Rockland on a shopping trip last Thursday," "Mr. and Mrs. Jones of Smithfield were the weekend guests of Mr. and Mrs. Rodney Alexander," "Peter Kloski has a new Farmall tractor"), a segment of the paper which serves as a communicator of important social facts for the rural readership. As town clerk he issues birth, marriage, and death certificates; dog, hunting, and fishing licenses; and records all property assessments. As a result of this dual position his contacts with the public extend throughout the township and, due to his "friendly, helpful, and talkative" man-

ner, he is on personal terms with a great many people. Over a period of twenty years he has developed a wide arc of independent supporters.

Lee is assured of the personal loyalty of sufficient number of individuals to be elected to any position on the town board. However, his supporters are not organized and are not independent of other leaders of the invisible government. Moreover, by his simultaneous association with the invisible government of the township and by his attacks on village government, there are pockets of resentment against him in the township (particularly in the poor road areas) and in the village. Hence he has not been able to set himself up as an independent force in local politics, and continues his close identification with the Republican committee.

Lee has supported his position on the Republican committee by the political uses to which he has put his paper in state elections. Candidates for the state legislature and for the national Congress approach Lee directly for the support of his newspaper. In concrete terms this means carrying the picture of the candidate and a front-page news story on the virtues of his character and accomplishments. When these candidates visit the community, they do so under the auspices of Lee, who introduces them to friends and newcomers and to all those who transact business with him in his capacity as editor and clerk. This link between Lee and county and state candidates at election time, and the potential power and prestige by association which is implied by such connections, supports his position in local political circles.

In addition, however, as clerk of the board Lee is the supervisor of township elections. He sees to it that ballots are printed and distributed to each of the five voting districts in the township. He does these chores personally and in doing them comes in contact with those who officiate at the polls in each of the districts. He has known these people for a long time and has had a voice in their selection. It is through them that he gauges political sentiment in each of the districts and is kept informed of voting trends on election day. In this capacity he serves a positively useful purpose for the party committee and simultaneously supports his own position within it.

As a result of these circumstances Lee is a force, but not an independent one, in township politics and in the Republican committee. The opposition both within and outside the committee has not been able to dislodge him. For lack of an independent and coherent organization of his own, he must express himself politically through the Republican committee. He does this through a relationship with Howard Jones, who invisibly connects both the visible and invisible governments of the village and town—in the village through Flint and in the town through Lee. The invisible government has its key in the person of Jones.

Jones, a name familiar to the community for a hundred years, is the second son of a man who made the name important as a cattle dealer in the preceding generation. Howard Jones entered the feed business in 1918 in partnership with an older man, Richard Hilton, who now plays only a minor part in the business and community. Since 1918 the business has expanded to include building supplies, farm implements, machinery repairs, lumber, hardware, and an extensive delivery service. The business employs six to eight workers and a bookkeeper. Local competition consists of a Grange League Federation outlet which does one-tenth the business of Jones and Hilton, and which has no local connection to the Grange.

The line of supplies merchandised by the firm and the repair and feed grinding services which it offers are sufficiently broad to meet the needs of village and rural nonfarm residents as well as farmers. A large proportion of home repair and construction materials business and a great proportion of the available farm business is handled by the firm. A substantial portion of the business is conducted on short-term credit, and perhaps 5 to 10 per cent is conducted on long-term credit. No interest is charged on extended credits. Cash payments within thirty days receive a 1 per cent discount. During the 1920's and particularly during the 1930's the firm "carried" a substantial number of farmers who are successful today, especially the Polish farmers, who now uniformly state that Howard Jones was "the only man who trusted us when we first came." The firm carries mortgages on a number of farms and is known to have foreclosed only once (on an outsider).

The business is located in the village and is a focal point for farmers who come to the village. Any farmer who does business with the firm makes a trip to the "mill" at least every week or two. On a rainy day there is a congestion of traffic around the mill and the farmer regards his visit as much a social as a business occasion. He wants to talk and to meet friends. He wants to know how other farmers are doing, "how much young heifers are bringing," whether grains are "going up or down," and he wants to discuss milk prices, farming practices, and new types of machinery. At the mill he has an opportunity to do this with other farmers and with the proprietors.

Jones has an intimate knowledge of the affairs of the farmers who are his customers. He knows what their indebtedness is, what their long-range expansion plans are, what their seasonal needs are, and what their family life is like (i.e., whether the wife is a helpmate, which sons are interested in farming, what "quality" people they are).

It is generally acknowledged and has been demonstrated that Jones is capable of securing a great many farm signatures on petitions. He is in close contact with one or two outstanding farmers in each of the main farm neighborhoods and it is through these farmers that he circulates petitions and information. When it is necessary to have a farm representation at a public hearing in the county seat or at a town board meeting, Jones is capable of assuring that representation. It is said that "he can have fifty farmers in the village inside of a half-hour, rain or shine." In important elections he takes an active part in getting out the farm vote. In purely local elections, unless there is a "contest," his activities are not publicly visible.

As a result of his extensive and peculiar relationships with the farmers of the township, Jones is a power in town government. He expresses this power both positively and negatively through Lee. Lee, who plays a major role in the nomination of township candidates, must consult with Jones before Republican party nominations become official. In village government the position analogous to Lee's is held by Flint, and these two men as individuals embody the village-rural clash of interest. Aside from immediate personality differences between the two, Lee attacks the village board as penny pinchers (while alternat[e]ly attacking them as "money grabbers"), as poor businessmen, and for dereliction of duty. While engaging in such attacks, Lee in his private activities carries out some of the functions of village government and hence his attack cannot be construed as an attack on the village at large.

Flint and others on the village board focus their attack on Lee on the cost of town government (inefficiency of the clerk, poor administration) to a village constituency which derives no benefit from town government. This attack, however, is veiled, since an attack on town government can easily be construed by farmers as an effort to reduce expenditures on roads, the most immediate and visible consequence of the existence of town government. Farmers, who are viewed in the popular mind is providing the main economic base of the town, are the one group in the town whom no one consciously offends. Ironically, . . . it is these farmers who prevent the town board from making expenditures on village activities since they can see no direct benefit to themselves from town investments in the village. In

this sense, then, Lee and Flint stand as symbols of the village-rural conflict.

Jones stands as a higher power in this conflict. He too, in a personal and political way, is involved in the conflict. He has economic and property interests in the village and for fifteen years up to 1949 was its mayor. In village affairs, as the most successful businessman in town, he accepts the ideology of the village board. Due to his peculiar position, however, he has personal and political extensions into the township. Good roads are important to the conduct of his business and farmers are his most important customers. In a very real way Jones's position embodies all the elements of the conflict and this fact places him in a dual position. The manner in which he resolves this conflict with respect to his own position in local politics provides the basis for understanding how a balance is maintained within the invisible government.

Jones practices a knife-edge aloofness from the conflict between Lee and Flint and all that it represents. Neither Flint nor Lee takes his conflicts to Jones for resolution. Hence it is a mutually respected traditional practice to avoid a "showdown battle," and the effective Republican committee maintains its coherence and control within the framework of these differences. The independent strength which Jones has among farmers, not to mention his personal wealth and prestige, enhances his position in relation to Lee, who also has strength among farmers; because of this, Lee is satisfied to be regularly renominated to the clerkship, while tacitly agreeing not to upset the balance of forces in the invisible government.

As a result of this intricate constellation of relationships, Jones is the controlling figure in both village and town government. However, due to the village-rural conflict and his own dual position in relation to it, he must remain publicly anonymous and exercise control invisibly. He cannot appear to commit himself overwhelmingly in the village-rural conflict or he would become identified with one side and lose the support and control of the other. The effective Republican committee would be split. It is in this sense that Jones is the invisible government over the village and town, and it is his relationship with prosperous farmers which makes it possible for the board to act on the issue of roads.

The Dominance of Prosperous Farmers

Prosperous farmers have tended to dominate town government less by occupying its formal positions than by acting (successfully) as a pressure group. It is possible that they could fill the positions of one or both board members and even of town supervisor since, if they indicated an interest or a desire, they could easily secure the nomination. In practice, however, prosperous farmers have no desire to occupy their time with the regular official meetings of the board. These meetings are dull, lengthy, and require a type of activity which is alien to the productive "get-things-done" attitude of the prosperous farmer. Melbin became town supervisor while he was still a struggling hill farmer and kept the position even after he became prosperous because he had larger political ambitions. The Polish member, Kinserna, holds the position less as a prosperous farmer than as a Pole who see it as an avenue to social acceptance in a dominantly "American" environment. When prosperous farmers happen to be on the board they seem to be there for reasons other than openly influencing board policies in favor of the group they represent.

Prosperous farmers are interested in good roads as an adjunct to their business operations and because a good road fronting their property enhances the value of that property. As a consequence of this specialized interest, they become interested in town government only on those occasions when road policies are under consideration. These occasions are rare, once in a year or two and sometimes not for

five years. In the intervening years their roads are maintained on a seasonal basis to their satisfaction or, if not, they approach the town supervisor personally "to see that something is done to get my road graded and oiled."

When road policies are under consideration before the board, prosperous farmers organize delegations to attend such meetings for the purpose of exerting pressure to influence decisions. This was done in 1951, when the board was considering a state-supported ten-year road development plan for rural townships. State legislation provided for the state to bear 75 per cent of the program's cost and stipulated that local boards hold public hearings on the plan. Springdale's town board held such a hearing which was attended by about one hundred people. After this hearing, the board decided, but not in a decisive way, not to participate in the program. The farmers "heard" that the board was ready to jettison the plan, and at the next meeting of the board four prosperous farmers along with the state highway engineer came "to make sure this program is adopted." At this meeting the board reversed its decision under the pressure of the prosperous farmers. The first question in the protocol below is by Stevens, the road superintendent, and is directed at Lashly, the state engineer:

> Stevens asks what about construction of bridges, etc.; the law has no provisions for that sort of thing. Lashly brushes this off, says his candid opinion is that the town should adopt the program. Fridel announces that we (sweep of hand indicating Best, Burdin, and Havland, all prosperous farmers) are here to make sure this program is adopted. Fridel adds, "I understood that the town board was opposed to going in on the program." (Woodhouse, Calvin, Elson, board members weakly say, "No, no.") Fridel continues, "This is the first town board meeting I've ever attended." Elson says if he likes it he should come more often. Fridel says he doesn't want to butt in but this sort of thing (roads) is in his line. Calvin says Fridel misunderstands—this is a public meeting—they like to hear all sides. (All this in

a very friendly fashion.) There is much joking about widening roads—who will pay for fences that have to be set back. Lashly says if roads are being improved people are pretty cooperative. Then Lashly says that if the town is going to get into the program they will have to have a resolution. Calvin asks, "What do you fellows want to do about it—do you want to go in?" Elson says, "Don't see why not." Woodhouse says that the picture has changed completely since the meeting in the school, and adds that Butts, the state representative at the public hearing held at the school, had said that the road project had to be continuous over ten years, but now he knows it can be spread around and he is all for it. Then followed a discussion on whose road would be fixed first under the program—danger of favoritism. Best, contributing for the first time, said, "No problem here—we're a peaceable bunch." Lashly asks, "How are you going to satisfy people whose roads won't be built till 1958?"

With this and only this action, since there is no other public record on acceptance of the plan, the board entered the ten-year road plan which shows that in spite of its low-tax, low-expenditure ideology the board can be forced into programs which are costly, if it is urged to do so by the prosperous farmers.

In matters other than roads the prosperous farmers leave the board to its various ceremonialisms and do not interfere. But it is precisely on the issue of roads that the nexus between Howard Jones and the farmers, especially prosperous ones, find its meaning. Farmers need good roads for their daily deliveries of milk, and the value of farm property is related to the quality of the road on which it is located. At this point the business and political interests of Jones coincide with those of the farmers. These farmers are his customers and their roads are traveled by his delivery trucks. However, as the protocol above suggests, not all roads can be fixed equally well or at the same time. The prosperous farmers make sure that their roads get preferential treatment. Jones, however, cannot identify himself too closely with one segment of farmers since they are all his customers; for this

reason, even though he is in favor of road expenditures, he does not play a visible part in promoting them. His interests are expressed through the prosperous farmers in this as well as other political activities already mentioned. Hence he is able to continue as the main force in the invisible government of the town as well as of the village even when these governments exclude large segments of the population which are important to him in his business.

The Excluded Groups

Prosperous farmers represent only a portion of the constituency of the town board. One third of its constituency is made up of residents of the village; another third is composed of rural-dwelling industrial workers and shack people; the last third is composed of prosperous farmers and traditional farmers.[2] The village constituency has little or no interest in township affairs except with respect to the tax rate, which at worst is grumblingly accepted along with the low tax rhetoric. The only two groups who are psychologically located in township affairs are the traditional farmers and the prosperous farmers. The industrial workers are scattered and isolated and if they are active are oriented to village activities. The shack people have psychologically abdicated from the community and, in their lack of illusions caused by their psychology of resentment and lack of vested interests, are aware of the various public screens of politics. Their resentment results only in private and unorganized mutterings and complaints, since their time and attention is absorbed with too many other private matters concerned with daily living and pleasures.

The traditional farmers are a minority of the farm community, representing

2 *Three small settlements (Clinton, Pelham, and Hendy's Hollow) located on the periphery of the township have their psychological locus in communities in adjoining townships. This group comprises about one-fourth of the voting population but takes no part in village or township activities. However, they constitute an important segment of the voting population. . . .*

about a third of all the farmers. Since they are a small group who by the standards of prosperous farmers are not successful and since they are apt to represent lowly assessed property, they do not constitute a force in town government. Their lack of success tends to disqualify them from having a political voice even though several may be board members. In matters of road maintenance their voice, when heard, carries no weight. The road superintendent who may come from this group is a symbolic figurehead with no voice in determining which roads are to be maintained and improved. At best he is able to do an occasional favor (a free load of gravel, clearing a driveway) for a traditional farmer who may be a personal friend. With this exception, the traditional farmers as a group do not benefit from township government.

The ceremony of selecting nominees from both the village and the country and from different geographical areas of the country gives the illusion of representation for all groups. The Polish group is represented on the board by a prosperous Polish farmer who serves the ceremonial function of being a representative of the Polish group at the same time that roads in the Polish areas are among the worst in the township. The political biases of the board are revealed in the condition of specific roads and in the location of good roads. These biases reflect those forces in the community, the prosperous farmers, who can make the board act. However, the excluded groups are not always willing to tolerate the results of road decisions, and because of this the board and the invisible government must cope periodically with their accumulated resentments.

D. The Small Group

The Supreme Court as a Small Group

Eloise C. Snyder

Introduction

The Supreme Court as a political and social force and as a collection of great individual justices has long been a topic of scholarly research.[1] More recently analyses of the Supreme Court have been made by Jessie Bernard and C. Herman Pritchett.[2] The present study is analytical but differs from preceding studies in that it deals with the Supreme Court as a small group and attempts to discover what group processes are present as the justices solve the important problems brought before them. Specifically, this study attempts to determine whether or not the Supreme Court, a small group charged with the important duty of national decision making, becomes divided into subgroups or cliques of justices. If cliques of justices are found to be in existence, the present study is concerned with how changes in group alignments occur, how the court "ingests" or assimilates new members, and

[1] *Among others see* Fred Rodell, Nine Men (*New York: Random House, Inc., 1955*); John P. Frank, Mr. Justice Black (*New York: Alfred A. Knopf, Inc., 1949*); Felix Frankfurter, The Business of the Supreme Court (*New York: The Macmillan Company, 1927*).
[2] Jessie Bernard, "*Dimensions and Axes of Supreme Court Decisions,*" Social Forces, *Vol. XXXIV (October, 1955),* 19–27; C. Herman Pritchett, The Roosevelt Court (*New York: The Macmillan Company, 1948*); C. Herman Pritchett,

Civil Liberties and the Vinson Court (*Chicago: University of Chicago Press, 1954*).

Eloise C. Snyder, "The Supreme Court as a Small Group," *Social Forces* (published by the University of North Carolina Press), Vol. XXXVI (December, 1957), 232–38. Reprinted by permission.

how new members find their position in the group.

Since the Supreme Court is virtually a battleground for every important social conflict, acting as judge not only of the citizens but of the government itself, the analysis of the Court as a small group would appear to be significant.

Methodology

In this study the nine justices, who composed the Supreme Court for whatever period of time they existed as a stable, unchanging body, were conceived of as constituting a small group. Each time one of the justices was replaced, due to either death or retirement, a new group was conceived of as being initiated. Therefore, rather than analyzing the data in terms of a specific year such as the 1949 or the 1950 Court, in this study they were analyzed in terms of groups of justices. Thus the Court from 1949 to 1953 was viewed as a single small group since the same justices composed the Supreme Court for this period of time.

The method used to determine whether or not the Supreme Court contains cliques of justices was based upon the responses of the justices to the cases heard by them during their stays with the Supreme Court. A clique was considered to be in existence when a group of two or more justices consistently tended to respond together in opposition to the other members of the Court.

Data for the present study were gathered from Volumes 257 to 346, inclusive, of the *United States Reports,* published by the United States Government Printing Office, in Washington, D.C. The data included the responses of the justices to all cases heard by the Supreme Court from 1921 to 1953 involving one or more of the amendments to the Constitution of the United States.[3] Over this period approxi-

3 *The results of case analyses based on each amendment separately showed no significant difference from the results of the analysis of all amendment cases treated collectively. Therefore all amendment cases in this study are treated as one category.*

mately 1,148 amendment cases were decided by the Court, presenting approximately 10,332 individual opinions to be analyzed.

These 10,332 individual opinions were the resultants of the extensive considerations given by the justices to the cases argued before the Court. For each justice this involved both listening to a detailed case presentation and then attending a session which was held exclusively for the justices. The purpose of this "closed" session is to permit a "thrashing out" of the various facets of the case in an attempt to reconcile any conflicting points of view held by the justices. At the conclusion of this session each justice presented his final opinion regarding the case under consideration and the decision of the case was based on a majority opinion agreed upon by five or more of the nine justices. In this study opinions were grouped according to the individual justices who rendered them and were classified on the basis of consensus (agreement) with or dissent (disagreement) from the majority decision of the court. A consensus opinion was defined as one in which the justices responded in any of the following ways:

1. Joined with the majority decision;
2. Agreed with the majority decision but without a separate opinion;
3. Agreed with the majority decision but with a separate opinion, showing that although a different line of reasoning was employed, the decision was the same.

A dissenting opinion was defined as one in which the justice responded in either of the following ways:

1. Dissented from the majority decision without a separate opinion;
2. Dissented from the majority decision with a separate opinion.

Cases in which a justice neither dissented nor concurred, had no opinion, did not participate, or, in a complex case, dissented on one point and concurred on another, were considered to be neutral and classified as such.

As previously stated a clique herein is defined as a group consisting of two or more justices who tended to respond consistently together, that is concur or dissent, in opposition to the other members of the Court.

A new justice was considered as such from the time he presented his first opinion to the Court until another justice, newer than he, presented his first opinion.

The above grouping of opinions and classification according to consensus or dissent constituted the basis of analysis used in determining some of the group behaviors reflected by the Supreme Court from 1921 to 1953.

Results

Cliques.   The Supreme Court of the United States showed more agreement than disagreement in deciding the cases brought before it; however, when disagreement did occur, it consistently was displayed in given patterns of dissent by justices who tended to respond together to the exclusion of the other members of the Court. These groupings of justices are herein viewed as constituting clique formations and the Supreme Court was found to contain some three cliques of justices. The first is here called "clique *A*" and the second, "clique *B*." Although these two cliques agreed on many decisions, when disagreement was displayed, these two cliques usually were in opposition. The third clique apparently did not have as fixed a point of view as either clique *A* or *B,* because this third clique acted in a pivotal manner, voting on some occasions with clique *A,* and on others with clique *B*. This clique is therefore called the "pivotal clique." A listing of the specific justices composing each of the cliques is presented in Table 1.

Clique Function.   On the basis of the content of the opinions rendered by the cliques with respect to specific cases, it would have been acceptable twenty-five years ago to refer to clique *A* as the more "liberal" clique and to clique *B* as the

more "conservative." However, since that time the implication of these terms has changed considerably, and thus, in order to eliminate difficulties of interpretation, these terms are operationally defined as follows:

LIBERAL: a state of *readiness* to accept "new" constitutional interpretations.
CONSERVATIVE: A state of *reluctance* to accept "new" constitutional interpretations.

Thus, the clique *A* point of view tended to be the more dynamic and changing ideology, while the point of view of clique *B* tended to be more static and, to a great extent, the resistor of new ideology. In this sense, clique *A* functioned in such a manner as to facilitate the newer legislation, while clique *B* tended to act as a brake on current legislation. Here then are two opposing forces—one using all of its power to pull ahead into newer judicial interpretations and the other using all of its power to constrain and pull back from these new judicial interpretations.

Pivotal Clique: A Decisive Factor. In this ideological tug of war, cliques *A* and *B* frequently tended to cancel each other's power. This increased the effect of the power of the pivotal clique, for what generally occurred was that the pivotal clique, by adding its weight to one or the other of the two opposing cliques, was able to break this ideological stalemate and give victory to that clique with which it aligned. Thus it is apparent that since the two cliques tended to commit themselves to mutually opposing points of view, the pivotal clique held the potentiality of determining the victor. Therefore, of the three cliques the pivotal clique was considered to have had the greatest amount of effective power.

Cliques and Politics.   It has often been feared that political affiliation might constitute a dangerous bias in this, the highest tribunal of the United States. However, the results of this study tend to dispel this fear, for there appeared to be no relationship between the membership

TABLE I. CLIQUE LISTINGS FOR EACH GROUP OF JUSTICES FROM 1921 TO 1953*

Group	Clique A	Pivotal Clique	Clique B
1921–22	Holmes (R), Brandeis (D), McKenna (R)	Pitney (R), Clarke (D), Day (R), Taft (R)	Van Devanter (R), McReynolds (D)
1922–23	Brandeis (D)	Holmes (R), Van Devanter (R), Taft (R), McReynolds (D), *Sutherland (R)*, McKenna (R), Pitney (R), Day (R)	
1923–25	Holmes (R), Brandeis (D)	Van Devanter (R), Taft (R), McKenna (R), *Sanford (R)*, Butler (R)	McReynolds (D), Sutherland (R)
1925–30	Brandeis (D), Holmes (R), *Stone (R)*	Sanford (R), McReynolds (D), Van Devanter (R), Taft (R)	Sutherland (R), Butler (R)
1930–32	Brandeis (D), Holmes (R), Stone (R)	*Roberts (R)*, *Hughes (R)*	Van Devanter (R), Butler (R), Sutherland (R), McReynolds (D)
1932–37	Brandeis (D), Stone (R), *Cardozo (R)*	Roberts (R), Hughes (R)	Van Devanter (R), Butler (R), Sutherland (R), McReynolds (D)
1937–38		Brandeis (D), Cardozo (R), Stone (R), Hughes (R), *Black (D)*	Roberts (R), Sutherland (R), McReynolds (D), Butler (R)
1938–39	Black (D)	Brandeis (D), Cardozo (R), Stone (R), Hughes (R), *Reed (D)*, Roberts (R)	Butler (R), McReynolds (D)
1939–39	Black (D), *Frankfurter (D)*	Brandeis (D), Stone (R), Hughes (R), Reed (D), Roberts (R)	Butler (R), McReynolds (D)
1939–40	Black (D)	Reed (D), Frankfurter (D), Stone (R), *Douglas (D)*	Hughes (R), McReynolds (D), Roberts (R), Butler (R)
1940–41	Black (D), Douglas (D), *Murphy (D)*	Stone (R), Frankfurter (D), Reed (D)	Hughes (R), Roberts (R), McReynolds (D)
1941–43	Black (D), Douglas (D), Murphy (D)	Reed (D), Frankfurter (D), Stone (R), *Byrnes (D)*, Jackson (D)	Roberts (R)
1943–45	Black (D), Douglas (D), Murphy (D), *Rutledge (D)*	Stone (R), Reed (D)	Jackson (D), Frankfurter (D), Roberts (R)
1945–46	Murphy (D), Rutledge (D), Frankfurter (D)	Black (D), Douglas (D), Jackson (D)	Reed (D), Stone (R), *Burton (D)*
1946–49	Murphy (D), Rutledge (D), Douglas (D), Black (D)	Frankfurter (D)	Jackson (D), *Vinson (D)*, Reed (D), Burton (D)
1949–53	Black (D), Douglas (D), Frankfurter (D), Jackson (D)	Burton (D), *Clark (D)*, Vinson (D)	Minton (D), Reed (D)

* In this table, when the name of a justice appears in italics it means that he was a newly appointed justice on that court. The symbol (R) or (D) after the name of each justice means that he was appointed by a Republican or Democratic President, respectively.

of a clique and the political affiliation of the Presidents who appointed the justices. It was noted, for example, that the well-known combination of Justices Holmes and Brandeis, who for a number of years were both members of clique *A,* reflects Republican and Democratic appointments, respectively. This fear is further disproved by the fact that, although the Supreme Court from 1946 to 1953 consisted of justices all of whom were appointed by Democratic Presidents, the three cliques still were found to be very much in evidence.

Cliques and Presidents. In 1937, President Franklin D. Roosevelt asked for authority to increase the number of judges in the Supreme Court. It was feared that this would enable Roosevelt to "pack" the Court with men whose ideologies tended most to favor Roosevelt's own ideology and thus bias this important judicial body. However, in this study it was found that very little relationship existed between the cliques of justices and the particular ideologies of the appointing Presidents. For example, Justices Brandeis, McReynolds, and Clarke were all appointed by President Woodrow Wilson, yet Brandeis was more or less consistently found in clique *A,* McReynolds in clique *B,* and Clarke in the pivotal clique. Further, since 1940, when the Roosevelt appointees numerically predominated in the Supreme Court, at no time did they, as a group, tend to be members of any one clique. It is noted in Table 1 that from 1940 to 1943 the Roosevelt appointees were found in two separate cliques, namely, the pivotal clique and clique *A,* and from 1943 to 1953 they were found to be members of all three cliques.

Therefore, although there were cliques of justices in the Supreme Court, these cliques apparently were not biased by the specific President appointing the justices. This, at least to some degree, would appear to dispel the fear that the appointment of a majority of the justices to the

Supreme Court by one specific President would bias this high tribunal.

Clique Membership. Since cliques of justices were found to exist in the Supreme Court, it is now the concern of this study to attempt to discern how changes in group alignments occur. It was observed that some justices, such as Justices Pitney, Taft, and Sandford, were more or less consistent members of the pivotal clique, while others were found in clique *A* or *B* during most of their terms on the bench. Justice Black, for example, was a member of clique *A* from 1938 to 1953 with the exception of 1945 to 1946, when he was a member of the pivotal clique. This implies that Justice Black, along with Justices Holmes, Douglas, Murphy, and Rutledge, who also displayed this type of alignment, was a relatively consistent member of that clique which sought to explore newer judicial interpretations. Justice McReynolds, on the other hand, from the time of the first group of justices covered in this study, which was in 1921, until he left the bench in 1941, was consistently found in clique *B,* with the exception of two occasions, namely in 1922–1923 and in 1925–1930, when he was found in the pivotal clique. This implies that Justice McReynolds, along with Justices Sutherland, Butler, and Burton, who also displayed this type of alignment, was a relatively consistent member of that clique which sought to act as a brake on the exploration of newer judicial interpretations.

Most justices were relatively consistent members of a specific clique. When a change in clique membership did occur it did not tend to be radical, for it is noted in Table 1 that most change was from the liberal or conservative cliques (i.e., *A* or *B*) to the pivotal clique, or vice versa, and not from the liberal clique directly to the conservative (i.e., *A* to *B*) or vice versa. In fact, in the thirty-two years covered by the study, only two radical changes in clique membership were noted. The one occurred when Justice Frankfurter, who in 1943–1945 was a clique *B* member, directly moved to clique *A* in 1945–1946. The second occurred when Justice Jackson, who in 1946–1949 was a member of clique *B,* moved directly to clique *A* in 1949–1953. These two justices, namely Frankfurter and Jackson, were the only justices who made such radical changes in group alignment.

Justices Frankfurter and Jackson were also found to be exceptional in two other respects. First, these two justices displayed the maximum amount of repeated clique fluctuation, and secondly, they represented the only changes in coalition membership which ran from clique *B* to clique *A.* This is to say that the direction of clique change generally was from clique *A* to clique *B,* that is from the more liberal to the more conservative clique, although it is important to note that when these changes did occur, in each case the justice spent an intervening period as a member of the pivotal clique prior to becoming a member of clique *B.* This seems to indicate that it apparently was easier for a justice to change from the liberal clique toward the conservative clique and relatively impossible to join the liberal ranks having once been a conservative.

These alignment changes from clique *A* toward clique *B* were exemplified by several justices such as Justice Brandeis, who had been a clique *A* member for sixteen years when he changed to pivotal clique membership for [his] remaining two years on the bench and also for Justice Hughes, who had been a member of the pivotal clique for the first nine years of his term when he changed to clique *B* for the remaining two of his term. Justice Reed also reflected this tendency. He, after seven years as a member of the pivotal clique, switched to clique *B* for the next eight years, at which period this study concluded with Justice Reed still in clique *B.* Justice Stone probably presents the most pertinent example of this type of clique membership change, for Justice Stone began as a clique *A* member but after twelve years of membership, he joined the pivotal clique. However, he did not stop here, for after eight years in the pivotal clique, Justice Stone then moved on to clique *B,* where he remained for his final year with the Court.

This raises the serious question of why was it apparently easier for a justice to change from the liberal toward the conservative clique rather than vice versa? It may be that there is a tendency for one's viewpoint to become more conservative as one grows older. However, this was not found to be the case in this study, for the justices' points of view *per se* reflected little change. Rather, the Supreme Court itself, as a collective body of justices, was found to reflect a highly dramatic conceptual framework. It appears that, with progressive changes in the personnel of the Court, the conceptual framework of this body changed so much that an opinion which was once considered a clique *A* point of view, without changing, suddenly was found to be a neutral or even a clique *B* point of view. This implies that an opinion which was considered "liberal" in 1930, might well have been considered "conservative" in 1945. In this sense, it appears that Justice Brandeis, without altering his views, became automatically realigned with the pivotal clique rather than with the liberal clique on the basis of the dynamics of the group itself. It is also conceivable that this dynamic element was so forceful by the 1945–1946 Court that the responses of Justice Stone, previously a clique *A* member, were suddenly too conservative even for the pivotal clique and rather more consistent with clique *B* responses.

It was noted, however, that some justices did not find it necessary to give up their clique *A* membership, for such justices as Black and Douglas were relatively consistent clique *A* members along with Justices Murphy and Rutledge, who never joined any other clique. This would seem to indicate that these justices were able to alter their views at the same rate of speed as the changing views of the Court itself, and thus by keeping pace with the Court's changing conceptual framework they were able to remain the liberal clique.

Having examined some of the group processes evident in the Supreme Court, it is now the concern of this study to examine how the Supreme Court assimilates new members and how these new members find their places in this already established and functioning group.

The Newly Appointed Justices. As previously stated, a justice was considered new from the time he presented his first opinion in the Court, until another justice, newer than he, presented his first opinion. There were nineteen newly appointed justices on the Courts covered by this study. Five of these new justices initiated their terms by aligning with clique *A* and three with clique *B*. The remaining eleven justices, however, aligned with the pivotal clique. This tendency for the newly appointed justice to initiate his term in the pivotal clique may have resulted from any or all of the following factors:

First, it may have been that the new justice, entering this already established body, lacked the assurance necessary to defend an extreme stand in constitutional interpretation and therefore found it more comfortable to respond as a member of that clique which reflected the more neutral point of view. It is true that some justices had previous judicial experience, but many did not. And in respect to those who had, few had ever served on a court of such high national esteem. In this respect it is not altogether inconceivable that the new justice to some degree might have experienced a lack of assurance and thus responded in a neutral manner.

Secondly, it may have been that the new justice entering this notable group of men was not immediately able to attain an "in-group" feeling, and, therefore, feeling like a "somewhat lesser member," he may have remained neutral rather than show any consistent identification with either of the two already established cliques.

Thirdly, it may have been that the new justice entered the Court without a fixed liberal or conservative point of view and thus was afforded the luxury of flexibility —that is, identifying on some occasions with clique *A* and on others with clique *B*.

Whatever the underlying factor, the new members of the Supreme Court were assimilated into the Court as members of the pivotal clique. This is important to the extent that it suggests that the men with the least amount of experience in the Supreme Court immediately tended to become members of that clique which, as has previously been pointed out, frequently held the potentiality of determining the victor, and, therefore, was viewed as having the greatest amount of effective power. This is clearly shown since the new justices apparently did not find it necessary to dissent as frequently as the older justices. In fact, the average number of dissents for the newly appointed justices was only 4.8 as compared with 7.3 for the older justices.[4]

It was further noted that, although the new justices started their terms in the court by aligning with the pivotal clique, most of them, after a period of time, became members of clique *A* or clique *B*. Thus, after acquiring experience, these men tended to align with a clique which, as previously stated, was found to have a lesser amount of effective power.

In this respect it was noted that Justices Sutherland, Butler, and Roberts, after starting as pivotal clique members, finally joined clique *B*, while justices Black and Douglas joined clique *A*. Justice Jackson also began as a pivotal clique member and finally aligned with clique *B* and clique *A* at different times.

This tendency for a newly appointed justice to align with clique *A* or *B* after initiating his term with the Court as pivotal clique member may have reflected any or all of the following processes:

First, it may have been that, after gain-

---

4 *Excluding three groups of justices in which Justices Stone, Cardozo, and Burton were new justices, the average number of dissents for the new justices is 2.9 as compared with 6.9 for the remaining older members.*

ing some experience with this, the highest decision-making body in the United States, the justice finally acquired an assurance which enabled him to "take a stand" with one of the two cliques which reflected a more extreme point of view.

Secondly, it may have been that after functioning for a period of time with this notable group of men, the new justice finally identified with one of the two opposing cliques on the basis of personalities involved. In effect, he may have been influenced by a certain personality which tended to mold his thinking and thus enable him to align with that clique.

Thirdly, it may have been that the experience of functioning with the Supreme Court itself created in the justice an unassailable point of view so that the new justice ultimately may have found himself unable to respond in a manner which might have suggested a neutral point of view.

Whatever the underlying principles, the fact remains that the newly appointed justice tended to be "ingested" by the Supreme Court through the pivotal clique and then, after a period of functioning with the Court, found his place in the group by joining one of the two opposing cliques.

Summary

This study was undertaken in an attempt to examine the Supreme Court as a small group. Certain patterns of behavior were noted as follows:

The Supreme Court contained three cliques of justices. The first, called clique *A,* was the more "liberal" and acted in such manner as to facilitate "newer" constitutional interpretations; the second, called clique *B,* was the more "conservative" and acted as a brake on "newer" interpretations; the third clique reflected a middle point of view, aligning with clique *A* on some occasions and with clique *B* on others, and thus was called the pivotal clique. Since cliques *A* and *B* were opposing forces, they tended to cancel each other's power, which allowed the

pivotal clique to break this ideological stalemate by aligning with one of them and in this manner determine the victor. The pivotal clique, therefore, was considered to have had the greatest amount of effective coalition power.

Membership in the cliques tended to be determined by ideological principles and not by political party considerations. This tends to dispel the fears that the political affiliations of the justices or the appointment of a majority of the justices by one specific President might bias this high tribunal. Both of these hypotheses were tested and found to be unsubstantiated.

Changes in clique membership did occur, but these changes did not tend to be radical. Membership change appeared to run from the more "liberal" clique *A* to the "neutral," pivotal clique and in some cases even progressed to the more "conservative" clique *B*. The majority of these changes did not reflect a change in the justices particular point of view *per se,* but rather were brought about by the dynamics of the Court itself. This dynamic element within the Supreme Court resulted from the progressive additions of new justices to the Court which tended to broaden the conceptual framework of the Supreme Court as a group to the extent that what was considered to have been a liberal view in 1921 might well have been considered conservative in 1953.

The Supreme Court tended to "adsorb" or assimilate new members through the pivotal clique. However, after a period of functioning with the Court, the new justice found his place in the group by joining one of the two opposing cliques. This is important in that the new, "inexperienced" justice tended to be a member of the clique which had the more effective clique power but, after acquiring experience with the Court, tended to become a member of a clique which had the less effective clique power. This is clearly shown in that the new justice did not find it necessary to dissent as frequently as the older member of the Court.

*   *   *

E. Language, Culture, and Politics

Language and Politics in India

Paul Friedrich

Of the many theoretical problems in the rapidly developing field of language and culture, the establishment of a common language for a multilingual state is probably fraught with the deepest political implications. Linguistic unity may conduce to unity in other phases of culture; for example, the presence of an upper class speaking a fairly homogeneous dialect of English certainly increased the national integration of the Congress Party during India's struggle for independence. On the other hand, animosity of political or economic origin may attach itself to the palpable symbols of linguistic difference. Starving Indians in the industrial slums of Bombay have knifed each other "because" one speaks Marathi, the other Gujarati. India today provides an egregious case of linguistic diversity combined with weak chances for any one of the potential national languages. The salient point is that this weakness and diversity appear to be growing. Both the people of the culture and scientific observers consider the combination a disruptive "social problem" about which something should be done. As with food supply and population growth, difficulties are increasing more rapidly than solutions are being formulated or effected. In short, the situation is one of possibly tragic drift.

To examine the problem, we should first define some of the principal terms. "National state" means a fairly large population on a bounded territory, united by a standing government and bureaucracy, by economic organization, some shared customs and values, and most importantly,

by a sense of self-identity as a body politic with a tradition. This definition fits India rather imperfectly, because India is composed of numerous seminational states, each with its own dialects, ethnocentric prejudices, and distinctive profile. By "language" is meant a system of mutually intelligible vocal symbols by which the members of a society communicate. "Written language" is a special kind of language. "Dialect" is the speech system of a regionally or socially defined group, marked by a combination of shared linguistic features; such dialects may form a chain, so that speakers of widely separated links cannot understand one another.

In the anthropological sense, language is a part of culture, because it too is a historically derived system of conscious and subconscious patterns shared and transmitted by the members of a particular society. On the other hand, language is unique because it is a means of communication—in part as a code, in part as a symbolic organization of experience—that is interwoven in the most pervasive way with other cultural subsystems, such as that of politics. Every known society possesses a fully developed language, but many virtually lack other systems, such as music or politics. In addition language plays a singular role in the processes by which individuals and groups define themselves and are defined by others. The rise of nationalism in the modern period is often linked with questions of linguistic status and linguistic boundaries. A primary objective of this paper is to show

Paul Friedrich, "Language and Politics in India," *Daedalus* (Published by the American Academy of Arts and Sciences, 280 Newton Street, Brookline Station, Boston, Massachusetts 02146), Vol. XCI, No. 3 (Summer, 1962), 543–559. Reprinted by permission.

how language is related to political dynamics in one particular country.

India, which now numbers over four hundred million, is exceeded in population only by Communist China. Its social problems have increased in proportion to this quantitative change. Linguistic diversification also tends to increase with the social isolation of speech communities. Most Indians still live mainly in villages, cross-cut by hundreds of subcastes in patterns of sociolinguistic segmentation that have no close parallel elsewhere. Of these villagers, it is the women, linguistically the most conservative, who are responsible for the primary language influences on the children. Even the upper-caste child is often cared for by monolingual, lower-caste ayas. The leading novelist in Malayalam has grown wealthy by his writings and traveled widely in Europe and the Orient; but his wife does not speak English, and has only once gone farther than a mile from her husband's home and her nearby matrilineal household. The extensive migration and labor movement within India does not much counter narrow circumscriptions by caste and region. Linguistic homogeneity may be increased through the mass media, but most Indians have no radio, and are still infrequently exposed to movies or public broadcasts (though the latter are gaining influence).

The problem increases with the number of languages and their relative size and importance; thus Mexico's forty-odd Indian languages, spoken mainly by tiny minorities, do not threaten the national status of Spanish. India, on the contrary, recognizes fourteen languages for official purposes; all but three of them (Sanscrit, Assamese, and Kashmiri) are spoken by over ten million persons, and five are spoken by over twenty-five million (Telegu, Tamil, Hindi, Bengali, Marathi).[1] In addition, almost

one-tenth of the population (thirty-two million) speak dozens of other mother tongues belonging phylogenetically to four categories: Indo-European, such as Nepali; Dravidian, such as Tulu; Austroasiatic (Munda branch), such as Ho; and, fourth, a great number of "non-Indian" languages, notably English and Persian. *The Census of India* cites twenty-four tribal languages spoken by one hundred thousand or more, and 720 minor languages and dialects with less than one hundred thousand; of the sixty-three non-Indian languages, English has the most mother-tongue speakers, with 171,742. At least six nonofficial languages are spoken by over one million, and two of these, Marwari and Sindhi, by only a few hundred thousand less than Assamese. The other big minority groups are, in millions: Santali, 2.8; Ghondi, 1.2; Bhili, 1.2; Mewari, 2; Jaipuri, 1.5.

The big official languages are absorbing the minority languages and also impeding the development of a national one; the Ho agriculturalist is learning a regional dialect of Hindi, but the Tulu is learning Kannada, while neither is learning English. Many who speak India's minority languages, especially the refugees from Pakistan, are now in various stages of transitional multilingualism marked by a reshuffling of dialects, considerable linguistic interference, and increasing submergence to the official languages. These minorities often resent the lack of official recognition; their case contrasts unfavorably with that of Rhaeto-Roman, a national language in Switzerland, although

---

[1] *The states are (with population in millions as of the 1951 census, and the language, in parentheses): Andhra (31, Telegu); Assam (5, Assamese); W. Bengali (26, Bengali); Bihar (38, Hindi); Bombay (46, Marathi and Gujarati); Madhya Pradesh (26, Hindi); Madras (29, Tamil); Orissa (14, Oriya); Punjab (16, Punjabi, Hindi); Uttar Pradesh (63, Hindi); Rajastan (15, Rajastan, Hindi); Jammu and Kashmir (4, Kashmiri, Urdu); Mysore (19, Kannada); Kerala (14, Malayalam). Note that five states are all or mainly Hindi-speaking. Telegu and Kannada, Malayalam and Tamil form two sets of closely related Dravidian languages. Most of the Indic languages listed are also very closely related, about as far from one another as the Scandinavian languages. Bengali has about eighty million speakers if we count the community in Pakistan. S. Sarkar, Hindustani Yearbook (Calcutta, 1959), pp. 402–407.*

spoken by only 1 per cent of the population.

The neglect of the minority languages on the part of the Indian government has further political implications. It is known pedagogically that children learn more rapidly and with less inner conflict if they first acquire literacy in their mother tongue. The present policy of immediate assimilation to the alien official language is bound to engender ambivalence and status conflict, for linguistic factors become inextricably enmeshed with political ones. India's sense of national unity might be reinforced by using minority languages in the elementary grades, by research into the geography of dialects, and by the reconstruction of linguistic protohistory; but comparatively little is spent on such activities. This is not to mitigate the significance of the stopgap government programs for intellectual exchanges between states, or the mushrooming interest in scientific linguistics, strongly supported by many universities, state governments, and financial magnates.

Linguistic problems tend to emerge as a symbolic reflex of almost any other conflict. Many Indians feel that the so-called "linguistic question" is itself abnormal and counter to the ethos of their culture; people are hungry and anxious about getting employment and providing for their families, so they get exasperated by language differences. The necessity of struggling for jobs with persons of different speech communities intensifies economically based animosities. Naturally, the Communist party of India has frequently exploited linguistic differences, since they weaken the central government and allow the Communists to identify themselves with "the people"; but the party line has varied greatly the last twenty years.

A spoken "natural" language is far more likely to attain national status, since the majority of a population is seldom sufficiently familiar with dead languages to make these immediately practical. But two extraordinary cases provide a contrary precedent. Hebrew, primarily a lit-

urgical language for over two thousand years, was reinstituted politically by the Israeli state in 1948. At least three factors account for this, and none of them obtains in India: first, the presence before 1948 of a Hebrew-speaking base population; second, the high literacy rate; third, the extraordinary patriotism bred of a profound sense of national mission, shared suffering under the Nazis, and a common Arab enemy of overwhelming numbers. Finally, modern Israeli Hebrew is strictly speaking a constructed dialect with a Biblical base and many recent accretions from other languages.[2] The second contrary case is presented by China. Written Chinese serves as a national code for the literate section of 618 million people speaking various dialects of at least seven mutually incomprehensible languages (for example, Cantonese, Peiping), as well as dozens of other Sinitic and non-Sinitic dialects. But special factors account for the vitality of the complex system of written ideographs: militant patriotism, the practicality of an existing supraregional language, the link to China's ancient, verbal culture, the aesthetic and moral connotations of calligraphic training.

Sanscrit is sacred to most Hindus. Since the Vedic hymns (c. 1500 B.C.) it has served in various related forms as a vehicle for metaphysics, the national epics, the laws of Manu, or the immortal poetry of Kalidasa. All literate Indians are more or less familiar with this spiritual lore and most revere it; orthodox Hindus know some by heart and may devote their declining years to reading and reciting aloud from the *Bhagavad Gita* and other repositories of wisdom. The grammarian who formulated the rules of Sanscrit over two thousand years ago today enjoys the status of a saint in the Hindu system. To a limited extent, written Sanscrit unites the educated Indians, especially the literati; hundreds of words and phrases are comprehended from the Indian Ocean to the

[2] E. Y. Kutscher, "The Role of Modern Hebrew in the Development of Jewish-Israeli National Consciousness," *PMLA* (1957), 38–42.

Himalayas, and a much smaller scatter of items are understood even by those who cannot read.

The case of Sanscrit, however, while analogous to Hebrew and written Chinese, differs significantly on many counts. India exhibits a degree of cultural pluralism that staggers the imagination. The Christians and the Muslims, who constitute about 15 per cent of the Indian population and up to half the population in the deep south, are sharply divided into innumerable subgroups. But they generally join to oppose Sanscrit. Even the Hindus are pitched against one another on the Sanscrit question; numerous copies of the sacred *Ramayana* epic have been publicly burnt by lower-caste organizations because of a racist interpretation of the dark-skinned monkeys in the text. Many Tamil intellectuals will not even consider studying Sanscrit because of its "Aryan" connotations. Hatred of the Brahmins because of their economic and political role is often linked with animosity toward Sanscrit, as in Bengal, Maharashtra, or Mysore. In addition, only a tiny subculture is really conversant with the language, and only a few thousand, centered in the Sanscrit colleges, can communicate freely using its complex inflections and luxuriant vocabulary. Since the great majority of Indians are still illiterate even in their mother tongue, it would seem a purely scholastic fantasy to suggest making Sanscrit *the* national language. Nevertheless, an influential, nationwide society is devoted to the cause.

* * *

. . . Just how many tongues can the average citizen be expected to control? Is multilingualism simply another type of lingualism or a qualitatively different phenomenon? Proficient, correct multilingualism on the part of individuals seems to be accompanied by a certain minimum of general intelligence, verbal aptitudes, and code-switching ability. At the societal level, it usually involves special familial or subcultural patterns for inculcating vocabulary and automatic translation habits, as exemplified by the intelligentsia of Bombay, who often speak English, Marathi, Gujarati, Hindi, and sometimes Sanscrit, or those of the Polish Jewry, speaking Yiddish, German, Polish, Russian, and Hebrew, with high fluency in at least three out of five. Multilingualism appears to be especially workable between typologically and genetically close languages, such as Tamil and Malayalam, Marathi and Gujarati, or Danish, Swedish, and Norwegian. On the other hand, widespread multilingualism between drastically different languages is rare—for example, the combination in much of Samarkand of Russian, Uzbek (a Turkic language) and Tadzhik (a variety of Persian). Many educated Malayalis in government service actually practice such an extraordinary range (e.g., Malayalam, Hindi, English, and Sanscrit), but their versatility can be explained through special schooling and career goals. All these aspects to the psychology of language learning suggest that one national or common language over and above the regional language might reasonably be considered the absolute maximum.

The basic fact remains that every member of every known culture speaks at least one language, but that no national state with full bilingualism—to say nothing of trilingualism—has ever existed. Thus, Switzerland, almost 100 per cent literate, deserves its illustrious reputation for language planning. But most Swiss villagers speaking French as their mother tongue are actually monolingual, and many educated Swiss know little Italian. Similar limitations to bilingualism may be adduced from other multilingual states, such as Paraguay (Spanish-Guarani), Canada (French-English), and the non-Russian republics of the U.S.S.R. Many Indians optimistically advocate a schedule of national trilingualism, combining the regional mother tongue with some combination of Hindi, English, or Sanscrit. But India will eventually have to combine the mother tongues with Hindi *or* English *or* Sanscrit. Even then she will experience difficulties in maintaining adequate competency, and she will be constantly threatened by communications breakdowns.

The general level of literacy also determines the acceptance of any language for national purposes. The demonstrable fact that all languages are equally perfect symbolic systems (with respect to phonology and grammar), and are equally capable of expressing any denotative information, should not be confused with the equally demonstrable fact that illiterate masses, whether primitive, peasant, or proletarian, are semantically hindered from playing a full role in the economic, social, and political life of a large nation. The presence of hundreds of botanical terms in some remote Hindi dialect does not mean that the speakers of it can make sense out of a governmental regulation. Educated Indians are passionately discussing what the average man—meaning the coolie, the peasant—wants to learn. But since the teeming masses are largely illiterate, even in their lower-caste dialects, the question of what second language they might want to learn is partly speculative, at least for the immediate future.

Some internal contradictions would be eliminated by focusing on the multilingualism to be promoted among the one hundred million literates and the fifteen million spiritual, political, and business leaders who must communicate between regions and nations. Politicians wax vociferous about the "common man" and hesitate to mention an "elite," partly because of the guilt and fear which they themselves feel about their own upper-caste status. Yet upper-caste leadership will probably endure for some time, irrespective of political transformations; the top leaders of even Kerala's well-known Communist party are all Nayars or Brahmins. In the modern West the ideals of the "common man" and of mass education have led to policy about a language for the entire population of a national state. Such democratic vistas are realistic in compara-

tively educated countries, but they seem unwise and illusory in India.

Elitist considerations are connected with status anxiety in a second way: that "speakers imitate the habits of their superiors" is a fruitful if somewhat uncritically accepted assumption in sociolinguistics. A standard language may evolve from a dialect of great geographical dispersal, much of it rural, so long as it is sufficiently prestigious; literary Russian in the nineteenth century exemplifies this. Standard Malayalam has developed largely over the past forty years from the dialect of the socially and intelectually dominant (but largely rural) Nayar caste; here, as with Russian, the literary work of certain prolific and popular writers has played its influential role. But the standards of a language usually derive from urban dialects, such as Parisian French or New Delhi Hindi; indeed, the sheer density of population in the cities makes them foci for linguistic change.

Hindi falls short of the mark as a standard national language because it lacks sufficient prestige. The official figure of 160 million "Hindi" speakers actually includes a plethora of Hindustani, Urdu, Punjabi, and other dialects, mostly spoken by illiterate peasants and often having less affinity with one another than with the neighboring dialects of other languages. As one of India's most influential writers on the question of a national language puts it: "The fact is that Hindi is not even a good *regional* language. There is a lot of synthesis yet to be done among the dialects of Hindi."[3] Many southerners feel that the Hindustan area itself is backward and dirty and that New Delhi is comparatively corrupt. To the average Bengali intellectual, Hindi is a lingo of the bazaars, although more status is accorded to its standard forms. As Tagore wrote in a short story, "But the hard fact was that my little Hindi happened to be picked up from the porters and bearers and would scarcely enable me to enter into intelli-

[3] *C. Rajagopalachari, in* The Hindu (*May 20, 1959*).

gent controversy with the Badraon prin- cess."[4] In an analogous sense, Berliners would not accept Munich Bavarian as standard German.

To the educated person, especially a man of letters, the prestige of a language is inextricably associated with the litera- ture in which the writers of the past have given expression to the genius of the tongue. Sparkling metaphors and sensitive characterizations can soften the resistance of proud minorities. For example, many Soviet citizens of minority states have ea- gerly learned Russian, the language of Pushkin and Tolstoy, despite their resent- ment of ethnic and political domination. English has also been appreciated in its own right by many Indian intellectuals; today romantic poets such as Byron are more fondly read in India than anywhere in the English-speaking world. Shake- speare is widely read in the schools. Once I was interviewing a prominent Malayali novelist who has always despised grammar in general and Sanskrit grammar in par- ticular. He alluded to the value of the "most unkindest." As I did not immedi- ately grasp the reference, my Nayar com- panion chimed in, "You know, the famous Shakespearean cut."

According to an almost universal con- sensus, the foremost literary language of contemporay India is Bengali, above all because it was the vehicle and in part the creation of Rabindranath Tagore. The Tamilians, on the other hand, possess one of the longest unbroken literary traditions of any of the world's living languages.[5] During the fifth and sixth centuries syn- dicates of bards in the principal cities created a glorious romantic and devotional poetry, full of imagination and realistic perceptions, and largely free of the dead- ening influence of Sanscrit models. A high point in this literature is signified by the two thousand poems of the *Eight Anthol-*

ogies, attributed to the "Third Academy" of Madras. The medieval poetry of Tamil- ians such as Ramanuja still occupies a primary place in Hindu traditions. On the other hand, although some date Hindi as a literary language by the fourteenth-cen- tury poems of Kabir, there are many others who claim that "as the channel of the main stream of poetry it was estab- lished only with the beginning of this cen- tury."[6] Hindi does have a literature that includes well-known contemporary names such as Prem Chand. But objective and weighty criteria tend to rank it below at least Sanscrit, Tamil, and Bengali. Cer- tainly most Indians having non-Hindi mother tongues would rank Hindi be- neath at least one other Indian language as well as English.

For the same reasons there is a reaction today against the imposition of an "in- ferior" recent idiom. Rajagopalachari, speaking before a packed and cheering mass meeting in Calcutta in 1959, said, "The new Hindi, as it continues to de- velop, is not a language but a burlesque. Self-styled Hindi lexicographers and self- appointed Hindi purists have been com- peting with one another in evolving all manner of fantastic and unfamiliar words and phrases."[7] To quote another leader:

> The strength of a language is as large or as poor as its literature. Precision and flexi- bility are essential for a language to be great and useful. It is well known that Hindi fails in these respects. The claim to greater political importance is absurd . . . if people speaking other languages prefer English and Sanscrit as furnishing greater knowledge, greater wisdom, greater enjoy- ment and greater continuity of enlightened life.[8]

Up to now the emphasis has been on the spontaneous acceptance of national languages. But they may be established

---

[4] *Rabindranath Tagore, "Episode of 1857," in* Stories from Bengal, *S. Dutt, trans. (Bombay, 1959), p. 14.*

[5] *A. L. Basham,* The Wonder That Was India *(London, 1956), p. 476.*

[6] *S. H. Vatsyayan, "Hindi Literature,"* Contem- porary Indian Literature: A Symposium *(New Delhi, 1957), p. 73.*

[7] *C. Rajagopalachari,* Tamil Culture *(1959), p. 210.*

[8] The Hindu *(May 20, 1959).*

also through political and military pressure; in Mexico the Spanish language was forced on the Indian population, linguist-friars following closely on the iron heel of the conquistador. The russification of minorities in the U.S.S.R. has been consistently backed by the power of the central government—not to be confused with the linguistic sophistication of Soviet policies on nationalities. But prestige and power never guarantee permanency, since a shift in political hegemony can lead very rapidly to linguistic change. Persian has virtually disappeared from India since its heyday under the Moguls, and English may eventually go the same way.

Political power and the national language are uniquely interrelated in India. Hindi was voted in *de iure* by a congressional majority of only one during the wave of patriotic fervor and anti-British sentiment that swept the country in 1947. The main factors in this victory for the Hindi faction were the geographical extent and numerical plurality of Hindi speakers, and the location of the capital in Delhi (Hindi dialects extend approximately from the Western Punjab to Bihar, and from the Nepal border south to Andhra Pradesh). All over India people responded to the passionate appeals of Mahatma Gandhi and others by studying Hindi. Today, with a considerable change in public opinion, the Indian central government is faced with the predicament of insufficient power and will to carry through a program that has been legalized.

Various events reflect these contradictions. The nominally powerful Language Commission has issued pronouncements on complete Hindization by 1965. On the other hand, Chatterji, India's most distinguished linguist, has produced a widely read dissenting opinion that resulted in a reconsideration of the majority report in 1959 and the appointment of Chatterji as president of a Sanscrit Commission, presumably to weaken the "Hindi fanatics" through this indirect line of attack. Delhi is influenced by numerous extremists, many incapable of discussing the language question in a rational manner, whether they are linguists, journalists, or political leaders. Indian fighters for national independence from the British have subsequently been insulted on the public rostrum as traitors because they were standing against Hindi. Many of the Dravidians and Bengalis who occupy key roles in the central government are exerting their influence against Hindization. Non-Hindi adults all over India are passively resisting Hindi for all practical purposes by not taking any active steps to acquire it. A final example of inner conflict comes from the All-India Summer School for Linguistics held in Madras in 1959, twelve years after the Independence. About half the students favored Hindi, most North Indians passionately so. Nevertheless, fewer than one-quarter could understand the Hindi speeches, and a public clash over the language question resulted in a social schism that ultimately affected most of the student body and some of the faculty. These disputants were linguists, supposedly enlightened as regards language. Some Indians say privately that they feel some dictatorial power is necessary to solve the language question, among others. But such power and the strategic vision to go with it are as yet absent.

Various fissures in India's culture may be growing rather than decreasing. One aspect of her linguistic pluralism has thrown into relief certain connections between language and politics. During British rule the political provinces almost never coincided completely with language boundaries. Thus Madras State included not only Tamilians but many people speaking Telegu, Malayalam, and Kannada, not to mention minority languages. The Bombay presidency included speakers of at least four major languages. The principal result of this lack of congruence was that persons of differing speech communities were forced to interact and therefore to apply the principles of intergroup tolerance that underlie so much of Indian life. Second, English tended to emerge almost automatically as the *lingua franca,* in politics especially. English enjoyed a comparatively neutral status, since it was for the most part the prerogative of a supraregional elite, members of which are often scattered over many states in a network of subcastes, reaping the benefits as political mediators and leaders. They usually control some combination of Dravidian languages, or Indic languages, and English; one fairly representative Mysore Brahmin knows Kannada, Tamil, Telegu, English, and some Hindi (plus Kodaku, his childhood language). Many such polyglot intellectuals and administrators have opposed the organization of "linguistic states," believing that the public support was basically the reflex of a provincial chauvinism that would rapidly accelerate the introversion of India's culture areas. But against this fading intelligentsia stand the lower-caste leaders, rising rapidly in the democratic atmosphere, and more prone to incite the largely monolingual voting masses by exploiting symbols of linguistic difference.

Gandhi and his followers had already harnessed linguistic self-determination to the Independence movement. This opened a veritable Pandora's box with which Nehru and others have not been able to cope very successfully. In 1948 the Linguistic Provinces Commission, appointed in the same year, stressed in its annual report the dangers of narrow regionalism. But by 1953 the central government had to organize the first "linguistic state" of Andhra (Telegu-speaking), after ceding to tremendous pressures that were climaxed by serious riots organized by the Communists after the fast to death of a Gandhian leader in Andhra—one of the first little whirlwinds of "passive resistance" that the Congress Party may continue to reap in the future. A States Reorganization Commission was appointed in 1954, submitted its report the following year, and recommendations began to go into effect after November 1, 1955. Despite various cautions and qualifications, it could be said that the cause of linguistic autonomy had won the day: the number

of states was cut to fourteen, or one-half the original number, plus six centrally administered territories.

Since the "reorganization of linguistic states," the feared consequences have indeed followed with great rapidity. English instruction has weakened, notably in greater Hindustan. The partial maintenance of standards is limited to non-Hindi areas, since it was stimulated by reaction against Hindi. The Hindi program has almost come to a standstill in some southern areas. More and more states are instituting their regional languages; in 1959 the Mysore universities went over to Kannada; almost all instruction at all levels in Uttar Pradesh, including Delhi, is or soon will be in Hindi. This is the academic side of India's more generalized and largely regional self-discovery that continues to be a profound national experience, leading at best to what might be called "constructive nativism," as in the resynthesis of areal dance forms, but coupled at its worst with provincial bigotry and cultural discrimination. Leaders have played increasingly on linguistic prejudices against intrusive job seekers from other states, leading indirectly to ramifications of a more serious character. Thus great numbers of (mainly Nayar) officials, expelled from Madras after the "reorganization," had to return to their native Kerala. The consequent piling up of ambitious and frustrated leaders in Kerala significantly influenced the Communist victory in the elections of 1957 (won through Nayar support), and also the defeat of the Communists in 1959 (after the Nayars withdrew their support).

The "reorganization of linguistic states" has raised a series of additional long-range problems. First, on a per capita basis the little states such as Assam (five million) are drowned out by Hindi-speaking aggregates such as Uttar Pradesh. Second, a political drift aptly called "the balkanization of the South and the consolidation of the North"[9] has been set in motion. Specifi-

9 *B. R. Ambedkar,* Thought on Linguistic States (*Aurangabad, 1955*).

cally, each of the four southern, Dravidian states is turning more to its own language—Tamil, Telegu, Kannada, or Malayalam. On the other hand, the huge Hindi-speaking states (Uttar Pradesh with sixty-three million; Bihar with thirty-eight million; Madhya Pradesh with twenty-six million) are becoming consolidated and tend to be joined politically by other states where Hindi is either spoken also or easily learned (Punjab, Rajastan, Jamnu and Kashmir, and Bombay).

The combined process of balkanization and consolidation rests in part on a logical non sequitur that has been conveniently overlooked by politically interested persons. The comparatively tenable principle of "one language for each state" (because of efficiency in administration, and so forth) does not mean that one must create a single state or an arbitrarily small number of states for each language. One leader has suggested a plan for breaking up the great nothern states into two or three smaller units each, centered around large cities serving as new regional capitals. As things stand at present, however, the organization of "linguistic states" has exacerbated the question of a national language while at the same time it makes some of the reasonable solutions less likely of success.

Finally, the principle of linguistic autonomy has proved unfeasible in Bombay and the Punjab because of the intense antagonism and inextricable intermingling of speech communities of commensurate strength; the Sikhs have been agitating with characteristic vigor for the official recognition of their writing system. The close juxtaposition of linguistic minorities does not necessarily produce fusion, despite the heat and friction of the urban industrial pot; thousands of caste groups living in diaspora in the big Indian cities have retained their mother tongue, endogamy, and religious practices for hundreds of years, in accordance with the deep-lying values that support social segregation, combined with various types of social interdependence. In 1958, for ex-

ample, I took part in a "test for dialect distance" between a Marathi and the member of a Marathi subcaste whose ancestors moved down into Andhra over six hundred years ago. India's multilingual cities, notably Bombay, would provide excellent laboratories for the study of linguistic interference.[10] Such interference, however, might be found to differ markedly from the same process in other parts of the world, where the tendency to form colonies and "quarters" is not reinforced by the values of a pervasive caste system (admittedly, there are some parallels in the Near East). The extreme "ghettoization" of India's cities means that urbanization and industrialization are not as favorable to the development of linguistic uniformity as is usually the case.

Perhaps the most compelling force for the spontaneous adoption of a language is its relation to political values. In some cases a speech community may lack such a political substructure and may be segmented into two or more political bodies (e.g., the linked dialects of Austria, German Switzerland, East Germany, West Germany, and Holland). Or a state with more or less homogeneous political values may lack a single national code; thus the German in Switzerland is closer to Swiss French with respect to a partly covert system of political meanings than it is to Berlin German. But as a usual rule national and linguistic boundaries tend to coincide; indeed, these two domains of culture may powerfully reinforce each other's development. India's linguistic pluralism, on the other hand, is paralleled by a political disjointedness than has largely the same causes. She was never united before the British conquest; even the Mauryan and Guptan dynasties brought together only various portions of the country, and a consciousness of "national unity under Akbar" is vague indeed in the Dravidian South. A superstratum of British legal and political ideas, while genuinely espoused by many Indians, still

10 *U. Weinreich,* Languages in Contact (*New York, 1953*).

lacks much in the way of integration with the various regional cultures. Also, any state or national government remains threatened by the possibility of massive mob action and the self-directed aggression of Indian "passive resistance."

What is the relation of the English language to Indian political values? Contrary to a widespread impression, the British followed a rather enlightened policy, without explicitly "imposing" their tongue. As early as 1832, however, they were seeking to produce individuals who would be Indian in blood, but English in opinion, morals, and intellect. During the late nineteenth century an anglicizing fashion swept upper-caste India because of the political and economic advantages of English, or because of ethnic shame (e.g., about nakedness, polygyny), and in part because of the intellectual appeal of English culture. An extensive system of nonprogressive schools achieved high proficiency in English through a combination of memorization by rote and active use in the classroom.

Today many Indians fully appreciate the advantages of this "window to the outside world." The regional languages themselves have become suitable for higher instruction only because of the new European learning. The languages of the mass media reflect public attitudes; over one million copies of English-language newspapers are sold daily, in contrast to fewer than four hundred thousand in Hindi. English enables Indians to attend international conferences with "dignity" (meaning elegance, sophistication). Even the Communist intellectuals are grateful for the "English language experience," which has brought them translations of Tolstoy and Gorky. But all these patterns are ironically counteracted by certain feelings. During a recent convention Malayalam writers were bitterly accused of "knowing all about world literature but completely ignoring their Tamil neighbors." Some Malayali defended themselves by blaming "the British yoke" for their ignorance. But both the accusation and the defense were couched in the language of Byron.

Above all the practical and logical advantages stands the unforgettable association with British rule. The great majority of Indians, from the illiterate *harijan* to the cultivated polyglot, feel that the national language must be Indian and not the flat, denotative code imported by a people who, despite their democracy and their Shakespeare, were primarily conquerors, imperialists, and exploiters of the native land. After one hundred and fifty years, less than two million Indians speak English (more have some smatterings). Powerful, informal pressures affect many Indians who prefer English to their regional languages; a brilliant Tamilian poet of my acquaintance is frequently made to feel uneasy by his fellows because English is the language "of his excitement." And bitter indeed is the psychological predicament of the young anglicized Indian who can speak only English. "It is doing violence to the manhood and especially to the womanhood of India to encourage our boys and girls to think that an entry into polite society is impossible without a knowledge of English. It is too humiliating a thought to be bearable."[11] Thus we see a negative value decisively influencing India's political destiny.

In conclusion, some Indians feel that the least harmful way out of the present difficulty might be an improved education in the regional languages and also in Hindi and English (selected according to circumstances), combined with a general attitude of tolerance and patience. Pressurized programs could stir up nativistic reactions beyond government control. Multilingualism itself should be regarded as a goal and a form of knowledge. It is hoped that language skills will continue to develop and be tried out in an experimental spirit, with leeway for the spontaneous drift of personality and culture. During the interim English might be explicitly rejected as a national language, while continuing in the status of an exist-

11 *Mahatma Gandhi,* Young India. *2.2.12.*

ing code, useful for national and international purposes. It would certainly accord with the Indian traditions of tolerance and religious reverence for "The Word" to adopt as a motto for the present: "Speak and let speak!"

In the welter of perspectives on political behavior, three dimensions are readily apparent: politics as *competition, conflict,* or *control;* politics as *power;* and politics as *communication.* The three subsequent chapters illustrate these dimensions, each in turn. Though they may overlap one another in fact, in theory they are clearly distinguishable. This, coupled with the frequency with which they have been used by modern political scientists in demarcating alternative approaches to the study of politics, accounts for our extended treatment of these dimensions of the diversity of contemporary perspectives on political behavior.

4

Competition, Conflict, and Control

One view of politics emphasizes its contentious nature. Man's desire to secure satisfaction for himself and for those with whom he agrees about how values should be distributed in society is often challenged—or even frustrated—by the countervailing efforts of others equally intent upon securing their own satisfactions. When such frictions develop, and rarely does hostility not arise over the distribution of scarce resources, man becomes involved in political combat and controversy and must attempt to defeat his opponents in the political wars.

Students of the political process in totalitarian as well as democratic systems have on occasion depicted this struggle in terms of the restraints inhibiting its more aggressive tendencies. Our concern in this chapter is to illustrate the characteristics of, and the restraints sometimes operative in, three forms of political stress: competition, conflict, and control.

The most apparent form of competition is that between contending parties organized primarily to wrest or keep power from an opposing body of similarly organized men. In American politics we find such competition dramatized in the Presidential election, which, according to democratic theorists, provides an opportunity for the electorate to chart the course of the nation by its choice between the candidates of the two major parties. Students of Presidential elections have observed, however, that too often in the past there has been no direct confrontation of candidates, let alone of principles, policies, or issues.

The election of 1960 provided an exception to the rule as, for the first time in American history, the voters had an opportunity to watch a series of nationally televised debates between the Republican, Richard M. Nixon, and the Democrat, John F. Kennedy. Theodore H. White, in his book *The Making of the President: 1960,* has caught the tense drama of the debates in the selection reprinted here.

White argues that the opportunity for public choice which was held out by the debates nevertheless was destroyed by the mass media themselves—television in particular—which encouraged the central actors to appeal to the audience rather than to rebut the opponent. Indeed, many journalists, pollsters, and political scientists felt that Kennedy won the debates—and the election—because Nixon made the mistake of reacting to Kennedy rather than projecting a positive image of himself. Nixon in effect lost the election because he attempted, however weakly, to dramatize in the television debates the competitiveness of the campaign. Kennedy was successful in appealing to the nation at large, intentionally ignoring the struggle that was taking place in the studio at the time.

In this sense the debates of 1960 illustrate the restraints operative on electoral competition in American politics. There have been a few instances of intense competition between Presidential candidates and parties—cases in which the alternatives have been sharply drawn and the future destiny of the nation hung in the balance. The most recent cases have been the campaigns of 1964, 1936, and possibly 1932 and 1928. In each exceptional case "the gloves have come off" and electoral competition in its unrestrained form has been evident. William Nisbet Chambers, in his analysis of the emergence of political parties in early America, catches the flavor of the first such contest between genuinely competing party philosophies in a Presidential election: the battle of 1800 between John Adams and Thomas Jefferson.

The "choice of 1800," as Chambers calls the campaign, was not only between the Federalist "ins" and the Democrat-Republican "outs," but between the socially conservative, mercantile, Anglophile Federalists and the low-tariff, low-tax, low-debt, free-press, egalitarian, Francophile Republicans. Jefferson and Aaron Burr, his running mate, stood for a change in American leadership, a change that, when it was accomplished, according to some historians, dramatically altered the course of American history.

The choice was also important because of its implications for the democratic process in America, in particular the nature of electoral activity and the character of American political parties. The Republicans represented a new type of political party, relying on what were in 1800 advanced techniques of organization, propagandizing, and disseminating of the party line. The Republicans built a grass-roots party, anticipating widespread popular suffrage and the role of the average citizen in actually determining the outcomes of Presidential elections by several years. (In 1800 each state set its own rules for selecting Presidential electors, and in many, such as New York, Pennsylvania, and South Carolina, the state legislatures rather than the people chose the electors.) In addition, state leaders in the critical uncertain states, through effective deployment of patronage and the election of loyal party men to the lower houses of the state legislatures, were able to ward off the influence of Federalist wealth in the coastal cities, which counted heavily in the upper houses of the state legislatures. Lastly, the election of 1800 dramatized the new power of the northern farmers as a group, shifting their allegiance from the Federalist to the Republican party and carrying with them the critical margin of Republican victory. Such shifting allegiances in Presidential elections have been noted throughout American history.[1]

[1] *See Wilfred E. Binkley,* American Political Parties: Their Natural History *(New York: Alfred A. Knopf, Inc., 1943).*

There was, of course, a peculiarity in the election of 1800. Because Jefferson and Burr received the same number of electoral votes and no specification of President and Vice President was made on the ballots, the tie had to be broken in the holdover, Federalist-controlled House of Representatives. The voting in the House was by state, with eight states controlled by Republicans, six by Federalists, and two uncertain. Because of the critical nature of the election, the Federalists chose to use their minority strength to forestall the easy election of Jefferson as President by the nine states necessary (a majority of the sixteen states in the Union at the time) until some *quid pro quo* could be exacted from the Republicans. Aaron Burr was the recipient of these obstructionist Federalist votes, thus splitting the Presidential ticket in a Congressional election settlement for the first and last time[2] in American history. After thirty-five inconclusive roll-call ballots, Jefferson secured the nine votes necessary, and the resisting Federalists accepted the outcome without any further perversion of the democratic process. Through this establishment of a precedent of peaceful interparty transfer of power, restraint upon political competition in America was forged early in the life of the Republic.

In the background, however, one can detect the evidence of another form of political competition—intraparty factionalism. Aaron Burr's willingness to serve the Federalist cause illustrated the flimsy basis of the party. The loose-knit American system, with its diffusion of authority among the several branches and levels of government, creates particular difficulty in securing party loyalty among political leaders having different constituencies and outlooks.

But though the constitutional system may reinforce or encourage it, intraparty factionalism has its roots in the conflicting objectives and tactics of party members. In recent years both the Democratic and Republican parties have been split internally—nationally and in many state, county, and city organizations—along lines of difference of opinion regarding party platform and/or issues of intraorganizational procedure, personality, or politics. At the state and local levels, especially in the more populous, industrialized states, the intraparty struggles have occurred between professional politicians, usually committed to a well-organized, traditional system for maintaining party power irrespective of any consideration of public benefit or public policy, and amateur politicians (those not dependent for their livelihood upon earnings from political activity), usually committed to particular causes irrespective of the impact of such causes on the maintenance or enhancement of power or the party to which they offer some degree of allegiance. The struggles vary in intensity, duration, and complexity from jurisdiction to jurisdiction and from party to party. Nevertheless, James Q.

---

2 *The Twelfth Amendment, ratified September 25, 1804, precluded any such future absurdity by requiring the specification of Presidential and Vice Presidential candidates.*

Wilson has ably presented what might be called a collective portrait of this struggle, and particularly of the amateur forces involved, by investigating activities within the Democratic party during the 1950's in three cities: New York, Chicago, and Los Angeles. The selection below analyzes the nature of the struggle against the old Tammany machine in New York City.

As Wilson points out, intraparty rivalry in New York City, and particularly insurgent opposition to the Tammany machine, has been a regularity of Democratic party affairs during this century. What distinguished the revolt of the 1950's was that the reformers concentrated on seizing control of the party organization, rather than simply altering the character of city leadership through municipal elections; the reformers of the fifties and sixties have sought, and in many cases successfully secured, control over the party offices at the district level. Moreover, recent reformers have not relied on the discovery of scandal, interborough factionalism, or Republican support to build a powerful antimachine force within the Democratic party; prior to the fifties all three elements comprised the basic ingredients of the reformers' political strength. In the fifties it was instead the new liberal force within the Democratic party generated by the 1956 Presidential candidacy of Adlai E. Stevenson that permitted the reformers to mount an increasingly successful internal assault on the district leadership in Manhattan.

Coupled with the existence of this mid-twentieth-century liberalism in the national party has been a change in the character of the Manhattan electorate. Alteration in the social structure of the city—the emigration of the clerical and blue-collar workers and their replacement by "highly educated young professionals"—made it difficult for the traditional party leaders to maintain the electorate's loyalty. The new arrivals to the city choose to become personally aware, and often active, in local politics; they not only refuse to vote for unimaginative, machine-backed nonentities, but they will work tirelessly without compensation to get out the vote for candidates who can provide intellectual leadership in city affairs.

Thus in New York City demographic change permitted an organizational revolution and redistribution of party power. But will the present reform movement survive? All such movements in the past in New York City (and many elsewhere) have been marked by the unfortunately episodic rise and fall of reform fortunes. One writer has described this historical tendency as the "life cycle of reform," stressing the almost inevitable decline in organizational strength of reform movements that tends to follow in the wake of their successes at the polls.[3] Will the seizure of the party apparatus by the reformers in 1961 prove sufficient to offset the difficulty reformers have in the past encountered in rallying the electorate on behalf of a reform movement already in control of municipal affairs?

The dynamics of conflict is even more apparent in communities than it is

---

[3] *James A. Reichley,* The Art of Government (*New York: Fund for the Republic, 1959*).

within parties. James S. Coleman in his monograph *Community Conflict* searches the literature on specific cases of controversy and local political hostilities in order to lay the groundwork for a general theory of conflict in the community setting.

His analysis provides a "portrait of the processes which are set in motion as controversy develops."[4] In the selection reprinted below, he examines this acceleration of hostility—the way in which conflict is generated and grows in any situation where disagreement over community issues exists.

Coleman sets forth a model which accounts for the intensification or escalation of conflict that often occurs with little or no extracommunity provocation. 1. Conflict shifts from specific issues to general ones. 2. New issues are injected. 3. Personal antagonism replaces heated argument over the issues. 4. The original issues become unimportant in what has become a highly personalized struggle. 5. The community at large tends to be drawn into the warring armies; parties indifferent to the struggle perforce become aligned with friends and associates more intensely involved in the struggle. 6. Even the leadership of the contending forces undergoes a transformation as extremists displace moderates. 7. Hearsay and rumors replace fact as the basis for opinion formation. 8. The grouping of like-minded persons in this polarized setting reinforces the conflict and makes settlement of differences a Herculean political task.

Coleman's model of conflict escalation appears to have a larger relevance than simply to community relations. International crises, squabbles within political parties, and interpersonal tensions in the extended family, social club, or work place all seem to follow the pattern of acceleration of hostility outlined by him. Thus it is of the utmost importance in terms of general social science to develop approaches to tension reduction and the control of what Coleman calls the Gresham's Law of Conflict—that "harmful and dangerous elements drive out those which would keep the conflict within bounds."[5]

Although these approaches are not discussed in the selection below, nevertheless Coleman elsewhere in his analysis points to the community's leadership as one major source of conflict inhibition. In line with this view, conflict management has been considered by some experts on human relations as one of the central functions of political leadership.

It is the political leaders who must shoulder the ultimate responsibility for managing and channeling conflict so that only beneficial effects will be felt. They hold special responsibilities in conflict management and prevention in the totalitarian system. If internal dissension becomes widespread or intensifies, the very sources of stability of the regime may be threatened; the

---

[4] James S. Coleman, Community Conflict (*New York: The Free Press of Glencoe, Inc., 1957*) *p. 3.*
[5] Ibid., *p. 14.*

officials of the ruling party, moreover, are in a particularly advantageous position for the total suppression of—or more likely the manipulation of—conflict to accomplish the objectives of the ruling clique. Raymond A. Bauer, in the selection below from his book *Nine Soviet Portraits*,[6] presents a fictional but realistic account of the Soviet Party Secretary, dramatizing the role and its strains on the incumbent. This portrait of the Party Secretary illustrates the burdens and opportunities of political leadership, which is every bit as complex in totalitarian systems as in Western democracies.

Bauer's analysis is essentially sociopsychological. He focuses on "the pressures and rewards . . . and the reaction of the [Party Secretary] as he attempts to pursue his own goals within the framework that the regime has created."[7] As a combination administrator-technician-troubleshooter concerned with maintaining production levels in his administrative district, the Party Secretary tries to avoid political entanglements, but he must pay considerable attention to the political environment within which he fulfills his administrative responsibilities. The Party Secretary, in short, reflects the central dilemmas of control and political leadership in his uncertainties about his career—and perhaps even his freedom.

These dilemmas are familiar to students of political leadership in totalitarian systems. The Party Secretary often uses his friends in the Soviet hierarchy to protect himself against the factional intrigue that abounds in the system. But the tactic can backfire: "When powerful figures in the party jockey for position at the top of the hierarchy, the reverse actions are felt in the lower stata of the operation."[8] As First Secretary Teplov muses, "It was risky to take sides, and it was risky not to take sides."[9] The stakes of this game of political chance are higher in totalitarian systems, where factional obstruction cannot be tolerated within the party. As a result, all life becomes infused with political overtones and implications; minor events assume a special importance to the individuals who must read every expression for hidden meaning. Moreover, the uncertainties of life are magnified. According to Third Secretary Shvartz, "one never knew in these days on whose side the gods would intervene,"[10] or, for that matter, why. Success in totalitarian party politics is a mystery to its own devotees.

Party officials are themselves captives of the system they collectively control. It is this aspect that gives the Soviet system its continuity and internal strength, but it also makes the system fail in terms of providing human satisfaction. The fears and frustrations of the party *apparatchiki* (officials) are transferred to the populace at large as the *apparatchiki* relieve their personal

---

[6] *The nine fictional portraits presented are drawn in large part from interviews, a review of documentary evidence, and a survey of Soviet literature.*
[7] *Raymond A. Bauer,* Nine Soviet Portraits *(Cambridge, Mass.: Massachusetts Institute of Technology Press, and New York: John Wiley & Sons, Inc., 1955) p. 180.*
[8] Ibid., *p. 60.*
[9] Ibid., *p. 69.*
[10] Ibid., *p. 69.*

sense of helplessness by tryrannizing one another and the citizens with whom they have contact.

There are important limits, however, to this freedom of action of the Soviet party officials. Witness, for example, the case of the party organizer in the shoe factory who was too zealous in the performance of his duties and had to be replaced. To clarify the restraints upon those in positions of control more fully, however, it is necessary to turn to a discussion of power—another dimension in the study of politics—which will occupy us in Chapter 5.

Suggestions for Additional Reading

Armstrong, John A., *The Politics of Totalitarianism: The Communist Party of the Soviet Union from 1934 to the Present.* New York: Random House, Inc., 1961.

Buchanan, William, *Legislative Partisanship: The Deviant Case of California,* University of California Publications in Political Science, Vol. XIII. Berkeley: University of California Press, 1963.

Coser, Lewis A., *The Functions of Social Conflict.* New York: The Free Press of Glencoe, Inc., 1956.

David, Paul T., Ralph M. Goldman, and Richard C. Bain, *The Politics of National Party Conventions,* rev. ed. New York: Vintage Books, Inc., 1964.

Duverger, Maurice, *Political Parties.* New York: John Wiley & Sons, Inc., 1954.

Eckstein, Harry, *A Theory of Stable Democracy,* Research Monograph, No. 10. Princeton Center of International Studies, 1961.

Kelley, Stanley, Jr., *Political Campaigning.* Washington, D.C.: The Brookings Institution, 1960.

Kornhauser, William, *The Politics of Mass Society.* New York. The Free Press of Glencoe, Inc., 1959.

Lazarsfeld, Paul F., *et al., The People's Choice,* 2nd ed. New York: Columbia University Press, 1948.

Lubell, Samuel, *The Future of American Politics,* 2nd ed. New York: Doubleday & Company, Inc., 1956.

McKenzie, Robert T., *British Political Parties.* New York: St. Martin's Press, Inc., 1955.

McNeil, Elton B., ed., *The Nature of Human Conflict.* Englewood Cliffs, N.J.: Prentice-Hall, Inc., 1965.

Michels, Robert, *Political Parties.* New York: The Free Press of Glencoe, Inc., 1949.

Moore, Barrington, *Terror and Progress U.S.S.R.: Some Sources of Changes and Stability in the Soviet Dictatorship.* Cambridge, Mass.: Harvard University Press, 1954.

Neumann, Sigmund, ed., *Modern Political Parties.* Chicago: University of Chicago Press, 1956.

Polsby, Nelson W., and Aaron B. Wildavsky, *Presidential Elections: Strategies of American Electoral Politics.* New York: Charles Scribner's Sons, 1964.

Ranney, Austin, and Willmoore Kendall, *Democracy and the American Party System.* New York: Harcourt, Brace & World, Inc., 1956.

Rapoport, Anatol, *Fights, Games and Debates.* Ann Arbor: University of Michigan Press, 1960.

Riker, William H., *The Theory of Political Coalitions.* New Haven, Conn.: Yale University Press, 1962.

Schelling, Thomas C., *The Strategy of Conflict.* Cambridge, Mass.: Harvard University Press, 1960.

Shubik, Martin, ed., *Game Theory and Related Approaches to Social Behavior: Selections.* New York: John Wiley & Sons, Inc., 1964.

Truman, David B., *The Congressional Party.* New York: John Wiley & Sons, Inc., 1959.

————, *The Governmental Process.* New York: Alfred A. Knopf, Inc., 1951.

Zeigler, Harmon, *Interest Groups in American Society.* Englewood Cliffs, N.J.: Prentice-Hall, Inc., 1964.

A. Campaigning for Office

Kennedy vs. Nixon: The T.V. Debates of 1960

Theodore H. White

Both candidates had had representatives in the CBS studio from 8:30 in the morning of the day of the debate.

Mr. Nixon's advisers and representatives, understandably nervous since they could not communicate with their principal, had made the best preparation they could. They had earlier requested that both candidates talk from a lectern, standing—and Kennedy had agreed. They had asked several days earlier that the two candidates be seated farther apart from each other than originally planned—and that had been agreed on too. Now, on the day of the debate, they paid meticulous attention to each detail. They were worried about the deep eye shadows in Nixon's face and they requested and adjusted two tiny spotlights ("inkies" in television parlance) to shine directly into his eye wells and illuminate the darkness there; they asked that a table be placed in front of the moderator, and this was agreed to also; they requested that no shots be taken of Nixon's left profile during the debate, and this was also agreed to.

The Kennedy advisers had no requests; they seemed as cocky and confident as their chief.

Nixon entered the studio about an hour before air time and inspected the setting, let himself be televised on an interior camera briefly for the inspection of his advisers, then paced moodily about in the back of the studio. He beckoned the producer to him at one point as he paced and asked as a personal favor that he not be on camera if he happened to be mopping sweat from his face. (That night, contrary to most reports, Nixon was wearing no theatrical make-up. In order to tone down his dark beard stubble on the screen, an adviser had applied only a light coating of "Lazy Shave," a pancake makeup with which a man who has heavy afternoon beard growth may powder his face to conceal the growth.)

Senator Kennedy arrived about fifteen minutes after the Vice President; he inspected the set; sat for the camera; and his advisers inspected him, then declared they were satisfied. The producer made a remark about the glare of the Senator's white shirt, and Kennedy sent an aide back to his hotel to bring back a blue one, into which he changed just before air time. The men took their seats, the tally lights on the cameras blinked red to show they were live now.

"Good evening," said Howard K. Smith, the gray and handsome moderator. "The television and radio stations of the United States . . . are proud to provide for a discussion of issues in the current political campaign by the two major candidates for the Presidency. The candidates need no introduction. . . ."

And they were on air, before seventy million Americans.

Rereading now the text of the first of the great debates (and of the following three also), one can find only a blurred echo of the emotions that rose from the performance, and the intense, immediate, and dramatic impact of the debate on the fortunes of the two candidates.

This, the first of the debates, was committed to a discussion of domestic issues—an area in which the Democrats, by their philosophy and record, make larger promises and offer a more aggressive attitude to the future than the Republicans. Kennedy, opening, declared that the world could not endure half-slave and half-free, and that the posture of America in the world rested fundamentally on its posture at home—how we behaved to each other, what we did to move American society forward at home, this affected not only us, but the world too: "Can freedom be maintained under the most severe attack it has ever known? I think it can be. And I think in the final analysis it depends upon what we do here. I think it's time America started moving again."

Nixon's opening statement, as it reads now in print, was one of good-willed difference: he agreed with Kennedy in all the goals Kennedy had outlined. He differed with Kennedy only in the methods to reach those goals. He lauded the progress made under the seven and a half years of the Eisenhower administration—hospitals, highways, electric power, gross national product, growth rate; were all moving at a rate, he said, never matched before in any administration.

The clue to what was happening can be remembered only in rereading the penultimate passage of Mr. Nixon's opening remarks:

> The final point that I would like to make is this: Senator Kennedy has suggested in his speeches that we lack compassion for the poor, for the old, and for others that are unfortunate. . . . I know what it means to be poor . . . I know that Senator Kennedy feels as deeply about these problems as I do, but our disagreement is not about the goals for America but only about the means to reach those goals.

For Mr. Nixon was debating with Mr. Kennedy as if a board of judges were scoring points; he rebutted and refuted, as he went, the inconsistencies or errors of his opponent. Nixon was addressing himself to Kennedy—but Kennedy was addressing himself to the audience that was the nation. In these debates, before this audience, there could be no appeal to the past or to the origins of any ethnic group—there could only be an appeal, across the board, to all Americans and to the future. This across-the-board appeal to all Americans had been Mr. Nixon's basic strategy from the very beginning—a generalized pressure that would fragment the minorities coalition of the Democrats. Yet here, before the largest audience of Americans in history, Nixon was not addressing himself to his central theme; he was offering no vision of the future that the Republican party might offer Americans—he was concerned with the cool and undisturbed man who sat across the platform from him, with the personal adversary in the studio, not with the mind of America.

Ten questions followed from the panel of television reporters who sat before the debaters: on the importance of a candidate's age; on the quality of decision in Presidential affairs; on farms; on taxes; on schools; on Congressional politics; on subversion; and on schools again. In each pair of answers, the same contrast repeated itself: the Senator from Massachusetts, ignoring the direct inquiry when it suited him, used each question as a springboard for an appeal to the mind and the imagination of the audience assembled before the countless sets. But the Vice President's mind and attention were fixed there in the studio. As one rereads the text, one finds him, over and over again, scoring excellently against the personal adversary in the hall beside him, yet forgetful of the need to score on the mind of the nation he hoped to lead.

The defensive quality of Mr. Nixon's performance (evident from his first enunciation: "The things that Senator Kennedy has said many of us can agree with. . . . I can subscribe completely to the spirit that Senator Kennedy has expressed tonight, the spirit that the United States should move ahead. . . .") can still be reconstructed from the texts. What cannot be reconstructed is the visual impact of the first debate.

For it was the sight of the two men side by side that carried the punch.

There was, first and above all, the crude, overwhelming impression that side by side the two seemed evenly matched—and this even matching in the popular imagination was for Kennedy a major victory. Until the cameras opened on the Senator and the Vice President, Kennedy had been the boy under assault and attack by the Vice President as immature, young, inexperienced. Now, obviously, in flesh and behavior he was the Vice President's equal.

Not only that, but the contrast of the two faces was astounding. Normally and in private, Kennedy under tension flutter[ed] his hands—he adjust[ed] his necktie, slap[ped] his knee, stroke[d] his face. Tonight he was calm and nerveless in appearance. The Vice President, by contrast, was tense, almost frightened, at turns glowering and, occasionally, haggard-looking to the point of sickness. Probably no picture in American politics tells a better story of crisis and episode than that famous shot of the camera on the Vice President as he half slouched, his "Lazy Shave" powder faintly streaked with sweat, his eyes exaggerated hollows of blackness, his jaw, jowls, and face drooping with strain.

It is impossible to look again at the still photographs of Nixon in his ordeal and to recollect the circumstances without utmost sympathy. For everything that could have gone wrong that night went wrong. The Vice President, to begin with, suffers from a handicap that is serious only on television—his is a light, naturally transparent skin. On a visual camera that takes pictures by optical projection this transparent skin photographs cleanly and well. But a television camera projects electronically, by an image-orthicon tube, which is a cousin of the X-ray tube; it seems to go beneath the skin, almost as the X-ray photograph does. On television, the camera on Nixon is usually held away from him, for in close-up his transparent skin shows the tiniest hair growing in the skin follicles beneath the surface, even after he has just shaved. And for the night of the first debate, CBS, understandably zealous, had equipped its cameras with brand-new tubes for the most perfect projection possible—a perfection of projection that could only be harmful to the Vice President. (In the later debates, Nixon was persuaded to wear theatrical makeup to repair the ravage TV's electronic tube makes of his countenance; but for this first debate he wore only "Lazy Shave.")

The scene of the debate, the studio of WBBM, had, further, been tense all day long, as furniture, desks, lecterns, background had been rearranged and then rearranged again for best effect. Nixon's TV advisers had been told that the background would be gray-scale five, a relatively dark tone; therefore they had urged their principal to dress in a light gray suit for contrast. Yet the backdrop, when they saw it, was so markedly lighter than they had anticipated that they insisted, rightly, it be repainted. Several times that day it was repainted—but each time the gray tone dried light. (The background indeed was still tacky to the touch when the two candidates went on the air.) Against this light background Nixon, in his light suit, faded into a fuzzed outline, while Kennedy, in his dark suit, had the crisp picture edge of contrast. The Nixon advisers had, further, adjusted all lighting to a master lighting scheme for their candidate before he went on the air; but in the last few minutes before the debate a horde of still photographers from newspapers and magazines were permitted on the set, and as they milled for their still pictures, they kicked over wires and displaced lights and television cameras from their marked positions.

There was, lastly, the fact that the Vice President had still not recovered from his illness, and was unrested from the exertions of his first two weeks of intense campaigning. His normal shirt hung loosely about his neck, and his recent weight loss made him appear scrawny. And, most of all, psychologically, his advisers now insist, he lacked the energy to project—for Nixon does best on television when he projects, when he can distract the attention of the viewer from his passive countenance to the theme or the message he wants to give forth, as in his famous "Checkers" appearance on television in 1952.

All this, however, was unknown then to the national audience. Those who heard the debates on radio, according to sample surveys, believed that the two candidates came off almost equal. Yet every survey of those who watched the debates on television indicated that the Vice President had come off poorly and, in the opinion of many, very poorly. It was the picture image that had done it—and in 1960 television had won the nation away from sound to images, and that was that.

The Vice President was later to recover from the impression he made in this first debate. But this first debate, the beginning of the contest, was, as in so many human affairs, half the whole. The second debate concerned itself with foreign policy and ranged from Cuba's Castro through the U-2 and espionage to the matter of America's declining prestige, and closed

on the first sharp clash of the series—the defense of Quemoy and Matsu.

The third debate resumed, like a needle stuck in a phonograph groove, with the subject of Quemoy and Matsu, hung there almost indefinitely, then broke away with Nixon's stern disapproval of President Truman's bad language, and went on to other matters, such as bigotry, labor unions, and gold outflow. This, according to all sample surveys, was Nixon's best performance in terms of its impact on the audience. This was the debate in which Nixon spoke from Los Angeles while Kennedy spoke from New York, and it was as if, separated by a continent from the personal presence of his adversary, Nixon were more at ease and could speak directly to the nation that lay between them.

The fourth debate was the dreariest— both candidates had by now almost nothing new left to say, and they repeated themselves on all the matters they had covered in the three previous debates. Curiously enough, the audience which had been highest for the first debate and dropped off slightly for the second and third, returned on the last debate to almost match the total of the first.

No accurate political measurement or reasonable judgment is yet possible on a matter as vast as the TV debates of 1960. When they began, Nixon was generally viewed as being the probable winner of the election contest and Kennedy as fighting an uphill battle; when they were over, the positions of the two contestants were reversed.

No reporter can claim any accuracy in charting the magic and mysterious flow of public opinion between the time a campaign starts and the ultimate tally of feelings at the polls; and so opinion seesawed back and forth for weeks, as it still seesaws back and forth now, long after the debates are over, as to what, specifically, the debates achieved in shaping the campaign and American opinion.

There were fragmentary and episodic achievements that no one could deny.

Any reporter who followed the Kennedy campaign remembers still the quantum jump in the size of crowds that greeted the campaigning Senator from the morrow of the first debate, the morning of Tuesday, September 27th, when he began to campaign in northern Ohio. His crowds had been growing for a full seven days before the debates, but now, overnight, they seethed with enthusiasm and multiplied in numbers, as if the sight of him, in their homes on the video box, had given him a "star quality" reserved only for television and movie idols.

Equally visible was the gloom that descended on Republican leaders around the country; they were angry with their own candidate, angry at his performance, angry most of all at his "me-too" debating style. At Nixon headquarters in Washington, the telephones rang incessantly, demanding that someone get to this "new Nixon" and convince him that only the "old Nixon" could win.

There were other measurable, hard political results. On the evening of the first debate, the Democratic governors of the Southern states were gathered for one of their annual conferences at Hot Springs, Arkansas. Except for Governor Luther Hodges[1] of North Carolina, they had until then viewed Kennedy with a range of emotions that ran from resigned apathy to whispered hostility. Watching him on TV that night, they too were suddenly impressed. We do not know whose idea it was to send Kennedy the telegram of congratulations which ten of the eleven signed that evening—but the enthusiasm and excitement of the telegram was not only genuine but a tidemark in the campaign. The Southern governors were with him now; and if they were with him, it meant that the machinery of their political organizations would be with him too.

It is much more difficult to measure the debates in terms of issues, of education of the American people to the tasks and problems before them. For there certainly

[1] *Hodges was later appointed Secretary of Commerce by President Kennedy.*

were real differences of philosophy and ideas between John F. Kennedy and Richard M. Nixon—yet rarely in American history has there been a political campaign that discussed issues less or clarified them less.

The TV debates, in retrospect, were the greatest opportunity ever for such discussion, but it was an opportunity missed. It is difficult to blame the form of the debates for this entirely; yet the form and the compulsions of the medium must certainly have been contributory. The nature of both TV and radio is that they abhor silence and "dead time." All TV and radio discussion programs are compelled to snap question and answer back and forth as if the contestants were adversaries in an intellectual tennis match. Although every experienced newspaperman and inquirer knows that the most thoughtful and responsive answers to any difficult question come after long pause, and that the longer the pause the more illuminating the thought that follows it, nonetheless the electronic media cannot bear to suffer a pause of more than five seconds; a pause of thirty seconds of dead time on air seems interminable. Thus, snapping their two-and-a-half-minute answers back and forth, both candidates could only react for the cameras and the people; they could not think. And, since two and a half minutes permit only a snatch of naked thought and a spatter of raw facts, both candidates, whenever caught out on a limb with a thought too heavy for two-minute exploration, a thought seemingly too bold or fresh to be accepted by the conditioned American mind, hastily scuttled back toward center as soon as they had enunciated the thought. Thus Kennedy's response to the first question on Quemoy and Matsu was probably one of the sharpest and clearest responses to any question of the debates; in that response, actually, Kennedy was tentatively fingering at one of the supreme problems of American statecraft, our relation with the revolution in Asia. Yet he was out too far with such a thought for a two-minute response[2] and, in succeeding debates, in reply to succeeding questions, he fuzzed the distinction between his position and Nixon's until it was almost impossible to tell them apart.

If there was to be any forum for issues, the TV debates should have provided such a forum. Yet they did not: every conceivable problem was raised by the probing imagination of the veteran correspondents who questioned the candidates. But all problems were answered in two-minute snatches, either with certain facts or with safe convictions. Neither man could pause to indulge in the slow reflection and rumination, the slow questioning of alternatives before decision, that is the inner quality of leadership.

If, then, the TV debates did little to advance the reasonable discussion of issues that is the dream of unblooded political scientists, what did they do?

What they did best was to give the voters of a great democracy a living portrait of two men under stress and let the voters decide, by instinct and emotion, which style and pattern of behavior under stress they preferred in their leader. The political roots of this tribal sense of the whole go as far back as the Roman Senate, or the beer-blown assemblies of the Teutonic tribes that Tacitus describes in his chronicles. This sense of personal choice of leader has been missing for centuries from modern civilization—or else limited to such conclaves of deputized spokesmen of the whole as a meeting of Tammany Hall captains, a gathering of Communist barons in the Kremlin or the dinners of leaders of the English Establishment in the clubs of London. What the TV debates did was to generalize this tribal

sense of participation, this emotional judgment of the leader, from the few to the multitude—for the salient fact of the great TV debates is not what the two candidates said, nor how they behaved, but how many of the candidates' fellow Americans gave up their evening hours to ponder the choice between the two.

There are many measures of the numbers of Americans who viewed the debates. The low measure is that of Dr. George Gallup, America's most experienced pollster, who sets the figure of Americans who viewed one or all of the debates at eighty-five million. The two most extensive surveys of audience were those made by NBC and CBS, the two great television networks. Their independent measures of the audience are so close that they must be taken seriously: NBC has estimated from its surveys that 115,000,000 Americans viewed one or all of the great debates; CBS has estimated the number at 120,-000,000. With or without issues, no larger assembly of human beings, their minds focused on one problem, has ever happened in history.

Even more significant than the numbers who viewed the debates was the penetration upon them of the personalities of the candidates; and on the effect of this penetration the public opinion samplers were unanimous.

There are any number of such surveys. The best localized survey (and that most respected by Nixon's television advisors) was performed in New York by a research-testing firm called Schwerin Research Corporation. The Schwerin Research Corporation, which operates a studio on Manhattan's West Side with scientifically selected audiences of three to four hundred people from the New York metropolitan area, is considered by some Madison Avenue experts as the best television-testing operation in the entire range of consumer goods advertising. Testing each debate in turn before its audiences, the Schwerin analysts reported that Kennedy outscored Nixon by 39 to 23 (balance un-

2 *For a full development of this two-minute answer, one had to wait for days, until Kennedy's extraordinarily lucid half-hour speech on Quemoy and Matsu in New York on Columbus Day, October 12th. That speech was heard only by a local audience, and its full text was reprinted, so far as I know, in only three newspapers in the country. It was as fine a campaign discussion of an issue of national importance as this correspondent can remember—yet its impact on the nation was nil.*

decided) in the first debate; by 44 to 28 in the second debate; lost to Nixon by 42 to 39 in the third debate (in which the contestants were separated physically by the space of the continent); and came back to win by 52 to 27 in the last debate.

The measurements of Dr. George Gallup coincide. After the first debate, 43 per cent of his respondents considered Kennedy to have been the best man, 23 per cent Nixon, 29 per cent considered them to have come off even, and 5 per cent were undecided. After the last debate Kennedy was held by 42 per cent to have won, Nixon to have won by 30 per cent, while 23 per cent considered the men even and 5 per cent were undecided.

There is, finally, the most extensive survey, that conducted for CBS by Dr. Elmo Roper. Sampling across the country, Dr. Roper estimated for CBS that 57 per cent of those who voted believed that the TV debates had influenced their decisions. Another 6 per cent, or over four million voters (by this sample), ascribed their final decision on voting to the debates alone. Of these four million voters, 26 per cent (or one million) voted for Nixon, and 72 per cent (or almost three million) voted for Kennedy. If these extrapolations are true, then two million of the Kennedy margin came from television's impact on the American mind—and since Kennedy won by only 112,000 votes, he was entirely justified in stating on the Monday following election, November 12th: "It was TV more than anything else that turned the tide."

B. Interparty Competition

The Choice of 1800

William Nisbet Chambers

Major elections under party systems provide prime opportunities for the expression of interests and opinions and for vast popular participation. They are also prime objects of partisan endeavor, for they are the means to the formal sanctions of power and office. Where parties offer significant options on which voters may base meaningful choices as to the men and policies that will govern them, elections may also be the fulcrums of popular decisions in a democracy. Such was the party contest of 1800 in America. Both parties saw the election as an ultimate test between the two great political bodies and their commitments on ideology and policy, and both were determined to rally their followings and seize the victory.

Many signs were favorable for the Federalists, although there were countersigns too. The "in" party had triumphed in the midterm elections, and Adams had finally brought peace with honor. Looking toward the Presidential contest, the wary Federalists had even reduced the army to peacetime strength in advance of the settlement with France. Yet many established party leaders were aging or edging toward retirement, and they viewed the new men who had come in with the Congressional victories as dubious replacements. Thus, for example, when Adams named the moderate spokesman Marshall to succeed Pickering at the State Department, high Federalists were aghast. Furthermore, the impact of the "repressive acts" was beginning to be felt, and sedition prosecutions had led, ironically, to doubling the num-

William Nisbet Chambers, *Political Parties in a New Nation: The American Experience, 1776–1809*, Chap. 8, "The Choice of 1880," pp. 150–69. Copyright © 1963 by Oxford University Press, Inc. Reprinted by permission.

ber of newspapers supporting Jefferson and the "out" party. Finally, in the mood of peace many Americans came to see the Federalists not as brave defenders but as headlong warmongers.

A caucus of Federalist Congressmen met in May, 1800. "By union," John Marshall warned, "we can scarcely maintain our ground—without it we must sink and with us all sound, correct American principles." Formal nominations were given to Adams and to Charles Cotesworth Pinckney, and the caucus firmly pledged the party's support to both candidates equally.

*   *   *

2

The Republicans entered the campaign united and resolute. By 1800 they had made Marache's boarding house in Philadelphia into an informal party command post. Members of Congress as various as Senator Langdon of New Hampshire and Representatives Macon of North Carolina and Randolph of Virginia stayed there. At "Marache's Club," as Randolph liked to call it, some forty-three Republican Senators and Representatives and several other partisans attended a caucus, also in May, 1800, to select the party's nominees. Once again Jefferson was obvious for President, and Gallatin could at last bring word from his father-in-law, Commodore James Nicholson, that conferences among Clinton, Burr, and other leaders in New York had cleared the way for Burr, who received the caucus nomination for Vice President. The Republicans also committed themselves firmly to an equality of votes, and the New York–Virginia axis at last seemed fixed.

Careful planning characterized Republican efforts throughout. Early in 1799 Jefferson had insisted that for success, "the engine is the press," and had called on "every man [to] lay his purse and pen under contribution." He suited action to his words by personally supervising the distribution of pamphlets and personally

soliciting funds, while urging others "to assess their friends also." At Philadelphia he dined or conferred with Congressmen who served as a national cadre, and he directed his always voluminous correspondence to the crucial concerns of party strategy.

In several states, new growths of Republican electoral organization developed from the seeds of national party action. Thus, for example, after an early election in New York, Burr traveled through Connecticut and Rhode Island to prepare the ground—labors in New York and Pennsylvania, of course, were already advanced. The Republicans in New Jersey began to organize committees throughout the state; Congressman Aaron Kitchell arranged for correspondence among "people of information and influence"; and a state meeting at Princeton issued an address exalting Jefferson and the elevation of the common man. The old-style politics which had favored the Federalists was giving way to organized coordination. In Virginia, where Monroe was now governor, a legislative caucus named a Republican ticket of electors; a Republican General Committee coordinated campaign labors, circulating printed or handwritten tickets which the voters could deposit at the polls; and the Committee also spread addresses to the citizens in the press. Only hesitant shoots of organization were apparent in North Carolina, but the Republicans at last had a newspaper, for Nathaniel Macon had brought Joseph Gales to Raleigh to establish the *Register* there.

Hindered again by the myopia of their notable leaders, the Federalists failed to read the signs. Although they followed Republican methods of organization to some extent in Virginia and Pennsylvania, elsewhere they generally relied on correspondence, occasional public meetings, and state gatherings of leaders, national patronage, and press propaganda. This last turned sharply on Jefferson, who was scourged as a Jacobin, the father of mulatto children, an "intellectual voluptary," a mad scientist whose estate ought to be called "Dog's Misery" because he practiced vivisection there, an atheist whose election would bring on the people of America "the just vengeance of insulted heaven." Voters were asked whether they would choose

GOD—AND A RELIGIOUS PRESIDENT;

or impiously declare for

JEFFERSON—AND NO GOD!!!

Such diatribes, however, did not make up for the Federalist failure to develop open organization comparable to the apparatus Republicans were establishing.

The Republicans also orchestrated a fortissimo propaganda attack. In a public letter-"platform" dispatched to Elbridge Gerry in 1799, Jefferson had taken his stand for "a government rigorously frugal and simple" and "the discharge of the national debt"; for a limited navy and for state militia forces for internal defense, except in case of "actual invasion"; for "free commerce with all nations, political connections with none," and against "joining in the [European] confederacy of kings to war against the principles of liberty"; for "freedom of religion, and . . . freedom of the press," and against "all violations of the Constitution" which would silence criticism "by force and not by reason." This summary of Republican "principles" was echoed again and again throughout the campaign, accompanied by specific blasts against the direct taxes and the Alien and Sedition Acts and by repeated praise of Jefferson as "our great Patriot." In addition, the themes of debt, taxes, and war were repeated in emotional reiteration, and popular prejudices were not ignored. A pamphlet called *The Family Compact of Connecticut* sought to expose the political machinations of the Congregational clergy beginning with "Dwight, Timothy—President of Yale, generally called the Pope." In Philadelphia, Beckley prepared several pamphlets for distribution north, south, and east, despite his own illness and the death of his only child.

Often emotional or personal, the Republican electoral appeals were still remarkably oriented to the great issues of the day. In addition, like Hamilton and the Federalists before them, the Republicans had in effect generated a program, a comprehensive set of policies which was patterned on their conception of the national interest and which appealed to broad and varied segments of the public. Only a very sleepy voter could have been oblivious to the choice before him.

3

The crucial states in the contest turned out to be New York (where Adams had won his margin in 1796), Pennsylvania (which the Republicans had to hold against Federalist maneuvering), and South Carolina (an essential hedge against trouble in Pennsylvania); and Jefferson and other Republican managers watched developments in these states closely. The time and procedures for choosing electors varied from state to state, and thus the struggles in each state were carried on as separate decisive events.

In New York, Burr was the driving force. He carefully arranged a city ticket of eminent men like Clinton, General Horatio Gates, and Brockholst Livingston to run for the legislature that would name the Presidential electors. He himself harangued in the city's taverns, guided an active finance committee, amassed an index of voters and their political histories, organized ward and precinct meetings, and worked at the polls. He also gathered together the forerunner of future partisan-personal machines, composed of cadre-followers who collaborated so efficiently that they became known as the "Myrmidons" or the "Tenth Legion." He cracked the problem of disfranchisement for many city workingmen under the state's property test for suffrage, by arranging for joint land tenancies which made each participant a legal owner. The whole effort found new resources which foreshadowed similar developments elsewhere. Many ambitious lesser merchants and would-be entrepreneurs were beginning to feel that their hopes for advancement were frustrated by Federalists in the interest of a few wealthy magnates. To encourage these disgruntled forces Burr and several associates had formed the Manhattan Company, chartered ostensibly to provide water for the city but granted sufficient powers to enable it to operate as a bank. Haughtily contemptuous of Burr's plebeian political tactics, the Federalists now found themselves also threatened by their own brand of politico-financial petard.

In the April elections the Republicans carried all twelve of New York City's state legislative districts over Hamilton's slate of Federalist mediocrities. They also ran well outside the city, and ultimately won a net majority of nineteen in the senate and assembly as a whole. Desperate, Hamilton maneuvered to change the rules in the middle of the game. Ignoring the fact that Federalists in 1799 had beaten down a proposal by Burr to name electors by popular vote, arguing bluntly that "in times like these it will not do to be over-scrupulous," Hamilton now urged Governor Jay to call a special session of the old Federalist-controlled legislature to authorize a new choice of electors by popular ballot. He hoped thereby to snatch New York from the Republicans after all. Disdaining to answer, Jay noted on Hamilton's letter: "Proposing a measure for party purposes, which I think it would not become me to adopt." The victory in the city had hinged on an average margin of 490 for Republicans over Federalists, but the whole of the Empire State's electoral vote would go to Jefferson—and Burr.

With Pennsylvania in the Republican column, Jefferson had declared, "we can defy the universe"—or at least the Federalists. In 1800 it appeared that the defiance could be effected, as Beckley (as chairman of the Committee of Correspondence for Philadelphia), Dallas, Gallatin, Leib, and others marshalled the Republican organization of committees throughout the state. Following the Republican

sweep in 1799, Governor Thomas McKean had removed Federalist officeholders by the score to make room for Republicans. He had commissioned Beckley, for example, as clerk of the Mayor's Court in Philadelphia and provided him with another subsidiary clerkship to pay him what he had drawn in the national House. It was an early version of the party-building "spoils system" which was later to run rampant in American politics, but McKean's patronage platoons marched to battle. There was no doubt that the Republicans had broad popular support also, and a Federalist observer lamented that by 1800 the state was dominated by "United Irishmen, Free Masons, and the most God-provoking Democrats on this side of Hell." Yet the Federalists labored to match Republican organization in Pennsylvania, and also maneuvered to keep the Keystone State from becoming the key to national Republican victory. Utilizing the resources of their holdover control of the Pennsylvania state senate, they first forced the Republicans to accept a choice of Presidential electors by the legislature instead of by popular vote. Next they refused senate concurrence in a Republican move to choose electors by a joint ballot of both houses of the legislature, in which the Republican preponderance in the more numerous lower house would have enabled them to name all fifteen electors. The Federalists thus compelled a final compromise which gave them seven electors to the Republicans' eight. The result scarcely represented the political balance in the state, as an overwhelming Republican victory in the Congressional elections was to reveal, but it neutralized Pennsylvania in the Presidential contest.

As all eyes turned South, the old Federalist bastion of South Carolina was experiencing a new frenzy of electioneering. Taking over active management for Jefferson and Burr, the Republican Charles Pinckney pressed his party's attack against "the Weight of Talent, Wealth, and personal and family interest" which favored the Federalists. He expected to lose

Charleston but labored to recruit back-country planters and farmers. Even so, he reported to Jefferson, he was amazed at the Federalist mobilization in the city:

> as much as I am accustomed to Politics and to study mankind this Election in Charleston has opened to me a new view of things. Never certainly was such an election in America . . . it is said that several Hundred more voted than paid taxes. the Lame, Crippled, diseased and blind were either led, lifted or brought in carriages to the Poll. the sacred right of ballot was struck at, for at a late hour, when too late to counteract it, in order to know how men [voted] the Novel and Unwarrantable measure was used of Voting with tickets printed on Green and blue and red and yellow paper and Men stationed to watch the votes.

The punctuation in Pinckney's report was archaic and whimsical, but Federalist tactics were indeed "Novel" (if not fraudulent), industrious, and modern—especially against the background of old-style politics in the state.

Yet when the legislature met, Pinckney managed tactics which provided a match for the Federalists. On the evening of the third day, the Republican members caucused and named a committee to prepare a list of electors. Each prospective elector was then interviewed for assurances of loyalty to Jefferson and Burr as well. A few days later the chairman of the caucus learned that a group of Federalists planned to attend a second meeting of the Republicans that night, presumably to propose a bipartisan ticket of Jefferson and the Federalist Pinckney. A note was promptly posted on the door of the meeting room stating that no caucus would be held. Meanwhile Charles Pinckney was firming his lines by promises of patronage if Jefferson was elected—promises Jefferson later honored. The day after the Federalist infiltration strategy had been blocked, the legislature named the electors for Jefferson and Burr by a majority of nineteen votes.

The crucial uncertain states of North and South had each gone for Jefferson and Burr by the same legislative margin, and despite a standoff in Pennsylvania the balance had been turned.

4

The total result was a clear indication of party discipline, although the Presidential outcome failed to reflect the full extent of the Republican triumph. The scattering of votes for the Vice Presidential post which had occurred in 1796 was entirely eliminated. Every elector who voted for Jefferson in 1800 also voted for Burr, and every Federalist elector but one (in order to assure Adams a lead) gave his votes for both Adams and Pinckney. The final tally showed seventy-three electoral votes each for Jefferson and Burr, sixty-five for Adams, and sixty-four for Pinckney.

The contest had been conducted throughout as a full-scale combat of settled national parties. Clear nominations had been made by parties; the emphasis in the public view had been on national party perspectives, positions, and slates of tickets; intense electioneering had been undertaken by partisan leaders and cadre; followings had been mobilized and groups had been joined together by party. It had become respectable to undertake party electioneering and act in the style of the "firm party man," as Noble Cunningham has put it, whereas in 1790 either might have been perceived as slavish or unpatriotic. To be sure, the Presidential results showed continuing sectional biases. All of New England's electoral votes went to the Federalists, and all tallies from the South except four votes from North Carolina were Republican, while once again the vote in the Middle Atlantic states was divided. Yet the Republicans were gathering support even in New England, and were to reduce their sectional dependence and emerge as a truly national party. More and more, parties were coming to act as nationalizing forces.

*   *   *

Nonetheless, the results of 1800 were produced, in part, by certain crucial defections from the Federalist cause. They came among previously Federalist artisanmechanic groups and even among entrepreneurial groups in cities like New York and Philadelphia. More portentously, previously Federalist farmers in prosperous Northampton, Bucks, and Montgomery counties in Pennsylvania, where John Fries had raised his rebellion against the land tax, swung sharply to the Republicans. Similar shifts occurred in many country areas in New York and New Jersey and in certain parts of New England. The intransigent, ultracommercial, prowar policies of the High Federalists had finally alienated numerous well-to-do agrarian conservatives who had once found their natural place in the Federalist following but who saw no virtue in a war for trade or in land taxes to pay military bills. In 1800 Adams's moderate appeal helped hold Federalist lines to some extent in the Presidential combat, but the lines broke sharply in the Congressional contests. When Jefferson, as Adams's successor, proved that Republicans could be moderate too, the Federalists lost still more of their old "country" support.

Yet the election was more than just party mobilization or group realignment. It was also a broad appeal to public opinion and to the electorate, a presentation of remarkably clearly shaped alternatives for electoral choice, and—in response—a decision as to who should govern and in what direction. It not only marked the apogee of the first American competitive party system, but also a profound shift in political alignments in the young American nation. For a dozen years Hamiltonians and Federalists had ruled, and now Jeffersonians and Republicans were in time to take over in a democratic transfer of political power, and keep the power for years to come. In this sense the election of 1800 was what V. O. Key has called a "critical election" in that it altered older alignments in the electorate and produced new alignments which were to persist through succeeding elections. Moreover, although Presidential electors had been chosen by popular vote in only five states in 1800, sharp party contention in the elections generally had brought voting to approximately 38 per cent of white adult males, a level not generally surpassed for some years to come. Perhaps Jefferson exaggerated when he called the democratic overturn "as real a revolution in the principles of our government as that of 1776 was in form." Nonetheless, most Federalists would have agreed, if wryly and with regret. Few national elections have been as decisive.

When the Congressional results were known, the bent of the electoral decision and the shift in party allegiances were brought home even more sharply. In the contests for the new House, the Republicans won sixty-six of 106 seats for an unprecedented majority, and also won control of the Senate for the first time by eighteen seats out of thirty-two. In the House elections the Republicans won strong majorities of the seats in every state outside New England except Delaware, which returned its lone Federalist member, and North Carolina and South Carolina, where the two parties boke even. In New England, the Republicans took both of Rhode Island's seats and actually carried six of Massachusett's fourteen places. In keystone Pennsylvania, the Republican candidates for the House carried the total popular vote by almost three to one. The attrition of "wavering," "kinkish," or "half-party" hopefuls had continued, and Republicans could be sure of their control.

There was, however, a curious flaw in the Presidential results. The exact equality in electoral votes for Jefferson and Burr meant, under the Constitution as it then stood, that the ultimate selection would be made by the House of Representatives. Furthermore, the issue would go to the old, Federalist-controlled House, not the newly elected one, and constitutionally the House had power to make either Jefferson or Burr President. The Republi-

TABLE I. PRESIDENTIAL AND CONGRESSIONAL RESULTS, 1800

	Electoral Vote, 1800		Congressional Elections, House	
	Jefferson and Burr	Adams and Pinckney	Republican Members	Federalist Members
New Hampshire		6		4
Vermont		4	1	1
Massachusetts		16	6	8
Rhode Island[a]		4[b]	2	
Connecticut		9		7
New York	12		7	3
New Jersey		7	5	
Pennsylvania	8	7	10[c]	3[c]
Delaware		3		1
Maryland[a]	5	5	5	3
Virginia[a]	21		17	2
North Carolina[a]	8	4	5	5
South Carolina	8		3	3
Georgia	4		2	
Kentucky[a]	4		2	
Tennessee	3		1	
	73	65[b]	66	40

[a] *States naming Presidential electors by popular vote.*
[b] *One elector from Rhode Island for Adams and John Jay; thus, Pinckney's total was 64 to Adams's 65.*
[c] *Before the Seventh Congress met in December, 1801, Gallatin resigned to become Secretary of the Treasury and was replaced by a moderate Federalist.*
Adapted from Edward G. Stanwood, A History of the Presidency from 1788 to 1897 *(Boston: Houghton Mifflin Company, 1898), p. 63, and Manning J. Dauer,* The Adams Federalists *(Baltimore: Johns Hopkins University Press, 1953), pp. 256–258, 328–331.*

cans had to face another ordeal before they could enjoy their victory.

Even so, enthusiasm ran high in the moment of popular triumph. Looking out of his window in the village of Dedham, Massachusetts, on the last day of 1800, Dr. Nathaniel Ames waxed apocalyptic. "Here ends the 18th Century," he exclaimed in his diary. "The 19th begins with a fine clear morning wind at S.W.; and the political horizon affords as fine a prospect under Jefferson's administration, with . . . the irresistible propagation of the Rights of Man, the eradication of hierarchy, oppression, superstition and tyranny." It was a large order, but everyone knew that both of the Ameses were a bit extreme.

*   *   *

5

The last session of the Federalist Congress met in Washington, the new "Capital City" on the stately Potomac. In fact, it was less city than scraggly village; the streets were less broad avenues than dusty trails in drought and mired paths in rain; and the scattered houses were jerry-built clapboard compared to Philadelphia's neat brick homes. Yet the unfinished capitol building looked to the beckoning West, and the nation looked to the future.

The immediate question was deciding on a President. In the show of party discipline in 1800, Jefferson had assumed that one or two electors would omit to vote for Burr and thus establish the Presidential priority, but now the holdover House would have to decide. Although the Federalists had a majority, they controlled delegations from only six of the sixteen states by 1801, while the Republicans by that time could count on eight, and two were divided or uncertain. It would take nine states to elect, and each state would cast one vote, determined by the majority of its representatives voting. Thus the Federalists could block a selection but probably not make one.

Excited rumors chased one another about the village. One reported that some Federalists were planning to name the President of the Senate as a Presidential replacement by legislation, perhaps only until new elections could be held—and a few Federalists did toy with this idea. Rumor also had Hamilton conspiring with Burr to make him a captive President by Federalist votes. This time, however, Hamilton eschewed such schemes; he feared Jefferson less than Burr, whom he privately called "truly the Cataline of America." Never exactly chained to principle, Burr was nonetheless not ready to go so far either, and he assured Jefferson that he aspired only to the Vice Presidency. Another Washington report had the Pennsylvania Republicans raising an armed band of fifteen hundred to murder any substitute executive—but, in fact, McKean was planning to call the militia only if a failure to name Jefferson brought civil disturbances. Somehow the nation was to survive the rumors as well as the genuine strains of the deadlock.

What most Federalists actually agreed on was to support Burr in order to produce a painfully prolonged standoff. Some thought the prospect of no election would induce frightened Republicans to vote for Burr, whom the Federalists would then control as the Republican party broke up. Deadlock also fitted the strategy Hamilton proposed, which was to secure commitments from Jefferson, and only then to make him President. Some years later, Jefferson remembered calling on Adams and the exchange that ensued, hotly on Adams's side: "Sir, the event of the election is within your own power. You have

only to say you will do justice to the public creditors, maintain the navy, and not disturb those holding offices, and the government will instantly be put into your hands." To this, Jefferson recalled replying: "I will not come into the government by capitulation. I will not enter on it, but in perfect freedom to follow the dictates of my own judgment."

To Adams's list Hamilton would have added the rest of his fiscal system and the army, but Gallatin was convinced at the time that Jefferson had "prove[d] decisively that he made no concessions whatever." He had been given election on what amounted to a platform, and he was determined to honor the popular choice.

Everywhere party heads were apprehensive and watchful. Maintaining close intelligence in the House, Gallatin totted up tallies of the probable vote, warned Republican Congressmen who were approached by Federalists with Burr-bait against bargains that might shatter "our party," worked through Samuel Smith of Maryland to sound Burr himself, and warned the New Yorker against hoping for any trade on the Presidency. In Virginia's capital, Monroe proposed "a chain of expresses" to travel between Washington and Richmond day and night. Meanwhile, Gallatin kept regularly in touch with McKean, Beckley, and Dallas in Pennsylvania, and with Monroe and others elsewhere.

The voting in the House began early in February and continued until February 17, through thirty-five inconclusive roll calls in all. Throughout, the tallies showed every New England state for Burr except Vermont, whose two Representatives cancelled one another out; all of the Middle Atlantic states for Jefferson except Delaware (for Burr) and Maryland (evenly divided); and all of the Southern or Southwestern states for Jefferson except South Carolina, whose holdover delegation was Federalist (all for Burr). Over all, Jefferson had only eight states to six for Burr, with the evenly divided votes of Vermont and Maryland not counted. Tension ran high:

Nicholson of Maryland (Republican) was brought to the House on his sickbed through a snowstorm to keep his state's tally from going to Burr, and Craik of Maryland (Federalist) was warned by his wife that she would divorce him if he voted for Jefferson. In a last maneuver the Federalist bulk also held firm and so denied Jefferson the essential total of nine states.

Finally the break came. The sole member from little Delaware, James A. Bayard, thought he finally had assurances from Samuel Smith that Jefferson would accede to Hamilton's conditions, and announced his intention to switch—"You can well imagine," he wrote to Hamilton, "the clamor and vehement invective to which I was subjected." Actually, after several desperate Federalist caucuses, a complicated scheme was worked out whereby Bayard and the Federalist representatives from South Carolina, Vermont, and Maryland refrained from voting, thereby allowing Republican votes in the latter two states to add them to the eight Jefferson had held throughout. Thus, on February 17, Jefferson carried ten states to four for Burr, with Delaware and South Carolina now blank. The long agony was ended, and yet no Federalist had to sully his party conscience by casting a ballot for the Republican chief. Within a half-month, Jefferson would be President.

In the final ratification of the popular choice, the new nation had demonstrated its growing political stability. It had for years been making its way to full acceptance of rational or legal patterns of authority in a modernized polity. In the beginning, however, it had depended for legitimacy also on the fatherly charisma of Washington, who in 1801, if he was not, like the dying emperors of Rome, "about to become a god," was at least revered as the patron saint of the republic. The emerging national consensus had also at the outset been strained by deep suspicion of opposition, and later by the alien and sedition fury. Yet Washington himself had supported the rules of republican conduct, insisting in his Farewell Address that "time and habit" were "necessary to fix the true character of government," and refusing to let his prestige become a passport to perpetual power; and the fear of opposition which had prompted the "Spirit of 'Ninety-eight" had begun to recede. By 1801, the nation was moving away even from its partial dependence on Washington, and toward full acceptance of the rational legitimacy of the Constitution, and of elections, decision by majority rule, and the counting of votes. The Federalists tried maneuver and bluff against Jefferson's succession to office (even these within the rules), but in the end they abided by the result and simply surrendered power to their opponents. Angered as they were at the outcome, they made no attempt at military resistance and threw up no further obstructions.

It was the first such grand, democratic, peaceful transfer of power in modern politics. It was an example of a procedure which many old as well as many new nations have yet to experience, which many defeated factions or parties have found it difficult or intolerable to accept, but one which 1801 did much to "fix" on the American scene.

Dejected and ill, as was his party, Adams rushed through a series of last-hour appointments. To maintain what partisan influence he could in the judiciary, which Federalist legislation had just enlarged, he signed commissions desperately into the hours of darkness of his last day in office—until midnight, according to legend, but only until nine o'clock, as Jefferson heard it. Early next morning Adams left for New England and home, not staying for the inauguration of his old Revolutionary friend as President. As he rode away from the unkempt capital village, the era of supremacy for the Federalist party vanished with him.

C. The Struggle for Organizational Control

New York: The Struggle for Power

James Q. Wilson

Late in the 1950's, Tammany Hall was challenged by a vigorous group of insurgents who styled themselves "reformers." It was an attack stronger and more sustained than any the regular Democratic party in Manhattan had withstood since the days of the Seabury investigation and the subsequent regime of Mayor Fiorello H. La Guardia. The leader of the Democratic party in New York County, Carmine G. De Sapio, was the principal object of the attack, and the issue was soon described as a choice between the "boss" and the "people." Unlike reformers in the past, however, these men and women were not attacking the regular party organization from the outside in general elections, nor were they relying on legislative investigations, newspaper crusades, or grand jury indictments. Instead, these reformers were challenging the regular organization from within, contesting primary elections in which control of the district and county leadership was at stake. The reformers were bent, not on changing the system from the outside, but on capturing the system itself.

By mid-1960, this new strategy of reform was no more than ten years old. Already, substantial gains had been registered. Since 1953, when the first "reform" club gained power (in the Ninth Assembly District), eight Tammany district leaders had been defeated and replaced by reform leaders, together with their female co-leaders. The Executive Committee of the Democratic County Committee of New York County has sixty-six members (thirty-three male and thirty-three female district leaders) who have a total of sixteen votes distributed among them (one vote for each assembly district, often split into halves or thirds to reflect the division of districts among leaders). In 1960, the reformers numbered sixteen of the sixty-six members and cast four and one-sixteenth votes.[1] In 1961, the reformers, running together with Mayor Robert Wagner in the Democratic primary, increased the number of seats they held on the county executive committe from sixteen to thirty and the number of votes from four and one-sixteenth to six and five-sixths—only a fraction more than one vote shy of absolute control of the committee, and theoretically enough for them to be a powerful force in naming the new county leader. The man they had sworn to defeat, Carmine De Sapio, had lost in his own fight to remain district leader in Greenwich Village and was thus no longer even a member of the executive committee. In the general election, Wagner easily defeated his Republican and independent opposition and was returned to office closely identified with the reform movement.

The political clubs which sustained these reform leaders were scattered throughout Manhattan and had, in the summer of 1961, a total of about eight thousand members. In addition to these, other "insurgent" reform clubs in Manhattan had

[1] *Cf. Wallace S. Sayre and Herbert Kaufman,* Governing New York City *(New York: Russell Sage Foundation, 1960), pp. 122–141, for a description of the formal party machinery.*

about five hundred more members.[2] These people were an extraordinary new force in Manhattan politics, and, to a remarkable degree, they had a more or less common set of characteristics, beliefs, and goals. It should be understood, however, that despite their many similarities, the reformers had important differences as well. Indeed, many reform leaders refused to consider their colleagues "true" reformers. . . . There were profound disagreements among them and a great variation in political styles, constituencies, attitudes, and goals. At the time, however, these differences were overshadowed by the victories they had won.[3] The momentum of

reform carried them along despite their differences. As that momentum built up over the years, the reform movement became increasingly outspoken, militant, and uncompromising. The later additions to the ranks of the reformers were, in many cases, far more doctrinaire than earlier entrants. . . .

The history of New York City politics has been the history of insurgency. It is the normal, not the exceptional state of affairs in the Democratic party, at least during this century. At times insurgent leaders have been part of or allied with a "reform" movement dedicated to changes in the forms and personnel of government; usually, however, insurgents have been fighting intraparty contests for power with no thought of fundamentally altering the rules governing city politics. In 1930–32, Professor Peel found 683 Democratic political clubs of various kinds in New York City and of these 120 were "revolt" clubs contesting with the regular neighborhood, district, and county organizations for power.[4] Since the middle of the nineteenth century, there have been a few strong Tammany leaders in Manhattan, such as William Tweed, Richard Croker, and Charles F. Murphy, who have enjoyed long periods of relatively undisputed authority, but at no time has the Tammany leader been completely free of intraparty opposition, and usually that opposition has been intense. Between the eras of the strong bosses there has usually been a sequence of weaker leaders who retained power for only three, four, or five years. The constant ecological change in which

2 *Some working definitions are in order. I shall speak of three kinds of Democratic clubs. "Regular reform" clubs are those whose district leaders are members of the "Reform Democratic Leadership Caucus" which was formed in August, 1960 (see [The] New York Times, August 5, 1960). Most, but not all, of those leaders had previously been identified as reform politicians because of their association with the New York Committee for Democratic Voters and because they had abstained in the September, 1959, vote for county leader and had signed the "reform manifesto" of February, 1959. The definition of reform clubs is made purposely broad so as to include all who have any claim to the title. . . . "Insurgent reform" refers to those reform-oriented clubs which have not captured the leadership of their districts but which have challenged the existing Tammany leaders. Both regular reform and insurgent reform clubs are part of the reform movement; the former hold power in their districts, the latter are out of power. "Tammany" clubs are those which have not been associated with the reform movement and whose leaders voted for De Sapio in the September, 1959, election. Excluded from this definition of reform clubs are those in Harlem under the leadership of Representative Adam Clayton Powell, Jr. Although these Negro leaders also abstained in the September county leader election, neither they nor the reformers consider them to be "reform." The conflict between Tammany and Harlem has been intense and significant, but unrelated to the reform issue. For a classic description of the nature of New York political clubs, see Roy V. Peel, The Political Clubs of New York City (New York: G. P. Putnam's Sons, 1935). The reform clubs are consciously endeavoring to break with the pattern Professor Peel described. . . .*

3 *The Manhattan insurgent reform clubs affiliated with the New York Committee for Democratic Voters in October, 1961, were:*

3d South . . . .New Chelsea Club for Democrats
15th South . .Heights Reform Club

In addition, there were nineteen clubs, none of which had won power in district leadership fights, in the other boroughs: eight in Queens, five in the Bronx and six in Brooklyn. This study is based almost entirely on the Manhattan clubs; resources were insufficient to examine the other boroughs. In any case, the reform movement is Manhattan-led and Manhattan-financed and, for the most part, Manhattan-staffed. Over three-fourths of the 124 members of the General Committee of the New York Committee for Democratic Voters were, in the summer of 1961, from Manhattan.

4 *Peel, op. cit., pp. 273, 334.*

one ethnic or nationality group has replaced another in the neighborhood, combined with the keen ambitions of rival
leaders who were lured by the high stakes
of politics, has made the post of Democratic county leader of Manhattan a tempt-
ing but insecure prize.

Complicating city politics has been the
struggle among the leaders of the five
county[5] organizations for pre-eminence.
Tammany, confined to Manhattan, has always had as rivals the Democratic party
organizations in Brooklyn and the Bronx.
An old battle cry of the Brooklyn organization has been, "don't let Tammany
cross the bridge"—that is, keep Tammany's
influence limited to Manhattan and maintain the independence of the organizations in the other boroughs. When Tweed,
Croker, and Murphy were leaders of Tammany, it tended to dominate the Democratic party in the city as a whole; when
lesser men were in office, Tammany had
to contend with strong, and sometimes superior, rivals in the other counties. As Professors Sayre and Kaufman point out, it is
largely a myth that Tammany has "run
New York City" or even that it has controlled the Democratic mayors of the city.
Tammany has controlled the mayor for
only about fourteen of the more than sixty
years since 1897. This period has been exceeded both by those mayors who owed
their election to the Brooklyn organization
and by those "Fusion" or good-government
mayors who were elected by reform movements. Brooklyn had dominant access to
the mayor for almost seventeen years, Fusion mayors were in power for eighteen

years, and anti-Tammany insurgents from
Manhattan have been in office for almost
thirteen years.

From time to time the normal pattern
of intraparty competition within Tammany and between Tammany and the
other county organizations has been caught
up in a reform movement. Reformers, who
generally have entered politics from a nonpolitical background in civic associations,
have capitalized on an accumulation of
public grievances against party government and on cleavages within the party
itself to win office for a reform mayor, usually by creating a "Fusion" party which
would campaign in alliance with Republicans and dissident Democrats. Reform or
Fusion mayors have won office in New
York three times in the last sixty years.[6]

Seth Low was elected mayor in 1901
after a special investigating committee of
the Republican-controlled state legislature
had made public certain scandals in
city affairs and after Rev. Charles Park-
hurst had dramatized the evils of "boss
rule" under Richard Croker. John Pur-
roy Mitchell, the second reform mayor,
was elected in 1913 at the peak of the
Progressive movement in the city. Tammany leader Murphy and his mayor were
relatively clean and able, but the nationwide reform sentiment was too strong to
be resisted, particularly when Mitchell
had the backing of President Woodrow
Wilson. Progressivism had already won
several procedural victories in New York
City, including the introduction of the direct primary and the extension of the
merit system in the civil service. The third
and most colorful reform mayor was, of
course, Fiorello La Guardia, who served
from 1933 until 1945. He came into office
on the wave of public indignation created
by the Seabury investigations of the regime of Tammany Mayor James Walker
and with the support of President Franklin D. Roosevelt.

---

[5] *New York City is composed of five boroughs:
Manhattan, Brooklyn, Bronx, Queens, and Staten
Island. Each borough also serves as a county, as
follows: Manhattan (New York County), Brooklyn
(Kings County), Staten Island (Richmond County),
and Bronx and Queens Counties. The governmental functions of both boroughs and counties
are quite limited. Party organization, however, is
very much tied to the county, and as a result
competition among the county or borough leaders
within the city is rather vigorous. For a comprehensive treatment of New York City government
and politics, see Sayre and Kaufman, op. cit.* (ED.
NOTE.)

[6] *The following material on reform mayors is
taken from Theodore J. Lowi, At the Pleasure of
the Mayor (New York: Columbia University Press,
1963), Chap. 8. . . .*

All of these early reform movements in New York City had certain features in common. First, they were triggered by a series of public scandals and exposures, often revealed by investigating committees sent down from the Republican legislature to embarrass the Democratic opposition in the city. Second, the Republicans were never able to take advantage of these opportunities by themselves; in each case they needed the support of independent and dissident Democrats who could be brought together in a Fusion-Republican coalition. Third, the City Fusion party, which was always a principal force in the reform movement, never endured. Low and Mitchell only lasted for one term each. La Guardia was able to survive despite the collapse of the Fusion party because he became the nominee of the American Labor party, which had been created in 1936 to provide a means whereby anti-Tammany Democrats could support Roosevelt in Washington and La Guardia in New York without giving aid and comfort to other Tammany candidates locally. Fourth, the local reform movement usually had powerful outside assistance from national Democratic politicians whom Tammany had alienated. In 1912 Tammany had, as usual, backed a loser, Champ Clark, instead of the winner, Woodrow Wilson, and Wilson threw his support to Mitchell, the anti-Tammany candidate for mayor. In 1932, Tammany opposed the nomination of Roosevelt in the Democratic National Convention, and thus Roosevelt, who had the backing of Edward Flynn's Democratic organization in the Bronx, threw his Presidential support to La Guardia the following year. Finally, the Republicans have always been disappointed by their support of the Fusion candidate, for his victory never produced that access to power and flow of patronage which the professional Republican politicians felt was their due. As a result, they refused to renominate Mitchell in 1917, and they tried to dump La Guardia in 1937.

The men and women who were at-tracted to the City Fusion party and the reform movement entered politics to defeat an enemy, to "clean up" government, and to replace bad men with good. Few of them had a positive program to offer beyond the procedural reform of the political structure. Further, they disliked the practice of politics and rarely remained active beyond the initial victories. For these and other reasons, reform never endured. As Lowi suggests, there has been a "reform cycle" in New York City: "Each time its onset was widespread, energetic, irresistible. But once there was a partial redress of the Democratic imbalance of power, the components dispersed. There has been no club core; no central bureaucracy; thus, reform has not been institutionalized."[7]

The reform movement of the 1950's and 1960's began with a reasonably clear realization of these problems. The leaders resolved at the outset that the Democratic party could not be "reformed" from the outside because, as a party, it could outlast any external enemy. Instead, the party must be captured from within. Reform must acquire control of the district clubs, staff the party hierarchy, and capture the party bureaucracy. The only way to insure that bad men would be replaced with good in government posts was to make certain that bad men were replaced with good in party posts.

La Guardia in New York and Roosevelt in Washington absorbed during the 1930's the energies of the young liberals, reformers, and intellectuals who were interested in a politics of principle. The Second World War diverted attention from local politics. After the war, veterans returning to New York and even younger leaders just then coming of age politically looked about for a means of reasserting the reform principle in city politics. La Guardia and Roosevelt had left office in 1945; the party, nationally and locally, had returned

[7] Ibid., *pp. 214–215. A similar point is made in Roy V. Peel, "New Machines for Old," The Nation (September 5, 1953), 188–190.*

to the hands of the conventional party leaders.

But the party these men now led was far weaker than the party of the 1920's. Reform, although not permanent, had left its mark. The merit system had drastically curtailed patronage. The hostility of Wilson and Roosevelt had deprived Tammany of federal patronage when the Democrats were in power nationally. When the Democrats were in power in Albany under Governor Herbert Lehman, Tammany managed to alienate itself from the full political resources of that office; Thomas E. Dewey, the Republican governor, went out of his way to attack the Democrats generally and Tammany in particular. Only under Democratic Governor Averell Harriman, who appointed Tammany leader Carmine De Sapio as his Secretary of State, did the Tiger[8] enjoy the full blessings of state patronage. Otherwise, Tammany was compelled to sustain itself during the Depression and war years largely through its control of the courts.[9] So low was its estate in 1943 that it was compelled for financial reasons to sell its headquarters building to a labor union and retrench to more modest rented quarters on Madison Avenue.

Further, ecological changes in Manhattan had proceeded to the point that it was doubtful whether any political machine, even one endowed with ample resources, could continue to govern without a radical redistribution of power internally. The influx of Negroes and Puerto Ricans and the exodus of Irish and Italians made a party organization led by Irish and Italians vulnerable to attack by new groups seeking recognition. Normal population movements out to less congested boroughs, such as Queens, and to the outlying suburban counties had been accelerated by land clearance programs which replaced older, blighted structures with either vacant land, new medium- and high-rental

apartments, or hospitals and other institutions.[10]

Land clearance has driven thousands of older residents out of the lower end of the West Side and the middle East Side, while the attractions of home ownership and a suburban style of life have drawn more thousands of Irish and Italians out of Greenwich Village and the lower East Side. The spaces vacated have often been filled by young married couples and single people for whom the attractions of life in Manhattan are worth the congestion and cost of living. This has been particularly true on the West Side. Reform politics has, in great measure, become possible because the class structure of Manhattan has undergone a fundamental change. It is coming to consist of three groups: the wealthy, often older, residents of the East Side, where new luxury apartments are rising at an incredible rate; the lower-income Negroes and Puerto Ricans of Harlem and East Harlem; and the highly educated young professionals, often married but frequently with few or no children, for whom Manhattan has an irresistible fasci-

10 *Manhattan Congressional districts all suffered a population loss between 1950 and 1960:*

Congressional District	1960	1950	Per Cent Decline
16	301,574	336,441	−10.4
17	260,235	316,434	−17.8
18	269,368	317,594	−15.2
19	301,499	336,122	−10.3
20	279,475	336,203	−16.9

The Twentieth District is on the West Side, where reform clubs are particularly active in the Third, Fifth, and Seventh Assembly districts. Part of the decline can be explained by land clearance. Sixty-two slum clearance projects were undertaken in New York City between 1950 and 1960, displacing an estimated 124,266 persons. The bulk of these were in Manhattan. [Census data from U.S. Department of Commerce, Bureau of Census, "Population of Congressional Districts: April 1, 1960." Supplementary Report PC[S]-2 (April 11, 1961). Land clearance data from [The] New York Times (September 6, 1960)]. A redistricting plan proposed by Republican leaders and passed by the state legislature reduced Manhattan's Congressional districts from five to three as a result of these population losses. [The] New York Times (November 11, 1961).

8 *The "Tiger" is the symbol of Tammany Hall.*— ED. NOTE.

9 *Cf. Sayre and Kaufman, op. cit., p. 541n.*

nation. Gone or leaving is the conventional middle class, composed of people of moderate or skimpy means, average education, a high proportion of children, and no particular commitment to the presumed cultural and social advantages of life in Manhattan. These people have moved to Queens, the upper Bronx, New Jersey, and even farther.

Almost all politicians, reform and Tammany alike, agreed that this change lies at the root of reform politics. A reform leader on the West Side spoke of the Fifth and Seventh Assembly districts as about "the only area left in Manhattan in which young, professional people can find decent homes in rent-controlled apartments— people with education and little money, predominantly Jewish." Greenwich Village, which thirty years ago was perhaps one-half Italian,[11] today is about one-third Italian. The new group is composed in part of bearded bohemians and social nomads, but more and more it consists of young middle-class families who regard the atmosphere of Village life as culturally and intellectually stimulating. The characteristics of the new group are graphically summarized by one observer:

> A growing number of the real residents hold down regular jobs [most often in what is now called "Communications" . . .], have husbands, wives, babies, and grocery carts. The main distinction in material possessions between them and the older Italian residents is that they have hi-fi instead of television sets. In the afternoon, they buy the *Post* instead of the *Journal-American,* and are likely to wear toreador pants or slacks instead of skirts and dresses when they wheel their babies into Washington Square Park. Many of them spent the protest years of their youth here, and when they closed that chapter with marriage, they decided to stay on.[12]

The areas of Manhattan vary considerably in the kinds of people attracted to them. Even though the older ethnic neigh-

borhoods were being broken down, the young people who were moving into the city tended to sort themselves out on the basis of income, occupation, and family status. This meant that the constituencies of reform clubs were not identical. Members of the VID [Village Independent Democrats] in Greenwich Village, for example, were younger than reform members in the Riverside or Lexington areas; fewer of them had children; and a greater proportion were in communications or the arts. The West Side, on the other hand, had more teachers and doctors, more married persons and fewer divorced individuals.

All of these factors contributed to the instability of the Manhattan Democratic party which was manifest throughout the postwar period. After La Guardia, each of the three mayors elected came, sooner or later, to a break with the Tammany leadership, but none except Wagner was able to serve as the rallying point for a new reform effort. William O'Dwyer became mayor in 1945 after serving as a gangbusting district attorney in Brooklyn. Soon he found himself in difficulties, in part arising from his own inability to master the role of mayor, in part because Tammany refused to accept his nominees for offices, and in part because of certain scandals which were uncovered. After less than five years in office, he resigned to become Ambassador to Mexico. Vincent Impelliteri, his successor, broke with Tammany and, in the special election of 1950, formed his own "Experience party" and defeated his Tammany opponent for the mayoralty. Tammany returned to power by backing Robert Wagner, son of the famous former Democratic Senator, in the mayoralty contest of 1953. Wagner was re-elected in 1957 by an overwhelming majority. However, Tammany's brief period of grace in the City Hall was cut short when Wagner, under heavy pressure from reform forces in the city, publicly broke with Tammany leader De Sapio in early 1961.

De Sapio had been chosen county leader in Tammany Hall in 1949. Democratic

---

11 *Cf. Caroline F. Ware,* Greenwich Village, 1920–1930 *(Boston: Houghton Mifflin Company, 1935).*
12 *Dan Wakefield, "Greenwich Village Challenges Tammany,"* Commentary *(October, 1959), 308.*

party leadership in Manhattan had been in a perpetual state of flux since Charles F. Murphy had left that post in 1924, and it was De Sapio's hope that he could rebuild the party's strength and consolidate his own position in part by making overtures to liberal and reform sentiment in the city rather than by following the policy of antagonizing them with deliberate rebukes. But the changing character of the electorate in Manhattan, the shortage of political resources, and the disfavor and disunity into which Tammany had fallen made this task exceptionally difficult. For a brief period, De Sapio scored some limited successes. During his early years in power, he was hailed in feature articles in national magazines as a "new-style boss," an "enlightened political leader" with an interest in civic reforms and improving the reputation of the party.[13]

Throughout this period, when De Sapio was establishing himself in Tammany and Tammany in turn was struggling with O'Dwyer and Impelliteri, young insurgents were active in various parts of the county on a limited scale. The returning veterans and the new reformers entered such organizations as the New York Young Democrats, the Americans for Democratic Action, the Fair Deal Democrats, and the Liberal party. Each of these groups became a focus for insurgent, anti-Tammany activity. Before 1956, however, these reformers were not a major force in the borough; that had to wait on the emergence of a set of prestigious state and national leaders who could extend the appeal of the reform cause.

The first two postwar reform efforts by the young liberals were the formation in 1949 of the Lexington Democratic Club on Manhattan's fashionable East Side to contest for the Democratic district leadership in the two halves of the Ninth Assembly District and the creation in the same year of the Fair Deal Democrats on the West Side to support Franklin D. Roose-

velt, Jr., in his contest for a Congressional seat. These two organizations not only were formed on opposite sides of the city, but they represented opposite philosophies of how best to attack the established organization. The Lexington Club leaders refused to join the Fair Deal Democrats. The former group took the position that it was first necessary to capture the assembly district leadership and become an integral part of the party before contesting for elective offices and that in so doing, one should not become closely identified with any public officials who were not firmly committed to reform. The Fair Deal Democrats, on the other hand, were prepared to wage a general election contest for various elective posts before capturing the local leadership and in the process were willing to form an alliance with such officials as Mayor O'Dwyer. This, of course, was the classic issue of reform: whether to fight the party or fight its candidates. Within a very few years the former approach became the dominant one in the reform clubs, and the Fair Deal Democrats, after some reversals at the polls, disintegrated.[14]

During this period De Sapio was able to stabilize his position as county leader. Although he had been defeated when Impelliteri won over Tammany's mayoral candidate and young Roosevelt won over its Congressional candidate, De Sapio now entered a period of successes. After the May, 1949, Congressional election, the rebel Tammany district leader who backed Roosevelt was removed. In the 1951 elec-

---

13 Cf. Robert Heilbroner, "Carmine De Sapio: The Smile on the Face of the Tiger," Harper's (July, 1954), 23–33.

14 *The Fair Deal Democrats were active in the victorious campaign of F. D. Roosevelt, Jr., in the special election of May, 1949, for the Congressional seat on the West Side vacated by the death of Representative Sol Bloom. The FDD also supported O'Dwyer for Mayor in 1949, after he had broken with the dominant De Sapio faction in Tammany Hall, and backed Robert Wagner for Manhattan Borough president in 1950. But it lost in local races for assemblyman and city councilman in 1949 and 1950. Roosevelt also had powerful support from the ADA, the Young Democrats, the CIO, a rebel Tammany leader, and the Liberal party. See Arthur D. Morse, "ADA's New New Deal," Survey (July, 1949), 351–355. . . .*

tions for district leaders, nineteen of the forty regular leaders faced challengers, but the regulars under De Sapio scored decisive victories in most of the contests. De Sapio followed this victory with a move which, by reducing the total number of Democratic district leaders in Manhattan from forty-one to thirty-five, eliminated three district leaders who had been close to De Sapio's enemy, Mayor Impelliteri. In January, 1952, he announced that Tammany would adopt certain reforms in procedure, including the direct election of district leaders and permanent personal registration. At the same time, the forces of Mayor Impelliteri abandoned their efforts to oust De Sapio. The following year, the Tammany candidate for mayor, Robert Wagner, won, and in 1954 Averell Harriman became governor of New York with Tammany support. De Sapio joined the governor's cabinet as chief patronage dispenser. Although by this time the reform candidates of the Lexington Club had won the district leadership in the Ninth Assembly District, reform had generally made little progress and De Sapio seemed firmly in control in the city and in Albany. In 1954 he completed his rise to dominance in the party by becoming the Democratic National Committeeman from New York.

Although De Sapio continued to encounter opposition to Tammany (in August, 1953, twelve of the thirty-five district leaders backed Impelliteri for mayor), by and large he was successful in dealing both with conventional party insurgents and with reform-minded club leaders. After Impelliteri's defeat by Wagner in 1953, nine Impelliteri leaders were dropped from Tammany. In the 1955 elections for district leader in Manhattan there were nine contests, but only one of these was a battle between a "reformer" and a "regular"; the rest were normal contests between ins and outs, and, of these, men backed by De Sapio won in almost every case.[15]

But beginning in 1956, the tide turned. De Sapio came under concerted attack by reformers in several parts of the borough, and by 1959 substantial reform victories had been won. The crucial events which seemed to have triggered this change were the candidacy of Adlai Stevenson for President in 1956 and the controversial state Democratic party convention at Buffalo in 1958. The former provided a national figure with whom local club leaders could identify; the latter created an issue and brought into the reform camp well-known Democratic leaders, principally former Senator Herbert H. Lehman.

By 1959, De Sapio's gains had been all but wiped out, his credit as an "enlightened" leader had been seriously impaired, and his brief run of electoral victories had been cut short. After controlling the primaries in 1951, 1953, and 1955 and electing Wagner in 1953 and Harriman in 1954, De Sapio began to suffer reversals. He failed in an attempt to "purge" Negro Representative Adam Clayton Powell, Jr., in the 1958 Congressional primary.[16] Harriman was defeated by Nelson Rockefeller for governor in 1958 and De Sapio's Senatorial candidate, Frank Hogan, lost badly to the Republican Kenneth B. Keating in what was elsewhere a strong Democratic year. The Buffalo convention which had selected Hogan left bitter feelings in the party and antagonized some of its "elder statesmen," notably Lehman and Mrs. Eleanor Roosevelt. In the 1957 primary, De Sapio himself was challenged in his own district by an insurgent reform candidate who made a strong showing and a Tammany leader was defeated by another reformer on the West Side. In the 1959 primaries, there were about twenty contests for district leader, seven of which were won by reformers and three by Negro

15 *The "reform" contest was in the Eighth District South, where Edward Costikyan defeated a regular, Connolly, who had been thrown off the ballot and was conducting a write-in campaign.* New York Times, *September 15, 1955.*
16 *On the Powell incident, see David Hapgood,* The Purge That Failed: Tammany v. Powell, *Case Studies in Practical Politics (New York: Holt Rinehart & Winston, Inc., 1959).*

(but not reform) insurgents led by Representative Powell. Only half the contests were won by regular Tammany leaders. De Sapio himself only barely defeated a reformer in his Greenwich Village district.

In 1960, De Sapio reluctantly supported John F. Kennedy for the Democratic Presidential nomination, probably as the only alternative to losing control over the delegation altogether. As it was, De Sapio's ally, State Chairman Michael Prendergast, was forced to give up his seat on the delegation to the anti-De Sapio leader, Herbert Lehman. Kennedy owed little to De Sapio for the support he received from New York. At the same time, the reformers sought to put Stevenson supporters on the delegation. New York Democrats, regular and reform, were in a poor position to rely on Presidential support in settling their intraparty contest.

The 1960 campaign was conducted under a temporary and imperfect truce, and scarcely had Kennedy won when De Sapio and the reformers exchanged heated attacks, accusing each other of bad faith. De Sapio promised a "purge" of all reform district leaders. Mayor Wagner, after much urging by reform leaders, publicly broke with De Sapio and urged his removal as county leader. The immediate cause of the rupture was the conflict between Wagner and De Sapio over who should be appointed by the city council to replace Manhattan Borough President Hulan E. Jack. Jack had been convicted and sentenced for improperly accepting funds while in office. The mayor's candidate, a Negro who was an independent Democrat (Edward Dudley, a justice in the Domestic Relations Court), was appointed over another Negro who had De Sapio's support.[17] The break with the Mayor cut De Sapio off from the patronage resources under the Mayor's control and the selection of a new borough president who

was obligated to the Mayor rather than the Tammany leader threatened De Sapio's access to patronage in that office.[18] Throughout this period, the new Democratic administration in Washington acted as if it were seeking a change in party leadership in the state and city by refusing to channel the federal patronage through either State Chairman Michael Prendergast or National Committeeman De Sapio.

Thus, by 1961 many of the classic elements of a reform movement were present in Manhattan politics. There had been a series of individually minor but cumulatively significant scandals in the city administration involving policemen, city inspectors from various departments, and the Manhattan Borough president. A Republican state legislature had sent an investigating committee to New York City and its findings, although not shocking, were sufficient to lead many prominent figures to call for a new city charter. Tammany had partially isolated itself from its allies. The Mayor had broken with it,[19] it had lost control of the borough president's office, and a Democratic President in Washington seemed to be withholding important federal patronage as a means of forcing a change in local party leadership (despite the fact that Tammany in 1960 had, untypically, backed a winner rather than a loser at the Democratic National

17 *Dudley defeated Assemblyman Lloyd E. Dickens by a vote of four to two. The vacancy was filled by the six city councilmen from Manhattan (five Democrats and one Republican). [The] New York Times (February 1, 1961).*

18 *Three Tammany district leaders had jobs in the borough president's office and there were "several hundred" low-paying posts as street workers in addition. [The] New York Times (February 1, 1961).*

19 *The mayor's break with De Sapio had one immediate effect. A bill in the 1961 state legislature, which had joint Democratic and Republican backing, would have created thirty-seven new judgeships in New York City if it had passed. These posts would have added greatly to De Sapio's patronage resources and thus strengthened his hand in dealing with intraparty strife. The bill failed of passage because Mayor Wagner refused to write a letter to the governor certifying that the city needed the posts. Had the letter been written, the bill almost certainly would have passed. It was widely believed that Wagner refused as a means of preventing De Sapio from getting control of these patronage resources. [The] New York Times (March 27, 1961).*

Convention). Weakened in its own borough, powerful rivals in other boroughs with strong organizations moved to extend their influence. Tammany district leaders, most of whom thought De Sapio able, were disturbed that his leadership had led to electoral defeat at the state level and that his name had become a symbol of bossism at the local level.

The opportunities for reformers could not have been better, but they proved difficult to seize. The 1961 mayoralty election was viewed as the decisive event for the reformers. Sworn to defeat De Sapio, they now had to choose whether to field a candidate of their own in the primary, endorse Wagner if he were willing to run, or do nothing. To do nothing, it was felt, would be fatal; the movement would disintegrate without a candidate. To accept a De Sapio candidate was impossible. But Wagner, until February, 1961, had *been* a De Sapio candidate who had personally endorsed not only De Sapio but every other regular organization county leader in the city. Several reform clubs passed resolutions declaring they would not support Wagner if he chose to run.[20] Efforts to settle on a reform candidate for mayor, however, were unsuccessful. Finally, at the very last minute, on June 22, Wagner announced he would run with a hand-picked slate of candidates for controller and president of the city council. Wagner knew De Sapio would not accept him; there is some doubt about whether he hoped for regular organization endorsement from the other four county leaders.[21]

But De Sapio had no trouble convincing the others that to support Wagner was to support reformers who had committed themselves to eliminating "bossism"—and not just in Manhattan.[22] In any case, the regular leaders announced their support for a rival slate headed by State Controller Arthur Levitt, the reformers endorsed Wagner, and the fight was on. After a bitter contest, in which he made full use of the epithet "boss," Wagner won resoundingly, defeating Levitt three to two and sweeping into party office as district leaders all the reformers who had run on his "line"—i.e., those who, by endorsing him and in turn being endorsed by him, appeared on the same line on the voting machine, enabling the voter, by pulling a straight-ticket lever, to vote for reformers as well as Wagner. The reformers elected fourteen new district leaders and re-elected sixteen and won the Democratic primary for four city council candidates in Manhattan and Brooklyn. Since only Manhattan district leadership seats are contested in the odd-numbered years, the regular organization in the other four boroughs remained intact. The victory in Manhattan, however, was substantial, but fraught with one ominous portent: the enemy De Sapio, who for years had served as a rallying cry and hence as a source of reform unity, was gone. He had lost his own district leadership to a reformer.

It must be understood that the reform movement *preceded* the uncovering of the scandals, the Buffalo convention, the inauguration of a Democratic President, the mayor's break with De Sapio, and the state investigations. The Manhattan reformers acquired, by these events, a set of issues with which to wage the fight, but their disaffection from Tammany and De Sapio was prior to and independent of these issues. For some, that disaffection sprang from nothing more than the personal ambition which drives young politicians to seek ways of rising in politics more quickly than the party ordinarily permits. But for others this disaffection was a revolt against

---

20 *Such sentiments were expressed by the Village Independent Democrats, the Riverside Democrats, the New Chelsea Club for Democrats, and others.*
21 *As late as June 19, three days before his announcement, Wagner was reported as conferring with Bronx Democratic leader Charles Buckley over endorsements. The day before, when his decision was still but a rumor, the belief was attributed to Wagner by newspapers that his ticket could be acceptable to both the reformers and the non-De Sapio regulars. [The] New York Times (June 18 and 19, 1961).*

22 *It is rumored De Sapio played a tape recording of a television program to the other leaders on which a reform leader had said that Buckley and others were "next" on the reform list.*

the very nature of politics and political organization. In Manhattan, an assault on Tammany became feasible because of the ecological changes, intraparty strife, organizational weakness, and tactical errors which afflicted the regular party. The antipathy to Tammany had always existed, and it was brought to a focus, not by De Sapio's actions, but by the entry of large numbers of new party activists anxious to support Adlai Stevenson for President.

D. The Dynamics of Controversy

The Escalation of Community Conflict

James S. Coleman

The most striking fact about the development and growth of community controversies is the similarity they exhibit despite diverse underlying sources and different kinds of precipitating incidents. Once the controversies have begun, they resemble each other remarkably. Were it not for these similarities, Machiavelli could never have written his guide to warfare, and none of the other numerous works on conflict, dispute, and controversy would have been possible.[1] It is the peculiarity of social controversy that it sets in motion its own dynamics; these tend to carry it forward in a path which bears little relation to its beginnings. An examination of these dynamics will occupy the attention of this [analysis].

One caution is necessary: we do not mean to suggest that nothing can be done about community controversy once it begins. To the contrary, the dynamics of controversy *can* be interrupted and diverted—either by conscious action or by existing conditions in the community. As a result, although the same dynamic tendencies of controversy are found in every case, the actual development in particular cases may differ widely. In the discussion below, the unrestrained dynamic tendencies will be discussed. . . .

Changes in Issues

The issues which provide the initial basis of response in a controversy undergo great transformations as the controversy develops. Three fundamental transformations appear to take place.

Specific to General.   First, *specific* issues give way to *general* ones. In Scarsdale, the school's critics began by attacking books in the school library; soon they focused on the whole educational philosophy. In Mason City, Iowa, where a city manager plan was abandoned, the campaign against the plan started with a letter to the newspaper from a local carpenter complaining that the creek overflowed into his home. This soon snowballed, gathering other specific complaints, and then gave way to the general charge that the council and manager were dominated by local business interests and had no concern for the workingman.

Most of the controversies examined

[1] *The one man who emphasized particularly the possibility of abstracting principles of conflict from particular situations of conflict is Georg Simmel, who wrote several essays on the subject. Unfortunately, Simmel never got around to writing a comprehensive theory of conflict, though he did set down a number of insights into particular aspects. See Simmel (1955) [all such references are given in full at the end of this article.—*ED. NOTE.] *Lewis Coser has brought together the best of Simmel's insights and elaborated on them (Coser, 1956).*

show a similar pattern. [Even those that do not are helpful, for they suggest just why the pattern *does* exist in so many cases. Political controversies, for example, exhibit the pattern much less than do disputes based primarily on differing values or economic interests. The Athens, Tennessee, political fight began with the same basic issue it ended with—political control of the community (Key, 1950). Other political struggles in which there is little popular involvement show a similar restriction to the initial issue.]

It seems that movement from specific to general issues occurs whenever there are deep cleavages of values or interests in the community which require a spark to set them off—usually a specific incident representing only a small part of the underlying difference. In contrast, those disputes which appear not to be generated by deep cleavages running through the community as a whole, but are rather power struggles within the community, do not show the shift from specific to general. To be sure, they may come to involve the entire community, but no profound fundamental difference comes out.

This first shift in the nature of the issues, then, uncovers the fundamental differences which set the stage for a precipitating incident in the first place.

New and Different Issues. Another frequent change in the issues of the dispute is the emergence of quite *new and different* issues, unrelated to the original ones. In the Pasadena school controversy, the initial issue was an increased school budget and a consequent increased tax rate. This soon became only one issue of many; ideological issues concerning "progressive education," and other issues, specific as well as general, arose. In another case, a controversy which began as a personal power struggle between a school superintendent and a principal shifted to a conflict involving general educational principles when the community as a whole entered in (Warner *et al.*, 1949, pp. 201–204). A study of the adoption of the city manager plan in fifty cities (Stone, Price, and Stone, 1940, pp. 34–38) shows that in one group of cities, designated by the authors "machine-ridden," the controversy grew to include ethnic, religious, political, and ideological differences. Political campaigns generally, in fact, show this tendency: issues multiply rapidly as the campaign increases in intensity.

There are two different sources for this diversification of issues. One is in a sense "involuntary"; issues which could not have been raised before the controversy spring suddenly to the fore as relationships between groups and individuals change. We see how this operates in an argument between two people, e.g., in the common phrases used to introduce new issues: "I hesitated to mention this before, but now . . . ." or, "While I'm at it, I might as well say this too. . . ." As long as functioning relations exist between individuals or groups, there are strong inhibitions upon introducing any issue which might impair the functioning. In a sense the stable relation suppresses topics which might upset it. But once the stability of the relation *is* upset, the suppressed topics can come to the surface uninhibitedly. We suggest that exactly the same mechanisms are at work in the community as a whole; networks of relations, however complex, act in the same fashion.

But in many other cases, illustrated best by political disputes, the diversification of issues is more a purposive move on the part of the antagonists, and serves quite a different function: to solidify opinion and bring in new participants by providing new bases of response. Again, this is evident in the two-person argument: each antagonist brings to bear all the *different* arguments he can to rationalize his position to himself and to convince his opponent. Just the same thing occurs in community conflict: each side attempts to increase solidarity and win new adherents from the still uncommitted neutrals by introducing as many diverse issues as will benefit its cause. Both these functions—increasing solidarity among present members and gaining new members—are vital;

the first aids in the important task of "girding for action" by disposing of all doubts and hesitancies; the second gains allies, always an important aim in community conflict.

The issues introduced must be very special ones with little potential for disrupting the group that initiates them. They are almost always "one-sided," in the sense that they provide a basis for response only in one direction, and they gain their value by monopolizing the attention of community members. In controversies where a challenge is offered to an incumbent administration, the issue of "maladministration" is, typically, a one-sided issue; the administration can only offer defense and hope that attention soon shifts elsewhere. In school controversies, the issue of Communist subversion in the schools is one-sided; as long as it occupies the attention of the community, it is to the advantage of school critics. In contrast, the issue "progressive education *vs.* traditional education" offers no differential advantage to either side (unless, of course, progressive education can be identified by its opponents as "communistic") until one group can prove to the majority of the community that one approach is better from all points of view. . . .

Disagreement to Antagonism. A third change in the nature of issues as a controversy develops is the shift from *disagreement* to *antagonism.* A dispute which began dispassionately, in a disagreement over issues, is characterized suddenly by personal slander, by rumor, by the focusing of direct hostility. This is one of the most important aspects in the self-generation of conflict. Once set in motion, hostility can sustain conflict unaided by disagreement about particular issues. The original issues may be settled, yet the controversy continues unabated. The antagonistic relationship has become direct: it no longer draws sustenance from an outside element—an issue. As in an argument between friends, a discussion which begins with *disagreement* on a point in question

often ends with each *disliking* the other.[2] The dynamics which account for the shift from disagreement to antagonism are two: "involuntary" and deliberate. Simmel explains the involuntary process by saying that it is "expedient" and "appropriate" to hate one's opponent just as it is "appropriate" to like someone who agrees with you (1955, p. 34). But perhaps there is a stronger explanation: we associate with every person we know certain beliefs, interests, traits, attributes, etc. So long as we disagree with only one or a few of his beliefs, we are "divided" in our feelings toward him. He is not wholly black or white in our eyes. But when we quarrel, the process of argument itself generates new issues; we disagree with more and more of our opponent's beliefs. Since these beliefs constitute *him* in our eyes, rather than isolated aspects of him, his image grows blacker. Our hostility is directed toward him personally. Thus the two processes—the first leading from a single issue to new and different ones, and the second leading from disagreement to direct antagonism—fit together perfectly and help carry the controversy along its course.[3] Once direct antagonism is felt toward an opponent, one is led to make public attacks on him.

Perhaps it would be fruitful to set down a little more precisely the "involun-

---

[2] *Conversely, a relationship which begins with two people agreeing in tastes and interests often ends with both liking one another. For a discussion of the process through which this occurs, see Merton and Lazarsfeld (1954).*

Georg Simmel notes the formal similarities between relations of positive and negative attachments, contrasting these with the absence of relationship. He suggests that the psychological processes generating antagonism are just as fundamental as those generating liking. Simmel also notes the difference between a negative relationship based on disagreement over an outside object, and one which needs no such object, but is directly antagonistic. See Simmel (1955, pp. 34, 36, et passim), and Coser (1956).

[3] *It should be emphasized that these suggestions for processes are highly tentative; systematic research into the psychological dynamics involved in these changing relations would contribute greatly to our knowledge about the development of controversy.*

tary" processes which we suggest operate to shift issues from one disagreement to a multitude, ultimately to antagonism. In a diagram it might look something like this:

> (1) Initial single issue.
> (2) Disrupts equilibrium of community relations.
> (3) Allows previously suppressed issues against opponent to appear.
> (4) More and more of opponent's beliefs enter into the disagreement.
> (5) The opponent appears totally bad.
> (6) Charges against opponent as a person.
> (7) Dispute becomes independent of initial disagreement.

Men have a strong need . . . for *consistency*. If I disagree violently with someone, then it becomes psychologically more comfortable to see him as totally black rather than gray.[4] This drive for consistency may provide the fuel for the generalization processes in Steps 3 and 4 above.

Apart from these "involuntary" or "natural" processes, the use of personal charges by the antagonists is a common device to bypass disagreement and go directly to antagonism. Sometimes consciously, often unconsciously, the opposing nuclei attempt to reach new people through this means, drawing more and more of the community to their side by creating personal hostility to the opponent.[5] In political disputes the degenera-

tion to personal charges is particularly frequent. V. O. Key notes that in the South, state political campaigns are often marked by candidates' personal attacks on each other. He suggests that such attacks grow in the absence of "real" issues (1950, pp. 194–200). This seems reasonable since the use of personal attacks may be an attempt to incite antagonism in cases where there is not enough disagreement for the natural processes of conflict to operate. In other words, the attacks constitute an attempt to stimulate controversy artificially—a "short-cut"—by bypassing a stage in the process which might otherwise let the conflict falter. Such actions would seem to occur only when community leaders need to gain the support of an otherwise apathetic community which has no real issues dividing it.

In another group of controversies, focused around certain value differences, the shift to personal attacks is sometimes immediate, and seems to be a result of real disagreement and incipient antagonism. School controversies often begin with personal charges against teachers or principals of moral impropriety, or, more frequently in recent days, subversion. Why is it that personal attacks in these instances succeed in creating immediate hostility within the community, while other kinds of personal attacks are viewed with disfavor by the community, that is, until the late, intense stages of controversy, when all inhibiting norms and constraints are forgotten? The reason may be this: When a personal accusation refers to behavior viewed as extremely illegitimate by community members it outweighs the norm against personal attacks. Presumably the community

---

[4] *One might speculate that this tendency would be stronger among those who tend to personalize easily; they move more quickly perhaps from specific disagreement to hostility toward the opponent as a whole. Feuds among hill people (who are highly "person-oriented"), for example, seem to bear this out. Thus the course of controversy may vary greatly in two communities, simply as a result of differences in "person-orientation."*

[5] *Whether or not persons previously neutral can be brought into the controversy seems to depend greatly upon the time at which they are confronted with the alternative. If the antagonists are too involved too early they are viewed with puzzlement and distaste and detachment by neutrals. The situation is much the same as confronts a man arriving sober in the middle of a drunken party: he cannot join in because these people are "too far gone" for him to experience the events of the party as they do. The similarity between an orgy of community controversy and a drunken orgy is more than superficial in this and other respects. People collectively "forget themselves" in ways they may be ashamed of later. One of the major questions of community conflict concerns*

the processes through which this "forgetting" occurs.

members put themselves in the place of the attacker and say, in effect, "If I knew these things to be true, would I feel right about speaking out publicly?" When the charges concern sexual immorality or political subversion, many persons can answer "yes" to such a question;[6] thus they feel unconcerned about making the kind of attacks that they would ordinarily never allow except in the heat of dispute.[7] These attacks, in turn, quickly create the heat that might be otherwise slow in coming.

Changes in content and character of issues constitute only one kind of change going on in the development of a controversy; at the same time, the whole structure of organizations and associations in the community is undergoing change as well. The nature of these changes is examined below.

Changes in the Social Organization of the Community

Polarization of Social Relations.   As controversy develops, associations flourish *within* each group, but wither *between* persons on opposing sides. People break off long-standing relationships, stop speaking to former friends who have been drawn to the opposition, but proliferate their associations with fellow-partisans. Again, this is part of the process of stripping for action: getting rid of all social encumbrances which impede the action necessary to win the conflict. Polarization is perhaps

---

[6] *It is a matter of the relative strengths of different values; some, like those against immorality and subversion, override the values against personal slander. If we knew the relative strength of certain social values among various segments of the population, we would be far better able to judge the course of controversy ranged around a certain issue. But we lack even methods for measurement.*
[7] *In contrast to "putting oneself in the place of the attacker," those who hold civil liberties to be of great importance evidently put themselves in the place of the attacked, and ask themselves how it would feel to be unjustly charged in this fashion. It appears that the* variations in relative values *between these two groups cause them to identify with opposing parties in a case of such charges. Thus they are immediately brought in on one side or the other in such a dispute.*

less pronounced in short-term conflicts, and in those in which the issues cut across existing organizational ties and informal relations. But in all conflicts, it tends to alter the social geography of the community to separate it into two clusters, breaking apart along the line of least attachment.

The Formation of Partisan Organizations.   In many types of community conflict, there are no existing organizations to form the nuclei of the two sides. But as the controversy develops, organizations form. In a recent controversy in Cincinnati over the left-wing political history of the city planning director (Hessler, 1953), supporters of the director and of the councilman who hired him formed a "Committee of 150 for Political Morality." This Committee used considerable sophistication in the selection of a name and in their whole campaign. Rather than remain on the defensive, and let the opposition blanket the community with charges of subversion, this Committee invoked an equally strong value—of morality in politics—and took the offensive against the use of personal attack by their opponents. This technique constitutes a way in which controversy can be held on a relatively high plane: by invoking community norms against smears, using these very norms as an issue of the controversy. If the norm is strong, it may keep the controversy "within bounds."

In general, as a dispute intensifies the partisans form *ad hoc* groups which have numerous functions while the controversy lasts: they serve as communication centers, as communication becomes more and more important within each side and attenuates between groups; they serve as centers for planning and organizing partisan meetings and other activities; and especially they can meet quickly—in a situation where speed is of utmost importance—any threat or challenge posed by the opposition.

The most common variation upon this theme is the union; in industrial disputes, the union is a defense organization *already* in existence; in a real controversy, it takes on all the aspects of the usual partisan organizations: secrecy, spirited meetings, pamphleteering, fund-raising.[8]

The Emergence of New Leaders. As partisan organizations are formed and a real nucleus develops around each of the opposing centers, new leaders tend to take over the dispute; often they are men who have not been community leaders in the past, men who face none of the constraints of maintaining a previous community position, and feel none of the cross pressures felt by members of community organizations. In addition, these leaders rarely have real identification with the community. In the literature they often emerge as marginal men who have never held a position of leadership before. A study of the fight against city manager plans pictures the leaders of the opposition as men personally frustrated and maladjusted (Stene and Floro, 1953, pp. 21–39). The current desegregation fights have produced numerous such leaders, often young, one a former convict, usually from the outside. (*Life,* 1954; *Southern School News,* 1956.)

The new leaders, at any rate, are seldom moderates; the situation itself calls for extremists. And such men have not been conditioned, through experience in handling past community problems, to the prevailing norms concerning tactics of dispute.

One countertendency appears in the development of these organizations and the emergence of their leaders. In certain conflicts, e.g., in Cincinnati, one side will be composed primarily of community leaders, men of prestige and responsibility in the community. Though such groups carry on the functions of a partisan organization, they act not to lower the level of controversy, but to *maintain* or raise it. As did the Committee of 150 (and the ADA in Norwalk, Connecticut, and other groups in other controversies), they attempt to invoke the community's norms against personal attacks and unrestrained conflict. Sometimes (as in Cincinnati) they are successful, sometimes not.

In the face of all the pressures toward increasing intensity and freedom from normal constraint this last development is puzzling. The source of the reversal seems to be this: in certain controversies (particularly those having to do with the accusation of subversion), one side derives much of its strength from personal attacks and derogation, that is, from techniques which, were they not legitimated by patriotism or sex codes or similar strong values, would be outlawed by the community. Thus, to the degree that such methods are permitted, the attackers gain; and to the degree that community norms are upheld against these methods, the advantage is to the attacked. The more the attacked side can invoke the norms defining legitimate controversy, the more likely it is to win.

Invocation of community constraints is almost the sole force *generated by the conflict itself* which acts in a restraining direction. It is a very special force, and which appears to operate *only* under the conditions discussed above. Even so, it represents one means by which some controversies may be contained within bounds of normal community decision making.

Community Organizations as the Controversy Develops. As conflict develops, the community's organizations tend to be drawn in, just as individual members are. It may be the American Legion, the P.T.A., the church, the local businessmen's association; if its members are drawn into the controversy, or if it can lend useful support, the organization will be under pressure from one or both sides to enter the controversy. This varies, of course, with the nature of the organization and the nature of the dispute.

At the same time there are often strong pressures, both within the organization and without, to remain neutral. From within: if its members hold opposing sentiments, then their disharmony forces the organization itself to remain neutral. And from without: the organization must main-

[8] *See Pope's (1942) graphic account of union operations in Gastonia, North Carolina, and Jones's (1941) discussion of union activity in Akron.*

tain a public position in the community which might be endangered by taking sides in a partisan battle threatening to split the community.

Examples of internal and external constraints on community organizations and leaders are not hard to find. In the Denver school controversy a few years ago, the county P.T.A. felt constrained to dissociate itself publicly from the criticisms of the school system made by their retiring president (Martin, 1951). In Hastings, New York, the positions were reversed: the school administration and teachers remained neutral while a battle raged over the P.T.A. election (McPhee, 1954). Similarly, in the strike in Gastonia, North Carolina, local ministers felt constrained not to take a public position (Pope, 1942, p. 283). If they had done so, the course of the strike might have been quite different as religious matters entered in explicitly. In some fights over the city manager plan, businessmen's associations tried to keep out because the plan was already under attack for its alliance with business interests (Stene and Floro, 1953, p. 60); and in at least one fluoridation controversy, doctors and dentists were reluctant to actively support the fluoridation plan, singly or as a group, because of possible community disfavor affecting business (Mausner, 1955).[9] In another case, union leaders who had originally helped elect a school board could not bring their organizations to support a superintendent the board had

appointed when he was accused of "progressivism" and favoritism to ethnic minorities. Their own members were too strongly split on the issue (McKee, 1953, p. 244). Ministers who were in favor of allowing Negro children to use the community house were influenced by the beliefs of influential members of their churches not to take a stand (*The Inquiry*, 1929, pp. 58–59). Even in Scarsdale, which was united behind its school board, the Town Club incurred disfavor with a minority of its members, who supported the school's critics, for taking as strong a stand as it did.

In sum, both community organizations and community leaders are faced with constraints when a dispute arises; the formation of a combat group to carry on the controversy and the emergence of a previous unknown as the combat leader are in part results of the immobility of responsible organizations and leaders. Both the new leader and the new organization are freed from some of the usual shackles of community norms and internal cross pressures which make pre-existing organizations and leaders tend to soften the dispute.

The immobility of organizations resulting from a lack of internal (or sometimes external) consensus is one element which varies according to the kind of issue involved. This is best exemplified by different issues in national politics: when the issue is an economic one, e.g., Taft-Hartley legislation, groups mobilize on each side of the economic fence; labor unions and allied organizations *vs.* the National Association of Manufacturers, trade associations, and businesses themselves. When the issue has to do with tariffs, the composition of each side is different,[10] but there is still a mobilization of organizations on both sides. Sometimes the issue

9 *There is some evidence that men in certain occupations are more sensitive than others to public opinion and thus less willing to commit themselves to either side and less able to hold on to a position of principle. On the Pasadena school board, the two members most sensitive to the mass mood were a retail merchant and an undertaker (both, it should be noted, like doctors and dentists, have a retail product to sell) (Hurlburd, 1950, pp. 31ff.). This and other evidence leads to the hypothesis that persons who have a clientele or set of retail customers in town cannot generally be trusted to stand up against a majority though they believe in the cause. Or even more generally, it seems that such men cannot start a controversy, since the initiator is always in a minority; neither can they continue against the initiator once he has gained the majority.*

10 *Sometimes labor unions and trade associations find themselves on the same side of the fence. The issue over an increase in watch tariffs saw the watchmakers' union and the manufacturers on the same side; both opposed a principle laid down by a tariff commission headed by the president of a steel company.*

cuts directly across the organizations and institutions in society, thus immobilizing them, e.g., "McCarthyism," which blossomed such a short time ago. Labor unions never opposed McCarthy—their members were split. The Democratic party never opposed him—its constituency was split. Few of the powerful institutions in the country had enough internal consensus to oppose McCarthy. As it was, he drew his followers from all walks of life and from all levels of society. The cross pressures resulting from lack of internal group consensus were reinforced by external pressures against opposing McCarthy, for all the values of patriotism were invoked by his forces. Almost the only organizations with neither internal nor external pressure against taking sides were the professionally patriotic groups like the American Legion and the DAR. If the issue had not immobilized labor unions and the Democratic party, then opposition to McCarthy would have been much more effective.[11]

The Increasing Use of Word-of-Mouth Communication. As the controversy proceeds, the formal media of communication—radio, television, and newspapers—become less and less able to tell people *as much* as they want to know about the controversy, or the *kinds of things* they want to know. These media are simply not flexible enough to fill the insatiable need for news which develops as people become more and more involved. At the same time, the media are restricted by normative and legal constraints against carrying the kind of rumor which abounds as controversy proceeds. Word-of-mouth communication gradually fills the gaps, both in volume and in content, left by the mass media. Street-corner discussion amplifies, elaborates, and usually distorts the news that it picks up from the papers or the radio. This interpersonal communica-

tion offers no restraints against slander and personal charges; rather, it helps make the rhetoric of controversy consistent with the intensity.

. . . It . . . remains to examine some of the reciprocal causations constituting the "vicious circles" or "runaway processes" so evident in conflict. These should give somewhat more insight into the mechanisms responsible for the growth of conflict.

Reciprocal Causation and the Developing Dispute

The inner dynamics of controversy derive from a number of mutually reinforcing relations; one element is enhanced by another, and, in turn, enhances the first, creating an endless spiral.[12] Some of the most important relations depend heavily upon this reciprocal reinforcement; if one or more of these cycles can be *broken*, then a disagreement already on the way to real conflict can be diverted into normal channels.

Mutual Reinforcement of Responses. Relations between people contain a built-in reciprocity. I smile at you; if you smile back, I speak to you; you respond, and a relationship has begun. At each step, my reaction is contingent upon yours, and yours, in turn, contingent upon mine.[13] If you fail to smile, but scowl instead, I may say a harsh word; you respond in kind, and another chain of mutual reinforcement builds up—this time toward antagonism. It is such chains which constitute not only the fundamental character of interpersonal relations, but also the

[11] *Interestingly, what is at one time an aid is at another time a hindrance; a movement with little organizational opposition also has little organizational support, and finds it difficult to become institutionalized without a coup.*

[12] *The dynamics of controversy is a topic for the theoretician in sociology; it comes as close as any area of social life to constituting a closed system, in which all the effects are from variables within the system. When a theory of controversy does exist, the sets of mutually reinforcing relations like those examined in this section will constitute the heart of the theory.*

[13] *Talcott Parsons (1951, p. 36), who studies this characteristic of interpersonal relations in detail, speaks of it as the "double-contingency of interpersonal relations." Parsons has a full discussion of this aspect of relations between persons.*

fundamental cycle of mutual effects in controversy. Breaking that cycle requires much effort. The admonition to "turn the other cheek" is not easily obeyed.

The direct reinforcement of response, however, is but one—the most obvious—of the mutually reinforcing relations which constitute the dynamics of controversy. Others, more tenuous, are more easily broken.

The Mutual Effects of Social and Psychological Polarization.   As participants in a dispute become psychologically "consistent," shedding doubts and hesitancies, they shun friends who are uncommitted, and elaborate their associations with those who feel the way they do. In effect, the psychological polarization leads to social polarization. The latter, in turn, leads to mutual reinforcement of opinions, that is, to further psychological polarization. One agrees more and more with his associates (and disagrees more and more with those he *doesn't* talk to), and comes to associate more and more with those who agree with him. Increasingly, his opponents' position seems preposterous—and, in fact, it *is* preposterous, as is his own; neither position feeds on anything but reinforcing opinions.

The outcome, of course, is the division of the community into two socially and attitudinally separate camps, each convinced it is absolutely right. The lengths to which this continually reinforcing cycle will go in any particular case depends on the characteristics of the people and the community involved. . . . It is these characteristics which provide one "handle" for reducing the intensity of community conflict.

Polarization and Intensity: Within the Individual and Within Each Side.   As the participants become psychologically polarized, all their attitudes mutually reinforcing, the *intensity* of their feeling increases. One of the consequences is that inconsistencies within the individual are driven out; thus he becomes even more psychologically polarized, in turn developing a greater intensity.

This chain of mutual enforcement lies completely *within* the individual. But there is an analogous chain of reinforcement on the social level. As social polarization occurs (that is, the proliferation of associations among those who feel one way, and the attenuation of association between those who feel differently), one's statements meet more and more with a positive response; one is more and more free to express the full intensity of his feeling. The "atmosphere" of the group is open for the kind of intensity of feeling that previously had to remain unexpressed. This atmosphere of intensity, in turn, further refines the group; it becomes intolerable that anyone who believes differently maintain association within the group.

These are examples of reciprocal causation in community conflict, as they appear in the literature of these controversies. They constitute the chains which carry controversy from beginning to end as long as they remain unbroken, but which also provide the means of softening the conflict if methods can be found to break them. It is important to note that these reciprocal relations, once set in motion by outside forces, become independent of them and continue on their own. The one continuing force at work is the drive of each side to win, which sets in motion the processes described above; it carries the conflict forward "under its own steam," so to speak. But reciprocal relations also affect the initial drive, amplifying it, changing it; no longer is it simply a drive to win, but an urge to ruin the opponents, strip them of their power, in effect, annihilate them. This shift in goals, itself a part of a final chain of reciprocal causation, drives these processes onward with ever more intensity.

Gresham's Law of Conflict.   The processes may be said to create a "Gresham's Law of Conflict": the harmful and dangerous elements drive out those which would keep the conflict within bounds. Reckless, unrestrained leaders head the attack; combat organizations arise to replace the milder, more constrained, pre-existing organizations: derogatory and scurrilous charges replace dispassionate issues; antagonism replaces disagreement, and a drive to ruin the opponent takes the place of the initial will to win. In other words, all the forces put into effect by the initiation of conflict act to drive out the conciliatory elements, replace them with those better equipped for combat.

In only one kind of case—exemplified best by the Cincinnati fight in which one side formed the "Committee of 150 for Political Morality"—"Gresham's Law of Conflict" did not hold. As we have said, it was to the *advantage* of that side—not altruism—to invoke against the opponents the community norms which ordinarily regulate a disagreement.

Yet a rather insistent question remains to be answered: if all these forces work in the direction of increasing intensity, how is it that community conflicts stop short of annihilation? After all, community conflicts *are* inhibited, yet the processes above give no indication how. Forces *do* exist which can counteract these processes and bring the dispute into orderly channels— forces which are for the most part products of pre-existing community characteristics, and may be thought of here as constituting a third side in the struggle. Primarily this "third force" preserves the community from division and acts as a "governor" to keep all controversies below a certain intensity.

In part the variations in these forces in the community are responsible for the wide variation in the intensity of community conflicts. Thus, a conflict which reaches extreme proportions in one community would be easily guided into quieter channels in another.

Certain attributes of the community's leadership, techniques which are used—or not used—at crucial points to guide the dispute into more reasonable channels, also affect the development of conflict. These methods, along with the pre-existing community attributes, constitute the means by which a disagreement which threatens to disrupt the community can be kept within bounds. . . .

References

Coser, Lewis, *The Functions of Social Conflict*. New York: The Free Press of Glencoe, Inc., 1956.

Hessler, William H., "It Didn't Work in Cincinnati," *The Reporter*, Vol. IX (December 22, 1953), 13–17.

Hurlburd, David, *This Happened in Pasadena*. New York: The Macmillan Company, 1950.

Jones, Alfred W., *Life, Liberty, and Property*. Philadelphia: J. B. Lippincott Co., 1941.

Key, V. O. Jr., *Southern Politics*. New York: Alfred A. Knopf, Inc., 1950.

Martin, Lawrence, "Denver, Colorado," *Saturday Review*, ("The Public School Crisis"), Vol. XXXIV (September 8, 1951), 6–20.

Mausner, Bernard and Judith Mausuer, "A Study of the Anti-Scientific Attitude," *Scientific American*, Vol. CXCII (February, 1955), 35–39.

McKee, James B., "Organized Labor and Community Decision-Making: A Study in the Sociology of Power." Unpublished Ph.D. dissertation, University of Wisconsin, 1953.

McPhee, William, "Community Controversies Affecting Personal Liberties and Institutional Freedoms in Education." Unpublished memorandum, Columbia University, Bureau of Applied Social Research, July, 1954.

Merton, Robert K., and Paul F. Lazarsfeld, "Friendship as a Social Process," in Monroe Berger, Theodore Abel, and Charles Page, eds. *Freedom and Control in Modern Society.* Princeton, N.J.: D. Van Nostrand Co., Inc., 1954.

Parsons, Talcott, *The Social System.* New York: The Free Press of Glencoe, Inc., 1951.

Pope, Liston, *Millhands and Preachers.* New Haven, Conn.: Yale University Press, 1942.

Simmel, Georg, *Conflict and the Web of Intergroup Affiliations.* New York: The Free Press of Glencoe, Inc., 1955.

Southern School News, Vol. III (October, 1956), Vol. 15.

Stene, Edwin K., and George K. Floro, *Abandonment of the Manager Plan.* Lawrence: University of Kansas Press, 1953.

Stone, Harold S., Don K. Price, and Kathryn H. Stone, *City Manager Government in the United States.* Chicago: Public Administration Service, 1940.

The Inquiry, *Community Conflict.* New York, 1929.

Warner, W. Lloyd and Associates, *Democracy in Jonesville.* New York: Harper & Row, Publishers, Inc., 1949.

E. The Politics of Totalitarian Control

The Soviet Party Secretary: A Vignette

Raymond A. Bauer

Teplov rubbed his eyes to keep awake. It was midnight and he wanted to go home to bed, but years of service in the Party apparatus had taught him the necessity of careful paper work. He was preparing an agenda for the meeting of the Executive Committee of the Raion Party Committee[1] in the morning, and this was no time to make mistakes. It was one of those periods in which any action could have the profoundest political ramifications. Teplov was a technician first, and a politician second, but in a time of crisis politics inevitably saturated all of life.

Stalin's picture still hanging on the wall symbolized the instability of Teplov's world, which would not be peaceful until another picture hung in its place. But whose picture would it be? And when

[1] *Raion: Minor administrative district immediately under the jurisdiction of the* Oblast, *which is the administrative unit immediately below the Republic.*—ED. NOTE.

would it happen? It was risky to take sides, and it was risky not to take sides.

Kornetsky, the sardonic Second Secretary, had chanced into the office one day as Teplov was putting a picture of Malenkov in his desk drawer. "We must be prepared for any eventuality, eh, Antip Trofimovitch? One must also be careful that he does not put in the same drawer the picture of two incompatible persons. This might prove to be a very serious business," Kornetsky had commented.

Teplov had looked up, angered. But he did not know how to respond to Kornetsky. He searched the Second Secretary's face for some trace of expression that would give him a clue as to what was on his mind. Kornetsky's teeth were fastened firmly on the huge pipe which he seldom smoked, but which was as fixed a feature of his face as his nose and ears. It gave his face a rigid, graven appearance that be-

Raymond A. Bauer, *Nine Soviet Portraits,* pp. 60–75. Copyright © 1955, Massachusetts Institute of Technology Press. Published jointly with John Wiley & Sons, Inc. Reprinted by permission.

trayed no feeling. Teplov muttered and slammed the drawer shut in embarrassment. If things turned out wrong, Kornetsky could use even so small an incident against him.

Many times in the course of the day, he looked at the door of the office and his name in reverse through the glass "A. T. Teplov, First Secretary, Baltinsk Raion Committee." When he did, the same unspoken question came to his mind that came when he looked at Stalin's picture. The sign painters weren't very skillful, but it took very little effort to scrape a name off the door and replace it with another—no harder than changing Stalin's picture on the wall.

But worrying about such things was a luxury a busy man could not afford. The life of the Raion was dependent on Teplov, and Teplov was dependent on the life of the Raion. If the Raion did not develop, flourish, and produce, he would have failed, and his career would be over. There was little he could do about the fight that was raging among the big shots, but his responsibilities to the Raion were many and immediate. He returned to his task, and was working furiously when he heard a tap at his door.

"Yes?" he called out, wondering who would be calling on him at this hour.

It was Shvartz, the Third Secretary, young, thin-faced, bookish-looking . . . probably, Teplov thought, because of his pince-nez, an incongruous affec[ta]tion for a Party worker. Teplov thought Shvartz looked like Trotsky with a shave. He was a good fellow, though, and a hard worker.

"Well, Antip Trofimovitch," Shvartz said, "I see you're still working."

Teplov gestured silently, drawing his hands across the pile of work on his desk with a single sweeping motion. "How about you?" he asked.

Shvartz grimaced. "I had a class for the four new Party candidates. I'm leading them patiently by the hand through the Short History of the Communist Party. A lazy bunch—I thought they'd go to sleep."

"Well, keep them at it," Teplov answered, and returned to the work on his desk.

Shvartz seemed unperturbed by being cut off so shortly by his chief. He said, "Good night. I'll see you in the morning," closed the door behind him and turned to leave the building. On the way out he noticed a small light bulb burning in one of the offices—and right in the middle of the campaign to save electricity, he groaned as he stepped inside for a moment to turn it off.

"A funny chap, the old man," Shvartz mused as he left the building. "You'd think he'd be more interested in the job I'm doing. Political education is an important part of the Party's work."

Teplov in turn was reciprocating Shvartz's compliment. He smiled slightly as Shvartz closed the door behind him. "A funny chap," he thought, "like one of the enthusiasts from the early thirties or even the twenties."

Teplov was interested in political education, but not in the way that Shvartz was. Teplov wanted the Party and Komsomol[2] members in the Raion to be sufficiently literate in the political classics and sufficiently up-to-date on the Party line so that they would not commit embarrassing errors. And he wanted Shvartz to keep the general populace at a sufficient level of apparent enthusiasm so that there should be no unfavorable reports going into the Center about morale in the Raion.

The Soviet state was built on deeds, not on words, but even a practical man had to have a proper respect for the role of persuasion. It took years of experience and a long process of ripening to appreciate the delicate balance to be maintained between persuasion and coercion. Many young men and women tended to regard persuasion as a façade. The young Party worker who read in the papers the endless telegrams from "workers' committees" pledging production goals and contributions often became cynical. He had been assigned the

2 *Komosomol: Young Communist League.*—ED. NOTE.

task of securing such "voluntary" actions. He would be told in advance by the Party what action should be taken. Then he would announce at the appropriate point in the meeting, "The adoption of such and such a program recommends itself to this meeting." Everyone understood "it recommends itself" meant "the Party wants." Nevertheless it was possible for the Party, in this manner, to direct affairs while retaining the façade of "democratic" action.

But some young Party workers never realized how this balance of coercion and persuasion worked. On Teplov's desk lay a note which read simply, "New Partorg[3] for shoe factory." If Shvartz tended slightly to overestimate the importance of words, the former Partorg at the shoe factory had underestimated it badly. He was assigned the task of securing a 10 per cent voluntary contribution to the state loan from the workers of the plant. With guileless naïveté he had posted an announcement that 10 per cent would be deducted from their pay envelopes . . . without an agitation program in the shop to explain the need of the State for the funds . . . without calling a factory meeting at which the activists among the workers could pledge the required amount. He was so gauche as to assume that everybody knew this was a formality and that it served no purpose. His action caused a furor in the Raion Committee. At Teplov's direction the head of the industrial section called the young man in, gave him a good dressing-down, and returned him full-time to his job of running a stitching machine in the factory. Now they would have to select a new Partorg—one with a greater sense of delicacy and of proper form.

Teplov's raw material for preparing tomorrow's agenda was the pile of crumpled slips of paper lying before him. It was difficult to keep in a supply of note pads. But for Teplov this was an item of utmost priority, and he used his connections in Moscow to make certain that two or three

times a year a small package of these pads would be sent to him. It seemed like a small item, but without them he was convinced that he would never be able to keep the affairs of the Raion straight. There was no telling when and where some matter of urgency would be called to his attention. He would scribble an elliptical note, understandable only to himself in most instances, tear off the slip of paper, and "file" it in his jacket pocket. In the course of days these slips would migrate from pocket to pocket, and through the various sections of his desk as he took action on these bits of business.

There was one slip in the pile before him which bore the legend, "Chairman, Broad Meadows Kolkhoz."[4] It had started out in his breast pocket, where he kept the note pad, two days before in the morning. He was on his way out of the building when he met the head of the agriculture sector, Nikitin. Nikitin was upset and agitated. He was running his hand around the back of his neck, inside his open collar —a gesture Teplov had long ago identified as meaning that there was trouble, and trouble for which Nikitin was afraid he himself might be held responsible.

"Antip Trofimovitch," Nikitin began, "you'll just have to call the Oblast office again about the chairman at Broad Meadow. They're two weeks behind in sowing, the buildings are in terrible shape, and half the chickens are sick. I can't do a thing with them. Always he gives me nothing but excuses. He should be replaced. We told them that last year."

Teplov nodded slightly, and pulled out his inevitable pad on which he made this brief notation. It was true that they had recommended replacing this chairman. Broad Meadows had been a problem for several years. The chairman was a former brigadier who had gone into service and had a good war record. He joined the Party during the war, and when he returned home the Raion Committee had recommended him for chairman of the

---

[3] *Partorg: party organizer.*—ED. NOTE.

[4] *Kolkhoz: collective farm.*—ED. NOTE.

kolkhoz. This was before Teplov's time, and he had since suggested tactfully to the Ministry of Agriculture that the chairman should be replaced. Well, this time he would be more firm.

But he couldn't let Nikitin get off that easily. He might get the idea that he could blame everything that went wrong in the agricultural sector on the kolkhoz chairmen. Anyway, he looked like he expected a bawling out. So Teplov gave him a thorough tongue lashing, ". . . passing the buck . . . don't expect me to bail you out of all your problems . . . should have worked more closely with him . . . making excuses is not planting grain." Nikitin grew red-faced, as several people passing by slowed their step to hear the dressing-down he was getting. At first he tried to stem the flow of Teplov's abuse with protestations of *"but,* Antip Trofimovitch." Teplov greeted each "but" with a fresh onslaught. It wasn't until Nikitin gave in and answered repeatedly *"Yes, Antip Trofimovitch"* that Teplov finally let him off.

The slip moved to the top of his desk that afternoon. He placed it there so that he would not forget to call the Ministry. The Ministry agreed to replace the chairman, and the slip moved to the top drawer of the desk with a number of other personnel problems that he had to take up with the head of the cadres section.

After that he called the head of the cadres section to his office and presented him with a list of positions which had to be filled in organizations under their jurisdiction. He instructed the head of the cadres division to prepare a list of recommendations from the card file, and then shoved the slip, along with the other notations on personnel matters, into his right-hand pocket.

Now, after its long migration it was back out on the desk top, where he had emptied his pockets and desk drawers in an effort to restore some order to his records. He made an entry on the agenda, under "Personnel," "Chairman, Broad Meadows." Above it, the list read: "Prin-

cipal, School #3, Director of Cooperative Store, Z. village, and Partorg, Shoe Factory." Then the slip and its companions were crumpled in one broad gesture and thrown into the waste basket.

He worked his way patiently through the pile of notes. There were a few production problems in several of the small factories in the Raion, but, thank God, not many. Nikitin, as head of the agricultural sector, would have to give them a report on the progress of the crops. Also a general propaganda and agitation program would have to be worked out in connection with the recent arrest of Beria. The editor of the Raion newspaper had taken his cue quickly, and, of course, printed the editorial that had been broadcast from Moscow. But the entire resources of the Raion would have to be mobilized.

Finally, about one-thirty, he finished. It was a warm July evening. Teplov wore a light coat as he walked home. His house was less than a quarter-mile from the office. Baltinsk, after which the Raion took its name, was a small provincial settlement. The streets were unpaved. There was a crude telephone connection with the nearest city. Electricity had been introduced only in the years after the war. As Teplov strolled along under the night sky, he was surveying his capital, for indeed this rural town was the center of the area over which he held sway.

But, now that he was no longer working, his feeling of uneasiness returned. The decision to seek a career in the Party apparatus was a risky one, although it hadn't seemed so to Teplov at the time. He was an engineering student, son of a foreman in a textile plant. His mother was a peasant who had come to the city to work in the same factory in which she met his father. It had seemed quite natural for him to enter the Komsomol, and quite natural for him to accept the assignments which were given him. Before he realized it, shortly after graduation he was no longer an engineer, but an "apparatchik," a member of the Party apparatus. First he was Party Secretary of the plant in which he had shortly before been a junior engineer; the head of the industrial sector in a Raion Committee; an interruption for the war, when he served as a political officer to a regiment and was wounded; and then he returned to be second, and, finally, First Secretary of the Baltinsk Raion. Teplov had not been a very distinguished youth. He was a little more energetic than average, a little above average in intelligence, and below average in imagination, but that was more an asset than a liability. He was very little concerned with politics, but quite intent on making a career for himself, and was entirely content to do what was asked of him in order to attain that goal. He was a technician-bureaucrat in a world of politics. As much as possible he tried to stay apart from factional struggles within the Party, and by a considerable adroitness at evading issues he managed to survive a full dozen years in the Party without becoming identified as anybody's man.

But tonight he was worried. It was comforting that he was not involved in any of the contending factions in the Party. He could be sure that he would not automatically be liquidated if the wrong faction won. But, at the same time, he could not be sure of the support of any of the factions either . . . and even though he had no one group of enemies, he did have individual enemies. Particularly he knew that he had enemies in some of the agencies in Moscow, and in some of the central Party offices.

Relations with the Center were always difficult for anyone with a responsible position in the provinces. Not only was the Center forever putting unreasonable demands on you, but they had completely fantastic notions of how to do a job best. Teplov was primarily concerned with his own self-interest and with compiling a record which would in the long run reflect to his credit. But he was strongly identified with his own Raion, and was convinced that neither he nor the country would prosper if the Raion were not in good running order.

Perhaps his worst enemy was V. N. Rashevsky, now a fairly high official in the Kremlin. Rashevsky had been head of the Oblast industrial sector when Teplov was appointed to head the Raion industrial sector. They had a number of arguments— an act of rare audacity on Teplov's part since he was little given to open displays of resistance.

While Teplov was away at war he heard that Rashevsky had been appointed First Secretary for the Oblast. Fortunately for Teplov, Rashevsky moved on to Moscow before he returned. There was little doubt that if Rashevsky had been Oblast Secretary at the time of Teplov's appointment, it would not have gone through.

Teplov rose in the Raion on the basis of his energetic work. But he continued to have his brushes with Rashevsky, who was now in the agricultural sector of the Central Committee.

On one occasion a division of troops was moved into Teplov's Raion. They were authorized to draw on Raion food resources for subsistence. It was quickly clear that the Raion's resources were inadequate. And they had to make the regular grain deliveries in addition! There would have been rebellion on all the kolkhozes, and the workers in the towns would have been short of food. Teplov carried the fight to the Oblast Committee, insisting that the regular deliveries be reduced accordingly, and the new Oblast Secretary took the matter up to Moscow. It was only later, after the matter had been settled in his favor, that Teplov heard that his old antagonist, Rashevsky, had been behind the original order. Incidents like these preyed on his mind.

Still in an uneasy reverie, he arrived at his house, a small, four-room structure, with two bedrooms, a kitchen, and a living room. His wife was sleeping in one bedroom and his two boys in the other. It was typical that he should return home after the family was asleep. He occasionally lamented how little he saw his family. But, except for being deprived of his company, they were well provided for. They were well dressed, housed, and fed. You could tell them by their more prosperous appearance if you saw them in any gathering. His boys, together with the children of the few highly placed officials in the town's two factories, were regarded with deference by their schoolmates. They were growing up with the self-assuredness and cockiness of the kids of well-off parents. Their mother indulged them, and the militia in the town were afraid to discipline them. Teplov paid little attention to them except on infrequent vacations, or when their behavior precipitated some special "scandal" in the town. Then he would lecture them severely. But they sensed that his concern was for the difficulties that their misdemeanors caused him personally, and they became only more skillful in having their way without having their escapades come to their father's attention.

Teplov slipped into bed, and dropped off to sleep. He did this so quickly and quietly that his wife, Elena, was not disturbed. He slept well. In fact he always slept well. He drained so much of his energy into his job that he had no trouble falling asleep even when he was worried.

Teplov knew nothing from the time he hit the bed until his wife shook him awake at eight o'clock in the morning. The children were already eating breakfast. He drew his clothes on mechanically and shuffled to the table. A glass of hot tea and a piece of rye bread sat before him. He gulped the tea and chewed the bread, and by his own exertions came awake gradually. As he passed from sleep to wakefulness, the voices of the boys advanced out of the background of his consciousness. They were engrossed in the model airplane that Sasha, the older boy, was building. But before Teplov could enter into the conversation, they were busily wiping their mouths on their sleeves, and hurrying off to school.

Elena had already left the table. She cleared a space in the sink, and poured hot water from the tea kettle into a shallow pan that stood beneath a small mirror.

Elena placed his razor beside the pan, and went to straighten out the bedroom while he shaved. She came through the kitchen several times while he was shaving, and commented on various household problems, but she seemed to address him only at such disadvantageous moments that he could only grunt through his clenched lips. He slipped into his jacket, said good-bye, and started for the office.

His driver was waiting outside the house sitting in the car and reading the copy of the Raion newspaper which he picked up regularly for Teplov every morning. They exchanged good-mornings, and Teplov got into the back seat. The driver handed Teplov the newspaper.

Teplov was doubly interested in the paper. On [the] one hand he was responsible for virtually everything that happened in the Raion. Therefore, he was anxious to see that it carried out policy properly. On the other hand, it told him of what was happening in the world outside the Raion. Of special interest were the items which Moscow sent out by radio to be printed verbatim. Occasionally when he had an evening to himself he would sit at home and listen to news stories and editorials being dictated at slow speed over the radio. Particularly in recent months the ponderous voice of the announcer would frequently intone statements reflecting the tremendous changes which were taking place: ". . . comma who has repeatedly committed antistate activities comma has been taken into custody period" . . . "the doctrine of one-man rule comma which is completely contrary to the principles of the Party comma must be replaced by collegial decisions" . . . "a series of benefits colon lowered food prices semicolon an ever-increasing standard of living semicolon . . . ." These dispatches were like the acts of some unknown being who would suddenly and violently intervene in Teplov's life, sometimes doing good and sometimes doing evil. *"Deus ex machina,"* Shvartz had commented to Teplov on one occasion when the arm of the secret police had opportunely removed a member of a ministry who was causing them great difficulty. Teplov listened attentively to Shvart's explanation, and for once was not bored with the Third Secretary's bookish references. He agreed with Shvartz that such events were very much like the timely appearance of the gods in a Greek play—but one never knew in these days on whose side the gods would intervene. He scanned the paper with mixed feelings of anticipation and anxiety, but there was little of interest.

As the car pulled up in front of the Raion headquarters, Teplov noticed an automobile sitting in front of the building. He recognized one of the chauffeurs from the shoe factory waiting in the car. For a brief moment he was puzzled, then he remembered that an inspector from the Chief Administration was expected. The factory had sent the car to the nearest railroad station to meet him. It was covered with dust from the hundred kilometers of dirt road that connected the town of Baltinsk with the railroad.

The inspector, Boris Aleksandrovitch Davidenkov, was waiting in Teplov's office. A round-faced, stocky man, his clothes marked him for a member of the Moscow bureaucracy, but their disheveled condition also showed the effects of his trip. He jumped up smiling, and pumped Teplov's arm warmly. "Just came in to see how the plastic soles are working out on the shoes, Antip Trefimovitch!" he said. "Needn't get scared. No charges of sabotage or anti-state activity." He guffawed loudly at his own joke.

Teplov grimaced and barely succeeded in looking amused. The inspector was a good fellow who caused no difficulty for the Raion, but his macabre jokes provoked little laughter from Teplov. However, his overactive sense of humor was coupled with a general talkativeness, and he brought Teplov many juicy bits of gossip from Moscow. For this Teplov was grateful. The bits of information he picked up from people like Davidenkov who traveled from place to place and brought the news that circulated by word of mouth in the big cities helped Teplov fill in the missing pieces in the pattern which he was constantly trying to put together from newspapers and radio.

"Good morning, Boris Mikhailevitch, I'm delighted to see you," Teplov replied. "I understand things are going fairly well with the plastic soles out at the shoe factory. They had a little trouble with the stitching machines at first, but I think that's pretty well in hand now. . . . But you can see for yourself when you visit the plant. Tell me, how are things in the Ministry?"

"So-so. Too many changes for comfort. But it looks pretty good. Looks like they're going to ease up on the pressure for once. At least you don't hear people going around screaming about raising the production quotas like they were before. Maybe we'll get a little peace."

"What's happening to my old friend Rashevsky?" Teplov asked.

"Oh, is he an old friend of yours?"—Davidenkov had missed the irony in Teplov's tone.—"Well, I guess you're in luck. The rumor is he's going to be head of the cadres division of the Central Committee. It looks like you're in for a promotion. Rashevsky's in with the right people now."

Teplov's head swam. There was no worse place to have an enemy . . . unless it was in the secret police itself, and even they were under attack these days. There was no worse place.

But his face and voice showed little of his feelings. The more you revealed about yourself and your weakness, the more weapons you put into the hands of your enemies. He rose and shook hands with Davidenkov: "I suppose you're in a hurry to get out to the factory. I hope you will drop in here afterward and let me know what you think of how things are going here. I hate to rush you out, but you'll miss the director if you don't hurry. He's due here for a meeting of the Executive Committee at ten o'clock."

Davidenkov shook hands, and left. Teplov took care of several bits of routine business, but the threat of Rashevsky lay in the back of his mind, and as time for the meeting came closer he found himself ever less able to concentrate on the problems immediately before him. Under ordinary circumstances the worst an enemy in the cadres division could do would be to get one demoted or, in extreme cases, removed from the Party apparatus entirely. But there were always jobs outside the apparatus, and it was rare to have the displeasure of even a powerful person follow one that far unless there was some political charge he could pin on you. But in a time of crisis everything was political. The mere fact that he was not strongly aligned with the dominant faction at the moment could be used to make it appear that he was unreliable; then anything could happen.

Shvartz arrived about five minutes early for the meeting. He was followed quickly by several other members of the Executive Committee. By the time the clock on the office wall struck ten all the members of the Committee were present except three: Kornetsky, the Second Secretary, Voronsky, director of the shoe factory, and Blonsky, the editor of the Raion newspaper.

Teplov gave an impatient glance at his watch. As he did so, his secretary opened the door and said: "Comrade Blonsky's secretary just called and said Comrade Blonsky will be here in a few minutes." That left just Voronsky and Kornetsky to be accounted for. Voronsky, he supposed, had been delayed by the inspector. "Does anyone know where Kornetsky is?" he asked of no one in particular. No one knew. It gave Teplov a particular feeling of uneasiness that Kornetsky should be absent. There were rumors that Kornetsky was a strong supporter of Rashevsky. He had been transferred to this Raion while Rashevsky was Oblast Secretary, and Teplov knew that there had been suspicious leaks of information. . . .

At five minutes after ten Kornetsky and Voronsky arrived together. Teplov's hand trembled slightly as he shook hands with Kornetsky.

"Sorry to delay things, Antip Trofimovitch," Voronsky said. "But Davidenkov got to my office at twenty to ten, and I couldn't get away sooner. Comrade Kornetsky was with me at the time and we were both help up. That Davidenkov is too damned talkative. We couldn't get away from him. He had to give us all the Moscow gossip before he would let us leave."

Teplov picked up a pencil and quickly began to make a series of notes. He had the impression that Kornetsky was watching him closely, and he was afraid that the tremor in his hand would betray his emotion. Writing kept his hand steady.

Kornetsky's flat voice came from between clenched teeth. "Yes, he told us the news about your old friend, Rashevsky. Big things are happening."

Teplov heard the tip of his pencil snap. For a moment he had no feeling. There could be no doubt but that Kornetsky's use of the phrase "old friend" was deliberate irony. Had Kornetsky heard the pencil break? It sounded to Teplov as loud as a rifle shot. He slipped it into his pocket. He glanced up at Kornetsky, but again the Second Secretary's face was a mask, with the huge pipe sticking out from his mouth. Damn it, muttered Teplov to himself, I wish at least he'd put some tobacco in that goddamned furnace.

"Yes," Teplov answered, "Rashevsky is a very excellent man. He will do a very good job. However, I believe we had better get on with the meeting, since Comrade Blonsky will be delayed for a few minutes."

Teplov turned to the chief of the cadres section. He was not a member of the Committee and ordinarily would not be attending the meeting, but since there were so many personnel decisions to be made, he was sitting in. Teplov asked him to present his recommendations. He began with the job of the Partorg in the shoe factory. He suggested a young foreman who had been a member of the Party for about three years. He had a good Party record, was an excellent worker, and seemed to be ambitious to move ahead in the Party.

Kornetsky objected: "He is a valuable worker. The shoe factory is one of the pilot plants developing the use of synthetic soles for the entire country. It cannot spare the services of so valuable a workman."

Teplov was dumbfounded. What was behind Kornetsky's protest? The job of Partorg in the shoe factory was not sufficiently important to take the man off his regular job more than part time. If it were a big factory with hundreds of Party members, Kornetsky's objection might make sense. Then there might be a full-time Party Secretary and he would have to be pulled off production. What, Teplov wondered, can Kornetsky be up to? Ordinarily he would have given Kornetsky a thorough dressing-down for such stupidity. But maybe this time there was more behind his protest than met the eye. Teplov turned his eyes questioningly toward Voronsky, the factory director.

Voronsky was flustered. He stammered and could not answer immediately.

Kornetsky cut in, and continued: "We must be extremely careful with our personnel decisions. At the present time even such an appointment as this may be reviewed by the cadres division of the Central Committee. But, of course, I defer to the judgment of Antip Trofimovitch."

Teplov began to perspire. So this is the game, he said to himself, he's going to make enough of a protest to get himself on the record, let me push the appointment through, and then use this as a lever to get me out by going to Rashevsky with it. Teplov fumbled for words, but before any could come to his lips, there was a noise in the hall, the door flew open, and Blonsky, the editor of the paper, bustled in. Blonsky was a short, round man, who waddled somewhat when he walked. This, coupled with the abnormal energy with which he propelled himself forward, gave him the appearance of an agitated duck. He was flourishing a sheaf of papers. "Sorry, sorry, gentlemen," he said. "Big

news from Moscow. I had to wait around to make sure the stenographers got it off the radio correctly. Here it is, Antip Trofimovitch." He tossed the papers down on Teplov's desk.

Teplov glanced at the dispatch. This time there was no mistaking the fact that his hand shook. The men in the room watched him, waiting for some comment.

Teplov read the dispatch aloud:

"A group of enemies of the Soviet state have been arrested for a plot to capture key positions in the Central Committee of the Party itself. These scoundrels, supporters of Lavrenty Beria in his antistate activities, had wormed their way into influential posts in the Party apparatus. They planned to effect their dominance over the Party by securing positions from which they could influence the appointments of personnel. A major step in this plan was to promote to the position of chief of the cadres section . . ." Teplov paused and stole a glance at Kornetsky. Kornetsky's pipe was not in its accustomed position. He had it in his hand and was stuffing it energetically with tobacco. Teplov continued: ". . . V. N. Rashevsky. Rashevsky, knowing that he could not escape from Soviet socialist justice, took his own life yesterday evening. All other members of this bandit clique are in custody."

Teplov put the dispatch down. "The rest," he said, "just gives some details. Well"—he paused—"I suppose we had better get on."

He turned back to the chief of the cadres section. "I think we can take that man as Partorg. Now, how about the rest of the list?"

The man continued his report, but Teplov found himself not listening to the words. How much politics were beyond one's control! How arbitrary, unpredictable, uncontrollable, unexpected were such events. How powerless one felt when the gods quarreled among themselves. What, he asked himself, was that expression Shvartz used. . . . Oh, yes, *Deus ex ma-*

china . . . like a god coming out of a machine, to lift the threat of politics from him and let him get back to the business of running the Raion.

He glanced again at Kornetsky. Kornetsky was sitting erect, as though listening attentively to the report. Clouds of smoke were billowing from his pipe, and his cheek worked spastically as he puffed furiously on the stem. Teplov reached into the top drawer of the desk, where he found a small knife. He retrieved his pencil from his pocket and began to sharpen it slowly and carefully, letting the shavings accumulate in a small pile in the middle of his desk.

5
Power

Since Aristotle first noted that "man is by nature a political animal" students of politics have considered power as the catalyst by which political leaders can secure compliance. Power, to mix the metaphor, is the lubricant of the body politic. To mix it further, power is also a magnet, for without it a political system would become atomistic, lacking cohesiveness and stability. In the last two thousand years this functional view of power has changed little, but there have been important refinements in our understanding of it. The selections below serve to highlight what appears to be a new face of power. But before discussing them it is necessary to clarify certain issues.

Though there have been several different definitions of power offered by political scientists and sociologists, its basic nature can be stated as follows: the ability of an individual or group to affect the behavior of others in conformance to his or its wishes. Using this statement as a working definition of what is admittedly an ambiguous term, it is possible to delineate several aspects of power. First, it is a *relationship* among men, not a characteristic, talent, or a quality possessed by them. There is no such thing as power among the powerful as there is money among the wealthy. Second, it is *issue-based:* power relationships cannot be evaluated as if they were indivisible. Each facet of a relationship has a separable power division; i.e., X has power over Y with regard to issue A but not issue B. Third, it is a *relative:* X has more power over Y than does Z. Moreover, power is *unevenly distributed* in society. There has never been a society in which all men have an equal amount of power over all others. Fourth, it is *situational:* it is a function of the circumstances surrounding its exercise. There are not likely to be power constants, even between the same men in comparable, but not exactly similar, situations. Fifth, power is based in part on the *acquiescence* of the influenced party: without the slaves' acceptance of slavery their masters would have little or no power over them. Sixth, *power leaves off where actual violence begins.* Once violence is used, it is apparent that there is no continued acquiescence in the original relationship. Power often involves the *threat* of force or violence, but according to several students of political science,[1] unless compliance is secured without the use of physical violence no power exists; there is only an attempt to influence.

In the interests of conceptual clarity, several different types of power must be distinguished. *Actual power* is exercised and is quite distinct from *potential power,* which is held in reserve for possible future use, but cannot always be readily converted into actual power. *Reputed power* is different from either of the above types. It is that power which an individual is reputed to have—i.e., his reputation as a powerful man. Power in general can be distinguished from *authority,* which is legally or formally sanctioned power, and *influence,* which is simply one kind of power, held or exercised by those who do not have authority, but who are close to—and heeded by—those in positions of authority. Leadership is another form of power—that of the leader, or recognized chief, who may or may not use his authority to control his followers.

The notion of power has been used in recent years as an *operational concept* in researching and theorizing about social relations. Testable hypotheses about the variables affecting the degree of power are often stated in terms of probabilities. Take, for example, the statement that "there is a high degree of probability that the greater the overall power of an individual, the greater is his power over any randomly selected individual." This proposition rests upon the idea that power is cumulative, a somewhat controversial assumption. Another example would be the statement that "there is a high degree of probability that the exercise of power will have its costs—costs incurred in part through the loss of potential power by the power-wielder." This rests upon the assumption that power, like capabilities in general, is depleted or expended as it is used, again a notion far from universally accepted by political scientists. Such uses of power as an operational concept have been increasingly evident in the literature of political science since the advent of behavioralism.

Yet there is a long tradition in political science—and one that has been continued in studies conducted by behavioral political scientists—of using power as simply an *organizing concept*—that is, one around which a study is organized but which is not itself directly employed in research or theory formation. One reason for this is that in spite of its importance in political behavior, it is difficult to assess or locate either actual or potential power empirically. (Indeed, most students using power as an operational concept have actually, but often unwittingly, analyzed only *inferred* power. For

[1] *See, for example, E. V. Walter, "Power, Civilization, and the Psychology of Conscience,"* American Political Science Review, *Vol. LIII (September, 1959), 641–642: "Violence is not the same as power; indeed, violence may be considered to be the failure of power. Ultimately, power depends on authority and voluntary obedience, which is based on persuasion, and persuasion, in turn, depends on convictions, ideals, and respect. Certainly force may be used in a domain of power to guarantee prescribed actions and to safeguard the limits of permitted behavior; nevertheless, sanctions, penalties, and the fear of punishment are merely braces and not foundations."*

example, from the changes in behavior on the part of the presumedly influenced party, the observer *infers* that the power was wielded by the presumedly influential party.) Thus here we will use power as an organizing
concept. This, we think, in no way detracts from the importance that must
be attached to power as a central concept in political science.

To return to our main theme, the new face of power is reflected most
vividly in its redistribution in many social settings that have been investi-
gated recently. The traditional model[2] of power distribution can be depicted
as follows:

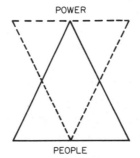

This is the pyramidal model of power distribution; the few at the top
socially have much power, while the many at the bottom have little power.
There is a concentration, or grossly inequitable distribution of power,
whether an organization, a community, or an entire society is being considered. In recent years this model has been challenged. There are several
arguments offered in opposition to it. The remainder of our comments in
this chapter place the illustrative selections we have chosen in the context
of this revision of the traditional conception of power.

Power relations have been partially inverted, according to many contemporary students. The process of democratization operating in the twentieth century has provided for greater popular participation and control in
all organized life. Partly as a reaction to this, leaders have begun to recognize
constituents or followers before making decisions affecting them. In terms
of the conception of the leader's power set forth by James C. Davies in the
selection below from his book *Human Nature in Politics*, the leader-follower
relationship has come to be recognized by both analysts and practicing leaders as a delicate and emotion-laden "marriage" of complementary "husband"

2 *The term "model" has been used in the social sciences in a variety of ways, ranging from*
simple analogies useful in providing understanding of complex phenomena, to complex mathe-
matical statements useful in predicting or forecasting developments. In this volume, "model"
means any general statement used to describe or predict by stating uniformities of relationships
among several persistently and regularly recurring phenomena. These general statments are
used in such a way that only those aspects of relationships that are essential to the description
or prediction are elaborated. Invariably the effectiveness of the model rests in large part on the
use of some concrete analogy to clarify the phenomena; in the model shown, power is viewed
as if it were a pyramid. In other cases, light is viewed as straight-line rays in optics and
molecules as billiard balls in physics.

and "wife." The followers identify with the leaders, but this does not grant the leaders any less dependence on their following. (Davies argues that it creates greater dependence.) Popular acceptance of the leader is conditioned in part on his success. The degree of which, moreover, is not for the leader, but for the followers to assess. And this they do by simply requiring leaders to act, to perform and to produce. Even in an autocratic regime, Davies argues, "the people are continually judging their dictators, monarchs, and Führers, and these judgments represent popular constraints upon the leader." In this sense there has come to be a recognition of the equalization of power at work in the leader-follower relationship.

If popular approval of leadership demands the action of leaders, as Davies argues, then the ability of leaders to carry out their will is the *sine qua non* of their success. Richard Neustadt argues that authority, the formal powers vested in public office, is its own best promoter. That is, the general authority of high office is a prime tool for the officeholder to carry out specific objectives under specific grants of power. The focus of his investigation is the Presidency of the United States, and his analysis explores the many ways in which the President can put his general authority to use in persuading others to comply with his wishes.

The President's problem is the same as that of anyone of authority—how to prevail over those who resist him and who have their own sources of authority to use as weapons in the struggle against him. Actually, what takes place between men of authority with differing opinions is more like negotiating than outright warfare. The *modus vivendi* is persuasive argumentation harnessed to certain actions that, like turns on a screw, tighten (or loosen) the hold that one official has on another. The bargaining is sometimes implicit as each threatens to act or attempts to bluff the other into submission. Even though the high office of the President is involved, the Chief Executive is frequently reduced to playing such a game in securing the cooperation of his own Cabinet appointees.

Neustadt points out the need for persuasion by men of authority in securing compliance by subordinates. This implication of limits on the superior's power, or the "upward flow of power restraints," has become a central notion in political and administrative studies during the last thirty years, dating back to Chester I. Barnard's idea about the restraints on executive authority developed in his classic *Functions of the Executive*.

Another recently recognized component of power is the role of experts and advisers in shaping the policy of public or private organizations. Power, as Harold Wilensky reveals in his study of labor union staff personnel,[3] is

3 *In* Intellectuals in Labor Unions: Organizational Pressures on Professional Roles, *Wilensky deals with staff experts in unions from the perspective of the interplay of individual and organization in the large private association. The study reports the findings of a survey of twenty-eight unions, in which Wilensky examined the factors affecting the outlook, functions, and degree of influence of different types of experts, taking into consideration the motives and organizational pressures affecting the experts and their role orientations.*

in the contemporary organizational world a product of knowledge, job assignments, ambition, and contacts. Without formal authority to make policy, the staff experts can nevertheless be highly influential in policy making. He can offer ideas, criticize the proposals of others, and narrow the range of alternatives to be considered. He can help to justify the leader's decisions (as necessary in union affairs as in government or business) and thus perform a critical role in crystallizing policy.

In discussing the variety of career lines that the staff experts follow, Wilensky notes that whether they are recruited from the union ranks or from the outside they are usually men who "sensed the moment, saw the possibilities of success, and seized the chance to climb aboard." These are the new men of power—the influential staff experts "on the rise" in government, in the universities, and in the corporate world. As James Burnham has noted in his book *The Managerial Revolution,* in the business world it is these managerial experts—rather than the investors, the entrepreneurs, the organization's official policy-making directorate, or even the publicly acknowledged chief, organization leader, or spokesman—who perform the most critical role in shaping the organization's destiny. Wilensky's analysis highlights a comparable reliance on staff experts in the control of union affairs, though he does not feel that technical knowledge is the main basis of the experts' power. Can we not likewise see in government and politics this stratum of non-elected, behind-the-scenes, influential advisers?[4] Where political know-how traditionally has been the source of political advisers' strength, today the breadth and depth of comprehension of public policy matters are almost as often recognized as the basis of the staff adviser's influence.

There has also been a substantial revision in the traditional concept of elite[5] dominance in a political or social system. The pyramidal or elitist model set forth in the earlier sociological works of Gaetano Mosca (*The Ruling Class*) and most recently presented by C. Wright Mills in *The Power Elite* has colored the study of community politics in particular, and only in the last ten years has there been developed an alternative concept of power distribution in the community.

The notion of elitist dominance in American communities has been hotly debated since the publication of sociologist Floyd Hunter's 1954 study of *Community Power Structure* in the city of Atlanta, Georgia. Hunter's work asserted the dominance of a business elite in running community affairs in Atlanta. This model stresses the stable, highly structured power hierarchy of individuals and groups under a dominant business elite that exercises far and away the greatest power in community political affairs. Several disbe-

---

4 *See, for example, several recent analyses of scientific experts operating in the American governmental sphere in Robert Gilpin and Christopher Wright, eds.,* Scientists and National Policy-Making (*New York: Columbia University Press, 1964*).
5 *Where a fairly small group of prominent men of similar social background and outlook collaborate in attempting to influence public policy, an elite can be said to exist.*

lieving political scientists have locked horns with the Hunterians, in particular Robert A. Dahl of Yale University and his former graduate students who subscribe to the view that the local political system is pluralistic; that is, composed of a diverse array of competing interests that act in large part as checks against each other's power.

It is neither possible nor worthwhile to review here either the controversy itself or the arguments offered by either side, but it must be noted that the political scientists have not only devised an alternative model of community power relations, but have also attacked the methods of sociological analysis, arguing that they predetermine elitist findings.

Political scientists have noted that persons interviewed often testify to the presence of a business elite even when there is limited empirical evidence to that effect. Edward C. Banfield, in a chapter from his book *Political Influence,* which explores the power structure of Chicago through the review of actual case studies, explodes what he calls this myth of elitist influence, the idea that a small coterie of business leaders secretly "runs" Chicago affairs.

Banfield's exploration dramatizes the difficulty of determining with certainty whether there is a ruling elite in Chicago. It is not really possible to know what is going on behind the scenes. Nevertheless, Banfield argues that elite dominance did not materialize in Chicago, and this, from his viewpoint, had both fortunate and unfortunate results. More important than any question of the moral or political implications of elitism, however, are the reasons Banfield offers for the downtown business clique's inability to control city affairs.

He cites three obstacles impeding elite dominance. First, there is always the distinct possibility, and in many cases the actual prospect, of conflict among the business leaders. Fragmentation of the elite very well may become increasingly likely as its power becomes more evident. Second, the maintenance of any system of control, however limited, requires an elaborate network of associations and the virtually continuous transmission of information requests and orders. Banfield believes that the metropolitan community in America does not provide the basis for such unimpeded communication; indeed, he argues that an elite's attempt to control community affairs would in effect overload the communications system and necessitate full-time involvement in political matters, leaving no time for strictly business concerns. There is little reason to believe that businessmen are presently so disinterested, or are likely to become so disinterested, in the management of their own firms. Third, organizations, the very instruments by which power is concentrated and through which community issues are resolved, often work against the consolidation of power or the resolution of differences of opinion. Organizations, in short, can be a divisive force in community affairs, and any metropolitan community is rife with outspoken organizations, many devoted to special interests and particular objectives. Even the seemingly "public-spirited" civic associations, in their frequent pleas for action in the community's interest as a whole, Banfield considers to be of little assistance in community management. He characterizes their efforts at public education and reform as "platitudinizing," or the enumeration of "plausible sounding, but essentially empty generalities."

In the course of demolishing the myth of elite dominance, Banfield reveals how difficult it is to prove that power is ever exerted by anyone. Indeed, as he notes, the absence of the richest men in Chicago from the settlement of important policy questions doesn't "prove that there is no 'they' behind the scenes." This matter is of central importance to our understanding of the concept of power, for it highlights a general methodological difficulty encountered in the empirical investigation of power: how to locate, observe, and accurately describe (not to mention measure) it in actual but covert use. And, of course, without such operationalism in the concept itself, it is hard to understand how the concept can advance empirical knowledge of the real world of power politics.

The problem is a general one in power analysis and has been increasingly apparent in recent years as power relationships have been more subtle and difficult to delineate in black and white terms. We have chosen to illustrate the problem with a selection dramatizing one aspect of the methodological problem of ascertaining when power or influence is exercised. The focus of this selection from John C. Wahlke, *et al., The Legislative System,* is the informal network of friendship ties in the legislature and the impact of such bonds on actual voting in roll-call votes. This selection attempts to test the assumption that friendship influences voting. Both houses of the legislatures of California, New Jersey, Ohio, and Tennessee were analyzed to confirm the assumption by determining social contacts, their sources, and their effects on legislative behavior.

As might be expected in considering the factors affecting legislative friendship groups, small, informal groups of usually no more than a dozen persons were found to exist; veteran legislators tended to belong to groups excluding freshmen; party lines were usually not crossed; and the formal structure of the legislature conditioned the pattern of such relationships. More important to our purpose, however, was the effect of friendship on legislative voting. It is here that we find the ambiguities of influence embedded. By examining the voting agreement for each possible pair of legislators in the lower house in California it was discovered that friendship did seem to have a significant effect on voting on controversial issues, though perhaps not as important as party identification in determining the vote of the entire chamber. Yet nothing in this elaborate analysis documents the power one friend exerts over another. Nor can it tell us which friend is influencing which, or whether there is a decision jointly reached to vote in agreement. Clearly, friendship is influential, but how influential is hard to say.

Thus, to summarize, in recent years the idea of power has been modified in several ways. From a simple notion of exertion of the will of a man in authority by the use of sanctions, threats of punishment, withholding rewards, or offering benefits, it has come to be recognized as resting on more subtle forms of persuasion. The limits on the power wielder have been stressed, as has the notion that subordinates and followers provide general constraints within which the effective political leader must operate. Power has come to be viewed as resting as much on expertise as on anything else. Moreover, the *reputation* for power has come to be recognized as something possibly quite different from *actual* power, and the general problem of finding power at all has been attacked by researchers in a variety of ways. All these refinements and innovations have rendered, in effect, a new concept of power: one characterized by ambiguity and imprecision, stressing pluralism and inversion, or equalization, in the democratic society.

This new face of power is in part explainable in terms of the communications process; that is, the realization of power can be assumed to occur in the flow of interpersonal and/or interorganizational messages, and can be wielded effectively only when clear, unequivocal meaning is transmitted between sender and receiver. To understand the new face of power, then, it is necessary to explore communications in the political process as a distinct aspect of political analysis.

Suggestions for Additional Reading

Agger, Robert E., Daniel Goldrich, and Bert E. Swanson, *The Rulers and the Ruled: Political Power and Impotence in American Communities.* New York: John Wiley & Sons, Inc., 1964.

Anton, Thomas J., "Power, Pluralism, and Local Politics," *Administrative Science Quarterly,* Vol. VII (March, 1963), 425–451.

Bachrach, Peter, and Morton S. Baratz, "Decisions and Nondecisions: An Analytical Framework," *American Political Science Review,* Vol. LVII (September, 1963), 632–642.

Bachrach, Peter, and Morton S. Baratz, "Two Faces of Power," *American Political Science Review,* Vol. LVI (December, 1962), 947–952.

Barber, James D., ed., *Political Leadership in American Government.* Boston: Little, Brown & Co., 1964.

Burnham, James, *The Managerial Revolution: What Is Happening in the World.* New York: The John Day Company, Inc., 1941.

Dahl, Robert A., *Who Governs? Democracy and Power in an American City.* New Haven, Conn.: Yale University Press, 1961.

Davies, James C., "Charisma in the 1952 Campaign," *American Political Science Review,* Vol. XLVIII (December, 1954), 1083–1102.

de Grazia, Sebastian; "What Authority Is Not," *American Political Science Review,* Vol. LIII (June, 1959), 321–331.

Fiellin, Alan, "The Functions of Informal Groups in Legislative Institutions," *Journal of Politics,* Vol. XXIV (February, 1962), 72–91.

Gilpin, Robert C., and Christopher Wright, eds., *Scientists and National Policy-Making.* New York: Columbia University Press, 1964.

Gouldner, Alvin W., ed., *Studies in Leadership.* New York: Harper & Row, Publishers, Inc., 1950.

Hunter, Floyd, *Community Power Structure: A Study of Decision-Making.* Chapel Hill: University of North Carolina Press, 1953.

Lasswell, Harold D., *The Comparative Study of Elites: An Introduction and Bibliography.* Stanford, Calif.: Stanford University Press, 1952.

Lasswell, Harold D., and Abraham Kaplan, *Power and Society.* New Haven, Conn.: Yale University Press, 1950.

Lasswell, Harold D., and Daniel Lerner, eds., *World Revolutionary Elites: Studies in Coercive Ideological Movements.* Cambridge, Mass.: Massachusetts Institute of Technology Press, 1965.

Leighton, Alexander, *The Governing of Men.* Princeton, N.J.: Princeton University Press, 1945.

Matthews, Donald R., *U.S. Senators and Their World.* Chapel Hill: University of North Carolina Press, 1960.

McConnell, Grant, *Steel and the Presidency: 1962.* New York: W. W. Norton & Company, Inc., 1963.

Mosca, Gaetano, *The Ruling Class,* Hanna D. Kahn, trans.; Arthur Livingston, ed. New York: McGraw-Hill Book Company, 1939.

Peabody, Robert L., and Nelson W. Polsby, eds., *New Perspectives on the House of Representatives.* Chicago: Rand McNally & Co., 1963.

Presthus, Robert V., *Men at the Top: A Study in Community Power.* New York: Oxford University Press, 1964.

Simon, Herbert A., "Notes on the Observation and Measurement of Political Power," *Journal of Politics,* Vol. XV (November, 1953), 500–516.

White, Ralph K., and Ronald Lippitt, *Autocracy and Democracy.* New York: Harper & Row, Publishers, Inc., 1960.

A. Leadership

Political Leaders and Followers

James C. Davies

Between Leaders and Followers

. . . Thousands of books have been written about hundreds of prominent political leaders—some five thousand, it has been estimated, on Abraham Lincoln alone. This writing would not be done were it not for the enduring fascination of great men, for not only writers but also readers. Perhaps no other single subject save sex has so preoccupied the human

James C. Davies, *Human Nature in Politics: The Dynamics of Political Behavior* (New York: John Wiley & Sons, Inc., 1963), Chap. 9, "Political Leaders and Followers," pp. 277, 278, 279–82, 285–88, 293–308. Reprinted by permission.

race, whether of high or low station, subtle or naïve, illiterate or educated. And the most prominent single category of great or at least prominent men is to be found in politics—as statesmen, agitators, theorists, polemicists, philosophers—or all of these wrapped in one man's life, as in the case of Thomas Jefferson, Lenin, Wilson, or Nehru.

The difficulty . . . lies in the typical ignoring of the basic fact of leadership, namely, that it involves universally a relationship between leaders and followers. Without this relationship there might be a society, but there surely would be no leaders and probably no politics either. A man who thinks he is Napoleon is ordinarily classed among the insane these days and confined to an institution, just as Napoleon was confined to Elba and then St. Helena. The reason for confining the real Napoleon was that, without his adoring public, he could not so irrepressibly wage war and conquer nations. In short, by removing him from France and his adoring public, he was made into somebody other than Napoleon.

Failure to appreciate the necessary relationship has led to an impossible dilemma, one of whose horns was polished by Thomas Carlyle and the other by Leo Tolstoi. Carlyle tended to see history with heavy emphasis on the role of the great man or the great devil—Cromwell and Frederick the Great being examples of the former and the "thin, acrid, incorruptible, seagreen" Robespierre of the latter. Tolstoi, in writing on the invasion of Russia by France, protests so much that Napoleon's role was insignificant that he raises him to prominence, almost without external confirmation, by repeatedly emphasizing Napoleon's triviality. Carlyle appeared to regard mankind as sheep and leaders as shepherds; Tolstoi would have called leaders wolves, as Jefferson indeed did.

The dilemma is a false one. Some leaders are shepherds, some are wolves, and some fit neither metaphor. But a man would not be a leader without a public which adheres to him and which looks to him for expression, guidance, and the making of most decisions in public affairs. Each is as necessary to the other (but not by analogy) as husband is to wife, and each is as necessary to the subject of leadership as husband and wife are to marriage. And yet virtually all discussions of leadership leave out the public half of the equation. If behavior is a function of the organism and the environment, so also (but not by analogy) is leadership a function of the leader and the public that follows him.

At least two reasons help explain the literary unpopularity of the popular half of the leadership concept. Leaders themselves, as men of nonaverage ability, find it easy to exaggerate their freedom of action and therefore their power. It is easier for them, in their self-image, to see themselves as governing rather than being governed, to see the broad extent rather than the broad limits of their power. Being chief of state over a large area of land is apt to make a leader feel he actually controls it and its people, whereas in reality even the most remarkable, gifted, and humane leaders are able to do little more than accelerate or hold steady or decelerate the rate of social movement through history. The track and the switches along the line are pretty much beyond the control of the locomotive engineer. The role of the engineer is greater than that of even his most travel-conscious passengers, but he is ahead of no one if the travelers get off and climb on another train.

The inevitable, understandable, even incorruptible narcissism of leaders is less excusably furthered by their biographers, most of whom seem to have only the vaguest theoretical awareness that leaders have any connection with anyone below the rank of Congressman, Member of Parliament, General of the Army, or the leading intellectuals of their age. The very central relationship of the leader to his broad popular following gets less mention than do the great man's childhood acquaintances and his close friends and enemies in public life. One does not have to agree altogether with Tolstoi to recognize that without their popular following leaders could not rule over more than a small segment of their nations. . . .

. . . It is indeed a paradox that the ruler is most powerful who represents the broadest range of followers among the people and that the one who governs without it thereby is not necessarily impotent but weaker. This relationship is an intricate and specific one, not readily transferable from one time to another, from one place to another, or from one leader to another. . . .

The most intellectually successful effort to conceptualize the leader-follower relationship is the work of a novelist. In his classic political allegory, *Mario and the Magician,* Thomas Mann gives to both leader and followers equal prominence. The followers do not become an impersonal mass, which a public never is but which social theorists are apt to convert any aggregation of more than fifty people into. The leader is not simply the embodiment of vast social forces. Both, as individuals, are in very intense interaction, the very aspect of leader-follower relationships which writers are most prone to ignore. If the discussion that follows falls short of Mann's brilliant symmetry and exquisite psychological insight, it is for lack of adequate facts about this powerful and subtle relationship—and a desire to abide by the ground rules of nonfiction.

What are the special characteristics of the relationship? It is like that between friends, work associates, brothers, husband and wife, and parents and children in its intimacy. Followers are incessantly curious about the personal life and welfare of their leader. They want to know what he eats, how long he sleeps, what he does for recreation, and what his wife is like. When he is ill they worry. When he is troubled they are troubled. When he triumphs, the victory is also personally their own. Again like these other relationships, the one be-

tween the leader and his followers is mutual and reciprocal. Followers depend on their leader and he on them, not just for direct support in their common political program but more personally.

To gain new strength for their unending task of governing, leaders periodically venture out into the sea of citizens, to be refreshed by the salty breezes that seldom penetrate a ruler's mansion or palace. On a popular tour, [Woodrow] Wilson was at first shocked and then braced by hearing a voice from the crowd yell, "Atta boy, Woody," an appellation no intimate of his would dream of using. Franklin Roosevelt was similarly buoyed up at a discouraging time during the depths of the depression. Jarred, jolted, often squeezed and twisted by well-wishers who want merely to touch him, a leader nonetheless needs this popular contact in the same sense that brother needs contact with brother, husband with wife, parents with children. As such the relationship is one instance of the basic social need.

The leader differs from his followers most markedly in his role: by and large he is the active and followers are the passive participants in the exercise of political power. That is, he proposes and the public ultimately disposes. The leader decides what to do and how to do it. The public decides whether he shall be permitted to do it. The latitude allowed the leader may be broad or narrow, but his power to effect anything enduring is constantly limited by the public's power to grant or withdraw support. This mutual interdependence of the roles of proposer and disposer obviously applies in societies where the process of popular responsibility is institutionalized by periodic elections. It applies, perhaps equally, in dictatorships, because a leader is in no more political interaction with those who are indifferent to him than he is with the mountains, the forests, and the rivers. By sheer coercion he may be able to elicit labor from many people, but this process is no more political than the relationship between a man and a mule or between a prison warden and a prisoner. The power that is exercised is not political. This, of course, is not to say that there is no politics in a dictatorship, but that dictatorships, to the extent that they rely on political means, are dependent on popular assent and support.

But an almost unique characteristic is the great distance separating leader and follower. If indeed it is intimate, it is for virtually all followers remote. Only a small fraction can ever establish even the thin strand of contact that is involved in attending a parade or other public meeting at which the leader appears. For others, the contact is indirect, mediated through the electronic equipment of radio and television and through the printed page. It is this great distance that apparently causes students to neglect the relation between a leader and his broad popular following, and to neglect the relation between leaders and their students and biographers. But thin though these strands are, their cumulative strength both ways is so great as to bind leaders and followers closely and strongly one to the other in their joint endeavors.

The relation between leader and followers is thus at once intimate and remote, with the unbelievably complex role of the leader as policy formulator, initiator, and executor being exercised within popular limits. What then resolves this paradox of a relation that in most other parts of society could not exist? Why do women sometimes swoon when they see their political leader gaze in their direction? Why have dictators like Perón occasionally received marital and often more casual sexual proposals from ardent female adherents? And why do some men and women cry when their beloved leader dies?

A standard explanation is that such people—which includes, in more or less intense form, all people in any modern nation at one time—are responding to a father or big-brother image and are emotionally tied to a surrogate father or brother. But the pattern of interactions, which is so varied from one nation to the next, does not quite fit this explanation. It makes a species into a genus. More appropriately the relation can be described as identification. To the extent that they interact with their leader, followers are putting themselves in his place. In their own minds they are becoming him. The style in which they do so may in some national circumstances resemble the relation between children and their parents, brothers, friends, or believers and their god. . . .

The special character of identification has to do with the remoteness of the intimacy. The followers identify not with their equal but with one whom they look up to as a man of superior virtue (energy, skill, intelligence, wisdom, compassion, patriotism, and other virtues). They identify with a possibly imperfect ideal who represents all that they are and all that they believe in politically. The leader is not what his followers are but what they would like to be. If they have particular enemies and friends in society, they expect their leader to share them, defeating the former and bringing victory to the latter. If they have particular aspirations for their country, the leader embodies these aspirations.

An implication of this is that the more completely a citizen has fulfilled his needs and hopes, and the freer therefore he is of frustrations and anxieties, the less likely he is to need to identify passively with a political leader. The weaker and more frustrated a citizen is, the more likely he will want to identify passively with a very strong, very wise, and virtuous political leader. Indeed a virile leader may politically arouse a following that has been hitherto impotent and withdrawn from the polity. If a citizen is frustrated and anxious enough, he will suffer from the same perceptual distortions of leaders that beset other facets of his outlook on life and will more likely make a god of his leader and devils of his and the leader's opponents. But no man in politics, whether citizen or politician, is altogether free of admiration for superiors. If successful citizens take a more realistic view of leaders because their need to identify is less, they will nevertheless identify in some degree. . . .

*   *   *

The Special Characteristics of Leaders

Thus far we have emphasized what binds leaders and followers together. Before taking up in more detail this relationship, . . . we may appropriately here consider what it is that sets leaders apart from followers—what causes them to become the living paradox of identifiers who are markedly distinct from the followers with whom they reciprocally identify.

. . . In terms of basic needs, political leaders are distinct from other prominent people, not in their desire for power but in their sheer enjoyment of the political process. They engage in politics because it is the way they can fulfill themselves most completely, a process related to their skills and capacities. To enjoy political life, one must have the abilities it demands, just as a sportsman needs good physical coordination, strength, endurance, etc. At this point we can emphasize the more common characteristics which distinguish the very heterogeneous category of political activists—the élite from which chiefs of state emerge.

Probably most of the characteristics distinguishing any elite group also distinguish the political elite. Not only business leaders, intellectual leaders, and professional leaders, but also political leaders tend to come from middle-class rather than working-class backgrounds.[1] A clear majority of the Presidents, Vice Presidents, and Cabinet members of the United States from 1789–1934 were the sons of professionals, proprietors, and officials. The rest were the sons of farmers or workingmen, but only 4 per cent were of wage-earning class origin, compared with some 36 per cent of the labor force in the wage-earning class as a proportion of the total popula-

tion. Some 95 per cent of these same high public officers before they entered politics had trained for careers as professionals, proprietors, and officials.[2] The overwhelming majority of the members of the German Cabinets of 1890–1945 came from either the aristocracy or the middle class, though only during the Weimar Republic were Cabinet members manifestly political officers.[3]

A study of the mostly political elite in Nigeria indicates the same tendency for the ruling class to come from a status group well above the bottom. A third of the topmost 156 elitists came from old elite families, most of these elitists being the sons of tribal chiefs. The others were of "ordinary stock." All but two members of the group had finished grade school, and 45 per cent possessed university degrees. Even in a period of rapid transition, which so upsets established status patterns, high-status backgrounds and education during childhood count heavily in Nigeria.[4] Upward social mobility almost by definition characterizes leaders in the modern political era. And in a political age, unless their fathers were in politics, they are moving up. A slim shred of evidence suggests that before entering politics, leaders had improved over the status of their fathers.[5] But in his study of United States Senators, out of the 180 who served in the ten years from 1947–1957, Matthews found that 15 per cent "were sons of politicians" and "another 15 per cent had one or more

[1] *Donald R. Matthews,* The Social Background of Political Decision-Makers *(New York: Doubleday & Company, Inc., 1954), Table 1, p. 23.*

[2] *Ibid., Table 7, p. 30.*

[3] *Ibid., Table 13, p. 49.*

[4] *See Hugh H. Smythe and Mabel M. Smythe,* The New Nigerian Elite *(Stanford, Calif.: Stanford University Press, 1960), pp. 74–92, esp. 78–83 and 87. Of the 156 interviewed, 113 were government officials (including ninety-six legislators), but only twenty-eight listed government and politics as their major occupation.*

[5] *R. M. Rosenzweig, "The Politician and the Career in Politics,"* Midwest Journal of Political Science, *Vol. I (1957), 163–172. The study was based on interviews of sixteen candidates for public office (mostly the state legislature) in Massachusetts. "Thirteen of the sixteen had higher status jobs than did their fathers. . . . This group of politicians was characterized by strong upward mobility" (p. 167).*

members of their families active in politics during their formative years."[6]

The major relevant point is that if they are more than usually upwardly mobile—which the data suggest but fail to demonstrate—political leaders are therefore apt to be marginal people, loosening old social and moral ties and tightening new ones, either in their movement from one major status group to another or within a major status category. And as marginal people, they are likely to suffer and enjoy the mental consequences of never quite being sure where they belong and what they value. Partly for this reason, they have an unusual desire for public acceptance.

It is reasonable to suppose also that leaders are extraordinary in their energy level. They are better able to work long hours, weekends, holidays, and when they should be asleep and others are. Some of this energy is employed in rising socially, part of it is employed in the simple enjoyment of politics, but part of it is also employed in gaining widespread popular acceptance. If a leader has no desire for this, perhaps he would never go into politics at all.

Alexander Hamilton is an instance of the man of low status, marginality, and high energy who leaped over numerous social barriers to high position, not just as a staff man for Washington but as a backstage politician in his own right. Born out in the periphery of British colonial society on a tiny island in the West Indies, he could not even claim legitimate birth. Moving in late adolescence to New York, a major center of British America, he jumped from King's College (now Columbia University) to Washington's wartime staff, to a brilliant marriage into one of New York's most distinguished families, and then into post-Revolutionary New York state and national politics. His energy was extraordinary, his mind sharp and cutting. He loved power and—it is reasonable to suppose—his hypersensitive

reaction to lowborn status combined with these other factors to boost him up and keep him forever seeking new heights. The reason he gave for not declining the challenge of Aaron Burr to a duel was that such apparent cowardice would ruin him politically in New York.

Theodore Roosevelt had many of the same personality characteristics that animated Hamilton, with the sole and gross exception of low status. Born into one of the best families in New York, he needed to seek no formal social status. Indeed his family were so sure of their own social supremacy that they considered it a degradation for Teddy to enter politics. Was he then, with his comfortable status, marginal or not? In his particular instance we cannot at one level find much evidence of genuine social easiness. With his poor physique and weak eyes, however, he experienced a kind of marginality: he always felt that he was on the edge of the world of the big and the strong. He spent his life trying to get into the middle and on top of this world. Even his bravery had a compulsive quality about it, as though he were really not even trying to prove himself to others but—in an extreme kind of marginality—to himself.

*   *   *

Ingredients of Success

*   *   *

The basic criterion for at least a continued tolerance of leaders is whether or not they succeed. Lord Charnwood pointed this out in comparing Lincoln and General George McClellan, the Democratic candidate for President in 1864. Charnwood invoked Dante and said that men were not first judged "according as they were of irreproachable or reproachable character; they were divided into those who did and those who did not."[7]

We must at least concede to the spirit of Plato's Thrasymachus and of Hegel

---

[6] Donald R. Matthews, *U.S. Senators and Their World* (*Chapel Hill: University of North Carolina Press, 1960*), *p. 49.*

[7] *Godfrey Rathbone Benson, Lord Charnwood, Abraham Lincoln (New York: Pocket Books, Inc., 1952), p. 312. This most penetrating biography was first published in 1916.*

that power must indeed be exercised, and effectively, in order for people to accept a leader. If there is any one necessary condition for judgment, it is this one, and for better and worse it is in many cases apparently deemed a sufficient criterion for judgment—among general publics and elites alike. If Hitler had at last succeeded in Germany in 1945—if Germany had been the victor in the Second World War—it is doubtful that his posthumous following would have been the relatively small one that it became. . . .

But the criterion of success is hard to apply and calls for continued reappraisal, by publics and elites, both during and after a leader's tenure of office. The standard plea for dictators, whether they built Autobahns or made the trains run on time or built bridges in Louisiana, is that they did something. . . .

* * *

The criterion of success can be more fully considered by comparing political with moral leaders, recognizing that Woodrow Wilson is on the borderline between the two categories. Socrates, Christ, and Gandhi were moral leaders whose marginal involvement in public policy in various ways resulted in their violent deaths as martyrs to principle. At least in their lifetimes the first two were hardly accountable as successful. They merely taught; they did nothing else; they stubbornly accomplished only their own death. Yet few people in the Western world would regard the lives and teachings of these three individuals, from the long-run standpoint, as anything less than triumphant achievements of civilization, a continuing process with which politics is inescapably concerned and for which the lives of these three are inescapable criteria.

Politicians are not judged by exactly the same set of standards as moral leaders, but moral considerations inevitably are involved, raising and lowering the reputations of individuals who may or may not have built roads and bridges, established social security programs, or won wars. . . .

But aside from moral aspects, the criteria for political success as such remain crude. In order to do something, leaders must have at least some awareness of the problems of their time. They probably must have more than the expressive awareness that William Jennings Bryan did of the farmers' problems, as only the mouthpiece for only one of several groups of discontented people of his time. Clear failures, the sort that are sometimes consciously blocked out of the memories of both their contemporaries and later generations, include men who were very dimly aware of these problems, like Louis XV, Nicholas II, and Buchanan and Harding. They also include those who, if aware, made no more than feeble efforts to solve problems. . . . All leaders who fail do so for more than one reason. There is never the Shakespearean tragic simplicity which can lay blame to rest in one grave of vaulting ambition or indecision or whatnot. And none of these leaders, a product of his time almost as much as his fellow countrymen, is altogether accountable for his failures, even though he had some freedom of action.

Our task in these pages is not finally to bury Caesars or to praise them but rather to understand them and judge them tentatively. . . .

* * *

. . . Let us categorize styles of rule more precisely, so that we more exactly know some of the bases for selection, retention, and adulation or condemnation of leaders by their publics. We must remember that some type of success is always presupposed: we remember but we do not honor Neville Chamberlain and James Buchanan—as failures rather than real leaders.

Leadership Styles and Responsibility

The basic stylistic distinction is between autocrats and what Friedrich and Brzezinski call heterocrats,[8] between rulers who

8 *See Carl J. Friedrich and Zbigniew K. Brzezinski,* Totalitarian Dictatorship and Autocracy *(Cam-*

rule themselves—are ultimate law unto themselves—and rulers who are responsible to some other persons or some other thing. The some other persons may include an entire populace, as in a democracy, or a small group of men, as in an oligarchy. The some other thing may be a concept, like the law of nature or of nature's God, or the nation's traditions or its written constitution. The basic distinction is between responsible and irresponsible rule, which is roughly equivalent to constitutional *vs.* unconstitutional rule.

*   *   *

It is appropriate at this point, before listing various kinds of rulers, to indicate that no ruler or ruling group exactly fits any typology, but each exemplifies to some degree different styles of rule. The statement applies even to the basic distinction between autocratic and heterocratic rule. No ruler acts altogether responsibly or irresponsibly. Even the totalitarian ruler has some limits to his power, established by the simple ability of people to refuse support, to take refuge in apathy. And even constitutional, responsible rulers do acts that are unprecedented. The American Constitutional Convention of 1787 was called to consider a revision of the Articles of Confederation; the Convention promptly proceeded to violate its instructions and to make a new, altogether unprecedented, unauthorized organic law.

Following a typology established by Max Weber, but not following it very strictly, I suggest that there are three major types of irresponsible rule and the same three types of responsible rule: the traditional, the charismatic, and the rational. Perhaps the archetypes of the traditional irresponsible ruler were the Russian tsars, who presumed to be exercising power according to long-established custom but for practical purposes recognized no superior earthly authority. Peter

the Great adopted the role of the Russian God's earthly emissary as the effective head of the church. When a delegation of churchmen came to ask that he appoint a head of the state church, Peter pointed to himself and said "here is your patriarch."[9] . . .

A major characteristic of this type of rule is that it is government by grace, a kind of paradoxical omnipotence derived from God, a magical interpretation of the nation's past which derives authority in a misty, romantic history. This style of rule ignores the origins of authority (sanctioned power) in a prior, often savage, and never misty test of strength and cunning, violence and fraud. It elicits apathy in part at least because the manifestations of rule are so often brutal and perhaps because the people fear they are themselves truly powerless and that God is indeed on the ruler's side. This apathy, rooted in the sheer struggle for survival, is mistaken for assent. When the apathy changes to antipathy in a revolution, such rulers are apparently often incredulous. The deep popular reluctance, indeed fear, of breaking with the past lends by default a precarious stability to such regimes.

The term "charisma"—miraculously given power—was transferred by Max Weber from its original religious meaning to politics. He described it as the "absolutely personal devotion and personal confidence in revelation, heroism, or other qualities of individual leadership."[10] The charismatic leader is thus one whose claim to rule is neither as a perpetuator of traditional values nor as one who resolves conflicting interests by reasonable and just means but as one endowed with superhuman powers to solve political problems. In the abstract, pure case he is seen by his

---

9 *Thomas G. Masaryk*, The Spirit of Russia (*London: George Allen & Unwin, Ltd., 1919*), Vol. I, *p. 62. Peter nevertheless was restrained by comparison with the early Soviet rulers. He favored religious freedom, saying that "the human conscience is subject to God alone." Ibid., p. 63.*

10 *H. H. Gerth and C. W. Mills, eds.*, From Max Weber: Essays in Sociology (*London: Routledge & Kegan Paul Ltd., 1948*), *p. 79.*

bridge, Mass.: Harvard University Press, 1956), pp. 3–4. I may be deviating somewhat from at least their vocabulary in my use of the term.

followers as being *all*-powerful, *all*-wise, and morally *perfect*. Perhaps Mahomet and Brigham Young; who were simultaneously prophets and political leaders, come close to the pure case.

One of the outstanding characteristics of charismatic rule is its mass base. Unlike the tsar or the palace revolutionary, the charismatic ruler is not content with gaining and maintaining control merely over the machinery of government—the police, administrative offices, legislature, and courts. He consciously seeks to gain control over the individual citizen—not just by the threat of force, but perhaps more significantly by appealing for affirmative and enthusiastic devotion. The leader seeks not passive acceptance of his rule but an active identification of the citizens' needs and expectations with his own and those of the nation. The political demands of individuals become uniform, at least on the manifest level, and are absorbed in and merged with the economic, social, and ethnic demands of the nation as these are expressed by the leader. A greater portion of the individual's life finds its expression in politics. The charismatic follower becomes an undifferentiated, cancerous cell on the body politic.

Like other styles of leadership, charisma is not a characteristic of leaders as such but a relationship between leader and followers. It depends both on the construction by a leader and his associates of an image of him as infallible, omniscient, and incorruptible and on a positive, active response to this kind of image building by those who are predisposed toward such leadership. The "compleat" charismatic follower is oriented in politics toward candidates, and in a particular way, rather than toward parties or issues. He tends to divide political figures on the basis of strength or weakness, omnicompetence or utter incompetence, righteousness or iniquity. He is unable to see any but good qualities in the leader he accepts or to see any good qualities in the one he rejects. Although strong liking for a candidate is not in itself evidential, for charismatics

the emotional attraction of a candidate is predominant and is coupled with the feeling that the leader is the incarnation of all virtues.

Pure charismatic followers, like pure charismatic leaders, are ideal types unlikely to be found in actual situations. There are doubtless some charismatic tendencies in all candidates for popularly elected office above the level of sanitation supervisor. The well-known panegyrics of those who introduce candidates at a public gathering as often as not are full of hackneyed phrases suggesting the power of their men to move mountains, stop the tides, and gain or regain Utopia within two weeks of taking office. There are doubtless some tendencies in all citizens to believe that the candidate of their choice is superhuman and that his opponent is infrahuman. For, campaign hyperbole aside, the phenomenon of strong leadership is perhaps only rarely divorced completely from the will to be or to follow a leader who will make no mistakes and suffer no defeats at the hands of malignant, real enemies and hostile, shadowy forces. In politics, neither St. George nor the dragon is ever quite dead.[11]

Charismatic irresponsible rule differs from traditional irresponsible rule in being highly individual and personal. If a Russian tsar could claim some kind of mystical historic justification for his irresponsible rule, the charismatic derives power and gains authority by his own unique attributes. Government is an act of sovereign grace, but the ultimate sovereign is not God or the spirit of the revolution or whatnot. It is the person of the ruler. In an era of predominantly charismatic rule in a nation, the people do not want to cling to the past. Having made the free jump into the future, they reject the past and what it stands for, focusing

11 *For an analysis of charismatic tendencies among voters in the 1952 Presidential campaign, when a military hero was elected, in the United States, see J. C. Davies, "Charisma in the 1952 Campaign,"* American Political Science Review, *Vol. XLVIII (1954), 1083–1102, where some of the above ideas were previously expressed.*

all their political loyalties on the person of the ruler, to whom they cling all the more intensely for having rejected the past. People who do attach themselves to such an irresponsible ruler, of course, have not thrown off the major part of their past.

When there has been a popular shift from passive acceptance of traditional irresponsible to charismatic irresponsible rule, a tentative step has been taken from apathy to some kind of passive political involvement. The public has at last and at least come to watch the political circus. With the passage of time this very likely means that the public will become critical judges of the performers. They could never have done this if they had stayed away from the show. There is additional hope of political maturation because, in contrast to the traditional irresponsibility of tsars, charismatic rulers are unable to transfer their own personal popularity to a designated successor, because their authority is derived from personal popular acceptance rather than from some mystic, supernatural, metahistorical force.

Julius Caesar was one of the archetypes of the charismatic irresponsible ruler. His eager cadre, with little hindrance from their chief, had statues erected of him—even temples built to honor him alone—and various festive days were established in his honor. For whatever reasons, he refused to accept the crown of kingship, which would have lent the aura of tradition to his rule—and possibly have diminished his personal authority. But he did permit himself to receive the reverence bestowed on gods, including chariots to carry his images.

Caesar's successors made a routine out of this personal investment with gracious authority and adopted as the verbal symbol of their power the name Caesar, which thus began its lineal descent down to the last tsar and last kaiser at the end of the First World War. When the later Caesars did this they were to a substantial degree losing the personal basis of their rule and becoming traditional rulers. They were to a considerable degree irresponsible but,

despite the symbols, no longer such unique and individual power figures. They wore the investments of Caesarly power like a garment that had been tailored for someone else.

The irresponsible charismatic with his antique prototype has had a renaissance in the twentieth century in the style of rule of Hitler and Stalin, whose cult of personality was a central theme of the "secret" speech which Khrushchev made to the Twentieth Party Congress in February, 1956. Not only was Stalin in his lifetime apparently regarded by his followers and seemingly by himself as a supremely competent ruler, he was supreme in other realms as well. A poem appeared in *Pravda* in 1936 that in part goes as follows:

Stalin

O, thou great leader of the peoples,
Thou who gavest man his life,
Thou who fructified the lands,
Thou who rejuvenated centuries,
Made chords sing and blossoms spring,
Our hearts love, our factories work;
In life around us is the strength,
O, father, of thy mighty hands.

Thou art the sun—my youth in bloom,
In hearts of millions reflected;
Thou hast from age-old gloom
My sleeping country resurrected.

And the disease has traveled to the Orient, to rationalist, Confucian, worldly China, which has no use for the spiritual, the supernatural. A poem appeared in *Women of China,* a magazine published in Peking, in 1961, entitled

In Praise of Mao Tse-tung

Mao Tse-tung,
Mao Tse-tung,
You are rain for the planting season,
Breeze for the hottest noon,
You are the red sun that never sets,
Wind for boats that need a sail.
If one never wants poverty to suffer,
He has to follow Mao Tse-tung forever.[12]

Another Chinese magazine reported that a man who suffered for thirteen years

12 *Both the Stalin and the Mao Tse-tung poems are quoted from* Atlas: The Magazine of the World Press, *Vol. I, No. 4 (June, 1961), 60.* . . .

from a gastrointestinal disorder was cured by obeying the prescription of a scroll which Mao gave him, the scroll admonishing "let your body give rise to a power of resistance which will struggle against and finally defeat . . . a chronic disease." The man recovered, finally being healthy enough to shout "it is the party and Chairman Mao that have given me a new life."[13]

Kwame Nkrumah, the Prime Minister of Ghana, like the ancient Caesars, is honored by statues and street names in his homeland. He has even outdone the Caesars, thanks to a technical advance after two thousand years, by appearing on postage stamps. An article in the Ghana press describes him thus: "Kwame Nkrumah has revealed himself like a Moses—yea, a greater Moses . . . with the support of all African leaders he will help to lead his people across the Red Sea of imperialist massacre and suffering." A newspaper cartoon in Accra in March, 1960, showed a man labeled "Africa" tied to a post, with "Christian settler" shooting at him. He cries "Kwame! Kwame!" and out of the sky, clad in a white robe, comes Nkrumah to the rescue, saying "Africa, oh Motherland." It is not quite clear whether Africa is Christ and Nkrumah is God, but the pictured scene scarcely implies that Osagyefo (the "great leader") is human.[14]

A third category of irresponsible rule is the rational or pararational. If the traditional irresponsible ruler founds his authority in the mystic and misty past or in divine sanction, the rational ruler who is irresponsible bases his in reason, more exactly in Reason, which in some manner has been revealed to him exclusively and in the name of which the irresponsible, rationalist ruler is sole interpreter—in a real sense, the embodiment of Reason himself. Notable instances have been the leaders of the French Revolution and the early part of the Russian Revolution. Such rule and also traditional irresponsible rule differ from charismatic rule because the source of authority lies somewhere outside the ruler himself. In fact, however, the authority of the rationalist irresponsible ruler is also personal, like that of the traditional and charismatic rulers, because ultimately there is no restraint on any of these rulers other than that which is self-imposed or which is the consequence of the public's ability to withhold support by being apathetic. The latter restraint to the irresponsible rationalist ruler is an obstacle like climate, topography, and natural resources—a natural phenomenon that has to be contended with and even turned to the ruler's advantage, but not an object of solicitude save as the means of achieving the ruler's purposes.

There is in actuality no pure instance of any of these three categories of irresponsible rule—quite apart from the very broad limitations imposed by the public's ability to withhold support. The pure case would be a ruler who was altogether free of any inner restraint, any inhibition of conscience, and whose knowledge of how to elicit popular support was so complete that he could make an entire populace into his willing instrument. But it may be that the irresponsible ruler who invokes traditional or rational sanction feels less restraint than the purely personal ruler. If one believes that whatever he does is effected with the blessing of a nation's past, its gods, God, or Reason, he may be better able to free himself from feelings of remorse, guilt, or of even the possibility of being in error than the charismatic ruler is.

* * *

Actual autocratic rulers . . . never fall neatly into one category or another. Each will in greater or less degree manifest some traditionalism, some charisma, some rationalism. If the tsars were traditionalists, they also in some instances (for example, Alexander I, who in a sense was Russia's

---

[13] *Quoted in the* Los Angeles Times (*May 16, 1961*).
[14] *The quotations and the cartoon appeared in the* BBC Listener, *No. 1685 (July 13, 1961), 46, 66.*

response to the Napoleonic image) manifest some charismatic tendencies and (again like Alexander) some rationalism along with the mysticism. If Hitler's rule was highly personal, it also appealed to the mystical folk spirit of the ancient Germanic race. And it had a strong appeal for those who thought there should be a more rational relationship between talent, performance, and reward than the rigidly class-based German society had hitherto allowed. The rationalist style of Lenin's rule, despite the early revolutionists' effort to deny the past and magic, could not avoid the popular imputation to Lenin of an historic role as a Russian and the possession of superhuman powers. Typologies such as the present one are useful if they help indicate relative emphasis. If they suggest a simple-minded purity of style they do a disservice, because styles of rule are far harder to isolate in actuality than are even such complicated stuffs as organic compounds in the chemical laboratory. The chemically pure charismatic has never existed.

After this discussion of various combinations of autocratic, irresponsible rule, we can now consider the heterocratic responsible counterparts.

Traditional responsible rulers are mainly responsible to the past, to a maintenance of both uniformity and continuity of present with past action. They are highly reluctant to do what has not been done or what the founding fathers, the great monarchs, or the great prime ministers of the past might disapprove of. Like Churchill, they do not feel that they have taken office in order to preside over the liquidation of anything great and glorious or indeed to change anything that has worked fairly well. Some examples include Charles II and George III of England, Franz Josef of the Austro-Hungarian Empire, possibly Wilhelm II, and surely Konrad Adenauer of Germany, the Ashanti chiefs of Ghana, such American Presidents as the two Adamses, McKinley, Taft, and Eisenhower. Like any other rulers,

these traditional responsible rulers may be vigorous and active, such as George III or Churchill or Wilhelm or Adenauer, but they are notably inactive when it comes to real innovation. They wish to restore the power of the king or of the empire or of their beloved fatherland, and they wish only such adaptation to changed circumstances as is absolutely essential in order for the monarchy or the empire or the nation to survive.

It is logically inconsistent to include charismatic rule in the responsible heterocratic category. Yet in actuality there are several rulers whose appeal has had an inevitably magic quality about it, with many followers believing the leader to be omnipotent, omniscient, and morally perfect, but with the leader himself being rather strictly self-limited in his actions. Some such rulers who have had considerable charismatic appeal include Andrew Jackson and Franklin Roosevelt in the United States, de Gaulle in France, and probably Bourguiba in Tunisia. Jackson was enormously popular but also had a clear sense that he could not do everything he wanted to. He was limited by the expectations of the middle class, the working class, and the western farmers who supported him so ardently and to whom he was so sensitive. He was also limited by a kind of gentlemanly code of his own that kept him from doing things in defiance of the Constitution or even of due legal process. In his fight with the Supreme Court, the veritable symbol of tradition in the United States, Franklin Roosevelt was only attempting to do what Lincoln and other Presidents had done—alter its composition by enlarging its membership. When he lost, he did not by guile, demagogy, or other autocratic process seek to reverse the emphatic rejection of his plan by Congress. He abode by the decision.

The deep suspicion of his most extreme opponents, who, like some of his ardent supporters, imagined him capable of anything, was a source of puzzled anger on Roosevelt's part because he was severely limited by a set of deeply inculcated values acquired at home, in preparatory school, and in college. These more effectively controlled him than did his extreme opponents. In the very critical, frightened months of 1933 when he first became President, he was probably more restrained from becoming a dictator by these values than by any interference on the part of Congress or any major segment of the public. Yet he retained a magical quality that not only contributed to his victories at election time but to a belief among some that he could do no wrong and could not fail in any of his enterprises, domestic or foreign.

Rational responsible rulers, the most desirable and perhaps least to be feared category, are inhibited by a "reasonable" outlook. It includes a healthy, reasoned respect for the value and inevitability of tradition or habit but is more immediately responsive to the unprecedented, perhaps nonrecurrent exigencies of the political dilemma of the era. The appeal is to thought more than to either habit or emotion or personal loyalties, and the leader presupposes an ability of people to respond to such an appeal. Among American Presidents, Jefferson is doubtless the most clear-cut instance, with Wilson and Lincoln exhibiting a style that was predominantly rational but less purely so than Jefferson's. Thomas Masaryk, the founder of Czechoslovakia, and Nehru, the father of modern India, are other instances.

The predominance of a rational style does not, of course, preclude less than rational actions. In a sense Jefferson's Declaration of Independence was a restrained piece of demagogy in its focusing of hostility on the British King rather than Parliament. And Jefferson was capable of decisively defeating a political enemy by every honorable political device he could employ, as in his attack on Aaron Burr in 1807. But probably no American President has depended so heavily on quiet discourse and persuasive appeal to reason in dealing with both Congress and the public. More responsible to what he thought reasonable and proper than responsive to the popular passion, he could be reluctant as a strict constructionist of the Constitution to purchase Louisiana, despite the manifest and widespread popularity of such a move—and later ignore widespread unpopularity in pursuing his policy of embargo and nonintercourse with Europe during the Napoleonic wars.

It seems evident not only that irresponsible autocratic rulers can exhibit in varying degrees all three styles of rule—traditional, charismatic, and rational—but that responsible heterocrats can show the same styles. It is also evident that no actual ruler who succeeds—that is, who does—can be altogether responsible or irresponsible. Even as the charismatic autocrat will limit the arbitrariness of his rule in the interest of staying in power, so even the traditionalist heterocrat will bend tradition slightly and the rationalist heterocrat on occasion act rather arbitrarily on his own authority, unauthorized by tradition, constitution, reason, or popular mandate.

B. Authority

The President's Power to Persuade

Richard E. Neustadt

. . . The Constitutional Convention of 1787 is supposed to have created a government of "separated powers." It did nothing of the sort. Rather, it created a government of separated institutions *sharing* powers. "I am part of the legislative process," Eisenhower often said in 1959 as a reminder of his veto. Congress, the dispenser of authority and funds, is no less part of the administrative process. Federalism adds another set of separated institutions. The Bill of Rights adds others. Many public purposes can only be achieved by voluntary acts of private institutions; the press, for one, in Douglass Cater's phrase, is a "fourth branch of government." And with the coming of alliances abroad, the separate institutions of a London, or a Bonn, share in the making of American public policy.

What the Constitution separates our political parties do not combine. The parties are themselves composed of separated organizations sharing public authority. The authority consists of nominating powers. Our national parties are confederations of state and local party institutions, with a headquarters that represents the White House, more or less, if the party has a President in office. These confederacies manage Presidential nominations. All other public offices depend upon electorates confined within the states. All other nominations are controlled within the states. The President and Congressmen who bear one party's label are divided by dependence upon different sets of voters. The differences are sharpest at the stage of nomination. The White House has too

small a share in nominating congressmen, and Congress has too little weight in nominating Presidents for party to erase their constitutional separation. Party links are stronger than is frequently supposed, but nominating processes assure the separation.

The separateness of institutions and the sharing of authority prescribe the terms on which a President persuades. When one man shares authority with another, but does not gain or lose his job upon the other's whim, his willingness to act upon the urging of the other turns on whether he conceives the action right for him. The essence of a President's persuasive task is to convince such men that what the White House wants of them is what they ought to do for their sake and on their authority.

Persuasive power, thus defined, amounts to more than charm or reasoned argument. These have their uses for a President, but these are not the whole of his resources. For the men he would induce to do what he wants done on their own responsibility will need or fear some acts by him on his responsibility. If they share his authority, he has some share in theirs. Presidential "powers" may be inconclusive when a President commands, but always remain relevant as he persuades. The status and authority inherent in his office reinforce his logic and his charm.

Status adds something to persuasiveness; authority adds still more. When Truman urged wage changes on his Secretary of Commerce while the latter was administering the steel mills, he and Secretary

Richard E. Neustadt, *Presidential Power: The Politics of Leadership* (New York: John Wiley & Sons, Inc., 1960), Chap. 3, "The Power to Persuade," pp. 33–43. Reprinted by permission.

Sawyer were not just two men reasoning with one another. Had they been so, Sawyer probably would never have agreed to act. Truman's status gave him special claims to Sawyer's loyalty, or at least attention. In Walter Bagehot's charming phrase "no man can *argue* on his knees." Although there is no kneeling in this country, few men—and exceedingly few Cabinet officers—are immune to the impulse to say "yes" to the President of the United States. It grows harder to say "no" when they are seated in his oval office at the White House, or in his study on the second floor, where almost tangibly he partakes of the aura of his physical surroundings. In Sawyer's case, moreover, the President possessed formal authority to intervene in many matters of concern to the Secretary of Commerce. These matters ranged from jurisdictional disputes among the defense agencies to legislation pending before Congress and, ultimately, to the tenure of the Secretary himself. There is nothing in the record to suggest that Truman voiced specific threats when they negotiated over wage increases. But given his *formal* powers and their relevance to Sawyer's other interests, it is safe to assume that Truman's very advocacy of wage action conveyed an implicit threat.

A President's authority and status give him great advantages in dealing with the men he would persuade. Each "power" is a vantage point for him in the degree that other men have use for his authority. From the veto to appointments, from publicity to budgeting, and so down a long list, the White House now controls the most encompassing array of vantage points in the American political system. With hardly an exception, the men who share in governing this country are aware that at some time, in some degree, the doing of *their* jobs, the furthering of *their* ambitions, may depend upon the President of the United States. Their need for Presidential action, or their fear of it, is bound to be recurrent, if not actually continuous. Their need or fear is his advantage.

A President's advantages are greater than mere listing of his "powers" might suggest. The men with whom he deals must deal with him until the last day of his term. Because they have continuing relationships with him, his future, while it lasts, supports his present influence. Even though there is no need or fear of him today, what he could do tomorrow may supply today's advantage. Continuing relationships may convert any "power," any aspect of his status, into vantage points in almost any case. When he induces other men to do what he wants done, a President can trade on their dependence now *and* later.

The President's advantages are checked by the advantages of others. Continuing relationships will pull in both directions. These are relationships of mutual dependence. A President depends upon the men he would persuade; he has to reckon with his need or fear of them. They too will possess status, or authority, or both, else they would be of little use to him. Their vantage points confront his own; their power tempers his.

Persuasion is a two-way street. Sawyer, it will be recalled, did not respond at once to Truman's plan for wage increases at the steel mills. On the contrary, the Secretary hesitated and delayed and only acquiesced when he was satisfied that publicly he would not bear the onus of decision. Sawyer had some points of vantage all his own from which to resist Presidential pressure. If he had to reckon with coercive implications in the President's "situations of strength," so had Truman to be mindful of the implications underlying Sawyer's place as a department head, as steel administrator, and as a Cabinet spokesman for business. Loyalty is reciprocal. Having taken on a dirty job in the steel crisis, Sawyer had strong claims to loyal support. Besides, he had authority to do some things that the White House could ill afford. Emulating Wilson, he might have resigned in a huff (the removal power also works two ways). Or emulating Ellis Arnall, he might have declined to sign necessary orders. Or he might have let it be known publicly that he deplored what he was told to do and protested its doing. By following any of these courses Sawyer almost surely would have strengthened the position of management, weakened the position of the White House, and embittered the union. But the whole purpose of a wage increase was to enhance White House persuasiveness in urging settlement upon union and companies alike. Although Sawyer's status and authority did not give him the power to prevent an increase outright, they gave him capability to undermine its purpose. If his authority over wage rates had been vested by a statute, not by revocable Presidential order, his power of prevention might have been complete. . . .

The power to persuade is the power to bargain. Status and authority yield bargaining advantages. But in a government of "separated institutions sharing powers," they yield them to all sides. With the array of vantage points at his disposal, a President may be far more persuasive than his logic or his charm could make him. But outcomes are not guaranteed by his advantages. There remain the counterpressures those whom he would influence can bring to bear on him from vantage points at their disposal. Command has limited utility; persuasion becomes give-and-take. It is well that the White House holds the vantage points it does. In such a business any President may need them all —and more.

This view of power as akin to bargaining is one we commonly accept in the sphere of Congressional relations. Every textbook states and every legislative session demonstrates that save in times like the extraordinary Hundred Days of 1933 —times virtually ruled out by definition at mid-century—a President will often be unable to obtain Congressional action on his terms or even to halt action he opposes. The reverse is equally accepted: Congress often is frustrated by the President. Their formal powers are so intertwined that neither will accomplish very much, for

very long, without the acquiescence of the other. By the same token, though, what one demands the other can resist. The stage is set for that great game, much like collective bargaining, in which each seeks to profit from the other's needs and fears. It is a game played catch as catch can, case by case. And everybody knows the game, observers and participants alike.

The concept of real power as a give-and-take is equally familiar when applied to Presidential influence outside the formal structure of the federal government. The Little Rock affair may be extreme, but Eisenhower's dealings with the governor—and with the citizens—became a case in point. Less extreme but no less pertinent is the steel seizure case with respect to union leaders, and to workers, and to company executives as well. When he deals with such people a President draws bargaining advantage from his status or authority. By virtue of their public places or their private rights they have some capability to reply in kind.

In spheres of party politics the same thing follows, necessarily, from the confederal nature of our party organizations. Even in the case of national nominations a President's advantages are checked by those of others. In 1944 it is by no means clear that Roosevelt got his first choice as his running mate. In 1948 Truman, then the President, faced serious revolts against his nomination. In 1952 his intervention from the White House helped assure the choice of Adlai Stevenson, but it is far from clear that Truman could have done as much for any other candidate acceptable to him.[1] In 1956 when Eisenhower was President, the record leaves obscure just who backed Harold Stassen's effort to block Richard Nixon's renomination as Vice President. But evidently everything did not go quite as Eisenhower wanted, whatever his intentions may have been.[2] The

[1] . . . *See Harry S. Truman*, Years of Trial and Hope, *(New York: Doubleday & Company, Inc., 1956), pp. 495–496.*
[2] . . . *For the public record on this matter see reported statements by Eisenhower, Nixon, Stassen,*

outcomes in these instances bear all the marks of limits on command and of power checked by power that characterize Congressional relations. Both in and out of politics these checks and limits seem to be quite widely understood.

Influence becomes still more a matter of give-and-take when Presidents attempt to deal with allied governments. A classic illustration is the long, unhappy wrangle over Suez policy in 1956. In dealing with the British and the French before their military intervention, Eisenhower had his share of bargaining advantages but no effective power of command. His allies had their share of counterpressures, and they finally tried the most extreme of all: action despite him. His pressure then was instrumental in reversing them. But had the British government been on safe ground *at home,* Eisenhower's wishes might have made as little difference after intervention as before. Behind the decorum of diplomacy—which was not very decorous in the Suez affair—relationships among allies are not unlike relationships among state delegations at a national convention. Power is persuasion and persuasion becomes bargaining. The concept is familiar to everyone who watches foreign policy.

In only one sphere is the concept unfamiliar: the sphere of executive relations. Perhaps because of civics textbooks and teaching in our schools, Americans instinctively resist the view that power in this sphere resembles power in all others. Even Washington reporters, White House aides, and Congressmen are not immune to the illusion that administrative agencies comprise a single structure, "the" executive branch, where Presidential word is law, or ought to be. . . . When a President seeks something from executive offi-

cials his persuasiveness is subject to the same sorts of limitations as in the case of Congressmen, or governors, or national committeemen, or private citizens, or foreign governments. There are no generic differences, no differences in kind and only sometimes in degree. The incidents preceding the dismissal of MacArthur and the incidents surrounding seizure of the steel mills make it plain that here as elsewhere influence derives from bargaining advantages; power is a give-and-take.

Like our governmental structure as a whole, the executive establishment consists of separated institutions sharing powers. The President heads one of these; Cabinet officers, agency administrators, and military commanders head others. Below the departmental level, virtually independent bureau chiefs head many more. Under mid-century conditions, federal operations spill across dividing lines on organization charts; almost every policy entangles many agencies; almost every program calls for interagency collaboration. Everything somehow involves the President. But operating agencies owe their existence least of all to one another—and only in some part to him. Each has a separate statutory base; each has its statutes to administer; each deals with a different set of subcommittees at the Capitol. Each has its own peculiar set of clients, friends, and enemies outside the formal government. Each has a different set of specialized careerists inside its own bailiwick. Our Constitution gives the President the "take-care" clause and the appointive power. Our statutes give him central budgeting and a degree of personnel control. All agency administrators are responsible to him. But they *also* are responsible to Congress, to their clients, to their staffs, and to themselves. In short, they have five masters. Only after all of those do they owe any loyalty to each other.

"The members of the Cabinet," Charles G. Dawes used to remark, "are a President's natural enemies." Dawes had been Harding's Budget Director, Coolidge's Vice President, and Hoover's Ambassador

Herter, and Leonard Hall (the National Republican Chairman) in The New York Times (March 1, 8, 15, 16; April 27; July 15, 16, 25–31; August 3, 4, 17, 23, 1956). See also the account from private sources by Earl Mazo in Richard Nixon: A Personal and Political Portrait (New York: Harper & Row, Publishers, Inc., 1959), pp. 158–187.

to London; he also had been General Pershing's chief assistant for supply in the First World War. The words are highly colored, but Dawes knew whereof he spoke. The men who have to serve so many masters cannot help but be somewhat the "enemy" of any one of them. By the same token, any master wanting service is in some degree the "enemy" of such a servant. A President is likely to want loyal support but not to relish trouble on his doorstep. Yet the more his Cabinet members cleave to him, the more they may need help from him in fending off the wrath of rival masters. Help, though, is synonymous with trouble. Many a Cabinet officer, with loyalty ill-rewarded by his lights and help withheld, has come to view the White House as innately hostile to department heads. Dawes's dictum can be turned around.

A senior Presidential aide remarked to me in Eisenhower's time: "If some of these Cabinet members would just take time out to stop and ask themselves 'What would I want if I were President?,' they wouldn't give him all the trouble he's been having." But even if they asked themselves the question, such officials often could not act upon the answer. Their personal attachment to the President is all too often overwhelmed by duty to their other masters.

Executive officials are not equally advantaged in their dealings with a President. Nor are the same officials equally advantaged all the time. Not every officeholder can resist like a MacArthur, or like Arnall, Sawyer, Wilson, in a rough descending order of effective counterpressure. The vantage points conferred upon officials by their own authority and status vary enormously. The variance is heightened by particulars of time and circumstance. In mid-October, 1950, Truman, at a press conference, remarked of the man he had considered firing in August and would fire the next April for intolerable insubordination:

> Let me tell you something that will be good for your souls. It's a pity that you . . .

can't understand the ideas of two intellectually honest men when they meet. General MacArthur . . . is a member of the Government of the United States. He is loyal to that Government. He is loyal to the President. He is loyal to the President in his foreign policy. . . . There is no disagreement between General MacArthur and myself. . . .[3]

MacArthur's status in and out of government was never higher than when Truman spoke those words. The words, once spoken, added to the General's credibility thereafter when he sought to use the press in his campaign against the President. And what had happened between August and October? Near-victory had happened, together with that premature conference on *post*war plans, the meeting at Wake Island.

If the bargaining advantages of a MacArthur fluctuate with changing circumstances, this is bound to be so with subordinates who have at their disposal fewer "powers," lesser status, to fall back on. And when officials have no "powers" in their own right, or depend upon the President for status, their counterpressure may be limited indeed. White House aides, who fit both categories, are among the most responsive men of all, and for good reason. As a Director of the Budget once remarked to me, "Thank God I'm here and not across the street. If the President doesn't call me, I've got plenty I can do right here and plenty coming up to me, by rights, to justify my calling him. But those poor fellows over there, if the boss doesn't call them, doesn't ask them to do something, what *can* they do but sit?" Authority and status so conditional are frail reliances in resisting a President's own wants. Within the White House precincts, lifted eyebrows may suffice to set an aide in motion; command, coercion, even charm aside. But even in the White House a President does not monopolize effective power. Even there persuasion is akin to

[3] *Stenographic transcript of Presidential press conference, October 19, 1950, on file in the Truman Library at Independence, Missouri.*

bargaining. A former Roosevelt aide once wrote of Cabinet officers:

> Half of a President's suggestions, which theoretically carry the weight of orders, can be safely forgotten by a Cabinet member. And if the President asks about a suggestion a second time, he can be told that it is being investigated. If he asks a third time, a wise Cabinet officer will give him at least part of what he suggests. But only occasionally, except about the most important matters, do Presidents ever get around to asking three times.[4]

The rule applies to staff as well as to the Cabinet, and certainly has been applied *by* staff in Truman's time and Eisenhower's.

Some aides will have more vantage points than a selective memory. Sherman Adams, for example, as The Assistant to the President under Eisenhower, scarcely deserved the appelation "White House aide" in the meaning of the term before his time or as applied to other members of the Eisenhower entourage. Although Adams was by no means "chief of staff" in any sense so sweeping—or so simple—as press commentaries often took for granted, he apparently became no more dependent on the President than Eisenhower on him. "I need him," said the President when Adams turned out to have been remarkably imprudent in the Goldfine case, and delegated to him even the decision on his own departure.[5] This instance is extreme, but the tendency it illustrates is common enough. Any aide who demonstrates to

others that he has the President's consistent confidence and a consistent part in Presidential business will acquire so much business on his own account that he becomes in some sense independent of his chief. Nothing in the Constitution keeps a well-placed aide from converting status into power of his own, usable in some degree even against the President—an outcome not unknown in Truman's regime or, by all accounts, in Eisenhower's.

The more an officeholder's status and his "powers" stem from sources independent of the President, the stronger will be his potential pressure *on* the President. Department heads in general have more bargaining power than do most members of the White House staff; but bureau chiefs may have still more, and specialists at upper levels of established career services may have almost unlimited reserves of the enormous power which consists of sitting still. As Franklin Roosevelt once remarked:

> The Treasury is so large and far-flung and ingrained in its practices that I find it is almost impossible to get the action and results I want—even with Henry [Morgenthau] there. But the Treasury is not to be compared with the State Department. You should go through the experience of trying to get any changes in the thinking, policy, and action of the career diplomats and then you'd know what a real problem was. But the Treasury and the State Department put together are nothing compared with the Na-a-vy. The admirals are really something to cope with—and I should know. To change anything in the Na-a-vy is like punching a feather bed. You punch it with you right and you punch it with your left until you are finally exhausted, and then you find the damn bed just as it was before you started punching.[6]

In the right circumstances, of course, a President can have his way with any of these people. . . . But one need only note the favorable factors giving . . . orders

---

4 Jonathan Daniels, Frontier on the Potomac (New York: The Macmillan Company, 1946), pp. 31–32.
5 Transcript of Presidential press conference, June 18, 1958, in Public Papers of the Presidents: Dwight D. Eisenhower, 1958 (Washington, D.C.: The National Archives, 1959), p. 479. In the summer of 1958, a Congressional investigation into the affairs of a New England textile manufacturer, Bernard Goldfine, revealed that Sherman Adams had accepted various gifts and favors from him (the most notoriety attached to a vicuña coat). Adams also had made inquiries about the status of a Federal Communications Commission proceeding in which Goldfine was involved. In September, 1958, Adams was allowed to resign. The episode was highly publicized and much discussed in that year's Congressional campaigns.

6 As reported in Marriner S. Eccles, Beckoning Frontiers (New York: Alfred A. Knopf, Inc., 1951), p. 336.

their self-executing quality to recognize that as between a President and his "subordinates," no less than others on whom he depends, real power is reciprocal and varies markedly with organization, subject matter, personality, and situation. The mere fact that persuasion is directed at executive officials signifies no necessary easing of his way. Any new Congressman of the Administration's party, especially if narrowly elected, may turn out more amenable (though less useful) to the President than any seasoned bureau chief "downtown." *The probabilities of power do not derive from the literary theory of the Constitution.*

C. Influence

The Influence of the Staff Expert

Harold L. Wilensky

Opportunities to Influence Policy

. . . The staff expert in a union—like the functionary in any private association —has many opportunities to influence "policy" at times and in ways far removed from formal or informal policy deliberations.

The union operates in a fast-moving, constantly changing situation. The executive in a democratic association must constantly adjust convention mandates, broad policy resolutions of official boards and committees, to cover new and unforeseen cases. To carry out organizational purposes, he must in fact change the purposes, adapting them to the needs of the moment. So, too, the functionaries who assist the executive, as they interpret and apply policy (even the executive's policy), can modify organizational purposes.

The staff expert gets his chance especially where official policy is loose, or the specificity of the problem as defined by the boss is low. In the role of "crystallizing agent," the expert affects the selection of means and makes decisions involved in execution. He articulates policy and gives it sharper definition; in doing so, he inevitably affects its direction. This occurs mainly when the expert is assigned to put something into words. He writes editorials, speeches, convention resolutions, and reports—all within the framework of New Deal-Fair Deal "policies," perhaps, but "there's always room to move around" in a framework so broad. In fact, he may have "a helluva time getting them [line officials] to participate in the shaping of the report." Or he writes up a wage program, a contract clause, a statement on government mobilization. Here he can expect closer scrutiny of the emphasis and tone, but, again, there is some leeway. There may be many hours of policy discussion, and he may be assigned to draft a statement, "boil it down." And in boiling it down he selects some things, eliminates others, gives this part a militant play, tones down another. Sometimes, instead of boiling it down, he may have to expand it. "He's the legalistic expert," said one informant, "and in interpretation of a clause, he'll set up a new policy. That's the only way I know how to put it. A three-word policy a lawyer will put into seven pages, and you get three or four different policies out of one. Read some of [an expert's] releases and you'll know what I mean."

The ambiguous character of "policy" and the gulf that divides "policy" from "execution" are seen most vividly when the necessity of speedy decision is combined with a heavy press of work. "There is a surprising amount of freedom," muses one expert. "Part of it, of course, isn't any great liberality; it's just that they're so damned busy they *can't* supervise." And decisions—policy or not—sometimes can't wait.[1]

It is true that the expert's influence on the content of official or semiofficial convention resolutions, press releases, editorials, and other "policy" statements is likely to exceed his influence on their implementation. The expert may sell the union officer on the "right" tariff policy for an after-dinner speech or federation resolution, but when free trade appears to threaten employment in an industry under jurisdiction the speech or resolution may be ignored. Nevertheless, these policy pronouncements, however loose, do upon occasion constitute a lever for expert influence. "As editor," says one expert, "I hewed close to CIO policy. Sometimes closer than they wanted me to! But they couldn't say anything—because they were supposed to be following CIO policy themselves."[2] An invocation of the union creed can sometimes be effective even where the issue is one vital to the union's interests:

> Even where it hurts, you can appeal to the total framework within which they [officers] have been operating for years. Our policy statements over the years have been antimonopoly. So when X was pressured by the industry into taking a stand upholding price collusion, I could point to their tradition and he would have to say, as he did, "Oh, I didn't realize its implications."

[1] *The experts working in small unions may have more frequent opportunity for exercising this sort of discretion. Such a union has a small headquarters staff; there is no raft of administrative assistants to keep things under control while the line officials are gone.*

[2] *Literal application of formal policy is a device frequently cited by experts who want to influence union race relations decisions.*

Whatever the channels of influence, and whatever the area of decision, the ways of influence in all unions are strikingly similar: "crystallize" the policy when the policy is loose, sharpen the definition of the problem when its specificity is low, fill the vacuum when the boss is busy or time is short, use official policy pronouncements as a lever.

In the final analysis, however, what counts is the cumulative effect of thousands of statements of opinion and fact flowing through all the channels of influence, formal and informal, direct and indirect. "Most of it is creating a climate," says one expert, "and the boss may not even know he's been influenced." Day by day the expert articulates trade union aims and aspirations; day by day he invokes the documents (whose content and tone he helped shape) as justification for union action along a broad front. It is plain that the expert supplies the leader with a set of comfortable justifications for union policies and rationalizes the leader's prior beliefs; but he also gives some coherence to these policies, and—through a steady influence in the nonbargaining areas—he helps broaden leadership understandings and interests, helps create and sustain leadership views of the role of unionism in a free society.

* * *

The Careers of Influential Experts

Many writers, on the basis of observation in a great variety of organizations, public and private, have noted in a general way the presence of an inner circle, a "kitchen cabinet" of key advisers who transcend the formal roles assigned to them. Many of these functionaries are technical specialists who have moved into the entire range of organizational decisions. Comptrollers in large corporations, Congressional committee staff experts, scientists in government and business, lawyers and economists in government agencies—all are seen to face the choice between a life of technical service and job advancement.[3] The role of the expert, all these studies suggest, is self-changing: if he is successful within his sphere of technical competence, if his advice is taken on matters where his specialized knowledge is relevant, he is likely to be chosen for tasks outside that sphere of competence, where his specialized knowledge may be irrelevant.[4]

The difficulty with these formulations is that they seldom make clear (1) from what these men of knowledge move—the precise nature of their initial competence; (2) to what they move—the functions fulfilled and skills developed in their new roles; and (3) the process by which their roles change. In the union case, an examination of some types of career lines will help clarify and explain this moving-in process. . . .

. . . The man of knowledge, wherever he begins his career, can become (at a local, state, regional, or national level) (1) a staff expert with High Influence and the beginnings of executive authority; (2) a "Braintruster-Confidant" or (3) a "House-

keeping Administrative Assistant"—both of whom have some executive authority; or (4) an elected or appointed line official who has power and wields formal executive authority.

1. *The High Influence Staff Expert.* This may be a Facts and Figures Man, an Internal Communications Specialist, or a Contact Man, though the Contact Man is the one most likely to rate high. A few of the High Influence Experts acquire some executive authority;[5] Their skills and functions shade off into those of:

2. *The Braintruster-Confidant.* This is the general adviser to the top officer. He may be called "Executive Vice President," "Administrative Assistant," or "General Counsel"; he may not even be on the official union staff. In all cases he has very high influence and operates in all areas of union decision. His authority and power rest upon his close personal, confidential relationship to the boss.

"Your power," says a retired Braintruster-Confidant, "stems from who you're representing. It's the kind of power Hopkins had with Roosevelt. Whether it's in a union or the government or a corporation, the chief executive officer has to have a couple people he can rely on. People who have no divided loyalties, who will do his bidding exactly and preferably who'll do his thinking for him, too. People who can be counted on to act exactly the way he would if he were around."

Sometimes, besides acting as general adviser and deputy to the boss, he does considerable trouble-shooting in the field:

X [braintruster] is Y's [officer's] alter ego in dealing with intraunion business. He represents him when he can't be there. He's Y's shadow, his right-hand man. He represents the maximum policy influence of any technician. . . . He's a diplomat and a trouble-shooter, a buffer and a fireman. He runs around for Y, he takes the heat off Y. . . . He's so good that he's developed an area of influence that is subdefinitive. He knows when to say yes and when to say no, when to press Y, when to keep

---

[3] *Marshall E. Dimock and H. K. Hyde,* Bureaucracy and Trusteeship in Large Corporations *(Washington, D.C.: U.S. Government Printing Office, 1940), p. 64; Stephen K. Bailey,* Congress Makes a Law: The Story Behind the Employment Act of 1946 *(New York: Columbia University Press, 1950), p. 64; A. W. Macmahon and John D. Millett,* Federal Administrators: A Biographical Approach to the Problem of Departmental Management *(New York: Columbia University Press, 1939), p. 464; B. Barber,* Science and the Social Order *(New York: The Free Press of Glencoe, Inc., 1952), p. 176; V. Thompson,* The Regulatory Process in OPA Gas Rationing *(New York: King's Crown Press, 1950).*

[4] *Note David Riesman's formulation of this theme: "The pressure toward social competence, with its concurrent disregard for technical competence . . . is typical for the emergence of a new pattern in American business and professional life: if one is successful in one's craft, one is forced to leave it." As the engineer, newspaperman, doctor, professor move up their occupational ladders, they " . . . must bury their craft routines and desert their craft companions. They must work less with things and more with people." David Riesman, Nathan Glazer and, Reuel Denney,* The Lonely Crowd: A Study of the Changing American Character *(New York: Doubleday & Company, Inc., 1955), pp. 154–155. . . .*

[5] *For instance, the Contact Man with the highest influence rating is viewed by his colleagues as an executive, not a staff expert. Faced with the allegation that the experts are moving in, several functionaries in one union denied it, citing in evidence the fact that the experts have to clear important matters with the General Counsel!*

quiet. . . . Strictly as a person he has important influence. He has a close personal relation —that's a large part of it. X is close enough to Y and experienced enough so people tend to trust his judgment. . . . He's worth ten years on Y's life.

The talents of the Braintruster-Confidant and the Contact Man are often described in identical terms. The distinction is one of degree; the former has more influence, has a closer personal relationship to the boss—a sustained, easy access the staff expert rarely achieves. Moreover, he is usually more visible and less anonymous in his operations; as deputy to the boss, he exercises some executive authority.[6]

3. *The Housekeeping Administrative Assistant.* Some of these are "pressure screeners" and in this their duties resemble those of the Braintruster-Confidant. Moreover, their relationship to the boss is close, their contacts with him frequent. But their work is far more routine, their influence typically less, their authority more circumscribed, and their operations generally more anonymous. The Housekeeping Administrative Assistant may be "sort of a personal secretary to the president"; like the private secretary in other unions he may channel the important mail, answer some of it, arrange appointments, protect the boss from unnecessary visitors and problems. He may combine the handling of administrative detail with financial functions; he may supervise the expenditures of the departments, act as watchdog over union properties.

In some unions there is a three-way split: one man (or set of men) handles the financial side; another the routine, nonfinancial administrative detail; a third acts in the Braintruster-Confidant role. In others one man or office combines aspects of all three.

4. *An Elected or Appointed Line Official.* Some men of knowledge acquire formal executive authority. In some unit at some level of the labor movement, they become president, vice president, secretary-treasurer, etc.; director of an operating department;

[6] *For a detailed description in similar vein of the Braintruster-Confidant role in government, see the references to Harry Hopkins in Robert E. Sherwood, Roosevelt and Hopkins, rev. ed. (New York: Bantam Books, Inc., 1950), esp. Vol. I., pp. 2–3, 6, 134, 220, 247–249, 260–266, 456–457; Vol. II, pp. 23, 44–47, 94–96, 232, 280, 368–370, 380–386, 442–450, 468–473, 520, 553.*

"International Rep.," or business agent. The extent of this is unknown. But I have the names in thirty-nine cases where it has occurred; and several respondents allege that it is on the increase in specific unions.

Thus there are four terminal points in the moving-in process: elected or appointed line official, housekeeping administrative assistant, braintruster-confidant, or staff expert with very high influence. All have acquired some executive authority; all possess managerial talent. From what beginnings do they move in?

The positions in which these men get their start (at any level of the labor movement) include: (1) staff expert recruited from the outside; (2) staff expert recruited from the ranks of union membership; (3) staff expert recruited from the outside who put in a brief ritual period in the rank and file; (4) professional or college man who enters as an organizer, paid or unpaid; (5) male private secretary; (6) private paid consultant; and (7) outside adviser with no paid connection with the union administration.[7]

* * *

. . . [I]t is possible to delineate a few necessary conditions for moving in. The following features . . . may occur in different sequence, be variously intertwined in any given case, and be of varying importance from case to case:

1. *Make prestigeful contact with the leaders of the unit into which one is moving.* Examples: A Socialist party or C[ommunist] P[arty] activist or leader contacts union with Socialist or C[ommunist] P[arty] leadership as organizer, consultant, etc. A lawyer risks his practice to defend unpopular unions, fight their cases. A government bureaucrat sticks neck out to fight for cause allied to labor's interests. A lawyer with good connections in a governor's office is hired as an area director in that state.

[7] *It is important to note that some cases are hired as administrative assistants from the start. Furthermore, in rare cases, the man of knowledge begins in a top executive post and moves down to staff specialist.*

2. *Get sponsor by demonstrating loyalty, indispensability to, or power over a leader or group of leaders.* Examples: A staff expert, organizer, special assistant, etc., moves up with a leader rising to power, assists in overcoming opposition. A professional offers free advice in early organizing struggles, wins confidence of leader who found advice useful. An outsider learns "where the bodies are buried," or shares in some malfeasance.

3. *Become expert in the workings of the organization.* This is an accomplishment of all the successful experts.

4. *Seize opportunities to broaden influence.* Examples: leadership vacuums left by succession or weakness of incumbents; war, depression, factional strife (each with their own heavy set of demands on officer competence).

Many of these men who moved in are people who sensed the moment, saw the possibilities of success, and seized the chance to climb aboard. From the ranks or not, "we took our lives in our hands and gambled on the union in the early days," says one. "And the officers know it." The interview explanations of how these men have moved in are replete with references both to "a good sense of timing" and a willingness to take a chance.

To say that the successful experts become "expert in the workings of the organization" is to point to the synoptic view that defines executive capacity. If the expert is a fellow profoundly immersed in his routine, a man whose intensity of vision destroys his sense of proportion, then all of the successful experts have ceased being experts. The good labor editor, as we have seen, comes to know the organization in all its aspects; "he needs to know how this particular sentence would affect this particular local, this particular personality." The labor lawyer has to check clause IVB-3a for gimmicks; to do the job right he must know its relation to other clauses, the history of the bargaining relationship, and more.

Even the most routine matter can provide occasion for spreading one's func-

tions. "We do letter writing, for instance," said one consultant:

> Just plain letter writing. These union officers are afraid of their grammar. They're afraid of not saying what they mean, so they bring in their letters or their speeches and want us to polish them up. So when you tell them, "Well, I wouldn't do it this way or that way," you have to tell them what way you *would* do it. . . . And pretty soon you're telling them what to do in negotiations, in all kinds of situations. . . .

The good specialist, in other words, becomes a specialist at large. By a gradual process, expert advice in one's area of special competence, if the action suggested is successful, evokes a demand for good advice in other areas as well. And the core knowledge required soon becomes a knowledge of the particular union—its personalities, politics, problems, traditions, and routines.

The moving-in process may necessitate the acquisition of a stronger personal identification with the incumbent officials of the particular union, and a decline in the intensity of any previous professional identification. But it does not necessarily entail a loss of craft competence. Some of the most powerful union lawyers, for example, retain considerable skill as legal technicians despite the increased demand on their competence in politics and interpersonal relations occasioned by their emergence in executive roles. This coupling of technical and political skills—seen, for example, in the convergence of wage workers trying to become experts and experts identifying as wage workers—is a clue to the basis of "confidence" between expert and boss.

*   *   *

The Channels of Influence

The Personal Relationship and Direct Access. There is no more widely and strongly held conviction among the union staff experts than the idea that their personal relationship with the boss—the "confidence" the line officials have in them, their informal contacts with key officers on and off the job—is the crucial determinant of their influence. Typical comments from functionaries in a variety of unions, new and old, large and small, indicate this.

A Contact Man: There's a great amount of that stuff that's not formalized. It's "pre-policy" discussion. . . . For [years] I've had lunch with [the top officer] 95 per cent of the time when he's in town. Much of the conversation is [the top officer] asking, "What do you think about this?"

Facts and Figures Man: [Line officials] come in and want a curbstone opinion. I've traveled all over the country and know most of the staff and many local union people. . . . They'll stop in and kick around their problems; they use me—just as another guy to talk to.

Ex-expert: I had [the top officer's] confidence for years. We'd make policy decisions whenever we talked in a sense. He'd think things out with me.

Many experts, to be sure, are not so favorably situated—either in personal resources or opportunity—that the boss "thinks things out" with them:

I'll be damned if I'm going to kill three afternoons a week at ———'s bar drinking whiskey with [a line official] or working on all-night poker games. I just couldn't do that—not only because I don't have the "technical" skills required, but because I couldn't do it and my job at the same time.

But attempts to deal with lower officials or the rank and file according to the impersonal norm are met with resistance. For instance, the staff expert just quoted —used to administrative procedures in government—describes his effort to maintain formality in his work relationships in the union setting:

The old-timers in the union don't know what to make of it. When they call in here and ask for Mike they get, "Just a moment, sir, Mr. ——— handles that problem," or they get the answer, "We'll have to check policy on that problem—as soon as we take it up in Thursday's staff meeting we'll let you know." They're used to a personalized service. They know Joe Blow in a depart-

ment in the International; they want the answer from Joe.[8]

This case—since departed from the union —later said he was working at this personal relationships problem by eating about three lunches a week with the proper people. Whether they find the process comfortable or not, the experts recognize the importance of the thousands of casual deliverances of opinion in sustained, direct, informal contact with the boss and other line officials.

Indirect Informal Channels: The Use of a Third Party. Some of the most effective informal channels of expert influence are indirect. If you can't reach the boss with a memo or through direct conversation, reach him through a third party.

The first channel is obvious:

You plant your ideas with one officer rather than another—and expect him to carry the ball for you. [Officer No. 2] is less harassed by broader union problems than [Officer no. 1]. He's also less conservative on some things. . . . There are times where it's best [No. 2] instead of [staff expert] present the case to [No. 1].

The use of a more influential staff expert—e.g., one who is temporarily in favor, or has not recently bothered the boss—is also common. When the expert has much contact with the local activists and lower line officials, he is also in a position to build up pressure from below if he encounters resistance in headquarters. "I get what I want anyway," says an Internal Communications Specialist, "by nurturing a demand from the field. . . ."

Less obvious are the expert-fostered pressures from the outside. Plant the idea with a government bureaucrat, a college professor, a politician who sees the boss in his more receptive moods. In return, feed him a little harmless "inside dope" that will help him in his work or prompt him

[8] *Informal sanctions such as kidding are directed against efforts at depersonalization. Headquarters colleagues say they needled the case quoted above: "Most other union people don't operate that way; why should we let him?"*

to bring up the problem when he sees the boss.

Another sub rosa area of influence stems from the demands the third party may put on the expert. How often this occurs is an open question, but these two examples illustrate the point. The first concerns government policy affecting the union:

> Someone in the White House wanted a real feel as to what's going on; they called in [union staff experts] informally. . . . The way they figured [in the White House] is why take it up with the officers—the kid is going to write it anyway. There are situations where the office boy is a more efficient source!

The second example concerns an arbitrator who similarly used the staff expert to feel out the union's position. Reams of data had been submitted, lengthy written testimony and argument concluded. "Nobody could go through this tremendous pile . . . nobody," reports a participant. So—

> Two or three days after the hearings were concluded, the arbitrator came to me [expert] and said, "I want to ask you to clarify this table for me" (it was the critical table—one on productivity). "Would it be right if I said you had an increase of productivity of 15 per cent?" Then, I happen to know, he went to the employer and asked if he would clarify this table. "Would it be right if I said there's been a 10 per cent increase?" After having felt us both out he gets the difference between 10 and 15 and he splits it, awards 12.5 per cent. Is that economic interpretation I made a matter of research or of policy? The fact is, it's a policy matter! . . . That's an area of decision on the part of the [staff expert] that never appears in the record. He'd never admit he's feeling us out. He's not going to [the union officer] and say what will you take; he goes to the [staff expert]. He's an honest man. I knew he wouldn't betray the fact that I didn't read the table for him but on the basis of what observations I could make, interpreted the officers' limits for him. In that brief moment and within those narrow limits, I as [staff expert] had an effect on the outcome.

Another third-party channel of influence—more important and more pervasive than the friendly outsider—is the female contingent in the headquarters building and around the boss. The well-known "office wife" who protects the busy executive from unimportant people, picks up after him, shares his secrets, knows his weaknesses—this figure is not confined to the business world.

> His secretary was one of my principal problems when I came on—creating a good relationship with her. She figured like most private secretaries, "If you don't tell 'em anything you can't get in any trouble." I had a helluva time finding out what was going on. It took her and me two years before she became convinced I could be trusted.

The union leader's private secretary can be a source of much grief for the staff expert, or she can be a powerful support. For it is her job to decide whom the boss will see, whose memo gets on top of the pile, whose problem gets mentioned at the most propitious moment. The secretary is a key point of transmission on the grapevine, and can slant the content of the rumors that pass along it. But the crucial facts that make her a force for the expert to contend with are these: (1) the white-collar girls in the union are typically among the few females on an almost all-male payroll; and (2) unions often recruit the wives and relatives of loyal unionists for the clerical jobs. These white-collar girls easily establish liaisons of friendship or marriage—if they don't already have relations of blood—with visiting line officials. They sometimes acquire a better "base" than the staff expert can build. In fact, there are cases in which the office girls have been able to invoke the ultimate sanction against a staff expert, i.e., get him fired.

Not only the office wife, but the wife at home—the expert's wife and the officers' wives and the wives of one's colleagues—may play a role as a channel of influence. This occurs where the off-the-job social life of the inner staff and line officials is close-knit. The expert's position may be much affected by the performance of his wife in these off-the-job cliques.

Smooth channel or rocklike blockade, the females with steady access to the boss must be counted as an important part of the communication system in the modern union; they often comprise for the expert an important indirect way to reach the top man.

In sum: the formal channels of influence are increasingly prominent in the work of staff experts in the larger unions. But typically, the aspects of bureaucracy we have discussed are not yet well developed: the division of labor, the definition of the job, the jurisdictional areas, and the hierarchy of authority remain fluid and loose.

As for autonomy within his sphere of competence, this is the exception, not the rule. In fact, the expert who moves out of his sphere of competence is more likely to acquire maximum leeway and autonomy. Hence the great load on the informal channels and ways of influence. To reach the boss, you cultivate his confidence in informal, direct contacts on and off the job; or you work indirectly through a third party who has his ear—other labor functionaries, local union activists, prestigeful outsiders, the female contingent at headquarters or in the inner-circle social clique.

*   *   *

A Managerial Revolution?

A "managerial revolution" is indeed going on in the American trade union, but it has not, save in rare instances, meant that indispensable technical knowledge is becoming the main basis for power. The managerial revolution in the union case occurs in these forms:

1. Unions have increased their employment of experts on and off the staff. Increasing use of experts, however, says nothing about their influence or power.
2. The trends in union structure, type of bargaining, degree of central control and

involvement with government put increased demands on leadership competence. The expert's chance to move in depends in part upon how these demands are expressed in the officer's administrative style.
3. Most top union leaders—now professional managers with reasonably secure tenure—are acquiring some expertise in their own right.
4. Some men of knowledge are moving into four types of executive or quasiexecutive position: High Influence staff expert, Braintruster-Confidant, Housekeeping Administrative Assistant, or line officer.

The staff experts who are able to make the most of the chance to move in are the Contact Men. They have the contacts and the political and human relations talents necessary to make maximum use of the informal channels for reaching the boss. The Facts and Figures Men, however technically indispensable the boss'[s] deficiencies make them, are less likely to win high influence. The leader is more impressed by men in his own image, men skilled in the arts of negotiation, consultation, interpersonal relations.

. . . Time of first service in the labor movement affects the influence position of the staff expert. The men who "grew up with the organization" have a better claim to a voice in its affairs, easier personal access to the boss. If they combine long service and the right functional type with a role orientation appropriate to the union's stage of development, high influence is even more likely—a point emphasized by looking at [the] influence . . . of the missionaries.[9]

*   *   *

[Looking at both high influence staff experts and other men of influence who

[9] *Wilensky defines "missionary" as one who "is oriented in his job towards some abstract concept of the labor movement; he is highly identified with an outside political or religious-political group." In the unions studied, he found a high correlation between the missionary role orientation and influence. Wilensky, op. cit., pp. 114, 205–207.* (ED. NOTE.)

have made good, we can draw a more dynamic picture of the road to influence.]

"Emerging in a crisis situation," "knowing where the bodies are buried"—these phrases capture the career patterns of two groups of outsiders who achieve executive or quasiexecutive posts in the labor movement. Two other types of careers begin in the ranks: the bona fide rank and file expert, and the synthetic rank and filer.

The man who can combine rank-and-file political experience with technical knowledge is in a good position to move in. Reasons for this can be seen in the features common to the careers of all those men of knowledge who have moved in, wherever and whenever they start and whatever position they climb to. The formula goes like this: make prestigeful contact with union people; demonstrate loyalty or indispensability to, or acquire some hold over a sponsor; seize opportunities to broaden your influence; in general, become expert in the workings of the organization. Why the successful expert must become "expert in the workings of the organization" is in part explained by the self-changing nature of the role of the expert: successful problem solving in areas within his sphere of competence tends to peg him as a problem solver in all areas. The expert who acquires intimate knowledge of the organization he works for can capitalize on this tendency of the role to broaden.

The imperatives in the process of "winning the boss'[s] confidence" present a series of paradoxes. The expert must (1) develop talents very similar to the political-executive-human relations skills of the union leader, but not offer him any serious competition; (2) be one of the boys, but still play the expert and maintain an aura of mystery; (3) avoid bothering the boss, but still see that tough decisions are made; (4) give unreserved loyalty to the boss and be dependent on him, but not too dependent.

This matter of dependence on the boss is crucial in understanding their relationship and the expert's chances for high influence. The nature of his acceptable alternative job opportunities, which are a compound of his own role orientation, the number and kind of job offers he gets, and the transferability of his skills; the ease with which he can be replaced; his connections on the outside and his "base" on the inside—the data suggest that all of these affect the influence of the staff expert because they affect his dependence on the boss.

The special prestige and influence of the outside consultant, the lawyer in particular, underscore the importance of factors which promote a sense of security and independence. The private practitioner can be seen as an epitome of the conditions maximizing expert influence in general. The lawyer, though it is easy to exaggerate this in the union case, has in some respects a special position. He has developed the device of the mystery more systematically than other experts, he has a unique fiduciary relationship, and he profits from the omnipresence of labor law. Above all, his success in the labor movement reflects his great power and prestige in the larger society.

D. Elites

The Mythology of Elite Influence

Edward C. Banfield

Many Chicagoans, including some who are generally well informed about civic affairs, believe that a little group of private persons whose names are in some cases unknown to the general public have ample power to decide any public matter whatsoever. These alleged "top leaders" are the multimillionaires who control the largest businesses, own the newspapers, and dominate the boards of directors of the civic associations, universities, hospitals, and other public service bodies. They are said to be at the top of a hierarchy of influence the lines of which are so well drawn as virtually to constitute a formal organization. When they give the word, lesser figures below them in the hierarchy —including other business leaders, as well as politicians, university heads, clergymen, and so on—are supposed to hasten to do their bidding. According to one business-man who knows his way around Chicago (he owns a firm that grosses more than one hundred million dollars a year), the city is run by only four men: "Do you know who really runs Chicago? Who has the real money and power? Four young men: Brooks McCormick of International Harvester; [William John] Hagenah of Wrigley's; Calvin Fentress, son-in-law of General Wood [Chairman of the Board, Sears-Roebuck Co.], you know; and Marshall Field, Jr. These four young men control the wealth of Chicago. Not many people know that."

The head of a Negro civic association set the number of "top leaders" a little higher. According to him, "There are a dozen men in this town who could go into

City Hall and order an end to racial violence just like you or I could go into a grocery store and order a loaf of bread. All they'd have to do is say what they wanted and they'd get it."

Sometimes the "top leaders" are regarded as a conspiracy of the rich to frustrate the workings of democracy.[1] More often, it is assumed that they exercise their influence for the good of the community. The "top leader"—according to this view—is rich enough to put aside his private advantage in most matters (certainly in all small ones), and he is accustomed, by training and position, to take a statesmanlike view of public questions. He may be the representative of a family—the Fields, McCormicks, Ryersons, Swifts, or Armours, for example—that has devoted itself to public service for generations, or he may be the head of a large corporation —Inland Steel, Sears-Roebuck, Field's department store, the Chicago Title and Trust Company, for example—that has a long-standing tradition of "civic responsibility." In any case, he is trusted to have good intentions. The Negro leader quoted above was confident that if the facts about racial violence were brought to the attention of the right men, they would give the necessary orders. It was reasonable for him to take their good will for granted: most of his organization's support came as gifts from corporations owned or controlled by them.

In Chicago, big businessmen are criti-

[1] *See Martin Meyerson and E. C. Banfield,* Politics, Planning and the Public Interest *(New York: The Free Press of Glencoe, Inc., 1955).*

cized less for interfering in public affairs than for "failing to assume their civic responsibilities." They themselves seem to agree with this view; those of them who do not exercise influence in civic affairs are apt to reproach themselves for failing in their duty. The general view seems to be that the "top leaders" ought to unite on some general plan for the development of the city and the metropolitan area.

Frequently, efforts are made in American cities to give official standing to the hierarchy of influence that is presumed to exist. The independent, unpaid planning commission, which is the organizational form into which the city-planning function has been cast in most cities, is, in intention (but not in practice), "top leadership" brought out from behind the scenes and made official. The assumption is that a plan can be carried into effect if—and only if—the principal private interests of the city agree upon it.[2]

It may be, as Norton E. Long has conjectured, that "top leadership" is talked about because people feel the need of a government that has power to solve community problems, to deal with community crises, and to make and carry out comprehensive plans. Where the politicians who hold the offices do not regard themselves as governors of the municipal territory but largely as mediators or players in a particular "game" (the great game of politics), the public finds reassurance in the notion that there exists a "they" who are really running things from behind the scenes.[3]

The notion that "top leaders" run the city is certainly not supported by the facts of [recent controversies]. On the contrary, in these cases the richest men of Chicago are conspicuous by their absence. Lesser business figures appear, but they do not act concertedly: some of them are on every side of every issue. The most influential people are the managers of large organizations the maintenance of which is at stake, a few "civic leaders" whose judgment, negotiating skill, and disinterestedness are unusual and, above all, the chief elected officials. Businessmen exercise influence (to the extent that they exercise it at all) not so much because they are rich or in a position to make threats and promises as, in the words of one of them, "by main force of being right."

These findings do not, however, prove that there is no "they" behind the scenes. Possibly, they were not sufficiently interested in what was at stake in these cases to bestir themselves. Or possibly they were well satisfied with what was done and saw no need to interfere. Or, again, they may, from considerations of policy, have restrained a desire to interfere (they may have thought interference "undemocratic" or "poor public relations"). Any of these theories, or all of them together, would explain the absence of "top leaders" from the scene and, incidentally, would leave open the possibility that in some future case—one in which their vital interests *are* at stake—they may issue the orders necessary to set in motion the lower echelons of the alleged influence hierarchy.

There is yet another possibility. It may be that the "top leaders" did not exercise their influence, or did not exercise it in earnest, for want of organization and that this want could easily have been supplied if they had cared to take the trouble. If, for example, the four young men who "have the real money and power" had got together for lunch one day and had talked things over, they might have set "policy" with regard to the Fort Dearborn Project [downtown redevelopment proposal], the Branch Hospital [proposed addition to Cook County Hospital], the Exhibition Hall [publicly constructed and operated convention hall promoted by the *Tribune* in the 1950's] and, for good measure, racial violence. If they had done so, their decisions (according to the theory) would have been quickly communicated down

2 See Robert A. Walker, The Planning Function in Urban Government (Chicago: University of Chicago Press, 1950), esp. Chap. 5.
3 Norton E. Long, "The Local Community as an Ecology of Games," American Journal of Sociology, Vol. LXIV, No. 3 (November, 1958), 255.

the hierarchy of lesser business leaders, elected officials, managers, and civic association professionals. That they did not get together for lunch was—on this theory—only a matter of "accident" or "mere circumstance." (One of the young men may perhaps have been confined to his home with a painful case of gout, while another was busy skiing in Switzerland.) On this theory, there was nothing to prevent the "top leaders" from running things except the difficulties that normally stand in the way of concerting the activities of four busy people. Their failure to exercise influence, then, is to be explained as "mere want of organization." This theory leaves open the possibility that the four young men may someday meet for lunch. If they do, presumably they will then run the city.

With such qualifications as these, the "top leadership" theory is widely held in Chicago. Probably no one with any knowledge of civic affairs supposes that the "top leaders" actually meet frequently to set policy and issue instructions to those beneath them in the hierarchy of influence. But there are many who think that the "top leaders" could do so if they wished and that, for the most part, it is "mere circumstance" that prevents them. The Negro leader quoted above and a white businessman were, in fact, trying to arrange a meeting of "top leaders" at which the Negro would present the case for ending racial violence. The white businessman intended to invite some "top leaders" to his home and to introduce the Negro to them there. Lack of communication between the white leaders and the Negro, and among the white leaders themselves, was, the businessman and the Negro believed, the strategic factor in the situation.

These theories are all plausible. It is unquestionably true that a very small number of men control the principal industries of the metropolitan area and, if they wish, can have a great deal to say about how civic associations and other private bodies are run. No doubt, any four of at least forty men could, if they acted together and if they exerted themselves fully, exer-

cise a great, and probably a decisive, influence. . . .

The political heads, even in the rather rare instances when they have decided policy preferences of their own, believe that they ought to be responsive to the wishes of the public and especially to the wishes of that part of the public which has the most at stake in the particular matter. As a rule, therefore, the "top leaders," if they were united and ready to back to the limit a project which was not obviously contrary to the interest of the community, would find the political heads ready to cooperate. And even if the political heads opposed [it], the "top leaders" might have their way, although perhaps not in the very short run. For if the twenty or thirty wealthiest men in Chicago acted as one and put all their wealth into the fight, they could easily destroy or capture the machine.

These remote and even fantastic possibilities are mentioned only to show that the notion of an elite having the ability to run the city (although not actually running it) is not inherently absurd. Indeed, if influence is defined as the *ability* to modify behavior in accordance with one's intention, there can be little doubt that there exist "top leaders" with aggregate influence sufficient to run the city.

What, then, accounts for their failure to do so? Are the factors that prevent the "top leaders" from exercising their full influence accidental features of the situation—are they "mere circumstance"—or are they an inevitable and necessary part of it?

Business leaders (including some who are at the top of the alleged hierarchy of influence) offer several explanations. Some say that big business is nowadays mainly run by managers rather than by owners. A generation or two ago, the principal enterprises in Chicago were run by owners who took a proprietary interest in the affairs of the community. Now the principal enterprises are run by salaried managers in behalf of stockholders, many or most of whom live in other places and who, even if they lived in Chicago, would probably have no common interest in anything except dividends. The managers of today do not identify with the city as fully as did the proprietors of a generation ago: for some of them, Chicago is only an interval in a career that will take them ultimately to New York, Washington, or Los Angeles. Even if the managers did identify fully with the city, they could not exercise as much influence as did the old proprietors because they are subject to boards of directors. "There are not a dozen men in this town who could commit twenty-five thousand dollars without asking a board," Don Maxwell, the editor of the *Tribune,* told an interviewer. "Colonel McCormick could do it, but I can't. There are three of us [trustees of the newspaper] instead of one; that's the difference."

Because his life history and his position in the firm are different, the whole mentality of the manager is different from that of the proprietor, according to this theory. Not only does he lack the proprietor's strong sense of responsibility to the community, but he also lacks his taste for power and for asserting his individuality. He does not want to "run" the community any more than he wants to "run" the business; he is essentially a staff man and a member of a management "team."

This explanation of the absence of effective "top leadership" is weakened by two circumstances. One is that there are still a number of large proprietors on the scene. Henry Crown [head of a construction supply firm] and Arnold Maremont [wealthy industrialist and corporate director], for example (not to mention the four young men who "have the wealth and power"), could commit millions of dollars without consulting a board of directors. The other is that many of the managers show both a very decided sense of civic responsibility and a marked taste for power, and are inhibited little, if at all, by their boards of directors. [Hughston H.] McBain, as head of Field's department store, could back the Fort Dearborn Project extensively without asking anyone's permission. [Holman D.] Pettibone, as head of

the Chicago Title and Trust Company, had the same freedom. So did the managers of the Inland Steel, Sears-Roebuck, and other large companies. That the *Tribune* was managed by three trustees rather than by a single proprietor did not prevent it from taking the lead in the promotion of the Exhibition Hall.

These objections are not conclusive, however. As James C. Downs [chairman, Real Estate Research Corporation] has pointed out, most of those who are now managers formed their standards under the tutelage of the proprietors of the last generation. (The trustees of the *Tribune,* for example, got their notions of a newspaper's role from Colonel McCormick, the proprietor who was their boss for many years.) In a sense, then, the present managers are anachronisms: they are living by the standards of the past. As they pass from the scene—and in another decade most of them will have passed from it—their places will be taken by men who will have no firsthand acquaintance with the ways of the old proprietors and who will always have been staff assistants, never dominating personalities.

This process, some say, has already gone so far that the prevailing ethos today is that of the staff assistant, not that of the proprietor as remembered by the manager who worked with him. This new ethos, it is said, has spread to those who, like the four young men who have the "real money and power," are from a legal standpoint proprietors themselves. Having absorbed the prevailing mood and spirit of the times—a mood and spirit set by the staff men whose style is in the ascendant— today's proprietors are utterly unlike those of a generation ago.

Whether from this cause or from some other, the significance of the businessman's civic activity may have changed even when its outward manifestations are the same as they were a generation ago. If today's manager does the things that were done by the proprietor of a generation ago, he may do them for different reasons. What the proprietor did because he believed it good for the community or for his business, the manager may do because it is good public relations. The proprietor was interested in objective results and was indifferent to what people thought. The manager, perhaps, is interested primarily in what people think and only secondarily in objective results. This may explain why Field's department store entered so readily into the Fort Dearborn Project, an undertaking that was of dubious advantage to the store or to the city. To be good public relations—to demonstrate that the store took an enlightened interest in the welfare of the community—it was not necessary that the Project be sound; it was only necessary that it be plausible.

The absence of effective "top leadership" is sometimes explained by defects of character on the part of those who are in a position to lead. Businessmen tell each other that it is only because they are selfish ("lacking a sense of responsibility to the community") or without vision that they do not make and carry out comprehensive plans for dealing with fundamental city problems. "The general attitude is: 'Leave it to the other fellow; send him a check and hope that it works out.'"

A businessman who thinks only of building his business and of making money for his stockholders is unfashionably "narrow." One who sends a check and "leaves it to the other fellow" is not much better. The man who is admired—the man of "broad" outlook—gives a large part of his time and energy and much of his stockholders' money to advance a variety of civic causes. The trouble is (the business community thinks) that there are not enough such statesmen at the top of the influence hierarchy. Most big businessmen, while acknowledging that they "ought" to "do more for the community," stop far short of doing what would be necessary to make and carry out a general plan for the development of the city. Accordingly, they are apologetic about not dealing with fundamentals like the race problem.

I see lip service given in a lot of businesses. But if they were thinking. . . . Hell, man, the Commercial Club would form one of these secret fifteen committees. They used to have one on prostitution. They'd talk facts to each other and get at it. . . .

. . . [Among businessmen] the most widely discussed topic is the current economic situation, and then politics, and then fishing, and hunting, and hobbies. So [race relations] is pretty far down the list. By and large, I don't think that very many people bring it up.

Many people told me at the ————— Club, after the presentation, "This is the most important meeting the Club has ever had." I heard no adverse comment. And it was pretty risky to put this thing up in strong black and white terms. We recruited quite a few. . . .

If it is defects of character that prevent big businessmen from concerting their activity to make "policy" for the community, then, as the quotation above suggests, exhortation or "education" may someday improve the situation. This, at any rate, seems to be the assumption on which much of the rhetoric at business luncheons rests.

There are, however, at least three other important circumstances which would radically limit the ability of a business elite to make fundamental decisions. These circumstances would exist if all big businesses were run by proprietors rather than by managers and if all of the proprietors were men of the "broadest" (i.e., the most community-serving) outlook.

1. There exist fundamental conflicts of interest and opinion among the business leaders. Even if only the few men at the very top of the alleged hierarchy of influence are taken into account, these conflicts are such as to make concerted action among them impossible. In part, the conflicts arise on purely business grounds: e.g., what is good for the owners of the downtown hotels is not good for the owners of the amphitheatre, and what is good for the owners of real estate on the north side of the Chicago River is not

good for the owners of real estate in the Loop. To suppose that these conflicts would be resolved if the "top leaders" met at lunch is naïve. Business is a continuing process of bargaining in which every actor tries to get into the position that is best for him; mutual advantage is constantly being discovered and bargains struck accordingly. There is no reason to believe, however, that bargains struck by "top leaders" around a luncheon table would represent any improvement in the situation from the standpoint of the community as a whole. There is, moreover, some presumption that where mutual advantage has not already been discovered, there is none to discover.

Where there is no mutual advantage, discussion can lead to nothing unless at least one party is willing to sacrifice his interest from a sense of "civic responsibility." Small sacrifices of business interests are made often, . . . but it is not to be expected that a great or vital sacrifice will be made. Yet little of importance can be done in the city without great or vital sacrifices of some interests.

Even where business interests are not at stake—even in those matters where all actors are sincerely motivated by public-serving ends—there are conflicts that make concerted action impossible. People hold different conceptions of the public interest, and even those who hold the same conception may disagree entirely in their judgments about probabilities.

Race relations, for example, might possibly be improved without impairing the vital interests of any big business. But the differences of opinion among "top leaders" on that subject probably run at least as deep as do the conflicts of business interest. The Negro civic leader who was quoted above may recruit some "top leaders" to his cause. But other "top leaders" will meanwhile have been recruited by the white civic leader whose complaint about "lip service" has just been quoted. This man, an executive of a utility company, fears that Chicago will someday elect a Negro mayor. It will then, he says,

be an intolerable place in which to live and do business.

2. Even if there were no such conflicts, the amount of communication that would be required to concert activity in making and carrying out a comprehensive plan would be so great that no time would be left for anything else. Even if there were, in fact, only four "top leaders" in Chicago, the communications problem would not be insignificant. (The problem would exist not only with respect to the four principals, but also—and mainly—within the vast empire which each of the four controls.) But Chicago, being a very large city, has a very large number of autonomous actors who would have to be taken into account; the number of these would certainly be not four but several hundred.

Even if there were a common purpose to which all would willingly subordinate themselves (which, of course, there is not), so many actors could coordinate their behavior only by exchanging a vast number of messages. The number of these would, of course, increase with the number of actors, with the complexity of the coordination required, and with the unwillingness of the actors to take direction from a common source.

The amount of communication that would be required to make and carry out a "policy" with regard to just one matter —race relations, for example—would probably overload the capacity of the influence hierarchy, even supposing its members were amenable to making "policy" on that subject. Anyone who has ever tried to get the key members of a large organization to enunciate a new policy and then to communicate the policy down the line to the "field" knows how many days of meetings with vice presidents, branch managers, supervisors, salesmen, and foremen are necessary and how many conferences must be held to prepare the way for each meeting. If this is the case within a single organization where there is agreement on a common purpose as well as morale and discipline, how much greater is the task where communication must go on outside

of a hierarchy and even outside of adher-
ence to a common purpose!

3. Once conflict has been overcome and
communication established, organization
is necessary to concert activity: a group of
"top leaders" who undertook to make and
carry out a plan for Chicago would constitute an organization *ipso facto*. But
organization, the evidence of this and
other studies suggests, soon becomes an
obstacle in the way of comprehensive action on fundamental matters. This is because the desire to maintain and enhance
the organization tends to displace the ends
for which it was formed: the organization
becomes unwilling to act on these ends
for fear that by acting it may weaken or
destroy itself. Not only this, but preoccupation with the maintenance or enhancement of the organization, or with the kind
of subject matter that is amenable to
being "acted upon by an organization"
rather than "thought about by an individual," tends to turn attention from these
ends altogether.

The civic associations . . . [have been]
generally ineffective because of their preoccupation with their own maintenance.
They [have] avoided controversy in order
to maintain themselves. Almost without
exception, they [have been] split down
the middle by the issues. . . . To avoid
being weakened (in the conventional formula, "loss of effectiveness"), they did not
take positions on important matters.
When the proponents or opponents of a
position found organization necessary,
they usually created *ad hoc* ones. If the
ad hoc organizations survived to become
permanent, they soon became as rigid as
the others: they could not go beyond the
fixed and narrow limits of the agreements
under which they came into existence;
sometimes they could not reach even to
these limits.

The civic organizations, then, are not
likely to deal with controversial problems
except in the few uninteresting cases
where virtually all members are on the
same side. They are likely not only to

avoid controversy but even to prevent its
arising.

The civic associations, moreover, may
get in the way of serious thought and discussion about fundamental problems.
When the problem is clear-cut and its
solution well understood, they may be an
instrumentality for getting something
done quickly. But with regard to the most
important problems—race relations, for
example—it is seldom at all clear what
ought to be done. The first need is for
persons of exceptional intelligence, information, and judgment to think out the
problems together and to come to some
general agreement about what ought to
be done. Organizations get in the way of
this. They feed on activity and publicity,
whereas serious discussion must be carried
on privately and without much regard to
immediate and practical results. As one
big businessman—himself the head of an
important civic association—explained to
an interviewer:

> Businessmen are giving more support to
> the Urban League but they are not ba-
> sically tackling the race relations issue.
> There are no forums where you can dis-
> cuss it and no vehicles. And you don't want
> to just stir up something irresponsibly and
> then not be able to follow through. When
> you study civic activity, where do you get
> the *reflective* aspect? People just want ac-
> tion. Most of them just grab an issue
> pronto and move on. I don't advocate the
> approach of Plato, but we do need men
> who can reflect. There is such a difference
> between seeing the need for a sewer or
> park and the delicate problems of human
> relations. This must be more delibera-
> tive. . . .
> There is the problem of how to set up
> the civic mechanisms. Where could I sit
> down in a group and not stir up the news-
> papers? It must be done carefully to be
> productive. Where can I sit down with
> prominent Negro leaders and find out what
> they want and what the reasonable solu-
> tions could be? This [racial and religious
> problem] is getting into a different sphere
> of problems. Most people say, "Hip, hip for
> the merit system" or "let's have more

parks." But these problems require more perception.

The staff people, who have the time and are paid to think, spend their time trying to raise money and to maintain the organizations. They just crystallize issues. Where can you get men of talent?

So much is done under the glare of publicity and so much of the publicity is inspired by the organizations themselves. They say, "In 1957 we did blah, blah, blah. . . ." Suppose you said to some people "Let's take a weekend in some hotel and talk things over." What a lack of enthusiasm you'd get!

I know I once spoke to a prominent woman civic leader. I said, "Let's just sit around and chew it over." She was interested for a while and then she lost her interest. It doesn't have quite the dramatic qualities that are needed. They want *action, progress. . . .*

This is not just true of businessmen. It is true because of organizations. Their lifeblood is specific actions. Philosophy has become obsolete, except in the Great Books course. There you can have philosophy. Of course, make sure you don't localize it— don't let it spread over into real activities.

People want to know, "What did you do?" If civic organizations said, "We talked," people would just laugh.

As this suggests, the tendency of the business leader to express his interest in civic affairs by participating in civic organizations focuses attention on those matters which make "good program material" for the associations (that is, matters on which there is general agreement and some prospect of immediate "accomplishment") and tends to withdraw from consideration matters which are too controversial or too difficult to be treated in the few minutes that are left after the monthly luncheon. In lieu of the really significant problems (which often cannot be made into "good program material" *because* of their significance), the civic association atmosphere tends to produce spurious problems. The rhetoric of the "civic leader" is full of plausible-sounding but essentially empty generalities. Here, for example, is the reply of a prominent Chicago attorney to an interviewer's question, "What are the most important things to be done in Chicago?"

I think that in general planning and every phase of civic and community activity should be better integrated and far more broadly based. . . . Planning in the physical sense. The use of land that is embraced in the metropolitan area. That includes the rehabilitation of community areas, a reorientation of land use—all on a comprehensive basis. And it also includes the planning of a political structure that will be comprehensive and inclusive. The present political structure is a hodge-podge. Also in the area of . . . the structure and functions and scope—ah—of those elements of the community organization which are strictly political. There are a great many voluntary agencies that have enormous responsibilities, that operate extrapolitically. And there should be a similar coordination of their functions, again on a broad, comprehensive area, wide basis . . . on the metropolitan area basis.

To a considerable extent, "civic leadership" consists of such platitudinizing. (The attorney who made this statement may have been tired or bored during the interview; perhaps in another mood he would have done better. But "civic leadership" often comes from men who are tired or bored.) When, as sometimes happens, such talk results in concrete proposals for action, these usually have to do with problems that are, if not altogether spurious, at least of secondary importance and, in any case, politically hopeless. Nevertheless, there is no denying that such activity serves a social function. In our society, everyone who has attained to a certain standing in the community is under some obligation to interfere in the conduct of public affairs in order to show that he is "civic-minded." Civic "activity" and civic "leadership" afford these people the opportunity to meet this obligation in ways that are, on the whole, innocuous.

The experience of Central Area Committee exemplifies rather well how the three factors to which attention has here been called limit the effectiveness of "top leadership" under even the most favorable of circumstances. The Committee . . . consisted of the heads of all the principal businesses having a large stake in the central area of the city. It was formed as an *ad hoc* committee because the civic associations, notably the Association of Commerce and Industry, could not deal with central-area problems without risking internal divisions that might "endanger their effectiveness." The circumstances under which the Committee was created were remarkably auspicious. It had the advantage of limited objectives (to protect real estate values in the inner city) that were of business importance to all of its members. There was available to serve as its full-time chairman the retiring head of the Chicago Title and Trust Company, Holman D. Pettibone, who knew the downtown business community intimately and who possessed extraordinary skills as a negotiator. The city was governed by an all-powerful political machine under Mayor Daley, whose general outlook and political situation disposed him to favor the general objectives of the Committee.

One would think that if there ever was an occasion when the "top leadership" of a big city would make and carry out a comprehensive plan, this was it.

In fact, . . . the Committee did not accomplish very much. It helped create an atmosphere in which the mayor was encouraged to move a little faster than he might otherwise have moved. It enlarged somewhat the area of agreement among its members, or, at least, it helped find terms on which they would compromise; no doubt this removed some obstacles that might have slowed the mayor, and no doubt it gave him incentive to press forward. The Committee did not, however, make a plan for the central area, nor did it cause the mayor to have one made. The big decisions with respect to such matters as the Fort Dearborn Project, the branch of the University of Illinois, and the Exhibition Hall turned mainly on considerations of parochial

and sometimes private advantage and not at all on any grand strategic conception laid down by Pettibone or other "top leaders." If there existed any guiding conception at all, which is very doubtful, it was in the minds of the mayor and of James C. Downs, a businessman (but not a "top" one) who functioned as an adviser to the mayor and not as one of a clique of "civic leaders."

Not only did the Committee fail to make a general plan for development, but it failed also to take a decided stand on those particular matters—the CTA[4] subsidy and the Fort Dearborn Project, for example—that were clearly of decisive importance to the future of the central city. . . . Conflicts of interest and opinion cut across the business community in so many directions that effective action was out of the question. But even if the business leaders agreed, there were others . . . who had contrary views and without whose cooperation no agreement could be carried into effect. Despite the energetic and talented efforts of Pettibone and others to bring all of the parties to these issues together, failures of communication were often decisive. (In the Fort Dearborn case, for example, the mayor and the sponsors seem never to have understood each other's basic positions.) And, . . . the Committee was prevented by considerations of organizational maintenance from doing some of the most important things that it was set up to do.

Although the businessmen, who have so much at stake in the metropolitan area, cannot themselves, because of the nature of their ends and the constraints upon their roles, make or carry out a plan for the area, they believe the local government can and should do so. One of the largest real estate men in Chicago told an interviewer:

I think that with the tremendous changes that have taken place in technology and living, it has become a matter of rebuild-

4 *CTA is the Chicago Transit Authority.*—ED. NOTE.

ing cities. And I don't think most of them [the very wealthy] visualize this. And for some reason or another—and this is awfully hard to see—neither do the public servants. The things the city is doing, with the exception of the expressways and the garages . . . amount to very little. It is a piecemeal program. Certainly the public servants are providing no leadership. And the one place where there should be leadership is in the Plan Commission, and they've done damn near nothing. What planning there is, is by small groups here and there and it is *forced* on the city. . . .

When the businessman tries to account for the failure of government to give the general direction he thinks is needed, he speaks of defects of organization—defects which in principle might easily be corrected and which are thus, in a sense, accidental or extraneous features of the situation—and of defects of character on the part of officials. These same factors are, of course, according to the mythology, all that stands in the way of informal government by a "power elite" of businessmen. But businessmen, even those of them who see clearly that business cannot formulate a plan for community development, often fail to see that government, for much the same reasons, cannot formulate one either. In the quotation above, the speaker complains of lack of leadership by public officials. When he was asked how he accounted for this lack, he said:

> Well, I think many of the wrong people are appointed and many of the good ones get discouraged. Here is a case in point. It happened very recently. The mayor said to Bach [the commissioner of planning], "Call a meeting and approve the 23rd Street site for the Convention Hall." So the Department of Planning calls a meeting and tries to put that over. If Bach had any guts, he wouldn't take that. He's too much of a Milquetoast guy.

The idea that there would be effective planning in Chicago if only the mayor had the "right attitude" or if only the planning commissioner had more "guts" is on a par with the idea that businessmen themselves could make and carry out a plan if only they had a stronger sense of civic responsibility. The fact is that some essential features of the political system, among them the structure of influence and certain deeply ingrained political habits and traditions, constrain all participants, the mayor no less than the planning commissioner, to act very much as they do. If the planning commissioner defied the mayor, he would at once be replaced by a commissioner who would not defy him. If the mayor had a planner's cast of mind (he would not have one, of course, for if he did he would never get to be boss in the first place), he would not be able to make the trades that keep him in office and give him power. To be sure, his power is great enough, thanks to the machine and to his ability to make the trades the planners deplore, so that he can exercise wide discretion in almost any matter. But being able to exercise discretion in almost any matter does not mean that he can exercise it in *all* matters. With respect to any one or two, or any few, moves, he is free. But if he wishes to stay in the game and to win, most of his moves, like most of the moves of the "civic leaders" and the businessmen in *their* games, must be determined by the exigencies of the game itself. Like them, he must act as the game requires or else get out of it.

E. The Study of Cliques—
Some Methodological Considerations

The Bonds of Legislative Friendship

John C. Wahlke, Heinz Eulau, William Buchanan, Leroy Ferguson

That legislative friendships play a part in the lawmaking process has received recognition by academic observers as well as participants. The structure and consequences of the ties of legislative friendship have been treated as follows:

> The need to do social favors involves an incessant vigilance for friends who have social graces and power. Their value may be justly estimated—that is, their value in the political exchange—and they must be held in corresponding regard and offered corresponding respect and political favors.[1]

> The relationships of a legislator with his fellow legislators do much to moderate the conflicts inherent in the legislative process and to facilitate the adjustments without which the process could not go on. Skill in handling such relationships, moreover, generates influence that is reflected in leader-follower patterns within the chamber.[2]

> Expertness in the art of parliamentary persuasion and manipulation [although] of the same stuff which underlies all interpersonal contacts . . . is hedged by written and unwritten canons of behavior, decorum, and practice; and it is informed by observation of the situation and the personalities involved. . . . Once reasonably well developed, this skill makes its possessor an equal among his legislative colleagues in fact as well as in theory.[3]

[1] *Herman Finer*, The Theory and Practice of Modern Government (*New York: Holt, Rinehart & Winston, Inc., 1949*), *p. 383*.
[2] *David B. Truman*, The Governmental Process (*New York: Alfred A. Knopf, Inc., 1953*), *pp. 344–345*.
[3] *Garland C. Routt, "Interpersonal Relations and*

Since it is within reasonable physical limits for one man to establish some sort of personal contact with forty-eight or even ninety-five others, it is possible and fairly common for one [U.S.] Senator, or a handful by concerted efforts, to affect materially the proceedings and decisions of the upper chamber.[4]

Compared to the extensive analysis of the effect of constituency, party, and group affiliation on legislative decisions, there have been comparatively few research efforts in this area. Part of the reason no doubt lies in the inaccessibility of data. The pair and clique connections among legislators may be ascertained only by research directed toward this end. For these are not individual characteristics, but rather reciprocal, transactional relationships. A's friendship with B, or his attachment to a clique consisting of C, D, and E, or his habit of looking to F for leadership or regarding with suspicion whatever G advocates—these are phenomena which demand, at a minimum, the description of two persons plus the nature of the relationship between them. They are role relationships, involving a "self," an "other," and some sort of expectation of behavior relating the two.

Research directed at this problem includes a unique study of the interaction

the Legislative Process," Annals of the American Academy of Political and Social Science, *Vol.* CVC (1938), 129–136.
[4] *David B. Truman*, The Congressional Party (*New York: John Wiley & Sons, Inc., 1959*), *p. 96*.

John C. Wahlke *et al., The Legislative System* (New York: John Wiley & Sons, Inc., 1962), Chap. 10, "The Bonds of Friendship," pp. 216–35, drafted by William Buchanan. Reprinted by permission.

of members on the floor of a senate, based on observations at periodic time intervals. Certain officers were seen to confer with high frequency, an informally recognized clique leader was in contact with a number of members, the minority leader appeared to be a go-between, and, in general, the number of contacts within parties was higher than between parties. "Such contacts," it was concluded, "are ingredients of the social cement which bound divergent factions of the senate together into a functioning whole."[5]

Utilizing the familiar "sociometric" technique of asking respondents to name persons who stand in a specified relation to them, Samuel C. Patterson was able to delineate several cliques of three to nine members within each party of the Wisconsin lower house. These appeared to be based on geography, tenure, earlier political alliances, seating in the chamber, or some combination of these elements. The cliques held together on certain votes and organizational decisions. Patterson concluded:

Friendship roles are functional in the legislative group. . . . Perception of friendship by members can be related to leadership in the sense that leaders will tend to be perceived as playing friendship roles by more members and nonleaders. . . . The legislator brings to the decision-making process not only his own sociological and psychological makeup and his multiple-group memberships, but also his informal associations within the legislative group. He is part of the informal social structure of the legislative group, and is affected by the norms of these informal groups in his own decision-making behavior.

Individuals who assume the legislative role have diverse backgrounds and diverse social, political, and economic experience, and different reference groups are salient for them. The informal friendship structure of the legislature tends to lessen such differences, to mitigate against the development of potential conflicts, to provide channels of communication and understanding

among members who share goals, and to facilitate logrolling.[6]

The existence of clique structures may be pursued by a third technique, using as data the recorded votes of legislators. The relationship between two or more members is expressed as the extent of their common agreement on certain legislative issues. Though complex mathematical techniques have been used to analyze the relation of many men linked by common characteristics and common viewpoints on many issues, we can learn a great deal without resorting to them.[7]

Legislators' Expression of Friendship Choices

The principal source of data for our analysis consists of responses to the question:

[5] *Routt, op. cit., p. 135.*

[6] "*Patterns of Interpersonal Relations in a State Legislative Group: The Wisconsin Assembly," Public Opinion Quarterly, Vol. XXIII (1959), 101–109.*
[7] *Beyle's pioneer exploration of "attribute-cluster blocs" [Herman C. Beyle, Identification and Analysis of Attribute-Cluster Blocs (Chicago: University of Chicago Press, 1931)] is analogous in certain respects to the more restrictive analysis of selected roll calls by Guttman scaling. It leads in its ultimate refinement to some form of factor analysis, as Duncan MacRae, Jr., has pointed out [Dimensions of Congressional Voting (Berkeley: University of California Press, 1958), p. 207.] Matrices setting out the relationships between persons in a group have been employed in intricate examination of the party system in Congress (Truman, The Congressional Party, op. cit.). In this last, Truman notes the comparability of sociometric choice and roll-call agreement (p. 44) and evaluates the techniques from Stuart Rice's Quantitative Methods in Politics (New York: Alfred A. Knopf, Inc., 1928) to date. High-speed computers have now made previously laborious techniques quite feasible. Among authors of papers (duplicated) which deal with these are MacRae (University of Chicago), Edward E. Cureton (University of Tennessee), Alan B. Wilson (University of California). The technique used later in this chapter —the calculation of percentage agreement between each pair of legislators—has been used as the first step in a cluster analysis of the U.S. Senate. David J. Fitch, Predicting Votes of Senators of the 83rd Congress, a Comparison of Similarity Analysis and Factor Analysis (Ph.D. dissertation, University of Illinois, 1958). See also Duncan MacRae, Jr., and Hugh D. Price, "Scale Position and 'Power' in the Senate," Behavioral Science, Vol. IV (July, 1959), 212–218.*

Now, who are some of your closest personal friends in the House (Senate)—I mean the members you see most often outside the chamber, at lunch or dinner or parties or social gatherings.

Since some of the conclusions we reach depend upon the way in which the data were gathered, it is important to call attention to certain features about the research technique:

1. It follows the traditional specifications for sociometric inquiry, except that it calls for a perceived relationship (who are your friends?) rather than a "choice" in the strictest sense (whom would you like for friends?).[8]

2. It asks for "extracurricular" relationships, and not for the names of members with whom the respondent agrees, votes, or interacts on the floor or in committee. Thus we are able to test for coincidences between these two kinds of behavior.

3. Of the 504 members of the four legislatures [California, New Jersey, Ohio, and Tennessee], 6 per cent were not interviewed, and another 3 per cent were not asked this question. Of the *remainder*—those who were given an opportunity to respond—13 per cent did not.[9] This included 2 per cent who refused to "name names" of other members, 6 per cent who evaded politely by saying they were friendly with "all the members" and 5 per cent who said they "had no friends" in the legislature. The last group included some, at least, who accurately described their status, for no other member named them. Nonrespondents of all types pose a

---

8 *For appraisal of the method and a summary of results, see Chap. 11, "Sociometric Measurement" by Gardner Lindzey and Edgar F. Borgatta in Lindzey, Handbook of Social Psychology (Reading, Mass.: Addison-Wesley Publishing Company, Inc., 1954), and Chap. 17, "Analysis of Sociometric Data," by C. H. Proctor and C. P. Loomis in Marie Johada, et al., Research Methods in Social Relations, Part II (New York: The Dryden Press, 1951).*

9 *This is exactly the rate of nonresponse encountered by Patterson. It was substantially the same in the four states, suggesting a potential ceiling on results from this method.*

problem in analysis of pair relations that is not present in other tabulation—one is never certain whether they might have reciprocated the "choices" other members extended toward them.

4. In asking such a question, some "cutting point" is established on the continuum that reaches from the respondent's most intimate friend to the persons he barely knows by name. Calling for a certain number (say five) when practicable, makes for ease in statistical analysis, but at the expense of accuracy in describing the perceptions of the respondent who sees three, or seven, members in substantially the same relationship to him. Refusal to set any numerical standard would encourage diversity of interpretation of the question. Our decision was to compromise: the question omitted a number, but interviewers were instructed to probe until five or six names were elicited, but to accept more or fewer if the respondent appeared to be referring to some clear standard of his own.

5. The word "friends" and the amplifying remark about dinners and social affairs give us our only information on the kind of relations elicited. We may extend this a little with our knowledge of the sort of arrangements characteristically made between peers in the same organization in our "shop-talking" society. Further inference that the relationship is of the sort suggested by other analysts—leadership, self-conscious manipulation, sociability as an item on the political exchange, coincidence of viewpoint, etc.—remains to be substantiated. What we do have is evidence of a closeness or linkage, a potential communication channel, between certain members that does not occur between others.

Certain hypotheses derived from the statements of legislators and scholars may be tested against the data at hand. The testing process cannot be a rigorous or conclusive one with the evidence we have, but we may at least determine whether the structure of relationships is of the sort that would promote or would inhibit the function hypothesized:

1. That the social linkages promote compromise and accommodation between legislators of differing persuasions.
2. That they stem from personal force or attractiveness ("skills," "graces," "arts"), which gives certain legislators a wide circle of influence.
3. That they link persons of like characteristics.
4. That they provide cues for decision making.
5. That they are reciprocal, and facilitate the exchange of influence.
6. That they follow the lines of force represented by the formal structure of the body.

Considered as categorical generalizations, it is evident that some of these (1 and 3, 2 and 5, for example) are not entirely compatible. Since they may exist as tendencies, however, it is quite possible for them to exist side by side. Such a generalized relationship as that of "friend" could serve several functions.

The Range of Individual Influence. The basic element in any pattern we may discern is the scope of the average individual's influence through his social relationships. Though interviewers encouraged respondents to give up to six names, some two-thirds of the legislators who listed some friends indicated that they did not have this many. Only one in ten voluntarily went above the scheduled six. . . . The larger proportion of the membership received one to four choices, and even allowing for the additional choices that might have been made by the non-respondents would not increase the norm substantially. The maximum number of choices received by any one person in the eight chambers ranged from eight to nineteen. . . . (The higher numbers were in the larger chambers in every case, of course.) All these evidences lead to the conclusion that legislative social circles are severely restricted in size, and are subject to an absolute limit rather than one

relative to the size of the chamber. The obvious source of such a limit would be the human capacities of time, energy, space, and attention in a busy legislative session—frailties that restrict the average member to perhaps three to five close friends and even the most gregarious to fewer than twenty. By contrast, the quality of "leadership," which does not necessarily demand personal contact, but may be exercised by example and embodied in reputation, recognition, and respect even when it is not dressed in the robe of formal office—this quality is virtually unrestricted in scope.

This limitation of a physical nature on the capacity of an individual to make friends is reminiscent of the early administrative concept of "span of control" which sets limits on the number of subordinates an executive can effectively supervise in person.[10] . . . Our numerical limits (which are quite comparable to Patterson's incidentally) are to some degree a function of the way the question was asked; a different technique might set higher and possibly more realistic limits. Making all due allowance for the crudeness of the measure, it seems unlikely that a legislator in any chamber can exert personal influence over a sustained period on more than a dozen members. Rather, it seems likely that whatever influence is exerted is brought to bear within small, interlocking, overlapping, permeable circles.

Some Correlates of Friendship

The contrasting propositions that social relationships will occur among members with similar characteristics and that they promote accommodation between members with different views may be examined by setting up opposing groups and determining the proportion of choice within and across group lines. The tendency to choose persons of like characteristics is called "homophily" and one measure

[10] *See V. A. Graicunas, "Relationship in Organization," in Luther Gulick and L. Urwick, Papers on the Science of Administration (New York: Institute of Public Administration, 1937), pp. 181–187.*

of it is *"h,"* which gauges the extent to which this occurs over and above the amount attributable solely to the relative sizes of the groups.

Tenure, which is in many respects the legislative equivalent of social status, suggests itself as a possible correlate of friendship choice. We might expect to find two tendencies: one for veteran legislators to choose within their own powerful subgroup; the other for freshmen to choose their seniors, using friendship as a channel of upward mobility.[11] . . . Veterans choose overwhelmingly within their own group. Freshmen do so to a considerably lesser extent, indicating that some of their choices are upwardly directed. Where veterans form a tightly knit group, freshmen are thrown back on friendships with their own classmates.

On the whole it appears that social life in the legislature performs about the same function it does elsewhere, providing companionship and status reassurance. Altogether, only 24 per cent of choices are made across the line that separates freshmen from veteran legislators. In every legislature stratification is more rigid in the large lower house than in the smaller senate. However, in the chamber with decidedly the largest proportion of new members, the Tennessee House (46 per cent), there is comparatively little ingroup choice on either side of the line. Our conclusions about the functional significance of "friendships" in accommodating and integrating new members into the life of the chamber must be limited. Wide variation is apparent: certain chambers have an "open-class" system, while others are rigidly structured, and we do not have enough cases to determine the institutional factors that might account for the differences. In general, since no chambers produced the negative *"h"* values that would indicate a concerted effort to "adopt" freshmen into existing

cliques, we may say that the social life of the legislature does more to reinforce existing differences than to acclimate freshmen to their new surroundings.

Party is a second natural boundary within the legislature, and one with more relevance to the political process than seniority. . . . Several phenomena are apparent:

1. Both the majority and the minority party tend to choose members of their own group to a large extent, with one exception —the small and stable New Jersey senate.

2. This tendency is greater among majority than among minority party members, again with one exception—the Ohio senate.

3. In-party friendship is more prevalent in lower than in upper houses.

4. Party exercises a much more regular and consistent effect than tenure, the range of *"h"* values being narrower and the differences between chambers smaller, though the values themselves are consistently high.

These findings, which may be summarized roughly by saying that only 18 per cent of all friendships are formed across party lines, suggest that interpersonal relationships are so structured as to be unlikely to perform one function suggested by several of the writers mentioned above—accommodating different points of view. Instead, they are more likely to *reinforce* team spirit and party competition.

We find here, as with tenure, that the senates have the more permeable party boundaries. The "clublike" atmosphere of the United States Senate and the loyalty of its members to the chamber as an institution have received considerable attention.[12] The size of the group compared to a house of four-hundred-odd members, has been credited as the important factor. Similar remarks about the clubbiness of

---

11 *Comparable tendencies have been found among college students, Lindzey and Borgatta, op. cit., p. 430.*

12 *Truman,* The Congressional Party, op. cit., *pp. 96, 314; Donald R. Matthews, "The Folkways of the United States Senate,"* American Political Science Review, *Vol. LIII (Dec., 1959), 1064–1089; William S. White,* Citadel *(New York: Harper & Row, Publishers, Inc., 1957).*

state senators when compared to lower house members occurred in our own interviews. State senates in the United States average less than half the size of the U.S. Senate, while lower houses in the states average 120 members—not much larger than the U.S. Senate. The absolute as well as the relative aspect of size should be taken into consideration along with length of service and other factors in any appraisal of the impact of structure on legislative decision making. Our data support the belief that small size, leading to a more integrated social system within the chamber, may blunt partisanship slightly.[13]

Friendships Among Legislative Leaders

The occupants of formal status positions in the legislature might be examined in the same way that party and tenure subgroups were, except that they constitute a rather small group for statistical manipulation. They have additional significance because of their power: if they constitute a clique, this is evidence that an informal channel exists for decision making. They may easily "consult" and perhaps "concur," to use the Wilsonian phraseology.

In general, legislative leaders are much more likely to be regarded as friends, as Patterson noted. Formal leaders of house and party receive nearly twice as many choices as do rank-and-file legislators,[14] with committee chairmen falling in between.[15]

Since each leader occupies a specified formal status, and there is a great deal of similarity among the eight chambers in their table of organization, we adopt a different technique of analysis. Here we examine the frequency with which a choice (in either direction) occurs between occupants of the same status position in all eight chambers. As representative of chamber leaders we used the elected presiding officer, the majority and the minority floor leaders. To represent chairmen we selected three, the heads of the finance, education, and judiciary committees, which appeared in all chambers, though not always by these names. From the rank and file we chose randomly three members of the majority and three of the minority. By totaling for the eight chambers the number of links between occupants of the same status, and expressing this as a proportion of the number of possible links, we may generalize about the intensity of social interaction between different parts of the typical legislative structure.[16] The data are given in Table 1.

It is apparent that there is a close relationship between the typical presiding officer and his majority leader, and also between these two officers and the chairman of the finance committee. The last, though technically at the second level of legislative organization, generally occupies

---

[13] *In the eight legislatures studied by Malcolm E. Jewell, "Party Voting in American State Legislatures"* [American Political Science Review, *Vol. XLIX (September, 1955), 773–791*], *the tendency, though slight and inconsistent, appears to be in the direction of greater party cohesion in the lower houses.*

[14] *The median for formal leaders is 5.3 choices, for rank and file, 2.6 choices. The former group is composed of presiding officers, party floor leaders and whips, and steering committee chairmen, a segment of the leadership corresponding approximately to Truman's "elective leaders"* (The Congressional Party, op. cit., *pp. 99–101*).

[15] *. . . One might reach the conclusion that persons who were widely chosen as "friend" reached legislative and committee office because of their* popularity. *That this is probably not the case is suggested by the fact that they did not make appreciably more choices than others and that they were no likelier to be chosen to fill vacancies in office that arose after the survey was made. It is safer to conclude that the additional choices they received are due to the prestige and visibility an office gives them.*

[16] *For example, take the speaker and majority leader. If both responded in a chamber, there are two possible choices, one in each direction. If both responded in all eight chambers, there are sixteen possible choices, and the number actually made is taken as a proportion of sixteen. If one of these officers in any chamber did not respond (whatever his reason), the number of possible choices is reduced to fifteen, and so on. Where one of the offices did not exist, possible choices are reduced from sixteen to fourteen, since this officer may neither choose nor be chosen.*

TABLE 1. PROPORTION OF POSSIBLE CHOICES AS "FRIEND" (IN EITHER DIRECTION) BETWEEN OCCUPANTS OF THE SAME STATUS POSITION IN EIGHT LEGISLATIVE CHAMBERS

	Majority Leader	Minority Leader	Chairman Finance	Chairman Education	Chairman Judiciary
Presiding officer	60%	10%	64%	21%	31%
Majority leader	X	22	25	45	30
Minority leader		X	0	0	0
Chairman, Finance			X	27	10
Chairman, Education				X	8

TABLE 2. PROPORTION OF POSSIBLE CHOICES AS "FRIEND" (IN EITHER DIRECTION) BETWEEN OCCUPANTS OF THREE STATUS LEVELS IN EIGHT LEGISLATIVE CHAMBERS

	Officers	Chairmen	Majority Members	Minority Members
Officers	31%	25%	7%	9%
Chairmen		15	12	5
Majority members			13*	3*
Minority members				11*

* These proportions are based on the sample of three members in each house, and are given for purposes of comparison with the rates for officers, rather than as reliable indices of majority-minority interaction.

a critical coordinative position due to his responsibility for the state's budget.

Table 2 shows on a similar basis the relationships between the two groups of officials, and within the two groups, and also the relations between these two official levels and the rank and file, both of the majority and the minority, as represented in our sample.

We find here a high rate of interaction among the chamber officers, and between them and the chairmen, but not among the chairmen to the same extent. We find minority members rather isolated except for their contacts with the minority leader, who accounts for most of their friendships in the officer level. (Computed separately, his interaction rate with minority members is 28 per cent, compared to 13 per cent between majority leader and majority members.) These differential rates have been sketched out in Figure 1, with the connecting links drawn wider where there is a high proportion of friendship choice. If these social channels bear policy communications, then majority members have the choice of two routes—via the chairmen or via their party leader—while the minority have

only one.[17] In general, the picture confirms the impression we gained from the earlier analysis: that informal, social relationships follow rather closely the formal, official structure of the legislature.

Friendships in the Decision Process

So far we have dealt with the consequences of these social relationships only by inference, concluding from an examination of their pattern and structure that they appear to be well adapted or poorly adapted to perform some function they have been reputed to perform. Now we shall try to appraise the effect of these friendship cliques on the actual lawmaking behavior of legislators and their resultant consequences for the society being governed. For this purpose we use an index which is entirely independent of the interview method—their votes on the bills before them.

This examination was confined to one of the eight chambers, the lower house

17 In view of the "mediate" character of the legislative party in Congress, Truman attaches considerable importance to the communication functions performed by its leadership structure. See The Congressional Party, op. cit., pp. 130–131.

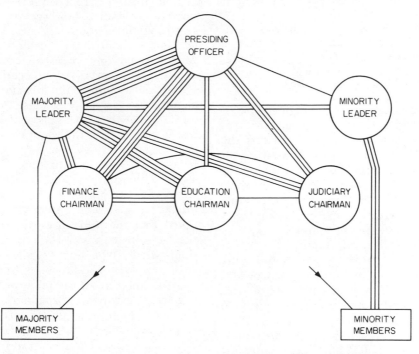

Figure 1. *Level of interaction between legislative officers, chairmen, and members. Based on cumulated friendship choices for eight chambers.*

(assembly) in California. The choice was dictated by three considerations: (1) there was a complete record of votes available; (2) recorded votes on the whole were meaningful indices of each individual legislator's contribution to the group's decision;[18] and (3) the California assembly presents a fluid environment where the interpersonal "friendships" studied would

be expected to play a part in members' voting decisions.[19] If we find these social relationships to be influential in California, it does not necessarily mean that they will be influential in every other legislature; but if we do not find them relevant here, it is rather unlikely that they will be effective elsewhere.

To compare our data on "choices" with voting records we need a generalized index of agreement between pairs of legislators on a variety of subjects. At the same time we may eliminate the non-controversial bills which neither require difficult decisions nor produce disagreements. Of the 4,250 roll calls in the 1957 session of the California assembly, 316 were selected which met the following specifications:

---

[18] *The importance of recorded votes varies from one legislature to another. Where the important decisions are made in caucus and followed by straight party-line votes, these record votes would be a poor indication of any member's contribution to the group's decision. Other practices that diminish the relevance of roll calls as an index of individual positions: automatic unanimous ratification of committee decisions; much time spent in committee of the whole, with heavy reliance on voice votes or standing votes; high rates of absenteeism; "carrying over" roll calls from one bill to the next, thus recording members as for or against who have actually left the chamber. None of these were common in the California Assembly in 1957. The record is not, of course, a perfect index of each individual's contribution to the decision. Nor do we assume that the vote indicates how a member "really" feels about the issue. . . .*

[19] *Parties were relatively weak, discipline negligible. Each member "carried" his own bills and lined up support for them by his own efforts. . . . In this situation one would expect ad hoc alliances and reciprocal arrangements to be of maximum utility to the individual member.*

1. More than 10 per cent (eight members) were on the losing side.

2. Where successive roll calls were on the same matter, at least five per cent (four members) shifted position.

3. Issues were substantive, not adjournment or housekeeping.

This procedure avoided judgment on the relative "importance" of the measures, except the judgment of the legislators that is implicit in the time and attention devoted to measures that were contested by amendments, motions for postponement, or reconsideration, and the various parliamentary tactics that make for many votes on contested bills and few on those not considered worth a fight.

For these 316 votes an index of agreement was computed for each pair of legislators, consisting of the number of times they voted the same way (either "aye" or "nay") divided by the number of opportunities for them to agree (i.e., the number of roll calls when neither was absent). The 3,081 pair-indices ranged in value from 27 per cent to 93 per cent, with 59 per cent as the mean.[20]

The Influence of Friendship.   The average of the agreement indices for those pairs of members who mutually chose one another as friends was 77 per cent; for those pairs linked by a unidirectional choice (i.e., *A* chose *B*, *B* chose other members or did not respond) it was 67 per cent; for the pairs who did not choose one another it was 58 per cent. It is apparent that members who are "friends" tend to agree in their votes.

20 *Each pair index was based on 316 comparisons and a percentaging operation made possible by a program written by Pete Tenney for the IBM 704 computer at the University of California. For advice we are indebted to J. O. Neuhaus of the Computer Center and Rod Frederickson of the Survey Research Center. The theoretical limits are 0, for no agreement, and 100 per cent, for perfect agreement. That the mean was 59 per cent, not 50 per cent, reflects the characteristic one-sidedness of legislative votes. Had more controversial, or less controversial, bills been included the mean would have been different, so it is also a function of the cut-off point.*

It is apparent from the earlier discussion of structure, however, that social groups conform to party lines, and it is necessary to control for the effect of party. At the same time we shall control for another structural division peculiar to the California assembly, the division of the membership into "Speaker's Coalition" and "Opposition" factions which occurs in connection with the contest to organize the assembly. These factions appear to have considerable stability over time. The data, with mutual and unidirectional choice pairs combined for the sake of stability, are given in Table 3. It will be noted that the differences are small but they are consistently in the expected direction, whether the linkages lie within or cut across party and factional divisions.

At the bottom of the table we subtract out to get a rough approximation of the relative influence of party, faction, and friendship, and we find that in percentage terms the social relationship has an effect comparable to the two political relationships. However, the numbers involved must be considered in evaluating their relative impact on the total process. If social relationships may be thought of as falling along a continuum from cordiality at one end to hostility or indifference at the other, our sociometric question (for reasons treated earlier) cuts the continuum near the "cordial" end. While friendship choices cover only a small number of pairs, a common party affiliation is shared by half the pairs. Thus a given level of voting cohesion resulting from common party has a greater impact on the total process than one resulting from friendships. Party cohesion also has a systematic effect, while friendship alliances may cancel each other out.

Conclusions

Returning to the hypotheses we may conclude:

1. There is evidence that where social relationships occur between members of different persuasions (as indexed by party

TABLE 3. RELATION OF FRIENDSHIP CHOICE TO PARTY VOTING IN THE CALIFORNIA ASSEMBLY
(PARTY AND FACTION CONTROLLED)

	(1) Voting Agreement Between Pairs of "Friends"		(2) Voting Agreement Between All Other Pairs		(3) Differ- ence: Col. 1 less Col. 2	(4) Weighted Mean of Cols. 1 and 2	
	Av.*	N†	Av.‡	N†		Av.	N†
Members of same party *and* faction							
1. Coalition Democrat	66.8	49	63.7	251	3.1		
2. Opposition Democrat	72.5	15	64.5	51	8.0		
3. Coalition Republican	75.8	55	69.1	246	6.7		
4. Opposition Republican	72.1	25	68.7	108	3.4		
5. Total (weighted)	71.8	144	66.7	656	5.1	67.6	800
Members of same party *not* same faction							
6. Democrats	68.8	17	60.5	283	8.3		
7. Republicans	65.0	21	61.6	407	3.4		
8. Total (weighted)	66.7	38	61.2	690	5.5	61.7	728
Members of same faction *not* same party							
9. Coalition	59.1	30	53.6	595	5.5		
10. Opposition	59.6	19	58.6	185	1.0		
11. Total (weighted)	59.3	49	54.8	780	4.5	55.0	829
Members *not* of same party *or* faction							
12. All combination	56.9	20	51.2	704	5.7	51.4	724
13. Column totals	67.4	251	58.2	2830	9.2	58.9	3081

Recapitulation (weighted averages)	Av.	N
Within party (Col. 4: line 5 + line 8)	64.7	1528
Between parties (Col. 4: line 11 + line 12)	53.3	1553
Difference (influence of party)	11.4	
Within faction (Col. 4: line 5 + line 11)	61.3	1629
Between factions (Col. 4: line 8 + line 12)	56.4	1452
Difference (influence of faction)	4.9	
Among pairs of friends (Col. 1, line 13)	67.4	251
Among other pairs (Col. 2: line 13)	58.2	2380
Difference (influence of friendship)	9.2	

* *Average of the percentage agreement between every pair of members choosing one another, either mutually or in one direction only.*
† *The number of mutual and unidirectional pair choices in the category.*
‡ *Average of the percentage agreement between all other pairs in the category; i.e., all members of the category who mutually ignored one another in the "friend" choices, taken as pairs.*

and faction) they do result in some accommodation, and perhaps compromise (as indexed by a common stand on the generality of issues). But the structure of social relations is such that it rarely links unlike legislators, so the effect on total output is almost negligible.

2. Whatever the personal qualities behind legislative friendships may be, they give their possessors only a limited range of consistent influence, due to physical limitations on interaction with more than about twenty persons. But qualities of "leadership" based instead on reputation may embrace a much larger segment of the body.

3. On all the criteria we examined (and presumably others as well) social contacts

occur more frequently between members with similar characteristics.

4. The higher agreement among mutual than among unidirectional pairs suggests that exchange of influence does take place.

5. Structural characteristics very strongly influence the location of social linkages. In general, these linkages reinforce the stratification of the chamber horizontally by tenure and officer status, vertically by party and/or faction.

To sum up, we may say that the political roles of a legislator, as a member of a party, an officer of the chamber, or chairman of a committee, are more compelling than his social role as a friend, a good fellow, and a dinner companion. The latter does have an effect in the one chamber where we were able to test it, but on the whole it was not large. So there are occasions when interpersonal social relations may account for otherwise inexplicable behavior on the part of certain members. But we must be careful, when we observe that X and Y appear to be bolting their party because of their cordiality toward Z on the other side of the aisle, that we do not overlook the fact that A, B, C, and D at the same moment may be hewing to the party line because of their friendship ties with each other and with E, their floor leader.

6

Communications

Contrary to the cliché, it is words that speak louder than actions, at least in the world of democratic politics. We have seen, for instance, that control over information is a critical element of power in a democratic society; and we may say generally that it is the expression of demands, rather than the use of force, that stimulates political response in democracies. This section explores the role of communications in the political realm. Before examining the relation between communication and political action, however, it is necessary to provide some background on the emergence of communications analysis as a subject of interest in political science.

The communications process has only recently been explored as a topic of import in political science. Professional awareness of it arose during World War II, when students of public opinion turned their attention to Axis propaganda and attempted to analyze its content and hidden meanings by calculating the frequency with which certain symbolic words occurred. In the postwar years this type of content analysis has fallen into general disuse, and only a few American students of Soviet propaganda continue to use the technique. The concern has turned instead to the more basic conception that the communications process is the fundamental medium of social interaction among humans.

That is to say, it has been recognized among political scientists, and social scientists generally, that the communications process—the transmission of interpersonal and/or interorganizational messages is, as one analyst has noted, "a link as essential in social systems as gravity is in the solar system."[1] Since this is the case, it has become desirable to examine (1) the meaning of language both in theory and in its particular use; (2) the generation and transmission of symbolic meaning in the social context; and (3) the neurological and psychological facets of perception, cognition, retention, and recall—all in order to develop new insights about, and new adaptations of, verbal communications in human problem solving that might be useful in the maintenance and improvement of social life. Out of these concerns have arisen special fields of inquiry in social science: philosophy of language, general semantics and linguistics, communications engineering in business,

---

[1] *Wilbert E. Moore,* The Conduct of the Corporation *(New York: Random House, Inc., 1962),* p. 59.

human experimental psychology, cybernetics, information theory, and computer design theory. Although none of these special areas of investigation is *directly* related to political science, each and every one has important implications for the study of politics. Indeed, almost every one of these new endeavors actually has been employed in some way in recent years in the study of political phenomena. But more important, taken together these areas of investigation, and the concerns that gave birth to them, highlight the significance and utility of examining any field of social action, politics included, in the light of an understanding of the communications process.

Actually a unified conception of the process has not been developed. Instead there have grown up several relatively discrete, partial concepts of communications. There is, for example, the analysis of the sociocultural meaning and implication of language, dramatized in political science by the study of symbolism and ideological overtones in political phenomena, such as free speech movements on college campuses or the "red specter" of international Communism. Secondly, there has been analysis of the method and effect of expression as they are related to the behavior patterns of senders and receivers, such as the studies of the use and effectiveness of public relations firms in election campaigns.[2] Thirdly, there has been study of the *frequency* of communication between different persons, groups, or nations to determine the intensity of mutual involvement of the communicating parties. For example, Professor Karl W. Deutsch has conducted and supervised studies of the changing volumes of international mail between nations to develop an index of the degree of their friendliness.[3] Studies have also been focused on the structural component of communications—the channels and networks through which messages flow. One famous study of opinion formation in a Presidential campaign, for example, stressed the informal network of communications that helped shape political attitudes; this study identified prominent, respected "opinion leaders" as the transmitters of ideas via the mass media to the populace at large.[4] A fifth type of analysis has concentrated on language *per se* as the primary component of communications. In the realm of political science this approach has been taken by students of the intrinsic meaning and logic of such political ideas as democracy, freedom, authority, and equality.[5]

[2] *See, for example,* Stanley Kelley, Jr., Professional Public Relations and Political Power (*Baltimore: Johns Hopkins University Press, 1956*).

[3] *Karl W. Deutsch, "Shifts in the Balance of International Communication Flows,"* Public Opinion Quarterly, *Vol. XXX (Spring, 1956), 143–160, and "Transaction Flows as Indicators of Political Cohesion," in Philip E. Jacob and James V. Toscano, eds.,* The Integration of Political Communities (*Philadelphia: J. B. Lippincott Co., 1964), esp. pp. 76–82.*

[4] *Elihu Katz and Paul F. Lazarsfeld,* Personal Influence (*New York: The Free Press of Glencoe, Inc., 1955*).

[5] *See, for example, Felix E. Oppenheim,* Dimensions of Freedom: An Analysis (*New York: St. Martin's Press, Inc., 1961); Thomas L. Thorson,* The Logic of Democracy (*New York: Holt, Rinehart & Winston, Inc., 1962); Carl J. Friedrich, ed.,* Nomos, *Vols. I–VII (New York: Atherton Press, 1958–1964).*

Although the above conceptions have not been integrated into one comprehensive theory of political communications, in recent years much emphasis has been placed on one type of theoretical statement: a model of the flow of messages in the communications process. This type of statement, an illustrative diagram and explanation of which we offer on p. 256, presents a simplified analysis of social or political communications flows as if they were embedded in electronic transmission systems.[6]

The model of the communications process delineates four major steps in the flow of messages, in any one of which distortion can take place. First, the sender, or message source, must sift and organize the environmental stimuli he receives in the process of developing background information upon which to base his message. In this stage of the process, distortion can set in as a result of (1) the source's faulty or biased scanning and screening of environmental stimuli; (2) his defective encoding, or forming of the message into transmittable form, defective possibly as a result of distractions; (3) his poor judgment in selection of the channels through which the encoded message is to be carried, channels which may not be appropriate in that particular instance.

In the second stage, the possibility of distortion arises as a result of noise potential in the channel carrying the message. Noise is the equivalent of static in the transmission of radio and television signals. In social and political communications, noise potential refers to the possible interference in the conveyance of messages between sources and destinations, resulting in distortion. When a President's State of the Union address is distorted in newspaper coverage then we can say that noise or static is present. All channels of communication have some noise potential.

In the third stage of message flow, the receiver, or destination, may distort the message through any or all of the following: (1) inadequate monitoring; (2) misinterpretation in decoding; (3) over- or underemphasis on certain elements as a result of crude volume and tone control in message reproduction. When certain messages are ignored, albeit accidentally, when language is misunderstood, or when unintended emphasis is placed on certain ideas, then the message—for example, a communiqué from an embassy to the U.S. Department of State offices in Washington—is distorted, and the reaction that follows is likely to be less than fully effective. It might be noted here that few if any receivers are able to pick up messages with perfect fidelity; there is an almost universal tendency for message destinations to distort as they deem necessary for accomplishment of their own objectives.

---

6 *Of course social or political communication never fully approximates electronic transmission or any other mechanistic or deterministic system. The utility of the model rests largely upon its delineation of probable, not necessary, similarities between electrical circuitry and human communications. This model, or any other general statement simplifying reality, should be viewed only as a more or less useful device for examining complex phenomena. If this qualification is applied, the diagram and its explanation should prove helpful in understanding the flow of messages in political communications.*

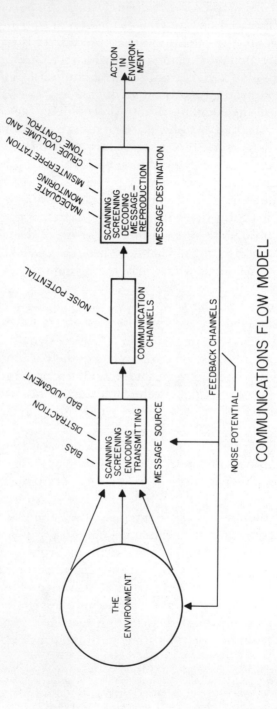

COMMUNICATIONS FLOW MODEL

The last stage of the message flow is the feedback directly to the source, as manifested in the form of the receiver's reaction, which in international communications might take such diverse forms as diplomatic approbation in a formally worded note, the expression of ominous warnings in the United Nations General Assembly, or the bombing of an embassy. These are fed back into the message-transmission machinery as they are absorbed into the environmental mix or spotted by other senders. The distortion in this fourth stage occurs when the intentions or meaning underlying the reaction are misinterpreted. As in the transmission from sender to receiver, distortion occurs wherever the original meaning is lost or altered in the process of communication.

This four-stage model is designed to highlight the origins of message distortion. It closely parallels other recently developed models of the political process that stress inputs, outputs, and the flow of political demands and rewards.[7] These can be used to identify the sources of instability in the disrupted flow of political currency. The communications flow model thus has important implications for the political process—though it does have shortcomings in political analysis. For example, although the model emphasizes message distortion, it provides no clear definition or way of measuring distortion in its various forms. Without this methodological refinement the model can tell us little about communications in concrete situations. In short, it is not readily applied empirically so that it can generate answers to the questions it raises.

In studying political communications, as a result, political science has often utilized simpler techniques of investigation. The selections we have chosen represent some of these approaches. They also illustrate how communications can, and do, affect political action in specific situations.

Eric Hoffer's discussion of "men of words," for example, deals with a central facet of the relationship between communications and political action: the frequent presence of persuasive intellectuals in the vanguard of mass political movements in this century. Hoffer notes that such leadership is critical to the development of discontent: by discrediting the established order, by laying the ideological groundwork for the new order, and by creating, perhaps unintentionally, a hunger among the people for new faith—the basis of fanatical mass action. Moreover, Hoffer notes that intellectuals, when alienated, are particularly dangerous threats to political leaders; their power of communication in effect can readily be turned to the destruction of the very regimes they sometimes have helped to establish. The recent case of the struggle between the Black Nationalists under the late Malcolm X and the Black Muslims under Elijah Muhammed dramatizes the potency of

7 *See, for example, Karl W. Deutsch,* The Nerves of Government (*New York: The Free Press of Glencoe, Inc., 1963*), *p. 258, and Lester W. Milbrath,* Political Participation (*Chicago: Rand McNally & Co., 1965*), *p. 28.*

intellectual differences in generating hostility and violence between the followers of different "men of words."

William C. Mitchell deals with the more common use of communications in politics—the political socialization of the citizenry. In the American context this function, whether performed formally in educational institutions or informally through the family, peer group, youth group, the mass media, or even the political party itself, is subject to conservative rather than radical or revolutionary influences. As Mitchell points out, this shaping of political attitudes in the young is controlled by and large by persons stressing conservative values of patriotism; traditional doctrines of law and order, consensus, and conflict avoidance; and the inherent superiority of the United States Constitution, free enterprise, and the American way of life. Only the family is likely (in certain special cases) to inculcate in children indifference or disrespect toward established authority. In all other socializing contexts the agents of opinion formation are almost invariably hostile toward fundamental change in the *status quo*. This "systematic bias" in communications patterns helps to account for widespread American lack of sympathy for radicalism of either the right or the left.

Another important effect of communications on politics is felt in the shaping of foreign policy, in which the press provides policy makers with information, ideas, and commentary on world affairs. In particular, Bernard Cohen singles out *The New York Times* as a source of knowledge, as well as a medium in which policy alternatives are analyzed and criticized. Unfortunately the *Times* conceives of its role, and thereby sets its criteria for reporting and analyzing foreign affairs, in terms of serving the needs of the metropolitan New York citizenry, not the policy makers of the nation. Yet in spite of this, it is clear that executive as well as legislative officials rely on the prestige press in the shaping of American foreign policy. No analysis of American policy on Southeast Asia or Latin America would be complete without a study of press reporting and opinions on Vietnam and the Dominican Republic affairs of 1964–1965. An understanding of the politics of American diplomacy in any crisis in the post-World War II years would require comparable attention to the role of the press in the policy-making process.

Politics and communications are also intertwined *within* any organization, since the system of power and decision making affects and is affected by the communications network through which the rules, orders, and norms of the organization are disseminated. This relevance of communications to "office politics" is most apparent, as indicated in Norton Long's essay, in the assimilation of new employees into the organization. "The recruit gets clued in on the office definition of the situation, a definition that may vary significantly between even relatively tiny, face-to-face groups sharing a few thousand square feet of floor space." By use of certain myths the individual is drawn into his appropriate role and status in the office political system. And in this indoctrination the men of power and authority in the organization, the influential old-timers, are in a good position to preserve their power through the exploitation of the communications network. "To a considerable extent the holders of power in an organization hold their power because they are able to get their definitions of the situation accepted by others." Of course communications about reward, punishment, and organizational purposes are also of critical importance to the new employee in limiting his freedom of action and conditioning his behavior as a participant in office politics. Moreover, he himself may utilize the communications networks in presenting to his superiors a favorable image of himself in order to influence their decisions regarding his advancement. In all these facets of organizational behavior, as well as in others noted by Long, communications and office politics are intertwined.

The recent interest in communications as a politically relevant phenomena has been in part sparked by a desire to explain political action in general, and power in particular, in terms of observable, motivation-revealing data—the interpersonal transmission of thought in patterned communications. In each of the spheres of political life discussed in the selections reprinted below, in each of the different political functions of communications revealed in them,[8] the analysis of communications provides at least implicitly a theoretical concept useful for an explanation and prediction of political behavior. In this sense the study of political communications is part of a larger emphasis on the development of a "scientific explanation" of political phenomena. The next, and final, chapter explores and illustrates this major aspect of contemporary political science.

[8] *These political functions are: ideological rationalization (Hoffer on "men of words"), political socialization (Mitchell on American citizenship), policy formulation (Cohen on the press in foreign policy making), and rule dissemination and indoctrination (Long on administrative communication). By political function we mean "the effects of action (in this case communication) of a member or members of a political system on the political character or actions of other members (or perhaps even on the totality) of the system to which they belong." For a further discussion of the concept of "function" see the discussion in Chap. 7, pp. 300–301.*

Suggestions for Additional Reading

Deutsch, Karl W., *Nationalism and Social Communications: An Inquiry into the Foundations of Nationality*. Cambridge, Mass.: Massachusetts Institute of Technology Press, and New York: John Wiley & Sons, Inc., 1953.

———, *The Nerves of Government*. New York: The Free Press of Glencoe, Inc., 1963.

Festinger, Leon, *A Theory of Cognitive Dissonance*. Harper & Row, Publishers, Inc., 1957.

Hall, Edward T., *The Silent Language*. New York: Doubleday & Company, Inc., 1959.

Hovland, C. I., I. L. Janis, and H. H. Kelly, *Communications and Persuasion*. New Haven, Conn.: Yale University Press, 1953.

Hyman, Herbert, *Political Socialization*. New York: The Free Press of Glencoe, Inc., 1959.

Katz, Daniel, *et al.*, eds., *Public Opinion and Propaganda*. New York: The Dryden Press, 1954.

Katz, Elihu, and Paul F. Lazarsfeld, *Personal Influence*. New York: The Free Press of Glencoe, Inc., 1955.

Key, V. O., Jr., *Public Opinion and American Democracy*. New York: Alfred A. Knopf, Inc., 1961.

Lane, Robert E., *Political Ideology: Why the American Common Man Believes What He Does*. New York: The Free Press of Glencoe, Inc., 1962.

————, and David Sears, *Public Opinion and Ideology*. Englewood Cliffs, N.J.: Prentice-Hall, Inc., 1964.

Lasswell, Harold C., and Nathan Leites and Associates, *Language of Politics: Studies in Quantitative Semantics*, South Norwalk, Conn.: George W. Stewart, Publisher, Inc., 1949.

Lifton, Robert J., *Thought Reform and the Psychology of Totalism: A Study of "Brainwashing" in China*. New York: W. W. Norton & Company, Inc., 1961.

Meier, Richard L., *A Communications Theory of Urban Growth*. Cambridge, Mass.: Massachussets Institute of Technology Press, 1962.

Merton, Robert K., *Mass Persuasion: The Social Psychology of a War Bond Drive*. New York: Harper & Row, Publishers, Inc., 1946.

Smith, M. Brewster, Jerome S. Bruner, and Robert W. White, *Opinions and Personality*. New York: John Wiley & Sons, Inc., 1956.

Wiener, Norbert, *The Human Use of Human Beings*. Boston: Houghton Mifflin Company, 1950.

A. Language and Action

Men of Words

Eric Hoffer

Mass movements do not usually rise until the prevailing order has been discredited. The discrediting is not an automatic result of the blunders and abuses of those in power, but the deliberate work of men of words with a grievance. Where the articulate are absent or without a grievance, the prevailing dispensation,[1] though incompetent and corrupt, may continue in power until it falls and crumbles of itself. On the other hand, a dispensation of undoubted merit and vigor may be swept away if it fails to win the allegiance of the articulate minority.

. . . A full-blown mass movement is a ruthless affair, and its management is in the hands of ruthless fanatics who use words only to give an appearance of spontaneity to a consent obtained by coercion. But these fanatics can move in and take charge only after the prevailing order has been discredited and has lost the allegiance of the masses. The preliminary work of undermining existing institutions, of famil-

[1] *Dispensation: regime or established order.*—ED. NOTE.

iarizing the masses with the idea of change, and of creating a receptivity to a new faith can be done only by men who are, first and foremost, talkers or writers and are recognized as such by all. As long as the existing order functions in a more or less orderly fashion, the masses remain basically conservative. They can think of reform but not of total innovation. The fanatical extremist, no matter how eloquent, strikes them as dangerous, traitorous, impractical, or even insane. They will not listen to him. Lenin himself recognized that where the ground is not ready for them the Communists "find it hard to approach the masses . . . and even get them to listen to them."[2] Moreover, the authorities, even when feeble or tolerant, are likely to react violently against the activist tactics of the fanatic and may gain from his activities, as it were, a new vigor.

Things are different in the case of the typical man of words. The masses listen to him because they know that his words, however urgent, cannot have immediate results. The authorities either ignore him or use mild methods to muzzle him. Thus imperceptibly the man of words undermines established institutions, discredits those in power, weakens prevailing beliefs and loyalties, and sets the stage for the rise of a mass movement.

The division between men of words, fanatics, and practical men of action, as outlined in the following sections, is not meant to be categorical. Men like Gandhi and Trotsky start out as apparently ineffectual men of words and later display exceptional talents as administrators or generals. A man like Mohammed starts out as a man of words, develops into an implacable fanatic, and finally reveals a superb practical sense. A fanatic like Lenin is a master of the spoken word, and unequaled as a man of action. What the classification attempts to suggest is that the readying of the ground for a mass

movement is done best by men whose chief claim to excellence is their skill in the use of the spoken or written word; that the hatching of an actual movement requires the temperament and the talents of the fanatic; and that the final consolidation of the movement is largely the work of practical men of action.

The emergence of an articulate minority where there was none before is a potential revolutionary step. The Western powers were indirect and unknowing fomenters of mass movements in Asia not only by kindling resentment . . . , but also by creating articulate minorities through educational work which was largely philanthropic. Many of the revolutionary leaders in India, China, and Indonesia received their training in conservative Western institutions. The American college at Beirut, which is directed and supported by God-fearing, conservative Americans, is a school for revolutionaries in the illiterate Arabic world. Nor is there any doubt that the God-fearing missionary school teachers in China were unknowingly among those who prepared the ground for the Chinese Revolution.

I

The men of words are of diverse types. They can be priests, scribes, prophets, writers, artists, professors, students, and intellectuals in general. Where, as in China, reading and writing is a difficult art, mere literacy can give one the status of a man of words. A similar situation prevailed in ancient Egypt, where the art of picture writing was the monopoly of a minority.

Whatever the type, there is a deep-seated craving common to almost all men of words which determines their attitude to the prevailing order. It is a craving for recognition; a craving for a clearly marked status above the common run of humanity. "Vanity," said Napoleon, "made the Revolution; liberty was only a pretext." There is apparently an irremediable insecurity at the core of every intellectual, be

[2] *G. E. G. Catlin,* The Story of the Political Philosophers *(New York: McGraw-Hill Book Company, 1939), p. 633.*

he noncreative or creative. Even the most gifted and prolific seem to live a life of eternal self-doubting and have to prove their worth anew each day. What de Rémusat said of Thiers is perhaps true of most men of words: "He has much more vanity than ambition; and he prefers consideration to obedience, and the appearance of power to power itself. Consult him constantly, and then do just as you please. He will take more notice of your deference to him than of your actions."[3]

There is a moment in the career of almost every fault-finding man of words when a deferential or conciliatory gesture from those in power may win him over to their side. At a certain stage, most men of words are ready to become time servers and courtiers. Jesus Himself might not have preached a new gospel had the dominant Pharisees taken Him into the fold, called Him rabbi, and listened to Him with deference. A bishopric conferred on Luther at the right moment might have cooled his ardor for a Reformation. The young Karl Marx could perhaps have been won over to Prussiandom by the bestowal of a title and an important government job; and Lassalle, by a title and a court uniform. It is true that once the man of words formulates a philosophy and a program, he is likely to stand by them and be immune to blandishments and enticements.

However much the protesting man of words sees himself as the champion of the downtrodden and injured, the grievance which animates him is, with very few exceptions, private and personal. His pity is usually hatched out of his hatred for the powers that be.[4] "It is only a few rare and exceptional men who have that kind of love toward mankind at large that makes them unable to endure patiently the general mass of evil and suffering, regardless of any relation it may have to their own

lives."[5] Thoreau states the fact with fierce extravagance: "I believe that what so saddens the reformer is not his sympathy with his fellows in distress, but, though he be the holiest son of God, is his private ail. Let this be righted . . . and he will forsake his generous companions without apology."[6] When his superior status is suitably acknowledged by those in power, the man of words usually finds all kinds of lofty reasons for siding with the strong against the weak. A Luther, who, when first defying the established Church, spoke feelingly of "the poor, simple, common folk,"[7] proclaimed later, when allied with the German princelings, that "God would perfer to suffer the government to exist no matter how evil, rather than to allow the rabble to riot, no matter how justified they are in doing so."[8] A Burke patronized by lords and nobles spoke of the "swinish multitude" and recommended to the poor "patience, labor, sobriety, frugality, and religion."[9] The pampered and flattered men of words in Nazi Germany and Bolshevik Russia [have felt] no impulsion to side with the persecuted and terrorized against the ruthless leaders and their secret police.

II

Whenever we find a dispensation enduring beyond its span of competence, there is either an entire absence of an educated class or an intimate alliance between those in power and the men of words. Where all learned men are clergymen, the church is unassailable. Where all learned men are bureaucrats or where education gives a man an acknowledged su-

[3] *Quoted by Alexis de Tocqueville,* Recollections *(New York: The Macmillan Company, 1896), p. 331.*
[4] *Multatuli (E. D. Dekker),* Max Havelaar *(New York: Alfred A. Knopf, Inc., 1927). . . .*

[5] *Bertrand Russell,* Proposed Roads to Freedom *(New York: Blue Ribbon Books, 1931), p. viii.*
[6] *Henry Thoreau,* Walden *(New York: Modern Library, Inc., 1937), p. 70.*
[7] *In his letter to the Archbishop of Mainz accompanying his theses. Quoted by Frantz Funck-Brentano,* Luther *(London: Jonathan Cape, Ltd., 1939), p. 65.*
[8] *Quoted by Jerome Frank,* Fate and Freedom *(New York: Simon and Schuster, Inc., 1945), p. 281.*
[9] *Ibid., p. 133.*

perior status, the prevailing order is likely to be free from movements of protest.

The Catholic Church sank to its lowest level in the tenth century, at the time of Pope John XII. It was then far more corrupt and ineffectual than at the time of the Reformation. But in the tenth century all learned men were priests, whereas in the fifteenth century, as the result of the introduction of [the] printing [press], learning had ceased to be the monopoly of the Church. It was the nonclerical humanists who formed the vanguard of the Reformation. Those of the scholars affiliated with the Church or who, as in Italy, enjoyed the patronage of the popes, "showed a tolerant spirit on the whole toward existing institutions, including the ecclesiastical abuses, and, in general, cared little how long the vulgar herd was left in superstitious darkness which befitted their state."[10]

The stability of Imperial China, like that of ancient Egypt, was due to an intimate alliance between the bureaucracy and the literati. It is of interest that the Tai-ping rebellion, the only effective Chinese mass movement while the Empire was still a going concern, was started by a scholar who failed again and again in the state examination for the highest mandarin caste.[11]

The long endurance of the Roman Empire was due in some degree to the wholehearted partnership between the Roman rulers and the Greek men of words. The conquered Greeks felt that they gave laws and civilization to the conquerors. It is disconcerting to read how the deformed and depraved Nero, who was extravagant in his admiration of Hellas, was welcomed hysterically by the Greeks on his visit in 67 A.D. They took him to their hearts as a fellow intellectual and artist. "To gratify him, all the games had been crowded into a single year. All the cities sent him the prizes of their contests. Committees were continually waiting on him, to beg him to

go and sing at every place."[12] And he in turn loaded them with privileges and proclaimed the freedom of Greece at the Isthmian games.

. . . It is not altogether farfetched to assume that, had the British in India instead of cultivating the Nizams, Maharajas, Nawabs, Gekawars, and so on made an effort to win the Indian intellectual; had they treated him as an equal, encouraged him in his work, and allowed him a share of the fleshpots, they could perhaps have maintained their rule there indefinitely. As it was, the British who ruled India were of a type altogether lacking in the aptitude for getting along with intellectuals in any land, and least of all in India. They were men of action imbued with a faith in the innate superiority of the British. For the most part they scorned the Indian intellectual both as a man of words and as an Indian. The British in India tried to preserve the realm of action for themselves. They did not to any real extent encourage the Indians to become engineers, agronomists, or technicians. The educational institutions they established produced "impractical" men of words; and it is an irony of fate that this system, instead of safeguarding British rule, hastened its end.

Britain's failure in Palestine was also due in part to the lack of rapport between the typical British colonial official and men of words. The majority of the Palestinian Jews, although steeped in action, are by upbringing and tradition men of words, and thin-skinned to a fault. They smarted under the contemptuous attitude of the British official who looked on the Jews as on a pack of unmanly and ungrateful quibblers—an easy prey for the warlike Arabs once Britain withdrew its protective hand. The Palestinian Jews also resented the tutelage of mediocre officials, their inferiors in both experience and intelligence. Britons of the caliber of Julian Huxley, Harold Nicolson, or Richard

10 *"Reformation,"* Encyclopaedia Britannica.
11 *René Fülöp Miller,* Leaders, Dreamers and Rebels *(New York: The Viking Press, 1935), p. 85.*

12 *Ernest Renan,* Antichrist *(Boston: Roberts Brothers, 1897), p. 245.*

Crossman just possibly might have saved Palestine for the Empire.

In both the Bolshevik and the Nazi regimes there [has been] evident an acute awareness of the fateful relation between men of words and the state. In Russia, men of letters, artists, and scholars share the privileges of the ruling group. They are all superior civil servants. And though made to toe the party line, they are but subject to the same discipline imposed on the rest of the elite. In the case of Hitler there was a diabolical realism in his plan to make all learning the monopoly of the élite which was to rule his envisioned world empire and keep the anonymous masses barely literate.

III

The men of letters of eighteenth-century France are the most familiar example of intellectuals pioneering a mass movement. A somewhat similar pattern may be detected in the periods preceding the rise of most movements. The ground for the Reformation was prepared by the men who satirized and denounced the clergy in popular pamphlets, and by men of letters like Johann Reuchlin, who fought and discredited the Roman curia. The rapid spread of Christianity in the Roman world was partly due to the fact that the pagan cults it sought to supplant were already thoroughly discredited. The discrediting was done, before and after the birth of Christianity, by the Greek philosophers, who were bored with the puerility of the cults and denounced and ridiculed them in schools and city streets. Christianity made little headway against Judaism because the Jewish religion had the ardent allegiance of the Jewish men of words. The rabbis and their disciples enjoyed an exalted status in Jewish life of that day, where the school and the book supplanted the temple and the fatherland. In any social order where the reign of men of words is so supreme, no opposition can develop within and no foreign mass movement can gain a foothold.

The mass movements of modern time, whether socialist or nationalist, were invariably pioneered by poets, writers, historians, scholars, philosophers, and the like. The connection between intellectual theoreticians and revolutionary movements needs no emphasis. But it is equally true that all nationalist movements—from the cult of *la patrie* in revolutionary France to the latest nationalist rising in Indonesia—were conceived not by men of action but by fault-finding intellectuals. The generals, industrialists, landowners, and businessmen who are considered pillars of patriotism are latecomers who join the movement after it has become a going concern. The most strenuous effort of the early phase of every nationalist movement consists in convincing and winning over these future pillars of patriotism. The Czech historian Palacky said that if the ceiling of a room in which he and a handful of friends were dining one night had collapsed, there would have been no Czech nationalist movement.[13] Such handfuls of impractical men of words were at the beginning of all nationalist movements. German intellectuals were the originators of German nationalism, just as Jewish intellectuals were the originators of Zionism. It is the deep-seated craving of the man of words for an exalted status which makes him oversensitive to any humiliation imposed on the class or community (racial, lingual, or religious) to which he belongs however loosely. It was Napoleon's humiliation of the Germans, particularly the Prussians, which drove Fichte and the German intellectuals to call on the German masses to unite into a mighty nation which would dominate Europe. Theodor Herzl and the Jewish intellectuals were driven to Zionism by the humiliations heaped upon millions of Jews in Russia, and by the calumnies to which the Jews in the rest of continental Europe were subjected toward the end of the nineteenth century. To a degree the national-

13 *Carlton J. H. Hayes*, The Historical Evolution of Modern Nationalism (*Peterborough, N.H.: Richard R. Smith, Inc., 1931*), *p. 294.*

ist movement which forced the British rulers out of India had its inception in the humiliation of a scrawny and bespectacled Indian man of words in South Africa.

IV

It is easy to see how the fault-finding man of words, by persistent ridicule and denunciation, shakes prevailing beliefs and loyalties, and familiarizes the masses with the idea of change. What is not so obvious is the process by which the discrediting of existing beliefs and institutions makes possible the rise of a new fanatical faith. For it is a remarkable fact that the militant man of words who "sounds the established order to its source to mark its want of authority and justice"[14] often prepares the ground not for a society of free-thinking individuals but for a corporate society that cherishes utmost unity and blind faith. A wide diffusion of doubt and irreverence thus leads often to unexpected results. The irreverence of the Renaissance was a prelude to the new fanaticism of Reformation and Counter-Reformation. The Frenchmen of the Enlightenment who debunked the Church and the crown and preached reason and tolerance released a burst of revolutionary and nationalist fanaticism which has not abated yet. Marx and his followers discredited religion, nationalism, and the passionate pursuit of business, and brought into being the new fanaticism of Socialism, Communism, Stalinist nationalism, and the passion for world dominion.

When we debunk a fanatical faith or prejudice, we do not strike at the root of fanaticism. We merely prevent its leaking out at a certain point, with the likely result that it will leak out at some other point. Thus by denigrating prevailing beliefs and loyalties, the militant man of words unwittingly creates in the disillusioned masses a hunger for faith. For the majority of people cannot endure the barrenness and futility of their lives unless they have some ardent dedication, or some passionate pursuit in which they can lose themselves. Thus, in spite of himself, the scoffing man of words becomes the precursor of a new faith.

The genuine man of words himself can get along without faith in absolutes. He values the search for truth as much as truth itself. He delights in the clash of thought and in the give-and-take of controversy. If he formulates a philosophy and a doctrine, they are more an exhibition of brilliance and an exercise in dialectics than a program of action and the tenets of a faith. His vanity, it is true, often prompts him to defend his speculations with savagery and even venom; but his appeal is usually to reason and not to faith. The fanatics and the faith-hungry masses, however, are likely to invest such speculations with the certitude of holy writ, and make them the fountainhead of a new faith. Jesus was not a Christian, nor was Marx a Marxist.

To sum up, the militant man of words prepares the ground for the rise of a mass movement: (1) by discrediting prevailing creeds and institutions and detaching from them the allegiance of the people; (2) by indirectly creating a hunger for faith in the hearts of those who cannot live without it, so that when the new faith is preached it finds an eager response among the disillusioned masses; (3) by furnishing the doctrine and the slogans of the new faith; (4) by undermining the convictions of the "better people"—those who can get along without faith—so that when the new fanaticism makes its appearance they are without the capacity to resist it. They see no sense in dying for convictions and principles, and yield to the new order without a fight.[15]

Thus when the irreverent intellectual has done his work:

14 *Pascal,* Pensées.

15 *Demaree Bess quotes a Dutch banker in Holland in 1941: "We do not want to become martyrs any more than most modern people want martyrdom." "The Bitter Fate of Holland,"* Saturday Evening Post *(February 1, 1941).*

The best lack all conviction, while the worst
Are full of passionate intensity.
Surely some revelation is at hand,
Surely the Second Coming is at hand.[16]

The stage is now set for the fanatics.

V

The tragic figures in the history of a mass movement are often the intellectual precursors who live long enough to see the downfall of the old order by the action of the masses.

The impression that mass movements, and revolutions in particular, are born of the resolve of the masses to overthrow a corrupt and oppressive tyranny and win for themselves freedom of action, speech, and conscience has its origin in the din of words let loose by the intellectual originators of the movement in their skirmishes with the prevailing order. The fact that mass movements as they arise often manifest less individual freedom than the order they supplant, is usually ascribed to the trickery of a power-hungry clique that kidnaps the movement at a critical stage and cheats the masses of the freedom about to dawn. Actually, the only people cheated in the process are the intellectual precursors. They rise against the established order, deride its irrationality and incompetence, denounce its illegitimacy and oppressiveness, and call for freedom of self-expression and self-realization. They take it for granted that the masses who respond to their call and range themselves behind them crave the same things. However, the freedom the masses crave is not freedom of self-expression and self-realization, but freedom from the intoler-

able burden of an autonomous existence. They want freedom from "the fearful burden of free choice,"[17] freedom from the arduous responsibility of realizing their ineffectual selves and shouldering the blame for the blemished product. They do not want freedom of conscience, but faith—blind, authoritarian faith. They sweep away the old order not to create a society of free and independent men, but to establish uniformity, individual anonymity, and a new structure of perfect unity. It is not the wickedness of the old regime they rise against, but its weakness; not its oppression, but its failure to hammer them together into one solid, mighty whole. The persuasiveness of the intellectual demagogue consists not so much in convincing people of the vileness of the established order as in demonstrating its helpless incompetence. The immediate result of a mass movement usually corresponds to what the people want. They are not cheated in the process.

The reason for the tragic fate which almost always overtakes the intellectual midwives of a mass movement is that, no matter how much they preach and glorify the united effort, they remain essentially individualists. They believe in the possibility of individual happiness and the validity of individual opinion and initiative. But once a movement gets rolling, power falls into the hands of those who have neither faith in, nor respect for, the individual. And the reason they prevail is not so much that their disregard of the individual gives them a capacity for ruthlessness, but that their attitude is in full accord with the ruling passion of the masses.

[16] *William Butler Yeats, "The Second Coming,"* Collected Poems (*New York: The Macmillan Company, 1933*).

[17] *Fyodor Dostoyevsky,* The Brothers Karamazov, *Book V. Chap. 5.*

B. Socialization and Opinion Formation

The Socialization of American Citizens

William C. Mitchell

Children are not born democratic nor American; they must be taught the tenets of both throughout their lives. Indeed, if Hobbes and Freud were correct, children are born with egotistical and aggressive drives that require either reduction or redirection and adaptation if society and government are to be realized. And as the demands of democracy are high, the molding of these assumed hostile natures into effective citizens cannot be an easy one. As Reinhold Niebuhr put the matter, "Man's capacity for justice makes democracy possible; but man's inclination to injustice makes democracy necessary."[1] Thus the task of making or converting man's "capacity for justice" into concrete motivations and behavior-sustaining democratic rule is a major task of the socialization process.

The concept "socialization," an old one in sociology,[2] is of very recent vintage in political science.[3] The notions conveyed by the term, however, are as ancient as Greek philosophy. Indeed, both Plato and Aristotle were greatly concerned over the training or educating of youth so as to preserve the social and political systems which they sought and defended. The phenomenon of political socialization, then, is an ancient one, but one that has not been adequately studied in contemporary social science.

Socialization, in short, has to do with the civilizing of the members of society. From the political scientist's point of view, the important aspect concerns the creation of citizens by instilling them with the desired ideals and practices of citizenship. Most often, the socialization process is thought of with relation to the young, for it is they who have so much to learn. Yet all members of society are in the process of learning all their lives. . . .

* * *

The Agents and Means of Socialization

No one is ever solely self-taught; teachers are always present in the learning situation. This is no less true in the political system than elsewhere. Becoming a citizen, a partisan, a government official, or a member of an interest group, all requires instruction from others even though it be informal and hardly a conscious or deliberate activity on the part of teacher or student.

Schools and Formal Education.   As might be expected in a complex society the size of the American [one], the agents of political socialization are many. For convenience we might approach the mat-

[1] *Reinhold Niebuhr,* The Children of Light and the Children of Darkness *(New York: Charles Scribner's Sons, 1944), p. xiii.*
[2] *For an excellent introduction to the study of socialization . . . see Frederick Elkin,* The Child and Society *(New York: Random House, Inc., 1960).*
[3] *This footnote was originally an extensive bibliography of socialization in political science. We here note two selections of particular interest. Herbert Hyman,* Political Socialization *(New York: The Free Press of Glencoe, Inc., 1959) and Lewis A. Froman, Jr., "Political Socialization,"* Journal of Politics, *Vol. XXIII (May, 1961), 341–352.—*ED. NOTE.

ter by first classifying the types of agents as either formal or informal and organizational or nonorganizational. Societies almost never allow the general socialization process to take place without having developed a set of formalized or highly institutionalized agencies of education. Thus, in all industrialized societies, a school system is a conspicuous element. And, from our point of view, the most important aspect and function of this school system is its role in making citizens out of the children entrusted to it. Indeed, the long history of public education in this country partially confirms the idea that schools are considered to or actually have a prime responsibility in citizenship training.[4] The elementary and secondary schools provide the most dramatic instance of political socialization, but hardly the only one. Universities and colleges also perform functions along these lines, and particularly state universities, which are required by state law to teach a certain minimum amount of political science or American history to the students. Another aspect of education in politics and the obligations of citizenship can be found in the requirement at many state universities that military training be a part of the male student's preparation for serving his country. Yet the colleges and universities of the country tend to treat the socialization process somewhat differently than do the primary and secondary institutions in that *knowledge* of politics is stressed rather than values and norms. But even this statement must be qualified, for the values and norms are more or less assumed to be democratic. Few if any professors of history, political science, or any of the social sciences, for example, ever deliberately educate students to believe that systems other than democracy are worthy. Fascism, Communism, and varieties thereof are almost never taught as exemplary

models for Americans. And while information about them may be conveyed, it is usually accompanied by condemnations. Indeed, the higher institutions of learning appear to operate on the belief that truth leads to greater faith in democracy. In any case, these formal institutions are important agents of political socialization in terms of developing citizenship. They are also important in another regard suggested above: that of equipping students with the knowledge and skills to become not merely citizens capable of performing the minimal duties of citizenship, but citizens capable of developing into future leaders for the polity. The fact that most of our leaders are college educated should come as no surprise.[5] Moreover, it may be assumed that many of their skills received their first sharpening during college years, either in the class room or in campus politics. The law schools, too, seem to play a profound role in the preparation of political leaders.

Mention should also be made of the specialized role engaged in by our public military schools, West Point, Annapolis, and the Air Force Academy, in developing skills which, though devoted generally to violence, are nevertheless an integral part of the polity. The military is employed by the state, not by private agencies. Obviously, military education contains a good deal of political socialization. In the United States this usually means that the future generals and admirals are taught to view patriotism as the highest virtue and party affiliation as bad. They are also taught that the politicians and politics itself are evil and useless or, at best, necessary evils. What is important to remember is that these military institutions, regardless of the content of the values and norms, do socialize their students.

The way in which the educational system implants the proper ideas and ideals in the young is a highly complicated one. It consists of both formal and informal

[4] V. O. Key, Jr., Politics, Parties and Pressure Groups, 2nd ed. (New York: Thomas Y. Crowell Company, 1948), esp. Chap. 21, and V. O. Key, Jr., Public Opinion and American Democracy (New York: Alfred A. Knopf, Inc., 1961), p. 315.

[5] Cf. Donald Matthews, The Social Backgrounds of Political Decision-Makers (New York: Doubleday & Company, Inc., 1954), pp. 28–29.

methods, and both conscious teaching and unconscious setting of experiences and examples. Among the formal means are, of course, the regular, formalized course offerings in civics, history, economics, and literature. In addition, the school uses symbolic occasions, including patriotic holidays and rites, to inculcate respect and affection for the country. Plays, pageants, and recitations are all a part of the process. Little children learn to pledge allegiance, to sing "The Star-Spangled Banner" and "God Bless America," and to recite the opening lines of the Declaration of Independence, the Constitution, the Bill of Rights, and the Gettysburg Address. Later on, the teenagers are taught to participate in politics through student government in their classrooms and the school assembly. Here they learn that governing is supposed to consist of elections and rational discussions. All this is done, however, within the close supervision of the school authorities. The students themselves really handle very little authority. In addition, the schools participate in providing such political experience as mock conventions of the political parties, "model United Nations" at the college level, or Boys' State or Junior Statesmen in some states, in which the boys learn how to elect officials and then meet government officials for a day or two. The young in some cities are allowed "to take over the reins of city government" for a day. All these techniques are meant to give understanding and appreciation through actual experience. Whether they do or not, we do not know.

The schools are the focal point of still another kind of experience for many children, an experience in politics stemming from their activities in peer groups during the off hours. Clubs of all sorts develop and are recognized by the school as legitimate organizations. It is in these clubs and informal groups of friends that the children learn American political values and norms. It is here that they learn authority, loyalty, and rebellion, plus something about the processes of accommo-

dation, conflict resolution, and leadership. How these lessons may be transmitted to adult political behavior is, of course, difficult to ascertain. But it is highly unlikely that such crucial experiences early in life will be forgotten or will be without effect. For they are the conditioning and reinforcing factors in the acquisition of values, norms, and attitudes.

In the United States, the school is the official agent of political socialization and, as such, occupies a strategic position in the communication and inculcation of political values and norms. It is of some significance, therefore, to determine *who* influences *what* is taught in the schools. In the United States, schools are locally controlled by elected officials called school boards, of which there are about two-hundred thousand members in the public elementary and secondary schools.[6] These men and women have great power, for they decide who the executive officers of the schools will be, who the teachers are, the course curriculum, the textbooks used, and what the school system will be used for outside the official school hours. In addition, they decide on matters of great importance to the teachers' career, such as their participation in the community, salaries, requirements, and the general standards of education in the local area. Who these people are, therefore, is a significant fact.

Most studies of school board members indicate a heavy preponderance of business and professional men, although these groups constitute but 15 per cent of the population. Form and Miller,[7] in summarizing the results of a number of studies conducted in several cities and states, and a national sample, concluded that the percentage of business and professional men on school boards totaled as high as 76 per cent in the national sample, while the percentage of laborers was only 3 per cent. In no case did the percentage of business

6 *William Form and Delbert Miller,* Industry, Labor, and Community (*New York: Harper & Row, Publishers, Inc., 1960*), p. 248.
7 Ibid., *p. 249.*

and professional groups drop below 66 per cent, nor did the total of working men rise over 6 per cent. Unfortunately, as the study did not distinguish between business and professional men, we have no information as to their distribution.

Also, as the relationship between social background and political values is not an easy one to establish, what we have to say on such relationships must be highly tentative. Nevertheless, businessmen and professional men do tend to vote Republican and to be somewhat more conservative than do the lower income groups. And while they may not dictate precisely what each teacher is to teach, it is highly unlikely that a school board composed of such men would long tolerate teachers and texts that departed sharply from the values and norms held by the school board as dear and essential to the welfare of America. Indeed there have been many instances in American history of the recent past that would suggest that deviant philosophies die a quick and most mortal death.[8] But, even if the board members themselves do not bring direct pressure to bear upon teachers to conform to their own values, the teachers often anticipate such pressure, and subconsciously, and sometimes quite consciously, conform. At the very least, they often shape their courses and discussions so that hostility will not be engendered. Thus statements on the United States and its politics are softened, and few criticisms are voiced of any severity. Thus civic *problems* are not really taught, and conflict is played down. Thus the role of radicals, unions, cooperatives, and socialism in our history is either ridiculed or passed over without comment. The student is generally taught only to revere, not to condemn, to be a "good" citizen, not a partisan making demands. The failure to do the latter tends to lend support to those who make up the bulk of the school boards. Not only does the Republican party tend to benefit from the treatment given politics in the schoolroom, but middle-class views of politics are also apt to prevail, all of which satisfies the school boards.

The Family.   No one would seriously disagree with the proposition that the family is the major agent of socialization in all societies. But while we are all familiar from personal experience, if not from academic study, with the role of the family in creating civilized beings, many of us, including political scientists, have forgotten how vital is the family in creating citizens. Our knowledge of the processes involved is not extensive, but there is reliable data on certain aspects of the process and particularly on the content of what is taught by the parents to their children. . . .

The family is apt to be crucial in the entire socialization process for the simple reason that the child spends most of his more formative years within its orbit. It is here that the child has his first experiences with power and authority. And authority . . . is fundamental in the polity whether it be in a family or a nation-state.

One of the better-known facts about the United States, for example, and one which distinguishes it from many other societies, is the looseness of the kinship system and the permissiveness with which children are raised by their parents.[9] The father is not usually a powerful authoritative figure either toward the wife or the children, as is the case in, say, Germany. In many situations, the whims and wishes of the child are indulged to the extent that the child learns little if any form of self-discipline. All this is done in the interests of democracy and personality development in which expressiveness and adjustment are regarded as prime virtues. At one time, "children were to be seen, not heard"—a maxim that has disintegrated today with a vengeance.

The child growing up in such an environment sees power diffused among at

[8] For an excellent contemporary history, see Robert W. Iversen, The Communists and the Schools (New York: Harcourt, Brace & World, Inc., 1959).

[9] Sister Francis Jerome Woods, The American Family System (New York: Harper & Row, Publishers, Inc., 1960), pp. 108–110.

least three persons: mother, father, and himself, and, perhaps, other children. Because he sees the mother on a more or less equal plane with the father as an authority, and his own wishes taken into account, he is likely to learn not only that power need not be respected, but that indeed it may even be manipulated.[10] Thus he soon learns to play the parents off against one another and thereby to gain his own ends. He will also note that he may be used by one parent against the other, and appreciate the bargaining strength he has acquired. All this means that the child views power not in mystical terms and unquestioned obedience, but as a pragmatic thing with which one can bargain. Thus rationality of action and skepticism about power holders are encouraged. It should also be noted that these two approaches to power are further stimulated by the practice of justifying the exercise of power by appeal to reason, either to the child or in front of him. When the child is expected to do some chore, for example, he is generally *asked,* not ordered, and provided with reasons for so doing. American children soon learn, therefore, to demand "why" when commands are given; likewise, parents soon learn to ask or request, not order.

The child learns not only how power and authority operate within the kinship group, but also acquires certain attitudes toward power holders outside of the family unit. Thus while parents and other elders may not be politically oriented, this attitude in itself, plus the comments on such authorities as the father's boss, the police, the politicians, and the bureaucrats, are apt to become internalized by the child as his own set of attitudes. Especially important in this regard are the stereotypes of such persons and the manner in which they are discussed before the child. The words "copper," "flatfoot," "politician," "boss," "political deal," and many others are not apt to convey favorable impressions of public authorities. Likewise, the behavior of parents before authorities will impress the child in striking fashion. Should the father talk back to the policeman who has flagged him down for speeding or should he defer to the officer, the child may respond in similar ways himself as an adult. The respect shown by a parent for public property is also preparation for the adult civic life of the child. These, then, are illustrations of a basic orientation that children learn from the parents, an orientation concerning one's rights and responsibilities as a citizen. In short, whether a child grows up to emphasize rights and demands on the government or to fulfill his own obligations is surely strongly influenced, if not actually determined, by early family experiences.

In America, authority tends to be minimized, and made pragmatic. Thus it should come as no surprise to discover that the child is taught to stress his own rights rather than his duties to the state. He is taught that government exists for the people, and is supposed to be run by them. He learns to question the actions of authorities who are regarded as "no better" than himself. And he learns to believe that politics is riddled with corruption. Following this same inexorable logic, however, he also learns that he must not despair, for he has "inalienable rights," and can pit one party against another, one official against another, one level of government against another, just as he did with his parents. But for all the pragmatic and sometimes unpleasant beliefs he amasses, he also acquires a firm belief in the greatness of America and its way of life, its riches, and its form of government. He acquires a lively if sometimes blatant sense of patriotism, but one that allows him to be something of a businessman with respect to winning profits from the government and the polity.

These basic beliefs are not the only products of the family socialization efforts. The child also acquires attitudes about daily politics, its personalities, policies, and parties. Indeed, according to the vot-

---

[10] *Erik H. Erikson,* Childhood and Society *(New York: W. W. Norton & Company, Inc., 1950) pp. 273–277.*

ing studies, the family is probably the chief influence on the voter. As V. O. Key, Jr., has written:

> The processes by which party identification is established and maintained are not well understood, but it is clear enough that the family is influential in building a sense of party identification. Commonly, 75 per cent or more persons vote as their parents did, and those whose parents were independents tend to be independents in high degree.[11]

Perhaps we can gain a more striking impression of the influence of the family on the voter if we quote from the responses of interviewees when asked about their party affiliations in a recent national poll.

> I'm a borned Republican, sister. We're Republicans from start to finish, clear back on the family tree. Hot Republicans all along. I'm not so much in favor of Eisenhower as the party he is on. I won't weaken my party by voting for a Democrat.[12]

The child's attitudes on the policies and politicians of the day are also likely to be accurate indicators of the parents' most recent pronouncements. And although the standards by which these matters are judged are not likely to be spelled out, they will become influential with the child, if only implicitly. How could it be otherwise with one who is still unable to reason on such indirect and complex matters?

Youth Organizations. Although American youth organize themselves in both formal and informal groups, they are also organized by their elders into groups having considerable relevance for political socialization.[13] Usually these organizations are set up for more general socialization, but all inculcate political values, norms, and information. For some, moreover, it is their *raison d'être*. Organizations such

as the Boy Scouts of America, Girl Scouts of America, Future Farmers of America, and 4-H Clubs of America are all generalized socializing groups, but each devotes much time to matters of political relevance. Other groups, including the Young Democrats and Young Republicans, are purely political in orientation. Still others, including the American Legion Baseball Leagues, are meant to provide recreation, attempting in the process to instill values and norms such as "competitiveness" and "good sportsmanship" that may serve to condition later political values and norms.

Each of these organizations inculcates ideal notions of citizenship and indoctrinates American values. Dominant values include: thrift, respect for private property, self-control, self-reliance, duty, good deeds, clean living, courtesy, productivity, and reverence for religion. Basically, these are the traditional values of the American middle class, and as such serve to rationalize and defend the *status quo*. In addition, the youth organizations also support the existing order by isolating youth from political conflict. American youth seldom learn or engage in the extreme forms of political behavior typical [of] the young of other countries. Nor are the youth of this country an active force in politics; their attentions are devoted rather to preparing for an occupation, and having a good time in the meanwhile—orientations that are supported by youth organizations.

If we look at some of these groups' activities, we can gain a better understanding of their possible impact. We have already noted that all these groups emphasize productive values and self-control rather than expressiveness, particularly political expression of the conflict type. The 4-H Clubs, for example, teach how to do things around the farm and in the household. The same is true of the Future Farmers of America. The Scout movement likewise teaches productive living, but perhaps is more oriented to the development of good citizens than are the farm organizations. Conservative values are instilled through the wearing of uniforms,

[11] *V. O. Key, Jr.,* Politics, Parties and Pressure Groups op. cit., *p. 234.*
[12] *Angus Campbell,* et al., The American Voter (*New York: John Wiley & Sons, Inc., 1960*), *p. 92.*
[13] *Bessie J. Pierce,* Citizens' Organizations and the Civic Training of Youth (*New York: Charles Scribner's Sons, 1933*).

the earning of "merits," the oath, and, above all, through the examples of their adult leaders who are generally from the middle class and value the American Way of Life. Active participation in the governing of the organization is also permitted on a limited basis by the leaders. In such participation the young members learn that they have a right to their opinions and to give them expression, but that they must also be well within the majority views. The importance of norms or rules of behavior and the conduct of meetings is also instilled. Ideas of social status are conveyed through the symbols of the ranks in scout troops and the system of rewards for achievement. In short, the members of all these organizations learn what is expected of them as ideal American citizens. By the bye, they may also learn many unintended facts, but the leaders do their best not to teach them contrary notions.

The role and function of private youth organizations become still clearer when we recognize the fact that they are largely under the control of the "better" people in the community. Although systematic data is not readily available, casual observation would seem to suggest that the schools are operated by the same groups of occupations, ethnic groups, religious affiliates, and civic-minded organizations among adults. In politics, these are the people most likely to vote Republican, to be conservative, Protestant, and to fall within the middle income range.

Political Parties. Most discussions of the functions of political parties suggest, if they do not prove, that parties serve to educate the citizenry.[14] How well they accomplish this function is debatable, but surely it is true that the parties do attempt to educate the citizens in their voter's role. Indeed, parties devote enormous amounts of time and energy, as well as other resources, in trying to communicate with the voters. And while their objective is obviously a self-oriented one—to

[14] *For a representative statement, see Dayton D. McKean,* Party and Pressure Politics *(Boston: Houghton Mifflin Company, 1949), p. 25.*

win elections—they also convey information in the process about issues, candidates, and the parties. They also disseminate norms and values for the voter to use in his own process of evaluation. And they generally exhort the voter to vote regardless of the direction of his vote. Thus, by encouraging citizens to take advantage of one of their basic rights, voting, they thereby contribute to the polity.

Parties in the United States are agents of citizenship only in a partial sense in that they do not exist to socialize, nor do they "teach" continuously. Rather, their actions are likely to be periodic or cyclical, mounting in frequency and intensity as elections approach, then suddenly diminishing and leveling off during the long interim periods. In short, they do not directly impinge on many of the citizens for any sustained period of time. Then, too, the parties are less concerned with the provision of factual data about political processes than with providing evaluative clues or perspectives. They train in partisanship.

But the inculcation of partisan values and information is not the only contribution made to political socialization. The American parties also teach and preach the superiority of our way of life. Both parties are nationalistic and both honor the political system that created and maintains them. Thus even while the parties may each have their partisan emblems and other symbols, they also have national heroes, display the national flag, sing the national anthem, pray for America and divine guidance, and claim to speak for the United States. Their candidates do not claim to be just Democrats or Republicans, but Americans first and party members second or third in the hierarchy of loyalties. In such ways do the parties socialize both for partisanship and integration.

The ways in which the parties accomplish these functions is, as was said above, somewhat unsystematic and erratic. Some are accomplished through the formal methods of campaigning and the distribution of literature. Much, however, is done informally and symbolically by the actions of officeholders. Moreover, each party is organized at all levels of government, but not evenly throughout the nation. Services are provided by party officials ranging from ticket fixing to legitimate help during crises. Many social events are utilized by parties, especially around election time, to educate the voters and maintain supporters. Clubs of all sorts are used to spread the word. To reach the young, each party has a Young Democrat or Young Republican affiliate, as the case may be. Thus conscious teaching and learning from experience in internal party activities serve to socialize those who have contact with the parties.

Interest Groups. Interest groups, like political parties, are also primarily concerned with "educating" the adults of the community.[15] And, like the parties, they are mostly interested in providing evaluative cues to their members and the publics outside their domain. As interest groups want to realize specific goals, usually to augment their own positions in society, they too teach value positions. What information is provided is dealt with as it relates to the goals or objectives of the group. Thus they maintain bulletins or newspapers with political sections or columns to keep members informed on the group's political action. Likewise, they publish and distribute special studies having to do with political affairs, and often engage speakers from public office and universities to inform them on political issues. Indeed, campaigns may well be run to encourage their members to participate in politics. To this end, books and lectures are provided to show how such activities can be accomplished. Apparently, the encouragement of political action by members is becoming increasingly popular. These groups, of course, have always engaged in politics, but have deceived themselves that only their opponents do so.

15 *David Truman,* The Governmental Process *(New York: Alfred A. Knopf, Inc., 1951), pp. 213–261.*

Some even run schools, as do the trade unions with COPE, or Committee for Political Education.

Interest groups cannot help but be agents of political socialization. They become so simply by being members of the political system. What distinguishes the modern interest group[s] from the old is the self-conscious manner in which the former approach their activities. They have become highly specialized bureaucracies in socialization. In still other words, interest groups are rationalizing those aspects of political socialization in which they are interested. Note the programs they conduct to "educate" the citizenry or public opinion to aid their cause. To accomplish the task, highly skilled technicians in mass communications are often employed at high cost.

Some interest groups, especially those which tend toward being patriotic, attempt to broaden the scope of their education by educating for civic participation and loyalty. These groups, of which the American Legion or the Daughters of the American Revolution are good examples, attempt to instill citizenship ideals, not just economic interests. The Legion, for example, conducts contests for school children in which essays on American history or patriotism are awarded for excellence as determined by the Legion. Likewise, they bestow civic commendations and awards to adults, awards that generally go to persons strongly identified with being a patriot and a conservative.

The Mass Media. In one sense, the mass media are simply a technical means of socialization. To treat them only as such, however, would be highly superficial. Those working with the mass media are, in fact, agents of socialization who have particular ideas of what should be conveyed to their consumers. In order to appreciate those in the mass media as agents of political socialization, we must, then, have some knowledge of who they are, of what their interests consist, and how they operate. Fortunately, students of public opinion have been quite diligent in collecting such data, and it is to their work that we will turn for most of what we want to know.[16]

By mass media we mean to include television, radio, newspapers, magazines, and books. These are the media that reach or are intended to reach large audiences, although considerable differences do exist in the sizes of the various audiences of each. Television, for example, influences many more Americans than do books. But whatever the differences, the numbers involved in even the smallest sphere are sizable.

One of the more crucial facts about the mass media is that they are largely and increasingly controlled by small numbers of people. For to own and operate a concern engaged in mass communications is a major task requiring great investments and technical skills. As a result, fewer persons are in control of most of the communications that go on in the country. Indeed, in terms of the numbers of publishers, television and radio stations, and newspaper publishers, there is less and less competitive activity. Even while there has been an increase in the daily subscriptions of newspapers, for example, the number of daily papers has dropped approximately 20 per cent during the year 1930–1947.[17] In 1953, the percentage of daily circulation held by owners of papers in two or more cities was 45.3 per cent.[18] The cities having competitive papers in 1954 represented only 6 per cent of the total number of cities with daily newspapers.[19] These figures suggest an increasing concentration of ownership. And, they

also suggest another hypothesis of considerable significance to the socialization process: namely, that mass audiences are receiving a more uniform set of political perceptions or images. Newspapers, of course, are hardly the only mass media providing such uniform images. All the media tend in that direction, just as all are becoming more centrally owned and controlled. But, unlike newspaper publishers, radio and television owners are restricted to some extent by government in the number of stations they may operate. On the other hand, there has been an increase in the number of jointly owned radio, television, and newspaper firms. As of 1957, 21.2 per cent of the radio and television stations were identified with newspaper ownership.[20] Likewise, in the area of book publishing, recent years have witnessed a number of mergers and thereby a reduction of the number of large publishing houses. To be sure, book publishers, unlike their newspaper counterparts, do put out a less uniform product, but its audience is, of course, far smaller and probably more sophisticated.

Regardless of who operates the mass media, it is imperative to study the content of their offerings to the public. We have already noted that there is a tendency to produce a uniform product. But we have not indicated what that content is nor the uniformities thereby contained. In the case of newspapers especially, the contents reflect an overriding concern for violence, sex, sentimentality, and the ignoble aspects of life generally. The amount of space—over time—devoted to political issues and news is not unusually great.[21]

The Process of Socialization

One of the less known areas of political socialization has to do with the *processes* of teaching and learning. We can only convey impressionistic notions of the techniques or methods and informal pro-

[16] *An excellent reader in public opinion is Daniel Katz,* et al., eds., Public Opinion and Propaganda (*New York: Holt, Rinehart & Winston, Inc., 1954*). *The primary professional publication is, of course, the* Public Opinion Quarterly.

[17] *Raymond B. Nixon, "Concentration and Absenteeism in Daily Newspaper Ownership," in* Bernard Berelson and Morris Janowitz, *eds.,* Reader in Public Opinion and Communication (*New York: The Free Press of Glencoe, Inc., 1953*), *p. 194.*

[18] *Clarence H. Schettler,* Public Opinion in American Society (*New York: Harper & Row, Publishers, Inc., 1960*), *p. 228.*

[19] Ibid., *p. 229.*

[20] Ibid.

[21] *William Albig,* Modern Public Opinion (*New York: McGraw-Hill Book Company, 1956*) *pp. 373–374.*

cesses.[22] If they should sound familiar to the reader, we shall have at least partial confirmation of their reliability.

How a person is taught and learns citizenship in a democracy is not likely to be a very clear picture, for many influences impinge upon the individual, and not all may be equal in their impact. Only one thing is certain: namely, that all of us are subject to both formalized teaching about politics and informal pressures to perceive and act in certain ways. No one group or institution employs a single procedure; all engage in many methods. Thus the schools formally teach history and civics and engage in rituals of respect for the nation. The teachers themselves act informally as symbols of power and authority for the students and even their parents. And, in the schoolroom, the teachers—unknowingly in some instances —convey political preferences via verbal and nonverbal expressions. In other cases,

[22] *Undoubtedly, we know more about political socialization in totalitarian than in democratic societies. Hardly a volume on the former is without chapters on schools, propaganda, and indoctrination, while very few books on American* politics *treat the same institutions and phenomena.*

they do so knowingly and openly. On the schoolgrounds, the child is socialized by the peer group with ideals of group behavior, and learns notions of authority, leadership, loyalty, bargaining, and conflict. All these "lessons in citizenship" are taught and learned informally without awareness of the process, as such, to its participants. Later in life, the adult citizen will have his political preferences constantly confirmed by the groups to which he belongs, even though he has no awareness of the acts of confirmation. And he may confirm these same preferences by an unconscious selective choice of the mass media.

Although political socialization is considered of paramount importance in this society as in all societies, it is a highly confused and unsystematic process. Both formal and informal techniques are employed by all the agents and agencies, with greater reliance placed on one or the other. The schools, for example, tend to formalize their methods and become very self-conscious about education. The family, on the other hand, socializes by example and imitation, both primarily informal and even unconscious means.

C. Mass Media

The Use of News in Foreign Policy Making

Bernard C. Cohen

Contradictory and ambivalent themes mark the approach of foreign policy officials to the press. . . . The negative attitudes toward the press and the strong depreciation of its standards and accuracy, the view that one cannot trust the newspapers or believe them or take them at face value, are all aspects of a cynical,

wary outlook suggesting that the official is relatively impervious to the contents of the press, that he regards it as something vulgar that he cannot rub out of his life but that he will not permit to upset the rhythm of his work and the order of his day. But as intense and as widespread as these feelings are, readership of the press and reliance upon its foreign affairs content are just as widespread and intense. Indeed, the evidence . . . suggests that the foreign policy maker typically takes more out of the press than any one of them readily admits to, or may even be aware of. The familiar saw, "All I know about foreign affairs is what I read in *The New York Times*," is meant as a confession of limited competence, and when it was uttered by a Presidential hopeful in early 1960 it earned the scorn of reporters; yet if the reference to *The New York Times* is meant generically, there is more truth in the statement than most practitioners feel comfortable with. The press is not wholly responsible for their education, to be sure, but it does serve them in some very important ways, supplying material that is not supplied elsewhere. What are some of the things that policy makers get out of the press that have a bearing on the foreign policy environment? And how well are the purposes that lead policy makers to communicate through the press actually served by these patterns of extraction from it?

Information

For the Executive. Although he is surrounded by official and unofficial private networks of communication designed to keep him informed, the policy maker in the State Department still turns to the press for basic factual information about the international political world he lives in—information from abroad as well as from his own immediate environment.[1] Why should this be so? What can he learn from this general public source that he does not get from his established internal sources of information? To a great extent the answer depends on how the internal

network of communication serves different needs or requirements of foreign policy officials at different levels and with varying functions and responsibilities. These officials have certain common requirements for information, and other needs that are functionally specific.

Except for the top foreign policy-making officials, there is a specialization of geographic area and/or function among the people in the State Department. The official network of communication from representatives abroad is designed to keep these specialists informed with respect to their own specialization. As a Departmental official pointed out, "The embassies do not attempt to cover the news; they assume that people in the State Department read newspapers." A former high-level official said the same thing: "Most of the information you get, you get from the newspapers. . . . In the State Department the internal flow of communication is specialized; the broad scope of developments is found in the newspaper." The same point was made by a foreign aid official: "Of course, government employees get their information from the newspapers. . . ." And from a former foreign aid official, "*The New York Times* is the primary information source for most of our foreign policy people." For the relatively few men at the top of the foreign policy establishment, the press also provides an independent report, outside the diplomatic channel, on what is happening around the world. The State Department long ago considered and gave up the notion that it might compete with the major news agencies by running its own network of news reporters around the world. Having taken that course, the Department became dependent on the wire services and on the major newspapers with their own staffs of foreign correspondents for its basic coverage of world events, and for an independent check on the more limited and private flow of intelligence within the Department. "*The New York Times* and other newspapers with their own correspondents abroad have angles that you

[1] *E.g., ". . . reporters who called to find out what the crisis men [the State Department's short-lived twenty-four hour Operations Center, the "crisis desk"] knew about last weekend's surprises—the Friday midnight revolt in Argentina and the Berlin border closing Saturday night—found that the center was getting its word from the press"* [The New York Times (*August 21, 1961*)].

may not be aware of as a consequence of reading only the official reports."[2]

Furthermore, the officials usually get their information sooner through the press than through official routes; owing to the coding and decoding procedures, official reports generally run behind press reports. Ultimately, of course, officials have to work with the information and analysis supplied by their own "reporters" in the missions abroad; but their contact with the rapidly changing contours of the international political world at any moment in time comes more through the press than through their own facilities. And the more rapidly the changes take place, the greater dependence there is upon the press. A close observer said that "in fast-breaking situations, the tickers beat cables by four or five hours—and in some cases by up to twenty-four hours." Another State Department official, who has the news tickers clipped and sent up to him steadily all day, concluded that "the State Department sources run about twenty-four hours behind the press." Radio news also has a competitive time advantage, in a limited situation: the early morning news round-ups often have later information than appears in the morning newspaper, and officials listen to them at home, some hours before they get a chance to see any of the same material on the tickers in the Department. It is not unusual, consequently, for an official to make a reference to a late radio news item in the Secretary of State's morning staff conference, or in other morning conferences within the State Department. Under these circumstances, the press cannot help but have some impact on the way the men at the top initially define international situations. "Your vision of the world," one of them said, "comes at you from the paper; it hits you at breakfast." The press's definition of the structure of international affairs, or parts of that

structure, may even become the prevailing definition among these top officials—indirectly, because it is the one so many other people accept; and by default, because these officials are physically unable to read everything that comes into the State Department through official channels.[3]

It may be misleading here, in any event, to discuss the press accounts and the diplomatic reports as if they were two wholly independent streams of intelligence. The men who write the reports in the embassies are like regular newspaper reporters in the sense that they too are responsive to developments "in the news," and what they send in to the Department some hours later may be their own reaction to things they have seen on the tickers, or it may be in reply to requests from Washington that were first stimulated by news reports. In this sense the press's definition of issues and the content of its news stories have a direct bearing upon the internal system of reporting. Furthermore, the local press in the foreign country has an impact on reporting from the field. In developing his own reports, the diplomatic official gathers his information from a variety of sources, prominent among them being the press of the country concerned. A Foreign Service officer reminisced: "The embassies find out what the government to which they are accredited is doing, via the press. . . . In ———— I used to mine the local newspapers all the time for my reports to Washington." In other words, the significance of the press is not merely that it gets to the foreign policy people sooner and perhaps over a wider range of issues, helping to define situations, but that in getting there first it also helps to shape the subsequent diplomatic reporting on the same issues. It does seem clear, in any case, that the reporting function of the diplomat—one of

---

[2] *A* New York Times *reporter once asked Under Secretary of State Sumner Welles, "Do you know anything we don't know today?" To which Welles replied, "Of course not, where do you think we get our information?"*

[3] *The Executive Secretariat screens, summarizes, and selects cables for the top three officers in the Department, in much the same way as the editorial staff of a newspaper makes its selections of material for the paper—ostensibly with "different priorities in mind," according to a close observer, but the process bears investigation.*

the classic triad of functions: reporting, representation, and negotiation—stands in need of re-examination in the larger context of the total flow of foreign policy information from abroad to foreign policy officials. There are some other points of similarity in the generally held conceptions of the diplomat and the foreign correspondent—for example, in the notions of desirable training, competence, language facility, and the like; but the smaller the difference, in practice, between regular journalism and diplomatic reporting, and the closer and more intimate the connection between them, the greater the significance that we must attach to the press in the stream of foreign policy intelligence, and the more relevant to the processes of policy making become the standards by which press coverage is made and measured.

For the foreign policy specialists, the desk men and others who work on a narrow front, the press also provides an independent and more rapid view of what is happening in their areas of interest. But since the internal flow of specialized material is great, the informational contribution that the press makes directly to their work is proportionately less. A desk officer described it this way: "There will be a story in *The New York Times* from time to time which is *news* to us, and about which there is nothing on the cables from ————. But it is usually the structural problem, not a particular event, that gives rise to this story." The press provides these people with other information, however; it tells them what is happening around the world in areas other than the one with which they are primarily concerned. Since they neither have access to, nor time to read, the official reports from all over the world, these specialists—up to, and sometimes including, the Assistant Secretaries of State—rely substantially upon the press for their broader knowledge of international developments. It would seem to be the case, however, that the narrower a man's area of specialization, and the greater the distance between him and the staff level in the State Department, the greater is his dependence on the press for his larger view of the world.

The press also provides the specialist with domestic political information. The specialist lives in a bureaucratic world, and he is familiar with the political struggles that accompany policy ideas and proposals along the route to decision. Of necessity, he acquires internal sources of information about relevant developments and possibilities in proximate bureaucratic units, but here too his intelligence becomes more tenuous with increasing distance. And so he turns to the press for information about things that are happening and proposals that are being considered elsewhere in the foreign policy-making structure of the government. Robinson, for example, reports how a *New York Times* story announcing an agreement between Senator [Mike] Monroney [D., Okla.] and the State and Treasury Departments on his resolution calling for an International Development Association stimulated renewed expressions of opposition from "a prominent financial official within the Administration."[4] Similarly, every announcement in the newspapers that Japanese peace treaty discussions might be in the offing evoked a wave of interested and critical participation from West Coast Congressmen who were concerned about a treaty solution to the fisheries problem.[5] Even the President keeps in touch with the administration of foreign affairs this way; a recent account described President Kennedy's phone conversation with a "top official" in which he discussed "a *New York Times* story dealing with expenditures of one of Chester Bowles' foreign journeys. Item by item, the President demanded explanations; the official, his brow wet with perspiration,

4 *James A. Robinson*, The Monroney Resolution (*New York: Holt, Rinehart & Winston, Inc., 1951*), p. 13.
5 *Bernard C. Cohen*, The Political Process and Foreign Policy (*Princeton, N.J.: Princeton University Press, 1957*), Chap. 12.

dealt with them as best he could."[6] A Foreign Service officer tactfully explained how the situation looked from high up in the State Department: "You cannot divorce foreign policy from domestic political situations and political events. By and large the traditional department methods of informing departmental officers do not suffice, so the press plays an important role in factually informing officers."

For the Congress. The Congressman's "need" for foreign affairs information is of a different order from that of the official in the State Department; his interests are rarely as specialized as the official's, and he rarely has to respond immediately to developments abroad. Despite this, the press is at least as important to members of Congress as a source of foreign policy information as it is to State Department officials, because the Congressman's alternative sources of information are not so extensive, and because for most Congressmen this is apparently the most congenial way of keeping broadly and generally informed.[7]

The legislative policy maker who is at all interested in foreign affairs is not much different from an attentive citizen in his dependence upon the press; he reads the newspapers to find out what is going on in the world. A Senator remarked, "I can't overemphasize the informational function of the newspaper. We have to get our information just as the citizen gets his." The

6 *Worth Bingham and Ward S. Just, in* The Reporter *(April 12, 1962), 21. Cf. also V. O. Key's discussion of the role of* The New York Times *and* The Washington Post *"as a means for supplementing the internal lines of communication of the sprawling federal establishment"* [Public Opinion and American Democracy *(New York: Alfred A. Knopf, Inc., 1961), p. 405]. In another example, Douglass Cater claims that during the U-2 crisis, officials were "communicating with each other via the news tickers" rather than through the NSC ["A Chronicle of Confusion,"* The Reporter *(June 9, 1960), 17].*
7 *Cf. Cabell Phillips, "The Mirror Called Congress," in Lester Markel, ed.,* Public Opinion and Foreign Policy *(New York: Harper & Row, Publishers, Inc., 1949); and Robert A. Dahl,* Congress and Foreign Policy *(New York: Harcourt, Brace & World, Inc., 1950), esp. Chaps. 1–2.*

absorption of legislators in the press is legendary; Congressmen are always to be seen in the lounges reading newspapers or the news tickers, and the Senators and Representatives who have a specialization or a reputation in the foreign policy field commonly begin their day by reading from two to six newspapers, spending as much as two hours on them. Staff specialists for these legislators are somewhat more introspective and articulate about the relative place of the press in the scheme of things than are the legislators themselves; this may be due in part to their better capacities for observation and generalization than the Congressmen possess, and in part it may be a projection of their own experiences. Among these staff people, remarks like the following are commonplace: "The newspapers are part of your life, your existence. Things just soak in from the newspapers. Then you may pick up bits in articles here and there. . . ." "The newspaper is *the* source of foreign policy information—especially *The New York Times,* which is better than the State Department." "On a day-to-day basis, of course, it is still the press that supplies the information." "The press remains the only way in which one can get the whole impact of the world around oneself." A State Department official with long legislative experience accounts for the endless reading of newspapers by Senators this way: "They are asked to comment on events, so they have to be up on them. . . . They are well posted on current problems."

The Congressman's dependence on his daily newspaper for his foreign affairs information is apparent in the inadequacy of his possible alternative sources of information. The links that Congress maintains with the State Department via the Foreign Affairs Committees of the two Houses provide additional, not alternative, sources of information. The Department's internal sources of information are not sufficient even for the foreign policy officials there; by the time the flow of classified information reaches the Committee members, it is more like a trickle—

intermittent, specialized, partial (for security reasons), except perhaps in the case of a very few and highly trusted Senators. A member of the House Foreign Affairs Committee suggested that executive sources of information are like frosting on the press cake: "The Committee, and the leadership on both sides, get briefed by the executive branch, so they get other information than what they get from the press." A leading Senator's staff assistant reported that "consultation with executive branch people only confirms what is seen in the press. . . . [The Senator] has said this many times." Further, some Committee members are distrustful of consultation with the executive branch, seeing it as a form of dependence on the executive and preferring the independence of press information. And among Representatives who are interested in foreign affairs but who are not on the Foreign Affairs Committee, there is disenchantment with the Committee, which further attentuates the flow of information from executive sources through this channel.

Congressmen even look to the press as a source of information on what is going on in and around the Congress. Matthews' observation to this effect[8] holds up in the foreign policy area, where the newspaper seems to be a convenient and economical substitute for the heavy investment required to read Congressional studies, reports, and hearings. One Senate staff assistant ascribed this pattern to Congressmen's being "primarily 'mouth and ear' men—i.e., they pay more attention to what they hear than what they read. Most of what they read is likely to be in the mass media." Congressmen even treat foreign affairs information in newspapers with the deference, and accord it the authority, that those on the "outside" (including reporters) commonly accord to the information that comes *out* of Congressional studies or deliberations. The newspapers often provide the material that enables

[8] *Donald Matthews*, U.S. Senators and Their World (*Chapel Hill: University of North Carolina Press, 1960*), *p. 206.*

legislators, according to their own testimony, to ask intelligent questions of witnesses during hearings. And according to a member of the House Foreign Affairs Committee, Committee members regularly bring newspaper clippings into their sessions to authenticate points and to clarify problems or raise them for questioning.

In all of these cases, the "press" referred to is the prestige press . . . modified scarcely at all by the addition of constituency newspapers. For most Congressmen, unless they are from eastern metropolitan areas, constituency newspapers are not a source of foreign affairs news, either because their coverage is relatively skimpy —"only the bigger papers have the facts"— or because they arrive in Washington too late. A midwestern Representative said, "No citizen or legislator could rely on any ———— [home state] newspaper as sources for policy or for broadly based knowledge as a citizen." When constituency newspapers do arrive, they are used for different purposes, which are amply summed up in this remark of a Democratic Senator's legislative counsel: "Local newspapers are read for their state political news, for their news about employment conditions, general or new business developments, and for what they say about the Senator."

It may seem obvious at this point, if it has not earlier, that the press serves foreign policy makers in both the executive and legislative branches as a basic, standard source of factual information about foreign affairs and also about political developments within the American government that are relevant to foreign policy. Yet it is of more than passing significance that even though the press gives the policy maker his "big picture" and a large number of his smaller ones, this particular service does not constitute one of the standards by which press roles or performances are defined or judged. The informational role of the press—its central function —is aimed at the citizen; even the reporters on the prestige papers, while they presume that the reading public is intelligent and well informed and may even include policy officials, generally have a relatively unspecialized public audience in mind as the group they are trying to serve.[9] (The participant roles of the press, on the other hand, which *are* aimed at the policy makers, are defined in political rather than educational terms; foreign policy interpretations and preferences of newspapermen, rather than substantive information, are introduced into the policy-making process.) Although many reporters see the foreign policy official as an important part of their audience, nowhere do newspapermen seriously argue that an important role of foreign affairs reporting is, or should be, the provision of information to officials. Thus the informational standards of the press, even the "prestige press," are set by the assumption that the chief market for everyday reporting is the citizen rather than the responsible specialist; the latter is, accordingly, fed a popular diet for breakfast, and with that initial intellectual nourishment he is supposed to go forth to his office and do battle with giants.

Ideas, Evaluation, Analysis, Interpretation

For the Executive. We can recall that most foreign affairs reporters and columnists are eager to be heard by policy makers; in their activist or reformist moments, they value participation as an important role for the press and as a useful outlet for their own interests and capacities. How much encouragement in this role do they get in practice from foreign policy officials (among whom we found very mixed attitudes toward newsmen and toward the press as an institution)? How well do these officials acknowledge the propriety of the correspondents' aspirations, as measured by the value they attach to their product? How open are the policy makers to the press as a source of intellectual stimulation and inspiration?

9 *A* New York Times *editor remarked, "We know we cater to a certain class of persons—defined as those people in the New York metropolitan area who for some purpose or other need to be informed."*

Policy makers quite obviously turn to the press not only for information but also for analysis and evaluation of developments and proposals, and sometimes even for new ideas on how to deal with the range of problems that confront them. Their attitudes toward the intellectual contribution of the columnists and reporters fall handily into three patterns, outlined below. The correlates of these attitudes are not readily apparent; in the data available neither political party nor rank in the policy-making hierarchy, the two most obvious variables, seems to make any difference in the receptivity of officials to ideas from the press. The implication seems to be that the differences are highly individual, much as we found competence in the handling of the press to be.

1. While men who are professionally involved in foreign policy decision making are quick to acknowledge their constant readership of foreign affairs analysts in the press, some of them are extremely reluctant to attach any great importance to the evaluations of these columnists or to admit that they contribute anything to the development of their own thinking. For instance, a former sub-Cabinet official described the effect of these writers as "mostly negative. They contributed very few constructive ideas." Another official of the same rank said that "none of them, Lippmann and the Alsops included," were important. "Their ideas had very little substance and merit. They were of trivial influence." There may be professional pride involved here—as in a Foreign Service officer's view that "it is damned infrequent that the Foreign Service would miss something"—as well as jealousy, an unwillingness to accord to any outside source the distinction of equality with, or superiority to, the thinking that goes on inside the foreign policy institutions. There may also be, in this attitude, a trace of suspicion that the columnists are grinding the axes of other, unidentified participants in the policy-making process.

2. A step above this negative position is occupied by officials who grudgingly acknowledge that sometimes the newspapermen do have something to say that is worthwhile. For example: "Occasionally some columnist will drop a new idea that will get picked up in Washington, but this doesn't happen too often." A former Assistant Secretary of State described his encounters with reporters in these terms: "Some of them would come to see you—even pester you. There would be an exchange of ideas. They often tried out a variety of ideas on you, most of which you wouldn't pay much attention to."

3. And then there are the officials who willingly give correspondents and columnists due credit for an important, if limited, creative role in the making of foreign policy. A number of high-ranking policy makers have said, in effect, that reading the columnists is part of their job, and that their columns have often been discussed at staff conferences.[10] An Assistant Secretary of State remarked, "Our policy is made by intelligent men who will read the views of . . . thoughtful and informed columnists." A Presidential adviser said that "the judgment of men like Lippmann, Reston, and Baldwin is valued because they offer interesting ideas from time to time." A foreign aid official reported that State Department personnel will "often times" draft arguments that take their line of reasoning from a recent article by one of the columnists; and a public affairs official in the State Department displayed a fresh newspaper clipping with some ideas on an educational exchange program, which the official was using as the basis of a memorandum proposing action along the same lines. The relevant attitude seems to be that good foreign policy ideas are scarce enough so that one should seek them out and exploit them wherever they may be found; if the

10 *See also Joseph M. Jones'[s] discussion of Lippmann's column of April 5, 1947, "one of the most consequential columns he has ever written." [The Fifteen Weeks (New York: The Viking Press, 1955), pp. 228–229.]*

columnists have the edge over academic or other outside specialists in this process—and it is not absolutely clear that they do have, although it seems so—it may be because they are easier to exploit, being right at hand and writing as if they were a part of the foreign policy establishment.

On balance, then, it appears that the press is a steady and somewhat fertile source of policy analysis and ideas, affecting even people who claim to be unaffected by it. One might entertain the proposition that the impact of the columnists' views is in inverse proportion to the number and diversity of competent specialists who take part in the competition over policy alternatives. Where the specialist market is thin, as it has been on many occasions in both foreign and military policy, the remarks of the columnists seem to weigh more heavily in the balance than they do where the competition is active and intense. (In the latter case, it is also more likely that the columnists will revert to a reportorial role, and concern themselves not so much with the substantive ideas at issue but rather with the fact of political competition and controversy involving those ideas.)

The press also provides the foreign policy official with another kind of evaluation, which is no less important for being less obvious. It is commonly understood that, in the political realm, what is *thought* to be true is often a more relevant source of political inspiration than what *is* true. A former State Department official who has always been a very close observer of foreign policy making put it this way: "The freedom of action of the diplomat is greatly limited; he has to work with the realities of the way people interpret events. The newspaperman is of the utmost importance in that field." A Foreign Service officer involved in high-level decision making in the State Department argued more explicitly that the policy appraisals made by persons outside the Department, representing a wider range of policy understandings, are themselves a vital part of the overall problem that is being considered within the Department: "In assessing a given situation, you can't rely exclusively on Foreign Service reporting, or on staff papers prepared below in the Department. You have to rely to a great extent on analyses from outside —from newspapers, editorial reaction, Congressional statements, etc.—all of which reach us via the daily press. These are not primary considerations in our decisions, but you can't leave them out." . . .

For the Congress.   Members of Congress and their staff assistants are almost unanimous in acknowledging the usefulness of the press, and especially the major columnists, as sources of ideas, insights, and interpretations in the field of foreign affairs. Unlike the State Department officials, the legislative personnel by and large lack a personal competence and expertise, lack their own resources for the analysis of foreign policy problems. They do have staff research facilities at their disposal, including the Legislative Reference Service of the Library of Congress, but these are not designed to provide the interpretations, the speculations, the new thoughts about current developments that are the daily food of politicians and the stock-in-trade of political columnists. The Congressman is interested in knowing what others are thinking about these unfolding events and their possibilities, as a convenient basis for locating and formulating his own thoughts. There are boundless examples of Congressmen absorbing the foreign policy ideas and reflecting the stimulation of columnists, ranging from the well-known relationship between [the late] Senator [Arthur] Vandenberg [R., Mich.] and James Reston to the daily and unremarked culling of ideas for policy speeches. Interestingly, the strongest and most explicit argument from anyone on the legislative side *against* the usefulness of the analytical content of the foreign affairs commentators came from a Senate staff person whose formative governmental experience in foreign affairs had been in the State Department.

Both Congressional and executive people agree that Congressmen are more susceptible to the foreign policy suggestions of columnists than are executive officials. In the eyes of officials, this susceptibility makes the press a desirable vehicle for exporting ideas to the Congress, in the hope of improving the chances for Congressional approval of executive policy proposals. It also heightens the executive officials' interest in the content of the columns, . . . because they learn what the Congressmen are reading and thus are likely to be thinking in the immediate future.

Foreign policy interpretation in the press has different implications for the policy-making system than are suggested by foreign affairs information in the press. We noted earlier that policy makers draw foreign policy information from a press that aims to supply it to nonspecialized readers. In the case of analysis and interpretation, however, the audience assumptions of the journalists are more in line with the uses made of their product, for the work of columnists in comment, evaluation, and analysis is explicitly aimed at the policy makers as well as at the ordinary citizen. . . . The interpretive function is generally regarded as an extension of the information role vis-à-vis the general reader, on the grounds that "the facts" are meaningless without some interpretation. But the functions of criticism, of advocacy, of asking unanswered questions, and of participating in the policy deliberations and in the exchange of policy ideas are all aspects of the larger participant roles, which assume a dialogue between the correspondents and columnists on one side and the government officials and legislators on the other. This is not to argue, though, that what is done deliberately and knowingly by reporters is therefore done well; indeed, the attention that commentators turn to policy ideas is generally as wandering, haphazard, and capricious as the attention that their brother reporters turn to accounts of foreign affairs events or developments. The same uncertainty of standards as to what is newsworthy lies behind them both.

* * *

By giving policy makers in both branches an insight into the political perceptions of men with important roles in the political process, the press helps to create common understandings or interpretations of political reality. There is thus some significance for the governmental—and hence public—debate on foreign policy in the fact that both executive officials and Congressmen draw on approximately the same sources for their wider knowledge of "what is going on in the world," and how important it seems to be. Certain kinds of behavior can thus be reasonably predicted, and mutual expectation can become the basis for policy planning. Despite the specialized and confidential character of the State Department's diplomatic channels of information, continuous and meaningful discourse among foreign policy-making officials in all parts of the government, at all times and at all levels, is possible within the bounds set by this independent source of information and intellectual structuring of policy.

D. Bureaucratic Politics and Organizational Behavior

Administrative Communication

Norton E. Long

One way of looking at administrative communication is to observe the process by which a new member of the organization discovers, relates to, and affects the communications net as he becomes socialized into the organization. Since the communication net has its being in and operates through individuals, the process by which new human material renovates or expands the organization is largely identical with that by which the communications net is continually recreated and altered. This essay will attempt to get at the communications net in a governmental organization by reconstructing the way in which a new member of the organization becomes progressively aware of the network of communications and becomes consciously and unconsciously involved in it.

The data for this essay derive largely from personal observation and experience and discussion with others who have reflected on their administrative experience. The value of the material will be largely its capacity to evoke a comprehensive picture of a wide variety of activities contributing to the communications network and give the picture some unification through the relevance of the picture to a particular actor. Hopefully the actor's group identifications and group determined definitions of the situation will give a more than merely personal dimension to what is described.

It may be stretching it to regard the image of the organization, the impressions of its procedures, and the congeries of related notions that the new recruit has as part of the organization's communications. Nevertheless, the pictures in the new recruit's head are part of those premises of value and fact that . . . constitute so large a part of the only partially controllable "given" of the human material entering an organization. Quite apart from the general organizational culture, the federal government, in the large, and its departments, in particular, contribute a vast number of intended and unintended cues to potential recruits. The smell of the post office, the recruiting posters for the marines, the television shows of the F.B.I. and T-men, the struggles with the income tax form, and the mixed assortment of stories in press and magazine all teach lessons from which the new recruit must somehow gain a preliminary definition of the situation that will confront him should he enter federal employment. These general messages may in the particular case be altered by personal acquaintance with those already in federal employ or by academic acquaintance with the subject through teaching and books.

At the entrance to federal employment the new recruit encounters a long and detailed form on which he is required to recite much of his biography, some of his relevant attainments, and a test of his political fitness, which he learns will be the subject of a corroborative government investigation. He will doubtless wonder just what use this information will or can be put to. Since he swears or affirms the truth of his statements he may well wonder if he is running the risk of perjury. Does the fact that I passed German for my Ph.D. mean I have a good reading knowledge of the language, or would saying that be, as I know in my heart of hearts, a lie? What difference does it make to my career whether I have a good reading knowledge of German? As the new recruit desperately scans the Attorney General's list and strives to remember whether in that ill-starred rebellious freshman year his name got anywhere it had better not, he wonders, if he is imaginative, how had I best answer this and what will the way I do cost me. If he has been coached by older hands, he may learn that his form, devised by an esoteric magic of the Civil Service Commission, will be transformed into a position on a civil service list with eligibility for certain classified positions.

When he takes his entrance exam, if the position to which he aspires requires an assembled examination, he will in many cases approach the examination with an array of knowledge as to what the Civil Service examiners will want on the examination. Instructors in exam schools and colleges will have drilled into his head the preferred doctrine and answers that will insure a good score.

The Civil Service examination and the relation of the Commission to the schools is perhaps the first piece of intended communication to the potential recruit. Course content and lectures may be and often are designed with an eye to helping the student pass entrance examinations. Contact between [the] Commission and the universities institutionalized through the Society for Personnel Administration and other groups concerned with professionalized personnel administration provides a two-way communication that influences both the education of recruits on the one hand and the body of doctrine of the Civil Service examinations on the other. In the past this has been a process highly oriented toward the point of view of staff to the neglect of line considerations. The mutual relation of Commission and academics has at times tended to produce a body of public administration dogma whose socialization was enforced by the system of examinations. The limited concern of line with recruitment and academic relations has biased the body of public administration education in a peculiar way. This is itself in large part a result of the isolation of the Commission and its counterparts in the agencies from line operations. For the new recruit this means a form of "academic" learning that quite often leads to expectations about the conduct of administration that have to be modified in practice or sometimes painfully unlearned.

The new recruit is frequently sworn in in a slovenly fashion that makes of this ceremony just a piece of meaningless routine. In all probability, little thought is given to how this might be used to communicate the symbolism of a value orientation that might be functional. However the matter of fact, unconcern may be preferable to the ritual that might be concocted by the D.A.R. or the American Legion should this particular piece of communication be taken seriously. At least it is interesting to consider the content of this particular communication in our general cultural unconcern with or inability to produce meaningful ceremony.

Not immediately following the swearing-in ceremony, but perhaps connected with its shoddiness, is the frequent delay in the process of papers, loyalty-security investigation, and the initial payment of salary. Just what is communicated to the new employee must vary from case to case. But in the main there must be an impression of a vast, shambling impersonality with little or no concern for the new recruit. This impression is rather confirmed than the reverse by the very human, very warm efforts of agency personnel to mitigate the impact of the "system" on the individual. At the very outset of his career the new recruit learns something about the "government," what you have to get used to and how to work the system. The account of the whys and wherefores will range from damnation of the treasury, the Budget Bureau, the Controller General, and Congress to a cynical acceptance of the fate of bureaucratic man. What seems most basically to get communicated is an appreciation of the necessity to work with the system and an initial feel for just how great a weight of irrational necessity one must learn to live with and manipulate.

The newcomer to the organization may be treated to a day of indoctrination or, if he is in a special category, to an extended period of orientation, taking weeks or even months. In the ordinary case the indoctrination will be in the hands of the personnel and training people with a few prestigious operating people as guest stars. Because of the felt necessity of keeping a

clear separation between the front and the back of the organization, the performance has often the same pious and platitudinous air as the lecture of a politician giving the inside story to a class of college sophomores. Occasionally a particularly charismatic agency figure may come across the footlights in a way to give the agency and its program some of the glow of his own personality. Often, however, the indoctrination is little more than the same kind of ceremonial routine as the swearing-in ceremony felt by both performers and audience as a manualized requirement to be gotten over with. The new employees, unless particularly starry-eyed, are eager to get really filled in, and they sense that by and large that this is done because in principle it should be. In the rare case where top management really has something to communicate it may do better. However, those who cavil would do well to listen to the inspiring D-Day addresses that somehow didn't measure up to the P.R., or [public relations] man's, hopes. The agency people who have the duty, who must instruct and inspire the oddly assorted crowd in Room 104, can testify to the frustrating sense of ineffectuality when you are told—communicate.

The new recruit in his unit or section is like a strange child in a new neighborhood. He may have been given a manual of internal procedure, a copy of the agency's statute, its last annual report, the information department's handouts, and the boss'[s] latest speeches, but these don't help much. He desperately needs to know the rules, who rates whom, what will get you fired, what are you really supposed to do. Like the freshman member of Congress, he needs, if only temporarily, a sponsor to fill him in. If it is only an old, motherly secretary who has been in the shop for years, he needs someone to give him those preliminary definitions of the situation that will tell him how the immediate group expects him to behave. The faces, the desks, the office geography begin to take on meaning. Virtually none of this comes from official communication. Again like a new child in a strange environment, the exploration moves from the immediate vicinity of the newcomer's desk to the strange territory beyond. This territory begins to take on shape as inhabited by lawyers, accountants, economists, the fieldmen, personnel, budget, and the like. The various offices with the glazed windows become the abodes of this or that human shape who takes on attributes through gossip and ascription. An ever-widening and -changing map of the bureaucratic terrain develops and is peopled with actors who grow faces as they are talked about and develop roles that are almost as clear as those in a play. In short, the recruit gets clued in on the office definition of the situation, a definition that may vary significantly between even relatively tiny face-to-face groups sharing a few thousand square feet of floor space.

As the recruit develops his conscious and largely unconscious sociometry of the organization, the "we" of his immediate identification acquires form and the "others" become differentiated both in their relation to the "we" and as grouped sets of actors having clear or shadowy parts in a system of action. These "others" are related to the recruit by direct contact, imputed relationships, and a comprehensive mythology that explains the action system in which he is involved. This mythology is one of the most significant communications ordering the conduct of the actors in the organization. The individual may have an individualized variant of the mythology, different groups within the organization will almost certainly exhibit variations of emphasis, but by and large what makes the organization hang together is the fact that somehow it socializes into its members a mythology explaining its system of action that gives the members more or less mutually compatible definitions of their situations.

. . . From a communications standpoint the meaning of anarchy is the existence of incompatible definitions of the situation. To a considerable extent the holders of power in an organization hold their power because they are able to get their definitions of the situation accepted by others. Rarely, however, do holders of power have freedom to deal radically with the definitions of the situation that are by and large the inherited collective habits of an ongoing organization and one of the products of its historically developed but largely unplanned system of interaction. At best, holders of power can work within the system, using it and incrementally changing it. More than this creates a revolutionary situation and shakes the existing order.

The importance of the mythology of the organization consists not only in its providing an account of the formal and informal structure of power and legitimacy, the celestial and infernal hierarchies, the powers of light and the powers of darkness, but equally in giving the individual a rationale for the self-assignment of role and tasks. The inhabitants of administrative organizations do not greatly differ from savages or convicts in their need to have the mystery of the forces playing upon them explained. Thunder and lightning, politics and power alike need to be made explicable, bearable, and perhaps manipulatable. The civilized savages of administration are equally in need of myths to reduce the painful uncertainties of the unknown. A more or less constant struggle goes on in organizations to alter the official and unofficial mythologies that define the situation for the members. Where these definitions vary beyond a point, as with the Communists, the coherence of the organization, its capacity to maintain itself as an order, may be threatened. Prerecruitment tests and a system of sanctions both formal and informal are designed to close the ears of the recruit to dangerous thoughts.

Much of what the recruit learns in an organization is communicated after the fashion of Benthams "dog law." He learns by the punishing effects of violating norms whose existence and whose particular application he discovers by their breach.

The uneasily felt menace of these sensed but unknown rules enforces the need for a rationale, a mythology to direct conduct, the more so that, except for the most routine behavior, much of the actor's conduct must be self-determined on the basis of his own appreciation of the situation.

There are perhaps, among many, three critical and separable though interrelated sorts of things the new recruit in the organization learns. At a fairly early stage he gets or thinks he gets enough knowledgeability about the folkways of the organization to get over the fear of being fired. This is almost the psychological equivalent of a child's learning to ride a bicycle. He can keep his balance without falling off. The ever-present sense of insecurity recedes, and within limits it is possible to experiment without the fear that the system will bite for some unknown reason. While the fear of being fired will be renewed from time to time, this initial communication of a sense of security is a critical stage in the recruit's socialization into the organization. Closely related to developing a sense for when you get fired, the organization's tolerance limits, is the knowledge of "how you make it." These two kinds of knowledge constitute the socialized folklore of the prevailing rewards system. The third critical piece of learning for the recruit is his development of some comprehensive rationale of organizational purpose and process that permits him to adapt his own discretionary activities to this in a fashion that to him seems to make sense.

Thus among the many communications that come to him are these critical ones: an instinctive sense of the limits of organizational tolerance, a more or less explicit theory of how people make it in the organization, and a general conception of organizational purposes and methods and their relationship to his own functioning. These three kinds of notions will alter over the recruit's career through time and organizational space. In fact, even in the same organization promotion or transfer may require a degree of relearning. Differ- ences in the position may, and frequently will, mean changes in the relevant data provided by the communications network. Some learning, however, is transferable, and the old hand fills in much more quickly than the rookie.

The three kinds of learning go on together both consciously and unconsciously as the newcomer settles into the organization. Much of what is communicated to him by his fellows is a set of routines that are standard for people in his position: who may one talk to and what manner to adopt. . . . The presentation of self in everyday life is transferable to the office where the new member learns and creates a part in an ongoing and evolving play. He is constantly looking for cues and constantly looks for, and with varying success gets, prompting, frequently contradictory prompting.

At an early stage, if he is sensitive, he will feel that within the vague limits of a general consensus there are rival definitions of the situation competing for his attention and allegiance. Most commonly there will be one, and perhaps more than one, emanating from sources of higher status than his own, his peer group's definition, lateral definitions from other parts of the organization, definitions coming up from lower status groups, and definitions beating in from the outside. Depending on his position in the organization he may be exposed to all these competing views, and their pull upon his particular view will be greater or less depending on his exposure and the plasticity of his own position.

Normally there are organization blinders that shield members' eyes from distracting and disturbing sights that might disrupt the steady progress of socialized routines. Fixity of work group location and intensity of interaction within particular units develop a protective tribalism that restricts external influences. To the extent that a work group definition of the situation develops it provides in addition to the locational and interactional factors a doctrinal screen that filters out much of the potentially disruptive communication and reorganizes data that cannot be ignored in ways compatible with and supportive of the accepted definition of the situation.

The face-to-face work group's attitude toward other differentiated parts of the organization is certainly one of the earliest pieces of communication for the newcomer. His position at entrance determines to a great extent the group membership which he will normally seek. His pattern of communication beyond this group will be considerably affected by group discipline. The group largely supplies the new member with his preliminary estimates and characterizations of the outsiders with whom he must deal. The informational needs of the member's job can produce patterns of contact and interaction that reduce the group's control over the members' definition of the situation. The foreman is the typical man in the middle, but there are other connectors whose role as information carriers and securers of intelligence puts them in a position of ambiguous identification.

The term "spy" is always unpleasant, even when used to describe that intelligence function which many groups will want performed to get the facts it needs to do its routine job, and quite as much to fill it in on the gossip, rumor, "the word" on which it depends for keeping up with the general orientation it feels necessary. One often hears in administration the remark "I have my spies." While said with a smile, it indicates a reality. Even in an organization that attempts to provide through established channels the information needed by its members to perform their jobs, this is seldom accomplished to the satisfaction of all the members of the organization. Often the most energetic and aggressive in the pursuit of organization goals are most sensitive in the pursuit of extra sources of information.

The new recruit at almost any level, if he has drive and ambition, becomes aware of the scarcity value of reliable sources of information. This information can be symbolized by a set of telephone numbers that, in addition to the weather and the time of day, give reliable information on things affecting the individual's job decisions and the larger enterprises with which he is concerned. The ability to secure such sources, even those required routinely, has its scarcity value. . . . Where the sources are the result of personal contacts and are to a degree privately possessed, they give their owner considerable value to others. The real or supposed contacts of individuals are a frequent explanation for staffing decisions.

The new member of the organization will have quite different interests in the development of his relation to the communications net depending on his conception of his personal strategy and role in the organization. This depends to quite an extent on the new member's conception of "how to make it" and what "making it" means to him. There is a great deal of difference between the upward mobile newcomer who regards his initial position as temporary and his face-to-face group relationship as merely a stage in a career, and the person who regards his initial position as a relatively permanent location and the esteem of his immediate associates as a highly significant reward.

One way of looking at the new member's participation in the communications networks that intersect the organization is to view their role as interest representatives. Another way which may seem less legitimately a part of a communications analysis is to see the new representatives as representatives of special skills or knowledge communicating these skills or knowledge to the organization.

In the simplest case, interest representation occurs where a member of the organization is chosen to represent or serve as a channel of communication with an interest. Thus a particular person may be recruited as representing organized labor, agriculture, real estate, Negroes, or many other groups of concern to an organization in the formation and execution of its policies. As a channel of communication the individual serves as a source of information for his organization and for his group. He also serves as a two-way instrument of diplomacy. A somewhat similar kind of communication and representative function is performed by organization members who are recruited because of their capacity to communicate with and represent governmental agencies of concern to the organization, such as the Bureau of the Budget or the Civil Service Commission, or sources of political power whose support or opposition is a matter of moment.

The interest or power group base provides a member of an organization with negotiable goods that can be cashed in for recognition, status, and rewards. Specialization in communication and within communication is one of the effective means of forwarding an organization member's career. Competition will occur between individuals and between groups to gain control of the channels of interest representation in the organization and to become the recognized interpreters of and spokesmen for a particular interest or center of power.

The representation of particular sources of knowledge differs in some ways from the representation of interests or agencies of power within the government. Nevertheless there is frequently keen competition to control the communication of particular kinds of knowledge within an organization or within the government. The general counsel's office is highly interested in seeing to it that it has a monopoly on the provision of legal information within the organization. The Bureau of Labor Statistics or the Census would like an exclusive franchise for their data. On the other hand, every organization with any drive toward autonomy is concerned with achieving control over the information it needs for decisional independence. Control over the communication of information requisite to key decisions is to an important degree control over the decisions themselves. This fact often plunges the most seemingly

harmless fact-gathering enterprise into the storms of politics.

Upward communication in the organization most obviously affects the new member in his attempt to "make it." How can he single himself out of the mass for favorable attention by his superiors without bringing upon himself the penalties for apple polishing or sticking his neck out. The written communication that travels up the hierarchy, the mixed-level committee, the extraorganizational social meeting, the political meeting, all can provide means of bringing the individual and his capacity to the attention of the relevant superiors. The formal channel of upward communication limits the individual's initiative in securing the most favorable consideration of his individual merits. Few who are ambitious and knowledgeable would trust solely to the evaluation of immediate superiors and personnel departments. The folklore of "how one makes it" will dictate the general strategy and tactics for the appropriate upward communication of the desired image. This drive for recognition is an important part of the psychological fuel of the organization.

The upward communication of images of the individual is paralleled by the upward communication of images of organization units (both central office and field) to the higher echelons. In a sense individuals and units are both trying to make it, and they are concerned with the most favorable presentation that they can make of themselves to superiors, to the public, and to those persons and groups that they believe can affect their fate. A major problem of superiors is to penetrate the public relations images presented to them by subordinates. Every report form is likely to be translated into a score card by subordinates who will figure out how to fill it out in a way they believe will give them the best score with their superiors.

Upward communication of favorable images is only one of a number of ways in which subordinates seek to influence superiors' decision making. Much of the new program and policies of the organization originate in the efforts of subordinates to perform their tasks, satisfy the wants of clienteles, and deal with changes in the situation that make existing routines unsatisfactory. Subordinates are in the position of attempting to manipulate superiors as rationers of the scarce resources of the organization and as legitimizers of program proposals. The . . . devices for securing superiors' attention run all the way from formal channels, the office grapevine, to leaks to the press and columnists, or even to stimulating Congressional inquiries as to why what you want to do isn't done. The line between the presentation of information and argument and the exercise of influence is difficult to draw. Subordinates have decisional needs that they must seek to get met by superiors. Superiors seek to confine the range of decisions and consequent delegations to force recurrent resort to them as a means of maintaining control. The struggle over the extent of delegation is inherent in the dilemma of delegation and control.

The communications net of the upward[ly] mobile new member of the organization expands upward and outward as he develops his sources of information and rumor. He discovers as he moves upward in the organization that he loses certain sources of information. Former peers passed by in the upward career become reticent. Others will frontily point out that you are no longer "one of the boys" and that you represent the brass or a different organizational interest. Where once one could cut in on the grapevine directly, it now becomes necessary to depend on one's secretary, an administrative assistant, or "a spy." Where before "what are they thinking?" referred to the brass, now it refers as much or more to the people down below. The new member having become an older member and an upper member begins to sense the problem of the upper level in securing information about those below and from those below.

The upward rise in the organization places the new member in a position where he must communicate with those below and with those above. A more or less conscious struggle goes on to capture his identification between his unit and the higher echelons. As has been so often pointed out, the man in the middle interprets each side to the other. To do the job of management he must successfully manipulate his unit while preserving his identification with management. This career point of the front-line supervisor is critical in the formal communications net. To be worth his salt to management the supervisor must be able to persuade his subordinates to honor the communications he transmits from above. To hold the esteem of his subordinates and thereby to do the job management wants done he must convince his subordinates of his identification with the interests of the unit and the group. At each level of organization this conflict of loyalties is likely to occur. Its impact on communication is obvious. Depending on the identification of the supervisor, communications will be biased to accomplish management objectives, unit objectives, the supervisor's objectives, or, in all probability, a varying mix of all three.

How the supervisor will behave in his role as a communicator relates closely to the values that motivate him and his conception of the appropriate strategy and tactics for their realization. Thus if he is an upward[ly] mobile careerist, the most effective indicator of his course of action is the folklore of the organization as to "how you make it." If he is an ideologically motivated individual concerned with a cause, there may be known patterns of behavior of people identified with his cause. In the case where the identification is with the work group, the more or less typical pattern of office feudalism emerges; the supervisor seeks to develop support for his autonomy and derives his satisfactions from the unit's job and the esteem of subordinates.

The higher the level an organization member attains, the more complex the net of communications in which he becomes involved and the more difficult the balancing of interests, programs, and loyalties. Functioning at one's own level . . . involves constantly higher abstraction and greater and greater difficulties of communication. The difficulties are, in part, those of getting the information at that distance from the firing line at all, or in any meaningful shape, and the impossibility of digesting the sheer mass of data flowing in to the point where it can be used for decision making.

The executive in the upper echelons is faced with a great gap between him and the working level of his organization. If he is sensitive and imaginative, he will realize that Tolstoi's graphic picture of Napoleon at the battle may well apply to him. How to get accurate information of what is going on, information both accurate and simplified to the point where it can be made manageable for decisions; how, out of all the possible courses of action, to get those before him that are worth considering, and that he rather than somebody else should consider, are the eternal questions.

Essentially, they shake down to the conflict between the organization as an historically developed system of human action and the organization as a conscious rational theory of how to accomplish certain objectives imposed on this historically developed system. The communications net is a product both of the formal habits of the existing administrative culture—the budget process, reporting procedures, administrative regulations—and the customs by which people have been socialized into

playing the American variant of the western game of administration—and of the informal communications nets that have grown up around the formal channels. To this more or less culturally determined pattern of communications—items much like the rest of the accepted folkways of how you run an institution—is added the attempt to dominate the historically developed routines, a net of communications that is determined by the theory of how the organization's purposes are to be attained in the light of its resources and human and material environment. In a sense, the attempt to set up a fully theoretically determined communications system is a demand to transform an historically developed system into an organization. This would mean that top management would try to impose its theory of organization purpose on the network of communications and dominate the important definitions of the situation at every level.

Such domination and control of communications is constantly called for in the name of carrying out the plans of management. In practice the demands seem always utopian. In practice it is difficult to develop and adopt a sufficiently comprehensive and specific theory whose communications implications can be made explicit. To the problem of developing an adequate theory is added the problem of developing sufficient power. Organizations of political importance become institutions; as institutions in a pluralistic society they become for the most part fatally involved in the noisy debate that pluralism itself engenders.

7

Approaches to the Science
of Politics

In the emergence of political science in the twentieth century, concern about the development of a genuine science[1] of politics has been expressed by many of the field's leading scholars. This section highlights this dimension of political analysis. Before exploring the readings it is necessary to comment upon some of the central obstacles that, so far at least, have blocked the full realization of a scientific approach to the study of politics. By examining such obstacles we may better understand the special efforts required to create a science of politics, a creation that may someday become a reality.

First, science demands objectivity in the reporting and analysis of facts. This is not easy to achieve in the social sciences because people perceive human behavior in terms of its implications for their own lives, and thus they tend to interpret data "reactively" in accordance with preconceived notions of what the facts ought to be. Sometimes this distortion is deliberate, but more often it is based on subconscious and rather subtle pressures of which the observer is not aware. All social sciences have acknowledged the problem, and different methods for overcoming it in empirical research have been used with varying success. It is almost universally recognized that such value distortion cannot be completely eliminated by any combination of methods, and that objectivity in empirical research is essentially an ideal to be striven for rather than an objective that must be achieved for work to be considered scientific in character.

Political science poses a special burden for researchers, because for several reasons it seems that value distortion is even more difficult to avoid here than in other social sciences. First, the data are especially value-laden, because political phenomena almost invariably have implications for the observer's preferences. Secondly, political analysis often requires looking *behind* action into probable motives generating behavior patterns. Although motives are not in the realm of observable phenomena, to overlook them in political re-

---

[1] *Science, though it is admittedly difficult to define, is commonly understood to include the following: (1) a body of systematically organized knowledge based on observation and classification of facts; (2) hierarchically organized general statements of uniformities and explanations; and (3) commonly accepted rules regarding the procedures for the induction of findings, procedures that permit replication in the testing of hypotheses.*

search would in many cases result in rather superficial analysis. But once one examines another's motives he becomes involved in the determination and interpretation of covert values, an effort that by its very nature cannot be considered legitimately scientific. Political science thus faces a hard choice in terms of research strategy. Thirdly, it is difficult for political scientists to maintain value-commitments in their private roles as citizens and voters and value-neutrality in their professional roles as observers and analysts in political research. Too often, they tend to lose sight of one or the other, becoming either indifferent citizens or prejudiced researchers. Indeed, because citizenship involves conscious choice among alternatives based on one's values, and research requires neutrality, political scientists have a burden in role-conflict unlike that shouldered by any other social scientists.

A second set of requirements of science relates to the establishment and development of theories. Scientific theory must explain and/or predict events; it cannot simply offer rationalizations for them after the fact or unsupported hypotheses regarding future developments. Moreover, it must be open to continuing refinement and correction by empirical testing. No theory is expected to stand as a final, perfect statement, however narrow or limited it might be. Thus its amenability to testing is of critical importance to its soundness *as a theory*. The concepts employed in its construction must be operationally defined—that is, formulated in such a way that they can be put to use in research. The propositions linking them must be based upon propositions of less generality and scope, verified and already generally accepted. Scientific theory construction does not permit the deliberate selection of only certain supporting generalizations and the rejection of incompatible facts or established theories. It cannot be patently, primarily, or intentionally argumentative.

In political science, theory has not worked this way, but rather has often been used to refer to basic ideas and statements that do not, and sometimes cannot, explain or predict phenomena. These usually have been cast in such a form that it is not at all clear how much of what they say pertains to explanation-prediction and how much to the desires and concerns of their authors. Witness, for example, one recent theory that the ubiquity of centralized power in federal systems in the contemporary world is a direct product of the ineffectiveness and instability of systems based on peripheralized or decentralized power. Its author explains that the peripheralized federal systems "fall gradually apart until they are easy prey for their enemies."[2] This theory incorporates ideas that are value-laden and not reducible to explanation or prediction free from its author's commitments. It is hard to separate

[2] William H. Riker, Federalism: Origin, Operation, Significance *(Boston: Little, Brown & Co., 1964), pp. 7–8. Riker's theory is perhaps the most advanced formulation of this idea. Any criticism implied in the above comments is intended to apply not so much to Riker's work as to the nature of the subject itself, which seems particularly open to criticism on the grounds noted.*

the descriptive idea of the durability of centralized federal power from the normative idea of its effectiveness.

Political science has developed a tradition of deliberately normative theorizing; many political theorists have tried intentionally to focus on value-laden propositions. Indeed, as noted in Chapter I, the transempiricist argument against behavioralism represents a major facet of contemporary political science, and one that is largely reflective of the tradition of non-scientific theory construction. For example, of six renowned essays written on political theory in the classic *Approaches to the Study of Politics*,[3] all six argued the importance of relying on this traditional normative theorizing. In short, theory in the study of politics has been commonly used to recommend change, to stipulate ideals, or to set standards by which to judge action. It is difficult to reconcile such usage with the role of theory in scientific investigation.

Theory in political science also leaves something to be desired in terms of self-correction. Traditional normative theory has regularly been derived deductively rather than inductively. It has offered few opportunities for testing, because neither its concepts nor its propositions are operationally stated or based on a full survey of already validated generalizations. It is often given as pronouncement, as a final draft in a completed work, not as a tentative and fragmentary formulation for future refinement. Moreover, it is not unusual to encounter theory offered purely as argument against existing beliefs, not designed for advancement of scientific investigation but for a frontal attack against intellectual enemies. In this sense it has too often served as simply a rallying banner for the conduct of normative debate in political science, action that may prove provocative to those concerned with the ethical aspects of politics, but that usually fails to advance the scientific pursuit of knowledge about political life. The discipline of political science is only beginning to alter its conception of theory to meet the demands of a scientific approach.

A third requirement of science is that facts and theories must be interrelated in such a way that theories attempt to explain facts and facts are gathered to help generate or test and possibly confirm novel, though necessary theories. Accumulated facts can and do create, change, or destroy theories, which, in turn, can and do alter the gathering and analysis of data that together is commonly called empirical research. This relationship can be called the fact-theory nexus, and represents a major challenge to both theorists and empirical researchers in all sciences because of the difficulty of

---

3 *Roland Young, ed.,* Approaches to the Study of Politics *(Evanston, Ill.: Northwestern University Press, 1958), Part II, pp. 113–214, essays by Norman Jacobson, Mulford Q. Sibley, Frederick M. Watkins, Robert G. McCloskey, Carl J. Friedrich, and Lindsay Rogers. It is particularly noteworthy that the remainder of this volume is devoted to the development of concepts, analytic systems, and community research design in the construction of a scientific approach to the study of politics.*

maintaining sufficient familiarity with and requisite skill in both realms to permit effective scientific inquiry.

Coupled with the fact-theory nexus is the use of intentionally simplified abstractions offered as *constructs* (such as the gene in genetics, the valence in chemistry, and anti-matter in nuclear physics) or *models* (such as the atom in physics, wave motion in optics and acoustics, and the magnetic field in electromagnetics). Such abstractions are of use in three ways: (1) to provide students with a groundwork for relating basic ideas regarding the subject under investigation; (2) to delineate those topics most fruitful for further theoretical and/or empirical inquiry; (3) to suggest new theoretical formulations or new ways to validate or verify old ones. Although such abstractions are frequently used in the development of a science, they may not be absolutely necessary. They function, along with the fact-theory nexus, to permit the self-correction of theory by guiding empirical verification and testing. Under no circumstances are such abstractions designed to avoid empirical investigation.

In political science the fact-theory nexus has too often been honored in the breach. Political scientists, perhaps even more than other social scientists, have often been unable to sustain commitments to both theorizing and research, tending to favor one or the other and thus creating an unfortunate gap in communications. As noted in Chapter I, in the early efforts to build the institutionalist mode of political inquiry great reliance was placed on the mere gathering and analysis of voluminous historical data. And specific facts —details of events, the individual peculiarities and distinctiveness of nations —still constitute the bulk of research matter. All too often such specificity has not been guided by theoretical considerations. On the other hand, political theorists have commonly worked in splendid isolation from empirical research. Robert K. Merton's notion of the need for middle-range theory[4] in social science is particularly relevant to political science; entirely too much effort has been spent by theorists in exploring unresearchable ideas, perhaps in subconscious reaction to the researchers' alienation from theory.

The danger of working in such a vacuum has not been completely overcome by the behavioralist innovation, in spite of the continuing argument for reliance on the fact-theory nexus in theory construction and research design. In particular, there has been a proliferation of behavioralist models, many of which offer no indication of the means by which they are related to research. Model building has become in the hands of some a favorite way of

---

[4] *"I believe that our major task today is to develop special theories applicable to limited ranges of data—theories, for example, of class dynamics, of conflicting group pressures, of the flow of power and the exercise of interpersonal influence—rather than to seek at once the 'integrated' conceptual structure adequate to derive all these and other theories. The sociological theorist exclusively committed to the exploration of high abstractions runs the risk that, as with modern décor, the furniture of his mind will be sparse, bare, and uncomfortable. . . ."* Robert K. Merton, Social Theory and Social Structure (*New York: The Free Press of Glencoe, Inc., 1957*), *p. 9.*

spinning out unsupported generalizations with no apparent relationship to theory or empirical validation. In such cases the construction of models undertaken in the name of science can stand in the way of the sound development of science.

Finally, a set of predictive laws is normally thought to be a necessary feature of a science. Theories can explain facts and facts correct theories only when facts are compiled and observed in terms of their similarities, or uniformities. Statements of uniformities, used as explanations of specific phenomena, are usually called laws, and because of their explanatory character they are also predictive. But a law requires some means of measuring the phenomena to which it is applied, and unless some measurement is used, the law cannot help to explain or scientifically predict specific developments.

Political science has never developed a body of scientifically useful laws, and perhaps part of the reason for this has been the reluctance (or inability) of political scientists to develop the means of measurement for many phenomena, such as power, loyalty, or hostility. Of course it is quite possible that these are not amenable to measurement, and this is one argument that transempiricists have used against the desirability or possibility of developing a science of politics.[5] Even the scientifically inclined have acknowledged the highly unpredictable nature of such phenomena and the difficulty of measuring important qualitative political characteristics. On such grounds alone, the development of predictive laws of politics will be long in coming. It should be noted, moreover, that the indiscriminate use of measurement and statistical data is not *ipso facto* scientifically justifiable; unless the right measures are used, and unless they make sense in terms of the phenomena, measurement in and of itself provides little in the way of truly useful work. But certainly, whatever the justification, the absence of predictive laws constitutes a serious handicap to the development of a science of politics.

Yet the efforts to build such a science have begun and are likely to continue in the future, with, in our view, increasingly positive results. In a sense these efforts consist of the steady advancement of methods and an increase in methodological sophistication in theory construction and research design. It is our purpose in this chapter to illustrate some of the more important aspects of this advancement, aspects that can almost always be found in the refinement of actual research design and methods. Because it is this that is of paramount importance here, we will not comment at length upon the substantive issues raised by the authors represented below.

The earliest effort at building scientific method in political analysis was through use of the comparative approach, dating back to Aristotle. In twentieth-century political science it has been used on occasion to permit the testing of hypotheses in different national or cultural settings. Seymour

---

[5] *Chapter I has provided a fuller discussion of the transempirical critique of the behavioral approach to political analysis.*

Martin Lipset's validation of the hypothesis that economic development is a prerequisite of democracy, for example, is based on a comparative analysis of many Latin American, European, and Asian democracies—both stable and unstable—and dictatorships. Lipset finds that invariably the more democratic nations of each region are economically better off than the less democratic ones.

A refinement of such comparative testing involves the use of statistical measures of differences in determining the causal or conditioning factors affecting outcomes. Donald R. Matthews and James W. Prothro have explored the social and economic factors conditioning differential rates of Negro voter registration in various counties of southern states by means of simple, partial, and multiple correlation and regression analyses, the procedures of which are explained by the authors in the article reprinted below. Cause-effect relationships have never been readily determined in the social sciences, and the methodological complexity of the Matthews-Prothro exploration provides evidence of this. Their analysis requires careful review in order to gain an understanding of the complications involved in using statistical measures for delineating contributing factors, or correlates, of political phenomena. The conclusions they reach are that Negro concentration has a clearly identifiable negative effect on registration, that there is *no* positive correlation between Negro registration and urbanization or industrialization, and—most striking—that there is a high negative correlation between it and white educational level. In conclusion they cite the need for examining political and legal factors in order to refine the explanation of the rate difference.[6]

The development of scientific explanation and prediction relies as much on the construction of theory as on the comparative and/or statistical testing of hypotheses. And in recent years theory construction has been closely aligned with the use of models and conceptual frameworks stressing at least implicitly the idea of systematic relatedness and symbiosis in political relations. Theories of international relations, of decision making, of legislative coalition formation, and of voting behavior have commonly assumed the natural interdependence of the components of a system of action. This is sometimes expressed in terms of "equilibrium," the delicate balance among the components of such a system in the *status quo*, the disturbance of which will set counteracting changes into motion to re-establish the balance on a new basis.[7] When France and Communist China successfully tested atom bombs, for example, the equilibrium in international relations was disturbed

---

[6] *This need was met by them in a subsequent article not presented in this volume. See the* American Political Science Review, *Vol. LVII, No. 2 (June, 1963), 355–367.*

[7] *The equilibrium is, of course, always being disturbed and re-established in fact, even if in theory the notion carries the unfortunate connotations of stability as normal and disruptive change as undesirable. The delicate balance is actually an abstraction useful in developing theories regarding social and political change, not a description of reality or a prescription in defense of the* status quo.

and a new one was established, with a new set of relationships developed between those two countries and all others.

One well-established systematic conceptual approach for theory construction is structural-functionalism, an approach originally developed by Talcott Parsons, who based it on the ideas of functionalism in biology. This approach is illustrated in Robert K. Merton's classic analysis of the political boss and city machine.[8]

In the structural-functional approach, the term "structure" refers to any patterned set of human actions that can be identified in terms of an agent or group of actors (called the structure) whose action provides the defining characteristics. For example, a political machine is a structure, as is a welfare agency, a family, a neighborhood, or a baseball team. In all cases it is the activity of the parts that serves to define the whole. In this sociological form of analysis a "function" is the effect that a structure has upon other structures or, in rare cases, upon itself. Normally it is directly related to certain actions performed by the structure. In the case of the political machine, getting voters registered and to the polls is a function; in the case of a welfare agency, it is funneling help to those who need it; in the family, rearing children; in a neighborhood, protecting the area from social, economic, and physical deterioration; in the case of a baseball team, coordinating the efforts of its members in playing according to the rules but in a continuing effort to win.

It is not at all uncommon for structures to perform certain functions that are not consciously selected by its members. These are called "latent functions," as distinguished from "manifest functions," such as those enumerated above. The city machine's provision of a channel of upward mobility for low-income ethnic minority group members is one latent function cited by Merton. Some people have argued that a welfare agency may in effect perform the latent function of building dependency among its clients. Likewise, a family may function to inhibit juvenile delinquency, a neighborhood to maintain segregation, a baseball team to permit the release of strongly competitive urges felt by its members. The jargon apparent in Merton's analysis, it should be noted, is common to virtually all structural-functionalism; it may be an endemic element of any effort to build a sophisticated theoretical foundation for any science of human behavior.

A science of politics would also seem to require conceptual rigor—the establishment of a formal set of terms, definitions, and relations designed to assist empirical research and theory formation. Such conceptualization has become standard for behavioral analysis in political science, though on occasion the terms and definitions are not always presented in a unified and integrated form. We have chosen for illustration a recent statement of con-

---

[8] *For a more advanced treatment of this approach, see Don Martindale, ed.,* Functionalism in the Social Sciences *(Philadelphia: American Academy of Political and Social Science, 1965).*

ceptual clarification and research design in a relatively new area of specialization in political science: civil-military relations. In reviewing Lewis J. Edinger's article, one should pay particular attention to the role of classification, terminological distinction, and the development of explicit research strategies in assisting theory building and research. Without such efforts at preliminary analysis or the predetermination of criteria for narrowing the range of investigation, neither theorizing nor research would efficiently yield scientifically fruitful results.

Some social scientists have argued that the primary test of scientific pedigree is experimentation. We disagree, but we do feel that it poses an important issue: How experimental can or should political science get? The limits of experimentation are central to any answer to this question, as are its possibilities and advantages. Richard C. Snyder provides what seems to us a fair review of these matters.

In a sense his analysis constitutes an implied review of the overall problem and the prospects for an empirical science of politics. The difficulties of experimentation are the difficulties inherent in developing a science in an area where human behavior is elusive and difficult to test and is "common-sensically" presumed to have certain characteristics. Perhaps experimentation is beyond the reach of political science in the foreseeable future. But suppose we insist on continuing the efforts to build such a science. Is a contradiction at work? We don't think so, but we do feel that these two aspects of the current approach dramatize the difficulties to be encountered in building a true science of politics.

Suggestions for Additional Reading

Almond, Gabriel A., "Comparative Political Systems," *Journal of Politics,* Vol. VIII (August, 1956), 391–409.

Benson, Oliver, "The Use of Mathematics in the Study of Political Science," in James C. Charlesworth, ed., *Mathematics and the Social Sciences,* 30–57. Philadelphia: American Academy of Political and Social Science, 1963.

Braithwaite, Richard B., *Scientific Explanation.* New York: Harper & Row, Publishers, Inc., 1960.

Brecht, Arnold, *Political Theory: The Foundation of Twentieth Century Thought.* Princeton, N.J.: Princeton University Press, 1959.

Catlin, George E. G., *The Science and Method of Politics.* New York: Alfred A. Knopf, Inc., 1927.

Easton, David, *A Framework for Political Analysis.* Englewood Cliffs, N.J.: Prentice-Hall, Inc., 1965.

Fiellin, Alan, "The Functions of Informal Groups in Legislative Institutions," *Journal of Politics,* Vol. XXIV (February, 1962), 72–91.

Guetzkow, Harold S., ed., *Simulation in Social Science: Readings.* Englewood Cliffs, N.J.: Prentice-Hall, Inc., 1962.

————, et al., *Simulation in International Relations: Developments for Research and Teaching.* Englewood Cliffs, N.J.: Prentice-Hall, Inc., 1963.

Hacker, Andrew, "Mathematics and Political Science," in James C. Charlesworth, ed., *Mathematics and the Social Sciences,* 58–76. Philadelphia: American Academy of Political and Social Science, 1963.

Janda, Kenneth, *Data Processing: Applications to Political Research.* Evanston, Ill.: Northwestern University Press, 1965.

Kaplan, Abraham, *The Conduct of Inquiry: Methodology for Social Science.* San Francisco: Chandler Publishing Company, 1964.

Key, V. O., Jr., *A Primer of Statistics for Political Scientists.* New York: Thomas Y. Crowell Company, 1954.

Lasswell, Harold D., and Abraham Kaplan, *Power and Society.* New Haven, Conn.: Yale University Press, 1950.

Lazarsfeld, Paul F., ed., *Mathematical Thinking in the Social Sciences.* New York: The Free Press of Glencoe, Inc., 1954.

Levy, Marion J., Jr., "Some Aspects of 'Structural-Functional' Analysis and Political Science," in Roland Young, ed., *Approaches to the Study of Politics,* pp. 52–66. Evanston, Ill.: Northwestern University Press, 1958.

Meehan, Eugene J., *The Theory and Method of Political Analysis.* Homewood, Ill.: Dorsey Press, Inc., 1965.

Mill, John Stuart, *Philosophy of Scientific Method.* New York: Hafner Publishing Co., Inc., 1950.

Mitchell, William C., *The American Polity: A Social and Cultural Interpretation.* New York: The Free Press of Glencoe, Inc., 1962.

Nagel, Ernest, *The Structure of Science.* New York: Harcourt, Brace, & World, Inc., 1961.

Parsons, Talcott, "Some Highlights of the General Theory of Action," in Roland Young, ed., *Approaches to the Study of Politics,* pp. 282–301. Evanston, Ill.: Northwestern University Press, 1958.

Popper, Karl, *The Logic of Scientific Discovery.* New York: Basic Books, Inc., 1959.

Toulmin, Stephen, *Philosophy of Science.* New York: Harper & Row, Publishers, Inc., 1960.

Winch, Peter, *The Idea of a Social Science and Its Relation to Philosophy* (New York: Humanities Press, 1959).

A. Comparative Analysis

Economic Development and Democracy

Seymour Martin Lipset

Economic Development in Europe and the Americas

Perhaps the most common generalization linking political systems to other aspects of society has been that democ-

racy[1] related to the state of economic de-

[1] *The main criteria used to define European democracies are the uninterrupted continuation of political democracy since World War I and the absence over the past twenty-five years of a major political movement opposed to the democratic*

Seymour Martin Lipset, *Political Man: The Social Bases of Politics* (New York: Doubleday & Company, Inc., 1960), Chap. 2, "Economic Development and Democracy," pp. 48–60. Copyright © 1960 by Seymour Martin Lipset. Reprinted by permission of Doubleday & Company, Inc.

TABLE 1. CLASSIFICATION OF EUROPEAN, ENGLISH-SPEAKING, AND LATIN-AMERICAN NATIONS BY DEGREE OF STABLE DEMOCRACY

European and English-Speaking Nations		*Latin-American Nations*	
Stable Democracies	Unstable Democracies and Dictatorships	Democracies and Unstable Dictatorships	Stable Dictatorships
Australia	Albania	Argentina	Bolivia
Belgium	Austria	Brazil	Cuba
Canada	Bulgaria	Chile	Dominican Republic
Denmark	Czechoslovakia	Columbia	Ecuador
Ireland	Finland	Costa Rica	El Salvador
Luxembourg	France	Mexico	Guatemala
Netherlands	Germany	Uruguay	Haiti
New Zealand	Greece		Honduras
Norway	Hungary		Nicaragua
Sweden	Iceland		Panama
Switzerland	Italy		Paraguay
United Kingdom	Poland		Peru
United States	Portugal		Venezuela
	Romania		
	Spain		
	U.S.S.R.		
	Yugoslavia		

velopment. The more well-to-do a nation, the greater the chances that it will sustain democracy. From Aristotle down to the present, men have argued that only in a wealthy society in which relatively few citizens lived at the level of real poverty could there be a situation in which the mass of the population intelligently participate in politics and develop the self-restraint necessary to avoid succumbing to the appeals of irresponsible demagogues. A society divided between a large, impoverished mass and a small, favored elite results either in oligarchy (dictatorial rule of the small upper stratum) or in tyranny (popular-based dictatorship). To give these two political forms modern labels, tyranny's face today is Communism or Perónism; while oligarchy appears in the tra-

ditionalist dictatorships found in parts of Latin America, Thailand, Spain, or Portugal.

To test this hypothesis concretely, I have used various indices of economic development—wealth, industrialization, urbanization, and education—and computed averages (means) for the countries which have been classified as more or less democratic in the Anglo-Saxon world and Europe, and in Latin America.

In each case, the average wealth, degree of industrialization and urbanization, and level of education is much higher for the more democratic countries, as the data in Table 2 indicate. If I had combined Latin America and Europe in one table, the differences would have been even greater.

The main indices of *wealth* used are per capita income, number of persons per motor vehicle and thousands of persons per physician, and the number of radios, telephones, and newspapers per thousand persons. The differences are striking on every score (see Table 2). In the more

"rules of the game." The somewhat less stringent criterion for Latin America is whether a given country has had a history of more or less free elections for most of the post-World War I period. Where in Europe we look for stable democracies, in South America we look for countries which have not had fairly constant dictatorial rule (See Table 1).

TABLE 2. A COMPARISON OF EUROPEAN, ENGLISH-SPEAKING, AND LATIN-AMERICAN
COUNTRIES, DIVIDED INTO TWO GROUPS, "MORE DEMOCRATIC" AND "LESS
DEMOCRATIC," BY INDICES OF WEALTH, INDUSTRIALIZATION,
EDUCATION, AND URBANIZATION

A. INDICES OF WEALTH

Means	*Per Capita Income*	*Thousands of Persons per Doctor*	*Persons per Motor Vehicle*
European and English-Speaking Stable Democracies	U.S.$ 695	.86	17
European and English-Speaking Unstable Democracies and Dictatorships	308	1.4	143
Latin-American Democracies and Unstable Dictatorships	171	2.1	99
Latin-American Stable Dictatorships	119	4.4	274
Ranges			
European Stable Democracies	420–1,453	.7–1.2	3–62
European Dictatorships	128–482	.6–4	10–538
Latin-American Democracies	112–346	.8–3.3	31–174
Latin-American Stable Dictatorships	40–331	1.0–10.8	38–428

Means	*Telephones per 1,000 Persons*	*Radios per 1,000 Persons*	*Newspaper Copies per 1,000 Persons*
European and English-Speaking Stable Democracies	205	350	341
European and English-Speaking Unstable Democracies and Dictatorships	58	160	167
Latin-American Democracies and Unstable Dictatorships	25	85	102
Latin-American Stable Dictatorships	10	43	43
Ranges			
European Stable Democracies	43–400	160–995	242–570
European Dictatorships	7–196	42–307	46–390
Latin-American Democracies	12–58	38–148	51–233
Latin-American Stable Dictatorships	1–24	4–154	4–111

B. INDICES OF INDUSTRIALIZATION

Means	*Percentage of Males in Agriculture*	*Per Capita Energy Consumed*
European Stable Democracies	21	3.6
European Dictatorships	41	1.4
Latin-American Democracies	52	.6
Latin-American Stable Dictatorships	67	.25

TABLE 2. (*Cont.*)

Ranges	Percentage of Males in Agriculture	Per Capita Energy Consumed
European Stable Democracies	6–46	1.4–7.8
European Dictatorships	16–60	.27–3.2
Latin-American Democracies	30–63	.30–0.9
Latin-American Stable Dictatorships	46–87	.02–1.27

C. INDICES OF EDUCATION

Means	Percentage Literate	Primary Education Enrollment per 1,000 Persons	Post-Primary Enrollment per 1,000 Persons	Higher Education Enrollment per 1,000 Persons
European Stable Democracies	96	134	44	4.2
European Dictatorships	85	121	22	3.5
Latin-American Democracies	74	101	13	2.0
Latin-American Dictatorships	46	72	8	1.3
Ranges				
European Stable Democracies	95–100	96–179	19–83	1.7–17.83
European Dictatorships	55–98	61–165	8–37	1.6–6.1
Latin-American Democracies	48–87	75–137	7–27	.7–4.6
Latin-American Dictatorships	11–76	11–149	3–24	.2–3.1

D. INDICES OF URBANIZATION

Means	Per Cent in Cities over 20,000	Per Cent in Cities over 100,000	Per Cent in Metropolitan Areas
European Stable Democracies	43	28	38
European Dictatorships	24	16	23
Latin-American Democracies	28	22	26
Latin-American Stable Dictatorships	17	12	15
Ranges			
European Stable Democracies	28–54	17–51	22–56
European Dictatorships	12–44	6–33	7–49
Latin-American Democracies	11–48	13–37	17–44
Latin-American Stable Dictatorships	5–36	4–22	7–26

democratic European countries, there are seventeen persons per motor vehicle compared to 143 for the less democratic. In the less dictatorial Latin-American countries there are ninety-nine persons per motor vehicle versus 274 for the more dictatorial.[2] Income differences for the groups are also sharp, dropping from an average per capita income of $695 for the more democratic countries of Europe to $308

[2] *It must be remembered that these figures are means, compiled from census figures for the vari-* *ous countries. The data vary widely in accuracy, and there is no way of measuring the validity of compound calculated figures such as those presented here. The consistent direction of all these differences, and their . . . magnitude, is the main indication of validity.*

for the less democratic; the corresponding difference for Latin America is from $171 to $119. The ranges are equally consistent, with the lowest per capita income in each group falling in the "less democratic" category, and the highest in the "more democratic."

Industrialization, to which indices of wealth are, of course, clearly related, is measured by the percentage of employed males in agriculture and the per capita commercially produced "energy" being used in the country (measured in terms of tons of coal per person per year). Both of these show equally consistent results. The average percentage of employed males working in agriculture and related occupations was twenty-one in the "more democratic" European countries and forty-one in the "less democratic"; fifty-two in the "less dictatorial" Latin-American countries and sixty-seven in the "more dictatorial." The differences in per capita energy employed are equally large.

The degree of *urbanization* is also related to the existence of democracy.[3] Three different indices of urbanization are available from data compiled by International Urban Research (Berkeley, California): the percentage of the population in communities of twenty thousand and over, the percentage in communities of one hundred thousand and over, and the percentage residing in standard metropolitan areas. On all three of these indices the more democratic countries score higher

than the less democratic for both of the areas under investigation.

Many people have suggested that the higher the *education* level of a nation's population, the better the chances for democracy, and the comparative data available support this proposition. The "more democratic" countries of Europe are almost entirely literate: the lowest has a rate of 96 per cent; while the "less democratic" nations have an average rate of 85 per cent. In Latin America the difference is between an average rate of 74 per cent for the "less dictatorial" countries and 46 per cent for the "more dictatorial."[4] The educational enrollment per thousand total population at three different levels—primary, post-primary, and higher educational—is equally consistently related to the degree of democracy. The tremendous disparity is shown by the extreme cases of Haiti and the United States. Haiti has fewer children (eleven per thousand) attending school in the primary grades than the United States has attending colleges (almost eighteen per thousand).

The relationship between education and democracy is worth more extensive treatment, since an entire philosophy of government has seen increased education as the basic requirement of democracy.[5] As James Bryce wrote, with special reference to South America, "education, if it does not make men good citizens, makes it at least easier for them to become so."[6]

---

3 *Urbanization has often been linked to democracy by political theorists. Harold J. Laski asserted that "organized democracy is the product of urban life," and that it was natural therefore that it should have "made its first effective appearance" in the Greek city-states, limited as was their definition of "citizen." See his article "Democracy" in the* Encyclopaedia of the Social Sciences *(New York: The Macmillan Company, 1937), Vol. V, pp. 76–85. Max Weber held that the city, as a certain type of political community, is a peculiarly Western phenomenon, and traced the emergence of the notion of "citizenship" from social developments closely related to urbanization. For a partial statement of his point of view, see the chapter on "Citizenship" in* General Economic History *(New York: The Free Press of Glencoe, Inc., 1950), pp. 315–38.*

4 *The pattern indicated by a comparison of the averages for each group of countries is sustained by the ranges (the high and low extremes) for each index. Most of the ranges overlap; that is, some countries which are in the "less democratic" category are higher on any given index than some which are "more democratic." It is noteworthy that in both Europe and Latin America, the nations which are lowest on any of the indices presented in the table are also in the "less democratic" category. Conversely, almost all countries which rank at the top of any of the indices are in the "more democratic" class.*

5 *See John Dewey,* Democracy and Education *(New York: The Macmillan Company, 1916).*

6 *James Bryce,* South America: Observations and Impressions *(New York: The Macmillan Company, 1912), p. 546. Bryce considered several classes of conditions in South America which af-*

Education presumably broadens man's outlook, enables him to understand the need for norms of tolerance, restrains him from adhering to extremist doctrines, and increases his capacity to make rational electoral choices.

The evidence on the contribution of education to democracy is even more direct and strong on the level of individual behavior *within* countries than it is in cross-national correlations. Data gathered by public opinion research agencies which have questioned people in different countries about their beliefs on tolerance for the opposition, their attitudes toward ethnic or racial minorities, and their feelings for multiparty as against one-party systems have showed that the most important single factor differentiating those giving democratic responses from the others has been education. The higher one's education, the more likely one is to believe in democratic values and support democratic practices.[7] All the relevant

studies indicate that education is more significant than either income or occupation.

These findings should lead us to anticipate a far higher correlation between national levels of education and political practice than we in fact find. Germany and France have been among the best educated nations of Europe, but this by itself did not stabilize their democracies.[8] It may be, however, that their educational level has served to inhibit other antidemocratic forces.

If we cannot say that a "high" level of education is a *sufficient* condition for democracy, the available evidence suggests that it comes close to being a *necessary* one. In Latin America, where widespread illiteracy still exists, only one of all the nations in which more than half the population is illiterate—Brazil—can be included in the "more democratic" group.

Lebanon, the one member of the Arab League which has maintained democratic institutions since World War II, is also by far the best educated (over 80 per cent literacy). East of the Arab world, only two states, the Philippines and Japan, have since 1945 maintained democratic regimes without the presence of large antidemocratic parties. And these two countries, although lower than most European states in per capita income, are among the world's leaders in educational attainment. The Philippines actually rank second to the United States in the proportion of people attending high schools and uni-

---

fected the chances for democracy, some of which are substantially the same as those presented here. The physical conditions of a country determined the ease of communications between areas, and thus the ease of formation of a "common public opinion." By "racial" conditions Bryce really meant whether there was ethnic homogeneity or not, with the existence of different ethnic or language groups preventing that "homogeneity and solidarity of the community which are almost indispensable conditions to the success of democratic government." Economic and social conditions included economic development, widespread political participation, and literacy. Bryce also detailed the specific historical factors which, over and above these "general" factors, operated in each South American country. See ibid., pp. 527–533 and 580ff. See also Karl Mannheim, Freedom, Power and Democratic Planning (New York: Oxford University Press, 1950).

[7] *See C. H. Smith, "Liberalism and Level of Information," Journal of Educational Psychology, Vol. XXXIX (1948), 65–82; Martin A. Trow, Right Wing Radicalism and Political Intolerance, unpublished Ph.D. thesis, Department of Sociology, Columbia University (1957), p. 17; Samuel A. Stouffer, Communism, Conformity, and Civil Liberties (New York: Doubleday & Company, Inc., 1955); Kotaro Kido and Masataka Suyi, "A Report of Research on Social Stratification and Mobility in Tokyo" (III), Japanese Sociological Review, Vol. IV (1954), 74–100. . . .*

[8] *Dewey has suggested that the character of the educational system will influence its effect on democracy, and this may shed some light on the sources of instability in Germany. The purpose of German education, according to Dewey, writing in 1916, was one of "disciplinary training rather than of personal development." The main aim was to produce "absorption of the aims and meaning of existing institutions," and "thoroughgoing subordination" to them. This point raises issues which cannot be entered into here, but indicates the complex character of the relationship between democracy and closely related factors, such as education. See John Dewey, op. cit., pp. 108–110.*

versities, and Japan has a higher educational level than any European nation.[9]

Although the evidence has been presented separately, all the various aspects of economic development—industrialization, urbanization, wealth, and education—are so closely interrelated as to form one major factor which has the political correlate of democracy.[10] A recent study of the Middle East further substantiates this. In 1951–1952, a survey of Turkey, Lebanon, Egypt, Syria, Jordan, and Iran, conducted by Daniel Lerner and the Bureau of Applied Social Research, found a close connection between urbanization, literacy, voting rates, media consumption and production, and education.[11] . . .

In the Middle East, Turkey and Lebanon score higher on most of these indices than do the other four countries analyzed, and Daniel Lerner, in reporting on the study, points out that the "great postwar events in Egypt, Syria, Jordan, and Iran have been the violent struggles for the control of power—struggles notably absent in Turkey and Lebanon [until very

recently] where the control of power has been decided by elections."[12]

Lerner further points out the effect of disproportionate development, in one area or another, for overall stability, and the need for coordinated changes in all of these variables. Comparing urbanization and literacy in Egypt and Turkey, he concludes that although Egypt is far more urbanized than Turkey, it is not really "modernized," and does not even have an adequate base for modernization, because literacy has not kept pace. In Turkey, all of the several indices of modernization have kept pace with each other, with rising voting participation (36 per cent in 1950), balanced by rising literacy, urbanization, etc. In Egypt, the cities are full of "homeless illiterates," who provide a ready audience for political mobilization in support of extremist ideologies. On Lerner's scale, Egypt should be twice as literate as Turkey, since it is twice as urbanized. The fact that it is only half as literate explains, for Lerner, the "imbalances" which "tend to become circular and to accelerate social disorganization," political as well as economic.[13]

Lerner introduces one important theoretical addition—the suggestion that these key variables in the modernization process may be viewed as historical phases, with

---

[9] *Ceylon, which shares the distinction with the Philippines and Japan of being the only democratic countries in South and Far East Asia in which the Communists are unimportant electorally, also shares with them the distinction of being the only countries in this area in which a majority of the population is literate. It should be noted, however, that Ceylon does have a fairly large Trotskyist party, now the official opposition, and while its educational level is high for Asia, it is much lower than either Japan or the Philippines.*

[10] *This statement is a "statistical" statement, which necessarily means that there will be many exceptions to the correlation. Thus we know that poorer people are more likely to vote for the Democratic or Labor parties in the United States and England. The fact that a large minority of the lower strata vote for the more conservative party in these countries does not challenge the proposition that stratification position is a main determinant of party choice.*

[11] *The study is reported in Daniel Lerner, The Passing of Traditional Society (New York: The Free Press of Glencoe, Inc., 1958). These correlations are derived from census data; the main sections of the survey dealt with reactions to and opinions about the mass media, with inferences as to the personality types appropriate to modern and to traditional society.*

[12] *Ibid., pp. 84–85.*
[13] *Ibid., pp. 87–89. Other theories of underdeveloped areas have also stressed the circular character of the forces sustaining a given level of economic and social development, and in a sense this paper may be regarded as an effort to extend the analysis of the complex of institutions constituting a "modernized" society to the political sphere. Leo Schnore's . . . monograph, Economic Development and Urbanization: An Ecological Approach, relates technological, demographic, and organizational (including literacy and per capita income) variables as an interdependent complex. Harvey Leibenstein's recent volume, Economic Backwardness and Economic Growth (New York: John Wiley & Sons, Inc., 1957), views "underdevelopment" within the framework of a "quasi-equilibrium" economic theory, as a complex of associated and mutually supportive aspects of a society, and includes cultural and political characteristics—illiteracy, the lack of a middle class, a crude communications system—as part of the complex. (See pp. 39–41.)*

democracy part of later developments, the "crowning institution of the participant society" (one of his terms for a modern industrial society). His view on the relations between these variables, seen as stages, is worth quoting at some length:

> The secular evolution of a participant society appears to involve a regular sequence of three phases. Urbanization comes first, for cities alone have developed the complex of skills and resources which characterize the modern industrial economy. Within this urban matrix develop both of the attributes which distinguish the next two phases—literacy and media growth. There is a close reciprocal relationship between these, for the literate develop the media which in turn spread literacy. But literacy performs the key function in the second phase. The capacity to read, at first acquired by relatively few people, equips them to perform the varied tasks required in the modernizing society. Not until the third phase, when the elaborate technology of industrial development is fairly well advanced, does a society begin to produce newspapers, radio networks, and motion pictures on a massive scale. This, in turn, accelerates the spread of literacy. Out of this interaction develop those institutions of participation (e.g., voting) which we find in all advanced modern societies.[14]

14 *Lerner, op. cit., p. 60. Lerner also focuses upon certain personality requirements of a "modern" society which may also be related to the person-*

Lerner's thesis, that these elements of modernization are functionally interdependent, is by no means established by his data. But . . . [it] . . . offers an opportunity for research along these lines. Deviant cases, such as Egypt, where "lagging" literacy is associated with serious strains and potential upheaval, may also be found in Europe and Latin America, and their analysis . . . will further clarify the basic dynamics of modernization and the problem of social stability in the midst of institutional change.

---

ality requirements of democracy. According to him, the physical and social mobility of modern society requires a mobile personality, capable of adaption to rapid change. Development of a "mobile sensibility so adaptive to change that rearrangement of the self-system is its distinctive mode" has been the work of the twentieth century. Its main feature is empathy, *denoting the "general capacity to see oneself in the other fellow's situation, whether favorably or unfavorably." (See pp. 49ff.)*

Whether this psychological characteristic results in a predisposition toward democracy (implying a willingness to accept the viewpoint of others) or is rather associated with the antidemocratic tendencies of a "mass society" type of personality (implying the lack of any solid personal values rooted in rewarding participation) is an open question. Possibly empathy (a more or less "cosmopolitan" outlook) is a general personality characteristic of modern societies, with other special conditions determining whether or not it has the social consequence of tolerance and democratic attitudes, or rootlessness and anomie.

B. Quantification and Statistical Analysis

Social and Economic Factors in Negro Voter Registration in the South

Donald R. Matthews and James W. Prothro

The vote is widely considered the southern Negro's most important weapon in his struggle for full citizenship and social and economic equality. It is argued that "political rights pave the way to all others."[1]

1 The New York Times (*January 7, 1962*).

Donald R. Matthews and James W. Prothro, "Social and Economic Factors in Negro Voter Registration in the South," *American Political Science Review,* Vol. LVII (March, 1963), 24–44. Reprinted by permission. (Extensive technical and bibliographical footnotes have been omitted.)

Once Negroes in the South vote in substantial numbers, white politicians will prove responsive to the desires of the Negro community. Also, federal action on voting will be met with less resistance from the white South—and southerners in Congress—than action involving schools, jobs, or housing.

Such, at least, seems to have been the reasoning behind the Civil Rights Acts of 1957 and 1960, both of which deal primarily with the right to vote.[2] Attorney General Robert F. Kennedy and his predecessor, Herbert Brownell, are both reported to believe that the vote provides the southern Negro with his most effective means of advancing toward equality, and recent actions of the Justice Department seem to reflect this view. Many Negro leaders share this belief in the overriding importance of the vote. Hundreds of Negro registration drives have been held in southern cities and counties since 1957. Martin Luther King, usually considered an advocate of nonviolent direct action, [has] remarked that the most significant step Negroes can take is in the "direction of the voting booths." The National Association for the Advancement of Colored People, historically identified with courtroom attacks on segregation, is now enthusiastically committed to a "battle of the ballots." In March, 1962, the Southern Regional Council announced receipt of foundation grants of $325,000 to initiate a major program to increase Negro voter registration in the South. The Congress of Racial Equality, the NAACP, the National Urban League, the Southern Christian Leadership Conference, and the Student Nonviolent Coordinating Committee are among the organizations now participating in the actual registration drives.

While the great importance of the vote to Negroes in the South can hardly be denied, some careful observers are skepti-

cal about the extent to which registration drives can add to the number of Negroes who are already registered. Southern Negroes overwhelmingly possess low social status, relatively small incomes, and limited education received in inferior schools. These attributes are associated with low voter turnout among all populations. The low voting rates of Negroes in the South are, to perhaps a large extent, a result of these factors more than a consequence of *direct political* discrimination by the white community. Moreover, the low status, income, and education of southern whites foster racial prejudice. Thus poverty and ignorance may have a double-barreled effect on Negro political participation by decreasing the Negroes' desire and ability to participate effectively while increasing white resistance to their doing so. Negro voting in the South is not, according to this line of argument, easily increased by political or legal means. A large, active, and effective Negro electorate in the South may have to await substantial social and economic change.

Despite the current interest in the political participation of southern Negroes, the literature of political science tells us little about the factors which facilitate or impede it. A theoretical concern as old as political science—the relative importance of socioeconomic and political factors in determining political behavior—is raised when one addresses this problem. Can registration drives, legal pressures on the region's voter registrars, abolition of poll taxes, revision of literacy tests, and similar legal and political reforms have a significant impact on Negro registration in the former confederate states? Or do these efforts deal merely with "superstructure," while the social and economic realities of the region will continue for generations to frustrate achievement of Negro parity at the ballot box? Social scientists owe such a heavy, if largely unacknowledged, debt to Karl Marx that most would probably assume the second alternative to be more valid. But the tradition of James Madison, recognizing the importance of

---

[2] *Note that this was written before the Civil Rights Act of 1964 and the Voting Rights Act of 1965 and before the accession of Nicholas deB. Katzenbach to the post of Attorney General.*—ED. NOTE.

social and economic factors, but also emphasizing the significance of "auxiliary" governmental arrangements, offers theoretical support for the former possibility.

A single article cannot hope to answer such a broad question, but we can attack part of it. In this article we offer a detailed analysis of the relationships between variations in rates of Negro voter registration in southern counties and the social and economic characteristics of those counties. While we shall not be directly concerned with political variables, the analysis has an obvious relevance for their importance. The more successful the explanation of the problem with socioeconomic variables, the less imperative the demand to examine political and legal factors. Alternatively, if we can account for only a small part of the variance with socioeconomic factors, the stronger the case for abandoning socioeconomic determinism and adding political and legal variables to the analysis.

The Data and the Approach

While the literature offers no comprehensive effort to account for variations in Negro voter registration in the South, previous studies of southern politics suggest a number of specific influences. Drawing upon this literature, we collected data on twenty social and economic characteristics of southern counties (counting Virginia's independent cities as counties). Some of these items, such as per cent of population Negro or per cent of population urban, could be taken directly from the U.S. Census. Others, such as per cent of nonwhite labor force in white-collar occupations or white and nonwhite median income, were derived from census figures but required calculations of varying degrees of complexity for each county. Still other items, such as per cent of population belonging to a church or the number of Negro colleges in each county, came from noncensus sources. Since our focus is on Negro registration, 108 counties with populations containing less than 1 per

cent Negroes were excluded from the analysis. All other counties for which 1958 registration data were available by race were included. This selection procedure gave us a total of 997 counties for the analysis of Negro registration and 822 for the consideration of white registration.

While this represents the most massive collection of data ever brought to bear upon the problem of political participation by southern Negroes, it is subject to several limitations.

To begin with, the measure of the independent variable is two steps removed from a direct measure of the voting turnout of individuals. Registration rather than voting figures had to be employed because they are available by race, whereas the number of Negroes actually voting is not known. This tends to exaggerate the size of the active Negro electorate since, for a number of reasons, some registered Negroes seldom if ever exercise their franchise. Moreover, voting lists in the rural areas are often out of date, containing the names of many bona fide residents of New York, Detroit, and Los Angeles, to say nothing of local graveyards. In some states, the payment of a poll tax is the nearest equivalent [to] voter registration, and numerous exemptions from the tax make lists of poll tax payers not strictly comparable to the enfranchised population. Finally, statewide statistics on voter registration (or poll tax payment) by race are collected only in Arkansas, Florida, Georgia, Louisiana, South Carolina and Virginia. In the remaining states, the number of registered Negro voters must be obtained from estimates made by county registrars, newsmen, politicians, and the like. Nonetheless, when analyzed with caution, the sometimes crude data on Negro voter registration can throw considerable light on Negro voting in the South.

The measure of the dependent variable is further removed from the actual behavior of individuals in that it consists of the percentage of all voting age Negroes who are registered to vote in each southern county. This employment of *areal* rather than *individual* analysis narrows the question we can examine. Rather than an unqualified examination of the relationship of social and economic characteristics to Negro registration, the effort must be understood to focus on the relationship of social and economic characteristics of given areas (counties) to variations in Negro registration among those areas. Accordingly, the data furnish no evidence of the sort afforded by opinion surveys directly linking political behavior to individual attributes. But they do permit conclusions linking varying registration rates to county attributes. Compensation for the loss of the former type of evidence is found in the acquisition of the latter type, which cannot be secured from surveys because they are conducted in a small number of counties. Our approach maximizes what we can say about counties, then, at the same time that it minimizes what we can say about individuals.

Another limitation stems from the fact that our measures capture an essentially static picture of both the characteristics of southern counties and of the relationship of their characteristics to variations in Negro registration. If data were available on Negro registration, at the county level, for earlier points in time, the analysis could be geared principally to rates of change. Only since the creation of the Civil Rights Commission, however, have adequate county registration data become available. We are necessarily limited, therefore, to an analysis based on *areal* rather than *temporal* variation.

A final limitation lies in the statistical approach employed here, which is that of correlation and regression analysis.[3] The coefficient of correlation (r) is a measure of the association between different variables when each variable is expressed as a series of measures of a quantitative characteristic. The value of the measure varies from

0 (no association between independent and dependent variables) to 1.0 (one variable perfectly predicts the other). A positive correlation indicates that as one variable increases, the other also increases; a negative correlation indicates an inverse relationship—as one variable increases, the other decreases. We shall first consider simple correlations, describing the association between per cent of Negroes registered and each of the social and economic characteristics of southern counties. In order to make a better estimate of the independence of these relationships, we shall also present partial correlations, which measure the remaining association between two variables when the contribution of a third variable has been taken into account. Finally, we shall employ multiple correlation (R) in order to determine the strength of association between all our independent variables and Negro registration.

While these measures are efficient devices for determining the strength and direction of association between the variables with which we are concerned, a caveat is in order. Correlations do not reflect the *absolute level* of the variables. Thus a given amount and regularity of change in Negro registration will produce the same correlation whether the actual level of Negro registration is high or low. Only for the more important variables will we look beneath the correlations to examine the level of Negro registration.

In the analysis which follows, we shall first consider the development of Negro registration and compare the distribution of white and Negro registration rates. Then we shall examine the correlations between a battery of social and economic variables and Negro voter registration in order to determine the extent to which the former are predictive of the latter for the South as a whole. The same social and economic factors will be correlated with the registration rate of whites to ascertain the extent to which the factors are related to voter registration in general, rather than to Negro registration alone. Finally,

3 *For a good discussion of correlation analysis, see* M. J. Hagood *and* D. O. Price, Statistics for Sociologists (*New York: Holt, Rinehart & Winston, Inc., 1952*), Chaps. 23 and 25.

the multiple correlation between all the social and economic variables and Negro voter registration will be presented, and conclusions and implications will be drawn from the analysis.

Negro Voter Registration: An Overview

Immediately after *Smith* v. *Allwright* declared the white primary unconstitutional in 1944, the number and proportion of Negro adults registered to vote in the southern states increased with startling speed (Table 1). Before this historic decision, about 250,000 Negroes (5 per cent of the adult nonwhite population) were thought to be registered voters. Three years after the white primary case, both the number and proportion of Negro registered voters had doubled. By 1952, about 20 per cent of the Negro adults were registered to vote. Since then, however, the rate of increase has been less impressive. In 1956, the authoritative Southern Regional Council estimated that about 25 per cent of the Negro adults were registered. Four years, two Civil Rights Acts, and innumerable local regis-

TABLE 1. ESTIMATED NUMBER AND PER CENT OF VOTING AGE NEGROES REGISTERED TO VOTE IN ELEVEN SOUTHERN STATES, 1940–1960

Year	Estimated Number of Negro Registered Voters	Per Cent of Voting Age Negroes Registered As Voters
1940	250,000	5%
1947	595,000	12
1952	1,008,614	20
1956	1,238,038	25
1958	1,266,488	25
1960	1,414,052	28

Sources: Derived from U.S. Census data on nonwhite population and Negro registration estimates in G. Myrdal, An American Dilemma *(New York: Harper & Row, Publishers, Inc., 1944), p. 488; M. Price,* The Negro Voter in the South *(Atlanta, Georgia: Southern Regional Council, 1957), p. 5; Southern Regional Council, "The Negro Voter in the South—1958," Special Report (mimeographed), p. 3; U.S. Commission on Civil Rights, 1959 Report and 1961 Report, Vol. I, "Voting."*

tration drives later, the proportion of Negro adults who were registered had risen to only 28 per cent. Of course the fact that Negroes held their own during this period is a significant accomplishment when one considers such factors as heavy outmigration, increased racial tensions stemming from the school desegregation crisis, the adoption of new voter restrictions in some states, and the stricter application of old requirements in other areas.

Figure 1 shows the 1958 distribution of southern counties according to level of voter registration for Negroes and whites. The point most dramatically demonstrated by the figure is that Negro registration is still much lower than white registration. In 38 per cent of the counties less than 20 per cent of the adult Negroes are registered, whereas less than 1 per cent of the counties have so few whites registered. Indeed, the most common (modal) situation for Negroes is a registration below 10 per cent of the potential; the most common situation for whites is a registration in excess of 90 per cent. Nevertheless, the range of Negro registration in the South is sizable; in a significant minority of cases, the level of Negro registration compares favorably with that of white southerners.

Social and Economic Correlates of Negro Registration

What accounts for the wide variation in Negro voter registration rates? The simple correlations between the per cent of the voting age Negroes registered to vote and twenty social and economic characteristics of southern counties are presented in the first column of Table 2.

Negro Concentration. In most political settings, the concentration of an ethnic or occupational group in a geographical area provides reinforcement of common values sufficient to produce more active political participation. But southern Negroes are in a peculiarly subordinate position. And the larger the proportion of Negroes in an area, the more in-

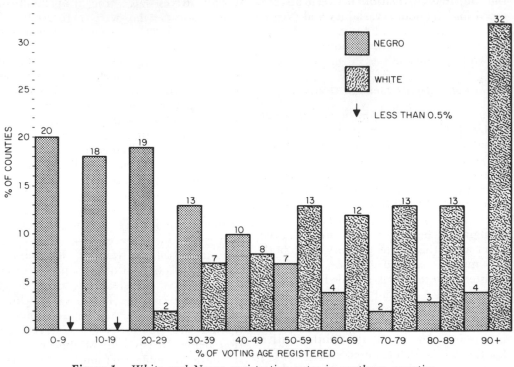

Figure 1.   *White and Negro registration rates in southern counties.*

tense the vague fears of Negro domination that seem to beset southern whites. Thus in virtually every study of southern politics the proportion of Negroes in the population has emerged as a primary explanatory variable.

It is not surprising, therefore, that the per cent of Negroes in the county population in 1950 is more strongly associated with the county's rate of Negro registration than any other social and economic attribute on which we have data. The negative value of the simple correlation (—.46) verifies the expectation that smaller proportions of Negroes register in those counties where a large percentage of the population is Negro. This does not mean, however, that the decline in Negro registration associated with increasing Negro concentration occurs at a constant rate. If the relationship between these two variables is examined over the entire range of southern counties, we see that increases in the proportion Negro from 1 per cent to about 30 per cent are not

accompanied by general and substantial declines in Negro registration rates (Figure 2). As the proportion Negro increases

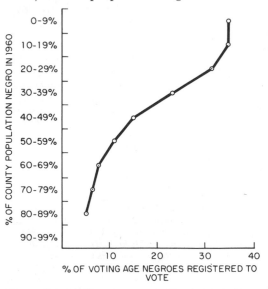

Figure 2.   *Median per cent of voting-age Negroes registered to vote by per cent of county population Negro in 1950: 11 southern states.*

TABLE 2. CORRELATIONS BETWEEN COUNTY SOCIAL AND ECONOMIC CHARACTERISTICS AND
PER CENT OF VOTING AGE NEGROES REGISTERED TO VOTE, BY COUNTY,
IN ELEVEN SOUTHERN STATES

County Characteristics	Simple Correlations (r)	Partial Correlations, Controlling for Per Cent Negro, 1950
Per cent of nonwhite labor force in white-collar occupations	+ .23	+ .15
Nonwhite median school years completed	+ .22	+ .01
Nonwhite median income	+ .19	+ .02
Per cent of total church membership, Roman Catholic	+ .15	+ .10
Per cent increase in population, 1940–1950	+ .08	.00
Per cent of labor force in manufacturing	+ .08	+ .09
White median income	+ .08	− .03
Per cent of population urban	+ .07	− .02
Percentage point difference in per cent population Negro, 1900–1950	+ .04	− .02
Per cent of total church membership, Jewish	+ .004	+ .01
Difference in white-nonwhite median school years completed	− .02	− .02
Difference in white-nonwhite median income	− .02	− .05
Number of Negro colleges in county	− .05	+ .01
Per cent of total church membership, Baptist	− .10	− .07
Per cent of population belonging to a church	− .17	+ .01
Per cent of labor force in agriculture	− .20	− .07
White median school years completed	− .26	− .15
Per cent of farms operated by tenants	− .32	− .13
Per cent of population Negro in 1900	− .41	− .01
Per cent of population Negro in 1950	− .46	—

Note: *No tests of significance are reported in this paper since the correlations are based upon a complete enumeration rather than a sample.*

beyond 30 per cent, however, Negro registration rates begin to decline very sharply until they approach zero at about 60 per cent Negro and above. There would seem to be a critical point, at about 30 per cent Negro, where white hostility to Negro political participation becomes severe.

One reason Negro concentration is such a powerful explanatory factor in analyzing southern politics may be that it is related to so many other social and economic characteristics of the region's counties. The simple correlation between per cent Negro in 1950 and per cent of farms operated by tenants is +.49; the correlation with nonwhite median income is −.40; with nonwhite school years completed, −.47; with per cent of the labor force in agriculture, +.30; with per cent of the total population belonging to a church, +.38. Such characteristics as these are in turn related to variation in rates of Negro voter registration. It is possible that these related factors rather than Negro concentration, viewed largely as an index of white attitudes, account for the −.46 correlation between per cent Negro and per cent registered to vote.

The partial correlations between Negro registration and Negro concentration, controlling separately for the contribution of all other county characteristics, reveals that this is not the case: Negro registration in southern counties goes down as the proportion of Negroes goes up, regardless of the other characteristics of the counties. Only one county characteristic is so closely related to both Negro registration in 1958 and Negro concentration in 1950 that the strength of their association drops when its contribution is taken into account—and this characteristic is an earlier measurement of the same independent variable. Controlling for per cent of Negroes in the population in 1900 reduces the correlation between 1950 Negro concentration and registration to —.21. Even with this control, the independent tendency of Negro registration to decrease in counties currently containing more Negroes is not eliminated, though it is reduced substantially.

Let us be clear on what a partial correlation does. It is designed to give us, as indicated above, the strength of association between two variables that remains after the contribution of a relevant third variable is taken into account. But when the third variable is introduced into the equation, so are all of the additional hidden variables that are associated with it. The magnitude of the partial correlation will accordingly be reduced not only by any contribution of the third variable to the association between the two original variables, but also by any contribution of factors that are associated with the third variable. This means that, when we attempt to examine the contribution of a third variable by computing partial correlations, we can be certain about its contribution only when the results are negative. That is, if the partial correlation is not much smaller than the simple correlation, we can be sure that the third variable is not responsible for the magnitude of the simple correlation. When the partial correlation is substantially smaller, however, we cannot conclude that the third variable *alone* is responsible for the magnitude of the simple correlation. It hap-

pens in the present instance that almost all of the county characteristics are similarly associated with Negro concentration in both 1900 and 1950. As a result, virtually all of the factors that contribute slightly to the correlation of Negro registration with 1950 Negro concentration are added to the contribution that 1900 Negro concentration makes to the correlation. The result is that Negro concentration in 1900 *and the hidden factors related to it* account for about half of the magnitude of the association between 1950 Negro concentration and Negro registration.

Before we conclude that Negro concentration at the turn of the century is as important as mid-century Negro concentration for current variations in Negro registration, we need to consider both the nature of the two measures and the detailed relationships of the variables. The two measures are of the same county characteristic, differing only in the point in time from which they were taken. And the characteristic they reflect cannot reasonably be thought to act directly on Negro registration. Today's lower rates of Negro registration in counties where Negroes constitute a larger portion of the population certainly do not stem from any tendency of Negroes to crowd one another out of registration queues! Even more evident is the fact that the percentage of Negroes in a county's population over half a century ago cannot have a direct effect on current rates of Negro registration. Both measures appear to be indices of county characteristics (most importantly, white practices and attitudes on racial questions) that are of direct consequence for Negro registration.

The 1900 measure was included in the analysis on the assumption that practices and attitudes produced by heavy Negro population may persist long after the Negroes have died or left for more attractive environs. Earlier research has suggested that Negro concentration around the turn of the century—when southern political practice was crystallizing in its strongly anti-Negro pattern—may be as important as current Negro concentration for rates of Negro political participation. Since the proportions of Negroes in different southern counties have not decreased at uniform rates (and have even increased in some counties), the measures at the two points in time afford an opportunity to test this hypothesis. And it seems to be supported by the fact that Negro concentration in 1900 is almost as highly (and negatively) correlated with Negro registration (—.41) as is Negro concentration a half-century later. This large simple correlation, added to the decrease in the correlation between 1950 Negro concentration and registration when 1900 Negro concentration is controlled, is impressive evidence of the stability of southern racial practices. The virtual absence of correlation (+.04) between Negro registration and the percentage point difference in the proportion of population Negro between 1900 and 1950 seems to point to the same conclusion.

It would be a mistake, however, to conclude either that 1900 Negro concentration is as important as 1950 Negro concentration for Negro registration, or that decreases in Negro concentration are not associated with increasing Negro voter registration. When we reverse the partialling process, and control for Negro concentration in 1950, the correlation between current Negro registration and 1900 Negro concentration disappears (it becomes —.01). The 1900 simple correlation accordingly seems to come from stable racial practices that in turn reflect a large measure of stability in Negro concentration and related county characteristics. The 1900 Negro concentration in itself has no autonomous relationship to present rates of Negro registration.

Moreover, decreases in Negro concentration are not as inconsequential as they would appear from the small simple correlation obtained from percentage point decreases. The lack of correlation seems to be an artifact of our crude measure. The largest percentage *point* decreases in

Negro population have occurred in counties with very high Negro proportions in 1900, and most of these counties still have heavy concentrations of Negro population. When one looks at the relationship between registration and decreases in Negro concentration, holding constant the proportion of the population Negro in 1900, several heretofore hidden relationships emerge (Figure 3). 1. In counties with heavy (over 70 per cent) Negro concentrations in 1900, decreases in the proportion Negro seem to make little difference—their Negro concentration was still relatively high in 1950 and the proportion of Negroes registered is negligible. 2. In counties with relatively few (less than 30 per cent) Negroes in 1900, rates of Negro registration tend to be high whether a decline in the proportion Negro was experienced or not. A decline in Negro concentration in these counties, however, is associated with a somewhat higher rate of Negro registration than in those counties where the division of the two races remained approximately the same between 1900 and 1950. 3. In counties with moderate (30 to 70 per cent) Negro concentrations in 1900, a decline in Negro concentration is clearly related to higher Negro voter registration. Moreover, the larger the decrease in the Negro population percentage, the higher the registration. The average county in this moderate group with a 30 percentage point decrease in Negro proportions has a voter registration rate double or triple that of the average county which did not experience significant change in the numerical balance between colored and white inhabitants.

The proportion of the county population which is Negro is the single most important social and economic factor for explaining its rate of Negro voter registration. The —.46 correlation accounts for about 20 per cent (r^2) of the variation in Negro registration rates, an unusually high explanatory power for any variable in the complex world of political and social relationships. But it leaves room for

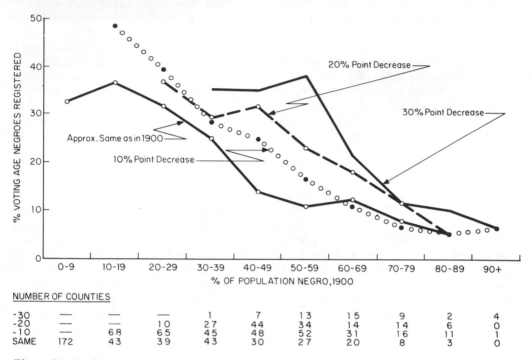

NUMBER OF COUNTIES

	0-9	10-19	20-29	30-39	40-49	50-59	60-69	70-79	80-89	90+
-30	—	—	—	1	7	13	15	9	2	4
-20	—	—	10	27	44	34	14	14	6	0
-10	—	68	65	45	48	52	31	16	11	1
SAME	172	43	39	43	30	27	20	8	3	0

Figure 3. *Median per cent of voting-age Negroes registered to vote, by county Negro concentration in 1900 and per cent point change since 1900.*

considerable fluctuation in registration rates unrelated to the per cent of Negroes in the population. This "unexplained" fluctuation may be the result of random and idiosyncratic factors, of political variables which have been excluded from this analysis, or the result of the operation of other social and economic factors. In the remainder of this paper we shall examine this last possibility.

Negro Attributes.   The higher the educational level, occupation, or income of a person, the more likely he is to participate actively in politics: these are among the more strongly supported generalizations in contemporary research on political participation. Moreover, these three factors are probably a pretty good index of the size of the county's Negro middle class. It is widely believed by students of Negro politics that the low rate of voter registration by southern Negroes is partly the result of a lack of leadership. Only

when there is a pool of educated and skillful leaders whose means of livelihood is not controlled by whites can sufficient leadership and political organization develop to ensure a relatively high rate of Negro registration in the South.

Our data support both lines of argument. The three largest positive correlations with Negro voter registration are per cent of the nonwhite labor force in white-collar occupations (+.23), the median number of school years completed by nonwhites (+.22), and the median income of nonwhites (+.19). These are simple correlations, however, and fairly small ones at that. It is quite possible that they are largely, if not entirely, the result of some third factor associated both with Negro registration rates and with Negro education, occupation, and income. The large negative correlation of Negro concentration with Negro registration suggests that the percentage of the population

Negro in 1950 is the most likely prospect as a key third variable. This expectation is heightened by the fact that it is also substantially correlated with Negro school years completed (—.47), income (—.40), and white-collar workers (—.23). When controls are introduced for per cent of Negroes in the population (see the second column of Table 2), the positive association of Negro registration with both income and education is reduced almost to the vanishing point. Thus Negro income and education levels are intervening variables, which helps to explain why more Negroes are registered in counties with fewer Negroes in their population. But in themselves, they have no independent association with Negro registration; in the few counties with large Negro concentrations but high Negro income and education, no more Negroes are registered than in similar counties with lower Negro income and education.

The explanatory power of our occupational measure—the per cent of the non-white labor force in white collar occupations—is also reduced when per cent of Negroes is taken into account, but to a much lesser degree. It be comes +.15. While this is a small partial correlation, it is one of the higher partials obtained in this study while controlling for the important factor of Negro concentration. The proportion of the employed Negroes in white-collar jobs does, therefore, have a small but discernible independent association with Negro voter registration.

Moreover, small increases in the proportion of Negro white-collar workers are associated with large increases in Negro voter registration (Figure 4), and these higher rates cannot be simply attributed to the registration of the white-collar workers themselves. A very small increase in the size of the Negro middle class seems to result in a substantial increase in the pool of qualified potential leaders. Middle-class Negroes are far more likely to register, and they in turn appear to stimulate working-class Negroes to follow their example. The average southern

county with 1 per cent of its nonwhite labor force in white-collar jobs has only 4 per cent of its voting age Negroes registered to vote; at 5 per cent white collar, 15 per cent of the Negroes are registered, and so on, each percentage point increase in white-collar occupation being associated with a 3 to 4 percentage point increase in voter registration. This trend continues until 12 per cent of the non-whites are in white-collar jobs and 42 per cent of the potential Negro electorate is registered. After this point, additional increases in the proportion of Negroes in white-collar jobs are no longer associated with increases in voter registration; indeed, voter registration actually declines as per cent white collar increases. Perhaps when the Negro middle class becomes fairly large, it tends to become more isolated from other Negroes, more preoccupied with the middle-class round of life, less identified with the black masses. A sharpening of class cleavages within the Negro community may lead to some loss of political effectiveness. Even so, this decline in effectiveness is not enough to wipe out the added increment from jobs to registered votes; it merely declines from three or four votes for every white-collar job to about two.

Despite the independent association of Negro white-collar employment with voter registration, the correlations between Negro registration and Negro education, income, and occupation are far smaller than many of the correlations between Negro registration and the characteristics of the white-dominated community. The level of Negro voter registration in southern counties is far less a matter of the attributes of the Negro population than of the characteristics of the white population and of the total community. The rest of our correlations, therefore, are with community and white characteristics rather than with Negro attributes.

The Agrarian Economy. It is widely believed that the South's relatively poor agricultural economy contributes to the low levels of Negro political participation

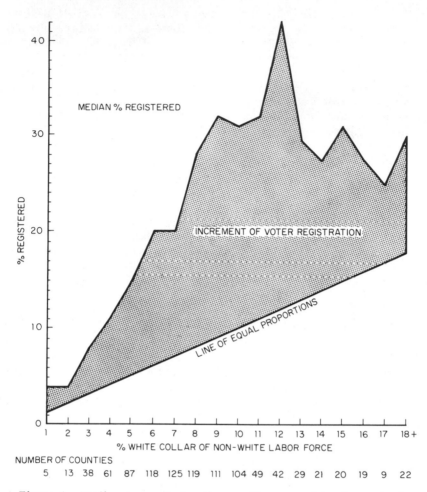

Figure 4. *Median per cent of voting-age Negroes registered to vote, by per cent of nonwhite labor force in white-collar occupations.*

in the region. People living in poverty are unlikely candidates for active citizenship anywhere. The Negroes' economic dependence upon local whites in the rural South serves as a potent inhibition to those few who are not otherwise discouraged from voting. Rural whites are both more hostile to Negro voting and in a better position to do something about it than their urban kin.

Our correlations tend to support this line of reasoning. Two measures included in the analysis reflect the degree to which a county has an agrarian economy—the per cent of labor force in agricultural employment and the per cent of farms

operated by tenants. The negative relationship of both these attributes to Negro voter registration (—.20 and —.32, respectively) indicates that Negro registration is lower in the old-style agrarian counties. But the region's Negro population is still primarily rural: the simple correlation between per cent in agriculture and per cent Negro is +.30; between farm tenancy and Negro concentration, +.49. Are these two characteristics of the counties still associated with low Negro voter registration when Negro concentration is controlled? The partial correlation between farm tenancy and Negro registration is —.13 when Negro concentration is controlled;

between per cent in agriculture and registration it is reduced even further, to —.07. There is, therefore, some tendency for Negro voter registration to decline as agricultural employment and farm tenancy increase, which holds true even when differences in Negro concentration from one county to the next are taken into account. Nonetheless, it is a far less important factor than Negro concentration and is no more important than the size of the Negro middle class as a factor explaining Negro participation and nonparticipation.

Urbanization and Industrialization. If the South's agrarian economy tends to discourage Negro registration and voting, then industrialization and urbanization should facilitate them. The urban-industrial life is more rational, impersonal, and less tradition-bound; both Negroes and whites enjoy more wealth and education; the Negroes benefit from a concentration of potential leaders and politically relevant organizations in the cities. The urban ghetto may provide social reinforcement to individual motivations for political action. Many other equally plausible reasons might be suggested why urbanization and industrialization should foster Negro registration. Our southwide correlations, however, cast serious doubt upon the entire line of reasoning.

The simple correlation between the per cent of the county population living in urban areas and Negro registration is a mere +.07; between per cent of the labor force in manufacturing and Negro registration the correlation is +.08. When partial correlations are figured, controlling for Negro concentration, the association between urbanization and Negro registration completely disappears, a fact which suggests that the initial +.07 simple correlation may be largely the result of the low proportion of the urban population which is Negro and associated factors. The partial correlation between per cent in manufacturing and Negro registration goes up slightly to +.09 when controls for Negro concentration are added. Partial correlations figured after controlling for many other social and economic variables do not significantly increase either correlation.

What accounts for these surprising findings? One possible explanation is the imperfections of the statistical measures we have employed. The 1950 census definition of "urban," for example, includes all places of two thousand five hundred plus the densely settled fringe around cities of fifty thousand or more. Many "urban" places in the South are therefore exceedingly small. From the potential Negro voter's point of view, it may make little difference whether he lives in a town of five thousand or in the open country, but one place is classified as "urban" and the other as "rural." Moreover, a county with a relatively small population concentrated in two or three small towns may possess a higher "urban" percentage than a very large county with a medium-sized city in it. A more meaningful classification of counties along an urban-rural dimension might possibly lead to different results.

It seems plausible to assume, however, that if urbanization does facilitate Negro

TABLE 3. MEDIAN PER CENT OF VOTING AGE NEGROES REGISTERED TO VOTE IN COUNTIES WITHIN STANDARD METROPOLITAN AREAS AND ALL OTHER COUNTIES, BY LEVEL OF NEGRO CONCENTRATION

Per Cent Negro in Pop. 1950	Counties in SMA's of Over 200,000 Pop.	Counties in SMA's of Less Than 200,000 Pop.	Counties Not in SMA's
%	%	%	%
0–9	25.0 (6)	28.8 (11)	37.8 (236)
10–19	45.0 (11)	30.0 (12)	35.7 (133)
20–29	30.0 (6)	35.0 (6)	32.2 (153)
30–39	24.0 (6)	23.8 (7)	23.8 (142)
40–49	—	15.0 (5)	15.9 (110)
50–59	—	—	12.0 (78)
60–69	—	—	8.1 (50)
70–79	—	—	5.8 (22)
80–89	—	—	5.0 (4)
Total Counties	(29)	(41)	(928)

voter registration, the effect should be particularly clear in the region's largest urban complexes. If the Negro registration rates of the seventy counties contained in the South's Standard Metropolitan Areas[4] are compared with registration rates for nonmetropolitan counties (Figure 5), we note that the "metropolitan"

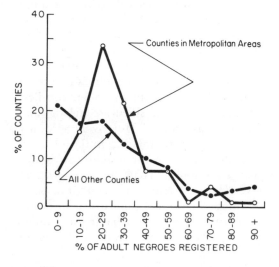

% OF COUNTIES

Counties in Metropolitan Areas

All Other Counties

% OF ADULT NEGROES REGISTERED

0-9 10-19 20-29 30-39 40-49 50-59 60-69 70-79 80-89 90 +

Figure 5. *Median per cent of voting-age Negroes registered to vote in metropolitan and other areas.*

counties are far more likely to have from 20 to 40 per cent of their voting age Negroes registered than the other counties. Moreover, there is a tendency for counties in larger metropolitan areas to have slightly higher registration rates than counties in less populous SMA's. However, the metropolitan counties have smaller concentrations of Negroes than the rural and small town counties. Do these relationships hold true when comparisons are made between metropolitan and nonmetropolitan counties with approximately the same proportion of Ne-

4 *The Bureau of the Census defines Standard Metropolitan Areas as a county or group of contiguous counties which contains at least one city of fifty thousand inhabitants or more. The contiguous counties must be socially and economically integrated with the central city to be included in the SMA.*

groes within their boundaries? Table 3 indicates that the answer is "no": there is no meaningful difference in the rate of Negro registration between metropolitan and nonmetropolitan counties when Negro concentration is controlled. Thus neither "urbanism" nor "metropolitanism," as crudely defined by the census categories, appears to be independently related to high Negro voter registration.

The very low correlation between per cent of the labor force in manufacturing employment and Negro voter registration appears to be the result of other considerations. The word "manufacturing" conjures up images of the "New South"—with belching smokestacks, booming cities, and bulging payrolls. For the South as a whole, this is a quite misleading picture. While manufacturing in 1950 was associated with somewhat higher income for both Negroes and whites (the correlation between per cent in manufacturing and median income was $+.19$ for both races), it was not primarily an urban phenomenon (the correlation between per cent in manufacturing and per cent urban was $+.08$), nor was it associated with rapid population growth (the correlation with population increase between 1940 and 1950 is $+.05$). Manufacturing was negatively correlated with school years completed by both whites and Negroes ($-.14$ and $-.05$, respectively). This kind of low-wage manufacturing centered in relatively stable, small towns is not very strongly associated with growing Negro voter registration. It is possible that the recent industrialization of the region— electronics as opposed to home production of chenille bedspreads, for example—may be quite differently related to Negro participation. So few counties have this new type of industry that they tend to be hidden by the bedspreads in a county-by-county correlation.

While our analysis should not be taken as the last word on the subject, it does strongly suggest that urbanization and industrialization are vastly overrated as facilitators of Negro voter registration.

Urbanization and industrialization may provide necessary conditions for high levels of Negro political participation but, by themselves, they are not sufficient to insure them.

White Educational Levels. If, as we have argued, Negro registration rates in the South respond far more to the characteristics of the white community than to the attributes of the Negroes themselves, then it seems reasonable to expect Negro voter registration to be positively correlated with white educational levels. Numerous studies have shown that racial prejudice and discrimination tend to be related to low levels of formal education. Where the whites are relatively well educated, there should be less resistance to Negro political participation and, therefore, more Negro voter registration.

Just the opposite is the case for the South as a whole. The correlation between median school years completed by whites and Negro voter registration is —.26, one of the largest negative correlations obtained in this study. When the education of whites in a county increases, Negro voter registration in the county tends to decrease.

How can we account for this unexpected finding? In view of the surprising nature of the relationship, the first expectation would be that it is merely a reflection of some third variable which happens to be related both to Negro registration and to white education. If so, it should disappear when other factors are held constant. But the correlation holds up surprisingly well when other variables are controlled: only one of the other social and economic characteristics of southern counties reduces the correlation at all. The third variable is, once again, Negro concentration in the population. With Negro concentration in 1950 controlled, the partial correlation between white educational level and Negro registration is —.15; controlling for Negro concentration in 1900 produces a partial correlation of —.16. While these are substantial reductions, the partial correlations are among

the largest obtained after controlling for the extraordinarily important factor of Negro concentration. The strong correlation (+.30) between Negro concentration and median school years completed by whites is almost as unexpected as the correlation between Negro registration and white education. The whites in the black belt counties tend to be better educated —at least quantitatively—than other white southerners. And, regardless of the percentage of Negroes in the population, fewer Negroes are registered in counties where whites have more education.

A second explanation for the negative relationship between white education and Negro registration might be that their relationship is curvilinear: at the lower educational levels, increases in white median school years might be associated with declining rates of Negro registration but, at higher educational levels, the relationship might be reversed. If this were the case, then the overall negative relationship would be a result of the generally low educational levels of the South, concealing the fact that the few counties with high white educational levels had the highest rates of Negro registration. Figure 6 suggests only a moderate tendency in this direction. As the number of school years completed by whites goes up through the primary and secondary grades, the proportion of voting age Negroes registered declines. In the very few counties in which the average white adult has completed high school or received some higher education, the trend reverses and Negro registration rates begin to increase. But the reversal is not sharp enough for the counties with the highest white education to reach as great a Negro registration as the counties with the lowest white education. Southern counties with extremely high white educational levels have only about average rates of Negro registration. The impressive fact revealed by Figure 6 is the near uniformity with which an increase in white school years is associated with a decrease in Negro registration.

Being unable to "explain away" our

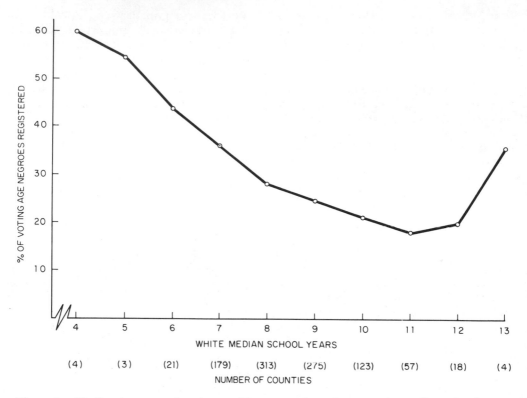

Figure 6. *Median per cent of voting-age Negroes registered to vote, by median school years completed by whites in county.*

finding entirely, either by examining the correlation for hidden third variables or by examining the regularity of the association, we must conclude that white education in southern counties is independently and negatively associated with Negro registration. Short of the highest levels, the more educated the whites the more actively and effectively they seem to enforce the traditional mores of the region against Negro participation in elections. The usual effect of an increase in average schooling for whites in the South as a whole appears to be to give the white people more of the skills that are needed to express effectively their anti-Negro sentiment. For example, the correlation between median school years completed by whites and the presence or absence of a White Citizens Council or similar organization is +.32. It seems to take considerably more formal education than the

average southern white receives to *alter* his attitude toward the Negro's place in southern politics.

White Religious Affiliation.   A variety of studies suggest that religion plays some role—either as independent or intervening variable—in the racial politics of the South. Churchgoers have been found to be less tolerant than nonattenders, and the South is a churchgoing region. Studies of Louisiana politics have found substantial political differences between the Catholic and Protestant sections of the state. It seemed worthwhile, therefore, to examine the correlation between white religious affiliation and Negro registration rates for the South as a whole.

We find that Negro registration rates are depressed as church membership among whites increases (—.17), despite the fact that white membership in different churches has different functions—Baptist membership is negatively related to Negro registration (—.10), while Catholic membership is positively related (+.15). On a southwide basis, the percentage of Jews in the county's total church membership is not significantly associated with Negro registration.

Granted that Catholicism is positively related to Negro registration, we can partial out the influence of Catholicism in order to determine the correlation between non-Catholic white church membership and Negro registration. This partial correlation is, as expected, slightly greater (—.23) than the simple correlation. But the negative correlation between white church membership and Negro registration disappears when Negro concentration is held constant. (The partial correlation is +.01.) Greater church membership among whites accordingly appears to be a reflection of other county attributes rather than an independent factor in relation to Negro registration. When we examine the correlations between church membership and all of our other measures of county attributes, we find very low correlations with all other variables except Negro concentration (+.38) and Catholicism (+.31). Apparently, then, white church membership *per se* is unimportant for Negro registration. White people in the kinds of counties with more Negroes and in predominantly Catholic counties are more often members of churches. In the former kinds of counties, fewer Negroes will vote regardless of non-Catholic church membership. Most non-Catholic churches presumably take on the racial attitudes of their localities; or, if they do not, they have little effect on those attitudes insofar as the attitudes are reflected in rates of Negro registration.

Per cent of Roman Catholics in the white church population appears to be by far the most important of our religious attributes of southern counties. And the relationship between Catholicism and Negro voter registration does not disappear when Negro concentration is controlled. (The partial correlation is +.10.) The presence of Roman Catholics, then, does seem to facilitate Negro voter registration on a southwide basis. Roman Catholic churches and priests presumably react less directly to other county attributes than most Protestant churches and their ministers; in any case, Catholicism is independently and positively related to Negro voter registration.

However, the concentration of Catholic population in Louisiana and the small number of Catholics in most other parts of the South dictate caution in accepting this explanation. For one thing, the distribution of Catholic percentages deviates so far from the assumption of normal distribution underlying correlation analysis that our southwide correlations may have been curiously and unpredictably affected. In the second place, the atypical political patterns of Louisiana—rather than Catholicism *per se*—may account for a large part of the correlation obtained. Only state-by-state analysis of the correlations can indicate if Catholicism is a genuinely independent and significant factor facilitating Negro registration throughout the entire South.

Negro vs. White Registration Rates

We have assumed that our analysis is of *Negro* voter registration rather than of voter registration *in general*. But this assumption might be incorrect: while Negroes register to vote in the South at a much lower rate than whites (Figure 1), the registration rates of the two races could be highly correlated with one another, both responding to the same social and economic characteristics of southern counties. The data permit two tests of this possibility: (1) an examination of the relationship between Negro and white registration; (2) a comparison of the relationships between county attributes and white registration with the relationships found between the same attributes and Negro registration.

The Relationship Between Negro and White Registration. To a limited ex-

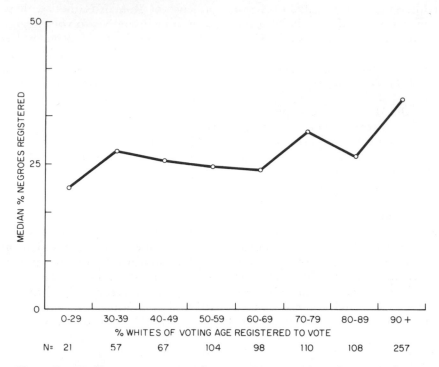

Figure 7. *Median per cent of voting-age Negroes registered to vote, by per cent of whites registered to vote in same county.*

tent, Negro registration does increase as white registration increases; their simple correlation is +.24. Figure 7 presents the relationship of Negro to white registration for every level of white registration. The detailed relationships depicted by the graph reveal that the lowest and the highest levels of white registration contribute most of the small correlation between the registration rates of the two races; if both of the extreme points were eliminated, the curve would be virtually horizontal, indicating that Negro registration had no relationship at all to white registration. Only when white registration is extremely high or extremely low, then, is it associated with the rate of Negro registration. For the broad middle range of counties with from 30 to 89 per cent of the whites registered—a group which contains over 70 per cent of all southern counties—Negro registration appears to be independent of white registration.

The Relationships Between Socio-Eco-

nomic Factors and Negro and White Registration.   Table 4 presents the correlations between the per cent of eligible whites registered to vote and the same twenty social and economic factors utilized in our effort to explain Negro registration. While these factors were chosen for their presumed relevance for Negro registration, the magnitude of the simple correlations in the first column of the table suggests that they are as strongly related to white as to Negro registration. When these simple correlations for whites are compared with those for Negroes in Table 2, however, we see that the direction of the correlation is reversed for fifteen of the twenty social and economic factors. Not one of the twenty variables is substantially and consistently related to both Negro and white rates of voter registration.

The reversal of relationships is so regular that social and economic attributes might appear to have opposite meanings

TABLE 4. CORRELATIONS BETWEEN COUNTY SOCIAL AND ECONOMIC CHARACTERISTICS AND
PER CENT OF VOTING AGE WHITES REGISTERED TO VOTE, BY COUNTY,
IN ELEVEN SOUTHERN STATES

County Characteristics	Simple Correlations (r)	Partial Correlations, Controlling for:	
		Per Cent Negro, 1950	Per Cent Urban, 1950
Per cent of nonwhite labor force in white-collar occupations	− .26	− .24	− .15
Nonwhite median school years completed	− .34	− .34	− .28
Nonwhite median income	− .19	− .17	− .08
Per cent of total church membership, Roman Catholic	− .09	− .08	− .03
Per cent increase in population, 1940–1950	− .06	− .04	+ .08
Per cent of labor force in manufacturing	+ .05	+ .05	+ .07
White median income	− .19	− .19	− .05
Per cent of population urban	− .25	− .24	
Percentage point difference in per cent population Negro, 1900–1950	+ .10	+ .11	+ .05
Per cent of total church membership, Jewish	− .03	− .03	+ .04
Difference in white-nonwhite median school years completed	+ .11	+ .07	+ .14
Difference in white-nonwhite median income	− .12	− .13	− .03
Number of Negro colleges in county	− .10	− .11	− .04
Per cent of total church membership, Baptist	+ .20	+ .19	+ .15
Per cent of population belonging to a church	+ .06	+ .02	+ .07
Per cent of labor force in agriculture	+ .21	+ .19	+ .06
White median school years completed	− .08	− .11	+ .03
Per cent of farms operated by tenants	+ .09	+ .05	+ .05
Per cent of population Negro, 1900	+ .03	− .12	+ .02
Per cent of population Negro, 1950	+ .10		+ .06

Note: *County characteristics are listed above in the same order as in Table 2 in order to facilitate comparison of Negro and white correlations.*

for Negro and white registration. Closer
inspection reveals, however, that the relationships are disparate rather than opposite.

The crucial variable for Negro registration is Negro concentration in the population, which not only furnishes the strongest simple correlation, but is also the
variable that most consistently accounts
for other apparent "influences" on Negro
registration. Indeed, Negro concentration
has generally been cited as the critical
factor in all dimensions of southern political behavior. Hence one immediately
suspects that all of the variables which
facilitate white registration must be positively correlated with concentration of

Negro population, which would thereby
stand as the dominant third factor for
both Negro and white registration. While
this familiar interpretation would conveniently account for the striking discrepancy
between correlates of white and Negro
registration, it is not supported by our
findings. On the contrary, *Negro concentration has a negligible relationship to
white voter registration.* Moreover, the
small simple correlation of Negro concentration and white registration (+.10)
drops to the vanishing point (+.06) when
urbanism is controlled.

No single variable is as important for
white registration as Negro concentration
is for Negro registration, but urbanism

emerges as particularly significant. Per cent of population urban—which proved inconsequential in the analysis of Negro registration—furnishes one of the strongest negative correlations with white voter registration, a correlation that is not affected when Negro concentration is controlled. And the same relationship is found if, instead of per cent of population urban, we use Standard Metropolitan Areas as our index of urban-rural difference; white registration is consistently higher in rural than in urban counties. Other county characteristics associated with urbanization—such as high income and education levels for whites and Negroes—are similarly related to low white registration. Perhaps the rural white resident finds politics more meaningful in a one-party region, where personality plays such an important role in elections. In any event, urban-rural differences are a key factor in variations in white voter registration.

Similar variations are found in the relationships of white and Negro registration rates to the other social and economic characteristics of southern counties. Average white education, for example, manifested a strong negative association with Negro registration—an association that held up under various controls so well that it led to novel conclusions. White education is also negatively related to white registration, but the correlation is extremely small and it is reversed when per cent of population urban is controlled.

Without an extended consideration of white registration, then, we can conclude that our analysis does apply to Negro voter registration in particular rather than to voter registration in general. The social and economic characteristics of southern counties have widely different meanings for Negro and white registration.

Conclusions

The proportion of voting age Negroes registered to vote in the former confeder-

ate states has increased more than 500 per cent since *Smith v. Allwright* was decided in 1944. Today, 28 per cent of the voting age Negroes are registered voters, a rate which is about half that of white adults in the South. In this article we have examined the statistical associations between selected social and economic characteristics of southern counties and Negro registration in an effort to ascertain the extent to which variations in Negro registration can be explained by the social and economic realities of the region.

The personal attributes of Negroes—their occupations, income, and education as reflected in county figures—were found to have relatively little to do with Negro registration rates. The size of the Negro middle class does appear to have an independent and positive correlation with Negro registration, but this correlation is small compared to those between Negro registration and the characteristics of the whites and of the total community.

The largest single correlation $(-.46)$ was between the per cent of the population Negro in 1950 and Negro registration. Differences in the proportion of the population Negro up to about 30 per cent are not associated with drastic reductions in the per cent of Negroes registered, but increasing Negro concentration above this figure seems to lead to very rapid decreases. Negro concentration in the past seems almost as important as Negro concentration today until one discovers that the close association of past with present Negro concentration accounts for the finding. Indeed, declines in Negro proportions in counties with populations from 30 to 70 per cent Negro in 1900 are associated with substantial registration increases over similar counties which have not experienced such change.

The presence of an agricultural economy and farm tenancy were found to have a small, independent, and depressing effect on Negro registration rates. Neither urbanization nor industrialization, on the other hand, seems to be associated with

Negro registration increases when other factors are controlled.

White educational levels were of about equal importance to the size of the Negro middle class and the existence of an agrarian economy. The more highly educated the whites in a county, the lower the rate of Negro registration—until the average white adult was a high school graduate or possessed some higher education. In these few counties, the rate of Negro registration was moderate. Up to the highest levels, increases in white educational levels apparently lead to more effective enforcement of the region's traditional mores against Negro participation in elections.

Another factor of about equal importance to all the others save Negro concentration is Roman Catholicism. The larger the proportion of Roman Catholics in a county, the higher the rate of Negro registration, regardless of what other factors are controlled.

When the same social and economic characteristics of southern counties are analyzed for their relationships to white voter registration, a radically different pattern is discovered. The direction of the relationship is reversed for most of the attributes with the shift from Negro to white registration, but more than a simple reversal is involved. The magnitudes of the correlations with white registration (disregarding direction of correlation) are quite different, and a different variable emerges as the most consistent independent correlate. Whereas Negro registration tends to increase in the counties—rural or urban—that have smaller portions of Negroes in their populations, white registration tends to increase in the more rural counties—regardless of the portions of Negroes in their populations. We can accordingly have some confidence that we are dealing with an autonomous set of relationships in our analysis of Negro registration in the South.

In all of the preceding analysis, we have examined the association between selected social and economic factors and Negro registration one at a time. While controls

for the impact of one social and economic factor on another have been introduced, we have not yet attempted to estimate the extent of the association between all the social and economic factors taken together and Negro registration. In order to do this, we have computed the multiple correlation coefficient between all twenty social and economic factors (plus the size of the Standard Metropolitan Area, if any, within which the county is contained—a qualitative variable for which simple correlations could not be obtained) and Negro voter registration. The correlation between all of the social and economic variables and county registration rates of Negroes is .53, which explains about 28 per cent (R^2) of the variation in Negro registration.

A multiple correlation of this magnitude demonstrates the great importance of social and economic characteristics for Negro registration. To explain over one-fourth of the variance in Negro registration—or any other significant political phenomenon—is no mean achievement in the current state of political science. But almost three-fourths of the variance remains to be accounted for. This leaves room for significant variation independent of social and economic forces that have been considered here. If political variables were added to the analysis, could still more of the variance in Negro registration be explained? If political variables do emerge as having an autonomous set of relationships to Negro registration, what is the comparative importance of political and demographic variables? Finally, if variations in state systems (social, economic, and political) were taken into account, could still more explanatory power be gained? A social and economic analysis has taken us a long way in our effort to understand Negro registration rates, but we still have a lot further to go. The massive bulk and complexity of our data require that an analysis of political and legal factors, of the relative importance of demographic *vs.* political variables, and of variations in state systems be reported separately. Our expectation is that, by an analysis of these additional factors, we can reduce the range of unexplained variation still further.

The application of our findings to the contemporary policy problem of how best to increase Negro voting in the South must be approached with the utmost caution. Our analysis deals with registration, not voting, and these are not identical forms of political participation. Our data deal with the characteristics of counties, not individuals, and the leap from the areal to the individual level is hazardous. Third, the analysis has been of variations in rates of registration and not of factors

which determine its absolute level. To find that an independent variable accounts for some of the variation in the dependent variable gives us no direct information on the size of the dependent variable. Fourth, correlations are not "causes," but merely associations; attributing causal relationships to variables which are correlated with one another is to engage in the drawing of inferences, which sometimes are spectacularly wrong. Finally, the bulk of our analysis has been restricted to one point in time, so that it does not directly produce predictions in which time is a key factor.

If these caveats are not forgotten but

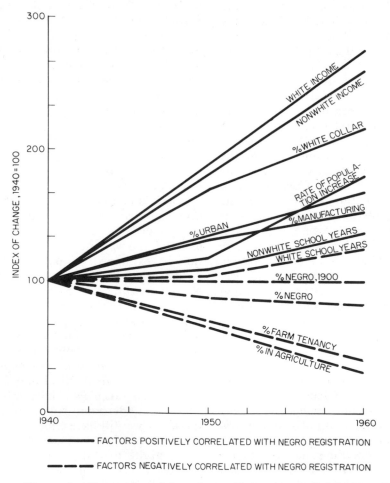

Figure 8. *Rates of social and economic change in the South 1940–1960.*

merely set aside, our correlations suggest that reformers should not expect miracles in their efforts, through political and legal means, to increase the size and effectiveness of the Negro vote in the South. The Negro registration rate is low, in rather large part, because of the social and economic characteristics of southerners—both Negro and white. These facts are not easily and quickly changed by law or political action. One cannot help but be impressed by the massive indications of stability in the situation—the extremely high negative correlation between per cent Negro in 1900 and Negro registration in 1958, the apparent failure of urbanization and industrialization to provide sufficiently favorable conditions for Negro political participation, the negative correlation between white educational levels and Negro registration, and so on.

At the same time, Negro registration has increased rapidly since 1944, and the social and economic factors we have considered account for only about 28 per cent of its 1958 variation. Changes in the southern society and economy strongly argue that Negro registration will continue to increase. In Figure 8, the trend since 1940 is presented for the variables we found to be most strongly related to Negro voter registration. *Every one of the variables positively associated with Negro registration is on the increase*—some have doubled in twenty years, and all but one have increased by at least 50 per cent. Only one of the factors associated with low Negro registration—white school years completed—is also increasing, and there is reason to believe that a good many southern counties will soon reach the stage where this factor may tend to facilitate rather than hinder Negro political participation. All the other factors negatively correlated with Negro registration (except, of course, per cent Negro in 1900) are declining rapidly.

The South's social and economic structure may be the reformer's major barrier —but it may also be a long-run cause for hope.

C. Functional Analysis

The Latent Functions of the Political Machine

Robert K. Merton

. . . In large sectors of the American population, the political machine or the "political racket" are judged as unequivocally "bad" and "undesirable." The grounds for such moral judgment vary somewhat, but they consist substantially in pointing out that political machines violate moral codes: political patronage violates the code of selecting personnel on the basis of impersonal qualifications rather than on grounds of party loyalty or contributions to the party warchest; bossism violates the code that votes should be based on individual appraisal of the qualifications of candidates and of political issues, and not on abiding loyalty to a feudal leader; bribery and "honest graft" obviously offend the proprieties of property; "protection" for crime clearly violates the law and the mores; and so on.

In view of these manifold respects in which political machines, in varying degrees, run counter to the mores and at times to the law, it becomes pertinent to inquire how they manage to continue in operation. The familiar "explanations"

Robert K. Merton, *Social Theory and Social Structure,* rev. ed., pp. 71–81. Copyright © 1957, by The Free Press, a corporation. Copyright 1949 by The Free Press. Reprinted by permission of The Free Press.

for the continuance of the political machine are not here in point. To be sure, it may well be that if "respectable citizenry" would carry through their political obligations; if the electorate were to be alert and enlightened; if the number of elective officers were substantially reduced from the dozens, even hundreds, which the average voter is now expected to appraise in the course of local, county, state, and national elections; if the electorate were activated by the "wealthy and educated classes without whose participation," as the not-always democratically oriented Bryce put it, "the best-framed government must speedily degenerate"; if these and a plethora of similar changes in political structure were introduced, perhaps the "evils" of the political machine would indeed be exorcized. But it should be noted that these changes are not typically introduced, that political machines have the phoenixlike quality of arising strong and unspoiled from their ashes, that, in short, this structure exhibits a notable vitality in many areas of American political life.

Proceeding from the functional view, therefore, that we should *ordinarily* (not invariably) expect persistent social patterns and social structures to perform positive functions *which are at the time not adequately fulfilled by other existing patterns and structures,* the thought occurs that perhaps this publicly maligned organization is, *under present conditions,* satisfying basic latent functions. A brief examination of current analyses of this type of structure may also serve to illustrate additional problems of functional analysis.

Some Functions of the Political Machine. Without presuming to enter into the variations of detail marking different political machines—a Tweed, Vare, Crump, Flynn, Hague are by no means identical types of bosses—we can briefly examine the functions more or less common to the political machine, as a generic type of social organization. We neither attempt to itemize all the diverse functions of the political machine nor imply that all these functions are similarly fulfilled by each and every machine.

The key structural function of the boss is to organize, centralize, and maintain in good working condition "the scattered fragments of power" which are at present dispersed through our political organization. By this centralized organization of political power, the boss and his apparatus can satisfy the needs of diverse subgroups in the larger community which are not adequately satisfied by legally devised and culturally approved social structures.

To understand the role of bossism and the machine, therefore, we must look at two types of sociological variables: (1) the *structural context* which makes it difficult, if not impossible, for morally approved structures to fulfill essential social functions, thus leaving the door open for political machines (or their structural equivalents) to fulfill these functions, and (2) the subgroups whose distinctive needs are left unsatisfied, except for the latent functions which the machine in fact fulfills.

Structural Context. The constitutional framework of American political organization specifically precludes the legal possibility of highly centralized power and, it has been noted, thus "discourages the growth of effective and responsible leadership. The framers of the Constitution, as Woodrow Wilson observed, set up the check and balance system 'to keep government at a sort of mechanical equipoise by means of a standing amicable contest among its several organic parts.' They distrusted power as dangerous to liberty: and therefore they spread it thin and erected barriers against its concentration." This dispersion of power is found not only at the national level but in local areas as well. "As a consequence, . . . when *the people or particular groups* among them demanded positive action, no one had adequate authority to act. The machine provided an antidote."[1]

[1] *Edward M. Sait, "Machine, Political,"* Encyclopaedia of the Social Sciences (*New York: The Macmillan Company, 1937*), *Vol. IX, 658b [italics supplied].*

The constitutional dispersion of power not only makes for difficulty of effective decision and action, but when action does occur it is defined and hemmed in by legalistic considerations. In consequence, there develops "a much *more human system* of partisan government, whose chief object soon became the circumvention of government by law. . . . The lawlessness of the extraofficial democracy was merely the counterpoise of the legalism of the official democracy. The lawyer having been permitted to subordinate democracy to the law, the boss had to be called in to extricate the victim, which he did after a fashion and for a consideration."[2]

Officially, political power is dispersed. Various well-known expedients were devised for this manifest objective. Not only was there the familiar separation of powers among the several branches of the government but, in some measure, tenure in each office was limited, rotation in office approved. And the scope of power inherent in each office was severely circumscribed. Yet, observes Sait in rigorously functional terms, "leadership is necessary; and *since* it does not develop readily within the constitutional framework, the boss provides it in a crude and irresponsible form from the outside."[3]

Put in more generalized terms, *the functional deficiencies of the official structure generate an alternative (unofficial) structure to fulfill existing needs somewhat more effectively.* Whatever its specific historical origins, the political machine persists as an apparatus for satisfying otherwise unfulfilled needs of diverse groups in the population. By turning to a few of these subgroups and their characteristic needs, we shall be led at once to a range of latent functions of the political machine.

Functions of the Political Machine for Diverse Subgroups. It is well known that one source of strength of the political

machine derives from its roots in the local community and the neighborhood. The political machine does not regard the electorate as a vague, undifferentiated mass of voters. With a keen sociological intuition, the machine recognizes that the voter is primarily a man living in a specific neighborhood, with specific personal problems and personal wants. Public issues are abstract and remote; private problems are extremely concrete and immediate. It is not through the generalized appeal to large public concerns that the machine operates, but through the direct, quasi-feudal relationships between local representatives of the machine and voters in their neighborhood. Elections are won in the precinct.

The machine welds its link with ordinary men and women by elaborate networks of personal relations. Politics is transformed into personal ties. The precinct captain "must be a friend to every man, . . . and utilize in his good works the resources which the boss puts at his disposal."[4] The precinct captain is forever a friend in need. In our prevailingly impersonal society, the machine, through its local agents, fulfills the important *social function of humanizing and personalizing all manner of assistance* to those in need. Food baskets and jobs, legal and extralegal advice, setting to rights minor scrapes with the law, helping the bright poor boy to a political scholarship in a local college, looking after the bereaved—the whole range of crises when a feller needs a friend, and, above all, a friend who knows the score and who can do something about it—all these find the ever-helpful precinct captain available in the pinch.

To assess this function of the political machine adequately, it is important to note not only the fact that aid *is* provided, but *the manner in which it is provided.* After all, other agencies do exist for dispensing such assistance. Welfare agencies, settlement houses, legal aid clinics, medical aid in free hospitals, public relief de-

---

2 Herbert Croly, Progressive Democracy (*New York: The Macmillan Company, 1914*), *p. 254, cited by Sait, op. cit., 658b.*
3 *Sait, op. cit., 659a [italics supplied].*

4 Ibid.

partments, immigration authorities—these and a multitude of other organizations are available to provide the most varied types of assistance. But in contrast to the professional techniques of the welfare worker, which may typically represent in the mind of the recipient the cold, bureaucratic dispensation of limited aid following upon detailed investigation of *legal* claims to aid of the "client," are the unprofessional techniques of the precinct captain who asks no questions, exacts no compliance with legal rules of eligibility, and does not "snoop" into private affairs.

For many, the loss of "self-respect" is too high a price for legalized assistance. In contrast to the gulf between the settlement house workers who so often come from a different social class, educational background, and ethnic group, the precinct worker is "just one of us," who understands what it's all about. The condescending lady bountiful can hardly compete with the understanding friend in need. In *this struggle between alternative structures for fulfilling the nominally same function* of providing aid and support to those who need it, it is clearly the machine politician who is better integrated with the groups which he serves than the impersonal, professionalized, socially distant, and legally constrained welfare worker. And since the politician can at times influence and manipulate the official organizations for the dispensation of assistance, whereas the welfare worker has practically no influence on the political machine, this only adds to his greater effectiveness. More colloquially and also, perhaps, more incisively, it was the Boston ward leader, Martin Lomasny, who described this essential function to the curious Lincoln Steffens: "I think," said Lomasny, "that there's got to be in every ward somebody that any bloke can come to—no matter what he's done—and get help. *Help, you understand; none of your law and justice, but help.*"[5]

[5] The Autobiography of Lincoln Steffens (*Chautauqua, N.Y.: Chautauqua Press, 1931*), p. 618.

The "deprived classes," then, constitute one subgroup for whom the political machine clearly satisfies wants not adequately satisfied in the same fashion by the legitimate social structure.

For a second subgroup, that of business (primarily "big" business, but also "small") the political boss serves the function of providing those political privileges which entail immediate economic gains. Business corporations, among which the public utilities (railroads, local transportation companies, communications corporations, electric light [companies]) are simply the most conspicuous in this regard, seek special political dispensations which will enable them to stabilize their situation and to near their objective of maximizing profits. Interestingly enough, corporations often want to avoid a chaos of uncontrolled competition. They want the greater security of an economic tsar who controls, regulates, and organizes competition, providing this tsar is not a public official with his decisions subject to public scrutiny and public control. (The latter would be "government control," and hence taboo.) The political boss fulfills these requirements admirably.

Examined for a moment apart from any "moral" considerations, the political apparatus of the boss is effectively designed to perform these functions with a minimum of inefficiency. Holding the strings of diverse governmental divisions, bureaus, and agencies in his competent hands, the boss rationalizes the relations between public and private business. He serves as the business community's ambassador in the otherwise alien (and sometimes unfriendly) realm of government. And, in strict, businesslike terms, he is well-paid for his economic services to his respectable business clients. In an article entitled, "An Apology to Graft," Steffens suggested that "Our economic system, which held up riches, power, and acclaim as prizes to men bold enough and able enough to buy corruptly timber, mines, oil fields, and franchises and 'get away with it,' was at fault."[6] And, in a conference with a hundred or so . . . Los Angeles business leaders, he described a fact well known to all of them: the boss and his machine were an *integral part* of the organization of the economy. "You cannot build or operate a railroad, or a street railway, gas, water, or power company, develop and operate a mine, or get forests and cut timber on a large scale, or run any privileged business, without corrupting or joining in the corruption of the government. You tell me privately that you must, and here I am telling you semipublicly that you must. And that is so all over the country. And that means that we have an organization of society in which, *for some reason,* you and your kind, the ablest, most intelligent, most imaginative, daring, and resourceful leaders of society, are and must be against society and its laws and its all-around growth."[7]

Since the demand for the services of special privileges are built into the structure of the society, the boss fulfills diverse functions for this second subgroup of business-seeking-privilege. These "needs" of business, as presently constituted, are not adequately provided for by "conventional" and "culturally approved" social structures; consequently, the extralegal but more or less efficient organization of the political machine comes to provide these services. To adopt an *exclusively* moral attitude toward the "corrupt political machine" is to lose sight of the very structural conditions which generate the "evil" that is so bitterly attacked. To adopt a functional outlook on the political machine is not to provide an apologia, but a more solid base for modifying or eliminating the machine, *providing* specific structural arrangements are introduced either for eliminating these effective demands of the business community or, if that is the objective, of satisfying these demands through alternative means.

A third set of distinctive functions ful-

6 Ibid., *p. 570.*
7 Ibid., *pp. 572–573.*

filled by the political machine for a special subgroup is that of providing alternative channels of social mobility for those otherwise excluded from the more conventional avenues for personal "advancement." Both the sources of this special "need" (for social mobility) and the respect in which the political machine comes to help satisfy this need can be understood by examining the structure of the larger culture and society. As is well known, the American culture lays enormous emphasis on money and power as a "success" goal legitimate for all members of the society. By no means alone in our inventory of cultural goals, it still remains among the most heavily endowed with positive effect and value. However, certain subgroups and certain ecological areas are notable for the relative absence of opportunity for achieving these (monetary and power) types of success. They constitute, in short, subpopulations where "the cultural emphasis upon pecuniary success" has been absorbed, but where there is *little access to conventional and legitimate* means for attaining such success. The conventional occupational opportunities of persons in (such areas) are almost completely limited to manual labor. Given our cultural stigmatization of manual labor, and its correlate, the prestige of white-collar work, it is clear that the result is a tendency to achieve these culturally approved objectives *through whatever means . . . possible.* These people are, on the one hand, "asked to orient their conduct toward the prospect of accumulating wealth [and power] and, on the other, they are largely denied effective opportunities to do so institutionally."

It is within this context of social structure that the political machine fulfills the basic function of providing avenues of social mobility for the otherwise disadvantaged. Within this context, even the corrupt political machine and the racket "represent the triumph of amoral intelligence over morally prescribed 'failure' when the channels of vertical mobility are closed or narrowed *in a society which places a high premium on economic afflu-*

ence, [power,] and social ascent for all *its members*."[8] As one sociologist has noted on the basis of several years of close observation in a "slum area":

> The sociologist who dismisses racket and political organizations as deviations from desirable standards thereby neglects some of the major elements of slum life. . . . *He does not discover the functions they perform for the members* [of the groupings in the slum]. The Irish and later immigrant peoples have had the greatest difficulty in finding places for themselves in our urban social and economic structure. Does anyone believe that the immigrants and their children could have achieved their present degree of social mobility without gaining control of the political organization of some of our largest cities? The same is true of the racket organization. *Politics and the rackets have furnished an important means of social mobility for individuals, who, because of ethnic background and low class position,* are blocked from advancement in the "respectable" channels.[9]

This, then represents a third type of function performed for a distinctive subgroup. This function, it may be noted in passing, is fulfilled by the *sheer* existence and operation of the political machine, for it is in the machine itself that these individuals and subgroups find their culturally induced needs more or less satisfied. It refers to the services which the political apparatus provides for its own personnel. But seen in the wider social context we have set forth, it no longer appears as *merely* a means of self-aggrandizement for profit-hungry and power-hungry *individuals,* but as an organized provision for *subgroups* otherwise excluded or restricted from the race for "getting ahead."

Just as the political machine performs services for "legitimate" business, so it operates to perform not dissimilar services for "illegitimate" business: vice, crime, and rackets. Once again, the basic socio-logical role of the machine in this respect can be more fully appreciated only if one temporarily abandons attitudes of moral indignation, to examine with all moral innocence the actual workings of the organization. In this light, it at once appears that the subgroup of the professional criminal, racketeer, gambler has basic similarities of organization, demands, and operation to the subgroup of the industrialist, man of business, speculator. If there is a Lumber King or an Oil King, there is also a Vice King or a Racket King. If expansive legitimate business organizes administrative and financial syndicates to "rationalize" and to "integrate" diverse areas of production and business enterprise, so expansive rackets and crime organize syndicates to bring order to the otherwise chaotic areas of production of illicit goods and services. If legitimate business regards the proliferation of small enterprises as wasteful and inefficient, substituting, for example, the giant chain stores for the hundreds of corner groceries, so illegitimate business adopts the same businesslike attitude and syndicates crime and vice.

Finally, and in many respects most important, is the basic similarity, if not near-identity, of the economic role of "legitimate" business and "illegitimate" business. *Both are in some degree concerned with the provision of goods and services for which there is an economic demand.* Morals aside, they are both business, industrial, and professional enterprises, dispensing goods and services which some people want, for which there is a market in which goods and services are transformed into commodities. And, in a prevalently market society, we should expect appropriate enterprises to arise whenever there is a market demand for given goods or services.

As is well known, vice, crime, and the rackets *are* "big business." Consider only that there have been estimated to be about five hundred thousand professional prostitutes in the United States, and compare this with the approximately two hundred

---

[8] *Robert K. Merton,* Social Theory and Social Structure, *p. 146.*
[9] *William F. Whyte, "Social Organization in the Slums,"* American Sociological Review, *Vol. VIII (February, 1943), 8, 34–39 [italics supplied].*

thousand physicians and two hundred thousand nurses. It is difficult to estimate which have the larger clientele: the professional men and women of medicine or the professional men and women of vice. It is, of course, difficult to estimate the economic assets, income, profits, and dividends of illicit gambling in this country and to compare [them] with the economic assets, income, profits, and dividends of, say, the shoe industry, but it is altogether possible that the two industries are about on a par. No precise figures exist on the annual expenditures on illicit narcotics, and it is probable that these are less than the expenditures on candy, but it is also probable that they are larger than the expenditures on books.

It takes but a moment's thought to recognize that, *in strictly economic terms,* there is no relevant difference between the provision of licit and of illicit goods and services. The liquor traffic illustrates this perfectly. It would be peculiar to argue that prior to 1920 (when the Eighteenth Amendment became effective), the provision of liquor constituted an economic service, that from 1920 to 1933 its production and sale no longer constituted an economic service dispensed in a market, and that from 1934 to the present it once again took on a serviceable aspect. Or, it would be *economically* (not morally) absurd to suggest that the sale of bootlegged liquor in the dry state of Kansas is less a response to a market demand than the sale of publicly manufactured liquor in the neighboring wet state of Missouri. Examples of this sort can, of course, be multiplied many times over. Can it be held that in European countries, with registered and legalized prostitution, the prostitute contributes an economic service, whereas in this country, lacking legal sanction, the prostitute provides no such service? Or that the professional abortionist is in the economic market where he has approved legal status and that he is out of the economic market where he is legally taboo? Or that gambling satisfies a specific demand for entertainment in Nevada, where it is one of the biggest business enterprises of the largest city in the state, but that it differs essentially in this respect from movie houses in the neighboring state of California?

The failure to recognize that these businesses are only *morally* and not *economically* distinguishable from "legitimate" businesses has led to badly scrambled analysis. Once the economic identity of the two is recognized, we may anticipate that if the political machine performs functions for "legitimate big business" it will be all the more likely to perform not dissimilar functions for "illegitimate big business." And, of course, such is often the case.

The distinctive function of the political machine for their criminal, vice, and racket clientele is to enable them to operate in satisfying the economic demands of a large market without due interference from the government. Just as big business may contribute funds to the political party war-chest to insure a minimum of governmental interference, so with big rackets and big crime. In both instances, the political machine can, in varying degrees, provide "protection." In both instances, many features of the structural context are identical: (1) market demands for goods and services; (2) the operators' concern with maximizing gains from their enterprises; (3) the need for partial control of government, which might otherwise interfere with these activities of businessmen; (4) the need for an efficient, powerful, and centralized agency to provide an effective liaison of "business" with government.

Without assuming that the foregoing . . . exhaust[s] either the range of functions or the range of subgroups served by the political machine, we can at least see that *it presently fulfills some functions for these diverse subgroups which are not adequately fulfilled by culturally approved or more conventional structures.*

Several additional implications of the functional analysis of the political machine can be mentioned here only in passing, although they obviously require to be developed at length. First, the foregoing analysis has direct implications for *social engineering*. It helps explain why the periodic efforts at "political reform," "turning the rascals out," and "cleaning political house" are typically short-lived and ineffectual. It exemplifies a basic theorem: *any attempt to eliminate an existing social structure without providing adequate alternative structures for fulfilling the functions previously fulfilled by the abolished organization is doomed to failure.* (Needless to say, this theorem has much wider bearing than the one instance of the political machine.) When "political reform" confines itself to the manifest task of "turning the rascals out," it is engaging in little more than sociological magic. The reform may for a time bring new figures into the political limelight; it may serve the casual social function of reassuring the electorate that the moral virtues remain intact and will ultimately triumph; it may actually effect a turnover in the personnel of the political machine; it may even, for a time, so curb the activities of the machine as to leave unsatisfied the many needs it has previously fulfilled. But, inevitably, unless the reform also involves a "re-forming" of the social and political structure such that the existing needs are satisfied by alternative structures, or unless it involves a change which eliminates these needs altogether, the political machine will return to its integral place in the social scheme of things. *To seek social change, without due recognition of the manifest and latent functions performed by the social organization undergoing change, is to indulge in social ritual rather than social engineering.* The concepts of manifest and latent functions (or their equivalents) are indispensable elements in the theoretic repertoire of the social engineer. In this crucial sense, these concepts are not "merely" theoretical (in the abusive sense of the term), but are eminently practical. In the deliberate enactment of social change, they can be ignored only at

the price of considerably heightening the risk of failure.

A second implication of our analysis of the political machine also has a bearing upon areas wider than the one we have considered. The "paradox" has often been noted that the supporters of the political machine include both the "respectable" business class elements, who are, of course, opposed to the criminal or racketeer, and the distinctly "unrespectable" elements of the underworld. And, at first appearance, this is cited as an instance of very strange bedfellows. The learned judge is not infrequently called upon to sentence the very racketeer beside whom he sat the night before at an informal dinner of the political bigwigs. The district attorney jostles the exonerated convict on his way to the back room where the boss has called a meeting. The big businessman may complain almost as bitterly as the big racketeer about the "extortionate" contributions to the party fund demanded by the boss. Social opposites meet—in the smoke-filled room of the successful politician.

In the light of a functional analysis, all this, of course, no longer seems paradoxical. Since the machine serves both the businessman and the criminal man, the two seemingly antipodal groups intersect. This points to a more general theorem: *the social functions of an organization help determine the structure (including the recruitment of personnel involved in the structure), just as the structure helps determine the effectiveness with which the functions are fulfilled.* In terms of social status, the business group and the criminal group are indeed poles apart. But status does not fully determine behavior and the interrelations between groups. Functions modify these relations. Given their distinctive needs, the several subgroups in the large society are "integrated," whatever their personal desires or intentions, by the centralizing structure which serves these several needs. In a phrase with many implications which require further study, *structure affects function and function affects structure.*

D. Conceptualization and Research Design

Military Leaders and Foreign Policy Making

Lewis J. Edinger

A survey of the literature of the last decade in the burgeoning interdisciplinary field which has come to be known—rather imprecisely—as civil-military relations, reveals a large number of descriptive and prescriptive, operational and theoretical studies, but little unity of focus or method. The interested shopper finds himself in a veritable department store filled with a wide assortment—including those in the bargain basement. Spurred on by wartime experiences and Cold War exigencies, historians and social scientists, physical scientists and journalists—above all in the United States—have covered reams of paper with discussions of the relationship between arms and men, war and peace, strategy and policy, defense and diplomacy. Displaying a great variety of analytical depth, breadth, and sophistication, some of these studies have advanced our knowledge of civil-military relations—particularly in contemporary America—while others have failed to survive changes in international politics and weapons technology. Some writers, both of conservative and liberal orientation, have focused on the "appropriate" role for the military in state and society; others have sought to remain detached from such normative questions in order to concentrate on microdescriptive phenomenal studies or more or less abstract macroanalytical theoretical models. Between the earthbound descriptive and prescriptive studies on the one hand, and the soaring theoretical efforts on the other, has loomed a wide gap, all to familiar to students of international relations, comparative politics, and public administration, waiting to be bridged—if bridged it can be—by empirical theories of civil-military relationships.

Most of the recent studies in the field have tended to deal with issues limited in time and space. On the whole they have been conspicuously ethnocentric in character, addressed in particular either to specific historical events or to contemporary problems of "national security" and its domestic and international ramifications. Conspicuously missing, as a number of observers have recently noted, have been cross-national comparisons of civil-military relations in different settings. The purpose of such comparative analysis is to reach generalizations about differences as well as similarities in space and time in order to identify significant cross-national patterns. It is not an easy task, and the "operational payoff" is uncertain. The complexity of the subject, the need for precise, rigorous analysis—including the inevitable "jargon"—may have discouraged competent scholars aware of the need for comparative analysis. It may be going too far to speak of an "almost complete absence of comparative studies of civil-military relations," as one scholar recently did.[1] But it is certainly true that "we know far too little about the comparative

[1] *Samuel P. Huntington, "Recent Writings in Military Politics—Foci and Corpora," in Huntington, ed., Changing Patterns of Military Politics (New York: The Free Press of Glencoe, Inc., 1962), p. 262. . . .*

Lewis J. Edinger, "Military Leaders and Foreign Policy Making," *American Political Science Review*, Vol. LVII (June, 1963), 392–405. Reprinted by permission. (Extensive technical and bibliographical footnotes have been edited or omitted.)

role of the military in various societies," to quote another recent study.[2]

* * *

The problems that confront the student of comparative civil-military relations are those of comparative analysis in general. There is the familiar dispute over the question of "uniqueness." At one extreme are the specialists, who insist that every case is unique and vehemently deny the validity of any generalizations; at the other are the grand theorists, systems analysts, and philosophers, who sometimes show little concern about empirical evidence to support their "logically consistent" assertions. Both groups are made unhappy by a third, whose members are fond of more or less impressionistic and often imprecise generalizations about "militarism," the "military mind," "garrison states," "warlords," and "warrior classes," about aristocratic and democratic, praetorian and mass armies, and so forth. Most of these grand generalizations tend to assume more than they explain. We are told that geography explains why military influence was traditionally weak in the British Isles and strong in the Continental European nations, but not why the opposite was apparently true of the Japanese Isles and the Asiatic mainland. It is said that German "militarism" was responsible for the outbreak of the First as well as the Second World War, but also that the extent of military influence in Germany was radically different in 1914 and in 1939. Was it difference in the personalities involved, in the "climate of opinion," or some combination of unexplained variables? Such questions obligate us to confront what seems to me perhaps the fundamental problem in comparative analysis, the problem of focus and method.

* * *

. . . Lack of common conceptualization is [also] a prevalent problem in the field.

2 *Richard C. Snyder and James A. Robinson,* National and International Decision-Making: A Report to the Committee on Research for Peace (New York: Institute for International Order, 1961), p. 86.

What exactly do we mean by "civil-military relations"? Is it self-evident and obvious and, therefore, is it casuistry to quibble? Everyone knows what is meant by "military"—so "civilian," I suppose, is that which is not? But if one examines the literature, it quickly becomes apparent that the concept "military" means various things to various men. Some writers try to define it—at least implicitly—but others do not even bother, relying on the "common sense" meaning of military. That seems to include anything from tribal warriors and former "liberation fighters" in newly independent states to "professional fighting men" in classical Sparta as well as contemporary Peru. More explicit definitions range from "armed forces" to "specialists in violence"; but these all too often obscure rather than clarify the distinction between military and civilian, as they speak of military men as "civilianized" and civilians as "militarized." For some scholars the military includes only the professionally trained career officer; others include all "regulars" (implicitly leaving a vast residual category of "irregular soldiers"); while still others conceive the military as an "ideal type" against which they evaluate the "professionalism" of what the dictionary calls "more or less skilled warriors." When international politics is seen as a struggle for power, and warfare but a continuation of that struggle by other means, it becomes difficult to perceive civil and military as dichotomous concepts. Confusion reigns over the distinction between "professional" and "nonprofessional" soldiers, between the military as a social group and the military as an institution, between "political" generals and uniformed "civilians." The conceptual problem is no nearer solution for such crucial terms as "defense," "national security," "warfare," and "militarism," all favorites among commentators on civil-military relations and yet all defined too rarely—or in such broad and vague terms as to be useless for compartive purposes. Many other examples could be cited, but I do not think it necessary to engage in further textual analysis. Rather, we face the question: what is to be done? The choice seems to lie between laboring, like Candide, in comparative security from doubts and criticism in one's little parochial garden, or to seek to move toward comparative generalizations by asking not only what, how, and why, but asking it in a consistent and unambiguous manner.

It is impossible to generalize about individual or group behavior without conceptualization, which permits us to order our data in order to trace patterns of similarities and differences. No matter how deep we dig for facts and how many documents we succeed in getting declassified, facts will never "speak for themselves" nor suggest answers to certain "why" questions without a guiding set of concepts to identify relevant and significant data. Conceptualization means deliberate and explicit dilution of the unique and specific situation. It is an inevitable risk we must take if we are to move toward comparative generalizations. It is the first, indispensable step which must be taken, though with great care. . . .

Military Elites and Foreign Policy: Proposal for a Conceptual Framework

Focus and Purpose. Wiser men may feel that I stray where they would fear to tread, but the present unsatisfactory state of comparative analysis in the area of civil-military relations impels me to move beyond the role of critic. Perhaps we can make some modest progress toward more systematic comparison if we concentrate on an aspect of the subject which is neither narrow to the point of insignificance nor so broad as to be lost in abstractions. The part which military elites may play in the making of foreign policy in modern, industrialized states seems to provide a promising focus for attempting a more systematic approach to civil-military relations, in the middle range between detailed description and soaring theory. By comparing the nature and extent of the influence of military leaders on the choice of alternative goals and policies by foreign policy makers in similar, but not identical settings, we may gain some new perspectives and move toward a more sophisticated examination of prevalent "common sense" and normative generalizations about civil-military relations in general. We may also contribute to a more systematic comparison of the nature of civil-military relations by identifying and comparing specific variables which appear to affect significantly the extent of military élite influence on foreign policy making. Though we limit our focus to modern, industrialized states, we may derive from such an investigation new insights into the role of "specialists in violence" in so-called "less-developed" states as well.

It may help to clarify my focus further if I list some questions which preliminary consideration of the subject has indicated to be relevant for the purposes of the proposed investigation:

1. Does the influence of military leaders on foreign policy making depend on factual or imagined threats to the community as perceived by the mass or elites; and, if so, how much?

2. What part do "myths" play in upholding the authority of military leaders?

3. Does the influence of military leaders on foreign policy making change with the external *involvement* or commitment of a state?

4. Does the influence of military leaders vary with the *status* of a state in the international political setting?

5. Is the influence of the military leadership related to developments in military technology and the "expertness" of the "professionals in violence"?

6. How is the social structure related to military influence? Does a conscious acceptance of military participation in foreign policy making vary with the socioeconomic homogeneity or a sharing of values of civilian and military élites? How do social mobility and broadening of the recruitment base for civilian élites affect the influence and composition of the military élite?

7. Is foreign policy making influenced by the desire of nonmilitary leaders and masses

to curb the influence—actual or potential—of the military leadership?

8. How is the nature of a political system related to the influence of the military leaders within it? Does military influence increase as popular compliance with authority becomes less voluntary? With democratization of the political decision-making system, does military influence depend increasingly on popular belief in threats from abroad (related to Questions 1 and 2), while in an autocratic system such influence depends primarily on personal and group ties between civilian and military élites?

These questions, suggested by new and old studies of civil-military relations, indicate some of the issues which may be encompassed by the focus of our investigation.

Fundamental Assumptions

1. The roles played by military leaders in developed and developing states are distinguished by functional dissimilarity, by a difference in kind rather than of degree. Only in modern industrialized states do we find a high degree of functional differentiation of military roles and tasks (leaving aside for the purposes of this analysis the role of the warrior in political systems other than sovereign states).

2. Historical evidence furnishes the most relevant data for the purposes of this investigation. . . . we should try to use a limited number of historical cases for the purpose of making comparative generalizations, relying most of the time "on nothing more scientific than the use of analogy, occasional insight, and judgment."[3]

3. The extent of military influence on foreign policy making may be assessed along a scale, one end of which might be called—with due credit to Harold Lasswell—the *Civilian State* (in which military influence is equal to zero because the military has no influence whatever on foreign policy making) and the other the *Garrison State* (in which military influence on for-

eign policy making is absolute because such policy making is entirely the prerogative of the military). The extent of military influence in decision making determines the position, on this dimension, of a particular civil-military relationship in the realm of foreign policy and vice versa. These polarities are to be understood as hypothetical constructs, not analytical abstracts (i.e., "ideal models"). They may exist in fact. Iceland, for example, is today a Civilian State, while Imperial Germany during the First World War and Japan during the second were Garrison States.

Major Concepts

1. *State.* A state is a human community that claims, on the whole successfully, a monopoly of the legitimate use of physical force within a given territory.[4]

2. *Military.* By the military I mean, for the purposes of this analysis, that group in the state which has legitimate, primary, and specific responsibility for the organized and planned employment of the state's physical force against other states. A military man, accordingly, is any legitimate member of this group—regardless of rank, dress, or position. When the military function is institutionalized, we may speak of a military establishment.[5]

---

3 *Karl W. Deutsch*, et al., Political Community and the North Atlantic Area: International Organization in the Light of Historical Experience (*Princeton, N.J.: Princeton University Press, 1957*), *p. 13. . . .*

4 *Max Weber, "Politics as a Vocation," in Hans Gerth and C. Wright Mills, eds., From Max Weber (London: Oxford University Press, 1946), p. 78.*
5 *This definition does not exclude the performance of other roles by the military—political education of conscripts, for example—but those are considered secondary functions only. The definition deliberately seeks to avoid a time- and culture-bound emphasis on professionalism, vocational "calling," corporate esprit, and commissioned rank which seems implicit or explicit in many current definitions of "the military." . . . Excluded from the military by my definition are guerrilla and resistance fighters, except when they are operating on behalf of and under the direction of another state. Excluded, too, are so-called "political" soldiers. Insofar as they are exercising primarily political functions, their tasks are entirely different in terms of the social system of the state, though their particular interpretation of their political role may well be influenced by previous military training and experiences. On the other hand, reserve officers on extended active*

A clear distinction between different types of "specialists in violence" seems an essential prerequisite for comparative analysis. . . . The chief distinction, it would appear, is one of functional specificity among the specialists in violence. In modern, so-called developed states we have a differentiation of functions between (1) the *military,* as a group of specialists in violence primarily, legitimately, and specifically concerned with the *interstate* application of force, and (2) the *police,* as a group of specialists in violence legitimately concerned first and foremost with the *intrastate* use of force for the maintenance of internal authority and stability in a state.

For the purposes of this analysis, we seek to distinguish clearly between military and police functions in a state and to identify explicitly those who perform the function which we have defined as that of the military. This is difficult, if not impossible, where military and police functions are relatively undifferentiated and the specialist in violence may perform both types of functions—as in the case of the European feudal nobility. Only when the specialists in violence are legitimately and *primarily* concerned with the application of force against other states can we speak of military men, as defined here. During the last century such differentiation of functions has existed only in modern, industrialized states. In states with relatively undifferentiated sociopolitical systems and relatively limited and uncomplicated external relations—such as contemporary Saudi Arabia—specificity of these functions is low (i.e., diffuse).[6]

3. *Military Elite.* By military elite I mean those comparatively few members of the military who—regardless of rank, service, or formal position—are *consistently* better informed and more influential concerning the policies and behavior of the entire group than the nonelite military mass. In general, the military elite is a positional elite, due to the hierarchical character of military organizations, and the formal military leaders are usually also the actual military decision makers—though not by any means invariably. Usually, the positional elite tends to command greater sources of relevant information and more explicitly recognized legitimate authority than its formal subordinates.

4. *Foreign Policy Making.* By foreign policy making I mean the more or less deliberate, conscious, and specific decision by the authoritative policy makers of a state to choose one particular course of action toward one or more other states over alternative courses that appear to be open to them. The decision-making unit may be an individual or a group; it may be formally or informally constituted. The important point is that policy making is a specific *choice* between alternatives, not the ratification of a previous decision. Although the distinction between foreign and domestic policy decisions may not always be clear and it may sometimes be difficult to delineate the boundaries of a decision-making group, these are not believed to be insurmountable difficulties.

5. *Military Influence.* By military influence I mean, for the purposes of this analysis, an asymmetrical relationship between the military and the nonmilitary in which the former more or less affect the policy decisions of the latter. That is, when we ask how "influential" is the mili-

---

duty and alien mercenaries are members of the military whenever their primary function is the legitimate application of force against other states.
[6] *This conceptual distinction between different specialists in violence obviously invites exceptions and objections. Like any analytical concept, it cannot be made either too restrictive or too loose, and qualitative judgment is unavoidable. Thus our concept demands qualitative judgment about the classification of paramilitary forces which may perform military and police functions interchangeably—such as the American National Guard*

—or simultaneously—such as the Nazi Waffen SS *in the Second World War, or the present West German "Border Police." As in the case of military men temporarily engaged in intrastate warfare against domestic opponents, or in "policing" an occupied state, a protectorate, or a colony, our emphasis on primary function must serve as the basis for qualitative judgment. . . .*

tary elite, we mean by influence something which in inferred from the behavior of the nonmilitary foreign policy makers, just as the influence of an advertiser is inferred from the behavior of consumers. For analytical purposes we must distinguish between *processes* and *channels* of military influence.

The process of military influence may take (1) the *direct* form of giving advice or participating in policy making in a face-to-face relationship between decision maker(s) and military leader(s), or (2) the *indirect* form of the conscious or unconscious adoption by the decision maker(s) of so-called "military factors" (values, interests, techniques) deliberately and consciously promoted by the military élite. In both instances, influence may be exerted by furnishing the decision makers with (1) *selective information* (the military élite acting as a source of "relevant facts") or (2) means and end values which orient the decision makers toward a desired course of action. That is, in Simon's words, "Influence is exercised through the control over the premises of decision."[7] For example, the German Schlieffen Plan

[7] *Herbert A. Simon,* Administrative Behavior, *2nd ed. (New York: The Macmillan Company, 1957), p. 223. See also Burton M. Sapin and Richard C. Snyder,* The Role of the Military in American Foreign Policy *(New York: Doubleday & Company, Inc., 1954), pp. 23, 32.*

for an attack on France established firm premises for German diplomatic decisions prior to the outbreak of the First World War. Diplomatic support for a specific military plan of operation seems also to have played a considerable role in pre-World War II British, French, and Japanese policy, as well as in postwar American Alliance policies related to the need for B-36, intermediate-range missile, and Polaris submarine bases, and in Pentagon demands for West German and Japanese rearmament.

The *channels of military influence* may be divided into formal and informal, direct and indirect channels.

1. *Formal channels* of military influence are those situated within the legitimate and authoritative policy-making structure of the state. Formal-direct influence may be exercised in face-to-face relations between military and nonmilitary leaders, as in the case of the participation of military men in key foreign policy making units (e.g., the Japanese Cabinet in the 1930's or the American National Security Council) or through direct access to key foreign policy makers (e.g., the formal privilege of the Chief of the German General Staff before 1914 to report directly to the Kaiser). Here we want to know the relevant formal decision-making units and to identify, if possible, the role military

	Direct	Indirect
Formal	Participation in or direct formal access to key policy-making units (Chief of German General Staff before 1914)	Access to key foreign policy-making units through formal nonmilitary intermediaries (US Service Secretaries)
Informal	Personal and/or group ties to authoritative and legitimate nonmilitary key foreign policy-makers (School or family ties)	Intermediary nonmilitary groups communicating preferences of military elite to authoritative and legitimate foreign policy-makers (Navy League)

Figure 1.   Channels of military influence.

leaders play in them at any given time, whether as expert advisers or representatives of military or service interests.

Formal-indirect channels of military influence allow influence to make itself felt through legitimate nonmilitary intermediaries. That is, the military participate indirectly in key foreign policy making units through such formal intermediaries as civilian defense ministers and service secretaries, parliamentary deputies, civil servants and—at least in totalitarian party states—party leaders. In extreme cases, such intermediaries may be no more than "front men" for the military élite.

2. Secondly, we have the *informal* channels through which military influence may flow outside the legitimate and authoritative policy-making structure of a state. These may be *informal-direct* channels, such as personal or group ties between authoritative and legitimate military and nonmilitary leaders (e.g., cliques, camaraderies, family ties, pre-service and in-service affiliations) which permit members of the military élite to communicate their preferences *directly* to nonmilitary foreign policy decision makers. *Indirect channels of informal influence* are the most difficult to identify and trace. They include alliances and ties between the military and nonmilitary elites which permit the former to communicate their explicit and implicit preferences to the foreign policy makers through informal intermediaries (e.g., leading members of powerful business groups, kitchen cabinets, political parties, and through spokesmen of such interest groups as naval and army leagues and veterans' organizations). Indirect channels of informal influence also include the broad channels of "public opinion" in its manifold forms.

The Extent and Intensity of Military Influence in Foreign Policy making

An Inventory of Relevant Analytical Variables

Several questions posed earlier in this paper sought to focus on a number of factors that may affect the extent and intensity of the influence of military leaders on foreign policy decisions. These factors we may now group into three major sets of variables: (1) external setting, (2) internal setting, and (3) military organization, technology, and techniques.

1. *External Setting.* By external setting I mean the *dominant* pattern of relationships with other states in the *relevant* international setting at the time a foreign policy decision is made. Geopolitically oriented analysts have stressed the importance of "natural" borders, island positions, and geographic features in discussing the role of the military in various states. . . . Whether and how much a modern state's international relationships affect the influence of military leaders on its foreign policy might be examined more carefully and explicitly by comparing evidence of such influence with the nature of the relevant external setting at the time of decision. To facilitate such a comparison we might classify a state's relationship with other states in terms of *general-dominant patterns* at the time of decision, as well as in terms of the *specific-dominant* relationship(s) with which the policy decision is concerned.

General-Dominant Pattern of Involvement. Unless a state is hermetically sealed off from all contacts with other states, its leaders obviously must make decisions about foreign relations. The general external setting provides stimuli to which some sort of response has to be made, whether it be in the form of a negative policy of inaction or isolation—as in the case of China in the nineteenth century— or a policy of deliberate involvement (which may take the form of belligerent competition or peaceful cooperation with states in the relevant international environment). However, what concerns us here is not the nature of these policy responses, but the extent to which the general external political environment requires foreign policy decisions. The extent, frequency, and intensity of the external contacts determine the *patterns of involvement* of a state, and it should be possible to assess the degree of such dominant and general involvement at any given moment of decision in terms of an *involvement-noninvolvement index*. For our purposes, such an assessment will have to be based upon rather crude qualitative judgments, but a more refined evaluation might enlist the aid of certain quantitative measurements. . . .

Specific-Dominant Relationship. Every foreign policy decision involves a dominant relationship with one or more other states, be it bilateral or multilateral. The decision may be to launch an attack, to cast a vote in an international organization, or to conclude a treaty of alliance. In each case, the nature of the particular relationship relevant to the decision taken may be described as more or less cooperative or more or less competitive and assessed accordingly in terms of a multidimensional *cooperation-competition index*. At one extreme we have a highly intimate and intense cooperative relationship which stops just short of amalgamation with one or more other states. Here agreement with the foreign policy makers of the other relevant states is at a maximum and to a large extent automatic. At the other extreme we have a highly intense competitive relationship, such as the state of belligerency usually labelled "all-out" war. In this case disagreement with the decision makers of the other state is at a maximum and so intense as to rule out any sort of agreement, as in the case of the United States' decision to declare war on Japan after Pearl Harbor. Between these extremes we have relationships characterized by a greater or lesser degree of cooperation or competition, by symmetry between powers more or less equal or asymmetry between superior and inferior, by stability or instability. Thus the Soviet decision to sign an agreement with Nazi Germany in 1939 was made against the background of an unstable, temporary, cooperative relationship between two more or less equal powers (symmetry), while the Soviet decision to sign a treaty with Finland in 1961

was based on a stable cooperative relationship between a superior and an inferior (asymmetrical). The United States' decision to come to the assistance of the Republic of Korea was made on the basis of an unstable competitive relationship with the Soviet Union, while France concluded a secret military convention with Tsarist Russia in December, 1893, against the background of a stable competitive relationship with a superior power, Imperial Germany.

In short, we seek to evaluate a state's external relations in terms of the *objective* nature of its association with other states. The subjective perception of such relationships by the decision makers and military leaders of a state is another matter, which we shall consider under the second set of variables that may affect the influence of military elites on foreign policy making.

2. Internal Setting. Earlier in this paper we asked whether threat perception, myths, and the general nature of a state's social and political systems may affect the influence of its military elite on foreign policy making. These factors might be examined more closely in terms of a set of variables which I have called the *internal setting*. I mean by this the *dominant* pattern of relationships within a state which affect the influence of the military elite upon foreign policy making at any given moment of decision. A great deal of the literature on civil-military relations puts primary stress on domestic political factors in assessing "military influence," but all too often by simply equating apparent agreement between military and nonmilitary leaders with military influence. (For example, the frequent assertion that Roosevelt allowed the Joint Chiefs of Staff to make important foreign policy decisions during the Second World War.) It is quite true, as we are frequently reminded, that the interrelationship between political and military factors—like that between foreign and domestic factors—is extremely complex in modern industrialized states, but we do not agree with those authors who conclude that this relationship therefore defies analysis. If it is possible to identify and isolate the interrelated variables which are said to affect significantly the relationship which interests us here, we may make explicit and, perhaps, testable some of the common assertions about domestic factors in civil-military relations —at least in the realm of foreign policy making. Keeping in mind that we are endeavoring to provide an itinerary or checklist of possibly significant variables, we might group those in the internal setting under several headings.

Degree of Military Accountability and Access to Decision Makers. A great deal of the literature on civil-military relations deals with the extent of nonmilitary authority over the military, that is, the asymmetrical relationship based on the superior's ability to gain compliance from the inferior. Generally, authors have taken the degree of military accountability and access to the nonmilitary policy makers in a state as valid criteria for measuring the extent of civilian control over the military. On the one hand, extreme nonaccountability and unlimited access [have] been attributed to German military leaders during the First World War; on the other hand, extremely high accountability but very limited access to nonmilitary decision makers are said to have characterized conditions in Germany and Russia during the Second World War. By examining specific criteria of nonmilitary authority, such as fiscal control over military expenditures and ultimate decision-making authority over military activities, it might be possible to make explicit the extent of such authority in a state when a foreign policy decision is taken.

Degree of Militarism. We are all familiar with assertions about the "typical" attitudes of a people toward war and peace and about the extent of "militarism" in a state. To make it possible to examine such attitudes more carefully, we need specific criteria for evaluating the degree of militarism at any given moment of decision. By *degree of militarism* I mean here the prevalence of certain kinds of elite and nonelite attitudes toward "military factors." The extent of elite and nonelite militarism might thus be assessed in terms of (1) attitudes toward the use of violence against other states (e.g., "preventive" and "just" wars, xenophobia and the perception of threats of aggression, force as a symbol of power and prestige);[8] (2) attitudes toward military leaders and the military function (e.g., to what extent are military authority and competence respected and accepted and in what areas of the social system? What are the images and expectations pertaining to relations between the military and nonmilitary?); (3) historical memories relating to war and peace, friendly and antagonistic states (i.e., "traditional" enemies or allies), military heroes, military history, etc.; (4) the existence of "legitimacy myths" supporting military authority (e.g., "defense of the national interest," "national security considerations," "capitalist encirclement").

Position of Military Leaders in the Sociopolitical Structure. Here we are interested in the extent of sociopolitical relations between military and nonmilitary élites. Is there a high degree of social cohesion (e.g., Imperial Germany), social conflict (e.g., Japan from 1922 to 1940), or simply a generally accepted social cleavage (e.g., [the] United States before 1939)? To what extent has the nonmilitary elite become allied with the military elite, to what extent has a military penetration of the nonmilitary elite positions taken place? To what extent are the military leaders economically dependent on the nonmilitary elites? What is the recruitment base of the military and what are the opportunities for social advancement for military leaders (e.g., ascriptive or achievement, mass or class base, warrior families, mer-

8 *Thus a number of writers have attributed the outbreak of war in 1914 to a general climate of insecurity, combined with a xenophobic attitude, among elites and masses in most European countries. On the other hand, Franco-British "appeasement" policies in the 1930's are said to have been based on fear of war, but not of aggression, among elites and masses in both these countries.*

cenary or citizen armies, élite or mass armies)?

Military Participation Ratio.[9] By the military participation ratio I mean the proportion of a state's human and physical resources which are devoted to military activities. That is, what percentages of the total national income, the national product, the productive labor force, technological resources, and communications network are allocated to the military function? Obviously, exact data for measuring such ratios are difficult, if not impossible to procure, but it should be possible in most cases to establish a rough estimate on the basis of available "open" sources.

The Political System. What are the patterns of policy making in general (e.g., authoritarian and monistic or libertarian and pluralistic, democratic or autocratic, homogeneous or heterogeneous)? How great is the ability of a state's policy makers to gain compliance with their decisions (e.g., political cohesion, homogeneity and consensus)? What means are employed to gain compliance with decisions (e.g., extent of compulsion or voluntary compliance, prevalent values concerning legitimacy of decision-making authority and degree of stability, manipulation, or voluntarism)? What is the role of élites, interest groups, and mass opinion in policy and decision making (e.g., communications flow: means, direction, and intensity; voting system; and voting participation)?

Principles and Practices of Foreign Policy. What have been the traditional means and ends of foreign policy and how deeply are they imbedded in the policy-making process (e.g., legalism, concepts of the national interest, traditional relations with other states, etc.)?

The Socioeconomic System. Size, mobility, literacy, distribution, homogeneity of the population, and other relevant data, such as economic resources, distribution of the labor force, the gross national product, per capita GNP, and growth rate of the GNP.

3. *Military Organization, Technology, and Techniques.* Perhaps the most obscure and, at the same time, most controversial question about the influence of military élites on policy making relates to the significance of the internal organization, technological development, and expertness of the military. Treatises on international politics and military affairs frequently contain assertions and assumptions about the impact of these factors on civil-military relations in various states, some claiming that it is negligible and others considering it all-important. By making more explicit the variables relating specifically to the preparation for and employment of physical force against other states we may be able to examine and compare their impact on foreign policy making in various settings—both by themselves and in conjunction with the other variables discussed previously.

Military Technology. By military technology, in this context, I mean the nature of the weapons systems that are actually and potentially available for use against other states at any given time. That is, we are above all interested in the type of weapons, "weapons-mix," and logistics systems which a state possesses or may possess in the immediate future (i.e., lead-time), rather than in so-called "strategic equations" relating its military capacity to that of other states.[10] For example, what was the significance—if any—of the British emphasis on naval power before 1914 for the role which the British military leadership played in the establishment of the *entente cordiale* with France? How important was the French and German "weapons-mix" of artillery and

---

[9] *I have borrowed the concept from Stanislaw Andrzejewski, who, in his book* Military Organization and Society *(London: Routledge & Kegan Paul, Ltd., 1954), employs it in a somewhat different sense and context.*

[10] *Not only are such "strategic equations" a matter of the external setting, but they are extremely difficult to ascertain objectively in any international relationship. Insofar as they enter "subjectively" into the consideration of the military and the decision makers, they should be considered in connection with the attitudes discussed under the internal setting.*

massed infantry for the influence of military leaders in these countries upon foreign policy? What bearing had the emphasis of French military technology on fortified positions upon French foreign policy decisions in the *interbellum* years? Did the American concentration on air-atomic power in the post-World War II years relate to the role which the Pentagon leadership played in the decision to rearm Germany?

Specificity of Military Functions. What concerns us here is the degree of functional specificity which is required to perform military functions in a state. How much skill and expertise is required, how long does it take to acquire it, and what sort of training is essential? To what extent and how rapidly can military skills be acquired by nonmilitary men, such as militia soldiers, reservists, and other "nonprofessionals"? To what extent are military and nonmilitary skills interchangeable, so that civilians can perform military functions on a part-time or temporary basis?

Military Structure. Here we are interested in the performance of military functions in a state. How are military decisions made and executed? What is the relationship between functional and structural specificity in the military establishment? In what manner are human and physical resources at the disposal of the military leadership exploited (e.g., the ratio of fire power to manpower or combat forces to total military manpower)?

Social Organization of the Military. This cluster of variables relates to some already touched upon under "internal setting," but here we focus specifically on the military as a social group or system, rather than as a subgroup of society. Some of the factors which appear to be relevant are the following:

1. The nature and composition of the military elite. What is the relationship between the formal and effective leaders? Are they more or less identical? If not, to what extent do the two sets of leaders diverge and what are the nature and

reasons for the divergence? Is there a dominant service?

2. What are the recruitment and mobility patterns for the military elite and the nature of the relationship among its members?

3. What is the extent of in-group sentiments and homogeneity relative to non-elite military men and nonmilitary elites? Are there service rivalries? Are there cliques, camaraderies, and other subgroups within the military elite, and are these linked to other elite and nonelite groups inside or outside the state? Is there a military counterelite or aspiring elite (e.g., "Young Turks")?

4. What is the extent of military elite authority over the military nonelite and to what extent is such authority accepted as legitimate by the military nonelite (e.g., discipline)?

5. What are the attitudes, images, and expectations of the members of the military elite relative to their own roles, those of other military men (both native and foreign), and those of the nonmilitary elites and nonelites? For example, do the military leaders perceive themselves as "guardians of the state" or arbitrators among other groups in the state? How do they view the internal and external political environment? In brief, is there a specific military code or philosophy that guides the behavior of the military elite in its relations with nonmembers and determines specific attitudes toward national and international politics (e.g., peace and war)?

Proposed Methodology

1. *The Collection of Data.* An inventory of variables is a sort of letter to Santa Claus: we tend to give free reign to our imagination and accumulate a long list of desired information. Wanting and getting, as children and scholars alike learn by bitter experience, are two different things. Ideally, the proposal I have put forward demands that we examine a very large number of foreign policy decisions in various settings, in which the preferences of a clearly identified military elite ran counter

to the manifest preferences of other individuals and groups participating in the decision-making process. In each case we would seek to identify the relevant decision makers and the variables pertinent to the role of the military elite in foreign policy making and then proceed to correlate outcome with variables. The facts of life, as always, force us to be satisfied with a good deal less than this ideal.

A survey of studies on the foreign affairs of the United States, Japan, and a number of European countries over the last century indicates that secondary data are available for the analysis of a considerable number of decisions participated in by the military leaders in modern, industrialized states. An inventory of this sort has obvious shortcomings. Secondary analysis is far from ideal and we shall be "biasing" our sample by proceeding in this manner. Inevitably, only some of the data we seek will be provided by such sources. I shall return to these problems shortly, but let me state at this point that I do not consider them insurmountable obstacles to a tentative exploration of comparative analysis within the proposed conceptual framework.

2. *Classification and Ordering of Data.* Henry James once said of one of his characters that "his mind contained several millions of facts packed too closely together for the light breeze of the imagination to draw through the mass." We have stressed the importance of adhering to a conceptual framework for the purposes of organizing our data, but concepts are more than mere pigeonholes for classification of information. They identify the relevant and the irrelevant, the important and the less significant information, and in the process of identifying and ordering our data, we cannot dispense with qualitative judgments derived from imaginative thinking. Whether we use high-speed computers or engage in old-fashioned counting, qualitative judgments are unavoidable. They need to be made as explicit and systematic as possible, however, and this we can do with the aid of our

conceptual framework. The codification of data is simply making more explicit and manageable the sorting of information that every scholar is more or less forced to engage in. Deutsch's proposed "profiles" for coding significant variables to permit their simultaneous inspection and comparison might be adopted in a modified form.[11] Quantitative measurements might make more explicit and manageable the sorting and comparing of information, and the keeping of a box score.

3. *Analysis of Data.* The object of the proposed investigation is not to draw a mathematically precise line from an unwarranted assumption to a foregone conclusion, but to search for general patterns and trends over time in the relationship between military and nonmilitary leaders in the field of foreign policy making. By comparing a considerable number of situations and decisions we may arrive at some meaningful generalizations about the military and nonmilitary influence in modern states. If we can correlate the outcome of each decision (in terms of the explicit military elite preferences) with the specific constellation of our three sets of major variables, we may arrive at some empirically supported hypotheses about the nature and extent of such influence in industrialized states.

Some Methodological Problems: The Author Tries to Anticipate his Critics

1. *The Individual Personality.* The question of the unique case as against the search for generalizations is one that has occupied historians and social scientists for a long time and is also crucial to our approach. I am presently engaged in an intensive analysis of a political leader and would be the last to deny the importance of individuals and their personality characteristics in the study of decision making. The properties of the individual and those of the setting in which he operates are

11 Karl W. Deutsch, "Toward an Inventory of Basic Trends and Patterns in Comparative and International Politics," *American Political Science Review, Vol. LIV (March, 1960),* 34–57.

complementary and interacting. If in the present proposal I tend to emphasize collective rather than individual attributes of the participating actors, this does not mean we should slight the role of the individual. I propose, however, that we consider it within the larger context of the suggested analytical framework. There are certainly instances where the personality of individuals is of considerable significance in arriving at decisions—we need only to think of Bismarck, Wilson, Hitler, and Stalin. But even in such cases one should not lose sight of the dog for the wagging tail, to make an outrageous mixture of metaphors. Not even the "great man" is—for methodological purposes—an island unto himself.

2. *Multiplicity of Categories and Variables.* It is to be expected that the proposed conceptual framework will be criticized for suggesting that we operate with an unmanageably large number of categories and variables. On the one hand, some will deny that enough data to permit meaningful generalizations can be found in historical records. On the other hand, as Harold Stein has warned, "all the relevant variables cannot be effectively isolated or precisely determined" in decision making.[12] Both points revolve around the question of relevance and completeness. Indeed, there is the danger that by trying to be exhaustive we may defeat our very purpose. We must exercise great care in attempting a multivariate analysis if we are to sail safely between the Scylla of monistic determinism and the Charybdis of anarchic indeterminism. If, at this point, I have deliberately put forward a tentative *itinerary* of possibly significant variables, it was done with the aim of helping us to identify and classify data which appear to be of possible relevance. Further research and analysis will probably result in eliminating, substituting,

and collapsing a number of these variables, as well as in the modification of the conceptual framework.

3. *The Use of Historical Data.* In proposing to make use of historical case studies we have to examine both the question of the relevancy and the adequacy of such data for the purposes of generalization. Again we confront the matter of the unique case. But here, too, comparison admittedly engages in a certain amount of obscuring—even distorting—of details in order to gain greater perspective. We cannot argue that something is unique unless we compare it with something else, and in that sense the argument against comparative generalizations seems to lose most of its strength.

The second problem in connection with the use of historical data relates to the relevance of such material for the purpose of making generalizations of even limited theoretical and operational contemporary significance. Students of civil-military relations have argued this point. Some insist that for the air-atomic age prenuclear experiences are entirely irrelevant in the study of civil-military relations. The impact of modern weapons systems is said to be truly "revolutionary." It seems to me that these assertions, while possibly true, tend to be unproven assumptions. It may also be that, while the weapons are new, "the concepts that guide their use are old."[13] Neither the character of modern weapons systems nor the apparent acceleration in the dynamics of political decision making in certain states *ipso facto* makes past experiences irrelevant. If nothing else, historical comparisons should help us to examine more closely the validity of the assumptions on both sides.

The problem of the adequacy of data remains. I have already pointed out that we are compelled to "bias" our sample of case studies by relying on readily available sources. We shall have to depend largely on secondary sources whose authors usu-

[12] *Harold Stein, "Case Method and the Analysis of Public Administration," in Stein, ed., Public Administration and Policy Development (New York: Harcourt, Brace & World, Inc., 1952), pp. xii–xvi.*

[13] *Louis Morton, "Historia Mentem Armet: Lessons of the Past," World Politics, Vol. XII (January, 1960), 155.*

ally have had entirely different criteria from our own for the selection and interpretation of their data. Nonetheless, I feel we can make, if not a virtue, at least a good case out of this necessity.

Fortunately, we now possess or will soon be presented with a number of historical studies, memoirs, and biographies which directly or indirectly concern the roles of the military in the foreign policy-making process of modern states. I have in mind broad surveys, such as the works of Alfred Vagts, and the recent collections of essays edited by Michael Howard, Kent Roberts Greenfield, and Harry Coles,[14] as well as various military histories and foreign policy studies. . . .

Perhaps we shall some day have available to us original case studies based on a common conceptual framework and methodology. They would certainly give greater weight to any generalizations and hypotheses. However, for present purposes, secondary analysis should permit us to proceed with data collection and speculative analysis.

4. *The Problem of Influence.* We cannot escape consideration of the crucial, yet so difficult problem of identifying and assessing influence—or rather, the effects of influence. In recent years this has been a problem of considerable concern to sociologists and social psychologists, as well as to political scientists, particularly in the area of community power structures and elite analyses, where "elites" are identified as the "influentials." Extraordinary difficulties attend the study of influence. Not only may the channels be direct and indirect, formal and informal, but the effects latent as well as manifest, anticipated as well as unanticipated—not to mention the problem of circularity of influence. . . . What March said a few years ago seems still true today: the empirical study of influence is as yet in its infancy.[15]

In the study of "civil-military relations" the effects of military influence have been exceedingly difficult to assess. Some authors seek to infer such effects from the spread of so-called "military values"—assumed to be universal—and speak of the "militarization" of society. Others refer to "civilian militarism" or "objective" and "subjective" civilian control—all of them concepts difficult to use for empirical purposes. More precise and reliable methods for gauging influence may gradually be developed, but for the purposes of this analysis we must beg these methodological questions and rely largely on secondary evidence of manifest military influence—an unsatisfactory, but apparently unavoidable method in the light of available data and analytical tools.

14 *Alfred Vagts*, A History of Militarism, *rev. ed.* (*New York: Meridian Books, Inc., 1959*) *and* Defense and Diplomacy (*New York: King's Crown Press, 1956*); *Michael Howard, ed.,* Soldiers and Governments (*Bloomington: University of Indiana Press, 1959*); *Kent Roberts Greenfield, ed.,* Command Decisions (*New York: Harcourt, Brace & World, Inc., 1959*); *Harry L. Coles,* Total War and Cold War (*Columbus: Ohio State University, 1962*).

15 *James G. March, "An Introduction to the Theory and Measurement of Influence,"* American Political Science Review, *Vol. XLIX (June, 1955), 463ff.*

E. Experimentation

Some Reflections on Experimental Techniques in Political Analysis

Richard C. Snyder

Can experimental techniques help the political scientist develop theories and select theories which need or deserve further refinement and preliminary testing?

The answer is yes, *provided* one does not aspire immediately to verification in the strict sense—the emphasis is on *exploration*—and provided one does *not* infer that our usual objects of inquiry must be discarded or other techniques replaced.
Kinds of Experiments.   Exactly what is implied by "experimental techniques"? Generally speaking, experimentation consists of a contrived series of observations of phenomena which are under more or less controlled conditions and which are repeatable and verifiable. Usually such observations are made in some sort of laboratory, where conditions can be more easily manipulated. The basic idea is, as we all know, that repeated exercises permit the researcher to vary certain factors while holding others constant (or as nearly so as possible) for the purpose of seeing what changes are induced as a result of the variance. (For those who take a puristic view of science, repeated controlled observation is the essence of the scientific method; there can be no scientific knowledge unless it is generated by this fundamental procedure.)

A number of possibilities are accessible to us because the basic idea can be expressed in many forms. Hence a crude classification is needed.

1. One important distinction has been suggested—quasi-experiments which permit some of the advantages of repeated observations under changing conditions in natural social settings without entailing the greater degree of control by the experimenter we associate with the laboratory. A prime example is Gosnell's classic study *Getting Out the Vote: An Experiment in the Stimulation of Voting* (Chicago: University of Chicago Press, 1927), which has not been replicated (to this writer's knowledge). Equally noteworthy is the fact that those committed to a more rigorous political science rarely cite Gosnell's work. Two other examples of interest to political analysts are [Muzafer] Sherif, *et al., The Robber's Cave Experiment* (Norman, Oklahoma: University Book Exchange, 1961) and [R. K.] White and [Ronald] Lippitt, *Autocracy and Democracy: An Experimental Inquiry* (New York: Harper & Row, Publishers, Inc., 1960). The former focuses on patterns of cooperation and conflict in a boys' camp; the latter focuses on patterns of leadership in after-school activity groups. A common characteristic of all these studies is that experimental controls are imposed on real-life situations, with the aim of disturbing spontaneous behavior as little as possible.

2. Artificial experimental situations, on the other hand, may be divided for our

Richard C. Snyder, "Experimental Techniques in Political Analysis: Some Reflections in the Context of Concern over Behavioral Approaches," in James C. Charlesworth, ed., *The Limits of Behavioralism in Political Science* (Philadelphia: The American Academy of Political and Social Science, 1962), pp. 102–11, 115, 117, 118–19, 121–22. Reprinted by permission.

purposes into two types: those which use computers and those which use human subjects. Both often involve *simulation,* that is, the attempt to induce realistic effects and to reproduce properties of reality.

Computer simulation of immediate interest to political scientists is exemplified in the successful effort to program national political campaigns and elections by Pool,[1] McPhee,[2] and others. Benson[3] has developed a computer simulation of international relations and diplomacy, and Coleman[4] has adapted his developmental model of community political conflict processes to a machine program. Essentially, the computer makes possible a much more complex set of starting conditions and variables whose interrelationships are expected to determine outcomes and a much greater opportunity to examine the different long- and short-term consequences of changes introduced at various stages. It becomes feasible to explore many more dynamic possibilities inherent in initial models, as in the case of the "campaign simulator," which permits the introduction of new voter appeals to see how opinion-formation processes are affected and how these, in turn, influence voting behavior. Pool reports considerable success in predicting the 1960 Presidential election. "Simulmatics," as his computer program is called, has been put on a semipermanent basis.

A second basic type of laboratory experimentation uses human subjects. In turn, these must be subdivided in order to reveal the range of choice:

(a) *Small, face-to-face groups.* Most of us tend to think first about the extensive literature and research on small groups when laboratory techniques are mentioned. It seems fair to say that this rapidly accumulating work has not yet been combed thoroughly and systematically by and for political scientists. Until recently, there were only a handful of examples of attempts at constructive political applications, and the general reaction has been a somewhat negative skepticism. Fortunately, two valuable books go a long way toward filling an important gap in our own literature: [Sidney] Verba, *Small Groups and Political Behavior: A Study of Leadership* (Princeton, N.J.: Princeton University Press, 1961); and [R. T.] Golembiewski, *Organization and Behavior* (Chicago: Rand McNally & Co., 1962). Both authors build bridges between a domain of psychological and sociological inquiry, on the one hand, and the interests of political analysts, on the other. Verba, in particular, discusses many of the problems which have caused the skepticism just mentioned, and it is therefore not necessary for me to repeat his major points. Together with Guetzkow's fine essay in [R. A.] Young, ed., *Approaches to the Study of Politics* (Evanston, Ill.: Northwestern University Press, 1958), the reader has a much more reliable introduction than has been available in the past.

* * *

. . . We must draw distinctions between kinds of primary groups—for example, a primary group actually embedded in a social milieu which performs a specific political function on a face-to-face basis (a jury) and a primary group associated with an institution which is thrown together sporadically without continuity (a clique in Congress). In turn, these two differ from a primary, or face-to-face, small group, which is a site for studying political phenomena—for example, husband and wife interaction over political issues.[5] So far as *experimental*

---

[1] *Ithiel Pool and Robert Abelson, "The Simulmatics Project," Public Opinion Quarterly, Vol. XXV (1961), 167–183.*
[2] *William McPhee, "Note on a Campaign Simulator," ibid., Vol. XXV (1961), 182–193.*
[3] *Oliver Benson, "Simulation of International Relations and Diplomacy," in H. Borko, ed., Computer Applications in the Behavioral Sciences (Englewood Cliffs, N.J.: Prentice-Hall, Inc., 1961).*
[4] *James Coleman, "The Simulation of Processes in Social Controversy," in Harold Guetzkow, ed., Simulation in Social Science (Englewood Cliffs, N.J.: Prentice-Hall, Inc., 1962).*

[5] *James March, "Husband and Wife Interaction over Political Issues," Public Opinion Quarterly, Vol. XVII (1953–1954), 461–470.*

small groups are concerned, it is important to note that, on the whole, the interest is to *produce* the phenomena to be observed—the assembled group plus its immediate operating environment *is* reality. This stands in contrast to the *reproduction* of phenomena and aspects of reality *indirectly* through various representational devices.

(*b*) *Simulation of institutions, organizations, systems, and processes.* It would be a mistake to assume automatically that if one saw a relatively small group of subjects going through certain motions in a laboratory that a small, face-to-face group experiment was under way. Neither primary groups nor face-to-face interactions are necessarily involved in observing social behavior under controlled conditions. Single business firms,[6] international systems,[7] or strategic encounters and diplomatic negotiations[8] can be simulated. To the extent that experimentation has entered a branch of political science, it has been mainly through the simulation of international relations. Simulation and one of its major species, "gaming," have become significant teaching[9] as well as research techniques, though only the latter will be discussed.

As already mentioned, simulation exercises *reproduce* some portion or aspect of reality—a "likeness" if you will. Because many kinds and degrees of likeness are

possible, still further distinctions among forms are indicated: relatively *realistic* and relative *nonrealistic; role playing* and *nonrole playing.* An example will illustrate both distinctions. If we used experienced officials, including Soviet experts, from the State Department and Defense Department to act out Soviet and American responses to a current problem—some phase of the Cold War or the negotiation of an inspection agreement—if, in constructing the "game," we employed all the relevant knowledge at our disposal, and if we asked the Soviet experts to take the part of the Soviet Union and act as real Soviet representatives would act, we would have a realistic, role-playing simulation. If, on the other hand, we created fictitious nations operated by nonexperts, if we built in only certain features of the international system, and if we presented the players with a minimal set of rules (for example, general objectives, modes of communication, and so forth), asking that they take off from a particular set of starting conditions and let actions and interactions flow as they will, then we would have a nonrole-playing, nonrealistic simulation. As a matter of fact, these overly simple descriptions differentiate between two actual simulation programs: the first kind has been undertaken by Rand[10] and the second by a group at Northwestern University.[11] The Rand version of gaming is more adapted to policy research, to determining how national policy makers might respond to various moves and situations and what alternative consequences will result from the interplay of political strategies. The Northwestern version is more adapted to basic research, to answering questions like: Under what conditions will coalitions form and how cohesive will

[6] *Harold Guetzkow and Ann Bowes, "The Development of Organizations in a Laboratory,"* Management Science, *Vol. III (1957), 380–402.*

[7] *Charles McClelland, "A World Politics Game" (San Francisco: San Francisco State College, International Studies Project, 1959, mimeographed).*

[8] *Herbert Goldhamer and Hans Speier, "Some Observations on Political Gaming,"* World Politics, *Vol. XII (1959), 71–83.*

[9] *Chadwick F. Alger, "Use of the Inter-Nation Simulation in the Undergraduate Teaching of International Relations," in Harold Guetzkow et al., eds.,* Simulation in International Relations: Developments for Research and Teaching *(Englewood Cliffs, N.J.: Prentice-Hall, Inc., 1962); Lincoln Bloomfield, "Political Gaming,"* United States Naval Institute Proceedings, *Vol. LXXXVI (1960), 57–64; W. Dill and J. Jackson, eds.,* Proceedings of the Conference on Business Games *(New Orleans: Tulane University Press, 1961).*

[10] *Joseph Goldsen,* The Political Exercise: An Assessment of the Fourth Round *(Washington, D.C.: The Rand Corporation, D-3640-RC, 1956, mimeographed).*

[11] *Harold Guetzkow, "A Use of Simulation in the Study of Inter-Nation Relations,"* Behavioral Science, *Vol. IV (1959), 183–191; Guetzkow, et al.,* Simulation in International Relations, op. cit.

they be? What will be the effects of distrust on communication patterns?

A further necessary distinction is between *more-programed* and *less-programed* simulations. Machine simulations are obviously programed by definition, but man-machine and man-man simulations differ with respect to how much is left to the participants to decide—the limitations incorporated in the rules, and/or whether some determinate "solution" is expected. Strategic gaming is, of course, a more programed type of simulation. The key difference lies in the availability of greater knowledge and "harder" variables (such as military factors) which programing requires.

(c) *Bargaining and negotiation experiments.*[12] Research into bargaining behavior has increased rapidly. While much of it has been focused on economics and economic theory, several projects have been inspired by, or are geared to, political analysis—notably international relations. It is here that some aspect or form of game theory is manifest in the design of experiments. To delimit bargaining from related phenomena, two characteristics may be regarded as essential: first, a conflict of interest (opposing needs) between parties cannot be satisfied separately, completely, or simultaneously—their fates are intertwined; second, a possibility of mutual gain through cooperation—gain meaning more than each party could achieve by going it alone. Bargaining experiments can be categorized as a variation under both (a) and (b) above, for face-to-face contacts among subjects may or may not be involved and exercises are not usually constructed as small group studies *per se.*

The purposes and designs of experiments vary, with the following targets of inquiry typical:[13] (1) a comparison of choice making in zero-sum and nonzero-sum game situations; (2) the relative significance of rational and irrational motivations on solutions reached; (3) effects of social-structural, personality, informational, and communication variables on bargaining strategies and payoffs; and (4) changes in strategies and payoffs through time as a result of learning and alteration of conditions or rules.

Though political content has not been built into bargaining experiments on any great scale, a leading exponent, economist Thomas Schelling [*The Strategy of Conflict* (Cambridge, Mass.: Harvard University Press, 1960)], is exploring his notion of "tacit" bargaining (indirect communication) between nations and a corollary notion of "prominent solutions." Schelling's general intent is to interpret or extend elements of game theory so as to embrace what he calls "mixed motive" conflicts in which nonmilitary strategic moves are interdependent under less limited conditions than are specified by the pure zero-sum version of the theory. Others (Ratoosh, Scodel, Willis, and Joseph) are also interested in applications to international relations. However, the basic structure of bargaining experiments is equally applicable to decision making within governments, and the role of bargaining in domestic policy formation is widely recognized though thus far not researched extensively.

One of the chief advantages of current work on bargaining is that it seems to provide a likely prospect of useful adaptation of game theoretic analysis to the political arena through the manipulation (and loosening) of conditions which hitherto have been too restrictive to be found often in real life.

12 *Thomas Schelling,* The Strategy of Conflict *(Cambridge, Mass.: Harvard University Press, 1960), esp. Chaps. 2 and 6; Sidney Siegel and Lawrence Fouraker,* Bargaining and Group Decision-Making: Experiments in Bilateral Monopoly *(New York: McGraw-Hill Book Company, 1960).*
13 *For example: Richard Willis and Myron Joseph, "Bargaining Behavior I: Prominence as a Predic-*
tor of Games of Agreement," Journal of Conflict Resolution, *Vol. III (1959), 102–113; Alvin Scodel, et al., "Some Descriptive Aspects of Two Person Non-Zero Sum Games,"* Journal of Conflict Resolution, *Vol. III (1959), 114–119; Alvin Scodel, et al., "Some Personality Correlates of Decision-Making Under Conditions of Risk," in D. Willner, ed.,* Decisions, Values, and Groups *(New York: Pergamon Press, Inc., 1960), pp. 37–49.*

Limits and Potentialities of Experimental Techniques

Even this sketchy discussion suggests there are a number of experimental modes to choose from once we admit the general technique to a place in a multiple strategy. I have glossed over some very difficult technical problems in the design and execution of experiments. In particular, there are problems of internal validation—for example, processes of change within human subjects resulting from the passage of time between trials—and external validation—for example, generalizability. I cannot begin to give these important factors the treatment they deserve. However, invalidating factors have been identified and ways of handling them have been proposed. Nothing could be worse for the development of politically relevant experimentation than naïve amateurism. At least three requirements enter, aside from statistical sophistication: (1) knowledge of the behavior to be produced or reproduced; (2) experience in rigorous use of the technique; and (3) imagination.

Are there unique advantages for the political scientist which would justify increased experimentation? I shall attempt to state my reasons for a qualified, yet strongly affirmative, answer to this question.

Limitations and Objections. The nature and significance of limitations on the utility of experimentation depend greatly on our keeping misunderstandings and false expectations to a minimum.

In order to clear the record, let me anticipate certain objections, knowing the reader might not raise them seriously in this form:

(a) *The richness of political reality is beyond the reach of the laboratory.*

Reply: If taken literally, this objection is both valid and irrelevant. The controlled experiment can never replace, say, a political ethnography, but *cultural elements* can be introduced. Although a surprising degree of richness can sometimes be produced, the primary aim of laboratory representations is to set key variables and their interrelationships *in motion* and to create, explicitly, imitations of and substitutes for the hidden explanatory or conditioning factors assumed to operate in life. Moreover, the experimental situation is usually designed to achieve *not actual effects* observed outside the laboratory but *equivalent kinds of effects* using the most economical representation of casual variables. For example, if we have reason to believe that the behavior of political actors is effected by their need to respond to voters or superiors or elite supporters, it is not necessary *for certain experimental purposes* to build in *all* of these possible sources of influence. Instead, *a validation function* can be injected which will accurately reflect the *gross impact* of a many-sided factor. Finally, it will be recalled that a quasi-experiment in a natural setting does permit the observer to impose "extras" on reality without fundamentally disturbing it.

(b) *Observing small numbers of people in contrived situations cannot tell us anything about the behavior of aggregates of large numbers or about institutional patterns.*

Reply: Again, by definition, yes, *unless* one draws a distinction between a small, face-to-face group experiment and one employing a small number of subjects. Apart from insights to be drawn from the former, complex organizational behavior can be simulated and nonface-to-face relationships can be reproduced artificially. Furthermore, because most small-group experiments *per se* have emphasized endogenous variables and nonpolitical behaviors, it does not mean that exogenous, political variables cannot be the focus of analysis. There is no reason *in principle* why a city council or a foreign office or a court cannot be imitated *in certain particular respects*. It is not numbers of participants by itself which is important, but the structural features and mechanisms we choose to manipulate. For example, we could watch the differential effects of precedent, group size, channels of communication, and allocations of power and responsibility on either group or organizational policy deliberations.

(c) No proposition concerning the real world can be directly tested in the laboratory.

Reply: At this stage of the game, and given the nature of political phenomena, probably not. However, two things must be added. First, "test" is an ambiguous word, and much depends on how propositions are stated—which goes to the word "directly." If by "test" one means rigorous proof, then clearly experiments will not do the job. If one adopts the position that *probing* theories—for example, disqualifying inadequate hypotheses or operationalizing variables—is required, then experimental techniques can help. As noted, the contrived situation is only one phase of a multiple strategy in which preliminary controls permit greater clarification than is possible by observation in natural settings. Second, there seems to be no way to test *directly* through experiment the proposition that legislatures assume relatively little initiative in external affairs as compared to the executive. But, if this proposition is logically derived from one (among others) which states that in complex organizations initiative tends to coincide with control over relevant information, then experimental exploration to discover the conditions under which the relationship between information and initiative holds or does not hold is feasible.

(d) Real world incentives cannot be simulated.

Reply: In effect, this says (1) that declaring war in a simulated international system does not have the consequences it does in reality, and (2) that epiphenomenal factors contaminate or destroy the validity of the experiment—the "gaming" really becomes a game for its own sake. This is a tricky question and one that implies conditions to be overcome. Is this sufficient reason not to use the technique as an adjunct to other research methods? To begin with, it is a warning not to base even tentative conclusions *solely on laboratory exercises* unless the behavioral situation is homologous. On the other hand, there are reasons for not overestimating the difficulty. Evidence indicates that subjects do become deeply involved in contrived situations and have a capacity for acting "as if" the exercise were actuality. And subjects can be pretested for general attributes deemed important in governing responses within the rules and parameters established by the experimenter. Thus, to put the matter in sharp perspective, the problem is not whether a college student acting as, say, a high-level policy maker really sees the world as the latter does, but whether, within the conditions imposed by the experimenter's theory, the college student is compelled to react to the same kinds of constraints which confront the policy maker. Artificiality of subjects' motivation will be directly related to the degree of role playing and programing manifest in a simulation. Generally speaking, we would not expect an average student to play President de Gaulle with much realism, though an expert might. To look at it from the other side, we know that political actors often must act contrary to their personal preferences. We do not, therefore, assert that the individual is incapable of being motivated *qua* policy maker. How far the incentive factor is a handicap depends in part on how the participants are chosen, on the purposes of the experiment, and on the experimenter's cleverness in devising ways of either inducing motivation or rendering inconsequential the lack of actual experience. This is one case where the proof of the pudding is in the eating—if equivalent effects are achieved despite the seeming lack of realistic incentives, then the lack is not fatal to the purposes of the exercise. The objection is plausible, but its a priori acceptance is not warranted and the limitation can be accommodated.

*   *   *

. . . we have a number of experimental modes to choose from once we admit the general technique may be a fruitful one.

1. As a heuristic procedure. Unless we are agreed that we either do not need bright ideas or that other ways—that is, the proverbial armchair—are cheaper or more productive, experimental exercises would seem to be a uniquely helpful source of new hypotheses. The world as given to us by direct sensory perception or indirectly by any of the familiar mediating filters is often confusing and complex—so much so that "hidden likenesses," patterns of uniformity, and key variables may be almost completely obscured. Experiments provide us with a simplified universe of observation and an opportunity for manipulation of what we suspect are crucial factors. . . .

* * *

2. Forced precision and explicitness in theory building. Implicit assumptions, "rubber" concepts, and tolerance of unspecific relationships among variables plague us all—indeed, it is often said that we get by with this sort of thing because we cannot, or will not, be called to account. One characteristic of laboratory and quasi-natural experiments is that we are compelled to make "bets," to choose a few among many possibilities for incorporation into the operating conditions and rules of the controlled exercise. Although the experimenter has options from which to choose, he cannot do everything, *and* he must have explicit reasons for his choices or he will not be able to evaluate results. It is difficult if not impossible to, say, inject all the twenty or thirty "elements of national power" usually mentioned in textbooks into the simulation of internation relations, or to avoid the problem of how one is going to define "democratic values" in a study of autocratic and democratic leadership patterns. The programing of a computer in order to simulate an election requires a limited number of crucial variables and hypothesized relationships among them.

* * *

3. "Probing" the elements of theory. Political science deals with an imposing realm of inquiry—a large variety of behaviors in a variety of contexts affected by many variables. Because we cannot do everything and because field research is difficult and expensive, anything which will improve the quality of our theory before it is committed to rigorous testing is welcome. A quasi-experimental approach embodies a series of trial-and-error explorations aimed at improving the definition and measurement of variables, the weeding out of less powerful variables, the elimination of competing hypotheses, and the clarification of interlevel relationships such as personality and political role. It is not that these are omitted from other forms of research; rather, we might gain by comparing techniques in terms of their cost, relative effectiveness at a certain stage of knowledge, and the time it takes to correct mistakes.

Given the complex institutional environment of politics, preliminary exploration might be an economical first step in a long-range research program focused on critical areas of ignorance. A few examples will illustrate. Attributes of individual decision makers—"personality" variables, including leadership traits—are regarded as operative factors in the formation of public policy. On the other hand, impersonal forces and roles, be they historical or bureaucratic or the like, are also felt to be determinants. So it is with situational components—the particular problem events which must be faced. At times all these (and others) may be affecting policy choices. To scan the multitude of locales where this set of factors and behaviors occurs and to pick out by inspection those which indicate different weightings for the factors appears very difficult indeed. From simulated decision-making structures and processes, two kinds of advantages could be expected: first, a clearer notion of the consequences of different operational definitions of organizational, individual, and situational variables; second, a basis for specifying the conditions under which one, or a particular combination, of these variables exerts a determining effect on decisional outcomes. To put it another way, we need to make preliminary judgments on which individual, organizational, and situational properties are significant, how they alter outcomes, and when they do so.

*   *   *

4. Change: emergent action situations. A most troublesome problem in political analysis—or social analysis generally, for that matter—is that so much of our research is timebound. We take snapshots at particular moments in time. If we analyze the Eighty-Fifth Congress, will conclusions hold for the Eighty-Third or the Ninety-First? More established action situations do exist, but, for the most part, we seem to be dealing with operating environments whose conditions are difficult to identify and predict. By the time academic research catches up with the observable results of change, something else is happening. There are several ways that experiments are useful in analyzing change. Accidents—unexpected events— can be introduced arbitrarily by the experimenter: the death of an important official (Archduke Ferdinand or Dag Hammarskjöld); a technological breakthrough in the form of an antimissile missile; or a crop failure. Developments can be rerun, something not possible in real life. Trials can be repeated over and over again, altering some factors and not others to observe the emergence of new configurations only dimly foreseen, to track various unfolding patterns.

Our grasp of changes in reality can be tested by comparing predictions within sequence of experimental runs and predictions of real events. The theory in each case might be the same or different—failures becoming an occasion for re-examination of explanatory hypotheses and successes (better than chance) becoming an explicit basis for greater confidence. Accumulations of experimental data permit blind, *ex post facto* predictions by neutral experts.

Concept and Subject Index

ABSTRACTIONS,
  in a discipline, 4–6
Abstracts, analytical,
  and hypothetical constructs: difference
    between, 342
Access to legislature,
  see legislative access
Advisers,
  basis of power in technical knowledge,
    200
  biases of, 104
  outside, 106–107
  power of in organizations, 199–200, 223–
    231
  qualifications of, 107–108
  role of in policy-making, 199–200
  variety of affecting decision-making, 96
  White House staff, 106
  see also staff experts
Amateur politicians,
  see politicians, amateur
Aristocracy,
  as a way of life distinguished from de-
    mocracy, 54–55
Attribute-cluster blocs,
  use of in legislative analysis, 243
Authority,
  attitudes toward stemming from sociali-
    zation in the family, 271
  definition of, 197
  uses of by leader, 198–199, 217–223

BEHAVIORALISM,
  definition of, 7
  in political science, 12–16
Bicameralism,
  limits on Congressional power, 34–35

"Blocs," legislative,
  primary characteristic of, 77

CAMPAIGNING,
  debates in, 151–157
  differences in among different party sys-
    tems, 59–60, 64–67
  in election of 1800, 158–161
Charisma,
  definition of, 211
  in responsible and irresponsible types of
    rulers, 210–216
  mass base of, 212
Check-and-balance system,
  effect of on differential access, 69–70
Civil-military relations,
  see military factor
Classical approach to political science,
  see traditional study
Classification, 301
  and conceptualization, 350
  see also taxonomy
Class differences,
  effect on politics, 97, 123–125
Clique,
  operational definition of, 127
  formation of in U.S. Supreme Court,
    125–132
Clique structure in legislative bodies,
  findings, 245–252
  hypotheses regarding, 245
  methodological difficulties of explora-
    tion, 242–243
Communications,
  flow model, 255–257
  functions of legislative leadership struc-
    ture, 248n.

Communications (*Cont.*)
  political functions of, 259n.
  through correspondence and press in a
    political campaign, 158–199
  upward, 291–292
Communications net,
  as a product of formal and informal or-
    ganizational demands and behavior
    patterns, 293
  role of in socialization of new organiza-
    tion members, 285–293
Communications process,
  definition of, 253
  effect on power relations, 203, 237–238
  informal channels of, 254
  study of, 253–254
Community conflict,
  see conflict, community
Comparative approach, 298–299, 302–309
Comparison, cross-national,
  need for, 340
Competition,
  as factor affecting party organizational
    power, 59
  in campaign debates, 151–157
  in the election of 1800, 157–165
Computers,
  use of in simulation, 354–356
Concepts as abstractions, 5
Conceptualization,
  definition of, 5
  explicit, 300–301, 340–352
Conflict management,
  see tension reduction
Conflict,
  community, 147–148, 176–185
  constraints on, invoked by community
    leaders, 181
  dynamics of, 147–148, 176–185
  escalation of, *see* hostility, acceleration of
  Gresham's Law of, 148, 184–185
Consensus,
  elements of in American politics, 37
  lack of in political science, 17–20
"Conspicuous industrialization,"
  definition of, 86
Constituencies,
  difference between presidential and con-
    gressional, 35
  safe, 72
Constructs, hypothetical,
  and analytical abstracts: difference be-
    tween, 342

Constructs, hypothetical (*Cont.*)
  illustrated, 297
Consultative function,
  role of meetings in, 95–96
Content analysis, 253
Correlation and regression analysis,
  limitations of, 312–313, 329–331
"Critical election,"
  definition of, 162
"Crystallizing agent,"
  role of staff expert, 223–224
Culture and politics, 99–100

DATA, historical,
  appropriate use of, 351–352
  reactive interpretation of, 294
Decision,
  definition of, 14
Decision-making,
  factors affecting, 95–97
Decoding,
  of messages in communications flow
    model, 255, 256
Democracy,
  as a way of life distinguished from aris-
    tocracy, 53–55
  factors conditioning existence of, 302–309
  operational definition, 303
Democratic revolution,
  effect on individualism, 55–56
Democratization,
  effect on power relations, 198
Despotism,
  characteristics, 56
  relation to equality, 56
Differential access,
  effects of, 26
  see also access to legislature
Discipline,
  ingredients of, 3–6
  political science as a, 16–20
Discretion,
  staff expert exercise of, 223–224

ECONOMIC development,
  advantages of Communist nations, 89–92
  and democracy, 302–309
  as an ideology regarding foreign aid, 85
  as type of foreign aid, handicaps for
    U.S., 89–92

Economic development (*Cont.*)
  as type of foreign aid, misconceptions regarding, 87–92
  relation to political change, 89–92
Elections,
  effect of in American democracy, 56–57
  in South, 58–67
  partisan, functions of, 157
  see also primaries, election
Electoral system,
  imperatives of on U.S. president, 33
Elite, military,
  definition of, 343
  social organization of, 349
  socio-political position of, 347-348
Elite dominance,
  myth of, 201, 232–241
  obstacles to, 201, 234–240
  traditional and contemporary notions of, 200–201
Empathy,
  definition of, 309n.
Empirical theory,
  in political science, 12–13
Encoding,
  in message transmission in communications flow model, 255, 256
Equal protection clause (of Fourteenth Amendment),
  and reapportionment, 45–46
Equality,
  evolution of idea of, 44–45
  ideal of, 52–53
  relation to despotism, 56
Experimentation, 301, 353–360
  absence of in traditional political analysis, 11
Experiments,
  limits and potentialities, 357–358
  types of, 353–354
  uses of, 359–360

Factionalism, intraparty, 147
  in New York City, 166–176
  in Soviet politics, 190
Factional machines,
  definition of, 67
  in political party organizations in the South, 61
Facts as abstractions,
  definition of, 5

Fact-value dichotomy, 12
Fact-theory nexus, 296–297
Feedback,
  in message transmission, 256, 257
Folkways,
  organizational, 289
Foreign aid,
  definition of, 84
  six types of, 84–92
Freedom,
  relation of to equality, 52–55
Friendship ties,
  and formal status in legislative bodies, 247–248, 249
  effect on voting, 202–203, 248–252
  informal network of in legislatures, 202–203, 242–252
Function,
  definition of, 300

Gaming,
  use of in simulation research, 355–356
Generalizations,
  in a discipline, 4–6
"Grand theory,"
  criticism of by traditionalists, 18
Group discipline,
  effect on newcomer's communication, 289–290
Group dynamics,
  in U.S. Supreme Court, 98–99, 125–132
Groups,
  differential rewards of, 98, 123–125

Heterocrats,
  as a type of political leader, 210–211, 215–216
Homophily,
  definition of, 245
  used as a measure of legislative behavior, 245–248
Hostility,
  acceleration of, 148, 176–185
Hypotheses,
  absence of in traditional political analysis, 17
  definition of, 5

Ideals,
  analysis of in traditional political science, 8–9

Identification,
of followers with leaders, 205–208
with parents in voting, 108–109
Ideologies,
definition of, 8
Immobilism,
of responsible community leaders in
emerging conflict, 182
Individualism,
ideal of, 54
its roots in democratic revolution, 55–56
Indoctrination,
function of, 259
Industrialization,
operational definition of, 306
tests of as a correlate, 305, 306
see also "conspicuous industrialization"
Influence,
channels for staff experts, 227–230
defined as one type of power, 197
difficulties confronting empirical analysis
of, 352
military, *see* military influence
of U.S. Congress, formal and informal,
33–34
of party, faction, and friendship in California lower house, 250–252
patterns available to staff experts in
unions, 226–227
range of individual, 245
Inputs,
in flow of political demands and rewards, 257
Institutional mode of traditional political science, 10, 297
Intelligence function, 278–279
role of the "spy" in, 290
Interest groups, 67–82
effect of prestige on differential access,
70–71
role of as socializing agents, 274–275
see also pressure group activity
"Invisible government," 98, 120–123
Issues,
illustration of public policy, 83–94
in community conflicts, 176–180

JUDICIAL intervention in political questions,
48–51
Judicial review,
effect on congressional power, 34

Juridical focus,
of traditional political analysis, 10–11
shift away from, 10–12

LANGUAGE,
and politics, 99–100, 133–143
definition of, 133
social functions of, 133–134
study of, 253–254
Latent functions,
definition of, 300
implications for reform, 338
of political machines, 331–338
Laws,
as generalizations, definition of, 4
Leader,
relation of to followers, 198–199, 205–
208
relation of to his advisers, 102–104
Leaders, political,
role of in conflict-management, 148, 185
role strains of, 148
Leadership, 204–216
defined as one type of power, 197
dilemmas of, 149
reliance on followers, 206–207
role strains of in totalitarian systems, 149
Legislative access,
differential distribution of, 68–69
dimensions of, 67–68
factors affecting, 68–81
formal, 68–74
informal, 75–81
Legislative analysis,
methods of, 243, 243n.
Legislative apportionment,
effect on distribution of differential access, 68
Linguistic diversity,
see multilingualism
Logical positivism, 12–13

MAIL-FLOW analysis, 257
Managerial revolution, 230–231
Manifest functions,
definition of, 330
Mass media,
concentration of control, 275
definition of, 275

Mass media (*Cont.*)
    role of as socializing agents, 274–275
    role of in policy making, 276–285
Mass movements, 260, 265
Measurement,
    problems of political science, 298
    role of in science, 298
Methodology,
    debate over in political science, 18
Militarism,
    degree of, defined operationally, 347
Military establishment,
    definition of, 342
Military factor,
    in political analysis, 339–352
Military foreign aid, 85–86
Military influence,
    alternate channels of, 344–345
    alternate forms of the process, 343–344
    definition of, 343
    external setting of, 345–346
    internal setting of, 346–348
    see also elite, military
Military technology,
    definition of, 348
    empirical dimensions of, 348–349
Models,
    abuse of, 297
    definition of, 198n.
    illustrated, 297
    message flows in the communications
        process, 255–257, 255n.
    types of, 198n.
Modernization,
    and linguistic diversity, 99–100, 139–143
    effect on political systems, 308–309
Motives,
    as a problem of political research, 294–
        295
Multilingualism,
    and political integration, 99–100
    practical problems of, 139–143
Multiple correlation analysis,
    illustration of use of, 311–313
Myths,
    role of in indoctrination, 258–259, 288

OBJECTIVITY,
    as an ingredient of scientific analysis, 294
Oligarchy,
    definition of, 303

One-man-one-vote,
    constitutional doctrine of, 45–48
"Opinion leaders," 254
Organizations,
    as a divisive force in community affairs,
        201, 236–237
    maintenance and enhancement needs of,
        238
Orthodox political science,
    see traditional study
Outputs,
    in flow of political demands and rewards,
        257
Overlapping membership,
    effect on differential access, 76–79

PARTIAL correlation,
    illustration of, 313–328
Patronage,
    see "spoils system"
Personality, cult of,
    in Soviet politics, 213
Persuasion,
    and coercion: delicate balance between,
        187–188
    role of in authoritative power relations,
        199, 217–223
Pluralism,
    as restraint on president, 32–33
    definition of in local political system, 201
    of congressional committee system, 42
Political analysis,
    art of, 27
Political campaigns,
    fund-raising in, 65
    illustrations of in 1800, 158–159
    propaganda in, 152
Political demands and rewards,
    flow of, 257
Political function,
    definition of, 259n.
Political leaders,
    as marginal people, 209
    middle class source of, 208
Political machine,
    and ecological changes, 170–171
    latent functions of, 331–338
Political party,
    as a nationalizing force, 161
    functions of, 59–60
    in the South, 58–67

Political party (*Cont.*)
models, competitive and noncompetitive, 59–60
new types in 1800, 145, 158
role of as socializing agent, 273–274
structure and cohesion of, effect on differential access, 70–71
Political questions,
U.S. Supreme Court's role in handling, 48
Political socialization,
see socialization, political
Political system,
definition of, 22n.
empirical questions regarding, 348
pluralist model of, 200–201
Politicians, amateur,
definition of, 146
normal commitments of, 146
Politicians, professional,
normal commitments of, 146
reliance on in a political campaign, 65–67
Politics,
definition of, 14
emphasis upon in behavioral analysis, 14–15
game of in community context, 118–122
Power,
actual, definition of, 197
as an operational concept, 197
as an organizing concept, 197–198
as catalyst in securing compliance, 196
aspects of, 196
definition of, 196
inferred, 197
limits on in totalitarian system, 148–149
methodological difficulties affecting empirical investigation of, 202–203
peaceful interparty transfer of, 146, 163–165
potential, definition of, 197
relation to violence, 196–197
reputed, definition of, 197
types of, 197
Predictive laws,
absence of in political science, 298
role of in science, 298
President,
ascendancy of in American politics, 39–42
electoral support for, 33
U.S., powers and roles of, 30–32
U.S., prestige of, 32–33

Presidential power,
and the constitutional separation of powers, 217
limits on, 32–33
role of status in, 217–218
Press,
informational role of, 277–282
intellectual role of, 282–285
relative influence of in foreign policy-making, 283–284
role of in policy-making, 258, 276–285
Pressure group activity,
in a community, 123–124
in the legislative arena, 67–82
see also interest groups
Primaries, election,
conduct of by political party organizations in the South, 60–61
Primary identification,
patterns of in voting, 108–113
Principles,
abuse of by traditionalists, 17
definition of, 5
Procedural reform
definition of, 9
Process mode of behavioral analysis, 15
Propaganda analysis, 253
Public opinion flow during a campaign, 154
Public policy orientation,
in traditional political science, 9–10
Pyramidal model of power distribution, 198
Chicago as illustration, 232–234
inversion of, 198

QUANTIFICATION,
emphasis upon in behavioralism, 15–16

REFORM,
life-cycle of, 147, 169
types of outlook in political science, 9
Reformist objectives in political science, 9
Representative government,
effect on individualism, 56–57
Research design, 300–301
"Revolution of rising expectations,"
definition of, 86
Roll call analysis of legislative voting, 243n.
and friendship ties, 248–250

Rules, legislative,
    effect of differential access, 72–74
Rulers,
    typology of, 210–211

SCIENCE,
    definition of, 294n.
    obstacles to the development of in politi-
        cal analysis, 13–14, 294–298
"Scientistic" tendencies of behavioralism, 17
Separation of powers,
    doctrine of, 22
    effects of on differential access, 68–69
    general effects of, 29
    political dimensions of, 68–69
Simulation,
    definition of, 354
    use of computers in, 354–356
    use of in research, 355
Small groups,
    use in predicting political behavior, 98,
        125–132
    see also group dynamics
Socialization,
    folklore of prevailing rewards system in,
        289
    organizational tolerance limits in, 289
    routines appropriate to, 289
Socialization, political, 258, 267–276
    agents of, 267–275
    American Way of Life, as stressed in,
        272, 273
    beliefs inculcated in, 271, 272
    citizenship concept in, 268–269, 272–273,
        274, 276
    conformity pressures in, 276
    definition of, 267
    methods of, 270, 273
    patriotism as a value inculcated in, 271,
        272, 273
    peer group role in, 276
    processes of, 275–276
    "systematic bias" in, 258, 269–270, 272–
        273, 275, 276
"Social lobby,"
    as a technique for developing overlapping
        membership ties and differential ac-
        cess, 79–80
    definition of, 79
    effect on freshman legislators, 80
    limited role of, 80–81

Social rank,
    effect on politics, 123–125
"Sociometric" technique,
    applied to organizations, 288
    applied to study of legislative behavior,
        243
Sovereignty,
    definition of, 11
"Specialists in violence," 343
"Spoils system,"
    early form of in 1800, 160
Staff experts,
    types of, 224–226
    see also advisers
State,
    definition of, 10, 133, 342
Statistical measures, 299, 309–331
    in indices of factors conditioning exist-
        ence of democracy, 303–306
Structure, social,
    definition of, 300
Structural-functionalism, 300
    illustration of, 331–338
Structural reform,
    definition of, 9
Subjectivity,
    in traditional political science, 10
Systems analysis,
    approach in behavioralism, 15

TAXONOMY,
    abuse of in behavioral analysis, 18
    as form of conceptualization, 6
Television,
    as a medium of political campaign de-
        bate, 155–156
    debates and effect on election of 1960,
        154–157
Tension reduction, 148
    need for in totalitarian systems, 148
    role of political leadership in, 148, 185
Terminology,
    debate over in political science, 18
Theory,
    and empirical research: interdependence
        of, 15–16
    definition of, 4, 296
    in political science, 4–5, 295–296
    middle-range, 297
    role of in science, 295
    self-correction of, 296

Threats,
  in authoritative power relations, 199
Traditional study of political science, 8–12
Transempiricist argument, 11, 296

UPPER class,
  role of in a democracy, 54–55
Urban majority,
  dimensions of, 43–44
Urbanization,
  operational definition of, 306
  tests of as a correlate, 305, 306

Utopian systems,
  definition of, 8

VALUES,
  definition of, 5
  in a discipline, 5, 12–13
  in political analysis, 294–295
  of legislator-politician: effect on differential access, 78–79
Value-relativism, 13
Variables,
  appropriate range of in empirical investigation, 349–350